Stanley J. Grenz is Pioneer McDonald
Professor of Baptist Heritage, Theology and
Ethics at Carey Theological College and
Professor of Theology and Ethics at Regent
College in Vancouver, British Columbia. He
is author of *Revisioning Evangelical
Theology, The Millennium Maze: Sorting
Out Evangelical Options, Reason for the
Hope: The Theology of Wolfhart
Pannenberg, Prayer: The Cry for the
Kingdom, Sexual Ethics, The Baptist
Congregation,* and *Isaac Backus: Puritan
and Baptist*. He has co-authored
*20th-Century Theology: God and the World
in a Transitional Age* and *AIDS: Ministry in
the Midst of a Crisis — A
Medical-Theological Perspective.*

THEOLOGY
for the
Community
OF GOD

THEOLOGY
for the
Community OF GOD

Stanley J. Grenz

**BROADMAN
&HOLMAN
PUBLISHERS**

Nashville, Tennessee

4228-01
0-8054-2801-1

Dewey Decimal Classification: 230
Subject Heading: THEOLOGY
Library of Congress Card Catalog Number: 93-26963

Library of Congress Cataloging-in-Publication Data
Grenz, Stanley, 1950–
    Theology for the community of God / Stanley J. Grenz.
        p.   cm.
    Includes bibliographical references and index.
    ISBN 0-8054-2801-1
    1. Theology, Doctrinal.   2. Evangelicalism.   I. Title.
BT75.2G74   1994
230'.046—dc20   93-26963
                                                           CIP

To
David S. Dockery
scholar, friend, and "kindred spirit"

Contents

 # Preface

During the last two decades, the church in North America has witnessed a renewed interest in theology. This interest has spawned a litter of new systematic theologies, as thinkers have sought to provide the intellectual resources for the Christian community as it faces the third millennium of its history. *Theology for the Community of God* arises out of this theological ferment.

Like many similar works, the following pages delineate the central themes of Christian doctrine in a systematic manner. Hence, after an introductory chapter, the discussion moves through the major divisions of systematic theology as it has been traditionally conceived: God (theology proper), humankind (anthropology), Christ (Christology), the Holy Spirit (pneumatology), the church (ecclesiology), and the last things (eschatology).

While sharing the common format, the book differs in certain crucial respects from other systematic theologies. One obvious difference is perspective. Every theology reflects to a certain degree the faith community which nourishes its author. *Theology for the Community of God* gives evidence to my location within the Baptist denomination and my participation in the broader evangelical trajectory. Consequently, the statement of systematic theology that follows is avowedly evangelical and unabashedly Baptist.

Above all, however, the book differs from recent theologies in the integrative motif—"community"—around which the discussion revolves. Like other statements of theology, the following chapters offer an outline of our Christian faith commitment. But my goal is to consider our faith within the context of God's central program for creation, namely, the establishment of community. I believe this understanding of the divine purpose offers a fruitful point of departure for theological discussion, because it lies at the heart both of the biblical vision and of the longings of humankind as we move into the emerging postmodern era.

As a result of its perspective and integrative motif, *Theology for the Community of God* comprises a preliminary sketch of the theology called for in my earlier, more programmatic book, *Revisioning Evangelical Theology* (Downers Grove, Ill.: InterVarsity, 1993).

The agenda set forth in both books is the product of my own theological odessey. My spiritual roots lie in the pious heritage of the Baptist parsonage in which I was raised. After experiencing a dramatic call to the gospel ministry, my educational track introduced me to the rationalist approach to theology espoused by my teachers, Gordon Lewis at Denver Seminary and Wolfhart Pannenberg in Munich. Consequently, when I began teaching in the early 1980s my approach strongly reflected the influence of my mentors, and their abiding influence is readily evident in this volume. During my first sabbatical leave (1987-88), I returned to Munich to study more closely the theology of my *Doktorvater*. The year marked an important milestone in my own thinking, as I discovered anew the importance of the pietist heritage in which I had been spiritually nurtured.

Since 1988, I have been seeking to integrate the rationalistic and pietistic dimensions of the Christian faith. In continuity with the training I received from my mentors, I acknowledge the crucial role of reason in the theological enterprise. At the same time, I am convinced that a personal faith commitment as nurtured in a community of faith—piety—is also significant in our attempt to understand and to pursue the constructive theological task. Thus, while theology may be an intellectual search for truth, this search must always be attached to the foundational, identity producing encounter with God in Christ. And it must issue forth in Christian living.

The book itself owes its impetus to an invitation in spring 1990 from David Dockery, then editor at Broadman Press, to write a one-volume text in systematic theology. Since then, David has returned to the Southern Baptist Theological Seminary, leaving the project in the capable hands of others at Broadman and Holman Publishers, especially John Landers and Steve Bond, to whom I express my gratitude. I am also indebted to Carey Theological College for providing an amiable context for my writing, as well as to the Carey support staff who have assisted me—Beverley Norgren, Heather Penner, and my teaching assistant, Jane Rowland. Finally, I thank the students and colleagues who have interacted with my ideas and challenged my thinking over the last thirteen years.

My hope is that this volume may provide a systematic context which will enhance the efforts of future students and colleagues in reflecting on our Christian faith, so that thereby the gospel may be served and, above all, that God may be glorified in the church. In short, I would hope that the following chapters might serve as a statement of theology for the community of God.

Stanley J. Grenz
Spring 1994

Introduction:
The Nature and Task
of Theology

We demolish arguments and every pretension that sets itself up against the knowledge of God, and we take captive every thought to make it obedient to Christ.
(2 Cor. 10:5)

Outline

Every Christian is a theologian. Whether consciously or unconsciously, each person of faith embraces a belief system. And each believer, whether in a deliberate manner or merely implicitly, reflects on the content of these beliefs and their significance for Christian life.

The biblical documents themselves provide the foundation for this close connection between faith stance and theological reflection. The Scriptures encourage us to think through our beliefs in order to understand the extent to which they express our personal and corporate commitment (e.g., Matt. 22:37; 2 Cor. 10:5; 1 Pet. 3:15). When we move beyond mere haphazard reflection on faith and consciously seek to articulate our beliefs systematically, we step into the discipline called "theology."

In this context the fundamental question arises: What exactly is theology? What task becomes ours when we begin to reflect systematically on faith and to seek to offer an ordered articulation of our beliefs?

The Theological Task

Basically, systematic theology is the reflection on, and the ordered articulation of faith. Hence, the reality of faith itself—our commitment to the God revealed in Christ—calls forth theological reflection. Because we are a people of faith, we readily engage in theology. The theological enterprise, therefore, functions within the life of discipleship; theology can be a spiritual activity. Before engaging in this task, however, we must look more closely at the intellectual discipline itself.

The Historical Development of Theology

We begin our attempt to understand theology historically, by noting how theologians at various stages in history have viewed their task. The ways in which Christian thinkers have understood both the term and the nature of the theological enterprise have changed over the centuries of Christian history.

Developments in the meaning of the term. The word "theology" does not appear in the biblical documents. Rather, ancient Greece formed the seedbed for its use. The word itself is formed from two other Greek terms, *theos* (God) and *logos* (word, teaching, study). Hence, etymologically "theology" means "the teaching concerning God" or "the study of God." The Greeks used the word to refer to the sayings of the philosophers and poets about divine matters, especially when viewed within the framework of knowledge of humankind and nature.[1]

Christian thinkers imported the central aspects of the Greek theological concern. Its presence is evident in Paul's encounter with the philosophers in Athens (Acts 17:16ff). Already in the first century Christian thinkers were theologizing in accordance with the Greek style. Even as late as the Middle Ages the Greek understanding of the theological enterprise remained influential among the theologians of the church. The early medieval thinkers understood "theology" as referring to the doctrine of God, which they regarded as one topic within the broader study of "dogmatics" or "sacred doctrine" (*sacra doctrina*).[2]

During the 1100s and 1200s, "theology" underwent a change in meaning. No longer simply the discourse concerning God, it now became the rational explication of divine revelation.[3] And with the rise of the universities, the enterprise was destined to become an academic, as well as an ecclesiastical discipline.[4] The term came to refer to a single, unified "science" focusing on knowledge of God. But it

---

1. For this latter point, see Frank Whaling, "The Development of the Word 'Theology,'" *Scottish Journal of Theology* 34 (1981): 292-93.

2. Emil Brunner, *The Christian Doctrine of God* (Philadelphia: Westminster, 1950), 89.

3. Yves M. J. Congar, *A History of Theology* (Garden City, N.Y.: Doubleday, 1968), 33. See also G. R. Evans., *The Beginnings of Theology as an Academic Discipline*, (Oxford: Clarendon, 1980).

4. Whaling, "The Development of the Word 'Theology,'" 300.

nevertheless remained "practical" (linked with Christian living), for theology retained its older character of "wisdom."[5]

In eighteenth-century Germany the understanding of theology shifted again. Christian thinkers replaced the concept of a unified, practical science with the multiplicity of the theological sciences[6] often divided into the now familiar scheme of biblical, systematic, historical, and practical theology.[7] Thereby "theology" was transformed into an all-inclusive word referring to the various aspects of the study of the Bible and the church. Friedrich Schleiermacher accepted the challenge of bringing the various theological disciplines into a unity.[8] He reorganized the several academic pursuits into a threefold curriculum division: biblical (the doctrine espoused by the various biblical authors and books), historical and systematic (the development of doctrine and the understandings of the contemporary church), and practical (the application of doctrine to church life).[9]

During this time, Christians were becoming increasingly aware that humans followed a number of separate religious traditions, each with its own belief system. Consequently, the term "theology" came to refer as well to the account of God in the various religions.[10]

Today Christians generally use "theology" either in the inclusive sense or in a slightly narrower manner, often interchangeable with what earlier thinkers termed "dogmatics." In North America the preferred designation for the latter is "systematic theology," or perhaps "constructive" or "doctrinal theology," although these terms may not be totally interchangeable.[11] Whatever the term used, the theological task encompasses the intellectual reflection on faith. Theology is primarily the articulation of a specific religious belief system itself

---

5. Edward Farley, *Theologia* (Philadelphia: Fortress, 1983), 77, 81.

6. Ibid., 49, 65, 77.

7. For a recent defense of the traditional fourfold scheme, see Richard A. Muller, *The Study of Theology* (Grand Rapids: Zondervan, 1991).

8. Friedrich Schleiermacher, *A Brief Outline on the Study of Theology* (Atlanta: John Knox, 1966). See also Farley, *Theologia*, 85, 94.

9. See Schleiermacher, *A Brief Outline of the Study of Theology.*

10. Whaling, "The Development of the Word 'Theology,'" 305-6.

11. In contrast to dogmatic theology with its focus on the presentation of the body of Christian doctrine, systematic theology moves beyond exposition to the larger question of the coherence of doctrine in the contemporary context and with all human knowledge. For a discussion of this distinction, see Muller, *The Study of Theology,* 125-28.

(doctrine). But it also includes reflection on the nature of believing, as well as declarations concerning the integration of commitment with personal and community life.

The Christian theologian seeks to set forth a coherent presentation of the themes of the Christian faith. Traditionally these include God (theology), humankind and the created universe (anthropology), the identity of Jesus as the Christ and the salvation he brought (Christology), the Holy Spirit and the Spirit's work both in the individual and in the world (pneumatology), the church as the corporate expression of Christian faith (ecclesiology), and the consummation of God's program for creation (eschatology).

The need for theology in the church. Theology as we know it developed over the centuries. Christians engage in theological reflection in response to the presence in the church of certain perceived needs, including what we may designate as "polemics," "catechetics," and "biblical summarization."[12] These needs span the centuries. They appeared already in the early church; in one form or another they have remained important throughout history; and they continue to command attention today.

(1) Theologians carry out their work because of the need to define the Christian belief system in the context of alternatives (polemics). This intention was prominent in the early Christian centuries, as the church faced doctrinal controversies. Thinkers employed theological formulations to differentiate orthodoxy from heresy.

The polemical factor was again of special importance during the Reformation. Christians who differed over questions of faith marked out their theological positions in order to define their own particular understanding of Christianity.

In the modern era, the importance of polemics has not abated, even though its context has shifted. We are now called to delineate our faith in the midst of many competing world views and religions. In order to understand how Christian commitment can be applied to the grave problems and needs of our world, we must become clear as

---

12. See Brunner, *The Christian Doctrine of God*, 93-96. Congar cites the church's need to speak to the pagan culture and the individual believer's need to reflect on faith in the pagan context. Congar, *A History of Theology*, 39, 40.

to the content of our message and how it differs from contemporary alternatives.

(2) The theological enterprise is also an outworking of the need to offer instruction to the people of God (catechetics). The task of teaching the faith to converts is especially important, for new believers must be instructed in the fundamentals of Christianity in order to become mature (Eph. 4:11-14).

From the beginning Christian leaders have acknowledged the importance of theology in the task of instruction. As early as the second century, the church devised elaborate summaries of doctrine as tools in teaching the many converts coming from pagan backgrounds. Since then the people of God have continually looked to theologians to assist them in fulfilling the pedagogical mandate to "make disciples of all nations. . . teaching them. . . ."

(3) The third impetus for the theological task arises from the need Christians have always sensed to bring the basic themes taught in the Bible into summary form (biblical summarization). In fact, this summarizing tendency is present already in the Scriptures. In the Old Testament era, the Hebrew people readily capsulized their understanding of the divine nature arising from their experience of, or encounter with the God who addressed them (Deut. 6:4-5; 26:5-9). The New Testament likewise contains summary theological statements, especially concerning the nature of salvation and the person of Christ (1 Cor. 15:3-8; Phil. 2:6-11; 1 Tim. 3:16). Taking their cue from these biblical texts, systematic theologians have traditionally attempted to bring together in systematic fashion the major biblical themes that focus on God's being and gracious salvation.

The understanding of theology as the summarization of biblical doctrine sports an impeccable pedigree within the history of the church. Yet since the Reformation many conservative theologians have treated this aspect as theology's central, if not sole function. And they have coupled the focus on biblical summarization with modern concepts of the nature of science. Just as the natural world is amenable to the scientists' probing, they assert, so also the teaching of Scripture is objectively understandable. As a consequence of this assumption, systematic theology becomes primarily the organizing of the "facts" of Scripture, just as the natural sciences are the systematizing of the facts of nature. We may call this the "concordance" or "propositionalist" approach.

Contemporary proponents of the concordance understanding of theology claim the heritage of the great Protestant scholastics[13] and the Princeton theologians of the 1800s. Following their forebears, they understand truth as propositional (consisting in a body of correct assertions) and unchanging. Consequently, propositionalists seek to emancipate theology from any one cultural context in order to produce a statement of truth that is timeless and culture-free.[14] For them, the correct theology is the one which best crystallizes biblical truth into a set of universally true and applicable propositions.[15]

Despite its ongoing popularity among conservative thinkers, the concordance model has been vigorously challenged. Neo-orthodox thinkers were especially relentless in asserting that revelation does not disclose supernatural knowledge; it is not the unveiling of a body of propositions about God. Rather, in revelation God encounters the human person.[16] In response to the neo-orthodox critique, conservatives rightly refuse to acknowledge a radical disjunction between "propositional" and "personal" revelation.[17] In so doing they emphasize a fundamental insight encapsuled by propositionalism: Our faith is tied to a divine revelation that has been objectively disclosed. God has communicated truth—himself—to us.

---

13. A theologian who is often connected with Reformed scholasticism and who through his link to the Princeton thinkers has exercised great influence on evangelicalism is Francis Turretin (1623-87). For a discussion of Turretin's contribution, see Richard A. Muller, "Scholasticism Protestant and Catholic: Francis Turretin on the Object and Principles of Theology," *Church History* 55/2 (June 1986): 193-205.

14. For a statement concerning the roots of this idea in the Princeton theologians, see David F. Wells, "An American Evangelical Theology: The Painful Transition from Theoria to Praxis," in *Evangelicalism and Modern America*, ed. George Marsden (Grand Rapids: Eerdmans, 1984), 85. Among the proponents of this biblically-focused, evangelical propositionalism none has been more untiring than Carl F. H. Henry, hailed as the most prominent evangelical theologian of the second half of the twentieth century. For a discussion of Henry's theology and significance, see Stanley J. Grenz and Roger E. Olson, *Twentieth Century Theology: God and the World in a Transitional Age* (Downers Grove, IL: InterVarsity, 1992), 288-97.

15. This feature of evangelical theology is noted by Wells, "An American Evangelical Theology," 86.

16. John Ballie, *The Idea of Revelation* (New York: Columbia University Press, 1956), 17-40.

17. See, for example, Millard J. Erickson, *Christian Theology*, three volumes (Grand Rapids: Baker, 1983), 1:196.

Despite its positive contributions, the concordance understanding of theology has one decisive flaw. It does not give adequate attention to the contextual nature of theology. Theological reflection always occurs within and for a specific historical context. Consequently, all theological assertions are historically conditioned. In contrast to the assumption of propositionalists, by its very nature theology is a contextual discipline.[18]

The contextual nature of theology renders the concordance model incomplete. But what comprises a fuller conception of theology?

The task of theology and the church. The contemporary interest in "narrative" offers one helpful insight that points toward a more adequate understanding of theology.[19] Narrative thinkers remind us that we must view theology in terms of its relationship to the story of God's action in history. This seminal assertion carries important implications.

One ramification is that we can pursue the theological task only "from within"—only from the vantage point of the faith community in which we stand. But why is this the case? Why is theology by nature a discipline of the church? The connection between theology and the faith community arises from a specific understanding of how Christian identity is formed.

Narrative theologians rightly point out that the revealed truth of God, which comes to us fundamentally in the narrative of God's actions in the world, forms the "basic grammar" that creates Christian identity. Truth establishes who we are—Christians, God's children. Rather than merely being a product of our experience, as certain strands of liberalism tend to argue, in an important sense this truth of God, this retold narrative, *creates* our experience.[20] The identity-creative experience, however, is not ours as individuals in isolation. Instead our identity arises within a community—within the fellowship of God's people in the church.

---

18. Several evangelicals have alerted their conservative colleagues to this reality. Hence, John Jefferson Davis, *Foundations of Evangelical Theology* (Grand Rapids: Baker, 1984), 67.

19. For a description of narrative theology, see Grenz and Olson, *Twentieth Century Theology*, 271-85.

20. See, for example, Pinnock's statement on evangelical theological method. Clark H. Pinnock and Delwin Brown, *Theological Crossfire: An Evangelical-Liberal Dialogue* (Grand Rapids: Zondervan, 1990), 45. This point is delineated in George Lindbeck, *The Nature of Doctrine*, (Philadelphia: Westminster, 1984), 80.

For this insight narrative theologians are indebted to recent voices within the human sciences. Thinkers in a wide variety of disciplines have attempted to move beyond the focus on the autonomous individual characteristic of the modern mentality in order to develop a more profound understanding of epistemology and identity formation. They theorize that the process of knowing and to some extent even experience of the world can only occur within a conceptual framework mediated by the social community in which a person participates. In the same way, personal identity is formed within social structures. We understand not only the world but also ourselves by means of an intricate web of traditions and beliefs. To the degree that it provides the categories or language in which we frame our questions and answers, this inherited web—this belief structure—shapes our lives. The web of belief is transmitted to us by the social group within which the ongoing process of identity formation occurs.[21]

The contemporary focus on community ties directly into the religious view of life. As Christians we assert that religious experience—an encounter with the divine—is foundational to our self-identity. According to the biblical tradition, the goal of the human-divine encounter is the establishment of a community of people who stand in covenant with God. We enter that community through our faith response to the proclamation of the salvific action of God in Christ, symbolized by baptism. Hence, the experience of encountering God together with the conceptual framework which facilitates it are mediated to us by a religious community—the church—through its symbols, narratives, and sacred documents.

The importance of the Christian community to the faith and identity of believers has important implications for our understanding of the nature of theology. Theology fulfills a role in the life of the people of God. Its purpose is ultimately "practical"; it is related to Christian life and practice.[22] The biblical narrative forms the foundation

---

21. Charles Taylor, *Sources of the Self: The Making of the Modern Identity* (Cambridge, Mass.: Harvard University Press, 1989), 25-40.

22. This understanding reflects points of contact with Niklas Luhmann's sociology of theology. For a sketch and appraisal of Luhmann's position, see Garrett Green, "The Sociology of Dogmatics: Niklas Luhmann's Challenge to Theology," *Journal of the American Academy of Religion* 50/1 (March 1982): 19-34.

for a conceptual framework by means of which we view ourselves and our experience of the world. Theologians function within the context of the Christian community by articulating the conceptual framework and belief structure we share.[23]

Theology, then, is the task of the faith community; it is a community act. Theology is the Christian community reflecting on and articulating the faith of the people who have encountered God in God's activity as focused in the history of Jesus of Nazareth and who therefore seek to live as the people of God in the contemporary world. Ultimately, then, the propositions of systematic theology find their source and aim in the identity and life of the community it serves. In fact, we need no other rationale to engage in the discipline than our participation in the church. And as Theodore Jennings rightly notes, theological reflection is reflection "on behalf of"—on behalf of a community, a tradition, a world.[24]

The Relationship of Theology to Other Concepts

Christian theology is the reflection on, and the articulation of the belief structure that gives identity to the Christian people. As an intellectual enterprise it is an academic discipline pursued within the faith community. But this raises the question concerning how theology differs from certain other activities included within the broader realm in which it is embedded. More specifically, what is its connection to the act of faith, which is foundational to Christian life, to the academic field of religious studies with which theology shares certain affinities, and to the several other intellectual disciplines which also attempt to speak about reality as a whole?

Theology and faith. If theology is reflection on faith, theology and personal faith are closely connected. Nevertheless, we must not confuse the two, for they differ in one important way.

---

23. So forceful have been recent voices setting forth the fundamentally practical nature of theology that Peter Slater finds a consensus among theologians that their discipline "serves the faithful, whether as individuals or collectives, and it does so properly when it enables them *to live* more faithfully." Peter Slater, "Theology in the 1990s," *Toronto Journal of Theology* 6/2 (Fall 1990): 289.

24. Theodore W. Jennings, Jr., *Introduction to Theology* (Philadelphia: Fortress, 1976), 179.

Faith is by nature immediate. It arises out of the human encounter with the person of God in Christ, mediated by the community's testimony to the divine revelation in Jesus. Personal faith, therefore, is our response to the call of God, which involves participation in the believing community.

Personal faith extends to all aspects of our psyche. It includes our intellect. In the faith-response we accept as true certain assertions concerning reality, and as a result we view the world in a specific way. Faith includes our will. It entails the volitional commitment of ourselves to Another—to the God revealed in Jesus Christ—and consequently we enter into a fellowship of commitment with the disciples of Jesus. And faith includes the emotions, for it is the heartfelt love for the One who saves us, which translates into affection for others.

Faith is also the focus of the theologians' inquiry. But their questions are not the existential queries concerning the presence of faith in a believer's heart readily asked by the church. Rather, they are the more academic questions concerning the nature and object of the believer's commitment: What doctrines do we espouse—what assertions do we accept as helpful reflections of the nature of reality? What is the nature of personal commitment—what does it mean to commit oneself? To whom are we committing ourselves—what statements express the nature of the God who is the author and object of our faith?

In this manner, the focus of theology rests on the intellectual dimension of the faith of the believing community. Theologians view faith as a subject for discussion and reflection. Insofar as their discipline entails verbal expression, they seek to isolate the specifically intellectual aspect of faith and then to illumine, clarify, and articulate it.

The distinction between faith and theology indicates that theology is a "second order" endeavor[25] over which faith takes primacy. Theology is called forth by faith; it arises as we seek to reflect on the reality of our faith and articulate its content.

---

25. See, Lindbeck, *The Nature of Doctrine*, 80.

This distinction likewise reminds us that professional theologians are not necessarily persons of greater faith than other Christians. Rather, they are those whom the church (often in conjunction with the academic community) has called to employ their powers of thought in service to faith.[26] They are to utilize their intellectual capabilities in order to understand the nature and content of faith and the application of Christian commitment to life. Professional theologians, therefore, are vocationally servants of the church, devoting their lives to assist in the task of speaking about the faith of the people of God. Nevertheless, to the extent that all Christians share in theological reflection, all participate in the theological task.

Theology and religious studies. The relation between theology and faith suggests that we ought not confuse theology with a related intellectual discipline—religious studies—even though both fields of inquiry focus on belief structures. Students of religion attempt to engage in a scientific observation of systems of belief. In approaching their topic, they emphasize objective and detached work. As far as possible, they seek to labor "from the outside," apart from personal adherence to the belief system under observation.

While not totally devoid of such aspects of scientific study as detached work and objective observation, the theologian approaches faith within the context of the believing community. Theology presupposes a faith stance and participation in the faith community on the part of the practitioner. Consequently, theologians speak about the nature and content of faith from the perspective of personal commitment. In contrast to students of religion, theologians do not seek to free themselves totally from their own faith commitment nor from their participation in the faith community in order to engage in their discipline. Rather, they carry out their work with a sympathetic attitude toward the tradition in which they stand.

Faith, then, marks the central difference between theology and religious studies. Theoretically, anyone could engage in the study of religion, whereas the theological task is limited to participants of the tradition under scrutiny. The academic study of Christianity is not

---

26. Brunner, *The Christian Doctrine of God*, 73.

limited to adherents of that tradition, but no one can claim to be a Christian theologian without being a practicing Christian.

Theology and the sciences. The overarching task of Christian theology is to present a specifically Christian understanding of reality, one which views the world through the eyes of faith in the God revealed in Jesus of Nazareth. This conclusion indicates that theology has some affinity with the natural and social sciences, insofar as scholars in both disciplines formulate understandings of reality. Theologians share with scientists a common area of exploration—the universe and especially the human person. And they employ the findings of science in their work.

Despite their common subject matter, the sciences and theology part ways in intent and method. Scientists test hypotheses and draw conclusions concerning the objects of their study by means of empirical observation of the universe. Theologians, in contrast, are not limited in their task to observation of the world, for theological knowledge also moves from the acknowledgment of divine revelation. In addition, theologians go beyond scientists in that ultimately their subject is God and God's relationship to creation. Theologians, therefore, are concerned about humankind and the cosmos—the objects of the scientists' probing—not as mere natural phenomena, but specifically as participants in "creation," that is, as related to the Creator.

Insofar as they speak of God and the totality of reality, the theologians' endeavors overlap with those of philosophers concerned about metaphysics (the study of reality beyond the realm of the physical or of empirical observation). In fact, theologians often employ philosophical categories as a context for their assertions. But theologians differ from metaphysicians in that they address their subject matter from a vantage point within the believing community. In contrast to the philosopher, the theologian seeks to present a specifically Christian understanding of reality which views the world through the eyes of faith in the God revealed in Jesus of Nazareth.

Theology and truth. While theologians pull into their purview reality as a whole and seek to describe it from the viewpoint of faith, no theological system encompasses reality in its fullness. The topics the theologian studies—God, the human person and the world as a whole—lie ultimately beyond the ability of the human intellect to grasp fully. Therefore, every theological system will have limitations. Nevertheless, the human mind can grasp something concerning reality, and therefore a theological system can to some extent represent truth.

In the task of setting forth truth, the theologian is facilitated by the use of what theorists of knowledge call "models." Important to a proper understanding of the role of models in the theological enterprise is the differentiation set forth in contemporary philosophy of science between "replica models" and "analogue models." Whereas replica models strive to reproduce the modeled reality on a smaller, more easily visualized scale, analogue models attempt to simulate the structural relationships of the reality modeled.

The model constructed by theology is of the latter type rather than the former.[27] Theological systems do not provide a replica, a "scale model" of reality. Their propositions are not univocal. Hence, no one system can claim to be exact verbal reproduction of the nature of God or of the human person and the world in relation to God. Rather, the theologian seeks to invoke an understanding of reality by setting forth through an analogous model realities which may be mysterious, even ineffable. In this process of understanding, a systematic theology can be helpful, insofar as it is an appropriate analogue model able to assist us in grasping the profound mystery of reality. In this sense, a theological system is always a human construct.

Christian theologians focus on the significance of Jesus of Nazareth for our understanding of God, creation, and history. They seek to assist the Christian community in articulating the importance of Jesus Christ to the divine program and the significance of our faith commitment to Jesus for all human life. To this end they construct an analogue model of reality viewed from the perspective of God's self-disclosure in Christ.

---

27. For a short discussion of the analogous nature of theology, see Davis, *Foundations of Evangelical Theology*, 48-50. For a more complete exploration of the nature of models in both science and theology, see Sallie McFague, *Metaphorical Theology* (Philadelphia: Fortress, 1982): 67-144.

Here again we see that theology is a second-order enterprise, and its propositions are second-order statements. Theologians formulate in culturally sensitive language the world view of the community that is constituted by the human response to the story of the salvific act of God in the history of Jesus.

The second-order nature of theology does not mean that theological declarations make no ontological claims. By its very nature, the conceptual framework of a faith community contains an implicit claim to represent the truth about the world and the divine reality its members have come to know and experience. For this reason, theology necessarily entails the quest for truth. Theologians enter into conversation with other disciplines of human knowledge with the goal of setting forth a Christian world view which coheres with what we know about human experience and the world. They seek to understand the human person and the cosmos as existing in relation to the reality of God. In so doing they attempt to fashion a fuller vision of God and his purposes in the world.[28] However, the ontological claims implicit in theological declarations come as an outworking of the intent of the theologian to provide a model of reality.

The Ongoing Nature of the Theological Task

Theology is a contextual discipline. Theologians do not merely amplify, refine, defend, and deliver to the next generation a timeless, fixed orthodoxy. Rather, by speaking from within the community of faith, they seek to describe the act of faith, the God toward whom faith is directed, and the implications of our faith commitment in, for, and to a specific historical and cultural context.

The fundamental Christian faith-commitment to the God revealed in Jesus is unchanging, of course. But the world into which we bring this confession is in flux. As a result, theologians function in a mediatorial manner. From the vantage point within the Christian tradition, they seek to assist the church in bringing the confession of faith in Jesus as the Christ into the contemporary context. They articulate this confession in the thought-forms of the culture they serve, and

---

28. Douglas F. Ottiti, "Christian Theology and Other Disciplines," *Journal of Religion* 64/2 (April 1984): 182.

they seek to show the implications, relevance, and application of the Christian confession to life in that society and that historical context.

The contextual nature of the discipline, therefore, mandates the use of contemporary thought-forms in theological reflection. For this reason, the categories theologians employ are by necessity culturally and historically conditioned, and the theologian is both a "child of the times" and a communicator to the times. Because the context in which the church speaks the Word of God is in flux—changing through time and location—the task of theology in assisting the church in formulating and applying its confession amidst the varied and changing flow of human thought and life never comes to an end. Like the church and the societies which it serves, theology is always *in via*—on the way. And the theologian is a pilgrim thinker ministering on behalf of a pilgrim people.[29]

Dangers in the Theological Enterprise

The understanding of theology charted above suggests several dangers which confront the Christian theologian. We must alert ourselves to three of these.

Substitution. Among the most insidious dangers is the temptation of substitution. Theologians too readily allow personal theologizing to become a surrogate for genuine, personal faith. We dare not replace commitment to the triune God and the living Christ with our doctrines about God and Christ. And we must avoid placing confidence in our abilities to develop a theological system, rather than in the God in whose service we stand.

Substitution can also take the form of a subtle drift away from theology into religious studies. Theologians sometimes make such a thorough-going attempt at objectivity that they lose from view the faith commitment to the triune God around which their vocation centers. The end result is to reduce Christianity to the status of being one religion among others, merely an object for academic study.

Dogmatism. As Christian theologians we are likewise faced with the temptation toward dogmatism. We run the risk of confusing one

---

29. See, for example, Daniel B. Stevick, *Beyond Fundamentalism* (Richmond, Va.: John Knox, 1964), 69.

specific model of reality with reality itself or one theological system with truth itself, thereby "canonizing" a particular theological construct or a specific theologian. Because all systems are models of reality, we must maintain a stance of openness to other models, aware of the tentativeness and incompleteness of all systems. In the final analysis, theology is a human enterprise, helpful for the task of the church, to be sure, but a human construct nevertheless.

Intellectualism. We must also caution ourselves against intellectualism. As Christian theologians we are tempted to see our task as ending with the construction of a theological system. In actuality, devising a "system," however important this may be, is not the ultimate purpose toward which the theologian strives. Rather, we engage in reflection on faith in order that the life of the believer and of the faith community in the world might be served.

Theological reflection ought to make a difference in Christian living. Doctrinal expression is designed to help clarify the ways in which Christian commitment is to be lived. It likewise ought to motivate Christians to live in accordance with their commitment. In short, theology must overflow into ethics. Whenever our theological work stops short of this, we have failed to be obedient to our calling.

Theological Method

As theologian, the goal of our engagement in intellectual reflection on the faith commitment of the believing community is the construction of a model of reality that can foster a truly godly spirituality that translates into ethical living in the social-historical context in which we are to be the people of God. Our task is the conscious reflection—within the context in which we live and minister—on the faith commitment we share as Christians. But how exactly do we engage in this enterprise?

Crucial to the development of a helpful theology is the employment of proper sources for the theological construction and the selection of a valid and beneficial integrative motif around which we delineate our theological system. To these aspects of our theological method we must now turn.

The Sources for Theology

Theology does not arise *sui generis*. Nor do theologians engage in this task without the aid of resources. Rather, each theological system reflects the use of certain norms which function as the specific sources employed by the theologian in carrying out the theological mandate. There is sharp disagreement among theologians, however, as to exactly what sources lie at our disposal. We must set forth our position in this context of loss of unanimity.

The Reformation debate. Although present in the church from the early centuries of the Christian era, the dispute over theological method first became acute during the Reformation. At stake in discussions since the 1500s has been the role of the Bible vis-a-vis other theological resources.

In the Middle Ages one proposal became the standard view in Roman Catholic thinking. This method posited two wellsprings of correct doctrine. The first norm, of course, was the Bible—more specifically, the Bible as canonized by the church and interpreted by the magisterium, the church's teaching office. The second norm was apostolic tradition as handed down through, and even augmented by, the church. These norms formed a twofold source of theological truth.

Foundational to the Protestant Reformation was a strong reaction against the medieval adherence to a twofold source of theology. Standing at the head of this shift in outlook, Martin Luther replaced the older view with a simpler, yet powerful approach focusing on *sola scriptura* ("Scripture alone"): The Scriptures are the sole primary source for theology. Later certain Calvinists, especially the English Puritans, refined Luther's position. The Westminster Confession of Faith, which formed the apex of Puritan efforts to delineate a proper recounting of biblical doctrine, declares that the final authority in the church is "the Holy Spirit speaking in the Scriptures."[30]

Contextualization and experience. The contextual nature of this discipline precludes any suggestion that theology is solely the con-

---

30. "The Westminster Confession of Faith," 1:10, in *Creeds of the Churches*, ed. John H. Leith, third edition (Atlanta: John Knox, 1982), 196.

struction or systematization of truth by appeal to the Bible alone. The process of contextualization requires a movement between at least two poles—the Bible as the source of the good news of God's action in Christ and contemporary culture as the source of at least some of the categories through which the theologian expresses the biblical message. Even though Scripture must remain the primary norm for theological statements, contextualization demands that we take seriously the thought-forms and mindset of the culture in which our theologizing transpires. Only then can we explicate the biblical message in language understandable in our specific setting.

Perhaps the most erudite twentieth century articulation of this modern two-norm approach is the well-known "method of correlation" proposed by Paul Tillich. His approach oscillates between the existential questions posed by philosophy and the revelatory answers set forth by theology. Through careful examination of human existence, theologians employ philosophy in order to raise the grave questions encountered by humans today. Then they draw on the symbols of divine revelation to formulate answers to the questions implied in human existence, which philosophy can discover but cannot answer. According to Tillich, the overall task of the theologian is to bring the questions and answers together in critical correlation.[31] The answers theology presents must be derived from revelation, but they must be expressed in a form which will speak to the existential concerns of human beings. Consequently, the theologian's goal is to articulate the answers of revelation in a manner that remains faithful to the original Christian message while being relevant to the questions asked by the modern, secular mindset.

An alternative to Tillich which has gained recognition in recent years is the so-called "Wesleyan quadrilateral." Theology, its proponents assert, appeals to four sources:[32] Scripture (the Bible as properly exegeted), reason (the findings of science and human reasoning), experience (individual and corporate encounters with life), and tradition (the teachings of the church throughout its histo-

---

31. Paul Tillich, *Systematic Theology*, three volumes (Chicago: University of Chicago Press, 1953), 1:22-28, 59-66.
32. Clark Pinnock, *Tracking the Maze* (San Francisco: Harper and Row, 1990), 170-81.

ry). Although seeing all four as valid, Wesleyans nevertheless tend to elevate one above the others, whether the Bible as the "norming norm"[33] or experience as the ultimate starting point for theological reflection.

The Wesleyan quadrilateral is not without problems. Perhaps its gravest difficulty lies in its appeal to experience as a theological norm separate from the other three. Tillich voiced a telling criticism of any method that elevates experience to normative status. Experience is not the source of theology, he argued, but the medium through which theology's sources are received.[34]

Rather than being its source, experience is in some sense the focus of the theological task. Theology is the reflection on faith, which as an act carrying implications for living is by its own nature experiential. Theologians utilize proper sources in order to construct an interpretive framework to assist in organizing and understanding our experience. Theology, then, is in some sense the critical reflection on Christian experience, for it seeks to account for and describe the encounter with God in accordance with specifically Christian categories.[35]

Carrying this consideration a step farther, we could say that experience cannot form a separate source simply because we never receive experience uninterpreted. It is always filtered by an interpretive framework or world view. In fact, because there is no "pure experience," the framework facilitates the reception of experiences. Hence, experience cannot serve as a source for theology separate from the world view which makes its reception possible.

Experience cannot be a proper source for theology finally, because any appeal to an unreflective individual experience is by its own nature wholly subjective. It lacks any canon by means of which it can be judged, both as to whether it is real or imagined and as to whether it is positive or negative, good or evil. Experience also

---

33. Donald W. Dayton, "The Use of Scripture in the Wesleyan Tradition," in *The Use of the Bible in Theology: Evangelical Options*, ed. Robert K. Johnston (Atlanta: John Knox, 1973), 135.

34. Tillich, *Systematic Theology*, 1:42.

35. For a lengthy discussion of theology as the giving of an account of Christian faith, see Gerhard Ebeling, *Dogmatik des christlichen Glaubens*, three volumes (Tuebingen: J.C.B. Mohr [Paul Siebeck], 1982).

leaves open the question of universalizability: Is such an experience normative for all persons, or is it merely a private, individual phenomenon?

Because we dare not confuse our experience of God with our fellowship with God, the human encounter with God is not the only object of the theologian's inquiry. Even though experience is not a separate norm for theology, it remains relevant to the theological enterprise.[36] Our experience is informative, for it helps us clarify the human relationship to God.

The threefold norm of theology. We conclude that as the attempt to articulate in a specific historical-cultural context the unchanging faith commitment of the church to the God revealed in Jesus Christ the theological task must be carried out with a view in three directions. The three sources or norms for theology are the biblical message, the theological heritage of the church, and the thought-forms of the historical-cultural context in which the contemporary people of God seek to speak, live, and act.[37]

(1) Of primary importance to the theological task is the Bible as canonized by the church. More specifically, the primary norm for theology is the biblical message. As theologians we must look to the *kerygma* as inscripturated in the Bible. Because faith is our response to the God who encounters us in his historical self-disclosure, our theology must take seriously the good news as proclaimed within the context of the ancient cultures. We must look to the trajectory of the proclamation of the story of God's salvific activity within the history of Israel, Jesus, and the infant church.

In complex prolegomena, some theologians preface their systematic-theological constructions with elaborate attempts to establish the resourcefulness of the Bible as the foundation for their dogmatic labors. To this end they argue for the divine nature of Scripture through a series of proofs, including appeals to externally verifiable

---

36. Despite his rejection of experience as a source for theology, Thomas nevertheless acknowledges this point. Owen C. Thomas, "Theology and Experience," *Harvard Theological Review* 78/1-2 (1985): 197.

37. For a similar delineation, see Gabriel Fackre, *The Christian Story* (Grand Rapids: Eerdmans, 1984), 40.

"miracles" (such as fulfilled prophecies) and to the Bible's own claims about itself.

All such attempts to establish the role of Scripture in theology, however, are ultimately unnecessary. In engaging in the theological task, we may simply assume the authority of the Bible on the basis of the integral relationship of theology to the faith community. Because the Bible is the universally-acknowledged foundational document of the Christian church, its message functions as the central norm for the systematic articulation of the faith of that community.

Consequently, the demonstration of the divine authorship of Scripture or its status as revelation need not constitute the prolegomenon to our theology. Sufficient for launching the systematic-theological enterprise is the nature of theology itself as reflection on community faith. And sufficient for the employment of the Bible in this task is its status as the book of the community, the source of the *kerygma*—the gospel proclamation—in the early communities and consequently in the contemporary community.

The Bible functions in the church as the Spirit-produced document through which the Spirit continues to speak. Therefore, we will reserve for pneumatology the fuller development of our doctrine of Scripture and biblical authority. Here we need only offer several remarks concerning the conjunction between theology and revelation.

Theologians have always viewed their discipline as in some way connected to revelation. We may define revelation as the divine act of self-disclosure which makes known God's essential nature. Ultimately, revelation stands at the eschaton, at the grand climax of human history. Nevertheless, the divine self-disclosure is a present reality, for it has appeared proleptically (in the manner of a foretaste) in human history.

Scripture is connected to God's historical revelation. Throughout the biblical era, each succeeding generation of the people of God found themselves confronted anew with the God who discloses himself. The Bible encapsules the foundational witness to God's self-revelation and the record of how the ancient faith communities responded to their awareness that God had acted to constitute them as his covenant people. In this way the biblical documents have functioned as the informing and forming canon for the people of God throughout the generations.

The Christian church, emerging as it did out of the older Hebrew community, was constituted by the events of the biblical narrative, especially the event of the coming of Jesus the Christ. In the New Testament documents the church preserved the memory of those grand foundational events together with the earliest responses to the revelation of God in Christ, which believers understood in the light and context of the Hebrew Scriptures.

The foundation of Christian theology lies in these paradigmatic events and their use in the community of faith as set forth in the Bible. The theologian's task is to assist the contemporary community in its responsibility to be the believing people in the world in which they are called to proclaim and live out the message that God has appeared in Christ for the sake of the salvation of humankind. Theologians facilitate this enterprise by appeal to the faith of the early community as found in the Bible.

The narratives and assertions of the early community as inscripturated in the Bible enjoy what we may call a "regulative" function.[38] The ancient believing community provides a cultural and linguistic framework, a constellation of symbols and concepts, by means of which contemporary members understand their lives and within which they experience their world.[39] Theologians explore, order, and systematize these symbols and concepts into a unified whole— a conceptual framework—for the sake of the community of faith which they serve. By appeal to the biblical documents they investigate the central questions concerning faith in the contemporary world: What does it mean to be the community of those who confess faith in the God revealed in Jesus of Nazareth? And how are we to verbalize and embody that confession in the contemporary context?

(2) Of secondary importance to the theological task is the flow of church history as it describes the conclusions of past theological discussions. The church has continually sought to express its faith in the God revealed in Jesus in the historical and cultural situations in

---

38. Lindbeck, *The Nature of Doctrine*, 18.
39. Ibid., 33.

which it found itself. This tradition remains significant for theologians today.

Past theological statements remain important insofar as they are instructive in our quest for a relevant theology. By reminding us of previous attempts to fulfill the theological mandate, they alert us to some of the pitfalls to avoid, and they point out some of the directions that might hold promise for our attempts to engage in the theological calling in the present.

Certain past formulations carry special significance, in that they have withstood the test of time. As "classic" statements of theological truth—milestones in the history of the theology of the church—these expressions have a special relevance for every age. We engage in the second order task known as theology as members of a community of faith that spans the centuries. Because we desire to participate in the one church of Jesus Christ—that is, to retain continuity with the entire body of the people of God—we must take seriously what has become the doctrine of the church throughout the ages. This doctrine is expressed in those formulations that have gained broad acknowledgement among Christians of many generations. It is likewise couched in the great theological literature of the centuries, which we therefore can read with profit in the contemporary situation.

Of course, past creeds and confessions of faith are not binding in and of themselves.[40] They must be tested by the Scriptures and by their applicability to our cultural situation. Nevertheless, the doctrinal statements that have withstood the test of time provide insight into the content of the beliefs of the church. They are valuable, however, only as we understand them within their historical and philosophical contexts. The intent of a creed, not its specific wording, is significant for contemporary theology. As Richard Muller notes,

> The history of Christian doctrine... ought not to be reduced to a
> list of formulae to be memorized for the sake of avoiding heresy. The
> issue in studying the formulae is to understand their interpretive rela-

---

40. Among evangelicals, Baptists have been an important voice in struggling with the problems surrounding creedalism. This denomination has generally stood against elevating any creed to binding authority.

tionship to the Christian message and the way in which they have served in particular historical contexts to convey that message and, in addition, to preserve it into the future.[41]

(3) Theology's tertiary source lies in the thought-forms of contemporary culture. Theologians have repeatedly looked to the categories of society for the concepts in which to express their understanding of the Christian faith commitment.[42] This task continues today.

Theology entails reflecting on Christian faith commitment in the world in which the church is called to live as the people of God. To fulfill this mandate—to speak in a manner understandable to contemporary society—theologians have an ongoing task of listening to culture.[43] Only by so doing are we able to construct theologies which can assist the church in expressing its world view in current thought-forms and in addressing current problems and outlooks. Likewise, if theology is to be truly systematic and meaningful, theologians must take into consideration the discoveries and insights of the various disciplines of human learning and seek to show the relevance of Christian faith for the human quest for truth.

Above all, however, the historical-cultural context of the faith community performs a crucial function for theology, especially in the matter that lies at the heart of theological reflection, identity formation.[44] The social community in which the people of God participate contains its own cognitive tools—language, symbols, myths, and outlooks toward the world—that facilitate identity formation

---

41. Muller, *The Study of Theology*, 114-15.

42. For example, theological explanations concerning the work of Christ have drawn from sociological and political realities of the surrounding culture. Hence, as Anselm so keenly noticed, the new feudalism of the early Middle Ages demanded a replacement of the older ransom theory of atonement (Christ was our ransom from the devil) to the newer satisfaction theory (Christ's death was a satisfaction offered for the honor of God offended by our sin). Later, when feudal society flowed into the era of national governments, the satisfaction theory gave place to the penal-substitution understanding (which views Christ as paying the penalty at God's bar of justice due us as offenders of the divine law). See Robert S. Paul, *The Atonement and the Sacraments* (New York: Abingdon, 1960), 66-72, 91-109.

43. For a discussion of theological use and study of culture, see Robert J. Schreiter, *Constructing Local Theologies* (Maryknoll, N.Y.: Orbis, 1985), 39-74.

44. For one evangelical attempt to take seriously the contribution of culture, see Richard J. Gehman, "Guidelines in Contextualization," *East Africa Journal of Evangelical Theology* 2/1 (1983): 29-30.

and the experience of reality. The message of the action of God in Christ is concerned with the creation of a new identity, namely, the redeemed person participating in the reconciled society, enjoying fellowship with all creation and with the Creator.

In order to facilitate the church in addressing this gospel message to the perceived aspirations of people, theologians must understand the identity-forming and experience-facilitating concepts of contemporary society. We must pay attention to the forces that shape identity in culture. We must listen intently to the ways in which our culture seeks to express the human drive toward identity-in-community. Thereby we can more capably reflect on the Christian faith commitment in order to sharpen its relevancy for the contemporary setting.

In summary, then, enroute toward the fulfillment of our mandate we must keep in proper balance the norms of *kerygma*, heritage, and culture. Although we can discuss them in isolation from each other, within the context of the theological enterprise the three are interrelated. As theologians we express the faith of the people of God by looking to the *kerygma*, the heritage of the church, and the contemporary cultural situation of the faith community. Our task is to articulate the biblical faith in continuity with the theological heritage of the church and through various cultural or philosophic forms in such a way that the message of the Bible and the faith of the one people of God comes to understanding in the present.

The Integrative Motif of Theology

In addition to working from specific sources, systematic theologians often order their presentation of the Christian faith around what we may call an "integrative motif." This concept serves as a systematic theology's central organizational feature, the theme around which it is structured. Such a motif is "integrative" in that it focuses the issues discussed and illumines the formulations of the responses to these issues. In short, the integrative motif is the central idea that provides the thematic perspective in light of which all other theological concepts are understood and given their relative meaning or value.[45]

45. Gerhard Sauter and Alex Stock, *Arbeitswesen Systematischer Theologie: Eine Anleitung* (Munich: Kaiser, 1976), 18-19.

Representative alternatives. Theological history has witnessed the devising of many integrative motifs. The great systematizer of the medieval church, Thomas Aquinas, for example, constructed his theology around the concept of the vision of God as the *telos* of the human person. Martin Luther's thinking revolved around justification by faith: The fundamental human quest for right standing before God finds its answer in the divine declaration of righteousness bestowed by grace on the sinner who receives God's provision by faith. The other great seminal theologian of the Reformation, John Calvin, focused his theological work on the glory of God: All of history and even our future eternity itself are the outworking of the decision God made before the creation of the world which in turn directs all events to the glorification of God. We could cite additional examples. John Wesley was captivated by the idea of responsible grace.[46] Friedrich Schleiermacher reflected on human religious experience. And Karl Barth centered on the nature of revelation, the self-disclosure of the triune God to the human person.

In the 1900s, thinkers proposed several possibilities. Certain fundamentalists and evangelicals looked to the dispensations of salvation history[47] or to the doctrine of Scripture as their unifying theological theme.[48] In mainline theological circles, the idea of process as derived from the philosophy of Alfred North Whitehead became highly influential.[49] Among the most widely employed themes in the 1970s and 1980s was that of liberation. Originally sounded within black theology in the United States[50] and in Latin American liberation theology,[51] its use quickly spread to thinkers in other groups. A related movement, feminist theology, utilizes the experience of women as the organizing principle for theological reflection.[52] More recently, narrative theology, which emphasizes

---

46. This theme is proposed by Randy L. Maddox, "Responsible Grace: The Systematic Perspective of Wesleyan Theology," *Wesleyan Theological Journal* 19/2 (Fall 1984): 12-18.

47. Lewis Sperry Chafer, *Systematic Theology*, eight volumes (Dallas, Tex.: Dallas Seminary Press, 1947-48).

48. Hence, Erickson, *Christian Theology*.

49. Marjorie Hewitt Suchocki, *God, Christ, Church* (New York: Crossroad, 1984). See also John Cobb, Jr., *A Christian Natural Theology* (Philadelphia: Westminster, 1965).

50. James H. Cone, *A Black Theology of Liberation* (Philadelphia: J. B. Lippincott, 1970).

51. Gustavo Gutierrez, *A Theology of Liberation* (Maryknoll, N. Y.: Orbis, 1980).

52. See, for example, Rosemary Radford Ruether, *Sexism and God Talk* (Boston: Beacon, 1983).

personal histories and the Bible as story, has gained attention even among conservatives.[53]

The kingdom of God. No theme has been as widely employed since the 1800s, however, as the concept of the kingdom of God.[54] Its broad acceptance is understandable, because the concept is readily visible in theology's foundational sources. The kingdom of God is a central theme in the synoptic gospels, which characterize Jesus' ministry as arising out of the expectations that developed during the Old Testament era of a coming divine reign. Throughout its history the church has employed the kingdom concept to express its understanding of the significance of Christian faith. And the theme has been used widely in contemporary theology,[55] for it offers important points of contact with the hopes of modernity.

Although a full delineation of the concept must wait until the ecclesiology section, a short definition is helpful here. The kingdom of God is that order of perfect peace, righteousness, justice, and love that God gives to the world. This gift is eschatological, for it comes in an ultimate way only at the renewal of the world consummated at Jesus' return. But the power of the kingdom is already at work, for it breaks into the present from the future. Therefore, we can experience the kingdom in a partial yet vital manner enroute to the great future day.

The most important contribution of kingdom theology is its orientation toward the future.[56] The concept of the kingdom of God reminds us that ultimately we engage in the theological task—we address theological questions—from the vantage point of the con-

---

53. George W. Stroup, *The Promise of Narrative Theology* (Atlanta: John Knox, 1973). See also Michael Goldberg, *Theology and Narrative* (Nashville: Abingdon, 1982); Gabriel Fackre, *The Christian Story* (Grand Rapids: Eerdmans, 1984).

54. As an example of the widespread influence of this concept, see the recently published doctrinal dissertation of the general secretary of the World Council of Churches, Emilio Castro, *Freedom in Mission: The Perspectives of the Kingdom of God—An Ecumenical Inquiry* (Geneva: World Council of Churches Publications, 1985).

55. The use of the concept of the kingdom has come under attack as being unreconcilable with the concerns of feminist theology. For a response, see Mortimer Arias, *Announcing the Reign of God* (Philadelphia: Fortress, 1984), xvi.

56. In recent years Moltmann and Pannenberg have been influential in focusing attention on the eschatological orientation of the kingdom. See Juergen Moltmann, *Theology of Hope* (New York: Harper and Row, 1965); Wolfhart Pannenberg, *Theology and the Kingdom of God* (Philadelphia: Westminster, 1969).

summation of God's activity in establishing his will and program for the world. In the chapters that follow we will seek to explore theology from this eschatological perspective. In our theological reflection, we will employ the concept of the eschatological kingdom, understood as God's ultimate goal for creation which is both the future of the world and is partially present now.

The community of God. Despite the appropriateness of the kingdom concept, alone it is insufficient to provide the integrative motif for theology. The focus on the kingdom raises a foundational question which it cannot answer: What is the divine reign that is coming and is already present among us? What is the world like when it is transformed by the in-breaking of the kingdom? Because the concept does not embody a complete and satisfactory answer to these questions, contemporary kingdom theologies have readily been seduced by the radical individualism of the modern era.

The modern Western fascination with individualism, however, is waning, especially within the human sciences. Many thinkers are realizing that our understanding of the human phenomenon must reflect a more adequate balance between its individual and social dimensions.[57] This awareness has led to the development of a new model of the relationship between the individual and society called "communalism," "communitarianism," or "culturalism."[58]

Communalists emphasize the importance of the social unit—the community—for crucial aspects of human living. Community is integral to epistemology, for example. Central to the knowing process is a cognitive framework mediated to the individual by the community in which one participates. Similarly, community is crucial to identity formation. Our sense of personal identity develops through the telling of a personal narrative, which, communalists declare, is always embedded in the story of the communities in which we live.[59]

---

57. Daniel A. Helminiak, "Human Solidarity and Collective Union in Christ," *Anglican Theological Review* 70/1 (January 1988): 37.

58. "Culturalism" is the term preferred by critic of the movement Robert J. McShea, *Morality and Human Nature: A New Route to Ethical Theory* (Philadelphia: Temple University Press, 1990), 89-148.

59. See, for example, Alisdair MacIntyre, *After Virtue*, second edition (Notre Dame: University of Notre Dame Press, 1984), 221.

Traditions mediated by communities, and not individuals, they argue, are the carriers of rationality. The community mediates to us the transcending story by means of which our personal narrative makes sense.

The larger community story also transmits traditions of virtue, common good, and ultimate meaning.[60] In this way, the community is crucial to the sustaining of character, virtue, and values. And it provides the necessary foundation for involvement in public discourse concerning matters of world view. Thereby the community of meaning contributes to the well-being of the broader society.

"Community" is important as an integrative motif for theology not only because it fits with contemporary thinking, but more importantly because it is central to the message of the Bible. From the narratives of the primordial garden which open the curtain on the biblical story to the vision of white-robed multitudes inhabiting the new earth with which it concludes, the drama of the Scriptures speaks of community. Taken as a whole the Bible asserts that God's program is directed to the bringing into being of community in the highest sense—a reconciled people, living within a renewed creation, and enjoying the presence of their Redeemer.

The eschatological community. In the following chapters we will add to the older motif of the kingdom of God the newer concern for community. Putting these two themes together yields as the integrative motif for our systematic theology the concept of "the eschatological community."

The kingdom dimension reminds us of the biblical assumption that history is meaningful. History is directed toward a goal—the kingdom of God or the presence of the will of God throughout the earth (Matt. 6:10). The concept of community fills the idea of the kingdom of God with its proper content. When God's rule is present—when God's will is done—community emerges. Or viewed from the opposite direction, in the emergence of community, God's rule is present and God's will is accomplished. We will explore this dialectic of kingdom and community as brought together by the concept of the eschatological community of God. This concept—the es-

---

60. E.g., Lindbeck, *The Nature of Doctrine*, 495.

chatological community—will function as the organizing principle governing our outline of Christian theology.

The Structure of the Theological System

In keeping with the classical confessional statements such as the Apostles' Creed, our systematic theology will follow a trinitarian structure. This approach is appropriate. As we have noted, because theology presupposes the presence of faith the theological enterprise develops from within the context of belief and the believing community. The faith presupposed by Christian theology is inherently trinitarian.

Our discussion, therefore, opens with the central doctrine of the Christian faith—God as the Trinity (theology proper). Here we explore the nature of the God whose goal is the establishment of the eschatological community. Standing in relationship with the sovereign, community-building God are God's moral creatures. The discussion of who we are as those God has designed and destined for community forms the subject of the second part (anthropology).

Part 3 focuses on the Second Person of the Trinity, Jesus the Christ (Christology). In this section we reflect on what it means to confess that this man Jesus is the eternal Son whose earthly vocation was to initiate community between God and sinful humans.

In part 4 (pneumatology) the Third Person of the Trinity, the Holy Spirit, comes into our purview. We explore the person of the Spirit followed by his work in Scripture and his role in effecting personal salvation understood in terms of community with God and others. Parts 5 (ecclesiology) and 6 (eschatology) view the Spirit's corporate and consummative work. In these chapters, we explore the activity of the Holy Spirit as God at work establishing community in history and ultimately in eternity, which is the divine goal for creation.

Theology and Ethics

The central task of the theologian is that of employing the theological sources in order to set forth a systematic reflection on, or articulation of Christian faith. But a systematic delineation of Christian doctrine is not the ultimate goal of the theologian's activities. To construction we must add application. Theological commitment must be applied to life—to the theologian's own Christian walk and to the life of the church—in order that faith can issue forth in discipleship.

The application of Christian commitment to life situations, therefore, likewise belongs to our activity as Christian theologians. At the same time, however, this application is the specific task of Christian ethics, which is an extension of the theological discipline. For this reason, the complete systematic discussion of the application of the Christian belief system to individual, corporate, and public life lies beyond the confines of this volume.

Part 1
Theology
The Doctrine of God

The first major affirmation of the Christian faith is our acknowledgment of God. Therefore the first focus of our systematic theology is the doctrine of God, the exploration of the reality of the God whom we have come to know in Jesus Christ. The delineation of the doctrine of God most suitably carries the title "theology," for this term connotes "the word concerning" or "the study of God" (*logos* + *theos*). For this reason, the doctrine of God is sometimes referred to as "theology proper."

Our construction of the doctrine begins with the foundational questions as to whether there is indeed a reality that corresponds to our word "God" and whether we can know this God (chapter 1). We examine the Christian testimony that we have come to know the true God, in that this God has given himself to be known. And we explore the Christian assertion that our acknowledgment of God illumines our experience of reality.

After setting forth the credibility of the Christian claim that we can know the God who is, we turn our attention to the major task of our doctrine of God. Our goal is to describe the one whom we have come to know in Jesus. We seek to declare what this God is like and how God relates to the world. Our description begins with the triune life of the God revealed in Christ (chapter 2). We conclude that the God we know is none other than the Triune One, the eternal community of Father, Son, and Holy Spirit, and consequently the God who is love.

Our study then moves to the character of the triune God (chapter 3). Because he is three-in-one, the God we know is internally and externally relational. On this basis we seek to understand God as the incomprehensible, self-determining, and free Person; the living Spirit who is the source of life; and the faithful "I Am," "the One who will be."

Our doctrine of God concludes with an examination of God's relationship to the world (chapter 4). According to Christian theology, the God we know is the Creator of the world. He orders all history toward his purpose. God directs his activities toward the establishment of community, which will be present in its fullness when God's sovereignty is fully displayed. This description forms the link to the second part of our systematic theology, anthropology, for it leads to the conclusion that creation derives its meaning from this purpose of the Creator as revealed in Jesus Christ.

The God Who Is

And without faith it is impossible to please God, because anyone who comes to him must believe that he exists and that he rewards those who earnestly seek him. (Heb. 11:6)

Outline

Knowledge of God in an Era of Agnosticism
   The Claim to Know God and Intellectual Agnosticism
      Epistemological agnosticism
      Logical positivism
      Agnosticism and the Incomprehensible God
   The Means to Knowledge of God
      Knowledge of God through reason
      Knowledge of God through religious experience
      Knowledge of God through God's self-revelation
   Knowing God
      Knowing God as subject
      Knowing God in history
      Knowing God and the concept of community

Foundational to our entire world view is our testimony that we have come to know the only true God. We understand ourselves, our experience, and even the world itself from the perspective of our acknowledgment of the God who chooses to be known by his creatures. This fundamental confession has marked the people of faith throughout history. Therefore, as we order our lives by means of reference to God we are linked with the faith community that spans the generations.

Despite its antiquity, our Christian confession does not enjoy universal acceptance. For this reason, before launching into our systematic presentation of the nature of the God in whom we have placed our trust (our doctrine of God), we must inquire into the possibility of faith. Our exploration will focus on two historically important questions which remain controversial today: Is there a God? And can humans know God? Our positive responses to these questions lie at the foundation of the construction of our systematic theology.

While logically separable, the discussion as to whether God is and whether God is knowable cannot be divided. If God existed but were not knowable, faith in him would be irrelevant to our lives. Conversely, the experience of knowing God, more so than any intellectual argument, confirms our claim that God exists.

The Reality of God in an Era of Atheism

God's existence is foundational to the faith of the Christian community. But God's reality is not self-evident. In fact, belief in God has come under attack from many quarters in the modern era. Many critics claim that God's existence is incompatible with empirical observations which confirm either the blindness and randomness of the natural forces that shape our universe or the presence of evil in the world. Others dismiss the God-hypothesis as philosophically suspect, being incompatible with human freedom[1] or linguistically nonsensical.[2]

Human questioning of the reality of God is not new. Already in the Old Testament wisdom literature we find evidence of the presence of this question among the thinkers of the ancient societies. The Book of Psalms, for example, tackles the problem head-on: "The fool has said . . . there is no God" (Ps. 14:1; 53:1). Yet, we ought not to equate the position of the ancient "fool" with the intellectual atheism of modern Western philosophy. The modern variety simply was not an option in the ancient Near East. The skepticism spoken of by the Psalmist did not focus on the intellectual, but on the moral or practical denial of God's existence; the fool *lived* as if there were no God.[3]

While many people today continue to live in accordance with the practical atheism of the ancient "fool," intellectual atheism has exercised a more visible influence on the Western philosophical climate. In the face of this challenge we boldly testify that "God is." We begin our quest for the foundation of our confession with an exploration of the historical trajectory that led to the modern atheistic challenge.

---

1. This is the case with atheistic existentialist philosophers. For a discussion, see Wolfhart Pannenberg, "Speaking of God in the face of Atheist Criticism," in *The Idea of God and Human Freedom*, trans. R. A. Wilson (Philadelphia: Westminster, 1973), 106.

2. Carnap, for example, asserts that in its metaphysical use, the word "God" is meaningless. Rudolf Carnap, "The Elimination of Metaphysics through Logical Analysis of Language," in *Logical Positivism*, ed. A. J. Ayer (New York: Free Press, 1959), 66-67.

3. Ludwig Kohler, *Old Testament Theology*, trans. H.A.S. Todd (Philadelphia: Westminister, 1957).

In the Era of the Bible: Which God?

Ironically, first century Christians were subjected to charges of atheism. Not only did their loyalty to Jesus preclude them from worshiping the gods of Rome, they denied the existence of the pagan pantheon (1 Cor. 8:5-6). As the accusation against the early believers indicates, the modern intellectual probing of the question, "Does God exist?" was not the primary debate in the ancient world. Instead, the biblical era was characterized by conflicts among rival tribal gods. The question of God's existence focused on determining which god was worthy of homage and service.[4]

The rivalry of the gods. The people of the ancient Near East venerated many localized, tribal gods. Further, they believed that events in the world revealed the relative strength of the various tribal deities. The strong god was the one who could perform mighty acts.

In keeping with the ancient understanding, the book of Exodus presents the plagues as signs indicating that Yahweh was stronger than the Egyptian gods; Israel's God could do wonders which the deities of Egypt could not imitate.[5] Israel's deliverance at the Red Sea became a further sign of Yahweh's power (Ex. 15:11-16). Forty years later Yahweh parted the waters of the Jordan River so that the children of Israel could enter the land of Canaan. This demonstration of power struck terror in the hearts of the Canaanites (Joshua 5:1). At a subsequent low point in Israel's history, Yahweh vindicated himself and his prophet Elijah on Mount Carmel (1 Kings 18).

To the ancient peoples one mighty act stood above all others, the provision of victory in battle.[6] They viewed military conflicts not merely as contests of rival armies, but as struggles between rival deities. A successful military venture evidenced the triumph

---

4. For a discussion of the development of the Israelite concept of monotheism, see Walther Eichrodt, *Theology of the Old Testament*, trans. J. A. Baker, two volumes (Philadelphia: Westminster, 1961), 1:220-27.

5. Elmer A. Martens, *God's Design: A Focus on Old Testament Theology* (Grand Rapids: Baker, 1981), 43.

6. Ibid., 41.

of the god of the conquering tribe, who by providing this victory had proven himself stronger than the deity worshiped by the defeated people. Hence, when the army of Assyria surrounded Jerusalem, the invading general taunted not only Israel but also their God, as he recounted the inability of the gods of the nations to protect them from the advancing conquerors (2 Kings 18:32-35).

This criterion, the provision of success in battle, led to a crisis when foreigners devastated the kingdoms of Israel and Judah. In response, however, the prophets offered an innovative claim: These defeats were not indications that Yahweh was unable to protect his own, but signs of his judgment on their sin.[7]

In the Old Testament, the determination that Yahweh was the true God led to an aversion against paying homage to any other god. The prophets declared that if Yahweh is indeed mightier than all rivals—if he is the God Almighty—then he alone is worthy of worship.[8] Their claim concerning the exalted status of the God of Israel motivated the prophets to speak out relentlessly against idolatry in the land. This critique was eventually successful, for the exiles who returned from captivity in Babylon were uncompromisingly monotheists. Only one God, Yahweh, was to be worshiped.[9]

The universality of God. Not only did the Old Testament respond to the problem of the gods, the prophets of Judah posed another far-reaching question: Is Yahweh merely Israel's tribal god, or is he also the God of all humankind? This issue carried far-reaching theological significance. Could only Israel worship Yahweh? Or was their God the only true God, so that all the nations of the earth should join in the worship of the Holy One of Israel?[10]

Although this burning issue was not resolved until the New Testament, the prophets anticipated the final answer. Zechariah,

---

7. Ibid., 197.
8. Ibid., 213-15.
9. Eichrodt, *Theology of the Old Testament*, 1:226-27.
10. Ibid., 219-21.

for example, pointed to a day when all nations would worship in Jerusalem (Zech. 14:16). His vision employed apocalyptic imagery to assert that Yahweh was the universal God and therefore to be worshiped by all the peoples of the earth.

The early church inherited the debate concerning the universality of God. At the Jerusalem council (Acts 15) the inclusivists won a decisive battle. The church leaders concluded that Gentiles need not become Jews in order to join the community of faith. The writers of the New Testament confirmed the Jerusalem decision. Paul, for example, declared that through Jesus Christ we know that there is only one God, who is God over all. The idols worshiped by other peoples are nothing (1 Cor. 8:4-7) or even demonic (1 Cor. 10:18-22).

In this manner, the ancient form of the query concerning the divine reality found its solution. The biblical community of faith responded to the question by affirming the supremacy and universality of Yahweh, the God of the patriarchs and the Father of Jesus Christ. He alone is worthy of worship throughout the entire world.

In the Christian Era: Does God Exist?

As the church expanded into the world dominated by Greek culture, the form of the question concerning God came to be altered. The older theological problem—Which tribal god is stronger and therefore to be worshiped?—became the intellectual question concerning the existence of God.

This change was a result of contact with the Greek philosophical tradition. The philosophers had embraced a type of monotheism, for they acknowledged a creator God beyond the pantheon the people worshiped. The proclamation of the gospel within this intellectual context raised the question of the relationship between the God of the Christians and the First Cause of the world whom the Greek thinkers acknowledged. In response to this new challenge, many Christian thinkers wedded the gospel with the theism of the philosophers. To facilitate this, they carved out a new, philosophical approach to theology.

In addition to espousing a type of monotheism, the Greek philosophers focused their attention on intellectual argumentation. They debated the possibility of setting forth intellectual proofs for theological beliefs, including the existence of the one, creator God, the First Cause. Christian thinkers adapted this concern. In the new setting the ancient question concerning the divine reality assumed the form of intellectual demonstrations of God's existence.

Initially the arguments Christian philosophers devised were not merely apologetic devices aimed against unbelief. More importantly, they provided intellectual confirmation of, and support for the faith stance that preceded intellectual reflection. Hence, Anselm of Canterbury could echo Augustine's famous dictum, "I do not seek to understand that I may believe, but I believe in order to understand."[11] However, with the pursuit of an intellectual demonstration of God's existence came the opposite possibility, that of skepticism and even atheism. When this occurred, the proofs devised by Christian philosophical theologians traded their catechetical intent for an apologetic purpose. "Faith seeking understanding" was replaced by an understanding that provided the prerequisite for faith. Beginning with the Middle Ages and into the Enlightenment, Christian thinkers developed three basic types of theistic proofs.

The ontological argument. A first group seeks to prove that God exists *a priori*, that is, independently of, or prior to our experience of the world. This proof is also called "ontological," because it claims to demonstrate God's existence by means of a consideration of the mere idea of God. Ontological proofs begin with a commonly-held definition and show that by necessity the God who corresponds to the definition must exist. Each of the two "classic" formulations, those of Anselm of Canterbury (AD 1033-

---

11. Anselm, *Proslogium,* in *St. Anselm: Basic Writings,* trans. S. N. Deane, second edition (La Salle, Ill.: Open Court, 1962), 7.

1109) and of the French philosopher Descartes (1596-1650), claim that by definition God cannot merely be an idea in human minds but must also exist in reality.

Anselm defined God as "that than which no greater can be conceived."[12] Either God exists only in human minds or he exists both in human minds and in reality. If we conceive of God as existing only in our minds and not in reality, this God is not "that than which no greater can be conceived," for we could conceive of a God that exists both in minds and in reality. The God who exists both mentally and actually is obviously greater than the God who exists only in our minds.

In his Fifth Meditation, Descartes argued from a somewhat similar definition, namely, God as the "supremely perfect Being."[13] If God does not exist in reality, he lacks one perfection, namely, existence. Hence, the God so conceived—as not existing in reality—is not the most perfect being.

Despite the erudition of its proponents, many philosophers reject the ontological argument. The medieval theologian Thomas Aquinas (1225-74), repudiated Anselm's presentation because it is *a priori*.[14] According to Thomas, no knowledge (hence, no knowledge of God) can arise apart from experience of the world, thus the Thomist adage, "there is nothing in the mind that is not first in the senses."[15]

The Lutheran philosopher, Immanuel Kant (1724-1804), responded to Descartes's formulation. Kant asserted that the ontological argument is invalid because it falsely presuppposes that existence is an attribute (or a "predicate"). Proponents of the ontological argument overlook an important quirk in language, he said. Words like "exists" and "is" function *grammatically* as predicates (the statement "God is" is grammatically valid). Yet they

---

12. Ibid., 8.

13. Rene Descartes, *Discourse on Method and The Meditations*, trans. Laurence J. Lafleur, Library of Liberal Arts edition (Indianapolis: Bobbs-Merrill, 1960), 120.

14. Thomas Aquinas, *Summa Theologica* 1.2.1, in *Introduction to St. Thomas Aquinas*, ed. Anton C. Pegis (New York: Modern Library, 1948), 22.

15. Maurice de Wulf, *The System of Thomas Aquinas* (New York: Dover, 1959), 22.

cannot function *logically* in this way. We add no new element to our knowledge when in enumerating the attributes of any object (including God), we add, "and this object exists."[16]

The cosmological and teleological arguments. The second type of philosophical proof seeks to demonstrate the existence of God *a posteriori*, that is, by drawing on evidence provided by sense experience. *A posteriori* proofs move from our empirical observations to the supposition of God as the one who lies behind the world. Some proofs purport to demonstrate that God must exist as the ultimate cause of the world (cosmological arguments). Others claim that God must exist as the cause of some aspect we observe in the natural world, most generally its apparent design or order (teleological arguments).

Thomas Aquinas developed a series of *a posteriori* arguments, often called "the five ways." These move from the empirical characteristics of the natural world to God as the cause of each aspect of creation. Creation is "moved" (in motion); God is the first mover. Creation is an effect which must have a cause; God is its first efficient cause. Creation is non-necessary (It need not exist); God has his own necessity and is the cause of the necessity of the world. Creation is gradated (Its various aspects are of varying value and good); God is the highest good or value to which this gradation points and is the cause of the relative perfection found in the things. Finally, creation is ordered (directed to an end or goal); God is the one who directs all natural things to their goal.[17]

Building on the post-Newtonian scientific outlook, William Paley (1743-1805) articulated a different teleological argument. He employed the widely-known analogy from the mechanistic watch. Just as this precise mechanical instrument proclaims the existence of the watchmaker, so also the design and intricate construction of the natural world gives witness to the existence of its Architect.[18]

---

16. Immanuel Kant, *Critique of Pure Reason*, trans. Norman Kemp Smith (New York: St. Martins, 1965), 500-506.

17. Thomas Aquinas, *Summa Theologica* 1.2.3, in *Introduction to St. Thomas Aquinas*, 24-27.

The validity of the *a posteriori* proofs is likewise contested. The British empiricist David Hume (1711-1776), for example, rejected all such arguments. He noted that all assertions must be based on empirical evidence. Sense experience, however, provides no direct knowledge or analogies concerning God's causation of the world. Consequently, we have no rational justification for extending the principle of cause and effect to God's relationship to the universe. In fact, Hume added, the connection of cause and effect is itself a human convention and not directly observable even in the natural world.[19]

Immanuel Kant built on Hume's argument. Causality, he argued, is one of the concepts within the structure of the human mind that make experience possible. It is one of the ways in which the mind organizes sense experience. Consequently, such concepts can have no bearing on objects which lie outside the realm of possible sense experience. Thus, it is inappropriate to talk about causality with respect to God's relationship to the world.[20]

The moral argument. A third philosophical proof begins with the human experience of being a moral creature. Kant offered a classic formulation of this approach. Each human being, he noted, lives with a sense of duty. Kant did not mean that all humans share a specific moral code, but that behind the various codes humans devise is a common feeling of being morally conditioned. God must exist, he concluded, if this experience of moral obligation is to have any meaning. In a truly moral universe virtuous conduct must be rewarded and wrongdoing must be punished. This requires a supreme power who guarantees the ultimate moral outcome.[21]

Hastings Rashdall (1858-1924) devised a somewhat different formulation of the moral proof. Ideals—standards and goals to-

18. William Paley. *Natural Theology* (New York: American Tract Society, n.d.), chapters 1-6.

19. David Hume, *Dialogues Concerning Natural Religion*, ed. Henry D. Aiken (New York: Hafner, 1969), 15-25, 47-56.

20. Kant, *Critique of Pure Reason*, 507-24.

21. Immanuel Kant, *Critique of Practical Reason*, trans. Lewis White Beck (Indianapolis: Bobs Merrill, 1956), 114-15, 126-139.

ward which people strive—exist only in minds, he noted. Certain ideals are absolute. These can exist only in a mind which is adequate for them, namely, in an absolute or divine mind.[22]

Like the other philosophical arguments the proofs from morality do not command universal reception. One critic, the French existentialist Jean-Paul Sartre (1905-1980), asserted that the world is devoid of any objective meaning or value. All that we have is individual existence. Any meaning, value, or essence in the world arises through the choices and commitments a person makes.[23]

Bertrand Russell (1882-1970) rejected the moral proof through an appeal to the concept of "value judgments." Any assertion of the form "X is good" is merely a statement about the speaker's personal perception, disposition, or desire. Consequently, all moral statements are purely individual, subjective, and relative.[24]

The Rise of Intellectual Atheism

In the Middle Ages the debate concerning the validity of the philosophical proofs was largely an intramural discussion among Christian theologians. In the post-Enlightenment context, however, the discussion shifted in focus, becoming a contest between belief and unbelief. This shift was indicative of a broader change within the cultural context in the West. As the modern era unfolded, Christians began to face the growing challenge of intellectual atheism with its philosophical denial of God.

Modern atheism asserts that the Christian postulate of God lacks intellectual credence. Although a recent phenomenon, its roots lie early in the history of the Western world. The door was opened when the Christian apologists linked Yahweh, the God of

---

22. Hastings Rashdall, *The Theory of Good and Evil*, two volumes (Oxford: Clarendon, 1907). 2:189-246.

23. Jean-Paul Sartre. "Existentialism," in *Existentialism and Human Emotions*, trans. Bernard Frechtman (New York: Philosophical Library, 1957), 15.

24. Bertrand Russell and F. C. Coppleston, "The Existence of God: A Debate between Bertrand Russell and Father F. C. Coppleston," in Bertrand Russell, *On God and Religion*, ed. Al Seckel (Buffalo, N.Y.: Prometheus Books, 1986), 123-46.

salvation history, with the First Cause of the world so important to the Greek philosophers. While bringing certain advantages, this link posed a danger. When thinkers began to question the necessity of postulating the existence of a First Cause in order to explain the world, they quite naturally also rejected the existence of the Christian God whom theologians declared to be the First Cause.

The intellectual rejection of the postulate of God emerged through several phases.

The critique of the First Cause. The foundational phase occurred beginning in the late Middle Ages and into the Enlightenment. During this era thinkers no longer found it necessary to appeal to God's existence in order to explain the physical world.

The medieval model of physics followed closely the thinking of ancient Greece. They explained the phenomenon of motion in the present ultimately by appeal to God as the ultimate cause of all movement. William of Ockham, however, perceived that the idea of first cause actually should be divided into two aspects, the original cause of the coming into being of all things and the agent ultimately responsible for maintaining motion in the present.[25] Ockham then denied the necessity of an eternally existing first cause in the temporal sense. Just as a human being today is generated from non-eternal human parents, he argued, so also the first creature in the temporal sequence of the world could have been generated from a non-eternal source.[26]

Isaac Newton's discovery of the law of inertia eliminated the other dimension of the idea of a first cause, God as the one who maintains motion in the present. According to this principle, unless acted upon by some other force each body will persist in its current state. But this means that once the universe was set in motion the need for God as the cause of motion ceased.

---

25. This characterization is based on Pannenberg, "Anthropology and the Question of God," in *The Idea of God and Human Freedom*, 82-83.
26. Ibid., 82.

From this point on, physics no longer required the postulate of God. Because scientists could explain the physical world without recourse to a divine agency, the supposition of God had become superfluous to their intellectual endeavor. Indicative of the new reality was the response of Pierre Laplace (1749-1827) to the complaint from Napoleon that his book on celestial mechanics contained no mention of God. The scientist boldly asserted, "Sire, I have no need of that hypothesis."[27]

The critique of the concept of God. The intellectual rejection of God was abetted through a second phase which entailed the questioning of the traditional concept of God.

The nineteenth century German philosopher, Johann Gottlieb Fichte (1762-1814), claimed that the Christian idea that God is a personal, infinite being is self-contradictory. To speak of God as a being, he noted, is tied to the notion of "substance." All substances exist in space. But placing God in space contradicts one of the crucial attributes of God, his infinity. Fichte noted that the same contradiction arises when we talk of God as person. Personhood entails being an "I" in contrast to other "I's." To assert God is a person, therefore, means to define God in contrast to other persons. But this denies God's infinity.[28]

The elimination of the idea of God. With the postulate of God eradicated from the realm of physics and the traditional concept of God under attack, thinkers in the third phase of the development of atheism sought to eliminate the concept of God.

In his book *The Essence of Christianity* (1841), Ludwig Feuerbach (1804-1872) determined to obliterate the postulate of God by explaining psychologically how this idea originally arose in the human psyche. Humankind is in actuality infinite, he ar-

---

27. Roger Hahn, "Laplace and the Mechanistic Universe," in *God and Nature: Historical Essays on the Encounter between Christianity and Science*, ed. David Clindberg and Ronald L. Numbers (Berkeley: University of California Press, 1986), 256.

28. Johann Gottlieb Fichte, "Ueber den Grund unseres Glaubes an eine goettliche Weltregierung," pp. 16-17, in *Saemmtliche Werke*, ed. J. H. Fichte (Berlin: Verlag von Veit und Comp., 1845), 5:187-88. For a discussion of this, see Frederick Coppleston, *A History of Philosophy* (Garden City, N.Y.: Image Books, 1965), 7/1:100-19.

gued.[29] Rather than acknowledging our corporate infinity, we project the infinite reality of humanity onto an imaginary heaven and call this projection "God."[30] Our concept of God is a dangerous illusion, Feuerbach cautioned, for in denying the greatness of our own human nature we have become alienated from ourselves.[31]

Feuerbach was optimistic that we would willingly reject the concept of God once we understood the origin of this erroneous idea. Friedrich Nietzsche (1844-1900) and Jean-Paul Sartre went a step farther and asserted that God *must* be rejected, because the concept denies human freedom. True freedom, in their view, entails the ability to make choices without boundaries. If God exists, he constitutes a boundary which curbs our freedom. Therefore, we must postulate the non-existence of God for the sake of freedom.[32]

Theology and the Modern Situation

In the face of the challenge Christian thinkers have continually attempted to mount a counterattack. Their efforts move in several directions.

The assertion of the uniqueness of Christianity. A first response to the modern situation has been the attempt to set faith, including the postulate of God, beyond the acids of intellectual scrutiny.

Contemporary proponents of this approach, often termed "fideism," stand in a great Christian tradition. In speaking concerning those who sought to wed Christian belief with Greek philosophy, the church father Tertullian (c. 155-c. 222) asked the rhetorical question, "What does light have to do with darkness? What does Jerusalem have to do with Athens?"[33] Over a millennium later the French philosopher Pascal (1623-1662) cried, "'God of Abraham,

---

29. Ludwig Feuerbach, *The Essence of Christianity*, trans. George Elliot (New York: Harper and Brothers, 1957), 22-23.

30. Ibid., 215.

31. Ibid., 230-31.

32. For this characterization of the existentialist position, see Pannenberg, "Speaking about God in the face of Atheist Criticism," in *The Idea of God and Human Freedom*, 106.

God of Isaac, God of Jacob' [Exod. 3:6], not of philosophers and scholars."[34]

Paradigmatic of twentieth century proponents of fideism and perhaps its most compelling expositor is Karl Barth. The Swiss theologian agreed with Feuerbach's critique. However, he claimed that it applies to natural theology and therefore to the philosophical doctrine of God. The Christian faith, in contrast, arises from a radically different source. In Christ, God has acted to reveal himself to us. This divine self-disclosure is unique, for in Christ God comes *to* humankind. The presence of the divine self-disclosure in Christ places Christian faith beyond the pale of Feuerbach's attack.[35]

In a manner reminiscent of Barth, some evangelical thinkers reject any attempts to rebut atheism through, and therefore to ground theology in, reasoned philosophical argumentation. Faith, they argue, comes through the hearing of the gospel, not by means of rational arguments directed toward the doubtings of unbelievers. The gospel message we proclaim is self-authenticating.

As influential as this position has been, most modern theologians have not accepted the Barthian eschewal of dialogue with intellectual atheism. Instead they have sought some point of contact between divine revelation and human intellectual reflection, which Barth so categorically rejected as merely an idolatrous striving after God.

The reformulation of the proofs. The assumption of a point of contact has given birth to a second, and quite opposite response to the modern critique of Christian faith. Some thinkers combat atheism by redoubling the intellectual attempt to demonstrate God's existence. The desire to engage intellectual atheism on its

---

33. Tertullian, "The Prescription Against Heretics" 5, trans. Peter Holmes, in *Latin Christianity: Its Founder, Tertullian*, volume 3 of *The Ante-Nicene Fathers*, ed. Alexander Roberts and James Donaldson, nine volumes (Grand Rapids: Eerdmans, 1976), 246. For a similar idea, see Tertullian, *Apology*, 46:14, trans. T. R. Glover, (Cambridge, Mass.: Harvard University Press, 1934), 205.

34. Pascal, *Pensees*, trans. A. J. Krailsheimer (Harmondsworth, England: Penguin, 1966), 913.

35. Karl Barth, "An Introductory Essay," in Feurbach, *The Essence of Christianity*, xxix.

own terms has led to reformulations of the philosophical proofs in the modern setting. Each of the three classical arguments has found champions among thinkers in the modern world.

The *a priori proof* reemerged in the work of Georg Hegel (1780-1831). He argued that the idea of God—God as the infinite in contrast to finite beings—is a necessary idea. The mind, he noted, cannot conceive of the finite without at the same time thinking of the infinite which bounds and determines the finite.[36] More recently Norman Malcolm (1911-) asserted that God must exist because by his very conception he cannot not exist. God's existence is by definition necessary existence.[37]

F. R. Tennant (1866-1957) offered an updated version of the *a posteriori proof*. He found in the evolutionary theories of Charles Darwin a pointer to the existence of God. Tennant appealed to a "wider teleology" within evolutionary nature. The cooperation of many strands have worked together toward the production of higher and higher levels of creatures climaxing in humanity, the moral creature. This universal cooperation, Tennant claimed, provides ground for reasonable belief.[38] More recently, the cosmologist Robert Jastrow has set forth the widely-held "big bang" theory as once again making the postulate of God intellectually respectable.[39]

Perhaps the most well known popular reformulation of the *moral argument* is that sketched by C. S. Lewis. In his book, *Mere Christianity*,[40] Lewis observes that the practices of all human societies reveal a universal code of morality, for certain conduct is universally praised while other actions are condemned. This phe-

---

36. G. W. F. Hegel, *The Phenomenology of Mind*, trans. J. B. Baillie, Harper Torchbooks/The Academy Library edition (New York: Harper and Row, 1967), 207-13. For a discussion of Hegel's thinking, see Pannenberg, *The Idea of God and Human Freedom*, 84-86.

37. Norman Malcolm, "Anselm's Ontological Arguments," in *Knowledge and Certainty: Essays and Lectures.* (Englewood Cliffs, NJ: Prentice Hall, 1963). 20-27.

38. F. R. Tennant, *Philosophical Theology*, two volumes (Cambridge, England: Cambridge University Press, 1928-30), 2:78-104.

39. Robert Jastrow, *God and the Astronomers* (New York: Norton, 1978).

40. C. S. Lewis, *Mere Christianity*, Macmillan Paperbacks edition (New York: Macmillan, 1960), 17-39.

nomenon indicates that behind the universe lies something which is more like mind than like anything else we know—something that is conscious, has purpose, and prefers one type of conduct to another. This Something is God.

The appeal to anthropology. Other modern theologians opt for an alternative between the fideism of Barth and the rationalism of philosophical theology. These thinkers seek to develop a reasoned response to atheism that falls short of claiming to be a conclusive proof for God's existence. They nevertheless believe that the Christian postulate is intellectually credible and therefore worthy of further consideration.

One widely employed mediating approach appeals to anthropology,[41] or the nature of the human person. Proponents argue that we cannot comprehend ourselves in our human subjectivity without the postulate of the divine reality. Rather, the human person presupposes God seemingly "by nature."

Important to the appeal to anthropology is the empirical difference between humans and other living things. Proponents often encapsule this distinction in terms such as "self-transcendence" or "openness to the world."[42] This difference forms the basis for postulating the reality of God. In contrast to the animals, the human creature is open beyond every particular form which the world takes.[43] Because no human alteration of the world is ultimately satisfying, we are dependent for fulfillment on a reality beyond the world. We call this reality "God."[44]

---

41. Although prominent first in the twentieth century, the connection between anthropology and theology is older. John Calvin, for example, in the opening paragraphs of the *Institutes* postulated a link between the two: "Nearly all the wisdom we possess, that is to say, true and sound wisdom, consists of two parts: the knowledge of God and of ourselves." John Calvin, *Institutes of the Christian Religion*, 1.1.1, trans. Ford Lewis Battles, *Library of Christian Classics* volumes 20-21, ed. John T. McNeill (Philadelphia: Westminster, 1960), 35.

Similarly, for Descartes the existence of the world outside the individual subject is guaranteed only by the existence of God, as he indicates in his Fifth Meditation. Rene Descartes, *Discourse on Method and Meditations*, trans. Laurence J. Lafleur, Library of Liberal Arts edition (1637, 1641; Indianapolis: Bobbs-Merrill, 1960), 124-25.

42. Wolfhart Pannenberg, *What is Man?* trans. Duane A. Priebe (Philadelphia: Fortress, 1970), 3-4.

43. Ibid., 9-10. See also Juergen Moltmann, *Man*, tr. John Sturdy (Philadelphia: Fortress, 1974), 4-7.

Christian Faith in the Contemporary Context

Christians in the Western world find themselves living in a complex situation. One unavoidable dimension of our context is the ongoing legacy of the historical path followed by the Western intellectual tradition. The intellectual atheism of the academicians remains undeniably a formidable force in the world in which we live. The legacy of this outlook has filtered into our general cultural ethos. Pressured by a scientific world view that leaves no room for religion, many people have discarded the concept of God. For them, God has become either the God-of-the-gaps for whom no gaps are left or a debilitating limitation on human freedom.

Other people have retained some semblance of belief in God while living as practical atheists. They go about the tasks of contemporary life with little need for recourse to God. Like the "fool" the psalmist mentions, they say by their actions—if not in their heads—"There is no God." For them God has become innocuous, or even totally irrelevant to life.

The pervasive residue of the intellectual rejection of the concept of God, however, does not exhaust our present situation. The West is also rapidly becoming a fertile field for a myriad of old and new religions. For some people, this proliferation of rival beliefs is but another intellectual problem that makes the Christian truth claim highly suspect. For others, however, the spiritual aridness of our intellectual climate has produced a new thirst for the divine. As a result, we are witnessing a rebirth of interest in the supernatural among the children of the Enlightenment. Yet the new supernaturalism is not necessarily informed by the Christian tradition. This suggests that we may once again be entering into an era akin to that faced by the biblical community, who proclaimed the reality of the God of Abraham and the Father of Jesus the Christ in a context of the rivalry of many "gods."

---

44. Pannenberg, *What Is Man?*, 10.

As theologians we are concerned primarily (but not exclusively) with the intellectual component of faith. For this reason, we cannot avoid the question as to whether the human experience of reality is best understood by appeal to the divine reality. John Calvin spoke on behalf of much of Christian tradition when he asserted, "it is certain that man never achieves a clear knowledge of himself unless he has first looked upon God's face, and then descends from contemplating him to scrutinize himself."[45]

As in Calvin's day so also today the task of Christian theology is partially apologetic. It includes articulating and exploring the Christian claim that we can understand ourselves and the world only as they are illumined by the acknowledgment of God. Consequently, we declare that our belief in God is not the product of a blind leap of faith. Nor is it merely a dogma accepted on the basis of some external authority. Instead, we are convinced that the recognition of God is integral to a full understanding of the universe and of humankind. As theologians we are concerned to clarify this conviction and show its intellectual credibility.

While undeniably intellectual in orientation, our attempt to offer a credible apologetic for the reality of God cannot be limited to intellectualization. Rather, ours must be a living demonstration, as we seek to embody our faith commitment in the way we conduct ourselves. This embodiment lies beyond the purview of theology, understood as the intellectual reflection on faith. Nevertheless, it is not beyond the concern of theology. Theology is directed toward an ultimately practical goal, namely, the translation of faith commitment into a life that brings glory to God.

While seeking to show the importance of the postulate of God for our understanding of ourselves and the world, we must also keep in mind that we are not setting forth the case for some mere generic God. As Christians, we assert that the God who is necessary for a proper understanding of all of creation has disclosed himself in Jesus of Nazareth. He is the God who raised Jesus from

---

45. Calvin, *Institutes of the Christian Religion*, 1.1.2, in volume 20 of the *Library of Christian Classics*, 37.

the dead and on behalf of whom Jesus will one day return in glory and judgment. This interest means that at every point our theology must be explicitly "Christian"; it must be an explication of the specifically Christian understanding of the nature of the divine reality as disclosed in Jesus. But this means as well that in the final analysis the confirmation of the conviction concerning the reality of God which we explore in theology comes only through God's demonstration of himself. Ultimately, this demonstration lies in the future, for it will occur only when Jesus returns in glory.

In the meantime, we continue to engage in the debate concerning the reality of God. In this debate the question of God's existence flows into the question of our knowing God. For us, the assertion "God is" finds its final confirmation in our glorious encounter with God in Jesus. Although the claim that God exists will remain open and debatable until the consummation of history, the Christian viewpoint gains heightened credence as God demonstrates his presence through the lives of the people who testify that they have come to know him. For this reason, our discussion of the contemporary possibility of faith must move to the question as to whether God can be known.

Knowledge of God in an Era of Agnosticism

Integral to our assertion "God is" is our testimony that we have come to know God. As Christians, we declare that the God whose reality illumines all creation and our human experience is the God who has made himself known to us in Jesus of Nazareth. In Jesus, we have come to know God. And only in knowing God can we finally give an affirmative answer to the question concerning the existence of God. But like the confession "God is," we testify that God can be known within a context in which many people dispute our claim.

The Claim to Know God
and Intellectual Agnosticism

In Western intellectual history, the question of God's existence has often been closely connected to another philosphical debate, namely, whether it is theoretically possible to know God. Just as some conclude that the postulate of the reality of God does not stand the test of credibility, others are convinced that it is incredible to assert that we can know God.

Epistemological agnosticism. The intellectual denial that God can be known is often termed "agnosticism." In one form, agnosticism is by nature non-dogmatic and intellectually open. In contrast to the ontological declaration of atheism—"God does not exist"—agnostics voice an appraisal of our meager human epistemological capability. They cautiously conclude that humans do not possess the capacity to know matters relating to God.

The Reformed theologian Louis Berkhof characterizes agnosticism as the belief that "the human mind is incapable of knowing anything of that which lies behind natural phenomena, and it therefore is necessarily ignorant of supersensible and divine things."[46] Because the human mind can only know objects that belong to the natural realm, the agnostic warns, we are by necessity totally ignorant of anything which lies beyond or behind the universe. We are unable to determine whether or not God is, and consequently we cannot know God.

The roots of epistemological agnosticism lie in the empiricism of David Hume and the transcendental philosophy of Immanuel Kant. Hume asserted that we derive all knowledge from sense experience. Because we cannot perceive the divine reality through the senses, we can never know that there is a reality who corresponds to the attributes we ascribe to God.[47] Kant postulated a distinction between noumena ("things-in-themselves" or objects as they actually are) and phenomena ("things-in-appearance" or

---

46. Louis Berkhof, *Systematic Theology*, revised edition (Grand Rapid: Eerdmans, 1953), 30.
47. Hume, *Dialogues Concerning Natural Religion*, 15-25, 47-56.

objects as they appear in human perception). Scientific or "pure" knowledge (knowledge that arises through the senses) can lead us only to things-in-appearance, never to things-in-themselves. Because God is never a phenomenon—never an object in our human perception—sense-based knowledge about God is impossible, he concluded.[48]

Logical positivism. Although perhaps not as influential as the agnosticism of Hume and Kant, a twentieth century philosophy known as "logical positivism" produced a more dogmatic and insidious rejection of the theoretical possibility of knowing God. According to logical positivists, all metaphysical statements—all assertions about any reality beyond the world of sense experience—are nonsensical.

Logical positivists appealed to one or the other of two axioms—"the verification principle" and "the falsification principle"—as the criterion for determining the truth of any assertion concerning reality. For a proposition to be considered a proper assertion, we must set forth the conditions under which we would judge the sentence either to be verified (proved true) or falsified (proved false). If, however, we cannot state what these conditions are, the statement is not an assertion about reality.[49]

We may illustrate this procedure with the statement, "God is love." The principle of falsification demands that we state the criteria by which we would declare the postulate to be incorrect. As Christians, however, we can conceive of no situation in which we would give up our assertion that God is love. That being the case, the logical positivist would rule the statement nonsensical.[50] In this manner logical positivism eliminated from the realm of proper human discourse all metaphysical statements.

Agnosticism and the incomprehensible God. The modern intellectual climate is permeated with skepticism about religious truth

---

48. Kant, *Critique of Pure Reason*. 507-14, 518-24.

49. See, for example, Moritz Schlick, "Positivism and Realism," in *Logical Positivism*, 86-95.

50. Anthony Flew, R. M. Hare, and Basil Mitchell, "Theology and Falsification," in *New Essays in Philosophical Theology*, ed. Anthony Flew and Alasdair MacIntyre (London: SCM, 1955), 96-106.

claims. Even if God exists, some people argue, he lies beyond the realm of human knowledge. Others simply reject as nonsense all assertions concerning a divine reality. In the midst of this context, we testify that we have come to know the living God. Yet in making this bold claim, we dare not miss the one valid reminder we should gain from agnosticism. Our encounter with skeptics ought to prompt in us the humble acknowledgment present within the Christian tradition that God is incomprehensible. Divine incomprehensibility is a biblical theme (e.g., Job 11:7-8; Ps. 97:2; 145:3; Isa. 40:28; 45:15; 55:8-9; 1 Cor. 2:11). But how are we to understand this theological declaration?

"God is incomprehensible" means that no human being can fully comprehend God or fathom the depth of the divine reality. Whatever knowledge we have about God is at best only partial. "God is incomprehensible" also means that no human can perceive fully God's essential being. God is hidden; God's essence is not totally displayed to us.

The acknowledgment that God is incomprehensible is related to an awareness that God is transcendent. Because he is beyond creation and comes to the world from beyond, God is always higher than our ability to fathom. Hence, the author of Ecclesiastes counsels, "God is in heaven and you are on earth, so let your words be few" (Eccl. 5:2).

While acknowledging that God is incomprehensible, we also adamantly maintain that God can be known. Our knowledge of God is always partial; yet when we know God we know him as he is. Jesus himself held out the possibility of our knowing God: "And this is life eternal that they should know you, the only true God and Jesus Christ whom you have sent" (John 17:3).

The Means to Knowledge of God

The possibility of knowing God raises the question of means. If we can know God, how does this come about? Christian thinkers offer a panorama of suggestions as to what forms the fundamental route to knowing God.

Knowledge of God through reason. Paralleling the long-standing attempt in Christian philosophical theology to demonstrate the existence of God, some thinkers hold open the possibility of coming to a partial, yet genuine knowledge of God through intellectual reflection. We can know God through philosophical or discursive reasoning.

Representative of the philosophical approach is the theological method of Thomas Aquinas. According to Thomas, God can be known through the divine works or "effects" evident to all through our sense experience of the world. Through this process we can draw certain conclusions concerning God. We may assert that he exists. And by employing the principle of analogy between creation and Creator, we can stipulate whatever must by necessity be true of God as the First Cause of the world.[51]

Building from the thinkers of the Middle Ages, Thomas proposed three ways by which we can draw conclusions concerning God from his effects. Following the *via causalitatis* (the way of causality) we can ascribe certain attributes to God on the basis of the perfections we observe in creation. These perfections must preexist in a more perfect way in God, for he is the cause of their presence in creation. Because God is perfect, the *via negationis* (the way of negation) instructs us to remove from our idea of God all the imperfections found in creatures and to assign to God the opposite perfection. Finally, the *via eminentiae* (the way of eminence) allows us to ascribe to God in the most eminent manner the relative perfections we discover in humans.[52]

Thomas readily admitted that deductive reasoning from sense experience does not yield all that we can know about God. To this natural knowledge of God the Christian theologian adds the propositions derived from God's revelation as handed down through the church. The additional knowledge of God drawn from the Bi-

---

51. Thomas Aquinas, *Summa Contra Gentiles* 1:29-34, trans. Anton C. Pegis (Garden City, NY: Image Books, 1955), 138-48.

52. Thomas Aquinas, *Summa Contra Gentiles* 1.30 [141-43]; *Summa theologica*, 1.13.1-5, in *Introduction to St. Thomas Aquinas*, 97-109.

ble and tradition includes God's triune nature and gracious work in saving humankind.

Thomas's theological method purports to yield a body of propositional truths, or doctrines, about God. As statements about the divine essence, they comprise actual "scientific" or objective knowledge concerning God. Although we generally link the Thomistic tradition with pre-Vatican II Roman Catholicism, not all aspects of Thomas's theological method are foreign to Protestantism. For example, certain contemporary evangelicals, building on the work of the nineteenth century Princeton theologians such as Charles Hodge, share Thomas's concern for a "scientific" theology.[53] Their goal, like his, is to derive a body of propositional truths concerning the divine reality from creation and Scripture.

Knowledge of God through religious experience. Although the Thomistic approach has been highly influential, it has not gained universal following. One prominent alternative suggests that we do not come to know God indirectly (through philosophical reflection and propositional truths) but directly, through some type personal religious experience. Theology, in turn, is not the ordering of scientific statements about God, but the intellectual reflection on our religious encounter. The theologian articulates what must be true on the basis of such experience.

Proponents of the theology of religious experience offer differing proposals concerning the nature of the paradigmatic encounter that mediates our knowing God.

Friedrich Schleiermacher (1768-1834) focused on the experience of God's immanence in the world. Lying behind Schleiermacher's proposal was his understanding of the three essential elements comprising the mental life: Perception gives rise to knowledge; activity issues forth in moral conduct; and feeling (understood not as emotion, but as intuition or awareness) is the particular faculty of the religious life. On this basis, he declared that the foundation of the religion lies in an intuition of the infinite

---

53. A. A. Hodge, *Outlines Of Theology*, reprint edition (1879; London: Banner of Truth Trust, 1972), 15.

within the finite, or a consciousness of the existence of all finite things in and through the infinite.[54] This intuitive consciousness gives birth to a sense of absolute dependence or "God-consciousness."[55]

Rudolph Otto offered a crucial alteration to Schleiermacher's suggestion. Rather than immanence, our foundational religious experience is the feeling of God's transcendence. The intuition of "the holy other" (the *mysterium tremendum*) results in a sense of awe-fulness, of overpoweringness, of being in the presence of the Holy Other, the Transcendent One.[56]

The Jewish theologian, Martin Buber, proposed a quite different religious experience—personal encounter—as lying at the foundation of our knowing God. He viewed God as the supreme person or the supreme "thou." Knowledge of God is unlocked and disclosed through particular persons, particular thou's. Consequently, in order to know God we must enter into relationship with others as persons. Buber termed these "I-thou" relations. We come to know God as we cultivate the "thou" in others.[57]

Many pietists and evangelicals elevate personal conversion as the way to know God. We encounter God as we are personally confronted with the living and present Christ, who radically alters our lives. Paradigmatic of such an experience is Paul's transformation on the Damascus Road or Augustine's conversion as described in his *Confessions*.

Other thinkers argue that the way to know God is through mystical experience. In such an encounter, the individual transcends the self and ascends to a union with the divine which supplants the duality between the self and God. According to the medieval mystical tradition, the way to union with God begins with withdrawal

54. Friederich Schleiermacher, *On Religion: Speeches to Its Cultured Despisers* 2.A.1, trans. Terrence N. Tice (Richmond, Va.: John Knox, 1969), 79.

55. Frederich Schleiermacher, *The Christian Faith*, ed. H. R. MacKintosh and J. S. Stewart (Edinburgh: T. & T. Clark, n.d.), 5-18.

56. Rudolf Otto, *The Idea of the Holy*. trans. John Harvey, (London: Oxford University Press, 1958), 1-13.

57. Martin Buber, *I and Thou*, trans. Ronald Gregor Smith (New York: Charles Scribner's Sons, 1958), 75-83.

first from sense experience and then from the mystic's own thoughts, ideas, and passions. In this state of emptiness the union with God can occur.[58]

Knowledge of God through his self-revelation. Not totally separable from either of these two major theological methods is a third alternative: We know God through his self-revelation. Theologians who elevate this as the means to knowing God offer differing proposals as to the locus of the divine self-disclosure.

As we noted in Thomas Aquinas, some theologians claim to find the divine self-revelation in creation. The Creator discloses himself in the world which he made. In support of their view, proponents appeal to biblical statements, such as the psalmist's assertion, "The heavens declare the glory of God" (Ps. 19:1-6). Or they cite Paul's claim that creation mediates to all persons some knowledge of God (Rom. 1:20). If God's revelation is found in creation, they reason, it follows that God can be known at least in part as we apprehend such revelation. Critics such as Karl Barth, however, point out that Paul's purpose is not to assert that God's revelation is present in creation but to point out that humans in fact do not apprehend God through it.

Other thinkers, including many evangelicals, suggest that the focal point of revelation is the Bible. Somewhat related to this view is the position articulated by Barth that God's self-disclosure is ultimately found exclusively in Christ.[59] Both these ideas will be explored in chapter 21, when we view Scripture as a work of the Holy Spirit.

Another group of thinkers look to history for the field of God's revelation. Some focus on the mighty acts of God in history, such as the Exodus, as comprising a special salvation history or a special history of the self-revelation of God.[60] Others, most notably

---

58. See for example, St. John of the Cross, *The Dark Night of the Soul*, trans Kurt F. Reinhardt (New York: Ungar, 1957).

59. Karl Barth, *Church Dogmatics*, trans. Geoffrey W. Bromiley, second edition (Edinburgh: T. & T. Clark, 1975), 1/1:119.

60. See, for example, G. Ernest Wright and Reginald H. Fuller, *The Book of the Acts of God*, Anchor Books edition (Garden City, N.J.: Doubleday, 1960), 17-29.

Wolfhart Pannenberg, claim that universal history or world history as a whole is the focal point of God's revelation.[61] This theme will likewise reappear in subsequent chapters.

Knowing God

Despite what appears to be a multitude of competing views, by the middle of the twentieth century theologians had come to somewhat of a consensus surrounding certain fundamental conclusions concerning knowing God.

Knowing God as Subject. The primary postulate discovered by modern theology is the realization that in the knowing process God is subject, not object. Bound up with this assertion are several important corollaries.

(1) "God is subject, not object" means that God cannot be made the object of human scrutiny. We do not approach God like we engage in the study of objects around us, namely, in an objective, scientific manner or at the whim of our own human will. Rather, we come to know God as God gives himself to be known. In the knowing process, therefore, the initiative comes from the divine side.[62]

Jesus reflected the importance of the divine initiative, when he declared, "All things have been committed to me by my Father. No one knows the Son except the Father, and no one knows the Father except the Son and those to whom the Son chooses to reveal him" (Matt. 11:27; see also 1 Cor. 2:9-16).

(2) "God is subject, not object" also means that there is a great difference between knowing God and possessing propositional knowledge about God. When we know God, we have more than merely a body of truths about God. More importantly, we know the living and personal God. The task of knowing God, then, does

---

61. Wolfhart Pannenberg, "Hermeneutic and Universal History," *Basic Questions in Theology*, trans. George H. Kehm, two volumes (Philadelphia: Fortress, 1970), 1:96-136. Wolfhart Pannenberg, "Introduction," in *Revelation as History.* ed. Wolfhart Pannenberg, trans. David Granskou (New York: Macmillan, 1968), 3-21.

62. John Baillie, *The Idea of Revelation* (New York: Columbia University Press, 1956), 19-40.

not focus on the possession of a list of statements about God, but on the enjoyment of fellowship with God.

That this is the case is readily evident. A body of propositions emerges from strenuous human effort, namely, the exercise of human reflection. True knowledge of God, in contrast, can arise only from an encounter with God. In this encounter God, and not the human person, is the active agent.[63]

Karl Barth was an important force in marking this distinction on the face of modern theological thinking. Barth even dismissed categorically any attempt to speak of a general human knowledge of God, for all such purported knowledge can only be the product of human efforts. Every attempt to deduce propositional statements about God's essence from the world is, therefore, ill-advised.[64]

Barth's contemporary, Emil Brunner, did not go as far in denouncing the philosophical approach to God. Nevertheless, he declared that the attempt to derive knowledge of God from creation (natural theology) is ultimately not helpful in the theological enterprise. Brunner admitted that a knowledge of the Creator forms part of our creaturely existence. But he concluded that this knowledge does not constitute knowing God truly, because such philosophical knowledge does not create communion with God.[65]

The position of Barth and Brunner has found an echo in the thought of many theologians since their day.

(3) Finally, "God is subject, not object" means that in knowing God the human person is the object, not the knowing subject. In this event we do not actively come to know God. Instead God grasps and knows us. Paul seemed to be reflecting this awareness when he remarked to the Galatian believers: "But now that you know God—or rather are known by God" (Gal. 4:9). The apostle finds an echo in James I. Packer's declaration, "What matters su-

---

63. Emil Bunner, *The Christian Doctrine of God*, trans. Olive Wyon (Philadelphia: Westminster, 1949), 14, 22.

64. Karl Barth, "No!" in Emil Brunner and Karl Barth, *Natural Theology*, trans. Peter Fraenkel (London: Centenary, 1946), 70-128.

65. Brunner, *The Christian Doctrine of God*, 1:121.

premely therefore is not in the last analysis the fact that I know God, but the larger fact which underlies it—the fact that *He knows me.*"[66]

Knowing God in history. This thesis—in the knowing process God is subject, not object—constitutes a first point in our answer to the question as to how God is knowable to humans. We know God insofar as God gives himself to be known. What we come to know in this process may include, but definitely goes beyond, a body of doctrines about God, for we know the personal God himself. And in this event God knows or makes claim to us.

The twentieth century emphasis on encounter, as helpful as it is, falls short of providing a full answer to the question concerning knowing God. It suffers from a debilitating shortcoming, namely, its inordinate emphasis on the individual in the present as the point of God's self-disclosure. Consequently, it is sorely in need of augmentation.

While the personal encounter with God does occur in the present, the present encounter is significant insofar as it is connected with the broader sweep of what God is doing in the whole of human history. Hence, we must place the present isolated moment within the context of the future and the past—within an awareness of what God will do at the consummation of history and what God has already done, especially in Jesus of Nazareth.

This observation links us with another emphasis widely acknowledged among contemporary theologians, namely, the focus on history and the kingdom of God.[67] Many theologians agree that whatever else may be said about the matter, the field of the divine self-disclosure is history. History has purpose and is directed to a goal—the final revelation of the glory of God.

Some theologians take this thesis one step farther. They add that there can be but one historical self-disclosure of God in the ultimate sense of the term and that the divine self-disclosure

---

66. James I. Packer, *Knowing God* (Downers Grove, Ill.: InterVarsity, 1973), 37.

67. For an explication, see Wolfhart Pannenberg, "Dogmatic Theses on the Doctrine of Revelation," in *Revelation as History*, 125-35.

stands at the end of the historical process, not at its beginning. Hence, God's self-disclosure is ultimately eschatological, for the final revelation of God will come only at the consummation of history (see 1 Cor. 13:12; 1 John 3:2). This event marks the full in-breaking of the reign of God. The eschatological reality is not merely future, however. It has already invaded our world in Jesus of Nazareth, who is the *telos* (goal) and meaning of history (1 John 5:20) and in whom the end is "proleptically" present, to use Pannenberg's term. Consequently, in Jesus the Christ we are confronted with and apprehended by God.

Knowing God and the concept of community. The contemporary accent on history and the kingdom yields an eschatological and christological dimension to our quest to know God. But even with this addition we have not yet fully overcome the highly individual focus characteristic of the emphasis on encounter. Hence, we have not arrived at the center of the answer to our query. Rather, we must invoke yet another concept, which capsulizes God's ultimate goal for the historical process and thereby points to the heart of our knowing God. The direction we will follow was outlined already in Brunner's theology. But more recent thinkers, especially the new communitarians and those who are exploring the role of narrative in identity formation, offer us much needed assistance.

Many human scientists have been exploring the thesis that our sense of personal identity develops through the telling of a personal narrative. Hence, finding ourselves means, among other things, finding the story in terms of which our lives make sense.[68] The narrative of a person's life is always embedded in the story of the communities in which the person participates.[69] The community is crucial in the process of identity formation, because it mediates to us the transcending story, bound up with which are

---

68. Robert N. Bellah, et al. *Habits of the Heart: Individualism and Commitment in American Life*, Perennial Library edition (New York: Harper and Row, 1986), 81.

69. See, for example, Alisdair MacIntyre, *After Virtue*, second edition (Notre Dame: University of Notre Dame Press, 1984), 221.

traditions of virtue, common good, and ultimate meaning, by means of which we construct our own narrative.[70]

The insights of the new communitarians are directly applicable to our query concerning God's goal for history and consequently how God brings us to know him. According to the Bible, God's program is directed to the establishing of a reconciled people from all nations to live within a renewed creation and enjoy the presence of their Redeemer God. This biblical vision of community is both the goal of history and the experience of each person who has come to know God.

The New Testament writers declare that to know God means to know Christ, or to be "united with Christ," to use Paul's motif. This union includes, but moves beyond, mental assent to a set of doctrines. It entails the embodying in one's beliefs, attitudes, and actions the meanings and values that characterized Jesus' own life. In the process of embodiment, the Christian community of faith is crucial. The believing community transmits from generation to generation and region to region the redemptive story, which it recounts in word and deed. In so doing it mediates to the believer the framework for the formation of personal identity, values, and world view.

In the final analysis, therefore, we know that we have encountered God in that we have been brought to share in community. We enjoy fellowship with God and participate in the people of faith. The fellowship that God intends for his creation begins in the present. But it is ultimately an eschatological reality, an enjoyment that will be ours in its fullness only at the consummation of history.

In subsequent chapters we will explore the theological implications and applications of the encounter with God as a community-inaugurating reality. Yet one conclusion is crucial to the present discussion. The participation in community with God, each other, and creation, which we enjoy partially in the present and fully in

---

70. E.g., George Lindbeck, "Confession and Community: An Israel-like View of the Church," *Christian Century* 107 (May 9, 1990): 495.

the eschatological future, forms the final answer both to the question concerning the possibility of knowing God and the question of God's existence.

The modern world challenges our claim that we have come to know the only God. We must meet this challenge on many fronts. Our answer must include the intellectual demonstration that the postulate of God best illumines our experience of our world and our own lives. But our response cannot end with an intellectual apologetic for faith. We must also embody our acknowledgment of the reality of God in the manner in which we live and in the way that we view ourselves. This embodiment entails participation in community—living in fellowship with God, others, and creation. In the end, only Christian living on this plane can confirm our testimony that we know God and therefore that God is.

The Triune God

May the grace of the Lord Jesus Christ, and the love of God, and the fellowship of the Holy Spirit be with you all. (2 Cor. 13:14)

Outline

Of the various aspects of our Christian understanding of God perhaps none is as difficult to grasp as the concept of God as triune. At the same time, no dimension of the Christian confession is closer to the heart of the mystery of the God we have come to know. In fact, what sets Christianity apart from the other religious traditions is the confession that the one God is Father, Son, and Spirit. As a consequence, no teaching lies at the center of Christian theology, if not of Christian faith itself, as does the doctrine of the Trinity. For this reason, the discussion of the triune God forms the appropriate beginning point for our delineation of the faith of the community of Christ.

The word, "trinity," is not found in the Bible. Nor is the theological concept fully delineated in the Scriptures. In the King James Bible, one verse (1 John 5:7) appears to contain an explicit reference to God as triune. But modern textual study has yielded the nearly unanimous consensus that these words were not part of the original document penned by the apostle. The absence of explicit reference to God as the Triune One in Scripture led Emil Brunner to this insightful conclusion:

> The ecclesiastical doctrine of the Trinity, established by the dogma of the ancient Church, is not a Biblical *kerygma*, therefore it is not the *kerygma* of the Church, but it is a theological doctrine which defends the central faith of the Bible and of the Church.[1]

---

1. Emil Brunner, *The Christian Doctrine of God*, trans. Olive Wyon (Philadelphia: Westminster, 1950), 206.

Brunner's point is well taken. The doctrine of the Trinity as we know it was formulated by the church during the patristic era. Hence, it was not an explicit aspect of the gospel proclaimed by the New Testament community. Nevertheless, the church was correct in coming to realize that understanding God as triune is a non-negotiable dimension of the gospel. The concept of tri-unity lies at the heart of the Christian understanding of God and therefore is necessary in order to maintain the central message of the Bible.

The doctrine of the Trinity is the product of a lengthy process arising from the experience of the people of faith. Therefore, to understand the special Christian view of God as triune, we must trace the historical trajectory that climaxed in the fixing of the doctrine.

Trinitarian Doctrine in Theological History

The journey that led to the development of the doctrine of the Trinity began in the Old Testament era. But the experience of the early Christians provided the immediate impetus that launched the quest for a more appropriate theological understanding of God. This venture reached completion through the work of the theologians of the church who eventually devised what came to be the commonly accepted formulation of the doctrine of the Trinity.

The Situation of the First Christians

The doctrine of the Trinity arose as the climax of an attempt on the part of church theologians to address certain foundational questions concerning the Christian faith. While the exact formulation of the doctrine remained elusive until at least the 300s, the questions themselves arose much earlier—in the situation of the first generation of Christians. Our formulation, "one essence, three persons," came as the climax to the theological attempts to respond to a problem which has confronted believers from the beginning of the Christian era. The faith of the early disciples required that they bring together three different strands of belief: the heritage of monotheism, the confession of Jesus' lordship, and the experience of the presence of the Holy Spirit.

The one God. As Jews, the early Christians claimed adamantly that the new movement was the continuation of what God had begun to do in the Old Testament era, as was foretold by the prophets. At the center of the Hebrew tradition bequeathed to the church was the belief in one God and the rejection of the worship of many gods found among the surrounding nations. The Old Testament community asserted unequivocally that there is but one God and that he demanded total loyalty: "Hear O Israel, the Lord our God, the Lord is one. Love the Lord your God with all your heart, with all your soul and with all your strength" (Deut. 6:4-5. See also Deut. 32:36-39; 2 Sam. 7:22; Isa. 45:18).

Viewing themselves as the continuation of the one people of faith, the early Christians resolutely maintained the tradition of monotheism they inherited from the Old Testament. The God they worshiped, these believers asserted, is the one and only true God, the God of the patriarchs.

Jesus' lordship. The early Christians continued the Jewish worship of one God. But they also knew that this God had revealed himself in Jesus, the head of the church and the Lord of all creation. Hence, the early church set forth a second, non-negotiable belief, the assertion of the divinity and lordship of Jesus (e.g., John 1:1; 20:28; Rom. 9:5; Titus 2:13).

At the same time, in keeping with the pattern set by the Master himself, his followers clearly differentiated between Jesus as the Son and the one whom he claimed to be both his and their Father (e.g., Rom. 15:5-6). In fact, it was just this dominical differentiation that led to the use of the terms "Father" and "Son" as the designations for the first and second persons of the Trinity.

Although not often found, the idea that God is Father was not totally foreign to the Hebrew Scriptures (see, for example, 2 Sam. 7:14; Jer. 31:20; Isa. 63:16; 64:8-9). The ancient people did not intend to imply thereby that God is strictly masculine, for they also spoke of God's motherly care. In any case, with Jesus the divine fatherhood took on heightened meaning. Our Lord spoke not only of God's parental care for creation and for his people, but also of the special filial relationship he sensed with the one he called "Abba." It was into participation in this sonship with the One Jesus knew as Father that the believers sensed they had been drawn. For this reason, the terms "Father" and "Son" came to be embedded in the theological language of the church.

The Spirit's presence. Not only did the early Christian faith consist of the confession of Jesus and the belief in one God, it also included the assertion that God is now present among his people through the Holy Spirit. This assertion was born out of an ongoing experience of a personal, divine reality within the Christian fellowship who was neither the Father nor the Son.

The New Testament gives evidence to a complex understanding of the Holy Spirit. The writers speak of the Spirit in personal terms. They employ masculine pronouns for what in the Greek language is actually a neuter term. They attribute to the Spirit aspects of personality, such as intellect, will, and emotion (e.g., 1 Cor. 2:10; 12:11; Rom. 8:26-27). In addition to seeing the Spirit as personal, the early believers also knew him to be divine. Their tendency to ascribe deity to the Spirit is evident in Peter's declaration to Ananias and Sapphira that in lying to the Holy Spirit they had lied to God (Acts 5:3, 4). Although they closely linked the Holy Spirit to the risen Lord (e.g., 2 Cor. 3:17-18), the early Christians also made a definite differentiation between him and both the Father and the Son. This is evidenced by the trinitarian formulations found in the New Testament (e.g., 2 Cor. 13:14).

Their situation, therefore, demanded that the early believers integrate into a composite understanding these three dimensions of their experience of God. These Christians confessed the one true God of the Old Testament. They proclaimed the lordship of Jesus of Nazareth who differentiated himself from his Father. And they knew the reality of the ongoing presence of God through the Holy Spirit who is distinct from both the Father and the Son. Discovering what conception of God could bring together these three strands challenged the minds of thinkers for the next four centuries.

Historical Development of Trinitarian Doctrine

The quest to find a means to bring together the confession of Jesus and the experience of the Holy Spirit with the heritage of belief in one God repeatedly enveloped the church in controversy. The historical process moved through two phases. The first focused on the relationship of Jesus to God, whereas the second concerned the nature of the Holy Spirit.

The deity of Jesus. The first question to which the church theologians devoted their attention centered on the relationship of Jesus of Nazareth to God. The earliest attempts to integrate these two aspects of the Christian confession came as responses to heresies concerning the nature of Jesus. Hence, the trajectory that climaxed in the formulation of the doctrine of the Trinity began in the early christological debates.

Among the first important attempts to respond to the various christological heresies that dogged the early church arose in the mid-second century. Its genesis lay in the desire among certain Christian thinkers, known as the "apologists," to find common ground between the gospel and the Greek philosophical tradition. The wedding of these two traditions led to a proposal known as the "logos Christology."[2]

As the name indicates, the logos Christology focused on the concept of the Word (Greek: *logos*), understood in the light of the Greek idea of the rational principle of the universe. This Word, the architects of the doctrine explained, is personal and was with God unexpressed in eternity. Twice the Word came to expression. At creation God spoke the universe into existence in accordance with the Word. And at the incarnation this creative principle appeared as the human Jesus.[3]

The architects of the logos Christology also looked to the concept of the Word for the answer to the question as to how the human Jesus could be divine.[4] The presence of the Word communicated God's own nature to Jesus, they reasoned, thereby constituting him as divine.

---

2. For a discussion of the logos Christology, see Paul Tillich, *A History of Christian Thought*, ed. Carl E. Braaten (New York: Simon and Shuster, 1968), 27-32.

3. Ibid., 29-32.

4. Ibid., 32.

Other thinkers, however, were not convinced. Critics perceived in the logos Christology an implicit bitheism (the belief in two gods). To them it marked a violation of the heritage of monotheism. Because they were motivated by an attempt to preserve the singular divine monarch, opponents came to be known as monarchians[5] (Greek: *mono + arche*, "one source of divinity").

The monarchians postulated two distinct alternatives to the question as to how Jesus could be divine. Theodotus, who came to Rome about 190 A.D., and Paul of Samosata, who was condemned in 268 A.D., offered an adoptionistic solution, called dynamic monarchianism[6] (Greek: *dunamis*, "power"). They theorized that the divine power descended upon the man Jesus, so that he was not ontologically God but merely the carrier of the divine power, an inspired man.

The modalistic monarchians, in contrast, asserted that the Father, Son, and Spirit are not separate realities, but "modes" through which the one divine being expresses himself.[7] Hence, the threeness does not belong to the essence of God throughout eternity. There are no eternal distinctions within the one God. Rather, "Father," "Son," and "Spirit" refer to God in his self-revelation. These distinctions are the ways in which the one God has chosen to be seen by human beings.

The opponents of one important early modalistic monarchian, Praxeas, saw in his teaching a heresy they termed "patripassionism." They accused him of declaring that the Father became incarnate in the Son, suffered, and died.[8]

A historically more influential form of modalistic monarchianism was attributed to Sabellius,[9] who came to Rome in 215. Sabellianism asserts that "Father," "Son," and "Spirit" refer to sequential divine expressions which are based on God's economic purposes. God's activities in the world began with the work of creation (the era of Fa-

---

5. J. N. D. Kelly, *Early Christian Doctrines*, revised edition (San Francisco: Harper and Row, 1978), 115.

6. Ibid., 115-19.

7. Ibid., 120-21.

8. Tertullian argues against this proported teaching of Praxeas in *Adversus Praxeam*. See Kelly, *Early Christian Doctrines*, 121.

9. Tillich, *A History of Christian Thought*, 67; Kelly, *Early Christian Doctrines*, 121-22.

ther), moved next to the life of Jesus (the era of the Son), and led finally into the church age (the era of the Spirit).

In response to the challenge of monarchianism, the orthodox theologians sought to come to grips with the nature of God in a manner that preserved the valid concern for monotheism that their opponents sought to protect. To facilitate this, the various proposals the church thinkers devised generally included some concept of subordination (the idea that the Son and the Spirit are to be ranked after the Father) with the Father seen as in some sense the source of divinity. Hippolytus and Tertullian, for example, postulated that the Father existed alone from all eternity. His solitariness, however, was not a bare numerical unity, for the Father carried multiplicity within himself.[10] More important for the subsequent debate, however, was the teaching of Origen (185-254 A.D.).[11]

Origen agreed that the Father is the source of the deity of the Son and the Spirit. But to describe the manner in which the Father shares his divinity with the Son, he borrowed a metaphor from human begetting. According to Origen, the Father generates the Son in an eternal movement, so that the Son eternally draws his life from the Father. Origen's concept of "the eternal generation of the Son"[12] marked both the climax of the early discussion and the beginning point for what followed.

The official christological dogma that provided a foundation for the doctrine of the Trinity did not arise from Origen, however. Rather its source lay in a theological struggle known as the Arian controversy.[13]

Like the monarchians, Arius, a deacon in the church in Alexandria, sought to protect the absolute uniqueness and transcendence of God. His concern, however, translated into a grave christological error. While agreeing with Origen that the Father begets or generates the Son, Arius could not conceive of this as an eternal movement

---

10. Kelly, *Early Christain Doctrines*, 111.

11. Ibid., 128-32.

12. For an example of his teaching see Origen, *De Principiius* 1.2.4, in *The Early Christian Fathers*, ed. Henry Bettenson (London: Oxforrd University Press, 1969), 231.

13. For a concise discussion of this controversy, see J.W.C. Wand, *The Four Great Heresies* (London: Mowbrays, 1955), 38-62.

within God. Rather, he suggested that the biblical verb "to beget" means "to make"—the Father *made* the Son, who therefore is a creature. As a creature whom the Father created out of nothing, the Word must have had a beginning: "the Son is not unbegotten, nor part of the unbegotten in any way...before he was begotten or created or appointed or established, he did not exist; for he was not unbegotten."[14] Like Sabellius, therefore, Arius believed that the trinitarian distinctions are external to God, that in his own eternal nature God is one, not three.[15]

Arius's Christology was opposed by the theologian Athanasius, who argued persuasively that the deity of the Son is necessitated by soteriology. If Jesus is not fully God, we do not truly receive salvation, for in salvation we participate in the divine nature: "The Word was made man in order that we might be made divine."[16]

At the First Ecumenical Council at Nicea in 325, the church unequivocally affirmed the full divinity of Christ. With the teaching of Arius obviously in view the council asserted that the Son is "begotten of the Father, of the substance of the Father, begotten not made, of one substance with the Father."[17] In short, the First Ecumenical Council placed the Son next to Father as being fully divine.

The deity of the Spirit. After Nicea another debate ensued that laid the corresponding pneumatological foundation for the doctrine of the Trinity. Like the christological debate that preceded it, the dispute had its roots in the teaching of Arius. The followers of the Alexandrian deacon not only postulated that the Son was the first creature of the Father, but that the Holy Spirit was the first creature of the Son.[18] Even though the Council of Nicea rejected Arius's Christology, many otherwise orthodox thinkers accepted the pneumatology that followed from it.

---

14. "The Letter of Arius to Eusebius," in *Documents of the Christian Church*, ed. Henry Bettenson, second edition (London: Oxford University Press, 1963), 39.

15. Tillich, *A History of Christian Thought*, 61-79.

16. Athanasius, *De Incarnatione* 54, in *The Early Christian Fathers*, 293. See also Athanasius, *Contra Arianos* 2.70, in *Early Christian Fathers*, 293.

17. See "The Creed of Nicaea," in *Documents of the Christian Church*, ed. Henry Bettenson, second edition, (London: Oxford University Press, 1963), 24.

18. Kelly, *Early Christian Doctrines*, 256.

The controversy itself is named for Macedonius, the bishop of Constantinople, who purportedly articulated the Arian pneumatology.[19] Once again Athanasius's teaching provided the foundation to meet the challenge. The church father argued that full deity of the Spirit, like that of the Son, is necessary for our faith.[20] Athanasius noted that the Holy Spirit is placed on equal footing with the Father and the Son in the baptismal formulas, apostolic benedictions, and trinitarian doxologies found in the New Testament and in early Christian literature.

Most importantly, as in his response to Arius, Athanasius showed that the deity of the Spirit is necessitated by soteriology. If the Spirit who enters our hearts as believers is not the actual Spirit of God, then we have no true community with God: "If we are made sharers of the divine nature through our partaking of the Spirit, it would be only a madman who would say that the Spirit is of created nature and not of the nature of God."[21]

The Second Ecumenical Council in Constantinople in 381 settled the question.[22] The church agreed with Athanasius, affirming the full deity of the Spirit.

From this point the orthodox understanding of God would need to view all three persons—Father, Son, and Spirit—as fully divine. Yet while the Councils of Nicea and Constantinople declared the full divinity of the Son and the Spirit along with that of the Father, the creeds did not answer the question as to how the three comprise the one God.

Formulating trinitarian doctrine. The challenge of devising an understanding of the relationship among the Father, Son, and Spirit was accepted by three theologians known as the Cappadocian fathers—Basil, Gregory of Nyssa, and Gregory of Nazianzus. Their efforts gave birth to what became the classic formulation of the doctrine of the Trinity.[23]

---

19. Ibid., 259.
20. See Tillich, *A History of Christian Thought*, 73-74; Kelly, *Early Christian Doctrines*, 257-58.
21. Athanasius, *Epistle as Serapionem* 1.24, in Bettenson, *The Early Church Fathers*, 296.
22. See "The Nicaeno-Constantinopolitan Creed," in *Documents of the Christian Church*, 25-26.
23. Kelly, *Early Christian Doctrines*, 258.

The goal of the reflection of these theologians was to find a middle ground between two dangers or heresies. On the one hand, they sought to avoid falling into the error of tritheism which views the Father, Son, and Spirit as three Gods. On the other hand, they could not move into Sabellianism with its suggestion that the three persons are merely modes of the revelation of the one God.[24]

In formulating a conception of God, the Cappadocians found two Greek synonyms helpful, *ousia* ("essence") and *hypostasis* ("center of consciousness" or "independent reality"). They declared that God is one *ousia* but three *hypostaseis*. The three "independent realities" share the same will, nature, and essence (that is, the one *ousia*). Yet each has special properties or activities.[25]

Building on the work of the earlier orthodox theologians, the Cappadocians maintained a subordination of order or dignity within the one divine reality. Ranking first is the Father, followed by the Son, and thirdly the Spirit. They connected this order with the special function of each of the three: the Father "generates," the Son "is generated," and the Spirit "proceeds." They added, however, that subordination in order does not lead to a subordination of essence among the three. On the contrary, Father, Son, and Spirit are equally divine.[26]

The Cappadocian formulation brought to a close the first chapter on the development of the doctrine of the Trinity. With it the church possessed a sophisticated statement of the Christian understanding of God. This conception preserved the Jewish heritage of monotheism, while acknowledging the full divinity of both the Son and the Spirit. At the heart of the Cappadocian formulation was the conviction that the trinitarian distinctions, Father, Son, and Holy Spirit, belong to the eternal nature of God. These distinctions cannot be relegated merely to God in appearance, God in salvation history, or God in our human perception.

---

24. For a short discussion of this, see Millard J. Erikson, *Christian Theology*, three volumes (Grand Rapids: Baker, 1983), 1:335-37.
25. Tillich, *A History of Christian Thought*, 77.
26. Kelly, *Early Christian Doctrines*, 264-65.

Trinitarian Doctrine in Post-Cappadocian Theology

The creeds composed by the ecumenical councils at Nicea and Constantinople and the formulation of the Cappadocian theologians provided the church with a fixed foundation for understanding God as triune. Yet, these conclusions did not end all discussion of the doctrine. On the contrary, the exact way of conceiving the three persons and the one God remained a source of contention.

Eastern and Western conceptions. Although the Cappadocian formulation was the standard for orthodoxy for all Christendom, the Eastern and Western churches soon developed differing outlooks concerning the nature of the Trinity. Basically, Eastern theologians tended to emphasize procession within the Godhead. Their Western counterparts, in contrast, focused more on the relations within the Trinity.

Several ideas were influential in the shaping of the Eastern outlook. Greek-speaking theologians built from the platonic philosophical concept of "emanation" and the difference the Cappadocians posited between the words *ousia* and *hypostasis*. At the heart of the Eastern understanding of the Trinity, however, was the subordination of the Son and the Spirit present in the East since the development of the logos Christology. Eastern thinkers viewed the Father as the source of divinity from whom the Son is generated and the Spirit proceeds in eternal movement. As a consequence of these ideas, theologians focused their gaze on the three individual members of the Trinity. The Father, Son, and Spirit possess the common essence of the Godhead, somewhat similar to the manner in which three human beings share the common essence of humanity. Eastern thinkers also tended to highlight the specific, individual workings of the Father, the Son, and the Spirit in the divine acts of creation and salvation. Because Latin, and not Greek, was the language of the West, Western thinkers were not fully cognizant of the nuances of the verbal constructions of their Eastern colleagues. To describe God they drew from the earlier work of Tertullian. This church father had been the first theologian to write in Latin, the first to use the word "Trinity,"[27] and the one who coined the well-known Latin formulation

---

27. For example, see Tertullian, *Adversus Praxean* 2, in *Early Christian Fathers*, 134.

tres personae, una substantia ("three persons, one substance"). Tertullian's description, however, served to complicate the matter. *Substantia* (the term Western theologians used to refer to the oneness of God) was the usual Latin translation of *hypostasis*, not *ousia*. And the word they used for the threeness in God, *persona*, was a theatrical term which meant "mask."

These difficulties of language were further compounded by the abiding influence of Athanasius. Prior to the innovative use of these terms in the Cappadocian formulation, this church father had understood *ousia* and *hypostasis* as synonyms.

Drawing out the implications of the Latin formulation, the theologians in the West emphasized the one divine essence or substance, rather than the threeness characteristic of the Eastern conception. Within the one substance they understood the threeness as relational. This is evidenced in the widespread use of the triangle as a symbol for the Trinity, which depicts each trinitarian member in reference to, or in relationship with, the other two. The fundamentally relational trinitarianism of the West led theologians to emphasize the joint workings of the Trinity in creation and salvation.

Paradigmatic of the Western understanding are the descriptions of the triune God developed by Augustine in his widely-read book *The Trinity*. In his explanation, Augustine appealed to the human person, for we display "vestages" of the Trinity because we are the image of God. The most central analogy is the triad of being, knowing, and willing.[28] From this central triad emerge three elaborations: the mind, its knowledge of itself, and its love for itself;[29] memory (the mind's latent knowledge of itself), intelligence (the mind's apprehension of itself), and will or love of itself (which sets the process of self-knowledge in motion);[30] and finally the mind as remembering God, knowing God, and loving God.[31] Each of these triads, but es-

---

28. Augustine, *Confessions* 13.1, trans. Vernon J. Bourke, volume 21 of *The Fathers of the Church*, ed. Roy Joseph Deferrari, eighty-one volumes (Washington: Catholic University of America Press, 1953), 417-18.
29. Augustine, *The Trinity* 9.2-8, trans. Steven McKenna, volume 45 of *The Fathers of the Church*, ed. Hermigild Dressler, eighty-one volumes (Washington: Catholic University of America Press, 1963), 271-78.
30. Ibid., 10.17-19 [310-13].
31. Ibid., 14.11-12 [425-30].

pecially the last one, are equal and essentially one; each casts light on the mutual relations of the three trinitarian persons.[32]

The filioque *controversy.* The differing conceptions of the Trinity which they described in the different languages they spoke led the theologians of each section of the church to misunderstand the intent of the formulation of the other. Eastern thinkers saw in the Western conception the heresy of Sabellianism, whereas their counterparts in the West feared that the East had fallen into tritheism. The differing outlooks toward the triune God gave rise to what is known as the *filioque* controversy, a theological parting of ways which contributed to the first and greatest schism in the church.

The focus of the controversy lay with the statement about the Holy Spirit found in the creed devised at Constantinople, but commonly referred to as the Nicene Creed. In its original wording the statement read, "We believe in…the Holy Spirit, the Lord and the Life-giver, that proceedeth from the Father, who with the Father and the Son is worshipped together and glorified together."[33]

In his influential book, *The Trinity*, Augustine went beyond the creedal formulation and taught that the Holy Spirit proceeds from the Son as well as from the Father.[34] A regional Spanish synod (the third Council of Toledo, 589 A.D.) incorporated Augustine's view into the Latin translation of the ancient creed, adding the word *filioque* ("and from the Son") to the description of the Spirit's procession.[35] Then in 809, a synod of Aachen (in Germany) gave its approval to this development,[36] adopting the altered Spanish version of the Latin text as the official creed for the newly constituted Holy Roman Empire.

Eventually the developments evoked a vigorous reaction from the Eastern church. In 867, the patriarch of Constantinople, Photius, leveled the charge of heresy against the leaders of the Western church

---

32. Kelly, *Early Christian Doctrines*, 278.

33. "The Nicaeno-Constantinopolitan Creed," in *Early Christian Documents*, 26.

34. The logic of Augustine's position is presented in Kelly, *Early Christian Doctrines*, 275.

35. For a discussion of the importance of these events, see Philip Schaff, *History of the Christian Church* (New York: Charles Scribner's Sons, 1899), 4:481-84.

36. Kenneth Scott Latourette, *A History of Christianity* (New York: Harper and Brothers, 1953), 304, 360.

for taking upon themselves the prerogative of tampering with an ecumenical creed.[37] In subsequent years the two positions solidified, the Eastern church rejecting what to them was an unwarranted inclusion of the *filioque* clause and the Western church defending the move.

Decline of the doctrine. The *filioque* controversy marked the last great debate over the doctrine of the Trinity. After the schism of the thirteenth century, other theological issues came to the forefront, crowding out further reflection on the trinitarian nature of God. With the subsiding of interest in the Trinity, the doctrine itself eventually came to be devalued.

Thomas Aquinas, for example, was more interested in setting forth what could be deduced from the world concerning the one God who is its First Cause than delineating the finer points of the doctrine of the Trinity. The situation remained unchanged by the Reformation. Luther disliked philosophical terms like "trinity," which had formed the basis for controversy in the church, although he did realize their descriptive value. Socinius and some of the radical Anabaptists simply rejected the doctrine of the Trinity on scriptural grounds; because they could not find it in the Bible, they declared the dogma to be inappropriate.

What at first was merely benign neglect became hostility in the Enlightenment. In the 1700s, thinkers deemphasized dogma as a whole (including doctrines such as the Trinity) in favor of the religion of reason. Because its purported foundation lay in special revelation and not in the general revelation accessible to all through reason, the doctrine of the Trinity was cast aside as a relic of a superstitious past.

The situation did not improve greatly when the Enlightenment gave way to the Romantic era. Friedrich Schleiermacher's lengthy delineation of *The Christian Faith* (750 pages of text in the English translation) does conclude with a discussion of God's triune nature. Yet the great theologian could offer only a skimpy 14-page treatment. Schleiermacher declared that the Trinity is "not an immediate

---

37. Justo L. Gonzales, *The Story of Christianity*, volume 1: *The Early Church to the Dawn of the Reformation* (San Francisco: Harper and Row, 1984), 264-65.

utterance concerning the Christian self-consciousness."[38] He then admits that he is not able to complete the task of constructing the doctrine.[39]

Recovery of the doctrine. Despite Schleiermacher's hesitations, the nineteenth century marked the first stage in the rediscovery of the doctrine of the Trinity. One significant theologian in this process was Schleiermacher's colleague at Berlin, George W. F. Hegel. Rather than an embarrassment, the concept of the Trinity is crucial to his conception of God.

According to Hegel, God is the Absolute Spirit, whose nature is to differentiate himself in order to determine himself. God accomplishes this self-differentiation through a dialectical process that unfolds under three determinations, corresponding to the three members of the Trinity.[40] Ultimately, however, Hegel's trinitarianism fell short of the patristic conception. For him, the reality of God is fully manifest only in the third mode, the Holy Spirit. As a result, only the Spirit—and not the triune God who is Father, Son, and Spirit—is God in the fullest sense.

In the twentieth century, Karl Barth was instrumental in elevating the doctrine of the Trinity to a significant place in theology. In fact, in his *Church Dogmatics* the doctrine functions as a type of prolegomenon. Barth's explication of the nature of God as triune forms the basis from which his systematic theology flows.

According to the Swiss theologian, revelation, which provides the foundation for theology, is a trinitarian event. The divine self-disclosure entails three moments: Revealer, Revelation, and Revealedness. These correspond to Father, Son, and Spirit.[41]

Since Barth, other thinkers have taken up the challenge to elevate the doctrine of the Trinity to the center of systematic theology. Among them, Karl Rahner, Jürgen Moltmann, and Wolfhart Pannen-

---

38. Friedrich Schleiermacher, *The Christian Faith*, ed. H. R. MacKintosh and J. S. Stewart (Edinburgh: T. & T. Clark, n.d.), 738.
39. Ibid., 751.
40. G.W.F. Hegel, *The Phenomenology of Mind*, trans. J. B. Baillie, Harper Torchbooks/The Academy Library edition (New York: Harper and Row, 1967), 766-85.
41. Karl Barth, *Church Dogmatics*, trans. G. W. Bromiley, second edition (Edinburgh: T. & T. Clark, 1975), 1/1:295.

berg have been the most influential.[42] Rahner's work has been foundational to the contemporary discussion. He set forth the important thesis that the immanent Trinity (God as the Triune One throughout all eternity apart from the world) and the economic Trinity (God as the Triune One at work in the world) are identical.[43]

Pannenberg's delineation ranks among the most highly developed statements of the doctrine.[44] He maintains that rather than relegating it to "footnote" status, we ought to place God's triune nature at the center of our theology. For Pannenberg—reminiscent of Barth—all of systematic theology is in some sense an explication of this central doctrine. At the same time, Pannenberg has been critical of the theological tradition from Augustine to Barth which views the trinitarian members as the internal relations within the one God. He claims that thereby theologians make God into a fourth "person" above the three members of the Trinity. Rather than speaking of the one God who is above the three, Pannenberg rightly argues that the one God is the three, and there is no God but the Father, Son, and Spirit.[45]

The Formulation of Trinitarian Doctrine

This outline of the historical development of the doctrine of the Trinity indicates that this aspect of the Christian conception of God is vital and central to our faith. But what actually does the doctrine declare? What does it mean to say that the God whom we have come to know is triune?

---

42. For a summary of several recent contributions as well as issues in the contemporary discussion, see John Thompson, "Modern Trinitarian Perspectives," *Scottish Journal of Theology* 44 (1991): 349-65.

43. Karl Rahner, *Theological Investigations* IV: *More Recent Writings*, trans. Kevin Smith (New York: Crossroad, 1982), 94-102.

44. For a summary and discussion of Pannenberg's position, see Stanley J. Grenz, *Reason for Hope: The Systematic Theology of Wolfhart Pannenberg* (New York: Oxford University Press, 1990), 46-54, 71-75.

45. Pannenberg articulates these themes repeatedly in his writings. See, for example, Wolfhart Pannenberg, "The Christian Vision of God: The New Discussion on the Trinitarian Doctrine," *Trinity Seminary Review* 13/2 (Fall 1991): 53-60.

The Content of Trinitarian Doctrine

We may summarize the actual content of the doctrine of the Trinity with four statements: "God is one," "God is three," "God is a diversity," and "God is a unity."

God is one. By the doctrine of the Trinity we are asserting that there is but one God. As Christians we are not polytheists—whether bitheists or tritheists—but staunch monotheists. We have come to know the God who is one. Consequently, our theological construction speaks of the one divine essence and of only one divine essence. The God whom we know is the one God confessed by the biblical faith community, whom the Old Testament people of God knew as Yahweh.

God is three. In affirming the doctrine of the Trinity we are confessing that the one God is three—the Father, the Son, and the Holy Spirit. Each of the three is deity, sharing together in, and together constituting, the one divine essence. The one God, therefore, is not an undifferentiated, solitary oneness, but subsists in a multiplicity, the three members of the Trinity. In fact, there is no God but the triune God; God is none other than Father, Son, and Spirit.

The divine threeness is not merely a matter of our perception of God. Nor are we merely speaking of God as he chooses to appear to us. Rather, the threeness of the one God is eternal; threeness is the way God actually is in his essential being. Like oneness, therefore, threeness belongs to the essence of God. The trinitarian distinctions are internal, and not merely external to the eternal divine reality.

Consequently, the distinctions within the one God are ontological. There are three—Father, Son, and Spirit—who together comprise the one God. Were the threeness of the one God not ontological, the Son and the Spirit would ultimately be lacking in full deity. As Athanasius rightly declared, in that case we could not participate in salvation.

Because the threeness of the one God is ontological it is also functional and economic. It belongs to the workings of the one God in the world. Just as there are three who together comprise the one God throughout all eternity, so also there are three—Father, Son, and

Spirit—who are at work in the world bringing about the one divine program for creation.

God is a diversity. The doctrine of the Trinity means that the one God is differentiated and hence is a diversity within unity. The three-ness of the one God means that the differentiations God has chosen to reveal to us are eternal, and they are internal to his nature. Father, Son, and Spirit actually belong to the divine essence throughout eternity. But further, these differentiations constitute actual diversity in the one God. The Father, Son, and Spirit are different from each other, and in the one God they differentiate themselves from each other. The differentiations in the one God represented by "Father," "Son," and "Spirit" constitute a diversity which is both ontological and economic.

Since the patristic era, theologians have viewed the ontological differentiations in terms of a double movement within the one God. They have described this movement by appeal to two terms, "generation" and "procession." These terms are, of course, metaphors, attempts to put in human words the ineffable essence of God. Nevertheless, they seek to assist us in reflecting on the nature of the God we have come to know.

"Generation" offers a means to differentiate the Father and the Son. The Son is generated by the Father. The Father is the one who generates the Son. "Procession" facilitates our differentiation of the Spirit from the Father and the Son. The Spirit is the one who proceeds from the Father (and from the Son). In short, the first member generates, the second is generated, and the third proceeds.

The ontological differentations facilitate an economic as well as an ontological diversity in the one God. Each of the three trinitarian members fulfills a specific role in the one divine program. The Father functions as the ground of the world and of the divine program for creation. The Son functions as the revealer of God, the exemplar and herald of the Father's will for creation, and the redeemer of humankind. And the Spirit functions as the personal divine power active in the world, the completer of the divine will and program.

God is a unity. Through the doctrine of the Trinity we affirm that, although differentiated from each other both ontologically and functionally, the three trinitarian persons comprise a unity that entails diversity. Like the divine diversity, the divine unity is both ontological and economic.

The economic unity of the three trinitarian members means that, despite their varying functions in the one divine program, all are involved in every area of God's working in the world. The divine activity is characterized by cooperation among the three members of the Trinity.

Although the Father is the ground of the creation of the world, the Son and the Spirit act with the Father in the creative task. The Son is the Word, the principle of creation, through whom the Father creates. And the Spirit is the divine power active in bringing the world into existence.

Likewise, although the Son is the redeemer of humanity, the Father and the Spirit are involved together with the Son in the program of reconciliation. The Father is the agent at work through the Son (e.g., 2 Cor. 5:18-19). And the Spirit is the active divine power effecting the process from the new birth to the eschatological resurrection.

Finally, although the Spirit is the completer of the divine program, he is joined in this eschatological work by the Son and the Father. The Son is the Lord who will return in glory. And the Father is the one who will be "all-in-all" (1 Cor. 15:28).

As these examples indicate, in each divine work the Father acts through the Son and by the agency of the Spirit.

The economic unity of the trinitarian members also means that each is dependent on the work of the others for the fulfillment of the one divine program. In sending the Son into the world, the Father entrusted his program, which includes his own rule or kingship and with it even his deity, to the Son (e.g., Matt. 11:27). The Father and the Son, in turn, have entrusted the completion of the divine program to the Spirit, who glorifies the Son—and through him the Father—in the world.

The functioning of the three trinitarian members in an economic unity reaches behind the economic Trinity, however. It points to the parallel truth concerning the immanent Trinity. The three members of the Trinity build an eternal, ontological unity in diversity. Thereby Father, Son, and Spirit together comprise the divine being and essence. Theologians sometimes employ the term *perichoresis* ("interpenetration") to refer to the interrelation, partnership, and mutual dependence of the trinitarian members not only in the workings of God in the world but even more foundationally in their very subsistence as the one God.

The New Testament (specifically, 1 John 4:7–21) suggests that the ontological unity which the three constitute and therefore which comprises the divine essence is *agape* (love). This does not mean, however, that love itself is God. In the original Greek, John's construction is carefully written, so as to state that "God is as to character love." While God is love, love cannot be God. Love is a relational term which presupposes someone who loves and someone who is loved. Therefore, love has no objective existence apart from being the relation between the lover and the beloved.

Helpful in understanding the theological significance of the biblical assertion "God is love" is Hegel's concept of the essence of "person." To be person, he asserted, means to be in self-dedication to another.[46] The application to the triune God follows, one which in embryonic form may actually date back to Athanasius.[47] The divine unity is comprised by the reciprocal self-dedication among the trinitarian members. This corresponds to the New Testament concept of *agape*, which may be defined as the giving of oneself for the other. Consequently, the assertion that love forms the foundation of the unity in the one God opens a window on the divine reality. The unity of God is nothing less than the self-dedication of the trinitarian persons to each other. Indeed, God is love—the divine essence is the love that binds together the Trinity.

The *Filioque* and the Relational Trinity

To us today the *filioque* controversy that eventually split the church may seem to be merely a spat over unimportant words. Yet,

---

46. G.W.F. Hegel, *Lectures on the Philosophy of Religion*, trans. E. B. Speirs and J. Burton Sanderson, three volumes (New York: Humanities Press, 1974), 3:24-25.

47. Athanasius wrote, "Since the Father has given all things to the Son, he possesses all things afresh in the Son." *Apologia Contra Arian* 3.36, in *A Select Library of Nicene and Post-Nicene Fathers of the Christian Church*, volume 4: *St. Athanasius: Select Works and Letters*, trans. Atkinson, ed. Archibald Robertson, second series (Grand Rapids: Eerdmans, 1975), 119.

apart from the grave ecclesiastical question concerning the propriety of the West in adding to an ecumenical creed, the disagreement over the propriety of the addition of *filioque* did carry theological importance.

From our vantage point, we are able to see the theological validity of both sides in the controversy that gave rise to the greatest schism in the history of the church.

On the one hand, the thinkers of the Eastern church were correct in their desire to retain the focus on the three trinitarian members—Father, Son, and Spirit—in the face of the overly relational emphasis of the Western model. By so doing they were in a position to avoid some of the theological traps to which their colleagues in the Western church have been susceptible.

For example, Eastern thinkers have been less likely to speak of "God" as a personal, acting agent in the world, and consequently to posit "God" as the "real" person above the three trinitarian members. Further, because they did not develop as strict a connection between the work of the Spirit and the work of Christ demanded by the *filioque*, Eastern theologians have been less likely to limit the activity of the Spirit to God's purposes in the salvation of humankind as mediated solely through the church. Eastern thinkers are in a better theological position to develop a Christian conception of creation which links God's work in making the world with his activity in saving it. Finally, the Eastern tradition has tended to view salvation in the broader sense of deification—our sharing in the divine life—rather than merely in terms of forensic (legal) righteousness or the forgiveness of sins.

On the other hand, the Western thinkers were not without warrant in concluding that a relationship must exist between the Son and the Spirit. The addition of *filioque* to the creed did have a basis in Scripture. The biblical writers do, of course, speak of the Holy Spirit as the Spirit of the Father or the Spirit of God. But in addition, Paul calls him "the Spirit of the Son" (Gal. 4:6) and "the Spirit of the Lord" (2 Cor. 3:17-18). And Jesus not only promised that he would petition the Father on behalf of his disciples, but that he would himself send the Spirit to them (John 15:26).

Building from this biblical foundation, the Western assertion of an intratrinitarian relationship between the Son and Spirit carries far-reaching theological importance. This relationship provides the theological foundation guaranteeing the continuity of the present work of the Spirit with the completed work of the Son. The Spirit is the Spirit of Christ. Therefore, the activity in which the Holy Spirit now engages is nothing less than the outworking or application of the work completed by Jesus of Nazareth.

In addition to this implication for the economic Trinity—the work of the triune God in the world—the Western model also has great importance for our understanding of the immanent Trinity—the dynamic within the one God in all eternity apart from the world. The trinitarian theologies of both East and West postulate two eternal movements within the one divine reality which give rise to the three persons. Nevertheless, the Western relational understanding appears to offer a stronger basis for understanding the eternal workings within God. It declares that the foundation of the inner life of the divine Trinity lies in the relationship between the Father and the Son, and that this relationship, in turn, is the Spirit, who is related to both of the other two.

The *filioque* controversy allows us to understand more fully the relational dynamic of the triune God. Two movements logically inhere within the one God. From the West, we learn that the second movement, the procession of the Spirit, is connected with both the Father and the Son. But the position of the East reminds us that ultimately both movements find their source in the priority of the Father.

(1) The first movement in the one God is generation. As Origen postulated, throughout eternity the Father generates the Son. This assertion emphasizes the priority of the Father in the triune God. The Father is the foundation of the divinity of the Son (and by extension, of the divinity of the Spirit as well). Yet, this movement does not only constitute the second member of the Trinity, who draws his life from the Father. Rather, as Athanasius noted, it also constitutes the first member, for without the Son he is not the Father.[48]

---

48. Athanasius, *Contra Arian* 3.6, in *The Early Christian Fathers*, 287.

Generation, therefore, leads to the differentiation between the first and second members of the Trinity. But the Father and the Son are also bound together. The bond between the two is the mutual love they share. Throughout all eternity the Father loves the Son, and the Son reciprocates that love. This love arises as well from the idea of generation. Out of love the Father generates the Son, and the Son in turn reciprocates the love of the One who generates him.

(2) The Father's eternal generation of the Son not only constitutes the first and second trinitarian members, it also leads to the third. As Augustine noticed, the love between the Father and the Son is the Holy Spirit, who is the eternal Spirit of the relationship between the Father and the Son.[49] Being the Spirit of the relationship between the first and second trinitarian members, he proceeds from the Father and from the Son, as the Western version of the creed declares.

The foundation for the triunity of God, therefore, lies with the eternal relationship between the Father and the Son. They share a fellowship of love, which is concretized in the third person. As a result, the Holy Spirit is the bond between the Father and the Son.[50] Therefore, the movement of generation which constitutes the Father and the Son leads logically to the movement of procession, which constitutes the Spirit as the Spirit of the Father and the Son.

Analogies to the Trinity

As early as the fourth century, Christians have proposed analogies from the natural realm to assist in our understanding the doctrine of the Trinity. Each analogy, although helpful to a limited extent, falls short of the intricacy of the Christian description of the divine reality.

One proposed analogy is the chemical formula, H_2O. Just as this compound can assume three forms—ice, water, or steam—so also

---

49. Augustine, *The Trinity* 6.5.7 [206-207]; see also 15.17.27 [491-92]; 5.11.12 [189-90]; 15.19.37 [503-504]. For the connection of this Augustinian idea to the Greek tradition, see Yves Congar, *I Believe in the Holy Spirit*, trans. David Smith, three volumes (New York: Seabury, 1983), 3:88-89, 147-48. For a contemporary delineation of this position, see, David Coffey, "The Holy Spirit as the Mutual Love of the Father and the Son," *Theological Studies* 51 (1990): 193-229.

50. Augustine, *The Trinity* 15.17.27-29,31 [491-94, 495-96]; 15.19.37 503-504].

the one God is three persons. This analogy, however, reflects a basically Sabellian understanding of the Trinity. Ice, water, and steam are simply three modes in which the one chemical formula can appear. Two other analogies are similar. A tree consists of three—root, trunk, and branch—yet there is but one tree. Likewise an egg is yolk, eggwhite, and shell. These analogies likewise have a fatal flaw. Neither reflects the dynamic movement by which the three trinitarian persons constitute one another and thereby dynamically constitute the one God.

All such analogies are reminders that the imprint of the triune God may be found in creation, as Augustine suggested. But nevertheless, nothing in creation is totally analogous to the one God who is the three-in-one.

The Theological Implication of Trinitarian Doctrine

The doctrine of the Trinity forms the foundation for the Christian conception of the essence of God. For this reason, it carries profound implications for our understanding of the divine reality.

Love as the Essence of God

As the apostolic writer indicates, the essence of God is love. The doctrine of the Trinity indicates how this is the case. Throughout all eternity the divine life—the life of the Father, Son, and Spirit—is best characterized by our word "love." Love, therefore, that is, the reciprocal self-dedication of the trinitarian members, builds the unity of the one God. There is no God but the Father, Son, and Spirit, bound together throughout eternity.

Love and the inner dymanic of God. When viewed in terms of its role in the doctrine of the Trinity, the term "love" offers a window on the profundity of the reality of God as understood by the Christian tradition. Trinitarian "love" describes God's inner life—God as God throughout eternity apart from any references to creation.

The explanation as to how love can be the essence of God lies in the triune nature of God as Father, Son, and Spirit. Love is a relational term, requiring both subject and object (Someone loves someone else). Were God a solitary acting subject, a person apart from Father, Son, and Spirit, God would require the world as the object of his love in order to be who he is, namely, the Loving One. But because God is triune, the divine reality already comprehends both love's subject and object. Consequently, the essence of God does indeed lie in the relationship between the Father and the Son (love) which is the Spirit.

Viewed theologically, therefore, John's statement, "God is love," refers first of all to the intratrinitarian relationship within the eternal God. God is love within himself: The Father loves the Son; the Son reciprocates that love; and this love between the Father and the Son is the Holy Spirit. In short, through all eternity God is the social Trinity, the community of love.

Love as the fundamental divine attribute. In that God is love apart from the creation of the world, love characterizes God. Love is the eternal essence of the one God. But this means that trinitarian love is not merely one attribute of God among many. Rather, love is the fundamental "attribute" of God. "God is love" is the foundational ontological statement we can declare concerning the divine essence. God is foundationally the mutuality of the love relationship between Father and Son, and this personal love is the Holy Spirit.

Because throughout eternity and apart from the world the one God is love, the God who is love cannot but respond to the world in accordance to his own eternal essence, which is love. Thus, this essential characteristic of God likewise describes the way God interacts with his world. "Love," therefore, is not only the description of the eternal God in himself, it is likewise the fundamental characteristic of God in relationship with creation. With profound theological insight, therefore, John bursts forth, "For God so loved the world that he gave..." (John 3:16).

Love and the Divine Holiness, Jealousy, and Wrath

The foundational attribute of God, the central and basic statement we can assert about the essence of God, is "God is love." There is no God but the Father and the Son throughout eternity bound together by love, a relationship concretized in the Holy Spirit. It is only within this context that we can understand the supposedly "dark" assertions concerning God, including his holiness, jealous nature, and wrathfulness.

In the twentieth century, many theologians asserted that holiness, which includes God's resolute disposition against sin.—and not merely love—must be ranked among the fundamental moral attributes of God. Brunner, for example, spoke of a "dialectic" or "paradoxical dualism" of holiness and love.[51] Louis Berkhof listed three moral attributes, which he saw as "the most glorious of the divine perfections": goodness (under which he subsumed love), holiness, and righteousness.[52] And the great Baptist thinker, Augustus Hopkins Strong, elevated holiness to "the fundamental attribute in God."[53]

In part this magnifying of holiness as a central divine attribute is motivated by the desire to protect God's prerogative in condemning unrepentant sinners and in turn to make palatable the doctrine of hell. Properly understood, however, love includes within it what this concern seeks to preserve. Simply stated, the presence of sin transforms the experience of the divine love from the bliss intended by God into wrath.

The possibility of experiencing love as wrath arises out of the nature of love itself. Bound up with love is a protective jealousy. As James I. Packer has noted, in addition to the sinful, vicious attitude we generally associate with the term, humans also display another jealousy, the "zeal to protect a love relationship or to avenge it when broken."[54] Packer then applied this to God: "Now Scripture consistently views God's jealousy as being of this latter kind, that is, as an aspect of his covenant love for his own people."

Genuine love, therefore, is positively jealous. It is protective, for the true lover seeks to maintain, even defend the love relationship whenever it is threatened by disruption, destruction, or outside intru-

---

51. Bunner, *The Christian Doctrine of God*, 163, 167, 183.

52. Louis Berkhof, *Systematic Theology*, revised edition (Grand Rapids: Eerdmans, 1953), 70-76.

53. Augustus Hopkins Strong, *Systematic Theology*, three volumes (Philadelphia: Griffith and Rowland, 1907), 1:296.

54. James I. Packer, *Knowing God* (Downers Grove, Ill.: InterVarsity, 1973), 154.

sion. Whenever another seeks to injure or undermine the love relationship, he or she experiences love's jealousy, which we call "wrath." When this dimension is lacking, love degenerates into mere sentimentality.

It is in this way that we can understand that the loving One is a jealous, wrathful God. Those who would undermine the love God pours forth for the world experience his love in the form of wrath.

God's holiness, jealousy, and wrath in the face of sin can be viewed in another manner as well. God's love for creation means that he is concerned that each person become all that God designed humankind to be. This forms the theological background for the repeated biblical injunction that we be holy (e.g., Ex. 20:3-6). But as humans reject the divine design, they suffer the outworking of their chosen wayward course of action. They remain the recipients of God's love, but experience that love in the form of wrath.

The final outworking of the rejection of God's love is a never-ending experience of the wrath of the eternal Lover. Hell, therefore, is not the experience of the absence of God's love. God loves his creation with an eternal love. Therefore God's love is present even in hell. But in hell people experience the presence of the divine love in the form of wrath. We will look more closely at this topic in chapter 24.

Love and the Other Moral Attributes

The declaration "God is love" forms the basis for our understanding of the so-called moral attributes of God. These include terms such as "grace," "mercy," and "longsuffering"—terms which speak of God's goodness. All such words, however, are best seen as various attempts to describe dimensions of God's fundamental character—love—as it is experienced by his creation. Because God is love, God is good—that is, gracious, merciful, and long-suffering—in all he does. Above all, because God loves, he seeks the salvation and renewal of fallen creation.

Trinitarian Doctrine and Christian Life

The doctrine of the Trinity is foundational to Christian theology. It is required for fidelity to the scriptural teaching concerning the self-revelation of the one God as Father, Son, and Spirit. It is likewise demanded by our desire to be faithful to the Christian experience of God's salvation. As Athanasius argued, the Son and the Spirit must be truly divine, if salvation is an actuality. At the same time, the unity of the Father, Son, and Spirit in the program of salvation is necessary, if we are indeed saved by the grace of the one God who has reconciled the world to himself.

In addition to its foundational theological importance, the doctrine of the Trinity is vital to Christian living. Two applications to our life as disciples will illustrate this fact.

Trinitarian Prayer

Our affirmation of the doctrine of the Trinity forms the foundation for the way we pray. In fact, we can enjoy renewed meaning and power in our prayer life as we grow in our understanding of the nature of the triune God who calls us to pray and who responds to prayer. Cognizance of the doctrine of the Trinity will facilitate a consciousness of whom we address in prayer.

The practice of some Christians is simply to address all prayer to Jesus. This, of course, is understandable, for we sense a closeness to our Lord who walked the earth and experienced the conditions of human existence. Others employ the general term "God" in addressing prayer. This too is understandable, for prayer is communication with God.

Yet, the doctrine of the Trinity suggests a more theologically mature manner of praying. Because God is triune—none other than Father, Son, and Spirit—our prayers ought to be addressed to the three trinitarian persons in accordance with both the purpose of the specific prayer we are voicing and the function of each trinitarian person.

As the New Testament itself confirms, we normally ought to address the Father in prayer. Jesus himself instructed his disciples to pray, "Our heavenly Father." And James reminds his readers that "every good and perfect gift comes from the Father" (James 1:17).

The doctrine of the Trinity reminds us that the Father functions as the ground and source, both of creation itself and also of salvation. Consequently, prayer is properly addressed to the Father as this glorious ground and source (Rev. 4:8-11). For this reason, in prayer we come before the Father. We praise him for who he is, thank him for what he has done, and petition him in the face of need, because he is the good and wise supplier of all that we lack.

Certain prayer, however, ought to be addressed to the Son. In prayer we can praise our Lord for who he is. Insofar as his work is completed, prayer addressed to the Son should also include thanksgiving for what he has done (see, Rev. 5:11-14). In addition, however, because the Son now intercedes for us, we can also thank him for this activity. And because we anticipate his return at the end of history, we can praise him in advance for what that event will mean. In this manner, we become the advance chorus of all creation that will publicly pay him homage as the Lord of all (Phil. 2:9-10).

As the one who completes the program of God, the work of the Spirit is ongoing. In this context, we can also address prayer to the third member of the Trinity. Although there is no direct biblical reference to prayer addressed to the Spirit, we can appeal to the long tradition of church liturgy and hymnology which leads us to approach the third trinitarian person. We will naturally offer our praise and thanksgiving to him. In addition, however, we may petition the Spirit in areas of his work in the world, although it is also proper to petition the Father to send the Holy Spirit to engage in such work.

At the same time, we must keep in mind that the Spirit acts as the "silent" member of the Trinity. Rather than drawing attention to himself, he manifests his presence by exalting the Son and the Father. Spirit-filled prayer, therefore, moves from the Spirit through the Son to the Father, for generally the Spirit prompts and empowers us to address our heavenly Father, through the name of Jesus.

Trinitarian Ethics

Not only should it affect the way we pray, the doctrine of the Trinity should influence the way we act. Our understanding that the God we know is triune forms the foundation for our Christian ethic.

Insofar as God is the ultimate model and standard for humankind, the essential nature of God forms the paradigm for the life of the Christian and of the Christian community (Matt. 10:39). At the heart of the Christian understanding of God is the declaration that God is triune—Father, Son, and Spirit. This means that in his eternal essence the one God is a social reality, the social Trinity. Because God is the social Trinity, a plurality in unity, the ideal for humankind does not focus on solitary persons, but on persons-in-community. God intends that we reflect his nature in our lives. This is only possible, however, as we move out of our isolation and into relationships with others. The ethical life, therefore, is the life-in-relationship, or the life-in-community.

The doctrine of the Trinity states further that the essence of God is love. Consequently, love stands as the ideal and the standard for human life as well.

God directs his love to all creation. The Triune One is concerned about all creatures and wills the best for creation. Therefore, our task is to seeking to reflect God's loving concern for all creatures in our natural environment, for the principle of love requires that human beings be concerned for the welfare of creation in the way that God is. For this reason, as Christians we ought to be at the forefront in promoting a sense of the true stewardship God has entrusted to humankind. We seek, in short, to live in community with the world of nature around us.

But humans are the special recipients of God's love. God loves each human being, and therefore he demands that we act justly. This forms the context for the repeated biblical intimation that God takes up the cause of the destitute and oppressed, and therefore he is on the side of the poor. God calls us to be his instruments in bringing about the divine vision of love, justice, and righteousness for all humankind. This task, however, must begin with the household of faith. The New Testament reminds us that as Christians our concern for humankind must begin "at home," that is, with the needs of sisters and brothers within the community of Christ (1 John 4:11). But it must not stop there. Rather, we must see the entire world as the object of our care and concern, just as the love of the triune God spills beyond the boundaries of the trinitarian members to encompass all creation.

The doctrine of the Trinity forms the heart of the Christian conception of God. Rather than being of secondary importance, this doctrine is central to our faith. The implications of this conception are immense. Above all, it suggests that God is himself relational. The Father, Son, and Spirit are the social Trinity. Therefore, community is not merely an aspect of human life, for it lies within the divine essence. To this relational heart of our conception of God we now turn.

3 The Relational God

> *We proclaim to you what we have seen and heard, so that you also may have fellowship with us. And our fellowship is with the Father and with his Son, Jesus Christ.*
> *(1 John 1:3)*

Outline

At the heart of the Christian faith is the affirmation that in Christ we have come to know the triune God. There is but one God, and this God is eternally none other than the Father, Son, and Holy Spirit. Consequently, at the heart of Christian theology is the doctrine of the Trinity. Yet our quest to speak about the mystery of the triune God leads us to probe further: What linguistic imagery provides a proper tool to assist us in conceiving of God?

Many theologians appeal to the concept of divine attributes in an attempt to pierce through the veil of mystery to the one, eternal divine essence. However, because God is triune—the Father, Son, and Spirit in eternal relationship—our quest to speak of the being and attributes of God actually constitutes an attempt to characterize the relational nature of God—God in relationship.

In the previous chapter our focus lay with the relationships among the three trinitarian members. Indeed, questions concerning the divine essence rightly begin with the intratrinitarian relations. But the relational God does not remain in isolation. Rather, from the internal divine dynamic our God enters into relationship with creation. For this reason we must also ask: What characterizes the manner in which the triune God enters into relationship with the world he creates? In inquiring concerning the "being" and "attributes" of God, therefore, we are asking about the relationships within the one God and also about the triune God in relation with us.

It is to the task of describing the one, relational God that we now turn our attention.

The Nature of the Relational God

The doctrine of the Trinity declares that God is relational. The one, true God is the social Trinity—Father, Son, and Spirit. Furthermore, the divine reality is eternally relational even apart from the world, in that the three trinitarian persons comprise the one God. But not only is the immanent Trinity relational, the triune God enters into relationship with the world he creates.

The relational focus forms the context for understanding certain aspects of the language the community of faith employs in speaking about the God we have come to know. Our task in this section is to explore the significance which God's relational nature carries for certain prominent theological terms.

God as (a) Being

Throughout theological history, thinkers have grappled with how best to define or conceive of God. Perhaps the most deeply ingrained conception among Christians views God as *a* being—albeit an eternal, uncreated being—who is both present within and exists beyond the world of created beings. This conception has a certain affinity to the anthropomorphic language about God employed by the Old Testament authors. Nevertheless, it owes its prominence as much to Greek philosophy—to the legacy of Plato and Aristotle—as to any biblical precedence it might claim.

The tradition of Plato was especially strong during the patristic era, as Christian platonists linked the God of the Bible to Plato's Form of the Good. During the Middle Ages Platonic theology gave way to Aristotle's conception of the divine being as the "unmoved mover." According to Aristotle, God is the static, final cause of all motion in the world. All things strive after him, but he himself remains unmoved by or undrawn to creation.[1] Whether influenced by Plato or Aristotle, Christian thinkers who built from the Greek philosophical tradition agreed that God is the highest being, the "impassi-

---

1. Aristotle, *Metaphysics* 1071b-1074, trans. Hugh Tredennick, volume 18 of the *Loeb Classical Library*, ed. G. P. Goold, twenty-three volumes (Cambridge, MA: Harvard University Press, 1965), 18:142-65.

ble" one who is eternally unchanging amidst the changing flux of the world of time.[2]

In the twentieth century, the classical postulate of the unchangeable God came under widespread attack. One important challenge arose from an influential movement known as "process theology."[3] Foundational to the newer outlook is the assertion that God is integrally involved with creation. God is not static, but active and affected by the events of the world. Process thinkers claim to provide a conception of God more appropriate to modern understandings of the workings of the universe. Yet despite important differences with the older conception, process theology continues to speak of God as an extant being among other beings. In the process conception God remains *a* being, one who glides through the historical process with his creatures and whose experiences are augmented by theirs.

Forming a more radical break with the classical conception are those theologians that reject the suggestion that God is a being among beings. One alternative, pantheism, boasts a long pedigree, especially among the religious traditions of the East. Pantheists speak of God as "the soul of the universe." This does not mean that the universe is God, as critics so often mistakenly suppose. Rather, pantheists describe the relationship between God and the world as analogous to that between the human soul and the physical body. Hence, God is the animating, or life principle of the world, which in turn may in some sense be seen as his body.[4]

Sometimes associated with pantheism is the proposal of Paul Tillich. According to Tillich, God is not *a* being, but "being itself" or the "ground of being." For Tillich this description is virtually self-evident: "If God is not being itself, he is subordinate to it."[5] Tillich

---

2. Brian Davies, "Impassibility," in the *Westminster Dictionary of Christian Theology*, ed. Alan Richardson and John Bowden (Philadelphia: Westminster, 1983), 288. See, for an example, Thomas Aquinas, *Summa Theologica* 1.2.3.

3. For a discussion of process theology, see Stanley J. Grenz and Roger E. Olson, *Twentieth Century Theology* (Downers Grove, Ill.: InterVarsity, 1992), 130-34.

4. Recently this idea has found echo in certain feminist writings. See, for example, Sallie McFague, *Models of God: Theology for an Ecological, Nuclear Age* (Philadelphia: Fortress, 1987), 59-87.

5. Paul Tillich, *Systematic Theology*, three volumes (Chicago: University of Chicago Press, 1953), 1:236.

understood this assertion to mean that God is the structure which lies behind reality and which is the ground of everything that is.[6]

The advent of the theology of hope in the late 1960s brought a quite different and highly innovative proposal. Its chief architects, Jürgen Moltmann and Wolfhart Pannenberg, sought to avoid speaking of God as an existing being among other beings. They sensed the importance of the atheist challenge that the traditional view of God was incompatible with human freedom. In the words of Pannenberg, "An existent being acting with omnipotence and omniscience would make freedom impossible."[7] To accomplish the needed transformation of theology, they shifted the focus of the answer to the question of God away from either the past or the present, that is, away from the idea of God as a being who exists throughout time. Instead of the past, they looked to the future to provide the "location" of God. In the words of Pannenberg, "The future seems to offer an alternative to an understanding of real which is concentrated entirely upon what is existing. For what belongs to the future is not yet existent and yet it already determines present experience."[8] Hence, God is "the power of the future."[9] But how can something which does not yet exist determine present experience? Pannenberg explains that humans who "are orientated towards the future...always experience their present and past in the light of the future which they hope for or which they fear."[10]

The future orientation suggested by thinkers such as Pannenberg and Moltmann provides a promising starting point for conceiving of the divine reality.[11] God is best conceived not as standing behind us or above us, but in front of us. For systematic theology, this basic outlook means that we no longer seek to answer theological ques-

---

6. Ibid., 1:238.

7. Wolfhart Pannenberg, "Speaking about God in the Face of Atheist Criticism," in *The Idea of God and Human Freedom*, trans. R. A. Wilson (Philadelphia: Westminster, 1973), 109.

8. Ibid., 110.

9. Jürgen Moltmann, *The Experiment Hope*, ed. M. Douglas Meeks (Philadelphia: Fortress, 1975), 51.

10. Pannenberg, "Speaking about God in the Face of Atheist Criticism," in *The Idea of God and Human Freedom*, 110.

11. For a description and appraisal of the contributions of Moltmann and Pannenberg, see Grenz and Olson, *Twentieth Century Theology*, 170-79.

tions from the perspective of the past—from the decisions God made before the creation of the world. Rather we engage in the theological enterprise by viewing reality from the perspective of the future— from God's ultimate goal for creation.

Although they may offer differing models of God, proponents of the contemporary emphasis on the social Trinity are in agreement at one crucial point. The traditional discussion of God as a being is no longer helpful. There is no God but the Father, Son, and Spirit. Therefore, our description of the divine reality does not refer to a God beyond the three trinitarian persons. Rather, in describing God we are describing precisely the Father, Son, and Spirit in their eternal relations.

God as Transcendent and Immanent

There is an additional noteworthy feature in the contemporary discussion of the divine nature. Despite their variety, nearly all of the suggestions—from Aristotle's "unmoved mover" to Pannenberg's "power of the future"—quite naturally speak of the divine reality in terms of God in relation to the world. What begins as a query as to whether the eternal God is an existing being quickly moves to the question of God's relationship to the world. This is true even of the Reformed tradition, which has played such an important formative role in evangelical theology. The Reformed emphasis on God as the Sovereign One defines God fundamentally in terms of his relationship to the world.

In a sense, the relational description of God—speaking of the divine reality in terms of God's relationship to creation—is inevitable. We have no other vantage point from which to view God than his gracious condescending to us in what we call "revelation." However, God's primary concern in revelation is not simply that we be able to formulate propositions concerning his eternal being. God's intent is that we understand who he is as the eternally relational, triune God and who he is in relationship to the world he has made, in order that we may enter into fellowship with him. Revelation, therefore, is the self-disclosure of God-in-relation.

From the beginning, Christian theology has characterized God and the world by appeal to two theological terms, "transcendence" and "immanence," which describe the two foundational aspects of that relationship. On the one hand, God is transcendent. God is self-sufficient apart from the world. He is above the universe and comes to the world from beyond. The Scriptures forcefully declare God's transcendence. The preacher cautioned his readers, "God is in heaven and you are on earth" (Eccl. 5:2). Similarly, before receiving his commission, the prophet Isaiah reported seeing the Lord "seated on a throne, high and exalted" (Isa. 6:1).

On the other hand, God is immanent in the world. This means that God is present to creation. He is active within the universe, involved with the natural processes and in human history. Paul emphasized this truth in his well-known speech to the Athenians. God "is not far from each one of us," he said, "'For in him we live and move and have our being'" (Acts 17:27-28). The Old Testament, especially the wisdom literature (e.g., Job 27:3; 33:4; 34:14-15; Ps. 104:29-30) repeatedly sound the theme of God being the sustainer of creation through his Spirit. Likewise, Jesus credited the natural processes such as sunshine and rain, the feeding of the birds, and the beauty of the flowers to the agency of his Father (Matt. 5:45; 6:25-30; 10:29-30).

In short, the God we know is immanent and transcendent. He is that reality who is present and active within the world process. Yet he is not simply to be equated with it, for he is at the same time self-sufficient and "beyond" the universe. In conceiving of God, therefore, we dare neither place him so far beyond the world that he cannot enter into relationship with his creatures nor collapse him so thoroughly into the world processes that he cannot stand over the creation which he made.

God as Spirit

Of the various descriptive words concerning God, perhaps none has gained more widespread acceptance than the assertion "God is Spirit." This affirmation can claim dominical foundation, for Jesus said: "God is spirit. Those who would worship him must worship him in spirit and truth" (see John 4:24). Yet we must ask, What actually does the faith community mean in affirming "God is Spirit"? What is "spirit"? And in what sense is this term a designation of the divine reality?

Hegel's conception of "spirit." Through his reappropriation of the term (German: *Geist*) G. W. F. Hegel inaugurated the modern discussion of "spirit" in philosophical theology.[12] The German philosopher claimed that *Geist* is fundamental to a proper understanding of both God and humans.

Hegel's term (*Geist*) combines the concept of rationality reflected in the English word "mind" with the dimension of the supermaterial bound up with our term "spirit." "Spirit," then, is not merely a substance or an existing thing, but an active subject, an activity, or a process. According to Hegel, all processes in nature and history form a unified whole which is the activity of God. Through them the divine reality takes on objective form and comes to full awareness of itself. This occurs particularly in human artistic, religious, and philosophical creativity. According to Hegel these are the self-manifestation of the divine Spirit. Hence, God comes to self-awareness through the world processes, especially through the human consciousness of God. In this sense, God is "Absolute Spirit," and human beings in turn are relative spirit.

Hegel's understanding of "spirit" as an activity rather than a passive or static being provides theology with a helpful insight. In fact, his view lies closer to the biblical concept of God as "spirit," than does the Greek conception which has dominated Christian theology.

The biblical conception of "spirit." The concept of spirit runs through the entire Bible. This biblical conception offers the foundation to our theological understanding of God as spirit.

Hebrew *ru'ach* means basically "breath" or "wind" and secondarily "the life principle in the human person." The development in meaning from "breath" to "life principle" arose quite naturally, for the ancient peoples knew that breathing was the normal sign of life. The Hebrews took this idea a step farther. They acknowledged that God is the source of the life principle in each human being, the presence of which was indicated by breath. The second creation narra-

---

12. For a discussion of Hegel's thought, see ibid., 31-39.

tive, for example, depicts God breathing into Adam's nostrils "the breath of life." As a result, "man became a living being" (Gen. 2:7).

The awareness that God is the source of the life principle led to a third meaning for *ru'ach*. "Spirit" is the divine power which creates and sustains life. It is the power of God which brings life into being and sustains life in existence.

The Greek term *pneuma* reflects a similar interconnectedness of meanings. It too refers both to "wind" and "breath." It too speaks of "life" for which breath is both the sign and the condition. And it too came to mean "the life-creating power."

These Hebrew and Greek words lie behind the biblical affirmation "God is Spirit," a declaration that affirms a vital dimension of the relationship of God to creation. By declaring "God is Spirit" we acknowledge that God is the source of all life. God is the one who bestows life on his creatures—on each living thing but most significantly on humans.

Theological implications. To say "God is Spirit" is to acknowledge that God is the source of created life. Yet this affirmation does not exhaust the significance of our confession. Lying behind God's relationship to the world as the Giver of life is a prior internal divine relationship, an eternal relationship within the triune God. To refer to God as Spirit means to understand God as the Living One. The triune God is dynamic movement.

Jesus himself gave indication of this vital internal divine relationship: "For as the Father has life in himself, so he has granted the Son to have life in himself" (John 5:26). This statement indicates that the divine vitality focuses on the relationship between the Father and the Son. The divine life is the eternal activity of the Father who as the fountain of deity generates the Son to share in his own divinity. The self-giving of the Father for the Son, in turn, is reciprocated in the Son's self-giving for the Father. This relationship between the Father and the Son comes forth as the third trinitarian member, the Holy Spirit. Because he is the Spirit of the Father and the Son, the Spirit is the essence of the triune God.

To say "God is Spirit," therefore, is to speak about the relational God. It is to acknowledge that throughout eternity the triune God is a vital dynamic. In this dynamic the Father generates the Son and through this act is constituted by his relationship to the Son. At the same time, the Father and the Son are bound together through their reciprocal self-dedication to the other (which is love). Finally, the dynamic of God is the Spirit proceeding from the Father and the Son, as the Spirit of that divine relationship between the first and the second trinitarian persons.

To say "God is Spirit" is to acknowledge that the vitality of the triune God overflows to creation. The God who is dynamic activity within the eternal trinitarian life relates to the world as the source and sustainer of created life.

God as Person

Not only do we as Christians speak of God as "Spirit," we also describe the one we have come to know as "Person." Unlike the assertion "God is Spirit," the confession "God is Person" cannot boast an explicit biblical text as its foundation. Nevertheless, many Christians believe that this statement naturally flows out of the biblical witness and capsulizes an important aspect of the God who has disclosed himself to us.

The philosophical concept of "person." Like the concept of "spirit," the idea of "person" was an important point of discussion in nineteenth century philosophical theology, especially among the German idealist thinkers.

The stage was set for that conversation by a disciple of Immanuel Kant, Johann Gottlieb Fichte. As we noted in our discussion of the rise of modern atheism (chapter 2), Fichte rejected the traditional conception of God as a person. According to the German philosopher, the concept of person always entails comparison. To be person means to exist over against a counterpart, which in turn means to be limited or finite. But God is by definition unlimited, and therefore God cannot be a person.[13]

---

13. Johann Gottlieb Fichte, "Über den Grund unseres Glaubes an eine goettliche Weltrügierung," pp. 16-17, in *Saemmtliche Werke*, ed. J. H. Fichte (Berlin: Verlag von Veit und Comp., 1845), 5:187-88.

Fichte's conclusion appeared to destroy the entire concept of a personal God—that is, until his challenge was taken up by G. W. F. Hegel. The great German thinker pointed out the flaw in Fichte's argument, namely, its mistaken understanding of the nature of person. According to Hegel, to be person does not mean to be limited by one's counterpart, but to be related to the counterpart. The essence of person lies in giving of oneself to one's counterpart—in sacrificing of oneself for the sake of the counterpart. Through this self-giving a person finds oneself in the counterpart.[14]

According to Hegel, in personal life—in the act of self-giving—the contrast between the person and the counterpart is overcome. Because personhood is determined by the extent to which this occurs, Hegel argued, the one who is most personal is actually infinite. Consequently, rather than the infinity of God being a contradiction to the personal nature of God, only the infinite God is fully person.

Personhood and God's relationship to the world. Hegel arrived at the confession of God as person through philosophical reflection on the meaning of the term itself. An alternative route lies in certain aspects of the manner in which God relates to the world. We affirm God is Person because he is incomprehensible, willful, and free.[15]

(1) First, the affirmation "God is Person" arises out of our experience of God as the incomprehensible one. We ascribe personhood to human beings on the basis of their relative incomprehensibility. We are all persons, because none of us is totally at the disposal of the knowing eye of another. No one ever fathoms totally the depths of the existence of another, for in the end each human remains mysterious or hidden. Before the rise of modern science, people extended the ascription of personhood to the myterious aspects of nature. The ancients personified unexplainable, and consequently awe-inspiring natural forces. They ascribed personal qualities to objects and pro-

---

14. G.W.F. Hegel, *Lectures on the Philosophy of Religion*, trans. E. B. Speirs and J. Burdon Sanderson, ed. E. B. Speirs, three volumes (New York: Humanities Press, 1974), 3:24-25.

15. For a somewhat similar delineation of this approach, see Wolfhart Pannenberg, "The Question of God," in *Basic Questions in Theology*, trans. George H. Kehm (Philadelphia: Fortress, 1970) 2:226-33; "Speaking about God in the Face of Atheist Criticism," in *The Idea of God and Human Freedom*, 112.

cesses, such as aspects of the weather, which they viewed as mysterious and hidden.

In an even greater sense, the one who enters into relationship with the world remains in the depth of his existence ultimately mysterious and beyond our ability to gain access through our innate ability to know. Because he is incomprehensible, God is person.

(2) The affirmation "God is person" arises from our experience of God as "will." We readily connect personhood not only with what we consider incomprehensible, but also with those aspects in our experience that appear to exercise will. Human beings are persons, for example, because we experience each other as self-determining, active agents. Humans have goals, purposes, and plans, and they act in the world, attempting to determine events. On this basis, the ancient peoples extended personhood to certain aspects of nature. They personified those forces which from their perspective appeared to be self-determining.

In a supreme manner, we experience God as "will." God is self-determining, lying totally beyond our control. God also has a goal for his creation, and he acts in the world to bring his purposes to completion. God, therefore, is Person.

(3) The affirmation "God is Person" arises out of our experience of God's freedom. Personhood is indeed connected with freedom. We speak of humans as persons, because they act beyond the total control of others. In fact, when we come under the control of another (such as through forced slavery) we cease to be persons in the eyes of others.

As Christians we acknowledge that God is totally beyond our control. God is free. And he is also source of our relative human freedom. Consequently, we speak of God as Person.

Personhood and God. However derived, the Christian declaration "God is Person" means that personhood belongs to the divine reality who confronts us. But it confirms as well the non-negotiable quality of human personal distinctions as well as the distinction between the divine and the human. Consequently, we affirm that when God acts to consummate the divine program for creation, our individual personhood as God's creatures will be confirmed for all eternity.

This anticipation forms a striking contrast to the conception proposed by certain other religions. These traditions describe God as impersonal, and as a consequence they speak of the final goal of human life in impersonal terms. Further, they teach that in the end personal distinctions will be eradicated. As a result, the ultimate goal of life is to lose one's personhood and merge into the all-encompassing Absolute. The Christian faith, in contrast, asserts that the triune God enters into a person-to-person relationship with his creatures which will never be dissolved.

The Name of God

The God we know is "Spirit"—the source and giver of life. The triune God is also "Person"—the source of the mystery, self-determination, and freedom of humans, with whom he enters into eternal relationship. As "Spirit" and "Person," our God also carries a name—the great "I Am."

In the ancient cultures, one's name was of utmost importance. Often it was intended to indicate something concerning the nature and character of its bearer. This was especially evident in human names. Hence, the naming of a child was a significant occasion. Sometimes parents gave a name in anticipation of the future role of its bearer. Other times the name expresses the hopes and aspirations of the family or community into which the child had been born.

In the Old Testament, the God of the Hebrews had a personal name, Yahweh. Scholars have not reached a consensus about the significance and rootage of this name. But it seems likely that it is linked to the verb *hayah*,[16] which carries a variety of related meanings, including "to be" or "to exist," "to arise" or "to appear," "to become," or "to happen" or "to come to pass."[17] More specifically, Yahweh is a derivative of the Qal, imperfect, third singular form of this verb, suggesting that Yahweh is "the one who will be."

---

16. Jacques Guillet and E. M. Stewart, "Yahweh," in the *Dictionary of Biblical Theology*, ed. Xavier Leon-Dufour, trans. P. Joseph Cahill, et al., second edition (New York: Seabury, 1973), 690.

17. Alexander Harkavy, *Students' Hebrew and Chaldee Dictionary to the Old Testament* (New York: Hebrew Publishing Co., 1914), 122.

The interpretation of Yahweh as "the one who will be" is confirmed by the only Old Testament verse that reflects explicitly on the name of God (Ex. 3:14). The setting of the text is significant. God has met Moses in the burning bush. There he has instructed him to tell the Israelites that their God is going to bring them out of Egypt and constitute them his people in the wilderness. Anticipating that his hearers will inquire as to the name of the God who has sent him to them, Moses, asks God what he should say in response to this query.

But why is Moses concerned that the people will demand to know the name of the God who had appeared to him? One possible explanation appeals to the importance among the ancient Hebrews of the differentiation between true from false prophets. The Torah provides the test: Any prophet who councils Israel to serve gods other than Yahweh is a false prophet and must not be followed regardless of what signs and wonders that person performs (Deut. 13:1-3; 18:20). Perhaps the future leader anticipates that the Israelites will employ the request for the name of God as a test to see whether or not he is a true prophet of Yahweh.

More probable is the suggestion that the actual question at issue in this incident is not so much that of God's name (which may or may not have been known prior to this time) but its meaning or significance. With this in view commentators have attempted to understand the response of God.

In his commentary, J. Phillips Hyatt sets forth the alternatives. On the one hand, perhaps the reply may be intentionally evasive; God simply avoids giving a direct answer. On the other hand, through his veiled answer God may intend to state something vitally important about his nature. The vagueness of the verb allows for at least four translations and hence four possibilities: "I am who I am"—God is the eternally existent one; "I Am because I Am"—there is no cause for God's existence outside of God; "I will be what I will be"—God is the master of his own destiny; "I am the one who is"—this God is the only one who truly exists. Hiatt himself leans toward the translation "I will be what I will be":

Most critics who comment upon this sentence agree that in Hebrew thought the emphasis is not upon pure or abstract being, but rather upon active being and positive manifestation of the Deity in activity. Specifically, the stress is upon God's presence with Moses and Israel; his "being" is a "being with," a divine presence. Hence, the fourth explanation above is more in harmony with Israelite thinking than the second and third.[18]

If the translation "I will be what I will be" is correct, the narrator's reflection on the name of God indicates that God is both the ultimate reality and an active agent in human affairs. In other words, the God who is the ultimate one is active and will be active in Hebrew history.

The Fourth Gospel provides the final commentary on the name of God. On one occasion Jesus boldly declared, "Before Abraham was, I am" (John 8:58, RSV). The Pharisees in his audience took our Lord's assertion to be blasphemous. But the gospel writer invites the reader to accept the Master's claim as true. In Jesus of Nazareth we do indeed encounter the great "I Am," the ultimate reality who is active in history from beginning to end.

The "I Am" invites us to participate in the community of disciples and thereby to enter into relationship with him and be constituted his people. This relational God is the Triune One. He is the Father who desires that we enjoy fellowship with him, the Son in whose fellowship with the Father we are called to share, and the Holy Spirit who as the bond of the divine fellowship brings us into participation in that relationship.

The Divine Attributes

We have concluded that the Triune One who is "Spirit," "Person," and the great "I Am" is a relational God. The God we know is the source of life. And he is active in sharing life in its fullness—the divine life—with his people. But we also desire to determine the characteristics of this God. What is God like? This quest raises the question of the divine attributes. Are there certain attributive statements that describe the divine character? Can we speak about the

---

18. J. Philip Hyatt, *Exodus*, in the *New Century Bible*, ed. Ronald E. Clements (London: Oliphants, 1971), 76. Hyatt's words are echoed by Noth: "the verb *hyh* in Hebrew does not express pure 'being,' pure 'existing,' but 'active being.'" Martin Noth, *Exodus: A Commentary*, trans. J. S. Bowden (Philadelphia: Westminster, 1962), 45.

God we know by ascribing characteristics to him as the one God, thereby expressing what God is like?

The Attributes and the Divine Substance

Classical Christian theologians often prefaced their delineation of the attributes by a discussion of the connection between the divine characteristics and the essence of God. Presupposing the Greek differentiation between substance and attributes, their descriptions often assumed that we can speak of God as a substance in which attributes inhere. They saw the divine attributes as characteristics which are indispensable to God's being and which therefore constitute God as God.

The medieval debate. While agreeing on this basic method, classical theologians differed as to exactly how the attributes inhere in the divine substance.

Characteristic of those medieval theologies that were especially influenced by the Platonic tradition was a first suggestion, often termed "realism." Philosophically, realism is the view which asserts that universals have a separate existence apart from individual objects.[19] Theological realists asserted that the divine attributes are individually real—they exist in and of themselves, even apart from their connection to the divine substance. Because the various attributes which belong to God are actual realities, God is the compound of the attributes that together inhere in him.

As the influence of Plato gave way to that of Aristotle, Platonic realism came to be altered. The resultant "modified realism" denied that the attributes have any objective existence apart from their presence in the divine substance. Modified realists proposed that rather than being self-existent the attributes *subsist* in the being of God. Consequently, God is the ground of the unity of his attributes.

On the surface the difference between the two views may appear insignificant. But when we probe deeper, we discover that it is not inconsequential. Modified realists were in agreement with the realists that the attributes are distinct from each other. (God's holiness,

---

19. William L. Reese, "Realism," in the *Dictionary of Philosophy and Religion* (Atlantic Highlands, N.J.: Humanities Press, 1980), 480.

for example, is not to be simply equated with God's love). In contrast to realists, however, modified realists viewed these attributes as co-extensive with the being of God. The implication of this change was far-reaching. It meant that the various attributes of God are never experienced in isolation from each other, as is possible if each of the attributes is an independent reality. Instead, we experience all the divine attributes together as one composite whole. Hence, for example, we never experience the wrath of God in isolation from the love of God. Each encounter with God is an experience of the one God who is always and in every circumstance both holy and loving.

A third group of medieval thinkers, the nominalists, whose ranks included William of Ockham, went beyond even the modified realists in their rejection of the Platonic view. Philosophical nominalism begins with the supposition that reality consists only in individual objects, and not in any supposedly existing universals.[20] Universals are not real entities. They are simply names we employ to refer to groups or classes of individual things.

For nominalist theologians this meant that our enumerations of God's attributes do not describe the divine substance at all. They are not descriptions of how God is within his own eternal reality. Rather, such statements reflect our own subjective concept of God. We employ them to speak about our understanding of the divine reality.

The doxological position. The question of the connection between the attributes and God's substance is no longer widely debated. Contemporary theologians have moved away from the substance/attribute nomenclature that underlay the earlier discussion. These theologians understand our statements about God more in terms of doxology than as propositional assertions. They are expressions of praise to the God who enters into relationship with us.[21]

John Calvin anticipated the contemporary emphasis on the doxological and relational character of our statements concerning the divine attributes. In commenting on Exodus 34:6-8, the Geneva reformer explained,

---

20. Reese, "Nominalism" and "Universalism," in the *Dictionary of Philosophy and Religion,* 393, 597.

21. See Pannenberg, "Analogy and Doxology," in *Basic Questions in Theology,* 1:211-38.

> Here let us observe that his eternity and his self-existence are announced by that wonderful name twice repeated. Thereupon his powers are mentioned, by which he is shown to us not as he is in himself, but as he is toward us: so that this recognition of him consists more in living experience than in vain and high-flown speculation.[22]

Rather than strict assertions intending to represent objective, "scientific" knowledge about God, the attributes are expressions arising out of our experience of the God who stands in relationship to humans and the world. These statements are an attempt to speak of God based on our encounter with him. Hence, descriptions in the form of attributes are designed to facilitate and to evoke praise from the community of faith. They facilitate the praise of those who have come to know God in a personal way.

If this understanding is correct, it points to the Archilles' heel of the scholastic understanding of the attributes. Whether realists, modified realists, or nominalists, the older theologians ascribed noetic intent to what are inherently doxological statements. However, contrary to the focus of scholastic theologies, attributive assertions do not impart knowledge of God's essence as a static reality or in isolation from world. Rather, our descriptions of the God we know are attempts to describe God-in-relation. Through such statements, we speak about the eternal relations of the triune God and the reality of God in relationship with creation, most importantly with us.

Certain conclusions of the previous chapters illume the doxological nature of attributive statements. As we have seen, God cannot be known merely by means of an intellectual grasp of various assertions that purport to describe his eternal nature. Thus, the various attributes theologians traditionally ascribe to God do not mediate the knowledge of God. God is known personally—as a person is known—through personal encounter, and never as an object which we scrutinize.

The traditional attributes of God function as a helpful reminder of the perfection of God in comparison to human beings and the universe. These attributes are doxological in orientation. They serve to

---

22. Calvin, *Institutes of the Christian Religion*, 1.10.2, in the *Library of Christian Classics* 20:97.

show forth the greatness of God, when we compare God with the universe he has made.

The Division of the Attributes

Theologians in the Protestant scholastic tradition tended to group the attributes of God into two or more basic categories. One widely-used partition divides them into the "incommunicable" and the "communicable" attributes. Louis Berkhof describes the first group as those attributes "for which there is nothing analogous in the creature."[23] Thus, the incommunicable attributes include all the divine characteristics which find no counterparts in creation, such as God's self-existence, immutability, infinity, and unity. The communicable attributes, in contrast, are those characteristics of God "to which the properties of the human spirit bear some analogy." These traits, which arise out of God's spiritual, intellectual, and moral nature, include knowledge, wisdom, veracity, goodness, holiness, righteousness, and sovereignty in will and power.

The classical description of the divine attributes as "incommunicable" and "communicable" presupposes a noetic understanding of attributive theological statements. It assumes that assertions concerning God assert propositional truths concerning the static divine essence apart from God's internal dynamic or his relationship to the world. But as we have seen, the attributes are fundamentally doxological assertions.

Despite our rejection of the classical understanding of the purpose of attributive assertions, we may nevertheless continue to divide our descriptive statements about God—our doxological descriptions of God's relationship to creation—into two categories. A first group of attributes speak about God's eternality. Hence, they describe God in his noetic and purposeful relationship to creation. The second group speaks of God's goodness, of his moral uprightness in all his dealings with creation.

We conclude, then, that the enumeration of the divine attributes is a proper result of our desire to describe God in relationship. The var-

---

23. Louis Berkhof, *Systematic Theology*, revised edition (Grand Rapids: Eerdmans, 1953), 55.

ious terms extol the greatness of God in comparison with creation. These doxological descriptions speak either of God's eternality or his goodness.

The Eternal God

Our assertion "God is eternal" is not easy to define. In Greek philosophy "eternality" referred to the timelessness of God as the one who exists totally beyond the temporal realm and who therefore remains untouched by events in time. Hence, "eternality" carried with it the idea of impassibility.

The Greek conception of eternality, however, does not square with our experience of God in the community of faith.[24] The biblical God sees, knows, cares, and responds to the plight of his creatures. The biblical community, therefore, did not claim to know a God who is impassible. Rather, they spoke of the one who is faithfully present through time. The experience of the people of faith means that we ought not to conceive of God's eternality as timeless impassibility but as omnipresence with respect to time. God is present in all time, and therefore all time is present to God.

Eternality and our experience of time. Our human experience of the temporal sequence provides insight as to how we may understand God's relationship to time.

We generally divide time into three aspects—past, present, and future. However, we are immediately cognizant of temporal events only in a limited sense. We have some sense of both the past and the future. But our knowing of the past—even our own past—is limited to memory, and we are cognizant of the future only through anticipation or hope. We know directly only what lies in our present. Therefore, we live in what we term the "present." Upon closer inspection, however, we discover that the present in which we live is a continually moving point which appears to travel with us through the temporal sequence. This vanishing present forms a bridge between the past we remember and the future we anticipate.

---

24. For a recent discussion of this, see, for example, Paul Fiddes, *The Creative Suffering of God* (New York: Oxford University Press, 1988).

Our experience of time assists us in understanding the divine eternality. As the point of our immediate cognition, the present constitutes a limited participation in eternity. Just as we are aware of present events in our personal world, so also God is cognizant of what occurs in the universe he made.

One important difference sets God's knowing apart from ours, however. Our immediate knowledge is finite. It is limited both by the finiteness of our "present" and by our finite capability to draw even events transpiring in our present into our perception. God's cognition, in contrast, is infinite. He is immediately and simultaneously cognizant of all events as themselves—whether they be in what we call "past," "present," or "future." In this sense, God is eternal with respect to creaturely time.

As a result of this difference, we ought to view our cognition in the light of God's. Through our "present" we participate in a finite manner in what for God is perfect and complete knowledge of the whole of the temporal reality.

Attributes related to God's eternality. Understood in this manner, God's eternality encompasses three related attributes, omnipresence, omniscience, and omnipotence.

First, we confess that God is *omnipresent*. The traditional understanding of "omnipresence" declares that God is near or present to all things. But to understand this attribute correctly, we must turn the definition around. Omnipresence means that all things are present to God in themselves, whether they be events in our past, our present, or our future. As this definition indicates, our affirmation of God's omnipresence is closely connected to our declaration that God is eternal.

Second, we declare that God is *omniscient* (all-knowing). The medieval theologians generally viewed this attribute in the abstract. For this reason, they debated whether God not only new all actual but also all possible events. We have concluded, however, that the attributes are relational terms. Consequently, in declaring "God is omniscient" we are not intending to make a claim concerning God's theoretical knowledge, but to affirm his perfect cognition of the world. God is cognizant of all things precisely because they are present to him immediately and as themselves. The divine mind perceives the entire temporal sequence—all events—simultaneously in one act of cognition.

Third, we confess that God is *omnipotent*. In the Middle Ages, theologians often conceived of this attribute as referring to God's theoretical as well as his actual power. This led to debates over obscure questions and apparent dilemmas, such as whether God could make a rock so heavy that he himself could not lift it. However, the doxological and relational significance of the attributes leads us to avoid conceiving of omnipotence as a statement concerning God in isolation. Rather, in declaring "God is omnipotent" we are speaking about God in relationship to the world. Through this term we acknowledge God's ability to bring to completion his design for creation.

Our confession of God's omnipotence is connected to our belief that he is omniscient, and it is eschatologically oriented. God's cognition of all things is not a disinterested, neutral knowing. Rather, God knows all things as the one who directs creation to its intended goal. He knows the world, therefore, as the one who exercises judgment over creation and who comes to the world in salvation. But judgment and salvation are eschatological realities. They belong to the consummation of God's program for creation. This means that God's omnipotence is likewise ultimately eschatological. God is all-powerful in that in the consummation, God makes all things new or brings about a new state of affairs. As he does this he is the omnipotent God who overcomes every evil for the sake of the good and replaces the old order with the new.

The Good God

The same God who relates to creation as the eternal one also comes to us as totally good. We describe this aspect of God's relationship to the world by means of the moral attributes.

Taken together, the moral attributes declare that God is perfect in all he does. Yet God's moral perfection may be best described as itself having two dimensions. At all times, God is totally upright, fair, just, and righteous in his treatment of his creatures; that is, he is holy.

At the same time God is gracious, benevolent, and long-suffering with us; he is compassionate.

Holiness. The various aspects of the fairness of God in all his relations with us are encapsulated by the several attributive words associated with the assertion, "God is holy." To understand God's fairness, therefore, we must look at the term "holiness," which theologians generally classify under the moral attributes.

The theological use is but one of three meanings of "holiness" in the Bible. In addition to moral uprightness, the word can also refer both to the divine transcendence and to God's uniqueness. Hence, God is holy, in that he is different from creation; he is beyond the world he made. Likewise, God is also holy, in that he is unique among, and set apart from all the gods; there is no God like our God.

"Holiness," however, is also an appropriate description of a dimension of God's moral character. God is holy, in that he is just and totally righteous in all he does. God is always fair with all creatures. Consequently, God seeks justice. And one day he will judge each human being according to his righteous standard.

Compassion. Holiness, understood in terms of justice or fairness, does not exhaust the way God interacts with his creatures. Were this the case, we could have no hope of salvation. But as James notes, "Mercy triumphs over judgment!" (James 2:13) Beyond the fair and righteous judgment of God, therefore, lies his grace. The various dimensions of God's mercifulness in his actions toward us as expressed in the several ascriptions associated with grace may be summarized by the confession, "God is compassionate." Several dimensions of the biblical teaching concerning the divine compassion are worthy of note.

The ancient faith community extolled God as being perfect in compassion. This forms a basic theological theme of the Old Testament (Neh. 9:17; Pss. 111:4; 116:5; 86:15; 103:8; 145:8; Joel 2:13; Jonah 4:2; Isa. 54:10). At the center of the faith of the Hebrew community stood a declaration of God's compassion, which the Book of Exodus describes as having its source in God himself. After revealing the divine name to Moses on Mount Sinai, Yahweh declares, "the compassionate and gracious God, slow to anger, abounding in love and faithfulness" (Ex. 34:6).

The Bible indicates that compassion characterizes God's response to the human predicament. Because of the divine love, the plight of God's creatures evokes his compassion. Because of his fidelity, God's people are the special object of this compassion (Jer. 31:20; Isa. 49:13; 63:9; Hos. 14:3). Yet, God's concern moves beyond Israel to encompass all creatures. As the psalmist declares, "The Lord is good to all; he has compassion on all he has made" (Ps. 145:9; see also Matt. 5:45; Rom. 11:32).

God graciously bestows compassion or mercy on us apart from our merit (Ex. 33:19; Dan. 9:18; Rom. 9:15-16,18). For this reason, God can be compassionate in spite of human rebellion (Dan. 9:9). Perhaps the most moving illustration of God's mercy on sinners is the parable of the prodigal son. While the son "was still a long way off," the father saw him "and was filled with compassion for him" (Luke 15:20).

The belief in a gracious, compassionate God likewise forms the foundation for the repeatedly expressed hope that at some future time God would again be compassionate to the people of Israel (Isa. 14:1; 54:7; Jer. 12:15; 30:18; 33:26; 42:12; Ezek. 39:25; Hos. 1:7; 2:23; Joel 2:18; Micah 7:19; Zech. 1:16; Mal. 3:17). Isaiah stands as an example of those who anticipated a day when they would experience God's compassion as an expression of God's everlasting kindness: "'In a surge of anger I hid my face from you for a moment, but with everlasting kindness I will have compassion on you,' says the Lord your Redeemer" (54:8).

Divine compassion leads to divine action (Isa. 63:7; Ps. 78:38; 2 Chron. 36:15). Israel did not view God's activity in history as belonging to a dead past, but as a living presence which held out the promise of a future renewal. This anticipation forms the context for the New Testament pronouncements of fulfillment. Zechariah's hymn at the birth of John the Baptist forms a lucid example. For this faithful servant, John's arrival was an act of God, who in this event was demonstrating his mercy and remembering the covenant with Israel (Luke 1:72).

According to the New Testament, however, the supreme act of divine compassion is the sending of Jesus Christ. God's loving compassion finds concrete expression in Jesus of Nazareth, for compassion lay at the heart of our Lord's understanding of his mission. In Jesus God has acted to make salvation available. Hence, Paul declares, God "saved us, not because of righteous things we had done, but because of his mercy" (Titus 3:5; see also Eph. 3:4-5). And Peter tells his readers that in God's "great mercy" he has given Christians "new birth into a living hope" (1 Pet. 1:3).

God intends that his loving compassion, which leads to divine action on behalf of God's creatures in the midst of their plight, leads all the peoples of the world together to offer praise to the glory of the one who has saved them. Hence, Paul writes to a multiracial church,

> For I tell you that Christ has become a servant of the Jews on behalf of God's truth, to confirm the promises made to the patriarchs so that the Gentiles may glorify God for his mercy, as it is written: "Therefore I will praise you among the Gentiles; I will sing hymns to your name." Again it says, "Rejoice, O Gentiles, with his people" (Rom. 15:8-10).

God as the moral standard. Not only is God morally perfect, he is the standard for morality. Rather than he himself being ruled by some moral concept, external to himself, God's disposition toward creation is the standard by which we will be judged and we are to judge all human conduct. John brings together the connection between God's character and our conduct: "This is how we know what love is: Jesus Christ laid down his life for us. And we ought to lay down our lives for our brothers" (1 John 3:16).

Ultimately the divine disposition and the divine being coalesce. As we noted in chapter three, God's essence and God's character are both love. Consequently, there is no dichotomy between God's own being and God's will, for God wills what God is. God wills what is right, and the "right" that God wills is nothing else but what characterizes God's own being as the Triune One.

The Practical Importance of the Attributes

Our confession of God as the eternal, gracious one is not merely theological theory. Rather, our descriptions of God's relation to the world carry important implications for Christian living. Our understanding of the divine attributes should lead us to joyful and awe-filled praise to our God. This point needs no elaboration, for it is bound up with the doxological nature of our assertions.

Less obvious is a further outworking of our discussion of the divine attributes. Our affirmation of God as the eternal and gracious one should lead us to bold prayer and bold action. The God we serve is faithful in bringing his creation to completion. All events are present to him, he is cognizant of all events, and he is capable of effecting his plan. This God invites us to cooperate with him in the completion of the divine program for history.

The means God gives us with which to cooperate with him are fervent petition and obedient action. In both of these activities we "rebel against the status quo"—that is, we refuse to acknowledge that the present state of affairs in our world is wholly in keeping with the divine plan. Through prayer and action we seek to allow ourselves to be instruments of the hands of the Holy Spirit to open the present to the in-breaking of the power of the future kingdom.[25]

Above all, the God of love responds to creation with compassion. The compassionate response of God to the world he has made provides for us the paradigm of what should characterize our cooperation with him in the completion of his program in the world. As those who claim to be Christ's disciples, we are to be emulators of our compassionate Lord, who revealed to us the merciful heart of the loving God. For this reason, compassion should characterize our attitude toward others as we pray and act.

This understanding is so well ingrained throughout the Bible that compassion is without question a central aspect of biblical piety. Job's rhetorical question "Have I not wept for those in trouble? Has not my soul grieved for the poor?" (30:25) indicates that such compassion was simply assumed to be characteristic of every member of

---

25. For a further discussion of this theme, see Stanley J. Grenz, *Prayer: The Cry for the Kingdom* (Peabody, Mass: Hendrickson, 1988).

the Old Testament covenant community. The New Testament reaffirms the same outlook. For example, James declares, "Religion that God our Father accepts as pure and faultless is this: to look after orphans and widows in their distress and to keep oneself from being polluted by the world" (1:27). Not only personal holiness—i.e., freedom from sin—but being compassionate toward others both in attitude and in action lies at the center of what the biblical people assumed to be normal religion.

In keeping with this, the New Testament writers repeatedly admonished the Christian community to be compassionate. Paul, for example, declares, "Clothe yourselves with compassion" (Col. 3:12). Likewise Peter commands his readers to be compassionate and sympathetic (1 Pet. 3:8). Elsewhere Paul forges the link between compassion and the example of Christ: "Carry each other's burdens, and in this way you will fulfill the law of Christ" (Gal. 6:2). Burden-lifting and sharing the load of others are important aspects by which believers follow the example of the Lord. And the Book of Hebrews offers specific ways in which the Christian community can live out godly compassion: "Remember those in prison as if you were their fellow prisoners, and those who are mistreated as if you yourselves were suffering" (13:3).

Perhaps the grandest illustration and admonition to the disciples of the Lord to be a compassionate people, however, is found in Jesus' parable of the good Samaritan. In narrating the story our Lord clearly sought to emphasize that this outcast individual, and not those who stood in traditional positions of leadership within the Jewish community, was compassionate to the man in need. The Samaritan saw the battered man lying along the road and "took pity on him," Jesus declares. It is interesting to note that the same verb the Gospel writers employed to speak of Jesus' outlook toward the needy is utilized here to describe the Samaritan. The emotion of compassion, so characteristic of the Master, was translated into action by the foreigner as he bandaged the wounds of the unfortunate traveler, took the injured person to an inn, and offered to pay the innkeeper to look after the needs of the battered Jew.

After delivering the parable, Jesus asked the expert in the law to whom he was speaking the crucial question: "Which of the three men was a neighbor to the man in need?" The response of his listener was significant: "The one who had mercy on him." This evoked Jesus' command, "Go and do likewise." Our Lord calls us to be a compassionate people. As imitators of God, we are to respond to persons in distress with action motivated by compassion.

Godly compassion, however, goes beyond what is humanly possible. It can only arise from love. But love in its full biblical sense must be created in us by the Holy Spirit. As Paul declares, love belongs to the fruit of the Spirit (Gal. 5:22). This conclusion brings us full circle to the essential nature of God. It is only as God shares with us his own essence—love—that we are able to engage in the work of the triune God in the world. This he does through the Holy Spirit who dwells within God's people.

The Creator God

He who was seated on the throne said, "I am making everything new." (Rev. 21:5)

Outline

The destruction of providence
God's Administration of His World
Preservation
Concurrence
Government

The Bible opens with the simple yet profound declaration, "In the beginning God created the heavens and the earth" (Gen. 1:1). This statement indicates that the triune God does not remain forever secluded within the eternal relations within the divine Trinity. Rather, the eternal God extends himself beyond the trinitarian life in order to bring into existence a universe which is other than God.

The deistic theologians of the Enlightenment tended to view God's creative activity solely as his establishment of the laws of nature in the past. Biblical faith, however, is richer. According to the Bible, God does not set the wheels of the universe in motion and then abandon it to run on its own. Instead, he enters into relationship with what he makes.

The faith community describes the fundamental relationship between God and the world by the terms "Creator" and "creation": God is the Creator of the universe, and the world is the creation of God. Theology articulates this faith assertion under the heading of the doctrine of creation. The related doctrine of providence focuses on God's activity in guiding the historical process with the goal of bringing to pass his intention for the world he creates.

God as the Creator of the World

As the Apostles' Creed suggests, our Christian confession of faith begins with the acknowledgment of God as Creator: "I believe in the Father Almighty, the Creator of heaven and earth." But what does it mean to confess faith in the Creator God? In what sense can we speak of creation as an act of God? And to what relationship between God and the world does this confession point?

The Creation of the World as the Act of God

The confession of the faith community, "God is the Creator of the world," suggests that in some sense the existence of the universe is a divine act. But how are we to understand creaturely existence as the product of the action of God? Two interrelated assertions provide the signposts along the way to an understanding of the confession of God as Creator: The creation of the world is both a free act and a loving act of God.

The free act of creation. One signpost along the path to a theological understanding of creation lies with the acknowledgment that God creates the world by an act of his freedom. Thus, God's creation of the universe is a free act, a non-necessary act. God is not driven to create, not forced by some sense of compulsion to bring the universe into existence.

That no sense of *external* compulsion lies behind God's act in creation is obvious. Were God driven by anything external to himself, this external reality would ultimately exercise sovereignty over the divine being.

Perhaps less obvious but no less valid is the assertion that creation is not the product of an *internal* necessity within God. Were creation the result of an internal divine compulsion, God's being would be bound up with the world. God would need the world to be who he is or to actualize his own essential nature. But if God is indeed the eternal and transcendent one, he must remain totally God in himself apart from the world, even though he is also immanent in the world.

The doctrine of the Trinity indicates how this can be the case. As we saw in chapter three, the essential character of God is love. Because God is triune, God's nature—love—is already actualized apart from the world in the eternal relationship between the Father and the Son, which is the Holy Spirit. God is fully himself within the divine Trinity apart from the world in that God is love within himself as the Triune One. Consequently, the existence of the universe comes about through a free act, and not by necessity. In this manner, the triune nature of God provides the foundation for the freedom of the divine creative act.

Closely bound to the assertion of the freedom of God in the act of creation is the widely employed but often misunderstood theological phrase "creation out of nothing" (Latin: *creatio ex nihilo*). The confession "God created the world out of nothing" is not a mere anthropomorphism. We ought not to picture God fashioning the world with no material at his disposal. Rather, the assertion declares that we need no additional principles beyond the triune God in order to explain the existence of the universe.

Creatio ex nihilo is reflected in the Old Testament picture of God's creative work. The Hebrew Scriptures portray the act of creation in a manner similar to the commands issued by an absolute monarch. Just as the king speaks and his commands bring about action, so also God speaks and his word accomplishes the intended result (e.g., Ps. 104:7). This is evident in the first creation narrative. At each stage in the making of the world, the narrator declares, "And God said...and it was so" (Gen. 1:3,6,9,14-15,20,24).

The portrait of creation depicted in the Old Testament forms a radical contrast to ancient conceptions which picture the creator as giving shape to some already existing reality. For example, the biblical view marks a contrast to the outlook of ancient Greece. According to Plato the world came about as the creator gave shape to an eternal, but unformed matter in accordance with the eternal ideas or "forms."

On the surface there appear to be certain similarities between the Greek understanding and the biblical picture of creation. Somewhat similar to the Platonic view, Genesis 2 offers a picture of God giving shape to matter. But the similarity is only apparent. The second creation narrative speaks of the creation of the first human and not of the world as a whole. Likewise, as we will see, Christian theology does affirm that God creates in accordance with a principle. But again the similarity to Platonism is only apparent. Rather than being external to God, as in the Platonic conception, according to Christian theology the principle of creation lies within the divine reality as the Second Person of the Trinity.

The biblical view of creation also forms a contrast to ancient Near Eastern mythology. These myths depict the world as the product of a battle between opposing forces in which a hero-god defeats a personified monster of chaos.[1] The Babylonian story, for example, describes the success of Marduk who prevails over Tiamat, the primordial mother who personifies chaos. The Hebrew Scriptures do incorporate the theme of creation as the victory of God over chaos, especially as personified by the sea monster, leviathan. But the presence of this idea is best understood as a polemic against elements in the world view of other cultures, not an actual depiction of the act of creation.

In setting forth the creation of the world, the Bible consistently avoids the suggestion that God employs any eternal principles apart from himself. The Creator calls the universe into existence as an act that originates in his own freedom.

Because creation is the product of the divine freedom, we may speak of the existence of the world as arising from God's free choice. On the basis of his own prerogative, God chooses to make the world with which to share his own existence. But the choice *for* creation is also a choice *against* the alternative, against the decision not to create. Hence, as Karl Barth observed, in creation God chooses "something" and rejects "nothing." God rejects the nothingness of the void. He willfully says "no" to non-existence.[2] Yet even this spurned nothingness ought not to be interpreted as a quasi-something with which God does battle and overcomes in creation.

Nor ought we to suggest that in creating the world God overcomes his own reluctance. The importance of this is evident from the parallel point: In addition to being a free act, creation is God's loving act.

The loving act of creation. The basis of the act of creation lies solely in God's love.

The doctrine of the Trinity likewise provides the foundation for understanding this dimension of the act of creation. As we have seen, God's essence is love. The dynamic of the Trinity is the love reciprocated between the Father and the Son, which is the Holy Spirit. This central dimension of the essence of God—trinitarian love—

---

1. For a discussion of this theme, see Bruce C. Birch, *Let Justice Roll Down* (Louisville, Ky.: Westminster/John Knox, 1991), 74-76.

2. Karl Barth, *Church Dogmatics*, ed. G. W. Bromiley and T. F. Torrance (Edinburgh: T. & T. Clark, 1958-1960), 3/1: 330-34, 344; 3/3: 289-368.

makes creation possible. The act of creation is the outflowing of the eternal love relationship within the triune God. The world exists because out of the overflow of his own character, which is love, the eternal God establishes an external counterpart, creation. Just as it is created in accordance with the very essence of God—love—this counterpart exists to be both the recipient of, and the mirror of, the divine love.

Because God is love, God is self-giving. Because God is self-giving, God willingly creates the world. This self-giving divine character, which is evident within the Trinity himself, forms the basis for the creation of God's external counterpart, the universe. However, as we noted above we must not see in this desire to create an internal compulsion placed on God which demands that he create. Rather, God's love is already complete within the Trinity apart from the act of creation.

Hence, precisely because creation is God's loving act, it is free, voluntary, and non-necessary. At the same time, precisely because God is love, the act of creation naturally flows out of the inner life of the Triune One. Because God is the trinitarian community of love, God need not create the world to actualize his character. Yet because God is love his creation of the world is fully in keeping with his character.

The Creation of the World as a Trinitarian Act

The foundation for the creation of the world lies in the triune reality of God. Because God is the Father, Son, and Spirit—the social Trinity characterized by love—the world exists as the outflow of the intratrinitarian relationships. Creation, therefore, is a trinitarian act. It is the result of the working together of all three persons of the eternal Trinity.

In the cooperative venture of creation, each trinitarian person fulfills a unique and specific role. This may be summarized by the classic theological assertion: The Father creates the world, through the Son, by his Spirit.

The role of the Father. The Father fulfills the primary role in the act of creation. He constitutes the ground of all that exists.

To affirm that the Father is the ground of the world is to acknowledge the Father as the ultimate, direct agent in the creative act. Hence, the church confesses faith in "God the Father, the creator...." In so doing, however, we are merely following the precedent set by the New Testament. Paul, for example, differentiates between the Father and the Son in the divine work of creation, and he attributes to the Father the function of source: "for us there is but one God, the Father, from whom all things came and for whom we live; and there is but one Lord, Jesus Christ, through whom all things came and through whom we live" (1 Cor. 8:6).

In what sense is the Father the ultimate or direct agent of creation? We may venture several points in answer to this query. The direct creative agency of the Father means that his will forms the foundation for the existence of all things. The world exists by the will of the Father. This is evident, for example, in John's vision of the living creatures giving glory "to him who sits on the throne." These creatures cry out, "You are worthy, our Lord and God, to receive glory and honor and power, for you created all things, and by your will they were created and have their being" (Rev. 4:11).

The Father is the direct agent of creation likewise means that he is the goal or *telos* of all things. Hence, in the text cited above Paul declares, "for us there is but one God, the Father...for whom we live...." Every creature exists for the sake of the Father, that is, for the praise of his glory. Creation around us quite naturally fulfills this divine intention. As the psalmist notes, "The heavens declare the glory of God..." (Psalm 19:1). God invites humans, his highest creatures, to glorify him willingly and consciously, and therefore most fully.

Finally, the direct creative agency of the Father means that he is the source of the existence of the world. In John's vision cited above, those who are offering praise to God declare that all creatures have their being in the Father. This theme finds echo in Paul's quotation from the Greek poets when he declared to the Athenians the nearness of God: "For in him we live and move and have our being.... We are his offspring" (Acts 17:28). Hence, all creation owes its existence to the Father.

The Father's function of the ground of creation is an overflow of his function as ground of the trinitarian life. The primary movement in the Trinity is the Father's eternal generation of the Son which flows from the love of the Father for the Son. Just as the Father generates the Son whom he loves and thereby eternally shares his deity with the Son, so also the Father freely makes the world and shares his existence with it. While acknowledging this connection between the trinitarian life and the creation of the world, we must keep in mind the great difference between the two acts. The intratrinitarian movement of generation is eternal, whereas the making of the world is temporal.

The role of the Son. Whereas the Father functions as the ground of creation, the role of the Son is that of being the principle of creation. Two themes, one arising from the Old Testament and the other from the New, form the biblical foundation for this declaration.

The Hebrew Scriptures do not reflect the New Testament's explicit portrayal of the Son as distinct from the Father. Nevertheless, the Old Testament provides an implicit foundation for the declaration that the Son is the principle of creation. The focal point of its contribution lies in the wisdom literature, especially in the hymn to wisdom (Prov. 8).

The hymn writer extols wisdom as being involved in creation. In fact, in the hymn personified wisdom claims to have been "the craftsman at his side" when God made the world (v.30). The central point of this section of the poem is obvious. The author lauds the ancientness of wisdom. Because it is present already at the beginning of God's work, wisdom predates even the creation of the world, and therefore the reader ought to live in accordance with wisdom. Yet the corollary of the argument is equally clear: Wisdom is the principle through which God fashioned the universe.

The hymn to wisdom, together with certain related texts, forms the basis for the development of a wisdom Christology in the early church. Nevertheless, in our appeal to this passage, we must be careful not to overstep what is exegetically warranted. In the final analysis, the text does not set forth the high view of the Son we find in the New Testament. Despite the high prerogatives it ascribes to the concept, the hymn describes personified wisdom as a "creature" of God. The hymn presents wisdom as itself having been fashioned by the eternal God, rather than participating fully in deity.[3] Consequently, for the explicit foundation for the assertion that the Son is the principle of creation we must look beyond the Old Testament to the New.

The New Testament theme that provides the foundation for our assertion concerning the creative activity of the Son is set forth most explicitly by John (John 1:1-3,10) and confirmed by Paul (Col. 1:16-17). In the opening verses of his gospel, John speaks of the involvement of the Word in the act of creation: "Through him all things were made; without him nothing was made that has been made" (v. 3). This Word, he adds, is incarnate in Jesus (v. 14).

The Greek term translated "Word" in the Johannine prologue is a multifaceted concept with rootage in both the Greek and Hebrew cultures. The Greek philosophers, especially the Stoics, postulated the reality of a rational principle lying behind all that is and uniting all things together. This principle is somewhat reminiscent of the Old Testament idea of wisdom. The Greeks termed this integrative, rational, ordering principle the *logos*.[4]

John's assertion finds echo in Paul's declaration, "all things were created by him" (Col. 1:16b). Although the apostle does not employ the term "Word" in this text, the logos-idea clearly lies behind his affirmation that in the Son "all things hold together" (v. 17). But the apostle enhances the concept by means of a teleological dimension: "all things were created...for him" (v. 16b). As the unitive principle of the universe, the Son is also the goal toward which all creation is directed.

Both authors carefully choose the same technical Greek construction to describe the Son's creative role. Specifically, they employ the phrase *di' autou* ("through him") which speaks of indirect agency, in contrast to direct agency, which is introduced by the preposition *hupo*.[5] Thus, these texts do not declare that the Word or Son directly

---

3. C. H. Toy, *Proverbs*, in the *International Critical Commentary*, ed. Samuel R. Driver, Alfred Plummer and Charles A. Briggs (Edinburgh: T. & T. Clark, 1977), 171-75.

4. H. Kleinknecht, "logo," in the *Theological Dictionary of the New Testament*, ed. Gerhard Kittel, trans. Geoffrey Bromiley (Grand Rapids: Eerdmans, 1967), 4:80-86.

5. A. T. Robertson, *A Grammar of the Greek New Testament in the Light of Historical Research* (Nashville: Broadman, 1934), 534.

created all things. Rather, he is the one *through* whom all things were created.

On the basis of these texts, we can conclude that the Son is not the direct, but the indirect agent of creation. The assumption implicit in the two passages is that the unnamed direct agent is God the Father, as is taught elsewhere in the Bible. Bringing these two principles together, we conclude that the biblical teaching is that through the Son, the Father creates the world. The Son is the *logos*, the unitive principle of all things, the principle of creation.

As in the case of our confession "the Father is the ground of creation," we now ask, What does it mean to say that the Son is the indirect agent and principle of creation?

Above all, the confession that the Son is the principle of creation means that he exemplifies the proper relation of creation to the Creator. The response that creatures owe to the Creator is based in the response of the Son to the Father. But this response finds its foundation in the eternal intratrinitarian relationship, which in turn is exemplified in the incarnate Word.

Throughout his life, Jesus displayed humble dependence on the one whom he called "Father." In fact, this was the primary characteristic of his response to his Father. As the one who lived in perfect dependency and obedience to the Father, Jesus is the incarnate Son. In a similar manner, all creatures ought humbly to acknowledge their dependence on the creative Ground.

Jesus' humble response to his Father has significance beyond the temporal life of the prophet from Nazareth. As the incarnate Son, Jesus is the revelation of the eternal response of the Son to the Father within the divine reality. Throughout all eternity the Son whom the Father generates responds to the Father in humble dependence and by reciprocating the Father's love. This filial relationship of the Son to the Father as exhibited by Jesus of Nazareth constitutes the paradigm for creation. Just as the Son humbly acknowledges the Father as the source of his life (John 5:26), so also all creatures are to look humbly to God as the fountain of their life.

As creatures follow the pattern exemplified by Jesus, they participate in the filial relationship the eternal Son enjoys with the Father.

Insofar as they respond to the Creator with the love he has bestowed on them by creating them to share in his existence, they reflect the eternal response of the Son to the Father who in love generates the Son from all eternity and thereby shares his deity with the Son. As this occurs, creation models itself after the pattern of the Son and demonstrates that the Son is indeed the one in whom "all things hold together" (Col. 1:17).

The role of the Spirit. The Father is the creative ground of creation and the Son is the principle of creation. The third member of the Trinity is likewise involved in the trinitarian act of creation. More specifically, we may speak of the Spirit as the divine power active in creating the universe.

The Hebrew faith community did not reflect the full pneumatology indicative of the trinitarianism of the Christian church. Nevertheless, the Old Testament provides the foundation for the declaration that the Spirit is the power of God in the creative act.

The first creation narrative pictures the Spirit of God as involved in giving form to the universe, for the Spirit broods over the void before God calls order out of chaos (Gen. 1:2; see also Job 26:13). In addition, based on the connection between "spirit" and "breath" we noted earlier in the Hebrew word *ru'ach*, the ancient Hebrews spoke of the divine Spirit as God's provision of life for creatures (Gen. 6:17; 7:22; Ps. 104:30) and especially for humankind (Gen. 2:7; 6:3; Job 33:4). The Spirit, therefore, is the power of God effecting creation.

Just as in the case of the Father and the Son, the function of the Spirit in creation is an outworking of his role in the eternal trinitarian relationship. As we have noted, the act of creation flows out of the inner life of God. The creation of the world comes as the outflowing of the eternal love relationship within the triune God. More specifically, the Father who eternally loves the Son creates the world in order that it might share in his existence and with the intent that the world reciprocate his love after the pattern of the Son's love for the Father.

The dynamic that binds the Father and the Son—the power of their relationship—is the Holy Spirit. In this sense the Spirit is likewise the essence of God, namely, love. This divine essence, the dynamic between the Father and the Son, lies behind the act of God in creating the world. Because he is precisely this dynamic and this love, the Holy Spirit is the one through whom the Father, the direct agent in creation, fashions the world. In other words, the Spirit is the personal power of God—the dynamic of love between the Father and the Son—by means of which all things exist.

The Act of Creation and the Sovereign Creator

As Creator, God rightfully enjoys a special status vis-a-vis the world which he made. Christian theologians capsulize this special status by affirming that God is sovereign over creation. Sovereignty entails ultimate governance. Ultimately God alone has the prerogative to declare what his creation should be. And his will alone should be the final norm throughout creation. Because he is the ground of creation, this status belongs most properly to the Father.

The biblical authors employ a forceful analogy from the ancient cultural world to speak of God's sovereignty. Just as the potter has the right to do with the clay as he chooses, so also God has the right to act toward creation in accordance with his will (Jer. 18:1-6; Rom. 9:21; see also, Isa. 29:15-16; 45:9; 64:8). The various biblical statements may focus on specific dimensions of God's sovereign working (Jeremiah uses the figure to refer to God's dealings with Israel, whereas Paul speaks of God's choice of nations), but the general principle nevertheless extends to realm of creation as a whole. Just as the potter deals with the clay as he will, so also as Creator, God has the right to act toward creation according to his own good pleasure.

Although free to govern creation according to his own purposes, God always acts in accordance with his own character, which is love. Indeed, the freedom of God as Creator is the freedom to fulfill his loving purposes for his handiwork. Consequently, in all he does, God seeks only what is best for the universe that he fashioned as the outflow of the divine love.

Yet we ask, To what extent can we truly confess that God is sovereign over creation? Given the undeniable presence of evil in the world, is God's will now being done "on earth as it is in heaven"? Two related distinctions are vital to our attempt to understand how we may affirm the reality of the divine sovereignty in a world tainted with evil. We must differentiate between the present and final realities of God's sovereignty, and between *de jure* and *de facto* sovereignty.

Present and final sovereignty. Strictly speaking God's sovereignty is an eschatological concept. It refers to the bringing to pass of the final goal God has for the world. This situation will emerge at the end of the historical process. When viewed from the vantage point of the eschatological end, therefore, God is fully and obviously sovereign.

When viewed from the perspective of present experience, however, it is not so obvious that God is sovereign. In fact, whether or not God is reigning over the world is presently an open question. In a sense, the present open-endedness of the divine sovereignty is implicit in the act of creation itself. The very existence of creation as a reality different from God raises the question of ultimate sovereignty: Is God sovereign over creation or is creation autonomous?

The question which is only implicit in creation is consciously raised by the actions and attitudes of humans. As the highest creation of God, we continually call God's rule in question. We act against the divine sovereign whom we should acknowledge and obey. The desire to be one's own sovereign loomed already in the first sin. The serpent tempted our parents by holding out the promise, "You shall be like God" (Gen. 3:5).

Wolfhart Pannenberg has correctly pointed out that as a consequence of the act of creating the world, the very deity of God is bound up with his sovereignty over the universe. A God whose will and design is never fulfilled is in the end not the ultimate reality. Consequently, the present questioning of God's sovereignty carries profound theological implications. It means that the deity of God is now being challenged. And unless God exercises sovereignty, history will have proven that God is in fact not God at all.[6]

---

6. See, for example, Wolfhart Pannenberg, "The God of Hope," in *Basic Questions in Theology*, trans. George H. Kehm (Philadelphia: Fortress, 1971), 2:239-44.

The connection between God's deity as the sovereign one and God's acting to demonstrate his sovereignty is rooted in the Old Testament. Asaph's experience of the arrogance and prosperity of the ungodly led him to question the reality of God (Ps. 73:3-14). Was God truly cognizant of the events in the world? Was he willing to act as sovereign? In the midst of his questioning, Asaph began to reflect on the situation from the perspective of "the sanctuary of God." This vantage point allowed him to contemplate the final destiny of the wicked (v. 17). In so doing, his faith was renewed. God will indeed one day take up the challenge and act. He will destroy the scoffers, proving himself to be the sovereign one (vv. 18-20, 27).

According to the Bible, therefore, God is not idle in the face of the challenge to his sovereignty. In fact, all of history is the arena of God's establishment of his will—his kingdom—and consequently his deity. Already God's claim to rulership has been borne to the world. Biblical history, beginning in the Garden of Eden and climaxing in the coming of the Son, is a testimony to the sovereignty of the Father. In the present God's rulership is being advanced and expanded by the work of the Holy Spirit in the world.

All God's activity in history, however, points toward the eschaton. This event will mark the final display of God's rulership. As Paul announces, "Every knee should bow,...and every tongue confess that Jesus Christ is Lord to the glory of God the Father" (Phil. 2:10-11). Elsewhere Paul declares that his doxological prophecy will become a reality when every enemy of Christ has been subdued and placed under the Father's sovereignty (1 Cor. 15:24-26).

In the strict sense, then, God is sovereign from the vantage point of the eschatological future. "Sovereignty" means that God is at work bringing to pass the final goal of his creative activity. But if God is sovereign in the future, we can affirm his sovereignty in the present as well. God is presently reigning in several senses.

God's present sovereignty means that the present situation is connected to the future fullness. If God is sovereign at the end of history, then all history is moving toward the great day when God acts in a final manner to bring creation to completion. Because our present moment is one point along the path enroute to the day of God's eschatological sovereignty, it too participates in the movement of history through which God is directing human affairs toward the accomplishment of his goal. In this sense, we may assert that God is always sovereign over creation. Even the evil we experience in the present does not escape the oversight of the divine one, for on that eschatological day the sovereign God will overrule the evil of our present for the praise of his glory.

God is sovereign in the present in another way as well. God will act definitively in the future to bring to pass his will throughout creation. But even now God's sovereign power breaks into the evil, sin, and imperfection of our present. Even before the end of the age, the powers of the kingdom are at work. Consequently, here and there we catch glimpses of that glorious future reality. Here and there we see God overcoming evil for good. Through such experiences we enjoy a foretaste of the culmination, the actual power of the future in the midst of the fallenness of the present.

De jure and de facto sovereignty. In addition to the differentiation between its eschatological and present expressions, another contrast is helpful in understanding God's sovereignty. This distinction may be capsulized by appeal to the Latin phrases, *de jure* and *de facto*.

De jure means what is predicated "by right" or "by law," what rightfully belongs to someone. *De facto*, in contrast, refers to what is actually the case, the actual state of affairs. Applied to God, we may say that at every moment God is completely sovereign *de jure* but not necessarily *de facto*.

When viewed from the perspective of God's status as creator, God alone may rightfully both claim and exercise sovereignty. Only God is sovereign *de jure*. In the actual situation in the present moments of history, however, God's complete will is not always evident. This is the case with respect to creation as whole, insofar as the universe is in bondage and groans awaiting its liberation, as Paul indicates. But most significantly, God's human creatures do not always live in accordance with his design or will for them. Insofar as we are not what God intends us to be nor do what God intends that we do, God is not now *de facto* sovereign.

Yet, this is not the end of the story. At the eschaton God will bring all creation into conformity with the divine design. Then he will not only be sovereign *de jure* but also *de facto*.

This is also not the entire story. Even now in certain ways certain humans do live in accordance with the divine design. And God is presently at work in history bringing about his eschatological purposes. To the extent that God is now actively bringing creation to its intended goal and creatures acknowledge, reflect, and obey the divine will, God becomes *de facto* sovereign in our present moments.

God's future. The double-sidedness of God's sovereignty forms the context in which we can understand the important contemporary question concerning the future of God. God is not merely the impassible, unmoved mover of Aristotelian theologies but is active in the world and the historical process. In this context we ask, To what extent is it proper to say that God has a future?

As is evident from our discussion of God's relationship to time, in one sense we must conclude that God has no future. We confess that God is eternal. The entire process of history is immediately present to him. Likewise, we assert that God is complete in himself apart from the world. Because God is not bound to creation, the processes of history neither actualize nor affect his eternal nature. From the perspective of eternity, therefore, God has no future.

At the same time, however, our discussion has rendered the conclusion that God's relationship to creation does have a future. At the eschaton God's rulership, and with it his deity, will in the final and fullest sense come to be. At that time, God's purposes will be fully actualized, and he will be "all in all" (1 Cor. 15: 28). Consequently, we can speak of the future of God, in the sense that God's relationship to creation has a future reality not yet realized in our present.

The Time of Creation

The differentiation between the future fullness of the divine sovereignty and our present partial experience leads us to inquire concerning the time of creation: When does God create the world?

Creation as past. In a sense, this question seems unnecessary. After all, because the world obviously exists, our inclination is to assert

rather matter-of-factly that the creation of the universe was a past occurrence. For this we can also claim biblical precedence. As the
opening verse of the Bible clearly states, "In the beginning God created the heavens and the earth" (Gen. 1:1). Nevertheless, in another
sense the question, "When does creation occur?" is appropriate and
necessary. And the answer is not so obvious.

On one level it is correct to assert that the creation of the world occurred in the primordial past, "in the beginning" of the temporal sequence. In this past sense, "creation" refers to God's free act in
calling the world into existence or in bringing forth something instead of nothing. In making this affirmation, however, we must be
careful not to place the event of creation within a temporal sequence
in the life of God. Augustine reminds us that God did not create the
world "in time," but "with time." That is, the act of creation marks
the beginning of time.[7]

Creation as future. In one sense, creation is an event in the primordial past. In another sense, however, creation is not a past but a future
event. The creation of the world does not merely begin the temporal
sequence. More significantly, it stands at the end of the historical
process. "Creation" indicates God's future completion of his work in
bringing the universe to its destined state. It is his act in making the
world in accordance with the divine design. Viewed in this manner,
the act of creation is not yet completed, for God is active in history
bringing about his world-creating work.

The understanding of creation as a future divine act lies at the
heart of the biblical message. Prophets in both Testaments anticipate
a day when God will transform the present universe into the perfect
reality he desires that we enjoy. Isaiah explicitly announces God's
intention: "Behold, I will create new heavens and a new earth. The
former things will not be remembered, nor will they come to mind.
But be glad and rejoice forever in what I will create." (Isa. 65:17-18).
The prophet then describes the perfection and harmony that will
characterize the new creation (vv. 18-25). What the Old Testament
prophet envisions finds echo and expansion in the vision of the apoc-

---

7. Augustine, *City of God* 11.6, trans. Marcus Dods, Modern Library edition (New York: Random House, 1950), 350.

alyptic seer, who reports seeing "a new heaven and a new earth" (Rev. 21:1).

The biblical hope is clear: God's creative activity is far from complete. At the consummation of history, God will fashion the universe in accordance with his design and purposes. In the meantime, the world now eagerly anticipates the eschatological renewal. As Paul declares, "The whole creation groans," longing for that day (Rom. 8:19-25). Hence, the universe is not yet what it will be. Nor is it fully what God intends it to become.

In addition to the explicit statements of the prophets, the futurity of creation is implicitly present elsewhere in the Bible. The early church fathers found the idea even in the first creation narrative. The late first or early second century document, the Epistle of Barnabas, is typical of many writings. Barnabas does not interpret the biblical account of the six-day creation followed by the sabbath as merely a statement about the primordial past. Rather, the biblical text encompasses the entire sweep of God's action in history climaxing in the eternal situation lying beyond the eschaton:

> Attend my children to the meaning of this expression, "He finished in six days." This implies that the Lord will finish all things in six thousand years, for a day with him is as a thousand years. Therefore, my children in six days, that is in six thousand years all things will be finished. "And he rested on the seventh day." This meaneth when his Son coming again shall destroy the time of the wicked man and judge the ungodly and change the sun and the moon and the stars then shall he truly rest on the seventh day.[8]

According to the author of this letter, even in the first creation narrative the act of creation refers to the eschatological renewal of the world.

Not only was this interpretation widely held in the patristic era, it has gained increased following in our day as well. The Old Testament scholar Gerhard von Rad, for example, concludes that the Priestly writers intended the reader to understand God's Sabbath rest on the seventh day of creation as the future, eschatological fulfill-

---

8. *Epistle of Barnabas* 15, trans. J. B. Lightfoot and J. R. Harmer, in *The Apostolic Fathers*, ed. Michael W. Holmes, second edition (Grand Rapids: Baker, 1989), 182-83.

ment.[9] We are to conclude from the creation narrative, therefore, that we are living in the sixth day, awaiting the dawn of the day of perfect *shalom*, the completion of God's creative activity.[10]

Creation and essence. These considerations lead us to two conclusions. On the one hand, the inauguration of the act of creation lies "in the beginning," when God called the world into existence. On the other hand, this act comes to completion only in the future, when God shapes creation into "the new heaven and the new earth." As a consequence, we must give primacy to the future eschaton, and not the primordial past, as the ultimate point of creation.

This assertion carries weighty implications. It means that the creation of the world is yet future. Only at the consummation of God's activity in history will the world take on its final shape and thereby reflect fully the destiny or design God intends for creation.

The future orientation of creation also carries a far-reaching implication for our understanding of "essence." In the final analysis, "essence" is an eschatological reality. If the act of creation ultimately lies in the future, the essence of all reality is likewise ultimately not found in the primordial past, but in the eschatological consummation of history.

The future orientation of the concept of essence is most significant for humankind. If the ultimate human essence lies in the future, then we must not look to the first human pair in the pristine past for the paradigm of essential human nature. Rather, our essential nature lies in the resurrected humankind in the future kingdom of God, which is revealed to us before the end of time in the resurrected Christ.

This has a grand consequence for our identity as Christians. As Paul indicates, our true essential nature is not disclosed in Adam, but in Christ. For "as was the earthly man [Adam], so are those who are of the earth; and as is the man from heaven [Christ], so also are those who are of heaven" (1 Cor. 15:48). Our ultimate identity, therefore, lies in the total Christlikeness which will be ours when through the resurrection, we come to "bear the likeness of the man from heaven" (v. 49).

---

9. Gerhard von Rad, *Genesis*, trans. John H. Marks (Philadelphia: Westminster, 1972), 60-61.

10. H. Paul Santmire, "The Genesis Creation Narratives Revisited," *Interpretation* 45/4 (October 1991): 372.

God as the Providential Administrator of the World

We have characterized the fundamental theological assertion concerning the relationship between God and the world by use of the terms "Creator" and "creation." The triune God is the Creator of the world; and the universe is the creation of God. But the divine act of creation, while including the primordial calling of the world into existence, ultimately is an eschatological event. Hence, the doctrine of creation encompasses the divine activity in bringing into being the new heaven and the new earth as envisioned by the biblical prophets and seers.

This conclusion naturally leads us to inquire concerning God's purposes for the world he is making and God's active directing of history toward the accomplishment of these purposes. Stated theologically, the doctrine of creation readily leads to the doctrine of providence.

"Community" as God's Purpose for Creation

Our assertion that God is the creator of the world leads immediately to the question concerning God's intention in his creative work. What purpose does the Creator seek to accomplish in and for the creation he is shaping?

As we noted earlier, the world exists as the product of the outflow of the divine love, the eternal relationship between the Father and the Son which is the Spirit. The Father intends that creation share in his existence and enter into the relationship the Son enjoys with him. Thus, as the product of God's essence (which is love) and as God's counterpart, the world exists in order to participate in the life of the social Trinity.

We may summarize God's intention for the world by employing the term "community." Just as the triune God is the eternal fellowship of the trinitarian members, so also God's purpose for creation is that the world participate in "community."

God's intent to establish community with creation is a central theme of the entire biblical message. From the narratives of the primordial garden, which open the curtain on the biblical story, to the vision of white-robed multitudes inhabiting the new earth, with which it concludes, the scriptural drama speaks concerning community. But what is the actual nature of the fellowship God is seeking to bring to pass? Taken as a whole the Bible asserts that God directs his program to the bringing about of community in the highest sense of the word—a redeemed people, living within a renewed creation, and enjoying the presence of their God.

The vision of community as spelled out in the biblical drama begins in the past. God states his intent already in the second creation narrative: "It is not good for the man to be alone"(Gen. 2:18). The goal of the divine activity throughout history is the bringing into being of the community envisioned by the Creator who took note of the solitariness of the first human in the Garden of Eden.

Central to the divine purpose of establishing community is the presence of God among his people. God's presence is a constant theme of the Bible. The Lord communed with Adam and Eve in the Garden. At various times and in various locations the patriarchs experienced the presence of God. To commemorate their encounters with him they built landmarks, altars, and memorials (e.g., Gen. 28: 13-17).

With a view toward the establishment of this focal dimension of community—God dwelling with his people—God elected and entered into covenant with Israel. God's intent is evident in the Exodus experience. The immediate goal of God's deliverance of Israel from the bondage of Egypt was the assembling of the people at Sinai. There God brought the Israelites into his presence in order that he might constitute them as his people (Exodus 20:2-3) and dwell in their midst. During the wilderness sojourn, God intended to make his abode among them in the tabernacle; like theirs, his house would be a tent. So important was the presence of God with Israel that when God proposed that the tabernacle not be built because of Israel's sin, Moses responded, "If your Presence does not go with us, do not send us up from here" (Ex. 33:15).[11] Later when Israel established fixed

---

11. For a discussion of the significance of this incident, see Edmund P. Clowney, "The Biblical Theology of the Church," in *The Church in the Bible and the World*, ed. D. A. Carson (Grand Rapids, Mich.: Baker, 1987), 25-26.

dwellings in the promised land, God also put his glory within a house, the temple in Jerusalem.

The Old Testament experience forms the context for the significance of Jesus Christ as Immanuel—God with us (Matt. 1:22-23). In Jesus, the divine Word became flesh and "tabernacled" among us (John 1:14). In him, God is present with humankind. Jesus promised that both he and the Father would take up their dwelling with his disciples (John 14:23), and he spoke of another Comforter who would be present among them (John 14:23).

Jesus' promise, understood within the context of the Old Testament hope, forms the foundation for the work of the Spirit. Since his out-pouring at Pentecost, the Holy Spirit facilitates the fulfillment of Jesus' assurance of his continual presence with his followers. The Holy Spirit comprises them individually and corporately as the temple of God. Because of the finished work of Christ and the continuing work of the Holy Spirit, therefore, God himself is among his people, even though our experience of that presence may be partial.

The grand fulfillment of God's program lies yet in the future. The biblical story does not end with Pentecost and hence not with the true, yet partial experience of the presence of God currently enjoyed by Christ's disciples. The drama of the Bible moves from the past into the future. It reaches its climax with the grand vision of the new heaven and new earth.

The future renewed creation was anticipated by certain Old Testament prophets. But it is developed more fully in the closing chapters of the Book of Revelation. The inspired author looked to an era beyond the present which will mark the completion of the divine program in human history. According to the seer, in the new order God himself will dwell with humans. Thereby he will bring to completion the ultimate divine design for creation:

> And I heard a loud voice from the throne saying, "Now the dwelling of God is with men, and he will live with them, They will be his people, and God himself will be with them and be their God. . ." The throne of God and of the Lamb will be in the city, and his servants will serve him. They will see his face, and his name will be on their foreheads. (Rev. 21:3; 22:3-4)

In addition to declaring the fullness of God's presence with his people, John's vision forms the climax of biblical anticipations of other dimensions of the eschatological community God is seeking to bring to pass. For example, the seer pictured the new order as a place in which nature will again fulfill its purpose of providing nourishment for all earthly inhabitants:

> Then the angel showed me the river of the water of life, as clear as crystal, flowing from the throne of God and of the Lamb down the middle of the great street of the city. On each side of the river stood the tree of life, bearing twelve crops of fruit, yielding its fruit every month. And the leaves of the tree are for the healing of the nations. No longer will there be any curse (Rev. 22:1-4).

Further, he described the eschatological reality as a great and beautiful city, the new Jerusalem (Rev. 21:9-21). In that city, the peoples will live together in peace and harmony. Consequently, as John's vision of a future eon characterized by a new community of reconciliation, fellowship, and harmony confirms, God's purposes for his people is that they be brought together into a corporate body, a human community, rather than remaining as isolated individuals.

According to the biblical vision, God's ultimate intention is not directed to a transpositioning of the individual believer to an isolated, individual realm of unending "eternal life" beyond the world and time. Rather, God's program focuses on the corporate human story and therefore on humans as potential participants in a new society in the future. In fact, Scripture consistently presents our eternal home in social, rather than individual terms. It is a great city, it encompasses many dwelling places, it is composed of a multitude of inhabitants, etc. Hence, it is a social reality. As Paul Hanson concludes from his study of the theme of community in the Bible,

> God's future reign was not construed in terms of a blissful union of the elect with God that removed them from the world of humanity, but as a reign of justice and peace that repaired all wounds and restored righteousness as the standard among humans.[12]

---

12. Paul D. Hanson, *The People Called* (San Francisco: Harper and Row, 1986), 510.

The social nature of God's intent is displayed likewise in the focal point of salvation history, the Christ event. Jesus came as the exemplar human being, the revelation of who we are to be. And the divine design revealed by Jesus focuses on our living in relationship with God and others. Jesus also came as the Messiah—a social figure—the fulfillment of the hopes and aspirations of the Hebrew people and by extension of all humankind. In the same way, his intent was not to fulfill an individual vocation for his own sake, but to be obedient to the will of the Father for the sake of humankind. Thus, in his death he took upon himself the sins of all. And he rose from the grave in order to mediate to us eternal life through our union with him.

The work of the Holy Spirit likewise has the establishment of a social reality in view. His outpouring at Pentecost was directed toward the establishing of the corporate body of Christ to be the one new people composed of Jews and Gentiles reconciled to each other (Eph. 2:11-22). During the present age the Holy Spirit is bringing together a people that transcends every human division—a people from every nation and every socio-economic status, and consisting of both male and female.

In short, the vision of the Scriptures is clear: The final goal of the work of the triune God in salvation history is the establishment of the eschatological community—a redeemed people dwelling in a renewed earth, enjoying reconciliation with their God, fellowship with each other, and harmony with all creation. Consequently, the goal of community lies at the heart of God's actions in history. And God's ultimate intention for creation is the establishment of community.

The Doctrine of Providence in Recent Theology

Our conclusions concerning the centrality of community to the biblical vision leads us to the central question of the doctrine of providence: Is God faithful in bringing his purpose to completion? Does God indeed order the events of history toward the goal of establishing community?

As Christians we believe in a God who is able to complete his work in the world. As a result, the doctrine of providence moves from the delineation of the nature of the divine purpose for the world to a reflection on this confession concerning the God in whom we place our trust.

The history of Christian theology has witnessed an ebb and flow in the importance theologians attached to the concept of God's providential ordering of the world. Thinkers have offered several differing ways of understanding this Christian confession. Nevertheless, a watershed in theological thinking came early in the twentieth century.

The classical position. From the Middle Ages through the 1800s, the doctrine of providence played an important role in theology. Thomas Aquinas provided the groundwork for the classic understanding of the doctrine. Providence, he declared, is "the exemplar of the order of things towards their end," which exemplar preexists in God's mind.[13] Building on this foundation, Protestant scholastic thinkers subsumed three subheadings—preservation, concurrence, and governance—under the doctrine of providence.[14]

(1) The Baptist theologian Augustus Hopkins Strong offered the classic Protestant definition of the first subheading. Preservation, he declared, refers to "that continuous agency of God by which he maintains in existence the things he has created, together with the properties and powers with which he has endowed them."[15] Proponents of the classic understanding claim that theirs is both the teaching of the Bible itself (e.g., Neh. 9:6; Heb. 1:3) and a necessary conclusion from the doctrine of creation. Because the universe as a created reality is not self-sustaining, proponents argue, it requires the ongoing activity of God in order to remain in existence.

(2) The second classical Protestant subheading of providence is "concurrence." We may define this doctrine as "the cooperation of the divine power with all secondary powers allowing them to act as they do within certain set spheres of activity." Understood in this sense, concurrence is a further outworking of preservation. If the continuous agency of God is needed in order to maintain in existence

---

13. Thomas Aquinas, *Summa Theologica* 1.22.1, in *Introduction to St. Thomas Aquinas*, ed. Anton C. Pegis, Modern Library edition (New York: Random House, 1948), 215.

14. See, for example, Louis Berkhof, *Systematic Theology*, revised edition (Grand Rapids: Eerdmans, 1953), 169-76.

15. Augustus Hopkins Strong, *Systematic Theology*, three volumes (Philadelphia: Griffith and Rowland, 1907), 2:410.

the things God has made, then for creatures to act as they do requires God's cooperation. Just as creatures cannot remain in existence without God continually upholding them, so also they cannot act without God's agreement.

Among classical Reformed thinkers, however, the exact nature of God's concurrence has been a point of grave disagreement, forming a dividing line between Calvinists and Arminians. Calvinists typically define concurrence as "the cooperation of divine power with all secondary powers *causing* them to act as they do."[16] Hence, these theologians emphasize the causal nature of the divine concurrence. In the Arminian view, in contrast, God's agency in concurrence is less active. Arminians speak of God as passive, as merely allowing creatures to act as they do.[17]

(3) "Government" or "providence proper" is the third subheading in the classical Protestant doctrine. It refers to God's teleological care and control over creation. Thus, Louis Berkhof speaks for the tradition in defining government as the "continued activity of God whereby he rules all things teleologically."[18] As Berkhof's definition indicates, the concept of government affirms that God directs creation toward his intended goals, so as to achieve the design for creation.

Although the idea of governance seems relatively simple, theologians have sought to delve deeper into the manner in which God exercises control over creation. Typical of many thinkers is the position offered by William Newton Clarke a leading Baptist liberal thinker at the beginning of the twentieth century. He divided the world into two dimensions—the physical and the moral—each of which reflects its own peculiar governance. God governs the physical world through uniform laws of physics, whereas he governs human beings according to moral law.

---

16. Berkhof, *Systematic Theology*, 171, emphasis mine.

17. Hence Pope takes the Calvinist position to task. W. B. Pope, *A Compendium of Christian Theology* (London: Wesleyan Conference Office, 1876), 195. The Arminian understanding is reflected in Wiley's assertion that concurrence "must be understood to mean, not merely that God conserves certain powers in nature as second causes, but that there is an immediate co-operation of God with the actions and effects of these second causes." H. Orton Wiley, *Christian Theology*, three volumes (Kansas City, Mo.: Beacon Hill, 1940), 1:480.

18. Berkhof, *Systematic Theology*, 175.

Clarke maintained that God administers the moral laws, in turn, according to several principles. One such principle is that of duty. Clarke wrote, "God who desires the right and good for all creatures requires the right and good from all his creatures. Hence for them right is duty and whatever is seen by them as right is required of them as duty."[19] Another principle is that of appropriate consequences: "Good works toward good and evil toward evil so that whatsoever a man soweth that shall he also reap." Clarke suggested that all humans find themselves governed by moral principles such as these. God's laws are written on the heart (Rom. 2:14-15), the human conscience acts as God's ally (Rom. 2:15), and God's system of rewards and punishments is everywhere operative.

Clarke's more conservative contemporary, Augustus Hopkins Strong, concerned himself with the related problem as to how evil fits into God's plan. Strong offered four principles according to which God directs even evil actions of humans to his intended goal.[20] First, God in grace sometimes prevents sin which would otherwise be committed (thus Gen. 31:2). Second, God often permits persons to do the evil which they desire to do simply by withholding "impediments from the path of the sinner." Third, God directs an evil act "to ends unforeseen and unintended by agents so that its course can be best controlled and least harm may result" (e.g., Ps. 76:10). Finally, God sets "the bounds reached by the evil passions of his creatures" (e.g., Job 1:12).

Providence in liberal theology. As the above discussion indicates, by the twentieth century providence had developed into a well-defined doctrine in conservative Protestant theology. But the concept fulfilled an equally important role in nineteenth century Protestant liberalism. Actually, we can differentiate between two types of liberalism with two quite different understandings of providence. The dividing line between the two lay with the infusion of Darwinian ideas into theological thinking after mid-century.

---

19. William Newton Clarke, *An Outline of Christian Theology,* twentieth edition (New York: Charles Scribner's Sons, 1912), 141.

20. Strong, *Systematic Theology,* 1:423-25.

A central characteristic of liberalism prior to Darwin was its emphasis on natural theology. As Langdon Gilkey noted, from the time of Francis Bacon in the 1600s through the first half of the nineteenth century providence was "perhaps the most secure tenet of natural theology." Creation appeared to point unequivocally to the providential care of the Creator. In the words of Gilkey, "in the examination of the structure of the world, the physical, geological, and even biological sciences seemed to uncover a marvelous 'fitting together' of things to one another and to their environment for their common good."[21]

Darwinism altered the faith of Protestant liberal theology. But it did not alter the important place subsequent liberalism accorded to the idea of providence. On the contrary, post-Darwinian liberals simply equated divine providence with the purposeful force which directed the evolutionary process. In this manner, rather than destroying the belief in providence, evolutionary theory had merely supplied a new understanding of the mechanism by which God orders creation to his intended goal.

The destruction of providence. The advent of the twentieth century—beginning with World War 1—brought a radically-changed situation. Since that catastrophic event, the truth of divine providence no longer has seemed so self-evident. On the contrary, the gloomy events of the century have served to exorcise from the human consciousness the idea of a God who is directing creation to an intended goal. The century that has known two world wars, the prospect of a nuclear Armageddon, and the growing threat of an ecological holocaust has led even theologians to the grim conclusion that God no longer appears to be governing the corporate affairs of humankind. A doctrine of providence which claims that all of history is moving towards a divine goal is difficult to maintain in the face of the reality of a world that appears to have spun out of control.

Consequently, the theological innovations which have sought to take seriously the new reality of the twentieth century have been marked by a definite waning in allegiance to the doctrine of provi-

---

21. Langdon B. Gilkey, "The Concept of Providence in Contemporary Theology," *Journal of Religion* 43/3 (July 1963): 171.

dence, at least as it has been traditionally understood. Neo-orthodox theologians rejected the idea of progress and sought to take seriously human sin. Existentialist thinkers limited truth to encounter. Neither approach has much room for any doctrine of providence that goes beyond God's care for the individual to describe a divine watchcare over the world process as a whole.

God's Administration of His World

The events of the twentieth century and the theological rearrangement of the doctrine of providence that these events have produced call into question the viability of the Christian confession of God as the providential governor of the world. How can we as theologians chastened by the realities of the twentieth century make sense of this classic Christian faith stance?

As significant as they may be, the events of the last hundred years do not call into question the providence of God. Rather, they demand that we think through clearly what this Christian confession actually means.

At its foundation, the doctrine of providence seeks to capsulize a fundamental Christian affirmation concerning the relationship of God the Creator to the world as his creation. To describe how this is the case, we must look again at the three subheadings of the classical doctrine in the light of the current situation.

Preservation. In its classical understanding "preservation" asserts that God continuously sustains the physical universe in existence. Historically this understanding arose out of the pre-Newtonian physics, which anticipated that the physical world would lapse into nonexistence without the continuous agency of God. With the demise of the older physics, the classical understanding of preservation has likewise lost its credibility. Yet, this does not mean that all concepts of the divine preservation of the world are obsolete. On the contrary, there is another, and for us more crucial dimension of existence that the confession of God as our preserver addresses.

More vital to us today than the purely physical understanding of God's agency in preservation is the confession that God is the one who preserves us in the face of the apparent meaninglessness of existence. Hence, when we confess God as the agent in preservation, we are providing the divine answer to the question, "Is there meaning to life?" The question of meaning arises both with respect to the existence of reality as a whole and individual existence.

"Preservation" constitutes the Christian answer to the question of the meaning of the whole. We confess that God provides the only ultimate meaning of creation. In so doing, he prevents the universe and its history from slipping into meaninglessness.

In the face of the apparent meaninglessness of the manifold variety of reality, we wonder if there is any meaning to the world. Atheistic existentialism answers this question in the negative: There is no objective, ultimate meaning; the only meaning is what human individuals create for themselves. Certain Eastern religions look for meaning apart from the world. They teach that we can find meaning only as we escape from the process of history.

In contrast to either pure subjectivism or mere escapism, the faith commitment of Christians is in the God who is the source of the goal for all creation and who orders all of history toward the completion of that purpose. In the face of evidence to the contrary, Christians believe that history is moving somewhere. God is ordering human affairs toward the establishment of the eschatological community. We believe likewise that God will bring creation to this goal. Consequently, for the Christian the whole of reality is meaningful.

Further, we believe that the eschatological goal of history is revealed in Jesus Christ. He is the *logos*, the meaning of history, for he is the exemplar of the purposeful relationship that can exist between creation and the Creator. We rest confident that God will bring history to its goal—community with him—because the one who guides history is the God who raised Jesus from the dead. He is the one who through the resurrection reestablished the community between Jesus and his Father which was broken on the cross.

"Preservation" also constitutes our answer to the problem of personal meaninglessness. As Christians we confess that God is the provider of meaning for our lives. Hence, he preserves us from personal meaninglessness.

Many people today experience life as a disjointed series of events. They find no structure which can mediate significance and continuity to day-to-day living. Consequently, they sense the dissipation of the self into a series of disjointed activities. And they believe that their personal experiences of evil preclude any hope for finding positive meaning to life.

In the face of the apparent meaninglessness of personal life, Christians confess faith in the God who preserves us by providing purposefulness for life. God gives meaning for personal life in that he provides the integrative focus for the seemingly unrelated activities and experiences of living.

God mediates meaning to us as we center our personal lives on Jesus Christ. For Jesus is the *logos*, the principle of unity, not only for the world as a whole but also for personal existence. Through commitment to Jesus as lord we find our lives centered on the integrating factor that can bring together the disjointed events of our lives.

The New Testament writers such as Paul describe this commitment to Jesus, and hence this centering of life on him, in terms of union with Christ. Such union entails not only mental assent to a set of doctrines, but also the embodying in our beliefs, attitudes, and actions the meanings and values that characterized Jesus' own life. In this process of embodiment the Christian faith-community is crucial. The believing community transmits from generation to generation and region to region the redemptive story, which it recounts in word and deed. In so doing it mediates to the believer the framework for the formation of personal identity, values, and world view.

Hence, our lives have meaning because of our union with Jesus. But union with Jesus means entering into community with the triune God and with all others who acknowledge Jesus as lord. Ultimately, then, God is the preserver of the meaningfulness of our existence in that through Christ he brings us to participate in his program for all creation, namely, the establishment of community. The goal of our existence is the enjoyment of eternal fellowship with the triune God in the renewed creation. Toward this goal God is ordering all the events of our lives, including even the trials we experience (e.g., Rom. 8:18; 1 Pet. 1:6-7; Jas. 1:2-4).

Concurrence. Like "preservation," the classical understanding of the second subheading of the doctrine of providence, "concurrence," was based on a now out-moded medieval physics. Concurrence as "the cooperation of the divine power with creaturely powers allowing or causing them to act as they do" made good sense in an era in which thinkers believed that the universe would come to a standstill without the continuous intervention of God as the first cause of motion.

Classical Protestant thinkers, of course, transferred the concept to the realm of will. They spoke of concurrence in terms of an ever-present and ever-acting divine will continually giving assent to, or causing the actions of human beings, whether these be good or evil. Despite this alteration, the underlying concept remained the same, for the human wills with which the divine will concurs are the intermediate causative agents of human action in the world. Consequently, with the passing away of the older view of the physical world, the older understanding of concurrence lost its appropriateness and explanatory power.

Despite the intervening shift in world view, our faith in the God of concurrence remains meaningful in the contemporary situation. More crucial than the understanding of concurrence as the permissive or causative influence of the divine will on human wills is the relationship of our confession of God as creator to the question of ultimacy. In the final analysis, "concurrence" is faith's answer to the question, "Who is ultimate?"

The experiences of contemporary living raise the question of ultimacy. It appears that each human being is an autonomous self, free to act in accordance with one's own purposes. And it appears that wicked people are free to do as they please unfettered and unchallenged. The Christian faith replies, however, that what seems to be the case in actuality is not. There is one ultimate reality. Even in their rebellion, human and cosmic agents remain dependent on God. Therefore, no kingdom of evil can attain ultimate status.

In addition to its negative function as a denial of the ultimacy of creaturely causative agents, concurrence serves a positive function.

Through it we affirm our Christian belief in God as the gracious one. Concurrence reminds us that God extends his goodness toward the undeserving, for he acts as the source or ground of our existence despite the rebellion of his creatures.

In addition, concurrence carries a special positive meaning within the context of Christian discipleship. The concurring God in whom we confess faith invites us to participate with him in the completion of his program for the world. Specifically, he calls us to pray and to work. As we are obedient to him, he "concurs" with our actions, sanctifying them and employing them for the sake of his kingdom. Thereby we enter into community with him and with other believers who have likewise responded to his invitation.

Government. Not only can we affirm "preservation" and "concurrence," but we can also continue to acknowledge the third classical subheading of providence, "government." When we assert that God "governs" his creation, we are expressing our certainty that God will bring both the world as a whole and our lives to their final goal. As Peter declares, God's power shields us for the inheritance he has in store for us (1 Pet. 1:5).

We ask, however, How is this possible, given the evil we experience in life? Here the concept of government provides an answer. This doctrine emphasizes the greatness of God in the face of evil. God governs the world in that he brings good out of evil, whether partially in this life or fully in the eschatological new creation.

The grand example of God's governance is the death of the incarnate Son. God used the atrocity of the crucifixion of the sinless Jesus as the means to bring salvation to the world. In the same way, God will attain the final goal for his world in part through the acts of rebellious human beings. For this reason even the tragedies of life can have good effects. At the consummation of history God will rectify all the evils and injustices of life (Rev. 20:4). On that great day, the dead will triumph over death, the oppressed will be victorious over oppression, and God will inaugurate his new order, the eschatological community.

Events of the last hundred years have made acute a dilemma that the faith community has always faced. The reality of evil calls into question the affirmation of God's care over his creation. Even the psalmist was perplexed as he saw the wicked prosper (Ps. 73:1-15). Because evil appears to be on the rampage while the righteous suffer, it seems that God is not ordering the affairs of the world.

Despite appearances to the contrary, the world historical process is going somewhere. God is directing human affairs to the final revelation of his sovereignty and the reordering of the universe in the new heaven and the new earth. In other words, all history is moving toward the establishment of community. In his time, God will act decisively. And even now he invites us to orient our lives around his on-going program. By means of allegiance to the God revealed in Christ we can exchange the disorder of life for a new order marked by community or fellowship with God, others, and all creation.

As those who confess faith in the triune God, we can be a people of hope. Hope is possible, for God will bring his purposes to pass and is using even the evils of life in this process. This is the message of the doctrine of providence (e.g., Ps. 73:16-28).

Part 2
Anthropology
The Doctrine of Humanity

Our doctrine of God concluded with the declaration that the triune God is the creator of the universe. The creator God is purposeful, for he fashions the universe with a goal in view. God's ultimate purpose is to establish community with his creatures.

The acknowledgment of God as Creator leads us naturally to consider creation—what God creates. In contemplating the universe, as Christians we are primarily interested in the special relationship God desires to share with the moral creatures he has made. This concern forms the context in which to understand humankind. Viewed from this perspective, Christian anthropology is an extension of the doctrine of God. In our doctrine of humanity we speak about human beings as creatures of God. We may encapsule our human identity as God's creatures in three postulates: We are the good creation of God, we are marred through our fall into sin, but we are also the object of God's redemptive activity.

Our status as part of God's good creation is the focus of the opening two chapters of our anthropology. We begin the discussion by looking at our origin, and hence our identity, as lying ultimately in God (chapter 5). In this chapter we appeal to the fundamental human experience of "openness to the world" as indicating that we are dependent beings whose origin lies both existentially and essentially in the Creator. As a result, our very existence stands as a testimony to the reality of God.

Next we turn our attention to human nature as designed by God (chapter 6). Here we explore the thesis that humans are unified beings with multiple capabilities. God created us with great value, for he designed us for community. And he desires that we reflect his own image.

From the lofty postulate that we are the good creation of God we turn to the sad declaration that we are marred. Rather than fulfilling the design God intends for us and living in accordance with our identity, we are sinful and separated from our divine origin (chapter 7). In this chapter we explore the human failure to live out our design to be the community who reflect the divine image. Since the wilful disobedience of the first humans, all of us have become accomplices. Because our failure leads to ultimate loss of community, we exist in a woeful and hopeless state.

We are not alone in this dialectic of being both responsible before God and capable of missing the divine design. Rather, we are related to another order of morally conditioned creatures, the spiritual hosts of angels and demons (angelology). In the final chapter of the section (chapter 8), we explore the nature of these realities which exert either positive or evil influence over human personal and corporate life. As they foster or undermine community, the spiritual forces either fulfill or deny their design as moral creatures of God.

The final anthropological postulate entails the story of God's activity to reconcile fallen humankind to himself and thereby to bestow on us a new identity in Christ. Reflection on this aspect of the Christian message takes us beyond the doctrine of humanity, for it encompasses the remaining four foci of systematic theology. Anthropology, therefore, sets the stage for all that follows.

5

The Human Identity and Our Origin in God

For in him we live and move and have our being." As some of your own poets have said, "We are his offspring." (Acts 17:28)

Outline

Humans are plagued with an identity problem. Scholars in a variety of disciplines pursue the question concerning the human identity. Psychologists, for example, speak of identity crises which vex individuals at various stages in life but which also contribute to personal development. Philosophers also seek to discover the essence of the human person. The nineteenth century pessimistic thinker Arthur Schopenhauer (1788-1860) supposedly bumped into a man while musing on this problem. When the angry recipient of his unintentional blow accosted him with the gruff question, "Who do you think you are?" the gloomy thinker responded wistfully, "Who am I? How I wish I knew."

We assert that at its core the human identity problem is religious in nature. The psychological experience of identity crisis or the philosophical ruminations on our identity are merely symptoms of a more profound enigma lying at the heart of the human situation in the world. Whether consciously or unconsciously, at the depth of our being we raise the question, "Who are we?"

Into this enigmatic situation Christians proclaim the good news that we have an identity. Our foundational identity arises from the fact that our ultimate origin lies in God. We are creatures of the one whom Jesus declared is our heavenly Father. As God's creatures we can know our origin and our destiny. In so doing we can begin to understand who we are. This origin and this destiny—and consequently our identity—are linked to our place in the creation that is God's handiwork.

Our Place in Creation

The question of the human identity is not unique to modern culture. The ancient Hebrews voiced the query, "Who are we?" The psalmist, for example, contemplated the vastness and majesty of the universe as created by God: "your heavens, the work of your fingers, the moon and the stars, which you have set in place." These reflections led the biblical poet to cry out, "what is man that you are mindful of him, the son of man that you care for him?" (Ps. 8:3-4).

As the psalmist's query indicates, one important context for responding to the question of our identity lies in the connection between humankind and the material universe. Who are we in relationship to everything else that is? In setting forth the Christian understanding of humankind, as theologians we must seek an answer to this question.

Humankind and the Cosmos in Changing Cultural Contexts

Since the beginning of human history, people have raised the question concerning our place in the cosmos. This query has evoked two quite different paradigmatic answers—the "premodern" and the "modern."

The "premodern" answer. The ancients responded to the question of human identity by setting forth an understanding of humans in accordance with what they perceived to be our assigned place within the created order. They viewed humans as creatures who enjoy a unique position in an orderly universe, which in turn serves as the context for designating our human identity.

Exemplifying the premodern world view, the psalmist found an appropriate response to his own query:

> ... what is man that you are mindful of him, the son of man that you care for him? You made him a little lower that the heavenly beings and crowned him with glory and honor. You made him ruler

over the works of your hands. You put everything under his feet (Ps. 8:4-6).

The biblical writer assigned a unique place to us. We stand above the material world, but under the spiritual beings who also populate the created order.

As Psalm 8 indicates, the Hebrews, like other ancient societies (and so-called "primitive" cultures today), pictured reality as ordered. God (or the highest God) stood at the apex, followed by the heavenly beings (or the gods), then humans, and finally the rest of creation—animals, plants, and inanimate objects. Not only is there order to reality, according to the ancient understanding creation provides a "home" for humankind. This sense of "belonging" included an assigned task: "You made him ruler over the works of your hands." Hence, in the older view humans could know who they are by virtue of their status within the wider whole of which they are an integral part and in which they are to function.

The modern answer. Modern cultures have largely rejected the ancient answer, substituting in its place a second response to the question of humankind in the cosmos. According to the modern world view, we find our identity not in any supposed status as creatures, but in our activity as creators. Consequently, the universe is not a "home" in which we naturally belong. Rather it is the material object of our human creative and transforming activity.

The modern answer to the question of human place in the universe may be on the wane. As we move into the postmodern era, many voices are crying for a revisioning of the modern world view. We are hearing increasingly loud calls for a new understanding of ourselves that would see humans not as separate and above, but as an integral part of the environment in which we live.

Despite the move toward postmodernity, there can be no wholesale return to the ancient world view. We simply cannot go behind the modern era. The growing ecological consciousness may serve to blunt some of the abuses of the environment that characterize industrial society. Nevertheless for most people there is no viable alternative to the continuation of the modern self-understanding which views the world as the material for our human transforming activity.

At the same time, the current concern for the environment and the desire on the part of some thinkers to develop new paradigms for our relationship to our environment offer Christians an opportunity. The changing cultural context demands that we articulate anew and afresh the biblical themes concerning the identity of humankind within a universe which is God's handiwork. Our challenge is to search out a theological answer to the question of human identity. We must develop a specifically Christian response to the question of identity which has perennially troubled humankind and which is being raised with new vigor in our changing context: Who are we in relationship to the world around us?

Christian Faith and the Insights of Anthropology

One propitious beginning point in our search for a Christian understanding of our relationship to creation lies in certain insights developed by a movement in thought generally referred to as "theological anthropology." Simply stated, this discipline is the attempt to discover the theological significance and apologetic value of the human self-understanding as propounded by the human sciences.

Theologians who follow this method employ the modern human self-consciousness, as depicted in the findings of anthropologists, in an attempt to develop a deeper understanding of the human person. Proponents of theological anthropology begin with the modern human self-awareness as a creator and the world as the material for our transforming activity. They then seek to discover the theological significance of this basic anthropological datum.

The concept of "openness to the world." The findings of contemporary anthropology have led certain thinkers to the concept of "openness to the world" as encapsulizing the basic situation of humans in the cosmos.

One proponent of this approach, Wolfhart Pannenberg, defines "openness to the world" as the "unique freedom of man to inquire and to move beyond every regulation of his existence."[1] As this definition suggests, the phrase "openness to the world" refers to the

---

1. Wolfhart Pannenberg, *What is Man?* trans. Duane A. Priebe (Philadelphia: Fortress, 1970), 3.

uniquely human ability to experience the environment always in new ways.

This specifically human possibility has a biological basis. Animals are bound to their environment by limitations set by heredity. Humans, in contrast, are not so closely restricted by inherited factors. Anthropologist Ashley Montagu expresses the generally acknowledged contrast by means of a comparison between humans and the other primates:

> And this essentially is the difference between the apes and man. The apes have pursued a developmental course which will ultimately lead to their extinction. They are too narrow, too specialized. They cannot compete with man. The human species on the other hand has pursued a developmental course which has been characterized by its plasticity and adaptability which have led mankind to the position in the world in which it now finds itself. Not "nature's sole mistake," at least not yet, but nature's most spoiled brat, perhaps: unquestionably nature's most promising child....
>
> This plasticity and adaptability which so conspicuously endowed man beyond all other animals with the ability to control so much of the world in which he lives is reflected both in the structure of his body and of his mind. Both are the least specialized of any to be found in the Order of Mammals to which he belongs. Now this is an extremely important point to grasp. That is that man biologically is both structurally and mentally the most plastic and adaptable animal in existence.[2]

The biologically based "plasticity and adaptability" of the human species gives humans an edge over other living creatures. More importantly, it also lies at the foundation of our lack of a biological "home" in the cosmos. Because we are adaptable, we enjoy the unique possibility of experiencing the environment always in new ways. This is what is meant by "openness to the world."

Our "openness to the world" also raises the question concerning our function in the universe. Other living beings have a discoverable "niche" in the biological framework. The human identity, in contrast, cannot be answered definitively by reference to biology. We

---

2. Ashley Montagu, *Man in Process* (New York: Mentor Books, 1961), 17-18.

cannot find a specific biological role that explains our purpose for existence.

"Openness to the world" also suggests that as humans we enjoy the possibility of transcending any finite ordering of our environment, any "world" we create. This is linked to our ability of self-transcendence, which makes us unique from the animals. In the tradition of Hegel, the German thinker, Max Scheler speaks of the spirit as the source of the capacity of each individual "to elevate himself above himself as a living being and, as it were, from a center beyond the spatiotemporal world, to make everything, including himself, an object of his knowledge."[3]

Because of this transendending capability, humans are never completely fulfilled by any one achievement or by any one "transformation" of the world we author. Rather, we are continually on the move to something yet undefined. That is to say, humans are never completely satisfied with the present. We are always seeking the new, the "future," the not-yet, that which surpasses the present. We are continually shaping and reshaping our environment in an unfulfilled attempt to create a "home" for ourselves. We sense what Arnold Gehlen calls an "infinite obligation."[4]

The theological significance of the concept. Several contemporary thinkers have ventured a theological interpretation to this basic anthropological finding by appeal especially to human adaptability.[5] Our "openness to the world," the authors of these studies argue, points to what may be called the "infinite dependency" of humankind. Because we are "open to the world," we are dependent on some reality that transcends the finitude of any expression of our "world."

The connection between "openness to the world" and "infinite dependency" is obvious. Because we have no niche in the biological framework, we simply can find no ultimate fulfillment in any one

---

3. Max Scheler, *Die Stellung des Menschen im Kosmos* (Munich: Nymphenburger Verlagshandlung, 1947), 48, as cited in George S. Hendry, *The Holy Spirit in Christian Theology*, revised edition (Philadelphia: Westminster, 1956), 102.

4. Arnold Gehlen, *Der Mensch* (Bonn: Athenauem, 1958), 349ff, as cited in Pannenberg, *What is Man?*, 9.

5. See, for example, Juergen Moltmann, *Man*, trans. John Sturdy (Philadelphia: Fortress, 1974). See also, Pannenberg, *What Is Man?*

"world" or environment we create for ourselves. This human incapability to be fulfilled by any structure of the world, in turn, drives us beyond the finitude of our experience in a never-ending quest for fulfillment. We are, therefore, dependent creatures. But our dependency is greater than the finite world can ever satisfy.

"Infinite dependence" suggests as well that humans are directed toward a goal "beyond the world." The fulfillment toward which the human person strives can never be found in any finite "world." Therefore, it must lie "beyond" the world, if it is to be found at all.

"Infinite dependency" readily points in the direction of God as the final answer to the human quest. The incessant drive beyond the world suggests that our very existence as beings who continually follow after an illusive, unrealized fulfillment presupposes something beyond every experience of the world. Because our world is always finite, the object of our infinite dependency cannot be found within the world. Rather, we are dependent for the fulfillment of our quest on Something beyond the world.

In this manner, articulators of theological anthropology move from "openness to the world" to the concept of "God" as the Source of our identity. Of course, the human sense of infinite dependency and of directedness beyond the finite confines of the world may in the end be nonsensical and meaningless. On the other hand, however, the fundamental human reality may actually point toward the Creator. The infinite, world-transcending Someone, who alone is the answer to our infinite dependency, proponents of theological anthropology conclude, is God. In short, anthropology itself suggests that our existence as humans presupposes an entity beyond the world upon whom we are dependent and toward whom we are directed for ultimate fulfillment.

In saying this, contemporary theologians are reasserting a fundamental declaration which has been present throughout the Christian tradition. Already in 397 A.D., Augustine declared, "Our hearts are restless until they find rest in thee, O God."[6] The sentiments of the

---

6. Augustine, *Confession* 1.1, trans. Vernon J. Bourke, volume 21 of *The Fathers of the Church*, ed. Roy Joseph Deferrari, eighty-one volumes (Washington: Catholic University of America Press, 1953), 4.

great church father find echo in the well-known declaration that there is a God-shaped vacuum in the heart of every person.[7]

The conclusions of theological anthropology suggest that the self-understanding of modern humans confirms the truth of these fundamental Christian theological affirmations. Within the cosmos we are the restless creatures that look beyond the material universe for ultimate fulfillment. We are designed to find our meaning and identity in relation to, and only in relation to God.

"Openness to the World" and General Revelation

The insights propounded by articulators of theological anthropology naturally lead to the question of general revelation. Is our human "openness to the world" a mark of the reality of God pressed in the heart of every human being? Has God so ordered the universe that he has indelibly left his stamp on the world and on the human person, so that all humans have access to at least a rudimentary knowledge of the divine reality? To some limited extent do all humans "know" the Creator God, because the very structure of human experience—our "openness to the world"—cries out his existence?

Before proceeding to discuss our origin in God, we must tackle this vital theological question.

The Question of "General Revelation" in Theology

The meaning of general revelation. Through a specific reading of several biblical texts (Ps. 19:1-4a; Rom. 1:18-2:16), the concept of general revelation has gained wide usage within many Christian theological circles. Before evaluating the propriety of the concept, however, we must become clear as to what it actually means.

Perhaps the most expeditious way to understand "general revelation" is by contrasting it with the related category, "specific" or "special revelation." The two forms of revelation differ in several ways.

As the designation "general" suggests, "general revelation" refers to that divine self-disclosure God has given to all humans or to hu-

---

7. This statement is commonly attributed to the seventeenth century French philosopher Pascal.

mans in general. "Special revelation," in contrast, comes only to certain "special" or "specific" persons.

Further, unlike special revelation, general revelation is that divine self-disclosure which is "natural" rather than "supernatural" or which is disclosed naturally rather than supernaturally. General revelation is communicated through nature—through the visible creation with its laws and through the moral nature of the human person. Because it is naturally available to all, humans can gain access to general revelation through reason. Special revelation, in contrast, is communicated supernaturally, whether directly by God or indirectly through God's messengers. Consequently, the employment of our natural powers of reason cannot put us in contact with it.

Finally, general revelation is "noetic" rather than "salvific." It is intended to mediate a general knowledge of God our Creator. The purpose of special revelation, in contrast, is to bring humans into fellowship with God our Saviour. In the words of the nineteenth century Princeton theologian Benjamin B. Warfield, general revelation is designed "to meet and supply the natural need of creatures for knowledge of their God," whereas special revelation is given "to rescue broken and deformed sinners from their sin and its consequences."[8]

Bruce Demarest pulls these themes together into a typically evangelical definition of the concept. General revelation is "that divine disclosure to all persons at all times and places by which one comes to know that God is, and what he is like. While not imparting saving truths such as the Trinity, incarnation, or atonement, general revelation mediates the conviction that God exists and that he is self-sufficient, transcendent, immanent, eternal, powerful, wise, good, and righteous."[9]

The place of general revelation in theological history. The division of revelation into the categories of "general" and "special" has had a checkered history. It has engendered broad recognition in one

---

8. Benjamin B. Warfield, *Revelation and Inspiration*, reprint edition (1927; Grand Rapids: Baker, 1991), 6.

9. Bruce Demarest, "Revelation, General," in the *Evangelical Dictionary of Theology*, ed. Walter A. Elwell (Grand Rapids: Baker, 1984), 944.

era, only to be discarded in the next. We may note five basic attitudes toward general revelation in theological history.[10]

(1) A first group of thinkers wholeheartedly embrace the concept of general revelation. They derive from this aspect of the divine self-disclosure a "natural theology," a body of truth concerning God available to all persons.

Paradigmatic of this position is the medieval theological system of Thomas Aquinas.[11] In fact, the idea of general revelation, while not unknown in the patristic era, first came to prominence in the Middle Ages with the work of the Roman Catholic scholastics.

The medieval theorists such as Thomas Aquinas were motivated in part by their concern to articulate a universal knowledge of God, a natural theology, on which to build the specifically revealed dogmas of the church. They argued, therefore, that God's self-disclosure in nature and in the human person provides the basis for the construction of a limited, but nevertheless true knowledge of God available to all humans through the use of our natural powers of reason. By looking at creation, human reason is able to discover a body of propositional statements—partial yet valid—about the nature of God.[12]

Thomas added, however, that natural theology building from general revelation is insufficient for a complete knowledge of God. Indeed, God's special revelation is necessary if we are to know the deeper salvific mysteries. These are given through the Christian faith, specifically through the Bible and church tradition.[13]

The medieval emphasis on natural theology and the corollary of an innate human ability to develop knowledge of God from the divine self-disclosure in nature suggested the validity of two avenues to truth. The first path, human reason, yields a body of truth to which the individual gives assent because this truth is demonstrated by argumentation. The second avenue is faith, which grasps those truths

---

10. For a somewhat similar characterization of the attitudes of theologians to the twofold division of revelation, see Demarest, "Revelation, General," 944.

11. Thomas Aquinas, *Summa Contra Gentiles* 1.2-4, trans. Anton C. Pegis, in *On the Truth of the Catholic Faith*, Image Books edition (Garden City, N.Y.: Doubleday, 1955), 1:61-68.

12. Ibid., 1.3.2 [63].

13. Ibid., 1.5 [69-70]. See also Thomas Aquinas, *Summa Theologica* 1.1.1, in *Introduction to St. Thomas Aquinas*, ed. Anton C. Pegis (New York: Modern Library, 1948), 3-5.

that are supernaturally revealed. According to the scholastics, these two paths to truth—reason and faith—can in principle never be in conflict. There can be no ultimate disagreement between the propositions demonstrated by reason and the higher assertions accepted by faith.[14] In short, general and special revelation are harmonious.

(2) The reaction to medieval theology in the Reformation formed the foundation for a second attitude toward the concept of general revelation. The Reformers accepted general revelation but rejected natural theology. They agreed with the schoolmen that God discloses himself in creation and that this revelation is available to all. But the Reformers set forth the bold thesis that sinful humankind is not able to know God through this general revelation.[15]

According to the Reformers, two factors, both related to human sin, account for the imperceptibility of general revelation. Our sin has obscured the revelation of God in nature. What was originally designed to be an orderly universe human sin has rendered disorderly. Sin, therefore, hides the revelation God has placed in the created order. In addition, we are unable to perceive the revelation in nature, because our sin has blinded us to the truth present in creation. We cannot see the truth God offers to humankind in nature.

This formed the basis for the Reformers' emphasis on the importance of special revelation. God's additional self-disclosure is necessary not only for our salvation, but even for us to see the revelation deposited in creation. Calvin expressed the Reformation position when he declared that the lenses of the gospel are required for an individual to be able to see the revelation of God in creation:

> Just as old or bleary-eyed men and those with weak vision, if you thrust before them a most beautiful volume, even if they recognize it to be some sort of writing, yet can scarcely construe two words, but with the aid of spectacles will begin to read distinctly, so Scripture, gathering up the otherwise confused knowledge of God in our minds, having dispensed our dullness, clearly shows us the true God.[16]

---

14. Thomas Aquinas, *Summa Contra Gentiles* 1.7 [74-75].

15. John Calvin, *Institutes of the Christian Religion*, 1.5.14, trans. Ford Lewis Battles, volumes 20-21 of the *Library of Christian Classics*, ed. John T. McNeill (Philadelphia: Westminster, 1960), 68-69.

16. Ibid., 1.5.14 [70].

Calvin's position has found echo in the writings of contemporary Reformed scholars. Leon Morris provides one example:

> It is special revelation that gives us the key to general revelation. Gordon H. Clark reminds us that, "The ancient Babylonians, Egyptians and Romans looked on the same nature that is seen by the modern Moslem, Hindu and Buddhist. But the messages that they purport to receive are considerably different." He goes on to say, "What the humanists and logical positivists see in nature is entirely different from what the orthodox Christian believes about nature." Without special revelation we would not know how to interpret general revelation. With it to guide us we can discern God's handiwork.[17]

(3) In the Enlightenment era, a third and quite opposite attitude toward general revelation emerged. Enlightenment theologians elevated reason to a position even higher than that accorded to the human power by Thomas Aquinas. They looked to reason and nature as the final arbiters of truth.[18]

Certain theologians of the Age of Reason concluded that general revelation—the self-disclosure of the supreme being in the laws of nature—was primary. Special revelation, if at all valid, was true insofar as it constituted a restatement of the truths available to human reason through general revelation. The Enlightenment's optimistic appraisal of our human ability to know God through reason formed the context for the agenda of nineteenth century liberalism.

(4) As the twentieth century began, a fourth attitude surfaced, namely, the questioning of general revelation as a source for knowledge of God. Karl Barth's radical attack on natural theology quickly became the most definitive modern critique of the concept.[19]

Barth's response arose in part from his understanding of the idea of revelation itself. According to Barth, revelation is not something which "is." It is not a body of truth waiting to be discovered. Nor is it something "out there" to which an individual comes. Rather in Barth's understanding revelation is a divine activity, God disclosing

---

17. Leon Morris, *I Believe in Revelation* (Grand Rapids: Eerdmans, 1976), 42-43.

18. This was the position of thinkers such as John Tillotson, John Locke, and Samuel Clark. See Arthur Cushman McGiffert, *Protestant Thought before Kant* (London: Duckworth, 1911), 195-210.

19. Karl Barth, *Church Dogmatics*, ed. G. W. Bromiley and T. F. Torrance (Edinburgh: T. & T. Clark, 1957), 2/1:63-178.

himself. Barth argued that the focus of revelation is Jesus Christ, for in Christ alone we are confronted with the revelation of God.

Placing Barth's view in the context of the distinction between general and special revelation yields the conclusion that for him, only special revelation is valid. According to Barth, what matters is our being confronted with the Word of God, which is Christ.

(5) More recently a fifth approach, the "blending" of general and special revelation, has emerged. The roots of the idea lie in the contemporary interest in salvation history (the idea that God discloses himself through his activity in history). On the basis of the thesis that God's self-disclosure is found in history as a whole the contemporary German theologian Wolfhart Pannenberg rejects as invalid any division of truth into general and special revelation.[20]

Pannenberg argues that there is but one self-disclosure of God. This revelation is "general," in that as history it is public. It is available to all who would discover the revelation present in the human story. At the same time, this one revelation is "special." It is the disclosure of God's saving activity.

The Theological Importance of "General Revelation"

The concept of general revelation has been and continues to be controversial. Despite the debate that surrounds its usage, however, the concept remains valid and helpful,[21] for it carries theological significance. Its importance lies in at least two directions. These are related to the two focal points of general revelation—the human person and the natural world.

Revelation in the human person. General revelation is a helpful theological concept in that it asserts that God has disclosed himself within the structure of the human person. Present to all humans is an internal testimony to God, a "revelation" apart from the divine action in public history.

---

20. For a discussion of this feature of his thought, see, Stanley J. Grenz, *Reason for Hope: The Systematic Theology of Wolfhart Pannenberg* (New York: Oxford University Press, 1990), 40.

21. For a plausible case for the use of the concept of general revelation, see Reinhold Niebuhr, *The Nature and Destiny of Man* (New York: Charles Scribner's Sons, 1941), 1:125-36.

Understood in this sense, the reality of general revelation is a logical conclusion from the idea of "openness to the world." As we saw earlier, we share a common dependency on something external to, or beyond any shape that we can give to our "world." The God-shaped vacuum within us, to which this dependency bears silent witness, is a testimony in the human heart to the reality of God.

As we have noted, "openness to the world" also indicates that we are directed to a goal beyond the world. We will discuss the theological implications of this observation more fully in chapter 7. Let it suffice here to say that the divine image, although marred, remains present to each person. By virtue of the fact that we are created beings, God has directed each of us to a common human destiny. Just as our common human dependency bears witness to the reality of God, so also the residue of the divine image within us is a dimension of general revelation. Our awareness that we are directed beyond the present stands as a silent witness to the reality of God for whom we are created.

One specific aspect of our sense of being directed beyond the world is the common human awareness of moral obligation, articulated by Kant (see chapter 2). In daily living we may suppress the sense of moral conditionedness. But it reemerges in the boundary situations of life, such as times of solitude or crisis. While falling short of forming the basis for a tightly reasoned proof for God's existence, this foundational moral experience forms a testimony to the reality of God present to each person.

Revelation in nature. General revelation is likewise a helpful theological concept in that it asserts that God has disclosed himself in the universe as a whole. Central to this assertion is the anthropological implication of the gracious benevolence of God toward creation.

While acknowledging that "the heavens declare the glory of God," the biblical writers are more concerned with the observable graciousness of God to all living creatures, even to humans in their rebellion against him. For the writers of Scripture, the focus of general revelation lies in such mundane matters as the regularity of the seasons and the provision of food for creatures (Ps. 136:25; Acts 14:17).

The theme of God's provision moves in two additional directions as well. On the one hand, God's care for creation is a sign that he desires to fulfill the longings of creatures, including the yearnings he has placed within human hearts (Acts 17:27). On the other hand, God's goodness extended toward us has practical importance. It calls us to mirror God's character by caring for others and for creation (Matt. 5:43-45).

In all these senses, God's benevolence constitutes a divine self-disclosure that is available to all. It stands as a constant testimony to the reality of God. The benevolent Creator made us in order that we should find in him the final answer to our quest for fulfillment. And he has implanted in us a purpose, namely, to imitate his character as we see it displayed all around us.

The "natural realm," therefore—creation itself and the structure of the human person—testifies to each human being concerning the reality of God.

The limit of general revelation. Although the concept of general revelation is valid and helpful, it is also limited. It is restricted in scope. What God has made available to all persons through general revelation does not provide the complete self-disclosure of God. On the contrary, general revelation functions only as a testimony to the presence of the God who is the reality standing both behind and within the world.

Hence, the heavens declare "the glory of God" (Ps. 19:1), not the deep mysteries of God's essence. Likewise, in creation humans perceive the eternal power and divinity of God (Rom. 1:20)—not the complete divine essence God himself. Thus, the natural world does not display God's "whatness" (the complete self-disclosure of the divine reality), but God's "thatness" (his presence to creation).

Because general revelation is limited in scope, it is also limited in its result and consequently in its potential use. Rather than bringing humans to know God, the testimony present in creation results in judgment and condemnation. As a result, general revelation does not offer us a firm foundation on which to build a systematic delineation of the nature of God.

The limited use of the concept is evident in the Bible itself. Even in the most definitive scriptural text on the subject (Rom. 1:18-2:16), general revelation plays a circumscribed role. Paul's main purpose is not to set forth the thesis that creation testifies to the reality of God. Rather, his point is that sinful humans suppress even the testimony heralded by the natural creation. Because of human sin, people do not in fact give ear to this available testimony.[22] Recast in the contemporary situation, his statement means that rather than following our inherent "openness to the world" to its intended goal—fellowship with God and the actualizing of our God-given destiny—human beings attempt to find fulfillment in themselves and in the finite "world" they create. To use Paul's conclusion, people become idolaters. This idolatry may take the blatant form of the veneration of carved images. Or it may come in the more subtle modern form of looking to our own creative ability for the satisfaction of our ultimate longings. In either case, all humans stand justly condemned before a holy God (Rom. 3:23).

Even for Paul, therefore, the concept of general revelation is subject to limitations. He invokes it to highlight human sin and divine judgment. The apostle does not appeal to general revelation to provide a sure foundation for a theological edifice.

God as Our Origin

As the concept of general revelation suggests, not only the natural world, but our existence as humans points toward God. Our biological adaptability and plasticity which give rise to "openness to the world" imply that we are "infinitely dependent" and directed beyond the world. For our ultimate identity we are dependent on a transcendent reality, the divine Creator.

When viewed theologically, "openness to the world" signifies our fundamental human creatureliness. In this way the modern concept returns us to the traditional theological affirmation of God as the or-

---

22. Barth, *Church Dogmatics*, 1/2:307.

igin of humankind. It also takes us back to the conclusion that humans are God's creatures. Because we are dependent on a transcendent reality, the ultimate origin of humankind lies beyond the world. Stated theologically, our origin is in God.

We now explore the wider significance of the theological affirmation that God is our origin. Specifically, the theological declaration—"Our origin lies in God the Creator"—carries significance for our human existence and our human essence.

The Existential Significance

Christian theology declares that our origin as humans lies in God our Creator. One dimension of this assertion is its existential significance, its meaning for our actual existence. Viewed from this vantage point, the confession "Our origin lies in God" means that God is the ground of human *existence*.

God as the ground of personal existence. The existential theme that God is the ground of existence has in view our individual, personal existence. This assertion means that we do not create ourselves. We did not and cannot choose to be. Nor does our actual existence in the world come from ourselves. Rather than being intrinsic to us or arising from our own being, our life is a derived life. We owe our existence to God the Creator. We *are*, simply because in accordance with his free graciousness and his gracious freedom God has bestowed existence on us.

Paul makes this point when in his speech to the Athenians he quotes from an ancient Greek poet, "For in him we live and move and have our being" (Acts 17:28). Each individual life—our very existence—occurs in the context of the reality of God.

The confession that God is our existential origin moves beyond mere physical existence, however. More importantly, it encompasses individual purpose. Not only personal life itself but also the meaning of our lives is not intrinsic to us. We derive personal meaning from a reality beyond ourselves, for God bestows meaning on us. And this bestowed meaning is related to the goal, purpose, or destiny God intends for us. This is the deeper meaning of Paul's statement that in God we "have our being."

As Christian theologians we add that in bestowing life and existence on us, God has not merely a general, ill-defined goal in view. On the contrary, his purpose is specific and particular. The Westminster Catechism aptly summarizes the divine purpose in the answer it offers to the first catechetical question: "The chief end of man is to glorify God and enjoy him forever."[23] God's purpose—God's desire—is that all creatures glorify the Creator. As those who are able to respond consciously to God, humans are to share in that great privilege. Glorifying God also means enjoying him, knowing the joy of relationship with the Creator. And this joyous glorification of God, while including the present, also spills over into the future, for it is directed toward "forever."

The future orientation of the answer of the catechism reminds us that God's design is linked to his sovereign rulership, which comes in its fullness at the eschaton. God's intention is that we participate in the eschatological kingdom, the glorious community of God with humankind. In addition, however, that eschatological community is to be a present reality, as even our lives manifest God's rule.

God as universal Father. Viewed in this manner, the affirmation that God is the origin of our existence forms the context for understanding the often misunderstood declaration that God is the universal Father. Correctly stated, the doctrine of the divine fatherhood asserts that as Creator, God is the ground or source of the existence of each human being. No one exists apart from the express will of God, who freely bestows life on human beings. As the ground and source of each, God is the Father of all.

The concept of God as universal Father is taught in Scripture. That believers are the children of God is an obvious biblical truth (John 1:12). Less evident is the fact that even rebellious, wayward creatures remain in some sense God's children. Nevertheless, a constant theme among the Old Testament prophetic writings is that even in apostasy Israel remains the object of God's love and the recipients of a special relationship with God.

---

23. "The Westminster Shorter Catechism," question 1, in *Creeds of Christendom*, ed. Philip Schaff, three volumes, reprint edition (Grand Rapids: Baker, 1977), 3:676.

Jesus' parable of the prodigal son extends the parameters of God's love beyond Israel and thereby forms one of the most graphic expressions of the divine fatherhood. Central to the parable is Jesus' depiction of the loving and forgiving heart of God. But our Lord also presents the lost, wayward, and foolish youth as ever remaining the son of his father, even while he was wandering far from his father's house. So too God continues to act as Father to all humans even in their sin, even when they refuse to acknowledge him.

The Old Testament wisdom literature extends the motif to what for us appears to be the most difficult case of all. Even the accuser himself, our enemy, Satan, is numbered among the heavenly sons of God, when, as the curtain lifts on the drama of the testing of Job, Satan and the angels present themselves before Yahweh (Job 1:6).

These biblical considerations raise the question, In what sense are we to understand the universal fatherhood of God? Our query brings us back to the subject of this section. Summarily stated, God is the Father of all, even of the wicked, insofar as he is the source of the existence of, and the author of the purpose or destiny for each creature. Even in our rebellion, we cannot escape the simple truth that we are not the source of our own existence. On the contrary, the origin of our life—our very existence as well as the destiny that alone can bring us fulfillment—is the God who bestows on us physical existence and "openness to the world." The universal identity of humankind, therefore, rests with the God who lies at the origin of our life.

The concept of the universal fatherhood of God carries important implications not only for how we view our identity, but also for our understanding of the reality of sin. God's universal fatherhood implies that sin is fundamentally a denial of our own legitimate Father. Sin severs what God designed to be a familial tie. But sin does not leave a person fatherless. On the contrary it entails the formation of an illegitimate familial bond. Hence, Jesus' stinging remark to the Jews: "You belong to your father the devil" (John 8:44). When humans forsake their divine family they enter the lineage of the chief rebel, Satan. Ultimately, therefore, sin exchanges the legitimate bond with God for an illegitimate family headed by an illegitimate "father," the father of lies himself (John 8:44).

As Creator—as the source of the existence and purpose of every living thing—God is the Father of all creatures. The universal fatherhood of God does not mean, however, that all persons acknowledge God as Father, whether in this life or in eternity. As we will see in our discussion of cosmic eschatology (chapter 24), the awful tragedy is that many who ought to share as members of the family of God fellowship with each other, creation, and their true Father, do in fact remain outside the divine community for all eternity.

The Essential Significance

In addition to its meaning for the existence of each human, the affirmation that our origin lies in God also carries importance for our understanding of the human essence we are to share. The statement "God is our origin" affirms that God is the source or the ground of the essence called "human." God has the prerogative to declare what it means to be human.

God's prerogative to determine the human essence is an outgrowth of his position as Creator. As the Creator, God is our fashioner, and therefore he alone has the right to declare what it means to be human. In the Christology section we will observe how Jesus as the true human reveals to us this divinely determined essence.

Beyond this general affirmation concerning God's prerogatives, to say that God is the ground of the essence of humanity has several practical implications for the Christian understanding. For example, it suggests that we are called to espouse a fundamentally "essentialist" world view. In contrast to the conclusion of certain pessimistic existentialist philosophers (e.g., Jean Paul Sartre), when viewed from the Christian perspective, life is not devoid of meaning. It is simply not the case that we are merely "thrown" into existence. It is not true that we must each create whatever meaning we can, or that we must devise our own essence through the choices we make. On the contrary, God has designed humankind with a purpose in view. Therefore, there is an objectively true human essence which God calls each human being to acknowledge, reflect, and actualize in life.

In addition, the affirmation that God is the origin of our essential humanity means that God is the source of value for all creation. Neither other human beings nor the human community has the ultimate prerogative to determine the value of anyone or anything that God has made.

This thesis should affect the way we view the natural environment. Creation is valuable not merely as the material for our human transformation, but because God values it for itself. From the beginning to the end of the biblical drama we find God valuing his creation. At its inception he called it "good." And it is this very earth that will be transformed in the eschatological renewal. God calls us to value the earth not for its utility but in accordance with the value he places on it.

The assertion "God is the source of value" is especially applicable to the realm of human value or the worth of individual persons. Our value is not merely a function of our perceived worth to another or to society. Instead, our value is based on the worth God ascribes to us. Rather than being the determiners of value, humans are commanded by God to acknowledge the value he ascribes to each person.

The issue of human value has specific application to several contemporary ethical questions that focus on human life and death. Christians are to espouse answers to all such questions from the standpoint of God, rather than the contemporary Western social community or the autonomous individual.

An important example is abortion. Many people today attempt to settle the question of the personhood of the fetus by appeal to the value either the mother or the wider human community places on that fetus.[24] However, no adequate response to the abortion issue can begin in this manner. A fetus does not become valuable only when he or she is "a wanted child" or when society chooses to acknowledge the unborn child as a person with rights. Rather, we must frame the discussion of abortion by asking, What value does God place on the new life developing in the womb? In so doing we conclude that God values all individual life.[25]

---

24. See, for example, Mary Anne Warren, "On the Moral and Legal Status of Abortion," in *Contemporary Issues in Bioethics*, ed. Tom L. Beauchamp and LeRoy Walters (Belmont, Cal.: Wadsworth, 1989), 211-20.

25. For a more detailed discussion, see Stanley J. Grenz, "Abortion: A Christian Response," *Conrad Grebel Review* 2/1 (Winter 1984): 21-30. See also Stanley J. Grenz, *Sexual Ethics* (Dallas: Word, 1990), 135-41.

In summary, our declaration, "God is the origin of humankind," arises as the theological interpretation of a foundational biological datum concerning humans, namely, our "openness to the world." Humans have a place in the universe: we are creatures with a special destiny in God's program. God created us to be the recipients of his special love and a special value. All humans share in that status, because God calls each one to participate in the destiny he has ordained for us. Our origin lies in God, for God is the source of both the existence and the essence of humankind as a whole and of each human person in particular.

Our Temporal Origin

In the confession, "Our origin is in God," we affirm that God is the source of our existence and our essence. For people today, however, the question of human origins does not focus on our essential nature or the beginnings of our personal existence. Rather, what generally first comes to mind is the question of our temporal origin.

The Question of the "First Human"

For many Christians a discussion of human origins invokes the question of the temporal origin of humankind: Was there a "first human"? In the modern era, scholars in many fields have debated the concept of a first human. Evangelical Christians, however, generally narrow the focus of this wider discussion to the long-standing debate concerning a historical Adam. Did humankind begin with a first person whom the Bible calls "Adam"?

The traditional position. Many Christians hold to what may be termed the "traditional" view. Proponents declare that Adam was a historical person, a specific human individual who formed the genesis of the human race. Many adherents also surmise (although perhaps not by necessity) that Adam came into existence through a specific divine creative act at a specific point in time.

Proponents of the traditional view appeal to several biblical texts.[26] They claim that the references to Adam scattered throughout

---

26. For an example of this approach, see Gordon R. Lewis and Bruce A. Demarest, *Integrative Theology*, three volumes (Grand Rapids: Zondervan, 1990), 2:26-47.

the Bible consistently treat him as a historical person (1 Chron. 1:1, Jude 14, Luke 3:38). Moreover, Paul's theological dichotomy between Adam and Christ (Rom. 5:12-21; 1 Cor. 15:20-22) requires that Adam be a historical individual in the same way that Jesus is. But above all, traditionalists appeal to the Adam story in the second creation narrative (Gen. 2-3), which they interpret as a historical account.

The mythical view. In the last two centuries, an alternative to the traditional view has gained adherents, even among evangelicals. We may characterize this newer position as the mythical view. Its proponents assert that Adam need not be understood as a historical individual, but is better seen as a symbol. On the question, For what or whom is Adam a symbol? articulators of the mythical view do not find agreement. Rather, thinkers put forth several suggestions concerning the identity of the referent in the Genesis story.

(1) One type of interpretation, which we may call "existentialist," views Adam as a symbol for everyone. "Adam" represents each individual human. Consequently, advocates suggest that the creation narrative intends to portray the course of events which occurs in the life of each person. The story of our lives is that of a fall, a move from innocency to sin.

Some "existentialist" interpreters understand the Genesis story as a description of the historical, personal fall experienced by everyone, generally at some point in childhood. Each human begins earthly life in a state of innocency. But eventually we all come to the point at which we begin to make ethical choices. When we reach this point, we fall from innocency into sin.

Other "existentialist" thinkers view the transition from innocency into sin not as occurring at a specific stage in life, but in terms of the point of moral decision-making in the face of temptation that we repeatedly encounter. The events of Genesis 2-3, therefore, transpire in each moment of decision. When confronted by a temptation or a moral decision, we begin in a state of innocence; with respect to the specific possible action we are existentially unaware of, or have no immediate experience of, good and evil. But when we yield to the temptation—when the sin is committed—we fall from innocency to guilt, just as the Genesis story depicts. In keeping with this view-point, Reinhold Niebuhr declares that Adam's story is "a symbol of an aspect of every historical moment in the life of man."[27]

(2) In addition to the various existentialist understandings, there is another mythical interpretation of "Adam," which we may call the "essentialist." The essentialist interpretation views Adam as a symbol for humankind as a whole. In this sense, the story of Genesis 2-3 is a type of historical representation. It speaks of the course of events which resulted in the current state of affairs in which we now find ourselves. Humankind began in paradise but fell into sin, even though that primordial fall cannot be traced to one specific historical human pair. As a consequence of the tragedy in our corporate history, all persons since that "beginning" find themselves sinful from birth.[28]

The underlying hermeneutical question. Because of the importance of the Adam story to our understanding of this biblical figure, discussions of the issue of the historicity of Adam often focus on the hermeneutical question concerning the intent of Genesis 2-3. Proponents of the mythical view of Adam suggest that the story is not simply historical narrative, but rather constitutes a theological statement in story form.

Evangelical thinker James Hurd summarizes the situation well in arguing for the mythical view. Concerning the hermeneutics of his position he writes,

> The Genesis record is not a strict "newspaper reporting" chronology of events, but rather is meant to set humans in their proper place in the cosmos—to espouse their ultimate meaning—to relate them, not to a mere string of naturalistic processes coinciding with known natural laws, but rather relate them to the creator.[29]

From his hermeneutical orientation, Hurd draws the obvious conclusion:

---

27. Niebuhr, *The Nature and Destiny of Man*, 1:269.

28. For an example of this approach, see Wolfhart Pannenberg, *The Apostles Creed*, trans. Margaret Kohl (Philadelphia: Westminster, 1972), 160-69.

29. James Hurd, "Anthropology, Theology, and Human Origins," *Journal of the American Scientific Affiliation* 33/4 (December 1981): 241.

> According to this view, Genesis does not force us to any particular scientific theory about human origins, but it does force to us a conclusion concerning the meaning of humanness, the relationship of humans to other humans, their corporate relationship to God, and their relationship to the cosmos.[30]

To the typical objection, namely, that if the Genesis story is not chronological newspaper reporting then other texts in Scripture likewise cannot be said to be reliable historical accounts, Hurd then responds:

> Even the most literal interpreters of the Biblical text are forced to draw a line between *history* and *allegory*; between enduring Biblical principles and culturally or temporally limited teachings....symbolism in Genesis need not detract from Biblical authority.... In this view, Genesis allows for any one of several scientific theories of human origin. It does not allow for pseudo scientific meanings for humankind that reject our grounding in God himself.[31]

Many evangelicals, however, have not found the hermeneutics of the mythical view either convincing or satisfying. This leads us to the ticklish related question of evolution.

The "First Human" and Evolution

In the minds of many, the question of the historicity of Adam and, by extension, the hermeneutics it entails leads quite naturally to the issue of evolution. To some extent this connection is valid. Those who accept the theory that humankind appeared on earth as the product of a process of evolution may find little compelling necessity to read in the Genesis story a narrative of a specific historical person named Adam. Those who deny that humans evolved from lower forms of life, in contrast, often base their rejection of the theory of evolution in the Genesis creation narratives—including the story of Adam—interpreted as the actual history of the beginnings of the universe and of the first human pair.

Considerations in the evolution debate. Although it is outside the scope of a systematic theology to interact explicitly with the evolu-

---

30. Ibid.
31. Ibid.

tion controversy, it is certainly in order for us to touch on a few guiding considerations for all Christians in approaching this issue.

(1) In discussing evolution we must keep in mind that the purpose of the biblical accounts and that of scientific theories may not always be identical. Although the following often-repeated distinction is an overstatement, it does help us see that the two disciplines are fundamentally different in intention: The scientist poses the question, "how?" and answers it in terms of cause and effect. The theologian, in contrast, asks, "for what purpose?" and responds by invoking conceptions concerning God's purposes, goals, and plans.

Leon Morris employs an everyday analogy to illustrate that the purposeful, personal answer sought by theology to questions concerning the universe is no less important than the scientific:

> In answering the question, why is the kettle boiling, one can speak of the striking of a match, the kindling of the gas flame, the increase of the temperature of the water and so on. The chain of cause and effect can be complete. But it is also possible to answer the question by saying, "because I want to make a cup of coffee." The second answer is just as true as the first. It would be foolish to deny the truth of the second on the grounds that the first can be demonstrated scientifically. The scientific explanation while true is not the only one. And it may be argued that it is not the most significant one. The personal factor is important.[32]

Some evangelicals have employed this distinction as a basis for embracing both the theory of evolution and the biblical doctrine of creation. Richard H. Bube, for example, offers this response to the question, Are evolution and the Bible mutually exclusive?

> It seems to me that at the present time the answer to this question is *no*. An evolutionary framework is as suitable as an instantaneous creation framework for expressing the basic truths of the Bible. Note what I am *not* arguing: (a) I am *not* arguing that instantaneous *fiat* creation is impossible (thereby limiting the omnipotence or God), and (b) I am *not* arguing that evolutionary process is an ultimately faithful description of God's creative activity (for there are still too many unanswered questions). What I *am* arguing is that an evolutionary-type description need not be ruled out *a priori* by biblical consider-

---

32. Leon Morris, "God's Dice or God's Purpose," *Christianity Today* 16/22 (August 11, 1972): 42 [1078].

ations, and that therefore the Christian has the freedom to pursue wherever biblical and scientific integrity lead in the future.[33]

We need not accept the theory of evolution in order to acknowledge that what Bube suggests is a genuine possibility.

(2) In approaching the evolution controversy we must realize that "scientism" (and its modern corollary, "evolutionism") is indeed in conflict with our Christian theological understanding of the universe. Scientism is the world view which arises from the assumption that science is ultimately able to provide the answers to all our human questions concerning life and existence. "Evolutionism," in turn, assumes that not only does the evolutionary process in and of itself offer the key to the question of our human origin but also constitutes the only way in which we can even frame the answer.

Given these presuppositions, proponents of scientism and evolutionism find no place in the discussion for any assertion concerning God's involvement or presence in the world. This is obviously incompatible with the biblical world view with its focus on the declaration that God is the Creator of the world.

(3) In this controversy we must keep in mind that in the final analysis it may be beyond the ability of scientific study to either prove or disprove the existence of a first human. By their very nature, temporal beginnings lie beyond the pale of the scientific method.

Adam as a historical person. The controversy over the process by means of which humans came to appear on the earth does not appear close to resolution. Scientific study will never determine conclusively whether or not a historical person existed who corresponds to the Adam of the opening chapters of Genesis. At the same time, the various biblical references to Adam suggest that the authors of Scripture considered him to be a person in history. Consequently, we have good reason to continue to affirm the traditional view.

For Christian faith, however, more important than the actual historical-scientific question concerning whether or not Adam was the first human is the theological significance of "Adam" as marking the

---

33. Richard H. Bube, "Creation: Understanding Creation and Evolution," *Journal of the American Scientific Affiliation* 32/3 (September 1980): 177.

beginning of humankind. It is to this significant dimension of the question of Adam we now turn.

Anthropology and Our Temporal Origin

Behind the question of the first human lies the broader topic of the temporal origin of humankind. Consequently, our discussion of "Adam" leads us back to our earlier affirmation, "Our origin lies in God."

As we concluded above, God our Creator determines what constitutes the human essence. He bestows value on humankind and on each individual human being. Viewed in this broader context, the question of the temporal origin becomes the question as to when this occurs: When does God create? When does God determine our human essence? And beginning when does God bestow value on us? Understood in this manner, the question concerning our temporal origin is actually twofold. It is a question both of essence and of existence.

The temporal beginning of humankind. Viewed essentially, we must pose this question in terms of the temporal origin of humankind as a whole. Beginning at what point does humankind receive value as those who are affirmed through the grace and love of the Creator? Theologically the answer to the essentialist question is "Adam." The temporal origin of humanity lies in Adam.

Regardless of how Adam actually appeared on the earth, God's purposes in creation reach a new plane with Adam. Beginning with this creature, God is at work in a special way on the earth, for he has determined a unique destiny for Adam and Adam's offspring.

Viewed theologically, then, humanity begins at a specific point in the history of the universe, namely, with the appearance of Adam on the earth. With Adam (or "homo sapiens") and solely with Adam, God enters into a special relationship or covenant. In this covenant God declares a new intention for creation, namely, that this creation—Adam and his offspring—fulfill a special destiny by being related to God in a way unique from all other aspects of the universe that God has made.

The temporal beginning of each person. Following from this essentialist answer to the question of our temporal origin lies the existentialist consideration. The existentialist context leads us to inquire concerning our temporal origin as individuals. We now ask concerning the genesis of individual life: Beginning at what point does what comes as the product of human conception become the recipient of value by means of the grace and love of the Creator? At what point does God look upon what is developing in the womb and acknowledge it as the object of God's grace, love, and special destiny? When does God enter into covenant with the developing human individual?

This question is traditionally posed in terms of the "soul," which will be dealt with in the next chapter. Therefore, we merely offer the question here. The answer must await our subsequent discussion.

The unity of humankind. Before leaving the topic at hand, however, we must touch on one further outworking of our discussion of Adam as the temporal origin of humankind. Our assertion that theologically the origin of humankind lies with Adam means that every human is the offspring of Adam and that all humankind forms a theological unity. The doctrine of the unity of humankind as arising from one fountainhead finds support in the Bible, in biology, and in other theological considerations.

Its biblical foundation lies already in the Genesis narrative. According to the story, after the fall Adam named his wife Eve, "because she would become the mother of all the living" (Gen. 3:20). In this manner, the narrator suggests that this couple became the progenitors of all other human beings. Paul echoes the Genesis assertion. In his speech to the Athenians he suggests that all nations ultimately sprang from Adam: "From one man he made every nation of men that they should inhabit the whole earth, and he determined the time set for them and exact places where they should live" (Acts 17:26).

The doctrine of the unity of humankind finds confirmation in the writings of modern biologists. Ashley Montagu, for example, expresses what is perhaps a consensus of his peers:

> And here the important fact requires to be stated that all varieties
> of man belong to the same species and without a doubt have the same

common human ancestors. This is the conclusion to which all the relevant evidence of comparative anatomy, haematology and genetics points. On genetic grounds alone it is virtually impossible to conceive of the varieties of man having originated separately as distinct lines from different anthropoid ancestors.[34]

Finally, the doctrine of the unity of humankind follows from the theological affirmation that God is the Creator. As we have seen, the creator God has the prerogative of determining the essence and value of his creation. In entering into covenant with Adam, God determines our human destiny and bestows the value of "human" upon all of Adam's offspring. Consequently, all humans share together as those whom God intends to participate in the one destiny. Therefore, we form a unity of essence.

The unity of humanity carries grave theological importance. It means that each of us stands before God as a participant in the one humanity. This common standing, in turn, entails several practical implications. It implies that all persons are equal in the sight of God. This principle provides the foundation for our response as Christians to ethical issues such as justice, racism, etc. The unity of humankind implies likewise that each person participates in the one fall into sin. Paul himself derives this point from the theological unity of all humankind in Adam (Rom. 5:12-21).

The discussion of this theological implication must await the treatment of sin in chapter 8. Before looking more closely at the sad reality of our sinfulness, however, we must describe another dimension of humans as God's good creation: We share a nature given by God.

---

34. Montagu, *Man in Progress*, 18.

6

Our Nature as Persons Destined for Community

So God created man in his own image, in the image of God he created him; male and female he created them. (Gen. 1:27)

Outline

The Image of God in the Bible
  The divine image in the Genesis creation narratives
  The divine image elsewhere in Genesis
  The image of God in the New Testament
The Theological Significance of the Image of God
  The divine image as a special standing
  The divine image as a special fellowship
  The divine image as an eschatological reality
  The divine image as a special community

In chapter 5, we explored the idea of our origin in God and its implications for our identity as humans. Our discussion moved from the concept of "openness to the world" as an expression of the modern self-understanding of humankind. This concept led us to assert that our identity ultimately can only be derived from a reference point outside the world. As Christians we know this transcendent reality to be God. We have an identity, therefore, because God our Creator is the origin of our personal existence and of the human essence we are called to share.

We now take this discussion a step farther, asking, What is this essence God intends for humankind? The focus of our inquiry is our essential human nature: Is there an essence all humans share? And if so, what characterizes the nature of humankind as God our Creator has determined?

These questions lead us to delve further into the insights offered by the Christian faith for a contemporary human self-understanding. In this chapter we set forth a theological perspective concerning our identity as creatures who are "open to the world." More specifically, in the following pages we describe our identity in the light of the nature of humanity. We discuss this identity first with respect to the essence of humankind and then under the rubric of the biblical-theological concept of the image of God.

Our Ontological Nature

Modern anthropologists characterize humans by appeal to terms such as "plasticity," "adaptability," and "openness to the world."

Does this "openness" indicate some sort of basic human nature that we all share? Do we begin life with a set of givens—an essence—which in part shapes and molds the choices we make and the actions we do? Or do we create whatever "essential" nature emerges by means of our choices and actions? Our first task in this chapter is to discover the stance of the Christian faith concerning this vital matter.

Autonomy Versus Determinism

In recent years thinkers working in several disciplines, including philosophy, the social sciences, and theology, have tackled the issue of autonomy and essence. The debate focuses on a crucial question: If we are creators and the world is the material for our transforming activity, are we fundamentally autonomous and free? Or is there some human essence which determines, at least in part, how we respond to this transformative challenge? At opposite ends of the spectrum of opinions on the question of autonomy and essence are "existentialism" and "eterminism."

The focus on autonomy. David Ray Griffin offers this summary definition of existentialism:

> The term *existentialism* is usually taken to the claim that existence precedes essence: no essence is to be found in the nature of things with which human beings should live in harmony. No natural law, no divine purpose, no objective importance, no hierarchy of values is inherent in the nature of things, to which we should conform. Rather, in the very act of existing we must create our own values, realizing all the while that they only seem important because we have chosen to make them so.[1]

As this description indicates, the existentialist option emphasizes autonomy. Proponents of this view declare that there is no foundational human essence lying beyond our experience of freedom. No human essence predisposes our choices or places boundaries upon our ability to choose. Rather, creative humans reach out into nothingness, as it were. Each individual is left free to decide what he or she is becoming. Consequently, each individual's identity is constituted by personal choices, rather than by some essential nature.

---

1. David Ray Griffin, *God and Religion in the Postmodern World* (Albany, N.Y.: State University of New York Press, 1989), 17-18.

The focus on essence. In contrast to the existentialist emphasis on autonomy, deterministic viewpoints elevate essence. Determinism asserts that humans possess no ultimate autonomy as such. Rather, factors over which we have no control determine how we employ our creative activity. Although we may appear to choose freely from among options, lying at the foundation of such choices are always certain motivating factors which are external to us and not under our control. According to determinism, therefore, creative humankind is the product of non-human forces. The choices we make are determined, even "predetermined."

Many people automatically connect these ideas with theological determinism, especially as it has appeared in certain forms of Calvinism. Indeed, insofar as Calvinists maintain that all events, including all human decisions, are ultimately understandable only in the context of God's sovereignty they are theological determinists. In the end, they declare, our choices are not expressions of human freedom but of God's sovereign determination.

Determinism is not limited to theological circles. In the social sciences, *behaviorism* develops empirical theories to explain behavior patterns and to predict future behavior patterns. Behaviorists theorize that future behavior will be caused by factors already at work.

Behaviorism is deterministic, for it suggests that human behavior is the consequence of the sum total of the influencing factors which act on a human being. In this way behaviorists exclude the possibility that our actions result from a free decision based on a neutral, self-determining will.

One of the most well-known representatives of behaviorism is B. F. Skinner (1904-). Skinner is especially important for his emphasis on the role of the social environment in shaping the behavior of individuals. In his widely read work, *Beyond Freedom and Dignity* (1971), the theorist offers a vision of a new society.[2] In Skinner's utopia we would cast aside concepts such as "freedom," which presuppose the "fiction" of the "autonomous individual." The ideal social order would employ a technology of behavior that reinforces

---

2. B. F. Skinner, *Beyond Freedom and Dignity* (New York: Bantam/Vintage, 1972).

those persons who have been induced by their culture to work for its survival.

In the second half of the twentieth century, another type of behaviorism, *sociobiology*, gained wide hearing. The Harvard zoologist, Edward O. Wilson, describes sociobiology as "the systematic study of the biological basis of all forms of social behavior in all kinds of organisms, including man."[3] As an "explicitly hybrid discipline," he adds, it incorporates knowledge from ethology (the naturalistic study of whole patterns of behavior), ecology (the study of the relations of organisms and their environments), and genetics. Its goal is to derive general principles concerning the biological properties of entire societies.

The motivation for the development of sociobiology did not come from a vision of a better society, however. Rather, the early theorists were seeking to plug a gap in the reigning biological theory—evolution. Darwinian ideas, such as the survival of the fittest and natural selection, suggest that life is totally competitive. This theory, however, cannot account for the phenomenon of altruism, why certain organisms help other members of their species. Because altruistic behavior reduces a specific organism's chance of survival, natural selection should have weeded it out long ago.

Proponents of sociobiology resolve this dilemma by theorizing that altruism is "genetic selfishness." Altruistic conduct may reduce one's own chance of survival. But insofar as it is directed toward the protection of nearby relatives, it increases the chance that some of one's own genes will survive. In other words, natural selection produces individuals that exchange favors, as it were, for the sake of the common genetic pool.

Underlying sociobiology is what Robert Wallace calls the "reproductive imperative."[4] This axiom stipulates that the ultimate goal of any organism is to reproduce as many offspring as possible and that the attempt to fulfill this goal will influence behavior patterns. Con-

---

3. E. O. Wilson, *On Human Nature*, Bantam Books edition (New York: Bantam Books, 1979), 16-17.

4. See Robert Wallace, *The Genesis Factor* (New York: William Morrow and Co., 1979), 17. Wallace entitles this chapter, "The Reproductive Imperative - or Why You *Really* Love Your Children."

sequently, sociobiologists suggest that when viewed from the vantage point of evolution the individual is meaningless. What is important in the final analysis is the genetic code or DNA, which is the unknowing driving force of the reproductive imperative. As Edward O. Wilson quips, an organism is simply DNA's way of making more DNA. Sociobiologists, therefore, postulate that evolutionary processes acting on genes shape human social patterns. Hence, genetic makeup influences behavior, which is subject to natural selection just as physical characteristics are.

Proponents of sociobiology assert that the charitable acts of human beings—like all human conduct—are rooted in biology and in genetic selfishness. In so doing, they present a highly deterministic understanding of action. Sociobiology gives little place to free will or choice. Instead all actions, including what appear to be acts of altruism, are actually the result of biological forces, especially the drive to advance the genetic pool which the individual shares.

The Christian perspective. Our Christian theological world view requires that we take a position between the extremes of existentialism and determinism.

In contrast to determinism, Christian theology upholds the personhood of the individual human being. As we saw in our discussion of God as person in chapter 5, bound up with the idea of personhood is the experience of mysterious freedom. To be "person" means to be beyond the total control of another. Humans are persons because in the final analysis we remain autonomous or self-determining (even though this self-determination may ultimately be finite and bounded). For this reason, to the extent that they uphold the personhood of all humans, advocates of the existentialist answer to the question of autonomy and essence provide a proper counterbalance to determinists. In this matter, the existentialist position coheres with Christian theology.

At the same time, we cannot go all the way with radical existentialists in their struggle against their deterministic antagonists. Existentialists err when they suggest that the human individual possesses unbounded freedom. On the contrary, our autonomy is limited. We do indeed make choices. But as determinists rightly point out, our choices are always circumscribed by boundaries.

The boundedness that characterizes our human experience of being an acting agent returns us to the idea of essence. We conclude that there is indeed a specifically human nature which is connected to the boundedness of human existence. But what belongs to our essential nature? To this question we now must turn.

Human Substances

We resolved the debate between existentialism and determinism by affirming that humans are creatures of freedom, albeit a limited freedom. Our experience of autonomy is indeed valid. Nevertheless, beyond autonomy lies an essential nature in accordance with which we act and make choices. Our freedom is bounded, and one dimension of this boundedness is the human essence that we share. These conclusions raise the ensuing question: How ought we to describe this human essence? What is our ontological nature?

The idea of substantial entities. Because of its connection with the Greek philosophical tradition, it is not surprising that Christian theology has included an enduring interest in matters of ontology (the study of being) and our knowledge of being. Beginning with the revival of Aristotelian philosophy among the medieval scholastics, theologians—including Protestant thinkers—have explored the ontological nature of the human person. Classically the debate has focused on the concept of human "substances," "substantial entities," or "constituent elements."[5]

The English term "substance" gains its philosophical meaning from its Latin derivation, *substantia*. The term is compounded from *sub* ("under") and *stare* ("to stand"), and hence carries the idea of "standing under." A substantial entity, therefore, is an ontological element that "stands under" or goes into the making of the human person.

Scholastic thinkers believed that they could perceive the presence of differing substances in the human person. The great American

---

5. For this term, see Lewis Berkhof, *Systematic Theology*, revised edition (Grand Rapids: Eerdmans, 1953), 191-92.

Presbyterian thinker of the 1800s, Charles Hodge, offered a phenomenological method of perception: "As we can know nothing of substance but from its phenomena, and as we are forced by a law of our nature to believe in the existence of a substance of which the phenomena are the manifestation, so by an equally stringent necessity we are forced to believe that where the phenomena are not only different, but incompatible, there the substances are also different."[6]

The trichotomist and dichotomist viewpoints. Scholastic theologians were convinced that the human person is a composite being consisting of several substances, each of which can be conceived of as standing alone. Hodge, for example, found himself driven to this conclusion by his phenomological method: "As, therefore, the phenomena or properties of matter are essentially different from those of mind, we are forced to conclude that matter and mind are two distinct substances; that the soul is not material nor the body spiritual."[7]

How many substances comprise the human person? Protestant theologians who stand in the scholastic tradition have gravitated to two basic alternatives.

(1) Trichotomists postulate that the human person consists of three substantial entities, "spirit," "soul," and "body" (*tri* = three). The simplest of the three aspects to grasp is the "body," for this term simply refers to the physical part of the human person. More difficult is the differentiation between "soul" and "spirit." Trichotomists see the "spirit" as that part of a human being which is capable of knowing God. The "soul," in contrast, is the seat of the personality. Thus, it encompasses our intellect, emotions, and will.

Contemporary trichotomists stand within a long theological tradition. They can claim as illustrious a forebear as the church father Irenaeus.[8] The position gained the support of several nineteenth century Bible commentators, including Franz Delitzsch.[9] Important twenti-

---

6. Charles Hodge, *Systematic Theology*, three volumes (New York: Charles Scribner, 1871), 2:42.

7. Ibid., 2:42-43.

8. See, for example, Irenaeus, *Adversus Haereses*, 5.6.1 and 5.9.1, in *The Early Christian Fathers*, ed. Henry Bettenson (London: Oxford University Press, 1969), 70-71.

9. Franz Delitzsch, *System of Biblical Psychology*, 2nd ed., trans. Robert E. Wallis (Edinburgh: T. & T. Clark, 1867), vii, 247-66.

eth century popularizers include the Chinese Christian, Watchman Nee,[10] who languished in a Communist prison until just prior to his death in the 1970s. Nee is known for his helpful writings on the subject of sanctification, which he constructed upon a trichotomist anthropology.[11] The trichotomist position has also won advocates among dispensationalists. In fact, this interpretation found its way into both editions of the Scofield Reference Bible.[12]

Two New Testament texts supply the surest foundation for the trichotomist understanding. Advocates see a reference to the threefold partition of the human person in Paul's benediction, "May your whole spirit, soul and body be kept blameless at the coming of our Lord Jesus Christ" (1 Thess. 5:23). A second crucial text distinguishes between soul and spirit as two separate substantial entities:

> For the word of God is living and active. Sharper than any double edged sword, it penetrates even to dividing soul and spirit, joints and marrow; it judges the thoughts and attitudes of the heart. (Heb. 4:12)

(2) More prominent among classic theologians is the dichotomist position.[13] Dichotomists assert that the human person is the product of two substantial entities, the immaterial (or inner) self and the material (or outer) self.[14] The material self is the body, the vehicle through which the person relates to the physical world. The immaterial self functions in two directions. It acts both as "spirit"—the capacity of the self to relate to God—and as "soul"—the capacity to relate to self and other selves.

Dichotomists argue that theirs, and not the more complicated trichotomist view, reflects the biblical teaching.[15] They point to the

---

10. E.g., Watchman Nee, *The Release of the Spirit* (Indianapolis: Sure Foundation, 1956), 6.

11. For his most complete statement, see Watchman Nee, *The Spiritual Man*, three volumes (New York: Christian Fellowship Publishers, 1968).

12. *The Scofield Reference Bible* (New York: Oxford, 1909), note 1 on 1 Thess. 5:23; *The New Scofield Referennce Bible* (New York: Oxford, 1967), note 2 on 1 Thess. 5:23.

13. For a statement of the classical dichotomist position, see Berkhof, *Systematic Theology*, 192-95. Variations on this classic theme are found in Millard J. Erickson, *Christian Theology*, three volumes (Grand Rapids: Baker, 1984), 2:536-38; and in Gordon R. Lewis and Bruce A. Demarest, *Integrative Theology*, three volumes (Grand Rapids: Zondervan, 1990), 2:144.

14. Lewis and Demarest, for example, assert that although each human is metaphysically one, this oneness includes outer and inner aspects. *Integrative Theology*, 2:144.

15. See Berkhof, *Systematic Theology*, 192-93; Erickson, *Christian Theology*, 2:527-30; Lewis and Demarest, *Integrative Theology*, 2:145-46.

seemingly interchangeable usage of the terms "soul" and "spirit" in the Scriptures (compare Gen. 35:18 and Eccl. 12:7; Heb. 12:23 and Rev. 6:9; Gen. 41:8 and Ps. 42:6; John 12:27 and 13:21; Matt. 20:28 and 27:50). For explicit support of their alternative, dichotomists look to several Bible texts which either teach or at least assume their simpler anthropological view. Especially relevant are verses which contrast the body with the soul/spirit. For example, Jesus charges his disciples not to fear those who kill the body but cannot kill the soul, but to fear the one who can destroy both soul and body (Matt. 10:28). Similarly James compares the deadness of faith without works to the body without the spirit (James 2:26). And the Old Testament preacher seemingly offers insight into our ontological nature when he writes, "The dust returns to the ground it came from, and the spirit returns to God who gave it" (Eccl. 12:7).

(3) Seeing the strength of both traditional positions, the erudite Baptist theologian of the early twentieth century, Augustus Hopkins Strong, offered what became an influential compromise. According to Strong, the human person is a "substantial dichotomy" and a "functional trichotomy."[16] The dichotomists are correct concerning the human ontology. The human person consists of only two substantial entities. But the trichotomist understanding also reflects a truth about the human essence, namely, that we have the capacity to relate to God (spirit), others or ourselves (soul), and the physical world (body).

Substantial entities and modern theology. In contrast to the consensus in the scholastic era that the human person is a composite being, modern theologians tend to reject any concept of multiple substantial entities.[17] They generally cite three main reasons for this rejection.[18]

---

16. Augustus Hopkins Strong, *Systematic Theology*, three volumes (Philadelphia: Griffith and Rowland, 1907), 2:486.

17. The movement away from dualistic anthropologies includes conservatives, as well as progressives. See, for example, the position developed by Anthony A. Hoekema, *Created in God's Image* (Grand Rapids: Eerdmans, 1986), 203-26.

18. For a discussion and critique of the modern rejection of the soul, see C. Stephen Evans, "Healing Old Wounds and Recovering Old Insights: Toward a Christian View of the Person for Today" *Christian Faith and Practice in the Modern World*, ed. Mark A. Noll and David F. Wells (Grand Rapids: Eerdmans, 1988), 78-83.

(1) Modern thinkers repudiate the older view primarily because they conclude that it is non-scientific. Finding no empirical basis for the idea that the human person is anything but a unity, they view the belief in a soul that can exist separate from the body as metaphysical speculation.

(2) Modern theologians also claim that viewpoints which see the human person as a composite being are more philosophical than biblical. Both the dichotomist and trichotomist positions, they argue, are the product of Greek—more specifically Platonic—influences on the theological tradition of the church. Some of these theologians have set the Greek philosophical tradition against the ancient Hebrew mindset. They call for a return to the outlook of the Bible, which predates the intrusion of Hellenistic thinking into the theology of the church.

The major problem modern theologians find in Platonism is its inherent dualism. The dualistic Platonic anthropology, they assert, contradicts the understanding of the human person disclosed in the Scriptures. The Dutch theologian G. C. Berkouwer capsulized the modern findings:

> We can say that in our times, under the influence of Biblical research, a fairly general consensus of opinion has arisen among theologians. They are increasingly conscious of the fact that the Biblical view of man shows him to us in an impressive diversity, but that it never loses sight of the unity of the whole man, but rather brings it out and accentuates it.[19]

More specifically, Berkouwer concluded that the apostle's use of words "radically excludes any idea that an essential anthropological dualism, an a priori ontic structure of higher and lower, dominates Paul's presentation of the Gospel."[20]

Critics claim that the dualism of Platonic thinking is theologically disastrous. It leads to a host of anthropological errors.

One such error is the elevation of one substance over the other. Modern theologians note that the tendency in both the dichotomist and trichotomist positions is to equate the human person with the im-

---

19. G. C. Berkouwer, *Man—the Image of God*, trans. Dirk W. Jellema (Grand Rapids: Eerdmans, 1962), 200.
20. Ibid., 206.

material part. Ultimately, we are "soul" or "spirit" and not body. This emphasis on the immaterial soul readily leads to an unbiblical deprecation of the body, that is, the physical dimension of existence.

In addition, Platonic dualism leads to a mistaken belief in the intrinsic immortality of the soul. Critics charge that in the end both the trichotomist and dichotomist views render the human person essentially immortal. Hence, dualists often speak of each human as "having an immortal soul." In the biblical view, in contrast, immortality is not limited to the immaterial part of the human person, but extends beyond the soul to include the body. And this immortality is not the possession of the soul; it does not belong intrinsically to the immaterial part. On the contrary, immortality is the goal of the entire human person,[21] as is symbolized by the tree of life in the Genesis narrative of the fall.

(3) In addition, modern thinkers reject the concept of multiple substantial entities because it is highly problematic. Specifically, any anthropology that sets forth the human person as a composite being raises the question as to how the substantial entities are able to interact with one another. We may cite, for example, the difficult question of the connection between mind and body, which has plagued philosophers since Descartes: How is it possible for the immaterial soul (the mind) to interact with the material body (i.e., the brain)?

One solution to the mind-body problem held among evangelicals carries the designation "dualistic interactionism" or "dualistic realism." The evangelical theologian James Oliver Buswell, Jr. described this view in the following manner:

> There are mental events and there are material events: and it is a daily experience that purposes in the mind release energy in the body and produce effects in the material world, just as events in the material world, through the sensory organs, produce events in the mental world.[22]

As Buswell's description indicates, dualistic interactionism is not so much a solution as merely a statement of the problem. It affirms

---

21. For a discussion of this thesis, see Oscar Cullmann, *The Immortality of the Soul or the Resurrection of the Body?* (London: Epworth, 1958), 36-37.

22. James Oliver Buswell, Jr., *A Christian View of Being and Knowing* (Grand Rapids: Zondervan, 1960), 126-28.

that the material and immaterial substances do affect one another. But it does not clarify how this occurs.

The contemporary wholistic alternative. Given the difficulties of composite descriptions of the human person, is there an alternative? In the place of the ontological terminology indicative of both the dichotomist and trichotomist anthropologies, modern thinkers tend to conceive of the human person as an ontological unity with multiple functions. We are capable of relating to the physical world and also of transcending ourselves. Rather than demanding two or three substantial entities to accomplish these quite different functions, however, they view them as capabilities of the one human person. We are physical beings who live and act in the physical world. Yet our existence and actions have ramifications beyond the given physical realm of the here and now.

We ought not to confuse the contemporary emphasis on the multiple functional capabilities of the one human substance with pure materialism. Proponents are not advocating that we see ourselves as nothing but impersonal matter. Thinkers today find the materialistic alternative to dualism problematic, for it is both reductionistic and scientifically questionable. Instead, the newer anthropology posits what some proponents call "dual aspect monism," which views interaction on the planes of the material and the immaterial as two different modes of the one human reality.

The Christian philosopher of science John Polkinghorne calls for a unitary anthropology. He couches the newer understanding of the human person within a vision of the entire cosmos. The universe is "a complementary world of mind/matter in which these polar opposites cohere as contrasting aspects of world-stuff, encountered in greater or lesser states of organization."[23] The human person, in turn, is a psychosomatic unity, an animated body, who "is able to participate in a noetic world of idea and purposes, as well as being able to act within the physical world."[24]

The more wholistic modern anthropology is supported by scientific findings concerning the fundamental interconnectedness of hu-

---

23. John Polkinghorne, *Science and Creation* (London: SPCK, 1988), 71.
24. John Polkinghorne, *Science and Providence* (London: SPCK, 1989), 33.

man functions with the physical body. Especially significant is the reciprocal connection between mental activities and the brain. The mutual dependency is evident, for example, in the fact that certain types of brain damage impair such mental functions as memory and thinking.

Despite its recent rise to prominence, wholistic anthropology is not a modern invention. The Bible itself espouses a similar viewpoint concerning the human person. Recent exegesis yields the conclusion that in the Scriptures the terms "soul" and "spirit" are neither designations of two constituent elements nor synonyms for some immaterial substance that inheres the physical body. Rather, both words can stand for the human person as an undifferentiated whole.[25] And they are both connected to the life principle present in living creatures.

This connection to creaturely life is evident in the two Hebrew terms *ruach* ("spirit") and *nephesh* ("soul"). According to Genesis 2:7, God breathed into Adam's nostrils "the breath of life" (*neshamah*), so that he became "a living soul" (*nephesh*). The life-giving action of the Creator constituted the one physical reality—the first human creature—a living person.

The Old Testament, however, does not view the life principle as the exclusive property of humans. We are, of course, "living souls." But the animals are also (e.g., Gen. 1:30). In fact, on at least eleven occasions the Old Testament declares that animals are or possess "soul," a term which in several references is clearly equated with the concept of life (e.g., Lev. 24:17-18; 1 Kings 3:11). In the same manner, the Genesis narrator reports God as saying concerning the impending flood, "I am going to bring floodwaters on the earth to destroy all life under the heavens, every creature that has the breath (*ruach*) of life in it" (Gen. 6:17; cf. 7:15). Hence, not only *nephesh*, but also *ruach* is connected with animals as well as humankind.

Further, the Bible presents God as the giver of the life of each individual, so that each human must look to God for life itself. Hence, the book of Numbers refers to God as "the God of the spirits (*ruach*) of all mankind" (Num. 16:22; 27:16). The Scriptures, therefore,

---

25. Berkouwer, *Man—The Image of God*, 200-201.

know of no aspect of the human person—such as the Greek concep-tion of the soul—that is intrinsically immortal. In fact, the book of Numbers can even speak of a "dead soul" (Num. 5:2, 6:6; 9:6-7, 10; and 19:13).

Consequently, *ruach* and *nephesh*, while distinct, overlap in meaning. W. D. Stacey describes the differences in nuance between them:

> When reference is made to man in his relation to God *ruach* is the term most likely to be used. . . , but when reference is made to man in relation to other men, or man living the common life of men, then *nephesh* is most likely, if a psychical term is required. In both cases the whole man was involved.[26]

Despite the shades of meaning that differentiate them, the two words, and especially the more common term *nephesh*, refer to the one human person. As Edmond Jacob concludes, "Nephesh is the usual term for a man's total nature. . . . Hence, the best translation in many instances is 'person.'"[27]

What is true of the Hebrew words carries over into the New Tes-tament employment of the corresponding Greek terms *psuche* ("soul") and *pneuma* ("spirit") to speak of the human person. From his study, Anthony Hoekema offers this succinct conclusion: "Pneu-ma, it is clear, may often be used to designate the whole person; it, like *psyche*, describes an aspect of man in his totality."[28]

The biblical terms indicate the weakness of both the dichotomist and the trichotomist anthropologies. Both understand the "soul" or the immaterial part as an ontological substance which is intrinsically immortal. In the Old Testament, in contrast, *nephesh* and *ruach* refer to animated creatures—especially, but not exclusively human be-ings—who are dependent on God for life itself.

But what about the Preacher's declaration, "the dust returns to the ground it came from and the spirit returns to God who gave it" (Eccl. 12:7)? Does this verse not offer a biblical foundation for a composite

---

26. W. D. Stacey, *The Pauline View of Man* (London: Macmillan, 1956), 90.

27. Edmond Jacob, "psyche," in the *Theological Dictionary of the New Testament*, ed. Gerhar-hard Friedrich, trans. Geoffrey W. Bromiley (Grand Rapids: Eerdmans, 1974), 9:620.

28. Hoekema, *Created in God's Image*, 214.

human consisting of multiple substances? Although we could indeed see a dualistic anthropology in this text, it is actually better interpreted in accordance with the dominant Old Testament meaning of *ruach*, namely, as referring to the life principle. The author is not declaring that the spirit is a specific human substantial entity which is the "real" person and which at death goes to be with God. Rather, the statement means that at death God, who as Creator is the source of all life, reclaims the principle of life that he loaned to his creature. At death, the Creator withdraws the life principle from the creature.[29]

We must follow the lead of both the Bible and contemporary thought and adopt a wholistic view of the human person. Foundational for any statement we make concerning the ontological nature of humankind must be the acknowledgment that each human is the creature of God and as a creature is finite and dependent in one's entire being. This means that God bestows on us the life principle (thus Gen. 2:7), which God can reclaim (which is the point of Eccl. 12:7). Consequently, we cannot single out some supposedly immortal, immaterial substance. There is no part of the human person which is intrinsically immortal.

While acknowledging the mortality of the whole human being, we must add that God's design or destiny for humankind is eternal life. He desires that we enjoy life forever in his presence. This is the explicit teaching of the New Testament concerning the future that awaits the child of God.

In fact, the biblical hope of resurrection forms the final confirmation of the correctness of a wholistic anthropology. The New Testament writers anticipate that believers will undergo a physical resurrection. Our mortal bodies will be transformed; they will put on immortality. As a result of this event, the child of God will live forever in some physical form. God's gift of eternal life, therefore, will be ours in its fullness at the eschatological resurrection.

Because the resurrection of the body is the gateway to eternal fellowship in the presence of God, the eternal life that God desires to

---

29. Michael A. Eaton, *Ecclesiastes,* in the *Tyndale Old Testament Commentaries,* ed. D. J. Wiseman (Leicester, England: InterVarsity, 1983), 150-51.

give us is not limited to one dimension of the human person. Rather than being merely the transformation of some supposedly immaterial substance, whether it be termed "soul" or "spirit," the promised eternal life encompasses the whole individual, including the body.

The assertion that our final destiny as designed by God is the future, resurrected existence means as well that our essential human nature ultimately lies in the resurrected believer that we are enroute to becoming. The resurrected reality is not that of a disembodied immaterial substance, but an embodied psychosomatic human person. Consequently, our essential nature is wholistic. The human person is by divine design one indivisible reality.

Death and the whole person. The ontological indivisibility of the human person carries implications in many directions. Perhaps none, however, is more controversial than its outworking for our understanding of death. Because death is properly a topic in the eschatology section of our systematic theology, we can offer only a few preliminary remarks here.

We have concluded that the human person is an indivisible being, finite and dependent on God for every aspect of one's existence. Consequently, death marks the end of one's life, for with the cessation of vital functions essential human existence has ceased. For this reason, God warns Israel, "Do not put your trust in princes, in mortal men, who cannot save. When their spirit departs, they return to the ground; on that very day their plans come to nothing" (Ps. 146:3-4). When death comes, God reclaims the life principle, and the existence of all persons—from the most humble peasant to the greatest prince—ends.

Death marks the end of life. Death's connection with sin means that it also marks the *tragic* end to life. Indeed, the Scriptures characterize death as an enemy of humankind and a power that through sin carries a "sting." Not only does it usher in the end of functioning among the living, death also calls into question the meaning of a person's entire life. For this reason much "Christian" talk about death as merely the door to a higher existence is unfortunate, if not detrimental.

The good news of the Bible, however, is that death is not the last word. God's destiny for us lies beyond death in the new creation. We will receive eternal life in its fullness—which is our destiny—at the resurrection, when the mortal puts on immortality (1 Cor. 15:50-54). Because our human destiny is eternal life, this destiny transcends death. Consequently, although it remains the last enemy, in Christ death is defeated. And one day it will be eternally destroyed (1 Cor. 15:25-26). Knowing this, even now we are confident that death cannot separate us from God's love (Rom. 8:35-39). Even in death the one who has been united to Christ is held by God's love awaiting the new creation in the resurrection.

The Origin of the Soul

According to the traditional anthropology the human person is a composite being, whether consisting of two or three substantial entities. The classical distinction between body and soul (and perhaps spirit) naturally leads to questions concerning the temporal relationship between these two dimensions. If the human person consists of a material substance joined with a immaterial substance, then how does this immaterial entity arise, and when does it become joined with the material substance? Is the soul created by a special act of God, or is it created together with the body through natural means at conception? In short, what is the origin of the soul?

Traditional alternatives. Thinkers who phrase the question of the origin of the soul in the classical manner generally adhere to one of three descriptions.

(1) The least widely-held alternative among orthodox Christian thinkers carries the designation *preexistence of the soul.* This view arose as an application of the Platonic supposition of immortality to the question of the origin of the soul. Simply stated, preexistence asserts that all human souls are already in existence before the creation of the bodies which eventually house them. Hence, a person's soul exists prior to the conception of the body, and this soul joins the body sometime in the womb or possibly at birth.

Some proponents of preexistence assert that the incarnation of a specific soul occurs only once. This has become the official teaching of the Church of Jesus Christ of Latter Day Saints (Mormons).[30] According to Mormon theology, before the creation of the world God begat a host of spiritual children. Through sexual intercourse, human parents procreate the body into which a spirit-child enters. For this reason, the Mormon Church emphasizes parenthood and family values. Faithful church members ought to have large families, in order to provide bodies for the many spirit-children waiting to be born.

Other adherents of preexistence believe that a soul can be incarnated into more than one body. Although each soul is an individual, each physical human may not be. This view was held by certain ancient Christian Platonists, such as Origen.[31] It reappears today in the idea of reincarnation prevalent among certain participants in the New Age movement.[32]

(2) More prominent among classical Christian theologians is a second position, anthropological *creationism*. This view boasts a long tradition within the Christian church, and it has been the major viewpoint within both the Roman Catholic and the Reformed traditions.

Proponents of creationism postulate that each human soul comes into existence by means of a direct creative act of God. Moreover, God creates a soul in close connection with the conception of the body, although the exact time may be uncertain.[33] Advocates appeal to several biblical texts which either teach or confirm this position (Isa. 42:5; Zech. 12:1; Num. 16:42; Heb. 12:9).

Early in the twentieth century Augustus Hopkins Strong articulated the major objection to creationism.[34] If the human person is taint-

---

30. This standard Mormon teaching generally draws from *The Pearl of Great Price*, Moses 3:5, and Joseph Smith, *History of the Church of Jesus Christ of Latter-day Saints, Period I*, ed. B.H. Roberts, second edition (Salt Lake City: Desert News Press, 1950), 6:308-312. For an example of the development of this doctrine, see Sterling M. McMurrin, *The Theological Foundations of the Mormon Religion* (Salt Lake City: University of Utah Press, 1965), 25-26,50.

31. Origen, *De Principiis* 2.9.2, trans. Federick Crombie, in *Tertullian; Minucius Felix; Commodian; Origen*, volume 4 of *The Ante-Nicene Fathers*, ed. Alexander Roberts and James Donaldson (Grand Rapids: Eerdmans, 1976), 4:290.

32. For references to the presence of this doctrine in the New Age movement, see Ruth A. Tucker, *Another Gospel: Alternate Religions and the New Age Movement* ((Grand Rapids: Zondervan, 1989), 331-32. For a critique of the New Age reincarnation teaching, see Douglas R. Groothuis, *Unmasking the New Age* (Downers Grove, Ill.: InterVarsity, 1986), 131, 150-52.

33. Berkhof, *Systematic Theology*, 201.

34. Strong, *Systematic Theology*, 2:493.

ed with original sin from birth and if God creates the soul directly, then God creates a tainted, sinful soul. In this manner, creationism makes God the direct author of evil.

(3) Perhaps the most widely held position among evangelicals is *traducianism*. Proponents assert that the unit human person produces after its kind, bodies generating bodies and souls generating souls. The union of husband and wife produces a unit human being consisting of body and soul. Consequently, the soul of the infant originates simultaneously with the conception of the body.

Like creationism, traducianism sports a long pedigree. Its presence in the church dates at least to the time of Tertullian, and Augustine ranks among its advocates. Traducianism has been the dominant position among traditional Lutheran theologians.[35] Although a Calvinist, the Baptist A. H. Strong also held to this alternative.[36]

Traducianists claim that their position best fits with certain biblical themes concerning humankind and human sin. Foundational to the traducian position are the otherwise difficult statements that speak of persons having been "in the loins" of their fathers. For example, the author of the book of Hebrews argues, "When Melchizedek met Abraham, Levi was still in the body of his ancestor" (Heb. 7:10). Because parents produce the unit human being, we can say that in a sense children are indeed present in the body of their father prior to birth.

Traducians appeal to this idea to account for the unity of humankind, especially our unity in sin. A vexing problem in the classical Christian teaching concerns how all humans justly participate in the effects of Adam's sin (1 Cor. 15:22; Rom. 5:12). Traducianists theorize that we were all present in the Garden of Eden when Adam sinned, for we were "in his loins." Because we were present in Adam, we actually sinned in Adam, even though we were not yet born. Consequently, God is just in condemning us, for we are guilty of a trespass in which we participated.

Finally, proponents declare that more readily than any alternative this teaching accounts for the declarations of Scripture concerning

---

35. Berkhof, *Systematic Theology*, 197.
36. Strong, *Systematic Theology*, 2:493-97.

the passing of the sinful nature or "the flesh" from one generation to the next. For example, Jesus declared to Nicodemus, "Flesh gives birth to flesh, but spirit gives birth to spirit" (John 3:6). According to traducianists, "flesh" here refers to the entire human person, body and soul, as generated in the corrupt state by the coming together of husband and wife.

Despite its popularity ,traducianism is not without its detractors. Critics argue that this view contradicts the concept of the "simplicity" or indivisible unity of the soul.[37] Because the soul is incapable of division, it is impossible that the soul of the child is derived from the souls of the parents. Equally problematic is the use of traducianism to explain the original unity of all human souls and the participation of Adam's offspring in the effects of his sin. If we were in the loins of Adam and consequently are culpable for his sin, then why are we guilty of only Adam's first sin, rather than of all the sins he committed prior to the birth of those of his children who became our ancestors? In fact, would not the traducianist explanation mean that by extension we ought to be held responsible for all the sins our parents committed prior to our birth?

The classical debate and the contemporary context. The older debate concerning the origin of the soul loses much of its urgency once we move beyond the classical understanding of the human person as a composite being. As we have seen, modern anthropology emphasizes human wholeness, rather than the distinction between substantial entities such as "body" and "soul." As a consequence of this shift in understanding, contemporary thinkers tend no longer to frame the question of the origin of the soul in the classical terms of the point at which an immaterial substance joins with the material substance.

Despite its apparent theological irrelevance, viewed in another sense the question of the origin of the soul has not vanished. For example, in the discussion as to when a fetus is a person the traditional categories, traducianism and creationism, still apply, albeit with significantly altered meanings.[38] Some assert that God determines direct-

---

37. Berkhof, *Systematic Theology*, 198.
38. See Stanley J. Grenz, "Abortion: A Christian Response," *Conrad Grebel Review* 2/1 (1984): 23-27.

ly the point at which a fetus becomes a person, and that this occurs sometime subsequent to conception. Such a position continues the basic idea of the older creationism. Their opponents, those who claim that a fetus is a person from conception, reflect the older traducian understanding.

Understood as referring to the personhood of a fetus, this reinterpreted question of the "origin of the soul" has important implications for ethical issues such as abortion and birth control.[39] For "traducianists" life begins at conception, making both abortion and any post-conceptive method of birth control immoral. "Creationists," in contrast, hold out the possibility that actual life begins at some later point and consequently that certain post-conceptive practices could be ethically permissible, so long as they are not questionable on other grounds.

The Soul and Our Ontological Nature

The biblical-theological term "soul" carries several meanings. It refers to the life principle and God's gift of life present in all his creatures, but especially in humans. The "soul" likewise constitutes the basis of the individuality of each human person, in that God bestows the gift of life on us individually. These meanings lead naturally to another: Above all, the "soul" refers to the human person as the recipient of a special destiny or design in God's program. That it points to this assertion is the abiding truth of the typical evangelical declaration, "Each person possesses an eternal soul." We each do indeed "have" an "eternal" soul, in that God desires that each human participate in a destiny which transcends the temporal world for it encompasses all eternity. God has placed within us an "openness to the world," an eternal longing that he desires to fulfill beyond any temporal experience.

With this in view, we return to the classical question of the temporal origin of the soul. The point couched in the query concerning exactly when God bestows the "soul" is the question, When does God bestow on us the potential for participation in the special human

---

39. See Stanley J. Grenz, *Sexual Ethics* (Dallas: Word, 1990), 126-41.

destiny? Christians assert categorically that this occurs in the womb. But can we enquire further?

Our consideration of the significance of the soul links "soul" with individuality. "Soul" means that God addresses a claim on us as individuals. The term means likewise that God directs his special love toward each of us as individuals. And "soul" suggests God invites us as individuals to participate in the potential human destiny. The term indicates that God calls us to actualize the one human destiny as individual persons. Hence, the concept of "soul" leads us to ask, When does God embrace what is developing in the womb as an individual?

In our search of an answer theology may be supplemented by the findings of biology. Although our personal genetic makeup is set at conception, first at implantation (when the growing zygote implants itself in the walls of the uterus) does the developing life reach the point of irreversible individuality. For this reason, implantation may well mark the point when God looks upon what is growing in the womb, acknowledges him or her as an individual human person, and enters into covenant with this new life. In any case, however, God embraces us even before we take on physical shape, indeed even before our parents know that we are in the womb. In the context of this conclusion the word of the Lord to Jeremiah takes on added significance: "Before I formed you in the womb I knew you" (Jer. 1:5).

Humans as the Image of God

With the possible exception of human sin, perhaps the single most debated topic of Christian anthropology is the meaning of the designation "image of God." Indeed no assertion moves us closer to the heart of our human identity and our essential nature than does the declaration, "We are created in the divine image." But how are we to understand this crucial Christian affirmation? And to what does "the image of God" refer?

The trail we must traverse in seeking an answer begins with an overview of the uses to which theologians have put this concept. From that vantage point we then return to the biblical texts that employ the phrase. These studies, in turn, provide the foundation for an attempt to delineate our human identity in terms of our creation in the divine image.

The Image of God in Theological History

Theologians throughout Christian history have wrestled with the question, What does it mean to say that we are created in the image of God? In what sense and in what ways are we like God? And as a consequence of these considerations, how did our fall into sin affect the divine image in us? Concerning this matter, three basic positions have emerged in theological history.[40]

The structural view. Perhaps the most long-standing interpretation of the image of God in the history of the church is the structural view. The church fathers provided the foundation for this position, but it received its classic expression in the writings of the medieval scholastics. Later it was challenged by the Reformers only to gain ascendancy again in the theologies of Protestant orthodoxy. And it continues to find adherents today, including among evangelicals.

The classic view understands the image of God primarily as an anthropological concept. Being a formal structure of the human person, the divine image is something we "possess," and it includes the properties which constitute us as human beings. Because the divine image constitutes us as human, we retain it even in our sinful, fallen state. Hence, it is a present reality, a resemblance to God that characterizes all humans at all times.

The precise characteristics—the human capabilities—bound up with our possession of the image of God include above all our rationality and moral nature, to which some proponents add our capacity for holiness.[41] The emphasis on rationality is a natural outgrowth of the persistent influence of Greek philosophy on Christian thought. Beginning with Plato the Greek thinkers were nearly all in agreement that reason was the highest and most distinctive human characteristic. No wonder, therefore, the early Christian theologians linked

---

40. For a somewhat similar delineation to what follows, see Erickson, *Christian Theology*, 2:498-510.

41. Berkhof, *Systematic Theology*, 203, 204.

our resemblance to God to our rationality and viewed the divine image in terms of our possession of the rational capability.

The focusing of the image of God on our rational nature landed theologians in a difficulty when they considered the biblical narrative of the fall. If our resemblance to God consists in our possession of rationality, how does the fall affect our status as the divine image-bearers? How can we be both fallen and yet in possession of this hallmark of our essential humanness?

Early proponents of the structural view solved this dilemma by appeal to what they considered to be a biblical distinction between the "image of God" and the "likeness of God" (Gen. 1:26). Typical of thinkers in the second century, Irenaeus (c. 130-c. 200) described the divine image as our rationality, moral freedom, and responsibility, which we retain despite human sinfulness.[42] The divine likeness, in contrast, is the "robe of sanctity" which the Holy Spirit had bestowed on Adam.[43] The first human lost the divine likeness in the fall, but in redemption God restored this "likeness-bearing spirit" to us.

The patristic distinction between the image and likeness of God formed a basis for the anthropology of the Middle Ages. According to the scholastics the image of God is a natural gift, which is ours by virtue of creation and belongs to our essential nature. The divine image is linked to our natural human powers, especially reason.[44] Because we cannot lose such powers without ceasing to be human, the scholastics argued that the image of God remains intact even after the fall. The likeness of God, in contrast, is a supernatural gift. It is the original righteousness God bestowed on Adam in the Garden, which enabled the first human to use his reason to control his "lower

---

42. For a discussion of Irenaeus's differentiation between the image and likeness of God, see J.N.D. Kelley, *Early Christian Doctrines*, revised edition (San Francisco: Harper and Row, 1978), 171.

43. Irenaeus, *Adversus Haereses* 3.23.5, in *The Apostolic Fathers with Justin Martyr and Irenaeus*, volume 1 of *The Ante-Nicene Fathers*, ed. Alexander Roberts and James Donaldson, American reprint of the Edinburgh edition (Grand Rapids: Eerdmans, 1975), 1:457.

44. This characterization of medieval theology is widely-held. See, for example, A. H. Cremer, "Image of God," in *The New Schaff-Herzog Encyclopedia of Religious Knowledge*, ed. Samuel Macauley Jackson, 15 volumes (Grand Rapids: Baker, 1977), 5:451.

powers"—the emotions and the appetites.[45] In the fall, Adam lost this likeness to God, this supernatural gift.

The relational view. The Protestant Reformers rejected as exegetically unwarranted and theologically injurious the distinction between the image and likeness of God, which lay at the foundation of the medieval view.[46] In its place Martin Luther offered a unitary view of the divine image. He argued that the image of God includes the idea of original righteousness that the scholastics relegated to the divine likeness. In fact, Luther even suggested that the image of God consists primarily, if not exclusively in that original righteousness. Consequently, Luther concluded that the fall marred the image extensively.[47] On this point, the other great Reformer, John Calvin, stood in fundamental agreement with Luther.[48]

While arguing that the fall has effaced the image of God, neither Luther nor Calvin seemed willing to deny completely the presence of the divine image in sinful humankind. Especially Calvin held out the possibility that there may yet remain traces, a relic, or a remnant of the destroyed image in sinful humans.[49] Yet both thinkers clearly emphasized that the image is now "frightfully deformed."[50] The fall perverted and distorted whatever capabilities of reason or volition we may have retained.[51] In rejecting the anthropology of Thomas Aquinas, they asserted that fallen humankind is not just *deprived*, but *depraved*.[52]

---

45. Thomas Aquinas, *Summa Theologica* 1.95.1, trans. Fathers of the English Dominican Province, revised Daniel J. Sullivan, volume 19 of the *Great Books of the Western World*, ed. Robert Maynard Hutchins (Chicago: Encyclopedia Britannica, 1952), 19:506-507.

46. In commenting on Genesis 1:26, Luther, for example, ignores the coupling of image and likeness and then marks its absence in v. 27. Martin Luther, *Lectures on Genesis*, in *Luther's Works*, ed. Jeroslav Pelikan, trans. George V. Schick, American Edition (St. Louis: Concordia, 1958), 1:55-68.

47. Ibid., 1:62-65.

48. E.g., John Calvin, *A Commentary on Genesis* 1:26, trans. John King, two volumes in one (London: Banner of Truth Trust, 1965), 93-95.

49. Hence Calvin concludes, "Still, we see in this diversity some remaining traces of the image of God, which distinguish the entire human race from the other creatures." John Calvin, *Institutes of the Christian Religion* 2.2.17, in *Library of Christian Classics* volumes 20-21, trans Ford Lewis Battles, ed. John T. McNeill (Philadelphia: Westminster, 1960), 20:277.

50. For Calvin's view, see ibid., I.15.4 [189].

51. Ibid., 3.3.12 [604-605].

52. Hoekema, *Created in God's Image*, 46.

Because they rejected the medieval anthropology, the Reformers were compelled to replace the structural understanding of the image of God that had grown to dominance over the first fifteen centuries of Christian theology. In its stead, they offered a relational understanding.

The anthropology of the Reformation does not perceive the image of God primarily as a formal structure of the human essential nature, but as a standing before God. The divine image is essentially a special relation with the Creator which Adam lost, but Christ restores.

In this sense, the relational understanding shifts our focus away from the present to the past. Instead of seeing the divine image as a possession shared by all human beings, its proponents look to the idyllic innocence of the Garden of Eden as the point when humans existed in the image of God. At the same time, the Reformers shifted the focus from anthropology to Christology. Christ is the bearer and restorer of the divine image. Therefore, he is the ultimate paradigm of the image of God. We participate in the divine image only insofar as the Spirit works christlikeness in us.

The relational understanding has found powerful echo in the twentieth century in the writings of the neo-orthodox theologians. Emil Brunner, for example, rejects the medieval focus on reason. Instead, he understands the image of God primarily as our being in "relation" with God. As free, self-determining selves, we are to respond freely to God and hence we are responsible before God.[53] On this basis, he differentiates between the formal and the material aspects of the divine image.[54] The formal dimension refers to the fact that we stand responsible to respond both to God and to others. This aspect, of course, is not lost through sin,[55] for we remain accountable even when we do not love God. The material aspect of the divine image, in contrast, consists of the proper response to God, which we have lost completely.[56] For Brunner, Christ is the true image of God in the

---

53. Emil Brunner, *The Christian Doctrine of Creation and Redemption*, trans. Olive Wyon (Philadelphia: Westminster, 1953), 55-56.
54. Ibid., 57-61.
55. Ibid., 57.
56. Ibid., 58.

material sense, and consequently through existence in him the image is restored to us.[57]

While important to neo-orthodox thinking, the relational view of the divine image has influenced other theologians as well. The traditional Calvinist theologian Louis Berkhof, for example, articulates a relational understanding, insofar as he defines the image as the original righteousness—the true knowledge, righteousness, and holiness—which Adam lost, but which Christ restores to the individual believer. Berkhof then slips into the structural view, however, for he adds that the image also refers to the natural constitution of the human person, especially our intellect and moral freedom.[58]

The dynamic view. The roots of the third viewpoint, which we may call the dynamic view, also lie in the thinking of the Reformers. To many thinkers Genesis 9:6 contradicts the Reformation emphasis on the destruction of the image of God through the fall. In his discussion of this text, Luther offered what would prove to be a far-reaching suggestion: Even though we have lost the image of God through sin, "it can be restored through the Word and the Holy Spirit."[59] But this restoration, which begins now and reaches completion only on the Last Day, is even higher than what was lost. The perfection of the divine image is the eternal life for which Adam was "fitted";[60] hence, it is God's intention and goal for humankind.

Calvin went even further than Luther in introducing a dynamic aspect into at least the restorative dimension of the concept. By emphasizing sanctification as the growth of the believer into advancing conformity to Christ, the Geneva reformer elaborated further Luther's thesis that the divine image is restored in us progressively.[61] The Reformers agreed that the renewal of the image will not be completed until the life to come.

---

57. Ibid.
58. Berkhof, *Systematic Theology*, 204.
59. Martin Luther, *Lectures on Genesis*, in *Luther's Works*, 2:141.
60. Ibid., 1:64-65.
61. John Calvin, *Commentary on II Corinthians 3:18*, in *Calvin's Commentaries: The Second Epistle of Paul the Apostle to the Corinthians and the Epistles to Timothy, Titus and Philemon*, trans T. A. Smail, ed. David W. Torrance and Thomas F. Torrance (London: Oliver and Boyd, 1964), 49-50.

Although ideas such as these form the genesis for the dynamic understanding of the image of God, proponents claim as their patron saint the early church father Irenaeus. Especially important is his idea of recapitulation: Jesus Christ has "recapitulated" our own history, and thereby he brought us to our intended goal.[62] Yet the actual impetus for the development of the dynamic understanding came in German romanticism, especially in the work of Johann Gottfried von Herder (1744-1803). Working from the idea of "openness to the world," his followers have posited a link between the biblical concept of the image of God and the future human destiny. This link introduces a dynamic dimension into the concept of the divine image. The image of God is a reality toward which we are moving. It is what we are enroute to becoming.

According to proponents of the dynamic view, the image of God is neither the present structures of the human person nor the idyllic past relation to God lost by Adam but restored in Christ. Instead, the concept directs us to the future. The divine image is the goal or destiny that God intends for his creatures. Hence, it is a future reality that is present now only as a foretaste, or only in the form of our human potential. Consequently, the focus of the idea is neither anthropology nor Christology, but eschatology. The image of God will one day be borne by resurrected humans in the new creation. As Daniel Migliore states, "Being created in the image of God is not a state or condition but a movement with a goal: human beings are restless for a fulfillment of life not yet realized."[63]

The Image of God in the Bible

For the foundation of their understanding of the divine image Christian theologians turn to the uses to which the biblical authors put the phrase. The number of explicit scriptural references to the concept, however, is admittedly small. The Old Testament occurrences of the term are limited to three passages in the Book of Gen-

---

62. See, for example, Irenaeus, *Adversus Haereses* 2.22.4, 3.16.6, in *The Early Christian Fathers*, ed. Henry Bettenson (London: Oxford University Press, 1969), 80-81.
63. Daniel L. Migliore, *Faith Seeking Understanding: An Introduction to Christian Theology* (Grand Rapids: Eerdmans, 1991), 128.

esis. And the New Testament contains only a smattering of references—one in James and several in the Pauline corpus. Despite the meager use of the phrase itself by the biblical writers, the image of God remains an important biblical concept.

The divine image in the Genesis creation narratives. The beginning point for the biblical understanding of the divine image is the Book of Genesis. Foundational to all theological treatments of the idea is the reference contained in the creation narrative of the first chapter:

> Then God said, "Let us make man in our image, in our likeness, and let them rule over the fish of the sea and the birds of the air, over the livestock, over all the earth, and over all the creatures that move along the ground." So God created man in his own image. In the image of God he created him, male and female he created them. God blessed them and said to them, "Be fruitful and increase in number; fill the earth and subdue it. Rule over the fish of the sea and the birds of the air and over every living creature that moves on the ground." (Gen. 1:26–28)

The Genesis narrative has formed the fountainhead of several theological ideas. It suggests that the presence of the image of God separates humans from other creatures, for only we are created in the divine image. Further, the narrator links the image of God to the special role that humans are to exercise within creation: "Rule over the fish of the sea and the birds of the air and over every living creature that moves on the ground." When read in the context of the prohibition God gave to Adam found in the second creation narrative (Gen. 2:16-17), the text also yields the conclusion that the divine image entails a special accountability humans have before God.

These ideas are interconnected. Humans are created with a special status, namely, with the task of being the divine image bearers. The special human calling includes the prerogative to choose to honor God's intention for us or to disobey God, and thus it entails a special accountability before God. The second creation narrative, however, takes the idea a step farther. It suggests that our special calling lies in our role in creation: "The Lord God took the man and put him in the Garden of Eden to work it and take care of it" (Gen. 2:15).

Contemporary biblical scholars generally look to the royal ideology of the nations surrounding Israel for the clue concerning the source of the idea of the divine image.[64] They note that the kings of the ancient Near East often left images of themselves in those cities or territories where they could not be present in person. Such images served to represent their majesty and power.[65] Gerhard von Rad draws the parallel to humankind as the image of God:

> Just as powerful earthly kings, to indicate their claim to dominion erect an image of themselves in the provinces of their empire where they do not personally appear, so man is placed upon earth in God's image as God's sovereign emblem. He is really only God's representative, summoned to maintain and enforce God's claim to dominion over the earth. The decisive thing about man's similarity to God, therefore, is his function in the non-human world.[66]

The parallelism to the ancient Near Eastern nations has led scholars to conclude that the terms "image" and "likeness" carry the sense of "representation." This conclusion undercuts the classical structuralist interpretation of the image of God. The terms "image" and "likeness" do not connote a mere aspect of the human person. It is rather in the whole of our being that we are somehow like God. Further, the royal background suggests that the image of God points more to our purpose than to the nature of our being, more to teleology than ontology.

There remains, however, one additional theme concerning the divine image in the first creation narrative. As many thinkers since Karl Barth have noted, this is a community-text.[67] The image of God is a social rather than an individual concept.

---

64. See, for example, Phyllis A. Bird, "'Male and Female He Created Them': Gen. 1:27b in the Context of the Priestly Account of Creation," *Harvard Theological Review* 74 (April 1981): 137-44.

65. Gerhard von Rad, "eikon," in the *Theological Dictionary of the New Testament,* ed. Gerhard Kittel, trans. Goeffrey W. Bromiley (Grand Rapids: Eerdmans, 1964), 2:392. See also Henri Blocher, *In the Beginning: The Opening Chapters of Genesis,* trans. David G. Preston (Leicester, England: InterVarsity, 1984), 81.

66. Gerhard von Rad, *Genesis,* trans. John H. Marks, in the *Old Testament Library,* ed. G. Ernest Wright (Philadelphia: Westminster, 1972), 58.

67. H. Paul Santmire, "The Genesis Creation Narratives Revisited: Themes for a Global Age," *Interpretation* 45/4 (October 1991):374.

The clue to the social dimension of the divine image is present in the Genesis text itself. The narrator explicitly links the plurality of humankind, which includes a plurality of sexes,[68] to a plurality found in the divine self-reference. God expresses his intent with the declaration, "Let us make man in our image." Of course, we ought not to read into the text a proto-trinitarian declaration (as many exegetes since Tertullian have erroneously argued). Yet, at the very least the plural pronouns do suggest something about the intent of the narrator. In the words of Derrick Bailey, these pronouns indicate

> that he envisaged God as associating others with himself in some mysterious way as partners in the act of creation, and that he regarded Man as constituted in some sense after the pattern of a plurality of supernatural beings.[69]

The fuller divine self-disclosure of the New Testament allows us to see in these words in Genesis an even more profound meaning. "They express," to follow through with the conclusion of Bailey, "the Creator's resolve to crown his works by making a creature in whom, subject to the limitations of finitude, his own nature should be mirrored." The plural self-reference, therefore, finds its outworking in the creation of humankind as a plural reality.

As a plural creation, however, humans are embodied, sexually differentiated creatures. This dimension of the creation narrative has led certain scholars to conclude that corporality is included in the concept of the image of God.[70] In a sense, the idea is not new. Even John Calvin sought to include the body in the divine image, albeit through its connection with the soul.[71] What is new, however, is the implication that procreation may possibly be a functional dimension of the image and consequently in some sense serve as an analogy to God's creative action.[72]

---

68. On this, see Grenz, *Sexual Ethics*, 34.

69. Derrick Sherwin Bailey, *Sexual Relations in Christian Thought* (New York: Harper and Brothers, 1959), 267.

70. Gerhard von Rad, *Old Testament Theology*, trans. D.M.G. Stalker, two volumes (New York: Harper and Row, 1962), 1:144-48; Walther Eichrodt, *Theology of the Old Testament*, trans. J. A. Baker, two volumes (Philadelphia: Westminster, 1967), 2:122-31.

71. Calvin, *Institutes*, 1.15.3, in *Library of Christian Classics* 20:186-88.

72. Blocher, *In the Beginning*, 93; Meredith Kline, *Kingdom Prologue* (1989), 30.

The divine image elsewhere in Genesis. In addition to this foundational passage, the Genesis narrator employs the concept of the image of God in two other contexts.

The first comes as a preface to the genealogy of Adam: "When God created man, he made him in the likeness of God. He made them male and female; at the time they were created, he blessed them and called them 'man.' When Adam had lived 130 years, he had a son in his own likeness, in his own image; and he named him Seth" (Gen. 5:1-3). This reference suggests that the image of God is a special resemblance humans—or at least Adam—exhibit to God.

Later, in outlining his covenant with Noah, God appeals to the divine image as the basis for the strict penalty he demands in cases of murder: "Whoever sheds the blood of man, by man shall his blood be shed; for in the image of God has God made man" (Gen. 9:6). Here the narrator suggests that the image of God endows human life with special dignity and worth.

The image of God in the New Testament. The New Testament Epistle of James follows this final Genesis text in drawing ethical implications from the idea that all humans share a special status: "With the tongue we praise our Lord and Father, and with it we curse men, who have been made in God's likeness" (James 3:9).

In contrast to these more universally human applications of the concept of the divine image, Paul places the idea in an explicitly christological context. To the Corinthians he writes, "The god of this age has blinded the minds of unbelievers, so that they cannot see the light of the gospel of the glory of Christ, who is the image of God" (2 Cor. 4:4. See also Col. 1:15). According to Paul, therefore, Christ is the image of God in the ultimate sense. For the apostle, our Lord is the divine image in that he is the one who reveals to us the glory of God (2 Cor. 4:6).

The christological reference point Paul finds for the image of God allows him to broaden the concept to include believers. We are already being transformed into the image of Christ so that our lives may reflect Christ's glory (2 Cor. 3:18). In fact, it is to conformity to Christ (who is the likeness of God) that God has destined us (Rom. 8:29). To this end, we must "put on the new self, created to be like

God in true righteousness and holiness" (Eph. 4:24). Even now we are experiencing the renewal of the image of our Creator, a reality which for Paul carries ethical implications: "Do not lie to each other, since you have taken off your old self with its practices and have put on the new self, which is being renewed in knowledge in the image of its Creator" (Col. 3:9-10).

Although we enjoy a foretaste in the present, our renewal is ultimately eschatological. It will be fulfilled only when God fully transforms us at the return of Christ (1 John 3:2). For this reason, Paul proclaims the hope that "just as we have borne the likeness of the earthly man, so shall we bear the likeness of the man from heaven" (1 Cor. 15:49). To this end, the apostle declares, we will be transformed through the resurrection (1 Cor. 15:50-53).

This biblical panorama leaves us with the impression that Paul, who draws out most completely the implications of the Genesis narrative, understands the whole purpose of God in terms of bringing into being a people who reflect the divine image. When the grand eschatological event draws history to a close, God will bring to completion what was his intention from the beginning.

The Theological Significance of the Image of God

The development of the concept from Genesis to Paul provides a foundation on which to construct a theological understanding of humans as the bearers of the image of God. Although it may be multifaceted in its connotations, at the heart of the divine image (or the synonymous term, "the divine likeness"[73]) is a reference to our human destiny as designed by God. We are the image of God insofar as we have received, are now fulfilling, and one day will fully actualize a divine design. And this design—God's intent for us—is that we mirror for the sake of creation the nature of the Creator.

Let us now expand our summary statement.

---

73. We agree with the consensus of modern scholarship that the Bible warrants no distinction between these two phrases, and hence the Reformers were correct in rejecting the scholastic dualism. For a summary of the arguments supporting the synonymous nature of the image and the likeness of God, written by a classical Calvinist, see Berkhof, *Systematic Theology*, 203.

The divine image as a special standing. Our divinely-given destiny begins with a special standing before God. As humans created in the divine image, we are the recipients of God's love. This means that each of us has special worth in God's sight (hence, Matt. 6:26). We are also the recipients of God's commands, which entails a special responsibility. Our responsibility is connected to the biblical concept of "dominion." Rather than reading this term against the background of the ideology of modern industrial society, however, we must place the concept within the context of the royal theology of the Old Testament.[74] God has entrusted to us a special task with reference to creation, namely, that we serve as his representatives. We are to reflect to creation the nature of God.

The concept of dominion suggests as well that we are living in a "secular" world, that is, a universe divested of lesser deities. There is but one God, and the entire world is the creation of that God. The Creator has given this creation to humankind to manage. But our management has as its goal that we show to creation what God is like. Consequently, we do not "manage" creation for our own purposes, but for the sake of that higher goal, namely, in order that we might serve as the mirror of the divine character.

The divine image as a special fellowship. Our divinely given destiny begins with a special standing before God, but it focuses on fellowship with God. God's intent is that we respond to his love by reciprocating love and to his commands with the obedience born from love. Only in this manner can we experience the true life for which God has called us into existence. This conclusion is present in embryonic form in the concept of "openness to the world," with its assertion that humans can find no permanent home in the world but are dependent on God for ultimate fulfillment. Consequently, "openness to the world" points to that enjoyment of fellowship with God which is the potential and the destiny our Creator has given us.

The divine image as an eschatological reality. In what sense is the image of God present in us? In one sense, it is correct to speak of all persons as being in the image of God. Primarily this assertion speaks of the universal human potential to actualize or live out the goal God

---

74. Santmire, "The Genesis Creation Narratives Revisited," 374-75.

intends for our existence. Each human is potentially a participant in the one destiny God has for us. As the above discussion indicates, this basic meaning has several connotations. It means that each person stands before God. God loves each person, and therefore each is the recipient of worth from the Creator. And God holds each one responsible. Potential participation in the common human destiny means likewise that God's desire is that each person respond to him in love and obedience and thereby live out the purpose of our existence. In short, all persons are potentially participants in that reality to which the concept of the divine image points.

Although in this sense we may declare that all persons are in the image of God, it is in Christ that the divine image is fully revealed. Christ is the image of God in the ultimate sense. It is he who reveals to us what God has created humankind to be. And it is he who brings us to participate in that destiny, in the sphere of truly human living. This theme, however, must await the Christology section for a fuller development.

By extension, the image of God is related to Christians in a special way. Those who are united to Christ share thereby in the image of God. This participation, however, is dynamic. Transformation into the image of God is a process which we experience beginning with conversion and lasting until the great eschatological renewal which will bring us into full conformity with the image of God. The discussion of sanctification in chapter 17 treats this theme.

The divine image as a special community. The eschatological dimension of the image of God as our divinely-given destiny leads us to a final and central conclusion. The divine image is a shared, corporate reality. It is fully present only in community.[75]

As we noted in the discussion of God as Creator (chapter 5), God's program for the world and hence for humankind as God's representative in the world focuses on the establishment of community. The foundation for the understanding of the image of God as a "community" concept lies in the creation narratives.[76] Implicit in Genesis

---

75. For a development of the philosophical basis for the social understanding of personhood, see Alistair I. McFadyen, *The Call to Personhood: A Christian Theory of the Individual in Social Relationships* (Cambridge: Cambridge University Press, 1990).

76. For a fuller discussion of the relationship of sexuality and community, see Grenz, *Sexual Ethics*, 35-37.

1:26-28 and more explicit in the second creation narrative is the theme that God creates the first human pair in order that humans may enjoy community with each other. More specifically, the creation of the woman is designed to deliver the man from his isolation. This primal community of male and female then becomes expansive. It produces the offspring that arise from the sexual union of husband and wife and eventually gives rise to the development of societies. What begins in the Garden of Eden finds its completion at the consummation of history. God's will for his creation is the establishment of a human society in which his children enjoy perfect fellowship with each other, the created world, and the Creator.

It is not surprising that ultimately the image of God should focus on "community." As the doctrine of the Trinity asserts, throughout all eternity God is "community," namely, the fellowship of Father, Son, and Holy Spirit who comprise the triune God. The creation of humankind in the divine image, therefore, can mean nothing less than that humans express the relational dynamic of the God whose representation we are called to be. Consequently, each person can be related to the image of God only within the context of life in community with others. Only in fellowship with others can we show forth what God is like, for God is the community of love—the eternal relationship enjoyed by the Father and the Son, which is the Holy Spirit.

Although the fullest expression of our participation in the image of God must await the eschatological transformation of human life in the kingdom of God, the New Testament envisions a present foretaste of the eschatological human community. The focus of this present experience, according to the New Testament writers, is the community of Christ. As the eschatological community, the fellowship of those who seek to reflect in the present the future reality of the reign of God, the church of Jesus Christ is the prolepsis, the historical foretaste and sign, of the image of God.

The theological foundation for the New Testament link between the image of God and the church as an expression of the future human community lies in God's intent in creation and his eschatological purpose for creation. The discussion above has touched on these themes. But a third theme must be mentioned as well. The New Testament writers employ a metaphor of the church as Christ's body with Christ as the head. According to the New Testament, Christ is the image of God (2 Cor. 4:4; Col. 1:15; Heb. 1:3). As Christ's body, however, the church shares in his relationship to God. By extension the church also shares in Christ's calling as the image of God. Through our connection with our Lord, we have been given the responsibility and privilege of reflecting the very nature of the triune God. And as a result of this same connection, Paul speaks of believers, the members of the church, as now being transformed into the image of God in Christ (1 Cor. 15:49; 2 Cor. 3:18; Col. 3:10).

In the final analysis, then, the "image of God" is a community concept. It refers to humans as beings-in-fellowship. Although present in other dimensions of social life, the focal point of community can only be the community of Christ expressed in his church, which ought to be the highest form of human fellowship in this age. As we live in love—that is, as we give expression to true community—we reflect the love which characterizes the divine essence. And as we reflect the divine essence which is love, we live in accordance with our own essential nature, with that for which God created us. In this manner, we find our true identity—that form of the "world" toward which our "openness to the world" is intended to point us.

Our Lord himself articulated this principle in his call for radical discipleship: "For whoever wants to save his life will lose it, but whoever loses his life for me will find it" (Matt. 16:25). The way to life comes through the giving of one's own life in relationship to Christ. Hence, we come to find our true identity—we come to exemplify our true essence—only as we live out the design and destiny God has for us. This design is that we participate together with others in the community of the followers of Christ. Thereby we together reflect the divine life itself, which life is present among us through the Holy Spirit, who is the Spirit of the dynamic of the triune God.

7 Sin: The Destruction of Community

For all have sinned and fall short of the glory of God . (Rom. 3:23)

Outline

The biblical basis for the Reformed view
The Reality of Original Sin
The Results of Sin: Our Human Situation
  Alienation
  Condemnation
  Enslavement
  Depravity

Throughout history thinkers have noted that humans are a strange paradox. We are a mixture of good and evil, of godly beauty and of demonic hideousness, of unlimited potential and of tragic failure. In theological terms, we are God's good handiwork, but we have fallen into sin.

We confess that humans are the good creation of God and "fearfully and wonderfully made" (Ps. 139:14, KJV). Repeatedly people reflect this goodness by doing good acts, engaging in self-sacrificial actions, and caring for others. More significantly, as God's creatures, we are capable of being co-creators with him. Our creative capabilities surface through various human cultural expressions, including art, music, and literature, but even the development of language itself. Above all, God designed us to be his image, to reflect to all creation his own character.

At the same time, we also confess that humans show forth the workings of evil. Although created to respond to God and to others, we readily grow self-centered and apathetic, closing ourselves up within our own little universes. Designed to imitate the Creator through our creative abilities, we readily misuse the good gifts God has bestowed on us, destroy what others have constructed, and plunder the good world God made to nourish us. Above all, rather than reflecting God's own character, we display the malice of the evil one. In short, we whom God intends to be the crown of creation are fallen creatures. This dark side of the human situation is what the biblical authors term "sin." They forthrightly declare what human experience through the centuries confirms, namely, that something has gone wrong in the universe and humankind stands at the center of the derailing of God's good intention.

235

For this reason, while emphasizing the "good news"—the essential goodness of humankind and our human identity as the creatures of God, theology cannot avoid declaring the "bad news"—the grim reality of human sinfulness. Despite the unpopularity of this topic in a society which seeks to set aside the concept of sin,[1] we must unabashedly assert the truth of the human tragedy. We must boldly declare this dimension of our Christian affirmation, because the concept of "sin" belongs to the biblical *kerygma*, it is a non-negotiable thesis of our theological heritage, and the category retains its ability to cast light on human self-awareness and experience in every generation.

Our attempt to reflect theologically on the Christian understanding of the dark dimension of the human reality and existence requires that we view sin in the light of several theological themes. We first inquire about the nature of the phenomenon itself: What actually is sin? Then we look at the biblical concept of the human fall into sin and the related idea of "original sin": In what sense did sin begin with Adam? How is it that we participate in the primordial human transgression? And do we stand condemned from birth because of the original sin? Finally, we conclude the chapter with a description of the abiding results of our human sin: What does the presence of sin mean for life now—for our standing before God and for our existence in the world?

The Nature of Sin

The writers of Scripture are uncompromising in characterizing of the tragedy of the human reality. The authors of both Testaments assert that we are sinners. But what is sin? And how ought we to understand the reality of human sinfulness today?

Biblical Terms for Sin

Our quest begins with a study of the terms the biblical writers employ to describe the human malaise.

---

1. See, for example, Karl Menninger, *Whatever Became of Sin?* (New York: Hawthorn Books, 1973).

Old Testament words for sin. Several Hebrew terms touch on the various dimensions of sin.[2] These include *ʿavah* ("bent" or "crooked"), *ʿaval* which refers to the lack of integrity and hence is generally translated "iniquity," *ʿavar* ("to cross over" or "transgress"), *raʿ* ("the rule of evil") and *maʿal* ("breach of trust"). To these must be added *pashaʿ* ("to revolt" or "refuse subjection to rightful authority"), which some scholars suggest describes the essence of sin or sin in its underlying motivation. The most widely used term to describe "sin" in the Old Testament, however, is *chatha*.[3] Basically this word means "to miss the right point" or "to deviate from the norm." Thus, it refers to "erroneous action." Yet, the root meaning of *chatha* does not lie in the religious realm. Underlying its theological meaning is its more fundamental use as a verb of movement—"missing the right point."[4] Hence, *chatha* can denote "to lose," as the opposite of "to find" (Prov. 8:35-36). Or it can carry the idea of inaccuracy in exercising certain abilities, as for example, in the narrator's use of the term in describing the left-handed soldiers of Israel: They "could sling a stone at a hair and *not miss*" (Judg. 20:16, emphasis added).

Although it is sometimes used in a purely non-religious manner, most occurrences of *chatha* in the Old Testament are theological.[5] As a description of the sinful human situation the term means "to depart from God's purpose" (or God's law) or "to miss the goal," whether ignorantly or deliberately (Lev. 4:2; Num. 15:28).[6] Generally *chatha* refers to specific actions, whether of thought, word, or deed.[7] Only rarely does it describe a state of being or existence.

New Testament words for sin. The New Testament writers likewise use several terms to describe the phenomenon of sin. These include *parabasis* ("the transgression of a boundary"), *parkoe* ("disobedience to a voice"), *paraptoma* ("falling where one should have stood upright"), *agnoema* ("ignorance of what one ought to

---

2. For a summary, see Robert B. Girdlestone, *Synonyms of the Old Testament*, second edition (1897; Grand Rapids: Eerdmans, 1973), 76-86.

3. Gottfried Quell, "hamartano," in the *Theological Dictionary of the New Testament*, ed. Gerhard Kittel, trans. Geoffrey W. Bromiley (Grand Rapids: Eerdmans, 1964), 1:271.

4. Ibid.

5. Ibid., 270.

6. Girdlestone, *Synonyms of the Old Testament*, 77.

7. Ibid.

have known"), *hettema* ("the diminishing of what should have been fully rendered"), *anomia* ("the non-observance of a law"), and *plemmeleia* ("a discord in the harmonies of God's universe").[8]

The Greek word *hubris*, which occurs occasionally in the New Testament (e.g., Acts 27:10, 21; 2 Cor. 12:10), parallels the Hebrew *pasha*. William Barclay offers a helpful definition of the term. *Hubris*, he writes, "is mingled pride and cruelty. *Hubris* is the pride which makes a man defy God, and the arrogant contempt which makes him trample on the hearts of his fellow men."[9] Hence, it is the forgetting of personal creatureliness and the attempt to be equal with God. In classical Greek, *hubris* carried greater significance than is evidenced in the New Testament. The ancient philosophers viewed it as the supreme sin, one which brought destruction and total ruin.

The most widely used term for "sin" in the New Testament, however, is the noun *hamartia* and its related verb *hamartano*. Similar to the Old Testament word *chatha*, *hamartia* means "to miss the mark." According to Gottfried Quell, writing in the *Theological Dictionary of the New Testament*, the word refers to "an offense in relation to God with emphasis on guilt."[10]

The New Testament usage of *hamartia* describes the human predicament as a complex situation. Similar to the central Old Testament understanding of the human malaise, *hamartia* can refer to sin as a specific act. But in addition, the New Testament authors speak of a power or force operative in the human sphere. As an alien reality which has us in its grasp, sin holds sway over individuals not merely externally, but also internally.[11] Consequently, *hamartia* also denotes the defective, internal dimension of the human person.

Both the Old and New Testaments, despite subtle differences in emphasis, view sin fundamentally as failure. As both *chatha* and *hamartia* suggest, sin is primarily "missing the mark" or "falling short." It entails our inability to be what God desires us to be, our failure to fulfill God's intention for us.

---

8. Richard C. Trench, *Synonyms of the New Testament*, ninth edition (1880; Grand Rapids: Eerdmans, 1953), 240
9. William Barclay, *New Testament Words* (London: SCM, 1964), 133.
10. Quell, "hamartia,' in TDNT, 1:275.
11. Barclay, *New Testament Words*, 119.

Sin and the Human Person

The biblical authors agree that all humans share in the sinful situation. We are all affected by, and participate in the human predicament. The biblical authors employ several themes to describe in greater detail this personal involvement.

Sin infects the core of our being. Repeatedly the Scripture writers link "sin" with the core of our being. Sinful acts arise from within us, from the center of our existence. Hence, sin dwells in our "hearts" or in our "flesh" (Mark 7:14-23; Matt. 12:33-37).

Just as "soul" and "spirit" do not refer to substantial entities that form part of our ontological nature, so also in this context we ought not to interpret *flesh* as referring to the specifically physical dimension of the human reality. Rather, both the Hebrew and the Greek terms translated "flesh" (*basar* and *sarx*) can refer to the whole human person in our moral weakness, in our tendency to sin or rebel against God in every area of life.[12]

The authors of Scripture assert that the human predicament results from the corrupt *heart* (e.g., Rom. 7:18; Eph. 2:3; Jer. 17:9). By this, they mean that sin has found lodging within us—in the core of our personal being.

The Scriptures teach that sin affects a person's entire heart. It infects our personal "control center." Paul describes this situation in vivid terms. He speaks of sin as causing "our foolish hearts" to be "darkened" (Rom. 1:21) and our minds to be "corrupt" (1 Tim. 6:5). Because of sin, the apostle declares, we cannot understand spiritual truths (1 Cor. 2:14; 2 Cor. 4:4), and our thinking has become "futile" (Rom. 1:21). In fact, our mind is even hostile to God (Rom. 8:7-8).

In infecting the human heart, sin has likewise corrupted our *affections*. Sinful humans are "enslaved by all kinds of passions and pleasures" (Titus 3:3). And because our deeds are evil, we love darkness instead of light (John 3:19).

The New Testament asserts that the sin which now resides in the core of our being enslaves its prey. It is a power that rules our lives, for our sinning gives evidence to our bondage to sin. Hence, Jesus de-

---

12. This position has recently been defended even by conservative theologians. See, for example, Anthony A. Hoekema, *Created in God's Image* (Grand Rapids: Eerdmans, 1986), 212, 216.

clares, "I tell you the truth, everyone who sins is a slave to sin" (John 8:34). And both Paul (Rom. 6:16-17, 20) and Peter (2 Peter 2:19) assert that we are slaves to whatever has mastered us.

Sin perverts goodness. By their claim that we are in bondage to sin, the biblical authors do not mean to suggest that we can never do what is right. On the contrary, they hold out the prospect that we do indeed engage in good acts, even "by nature." Hence, Paul declares that sometimes the Gentiles, "who do not have the law, do by nature things required by the law," thereby demonstrating that "the requirements of the law are written on their hearts" (Rom. 2:14-15).

Yet we must temper the claim that humans do good. Because of the perniciousness of sin, God's gracious provision of the law only heightens our sense of bondage to sin rather than facilitating us to live properly. Paul, for example, affirms this from his own experience. Sin seizes the opportunity the law affords. As the law defines what sin is, it arouses the desire to transgress (Rom. 7:8-11). In the same way, knowledge only serves to heighten our responsibility not to sin (James 4:17; John 9:41).[13]

Not only does sin work to pervert God's good provision of the law, even those good acts that we do readily fall under the evil impulse. Repeatedly we discover that despite our apparent good intentions, corrupt motives also lie behind the good things we do. Jesus suggests this in the parable of the Pharisee and the publican. A self-righteous attitude, rather than true piety, motivated what on the surface would appear to be a pious act—the Pharisee's temple prayer (Luke 18:9-14).

Sin is universal. Finally, the biblical authors assert that sin is universal. We all participate in sin. Drawing from a variety of Old Testament texts, Paul concludes his discussion of the human predicament with the categorical declaration, "for all have sinned and fall short of the glory of God" (Rom. 3:23; see also 1 Kings 8:46; Ps. 143:2; Rom. 3:10-20). Each of us is personally indicted in the sorry reality that plagues all humankind.

---

13. Girdlestone, *Synonyms of the Old Testament*, 85.

The Essence of Sin

The biblical writers do not sidestep the stark thesis that humans participate in sin. We are all caught in this awful reality. And the sin problem is radical: it infects the very core of our being. But can we say more? Can we pinpoint the essence of our malignancy? Christian thinkers have repeatedly sought to pierce to the root of sin. This attempt has often focused on the attempt to determine a root sin.

Sin as failure. Many theologians view *pasha^c* and *hubris* as providing just such a root motivation for sin. By appeal to these terms together with the narrative of the first sin, thinkers since Augustine have asserted that pride lies behind our deplorable situation.[14] Our human refusal to assume our assigned role as creatures of God, they postulate, results in humans setting themselves in the place of God. This has been our human tendency since the beginning, they add, for instead of obeying God, Adam and Eve believed the lie of the serpent and sought to become their own masters.

The claim that pride is the root sin does, of course, point to an important truth. Our human unwillingness to acknowledge God's sovereignty, which constitutes a fundamental rebellion against the divine rule, lies at the root of many sinful actions. However, we must be cautious lest we too quickly focus on *hubris* as the primordial sin and the motivation for all sin. The biblical writers themselves do not invest the concept with such exalted stature, but present sin as multifaceted. And they avoid speculating concerning the root of the various ways in which we fail to fulfill God's design.

If any term looms as the best candidate for the description of sin in its root reality, it is *chatha* or *hamartia*, not *hubris*. The biblical writers describe our human problem as "failure," not "pride." In its essential nature "sin" describes our inability, or even our set refusal, to fulfill God's design for us. Simply stated, we "miss the mark" and "fall short of God's glory."

Further, the focus on "pride" may actually betray a specifically male perception of the human condition. While women are not exempted from the tendency toward pride and rebellion, our contem-

---

14. For Augustine's position, see Augustine, *City of God* 14.13-14, trans. Marcus Dods, Modern Library edition (New York: Random House, 1950), 460-62.

porary situation suggests that pride is an especially strong temptation for men. In our society it is men who are most susceptible to prideful rebellion against God's intention.

Whereas humans may miss the mark in a willful, prideful manner, many women have discovered that they are more likely to fail God's ideal by too readily acquiescing to the domination of others. In their self-abnegation, women readily assume that the curse of Genesis 3 is their place in creation rather than a distortion of it.[15] In so doing, they fail to reflect God's declaration that humans as men and women are created good. The self-abnegation of many women is no less sinful, no less a way of failing to fulfill God's design, than is the pride of their male counterparts.[16] It is merely different.

We conclude, therefore, that the concept of pride describes an important dimension of sin, but does not constitute the root motivation for our sinful attitudes and actions. To discover the essence of sin, we must begin with the biblical concept of "missing the mark" (*chatha* and *hamartia*). These Hebrew and Greek terms indicate that the human situation is fundamentally that of "failure." We are sinners ultimately in that we "miss the mark." We fail to live in accordance with the destiny and design God intends for us.

Sin as disruption of community. Our understanding of sin by appeal to "failure," however, cannot stop here. Rather we must ask, What is the divine intention that we fail to live out? Here the concept of the image of God discussed in chapter 6 becomes once again important. If our divinely given design is that we be God's image bearer, we must understand sin as our failure to reflect the image of God.

At the heart of the concept of the divine image is God's ultimate intention that humankind show forth God's own character. As the Old Testament emphasizes and the New Testament confirms, sin lies in specific acts. The term designates any attitude or action that is ungodly, that does not mirror God, that fails to reflect the manner in which God would think or act.

---

15. See Rosemary Ruether, *Sexism and God-Talk* (Boston: Beacon, 1983), 184-89.

16. See, for example, Daniel L. Migliore, *Faith Seeking Understanding: An Introduction to Christian Theology* (Grand Rapids: Eerdmans, 1991), 130-31.

Behind individual acts of failure is a deeper way in which we are "in sin." As we noted in chapter 6, being in the image of God means reflecting the nature of God, who is the social Trinity. The divine image emerges in its ultimate sense, therefore, as humans show forth community—as we enjoy fellowship with God, with each other, and with the creation around us. Only then are we truly reflecting to all creation what God is like. This understanding of the intent of God means that sin is ultimately our human failure to live in community with God, each other, and the natural environment.

Sin is marked by the disruption of the community that God desires for us and consequently for all creation. This disruption is present whenever community is absent. Hence, sin is essentially both the lack of and the loss of community. Yet, the opposition between sin and community is even stronger. In its essence, sin is also whatever disrupts and seeks to destroy the community God intends to establish. Summarily stated, sin is the destruction of community.

As the absence of, and even the destruction of community, sin is "missing the mark." In our fallenness, we fail to live in accordance with our purpose. Such failure may be simply passive—as we do not appropriate our identity as participants in the community of God. Or it can be more active, taking the form of rebellious opposition to the divine purpose.

In either case, sin entails an improper valuation. In sin, the self rather than God becomes our criterion of value. We may simply refuse to see ourselves as God's good creation, or we may actually elevate the creation rather than the Creator as our sovereign. Sin's improper valuation extends to human relations as well. Insofar as we erroneously view ourselves as either better than or less than others, our sin leads to broken relationships and the sense of personal insecurity or insignificance. Sin likewise affects the way we view the creation around us, as we see nature as having value only insofar as it serves us.

The sinful destruction of community has been the human predicament from the beginning. The transgression of our first parents led to the unmistakable disruption of community. Their act brought alienation or estrangement where once had been only fellowship.

The innocent transparency in the presence of each other they had once known gave way to shame (Gen 3: 7). In addition, Adam and Eve now feared the face of the God who had lovingly created them (v. 10). And they now experienced the bitter reality that the world around them was no longer their friend (vv. 15, 17-19).

Sin as revealed in the gospel. The connection between sin and community suggests a final thought concerning sin's essence. Sin is most fully revealed in the light of the gospel, the message about Christit.[17] Paul indicates that the law brings sin to light, for the law defines what is sinful (Rom. 7:7). Yet, as he adds, this knowledge only gives sin occasion to ensnare us. To understand sin more fully, we must move beyond the law. We must view sin not only as the transgression of the law, but more importantly in view of the gospel message.

The revelation of sin through the gospel is connected with the radical nature of sin. The problem of sin is not merely external to us, but is a radical problem—it goes to the core of our being. Consequently, the solution to the problem must be equally radical.

This is the point of the gospel. The good news narrates the story of the depth to which God suffered on our behalf. The gospel narrative begins already in the Old Testament with the recounting of God's faithfulness in the face of the faithlessness of Israel. But it reaches its climax in the account of the sufferings of the innocent Jesus. As the Servant of Yahweh he reveals the radical lengths to which God in Christ has gone to deal with our condition, that is, to restore community with us. Indeed, as Paul writes,

> All this is from God, who reconciled us to himself through Christ and gave us the ministry of reconciliation: that God was reconciling the world to himself in Christ, not counting men's sins against them. And he has committed to us the message of reconciliation. We are therefore Christ's ambassadors, as though God were making his appeal through us. We implore you on Christ's behalf: Be reconciled to God. God made him who had no sin to be sin for us, so that in him we might become the righteousness of God (2 Cor. 5:18-21).

---

17. In the twentieth century, Barth emphasized this point. See, Karl Barth, *Church Dogmatics*, trans. Geoffrey W. Bromiley (Edinburgh: T. & T. Clark, 1956), IV/I:358-413.

Our sin—our breach of community—is serious, the gospel declares. It is so serious that it could only be overcome through the sacrifice of Jesus through which God has overcome our alienation.

The depth of sin is revealed in the gospel likewise in that the good news declares God's ultimate intent for humankind. His desire is that we be his image. Ultimately, the divine image is Christ, for he reflects perfectly the perfect character of God. Consequently, in that the gospel depicts Jesus as the one who lived out fully his vocation as the bearer of the image of God, this good news about Christ also exposes our own failure to fulfill God's design for humankind. As theologians throughout church history have asserted, only through Christ are we made cognizant of the depth of our own sin.

The image of God which Jesus Christ reveals to us, however, is the destiny to which God calls us. His purpose is that we show forth the character of God as the triune one, the community of love. Consequently, only when we live in the blessed reality of community can we perceive the evilness of sin. We understand best the lack of, loss of, and destruction of fellowship only when we are experiencing, even if only in a proleptic manner, the fellowship God desires for us.

Sin, then, denotes our human failure. We miss the mark of participation in the community of God which the Creator desires for his creatures. Sin is the lack of and the loss of community. While as the privation of God's good intentions, sin may be passive; sin is not merely so. It has an active, pernicious dimension, for it is also actual opposition to God's intent. Sin refers to whatever seeks to thwart God's plan and goal, namely, the establishment of community. Hence, it is whatever destroys true fellowship.

But where did sin come from? How is it that we are all caught up in this malevolent reality? This question moves us to our next point of inquiry, the question of original sin.

Original Sin

The Christian world view affirms that despite our being the handiwork of God, we are not what God desires us to be. By our own actions we have become flawed, so that we fail to live in accordance with the divine intent. All individual humans and all generations of humans participate in this problematical situation that the biblical authors refer to as "sin." In fact, the Book of Genesis indicates that this situation has existed "from the beginning." Although created good, from the first human pair onward throughout history humans have universally been caught in the snare of sin.

The biblical affirmation of the universality of sin raises a crucial question: How can this be the case? Where did sin come from? And how is it that we all participate in this failure? Questions about how sin entered the world of humankind and how all persons participate in the one human fate, arising as they do from the affirmation of the universality of sin, lie within the purview of the theological topic of original sin.

The theological concept of original sin, therefore, carries several connotations. It refers to the "original" or first sin. It denotes the depraved nature or "pollution" that forms the origin or source of our own sins. And it can encompass the origin or ground for the declaration of condemnation, the guilt that hangs over us. Although theologians do not always treat these aspects separately and despite the fact that there is a certain connectedness which binds them together, each dimension within the concept of original sin raises a somewhat separate question.

The Fall of Humankind—the Fall of Adam

The universality of human sin raises immediately the question of the presence of the predicament from the beginning of human life on the earth. Formulated in this manner, this is the question of original sin understood as the original human sin. If "all have sinned and fall short of the glory of God," then when and how did this "falling short" begin? Hence, we inquire about "the fall."

The question of the fall raises in the minds of many Christians the question of the fall of Adam. And this is right, for several biblical writings—especially the Genesis narrative of the fall and the Pauline typology between Christ and Adam—answer the question of the universality of sin by invoking Adam. On this basis, Christian theology has traditionally described the original human sin—that is, the first sin—as the sin of our first parents. Adam and Eve fell, and this event marked the fall of humankind.

The foundation for the traditional description of the fall lies in the narrative of Genesis 3. The drama begins with Adam and Eve in the Garden of Eden, then introduces the serpent as the tempter of Eve, moves to the eating of the forbidden fruit, and climaxes with the divine pronouncement of a curse. It is, therefore, to this text that we must turn first.

The garden. The Genesis narration suggests that Adam and Eve began their existence in an idyllic, seemingly perfect state. Having been created good, they were untainted by evil; they lived in innocency. Our first parents enjoyed fellowship with God, perhaps in that God regularly walked in the Garden in the cool of the day (Gen. 3:8). They savored community with each other, for they were naked and felt no shame (Gen. 2:25). And the first humans experienced harmony with the rest of creation, in that they ate of the trees of the field (Gen. 2:16) for which they cared (v. 15), and they were presumably friends with the animals Adam had named (Gen. 2:19-20). To this extent, therefore, our first parents were the bearers of the image of God (hence, Gen. 1:26-27), for they lived in community and thereby represented the character of God to creation.

While acknowledging the idyllic state that characterized life in the Garden of Eden, many theologians throughout Christian history have suggested that the first humans were not characterized by positive, chosen obedience to God and the fullness of eternal life. That is, they did not yet fully participate in the human destiny as designed by God. This observation carries immense significance. It means that Jesus in his positive obedience to the will of the Father takes preeminence over Adam in his innocence. Jesus lifts humankind to a higher plain than that enjoyed by the first human pair in the Garden of Eden.

Further, theologians often draw an important conclusion from the divinely given prohibition, "you must not eat of the tree of the knowledge of good and evil, for when you eat of it you will surely die" (Gen. 2:17). In their innocence, Adam and Eve did not full recognize the radical difference between good and evil. They had not yet been confronted with experiential knowledge of this distinction, nor did they personally know the sting of sin. Therefore, the words of the serpent ("when you eat of it your eyes will be opened, and you will be like God, knowing good and evil" [Gen. 3:5]), although pernicious questioning of God's benevolence, were not fully devoid of truth. By following the serpent's suggestion they would indeed gain a heightened awareness of the nature of good and evil, albeit to their detriment.

The first sin. The Genesis story teaches that in the midst of the bliss of the garden, the first human pair chose to disobey the divine prohibition and thereby plunged humankind into sin. Their downward plummet began with mistrust. The serpent subtly raised doubts concerning God's goodness. He suggested that God's command was not given for human benefit, but to withhold some good from them. And the serpent's words set before them the possibility of a heightened knowledge that he claimed God had reserved for himself. In this sense the Genesis story has a striking similarity to the myth of Prometheus, the Greek hero who conspired to steal fire from the gods, because the gods had deprived them of a good by withholding fire from humans.

The narrator, however, clearly avoids any such connotation. God's intent is to test, not deprive his creatures of good. In one sense, the presence of a divinely initiated test does lay the beginnings of human sin with the Creator. Indeed, God originates the possibility of sin in that the prohibition gives birth to choice. Yet the presence of choice is not itself evil. Choice becomes evil only when choice is invoked for the evil alternative. Hence, by employing the symbols of the tree and the serpent, in his probing of the foundations for the first sin, the narrator draws our attention away from the Lawgiver to the natural conditions of life in the Garden of Eden.

Consequences of the first sin. The narrator continues the story, however, with the sad reality of the consequences of disobedience. As we indicated earlier, above all they no longer reflected the grandeur of the divine image, for the idyllic community was shattered.

When they hear his footsteps in the garden, Adam and Eve know they are naked, grow fearful, and seek to hide from God, indicating thereby that the pristine fellowship with the Creator is broken. They likewise cover themselves from each other, indicating that their sense of guilt and shame has marred the former sense of human community. Community would be further defaced as the husband would now rule over his wife (Gen. 3:16). And through their act, the first humans lose the primordial harmony with creation. In this manner, they introduce enmity into creation itself. Enmity separates humankind and the serpent, who must live under the curse of God (Gen. 3:14-15). The ground is also cursed, so that the man now needs to work hard to receive the sustenance that nature had so freely provided (Gen. 3:17-19), a curse which is later repeated in the case of the first murderer (Gen. 4:11-12). And Adam and Eve are banished from the Garden of Eden (Gen. 3:23).

In that it destroyed the primordial experience of community, the sin of Adam and Eve marked the immediate marring of the divine image. In addition, their act disrupted the divine intent that theirs be an unending earthly experience of community. Now the principle of death is at work in their lives. God had warned Adam, "for when you eat of [the forbidden fruit] you will surely die" (Gen. 2:17). Because of the fall, the divine warning became a reality, for the principle of death entered their world: Adam would now toil "until you return to the ground, since from it you were taken; for dust you are and to dust you will return" (Gen. 3:19).

In the pages of the New Testament we discover a theological commentary on the warning of death God spoke to Adam. Because of sin, we experience the sting of death. This sting comes in stages. It begins with the present life which is characterized by our being "dead in trespasses and sins" (Eph. 2:1). At the end of our life on earth, we undergo physical death, as God reclaims the life principle. But one day death will come in its ultimate manner as the unredeemed experience final separation from the source of life, eternal banishment from God's kingdom (Rev. 20:14-15).

The biblical understanding of the introduction of death into human experience stands in contrast to a thesis many theologians propose today. They claim that death, understood in terms of the cessation of personal physical life, was already present, at least in principle, among humans prior to the fall. Death, according to this viewpoint, is a natural corollary of finite existence. Rather than something added to human nature by the fall into sin, human finitude entails being subject to physical death.

Reinhold Niebuhr, for example, affirms that in the biblical view humankind is "a created and finite existence in both body and spirit,"[18] and this in accordance with "God's plan of creation."[19] This finitude entails death, in that the Genesis "account assumes the mortality of man and does not include it as one of the several punishments which Adam must endure."[20] In support of this thesis he appeals to the significance of the tree of life in the Garden of Eden. In the Genesis story, eating of the tree would bestow immortality (Gen. 3:22), thereby indicating that human finite existence means that humans were subjected by nature to physical death.

Niebuhr's conclusion, however, runs contrary to the teaching of the church throughout its history. According to Paul, death is the result of sin (Rom. 5:12; 15:17; Rom. 3:23),[21] a view which Niebuhr himself finds shared by Athanasius, Irenaeus, Gregory, Thomas Aquinas, and Luther. In addition, the warning God gave to Adam in the Genesis account seems to contradict Niebuhr's thesis, for it included the threat of death (Gen. 2:17). But above all, Niebuhr's conception fails to reflect the parallel concept to death, the New Testament idea of eternal life. Eternal life means existing forever in fellowship with God in the new creation, in which death will be banished and human nature will be present in its fullness. Because that full existence excludes death, physical death cannot be a part of our human essence.

We are by nature finite. Human finitude, however, does not include death, although death may well illustrate and confirm it. On this basis, we may now draw a conclusion concerning the significance of human finitude. God's infinity refers to his self-sufficiency, that is, that he is not dependent on anything external to himself to be who he is. As humans, however, we are finite and consequently de-

---

18. Reinhold Niebuhr, *The Nature and Destiny of Man*, two volumes (New York: Charles Scribner's Sons, 1941), 1:12.

19. Ibid., 1:167.

20. Ibid., 1:174, 176. Niebuhr cites Gen. 3:17-19.

21. Niebuhr admits that this is the Pauline view. See ibid., 1:174, 176.

pendent on God for our very life. In fact, as the concept of "openness to the world" suggests, each of us is infinitely dependent. This dependency is not altered even in eternity. Even after death is abolished, we remain finite creatures, dependent for our life on the one who alone has life within himself (John 5:26).

The First Sin and the Sin of Humankind

The Genesis narrator answers the question concerning the source of the presence of sin in our world by telling the story of the fall of Adam. Paul echoes the primordial narrative, declaring that "sin entered the world through one man" (Rom. 5:12), with the consequence that "in Adam all die" (1 Cor. 15:22). The appeal to Adam, however, raises the theological question concerning the connection between the first or "original" sin and the sin of Adam's offspring. More specifically, we ask, How is Adam related to humankind as a whole, so that the effects of his sin extend to each of his descendants?

Historical suggestions. Since the Reformation theologians have grappled with this connection. Several answers set forth in the era of Protestant scholasticism continue to enjoy prominence among evangelical thinkers.

(1) A first understanding of the connection between Adam and his descendants was propounded by thinkers within the Reformed tradition in connection with covenant theology. At its foundation this view depicts Adam as the historical "federal" head of humankind, and therefore it is known as the *federal headship* view.[22] More specifically, Adam is the representative of humanity in the "covenant of works."[23]

---

22. See Louis Berkhof, *Systematic Theology*, revised edition (Grand Rapids: Eerdmans, 1953), 215.

23. The idea of a primordial covenant of works has been a controversial thesis within Reformed theology. It was articulated at length by the great Dutch theologian Herman Bavinck. It has been defended in America by many of the leading lights of the old Princeton school. See, for example, Charles Hodge, *Systematic Theology* (New York: Charles Scribner and Co., 1871), 2:117-22; William G. T. Shedd, *Dogmatic Theology* (1888; Grand Rapids: Zondervan, n. d.), 2:152-53; Berkhof, *Systematic Theology*, 211-18. Several recent proponents have proposed substituting the designation "covenant of creation." E.g., Meredith Kline, *By Oath Consigned* (Grand Rapids: Eerdmans, 1968), 27-29, 32, 37. For a recent rebuttal of the viewpoint, see Hoekema, *Created in God's Image*, 119-21.

Proponents of federal headship conceive of the primordial existence in terms of a legal compact which God entered with Adam, the first human being. In this agreement God declared that if Adam obeyed the command not to eat from the forbidden tree, he would enjoy continued life (cf., Rom. 7:10), whereas disobedience would result in death. Because of the focus on human obedience to divine command, the agreement is the covenant of works.

Further, this expression of covenant theology asserts that the covenant of works extended beyond Adam as a historical individual to encompass all humankind. All of us, therefore, participated in that primordial covenant. The connection between each of us and Adam lies in the idea of representation. God designated Adam to be our representative. As the designated representative—the federal head—of all humankind, Adam acted not only for himself, but also on behalf of each human being. Proponent Louis Berkhof explains: "Adam was constituted the representative head of the human race so that he could act *for* all his descendants."[24]

At first glance, the idea of federal headship may appear quite strange and opaque. Yet the concept operates at many levels of contemporary life. For example, modern democracies such as the United States employ the idea of federalism, for governments act continuously on behalf of the populous. Hence, within certain spheres of responsibility, both the President and the Congress of the United States serve as the designated representatives of the people. Consequently, their actions, such as a declaration of war, have grave and lasting effects on each citizen and even on future generations of citizens. In a similar fashion, proponents of federal headship assert that God designated Adam to act on behalf of all his descendants, whether for good or for ill, whether for life or for death.

(2) Other theologians, who can claim the legacy of Augustine, advocate what we may call the *natural headship* view. Proponents theorize that Adam was not our federal, but our "natural" head. We were all present in Adam when he sinned, they argue. In fact, each of us actually acted in Adam, and thus we are all rightly implicated for his sin, which is also our sin.

---

24. Berkhof, *Systematic Theology*, 215.

But how can these theologians claim that we actually sinned with Adam? In response, advocates of natural headship appeal to the traducian understanding of the generation of the soul, which we looked at in chapter 6. Even though Adam's children were not yet born when he sinned, they were present in Adam—in his loins—at the time of the fall.

(3) Despite their different perspectives, both the federal and natural headship positions presuppose that Adam was an actual historical individual. In recent years this assumption has fallen into disfavor, at least among modern theologians. Consequently, the theories concerning the connection between Adam and humankind which build from the historicity of Adam have likewise been questioned. In their place many theologians advocate a symbolic understanding of the connection which is based on the symbolic interpretation of Adam discussed in chapter 6.

As we noted in chapter 6, there are differences in viewpoint concerning the reference for the Adam symbol: Is Adam the race or each individual human? Despite differences among them, those who argue that Adam is a symbol do not read the Genesis narrative of the fall as the account of one man in prehistory. Rather, it is a non-discursive description of the experience of humankind or of every historical person. The application to the nature of the fall follows: Either corporately or individually, we experience the fall and thereby participate in it. The fall, therefore, is not an event in the primordial past but a reality that we either corporately share[25] or individually experience.[26]

For many thinkers, the symbolic interpretation provides the foundation for attractive alternatives to what often appears to be a superfluous choice between two equally uninviting theories. The most popular theory of the connection between Adam and humankind, the

---

25. This viewpoint has been advocated by many in the liberal tradition, including Schleiermacher and Tillich. Cf. Friedrich Schleiermacher, *The Christian Faith*, ed. H. R. MacKintosh and J. S. Stewart (Edinburgh: T. & T. Clark, n.d.), 296, 299-304; Paul Tillich, *Systematic Theology*, three volumes (Chicago: University of Chicago Press, 1951), 1:255-56.

26. This position has been advocated by existentialist theologians following Kierkegaard. See, for example, Søren Kierkegaard, *The Concept of Dread*, trans. Walter Lowrie (Princeton, N.J.: Princeton University Press, 1957); Niebuhr, *The Nature and Destiny of Man*, 1:269.

existentialist understanding which sees the story of Adam's fall as indicating the psychology of each personal sin, renders valuable insight into the nature of human sin. Each individual begins in a state of innocence with respect to specific temptations and in a state of ignorance with respect to knowledge of the result which yielding to temptation will bring. This situation is symbolized by the innocence and ignorance of Adam in the Garden. Before yielding to temptation, the act appears pleasing and promises certain positive benefits. This is symbolized by Eve's attraction to the fruit and to the serpent's statement. Once the act is done, however, the hidden sting is revealed. Only then are the detrimental aspects of the action experienced. At that point the sinner senses guilt and regret. This is symbolized in the Genesis story by the subsequent actions of Adam and Eve. Sensing guilt and remorse they seek to hide from God and each other.

Despite the valuable insight into the psychology of sin it embodies, this description, which we might label the existentialist view, has its own problems. Most crucially, it fails to see the significant differences between Adam's sin and the sin of each human being. For example, the Genesis narrative presents the first temptation as external, instigated by the serpent. The New Testament writers, in contrast, describe our plight as lying at the core of our being. Hence, James declares that even temptation itself has an internal component: "Each one is tempted when by his own evil desire, he is dragged away and enticed" (James 1:14).

Likewise Adam's sin differs from ours in the context in which it occurs. The Genesis story describes the first sin as committed by persons enjoying the pristine state of knowledge of, and fellowship with God, each other, and all creation. The fall was therefore indeed that—a fall from community. We, in contrast, begin in a quite different situation, which Paul describes as that of being "dead in trespasses and sins" (Eph. 2:1). We sin in the context of the prior loss of community.

Given these fundamental differences between the first sin and our own, we cannot accept the existentialist form of the purely symbolic interpretation of the narrative of the fall. If it is purely symbolic, the

Genesis story must either be concerned with the fate of corporate humankind or a symbolic narrative of individual human histories. Modern attempts to interpret the narrative symbolically, from Schleiermacher to Tillich, have tended to move from the supposition that sin is an ontological dimension of human existence. To view sin in this manner, however, calls into question the biblical declaration that God created us good and hence appears to make God the author of evil.

(4) Given both the attraction and the difficulties of the symbolic interpretations of original sin, certain contemporary evangelical theologians, most notably Donald Bloesch, have recently attempted to bridge the gulf between the traditional understandings and the newer thinking. To construct this bridge, Bloesch supposes that *Adam is both actual and symbolic*, both the historical first man and a symbol for everyone. On the basis of this double significance, Bloesch views the fall as both a historical event in the distant past and a reality experienced by each person. He declares that the fall is "a turning away from God in the life of every person within history." It means "being caught up in a rebellion against the Creator" which was "already in effect at the beginning of the race."[27] Bloesch explains:

> The lost paradise is…an unrealized possibility that was removed from man by sin. It represents not an idyllic age at the dawn of history but a state of blessedness or communion with God which has been given to the first man and all men at their creation but which is irremediably forfeited by sin.[28]

Perhaps in the final analysis Bloesch's suggestion does provide helpful insight into the connection between Adam and his offspring. We all experience an individual fall and thereby join a reality that predates our own existence. But to make use of this insight, we must remind ourselves that sin is related to community, as both the absence of and the destruction of human fellowship with God, with one another, and with creation.

---

27. Donald G. Bloesch, *Essentials of Evangelical Theology*, two volumes (San Francisco: Harper and Row, 1978), 1:107.
28. Ibid., 1:107-108. See also 1:118 nt. 53.

The reality of the fall. We need not understand in a literalistic manner the details of the Genesis narrative of creation and fall to note the point of the description. At the dawning of human history, humankind enjoyed an experience of community which, although not fully perfected (not equivalent with what will be ours at the consummation of the kingdom of God), was nevertheless real and on a level not present in the world since then.

Some theologians suggest that certain aspects of the life-styles and outlooks of non-Western peoples may heighten our ability to imagine what may have characterized the idyllic human existence at the dawn of human history. Thereby they attempt to raise the plausibility that there indeed was a primordial community. But we need not travel to primitive societies to contemplate the possibility of such a pre-historical paradise. We are living in an age of heightened concern for ecology, growing uneasiness with the myth of the autonomous individual, and the resurgence of religious belief. The presence of these factors is making it easier for us to postulate a world in the distant past in which humans were more cognizant of our fundamental connectedness with the living environment around us, our basic interrelatedness to each other, and our undeniable dependency on the Creator who is the source of life.

The Genesis narrative reminds us that the "first sin" transpired in the context of such a pristine innocence. Consequently, the original sin was the great destroyer. It shattered the fellowship humankind experienced at the infancy of our corporate story.

Because of the insidiousness of the changes wrought by the original human sin, once destroyed the primordial community remains forever lost. We simply cannot restore the fellowship that our ancestors squandered. Just as we cannot return to any prior era in history, so also we cannot return to "the beginning." We always start in the present and with the conditions of existence in our world as they now are. In this sense, the original sin is in a class by itself, and the effects of the original sin are always with us. This first sin has permanently tainted the world and has irreparably altered its human inhabitants. We no longer know the world, our co-pilgrims, our Creator, and even ourselves as friends, for community has given way to enmity.

Since the original sin in the distant past, all humans live out their days in the midst of the loss of community. In fact, we begin life in the state of sin. And because community does not emerge among us, all now fall short of the design of God. In this weaker sense, we all participate in the sin of our first parents. Yet we also participate in the first sin in a stronger sense. The original sin embodied the destructive nature of human failure in the ultimate sense, of course, for it marked the decimation of the pristine experience of community. But the destruction of community that marked the error of our parents characterizes our attitudes and actions as well. We too are guilty of destroying the semblances of community that here and there emerge within the human family. In so doing, we gain a glimpse of the awfulness of the primordial human sin and of God's righteous judgment on humankind.

We are indeed in a desperate situation. And we remain in the darkness, unless God intervenes to both restore fellowship with us and then ultimately to consummate his goal of community in the highest sense.

Original Sin and Guilt

The Scriptures declare, and experience confirms, that we are sinners. We "fall short of the glory of God," for we do not live in accordance with the principles of the community of God, and therefore we do not display the divine character in keeping with God's intent. We begin life in the state of alienation. And each of us becomes involved in the primordial sin of destroying community. Hence, we are both affected by, and participate in the sin of Adam. The connection between the first sin and our sinfulness raises another question: Does original sin entail original guilt? In other words, In what sense ought we to understand the sin of Adam as the ground for our guilt and condemnation before a holy God?

Viewed in traditional terms, this question becomes: Do we inherit both sin (understood as depravity or pollution) and guilt (the sentence of condemnation leading to banishment from God's presence)? This general query can be variously formulated. For what are we guilty—our own individual sins or also the sin of Adam? Do we begin life both sinful and guilty? Are we both depraved and condemned? Does hell await the children of Adam because of the sin he committed, or only because of the sins we commit?

Enroute to a response to these questions, we must first look at the broad sweep of theological history. We ask, How did theologians in the past view the relationship between inherited sin and guilt?

The question of guilt in theological history. The church has witnessed various attempts to understand the connection between sin and guilt under the theme of original sin.

The early Christian thinkers presented no highly developed concept of original sin. As J. N. D. Kelly noted, "While taking it for granted that men are sinful, ignorant and in need of true life, they never attempt to account for their wretched plight."[29] Justin Martyr did not point to inherited sin as the cause of our predicament, but suggested that demons are to blame.[30] Irenaeus suggested that Adam lost some God-given status, a loss which has consequences for all humankind. But the church father nowhere formulates a specific account of the connection between Adam's act and his offspring.[31]

Tertullian's traducian anthropology opened the way for a heightened idea of original sin. Yet, even he did not follow where his understanding of our presence in Adam might have led. Kelly concluded: Tertullian "is more explicit and outspoken about this sinful bias than previous theologians, in whose eyes corruption and death seem to have been the principal legacy of the Fall; but...his language...can hardly be read as implying our solidarity with the first man in his culpability (i.e., original guilt) as well as in the consequences of his act."[32] Origen did not account for the universality of sin by appeal to any historical act (such as Adam's sin), but by his theory of a pre-cosmic fall: All individual souls fell away from God prior to creation.[33]

---

29. J. N. D. Kelly, *Early Christian Doctrines*, revised edition (San Francisco: Harper and Row, 1978), 163.
30. Ibid., 166-68.
31. Ibid., 172.
32. Ibid., 176.
33. Ibid., 180-81.

With Augustine, however, the situation changed drastically. More than any of his predecessors, the bishop of Hippo vividly depicted our complicity with Adam.[34] Here the doctrine of original sin reaches full development.[35] For the foundation of this teaching, the great church father appealed to the idea of "natural headship." According to Augustine, original sin is the punishment we all bear for Adam's sin. This punishment is ours in that we participated in that first sin, for we were all potentially present in Adam when he transgressed the divine prohibition. This blight is perpetuated through procreation and results in condemnation. Simply stated, all were potentially in Adam, all sinned in Adam, all inherit the punishment for Adam's sin, and thereby all are condemned.[36]

Theologians after Augustine sought to mitigate what appeared to be the harshness of his position. Some proposed a viewpoint called "semi-Augustinianism" or more generally "semi-Pelagianism," because it incorporates aspects of the teaching of his arch-rival Pelagius. The semi-Pelagians asserted that all human beings are indeed tainted by Adam's sin and therefore inclined toward evil. Yet we are neither totally unable to do good nor involved in the guilt of Adam.[37]

The Reformation sparked a return to the stricter Augustinian view. John Calvin, perhaps the most articulate reformulator of Augustine's view, declared that both guilt and corruption have spread to all Adam's offspring, being transmitted from parent to child.[38] One of Calvin's followers, James Arminius (1560-1609) softened the seemingly harsh view of Reformed theology. To do so, Arminius reasserted the semi-Pelagian position that Adam's offspring do not share in the guilt of the sin of our first father. Arminius added a new dimension, however. He theorized that present to the individual is a special, "prevenient" grace from God. Prevenient grace makes it possible for us to overcome our inherited depravity. The Dutch

---

34. For this conclusion, see ibid., 364.

35. Berkhof, *Systematic Theology*, 244.

36. For a summary of Augustine's position and citations of primary references, see Kelly, *Early Christian Doctrines*, 363-66.

37. Berkhof, *Systematic Theology*, 245.

38. John Calvin, *Institutes of the Christian Religion* 2.1.5-7, in Library of Christian Classics volumes 20-21, trans. Ford Lewis Battles, ed. John T. McNeill (Philadelphia: Westminster, 1960), 1:246-50.

thinker wrote: "It is this grace which operates on the mind, the affections, and the will; which infuses good thoughts into the mind, inspires good desires into the affections, and bends the will to carry into execution good thoughts and good desires."[39] Above all, prevenient grace "commences salvation, promotes it, and perfects and comsummates it."[40]

It was left to a later generation of Calvinist theologians, including the English Puritans, however, to engage in a more definitive discussion of this question. The debate focused on the term "imputation."[41] Basically, this broad theological word finds its center in the mystery of the presence of sin in us and the working of the atonement: How does God see us as guilty in Adam and righteous in Christ? The Latin verb from which the English term is derived, *imputare*, has legal or forensic roots and means literally "to charge to one's account." In the context of original sin, imputation raises the question of how God justly charges Adam's guilt to our account.

According to the Augustinian idea of natural headship, God does not impute Adam's guilt to us, for each human sinned in Adam. Our guilt, therefore, is our own. The Reformed thinkers, however, including the architects of the Westminster Confession of Faith, tended to follow the federal, rather than the natural headship model, which views Adam as our representative in the covenant of works.

Certain theologians argued that the covenantal theory entailed a corollary—"immediate imputation." God imputed or laid to the charge of all Adam's offspring immediately—that is, directly and without any other considerations—both Adam's sin and his guilt. We may summarize what theologians assert by the phrase "immediate imputation" by the simple syllogism: Adam sinned; therefore, all are guilty.

---

39. James Arminius, "Letter to Hippolytus a Collibus 4, in *The Writings of James Arminius*, trans. James Nichols and W. R. Bagnall, three volumes (Grand Rapids: Baker, 1956), 2:472.

40. Ibid., 2:473. See also Arminius, "Apology or Defence" 8, in *The Writings of James Arminius*, 1:299-301. For a restatement of the Arminian view, see H. Orton Wiley, *Christian Theology*, three volumes (Kansas City, Mo.: Beacon Hill, 1952), 2:356-57.

41. For a description of the term itself, see Robert K. Johnston, "Imputation," in the *Evangelical Dictionary of Theology*, ed. Walter A. Elwell (Grand Rapids: Baker, 1984), 554-55.

Earlier the semi-Pelagians sought to mitigate the perceived harshness of Augustinianism and Arminius sought to do likewise with Calvinism. Now other Reformed theologians, beginning with the French thinker Josue De La Place (1596-1655)—known as Placeus—but including leading New England theologians such as Samuel Hopkins, Timothy Dwight, and Nathanael Emmons,[42] attempted to soften the blow of Reformed theology. In place of immediate imputation they offered a more moderate position, known as mediate imputation. Proponents agreed with the immediate imputationists that because of Adam's fall sinfulness or depravity is transferred to his children, and this through natural propagation. They also agreed that God imputed guilt to the account of each person. But they differed in their understanding of the grounds for the imputation of guilt. We are not guilty for Adam's sin; rather, God imputes guilt to us because of the presence of depravity in us. Hence, the mediate imputationists added a step in the imputation syllogism: Adam sinned; therefore, all are depraved; therefore, all are guilty.

Some theologians, however, especially the "New School" Calvinists in nineteenth century North America,[43] found even this position too harsh. Consequently, they attempted to soften it further with the addition of one more line in the syllogism. They agreed with the mediate imputationists that each person inherits the disposition to sin as a consequence of Adam's sin. The New School theologians, however, argued that the presence of depravity is not itself the ground for God's imputation of guilt to our account. Rather, the evil disposition leads to sin once the individual becomes morally conscious or makes moral choices. And it is this personal sin—rather than either Adam's sin or the presence of the sinful disposition itself—which constitutes us guilty before God. The syllogism had become more complex: Adam sinned; therefore, all are depraved; therefore, all sin; therefore, all are guilty.

Despite heroic salvaging efforts such as those of the New School Calvinists, ideas of imputation fell out of favor in the nineteenth cen-

---

42. Hoekema, *Created in God's Image*, 156.

43. For a sketch of this viewpoint, see Augustus Hopkins Strong, *Systematic Theology*, three volumes (Philadelphia: Griffith and Rowland, 1907), 2:606-607.

tury. In fact, liberalism had little sympathy for the entire Augustini-an-Reformed understanding of original sin. In the 1900s, however, thinkers resurrected the older tradition, albeit as those who were chastened by the impact of the liberal critique.

Neo-orthodox theologians, for example, attempted to develop a new concept of original sin which they thought remained true to the biblical emphasis on human sin while avoiding the scholasticism that the doctrine had fallen into since Augustine.[44] By means of the symbolic interpretation of Adam and the fall (discussed above), they affirmed the fall but avoided the question of inherited guilt and corruption. In postulating that each human begins in the state of Adam and then experiences a personal fall, these thinkers understood original sin as the universal human tendency to choose wrongly.

The biblical basis for the Reformed view. As this historical survey indicates, original sin poses the crucial theological question of the relationship between sin, depravity, and guilt. The dominant position in the Reformed tradition postulates that all Adam's offspring inherit both a depraved nature (the pollution of sin) and actual guilt. We therefore must look more closely at the biblical basis for this view. Our focus will be on Ephesians 2:3 and Romans 5:12-21, the texts which have traditionally formed the foundation for the link between original sin and inherited guilt.

(1) First, we explore Paul's statement concerning this matter which he wrote to the Ephesians. The translation found in the New International Version reflects the classic Reformed interpretation: "Like the rest, we were by nature objects of wrath" (Eph. 2:3b). More succinctly stated, Paul's point appears to be that as Adam's offspring we are from birth under the wrath of God, because of the guilt we have inherited from Adam. Is this indeed the correct rendering of the sentence?

Two phrases are significant in exegeting this verse, "by nature" and "children of wrath." Lying behind the English "by nature" is the Greek noun *phusei*, which here is in the instrumental case (instrumental of means). In his epistles, Paul uses *phusis* 11 times (comprising 11 of the 13 New Testament occurrences of this word). He

---

44. See, for example, Niebuhr, *The Nature and Destiny of Man*, 1:241-64.

sometimes employs the term to refer to nature itself, understood as the created order (1 Cor. 11:14). Elsewhere *phusis* means "what is natural" (Rom. 11:21, 24) or "what properly belongs to something" (Gal. 2:15; 4:8). As an extension of this meaning, in Ephesians 2:3, "by nature" suggests a state that has become a natural part of our existence or that is now "naturally" our situation.

What now belongs to us "by nature"? Paul declares, We are by nature "children of wrath" (Greek: *tekna orges*). There are two major possibilities concerning the meaning of this phrase. It may declare that we are "under the wrath of God," suggesting that Paul is here teaching the concept of original guilt. Or the phrase may be translated "wrathful persons" ("persons characterized by wrath"). So interpreted, Paul would thereby be setting forth a hallmark of human character.

The decision between the two interpretations rests largely with the word *teknon*. According to both the Bauer and Thayer lexicons this term has a special use when it occurs with abstract nouns.[45] In such cases *teknon* with the abstract noun may reflect a typical Hebraism, or Hebrew way of describing people, which would fit well with the Hebrew background of the author. In fact, Bauer lists this verse as one example of a Hebraism, together with "children of light" (Eph. 5:8) and "children of wisdom" (Matt. 11:19). In the latter two cases, *teknon* carries the idea of "persons characterized by...." If this phrase is indeed a Hebraism it could very well be translated "wrathful children," i.e., "persons who are characterized by wrath."[46]

Several further contextual considerations support the translation of *tekna orges* as "wrathful persons." Paul does not specifically declare here that *God's* wrath is directed toward human beings; instead, the concept of the divine wrath must be imported into the text. Likewise, the context of the verse focuses on *activities* of human beings and not their fate: "All of us also lived among them at one time, grat-

---

45. Walter Bauer, *A Greek-English Lexicon of the New Testament and Other Early Christian Literature*, trans. William F. Arndt and F. Wilbur Gingrich (Chicago: University of Chicago Press, 1957), 816; Joseph Henry Thayer, *A Greek-English Lexicon of the New Testament*, corrected edition (1889; Wheaton, Ill.: Evangel Publishing Co., 1974), 618.

46. Some may want to cite Romans 9:22 as a counter example. However, the genitive construction here is not parallel to Ephesians 2:3, for Paul does not use *tekna orges*, but *steue orges*.

ifying the cravings of our sinful nature and following its desires and thoughts." Activities in which human beings engage—"walked," "followed," "lived"—form the ground for Paul's conclusion, "Like the rest we were by nature children of wrath." In fact, apart from the phrase in question, the fate of human beings or our standing before God is nowhere mentioned in the context. Finally, whenever *teknon* occurs in the New Testament in conjunction with an abstract noun, the construction never implies the idea of being liable to the fate expressed in the abstract noun. If *tekna orges* here means we are the objects of the divine wrath, then this occurrence of the construction stands as an exception to its normal usage.

We conclude, therefore, that Paul may not be declaring that Adam's offspring are guilty because of his sin. Rather, he may simply be describing what characterizes us in our sinful state of affairs, namely, that we are wrathful people. Whatever may be the final outcome of exegetical considerations of this verse, however, its exact meaning is sufficiently in doubt to render it a fragile foundation for a doctrine of inherited guilt.

(2) Perhaps the most important foundational text for the idea of inherited guilt is Romans 5:12-21. Here, proponents argue, Paul is clearly asserting that all Adam's offspring are somehow guilty because of his sin.

We must acknowledge that this passage is not easy to exegete. The interpretive task is compounded by the fact that Paul never finishes the sentence he starts in verse 12. As the opening conjunction, "therefore" suggests, he begins with the intent of summarizing the argument of the opening chapters of the book: "Therefore, just as sin entered the world through one man, and death through sin, and in this way death came to all men because all sinned—" (v. 12). But after beginning in this manner, Paul digresses from the main theme in order to elaborate the point that death did indeed come to all persons. And he never returns to the exact spot from which the digression began.

Nevertheless, we can conclude from what follows in the text that Paul focuses on a comparison of the results of Adam's work with the results of Christ's as a way of summarizing the opening sections of the book. In the first three chapters Paul describes the universal sin-fulness of humankind. The description of the universality of sin leads to Paul's second point, the divine solution to our sin problem. In chapter five, Paul associates these two themes with two persons—Adam, whose disobedience brought sin into the world, and Christ, whose obedience makes righteousness available. Paul's point, then, is that Adam and Christ are similar because the results of their actions affect us. Adam's action resulted in the presence of sin and death in the world, whereas Christ's resulted in the presence of righteousness and life.

In our attempt to understand this passage, we must keep in mind that Paul does not view humankind as specific individuals who make choices which determine their destiny. Rather in keeping with the Hebraic mindset he presents humanity as a single entity, a solid mass as it were. Into this mass of humanity Adam's act injected sin as a power or force hostile to God, which in turn brings the reign of death. Christ's obedience, in contrast, injected righteousness as a power and with it the reign of life.

The text raises the question: How does the work of Adam (and of Christ) affect the individual? Clearly present is the idea that with Adam's sin came the principle that sin brings death. As this principle became true for Adam, so it is true for all human beings. But Paul posits a stronger connection between Adam and his offspring. He declares that just as the effects of the life which resulted from Christ's obedience extend beyond Jesus so also the affects of the death which resulted from Adam's sin move beyond Adam himself.

Consequently, the question remains: How do we participate in the results of the work of each? Despite the urgency of the query, we must conclude that in Romans 5:12-21 Paul simply does not address it. The Apostle asserts that Adam's sin leads to all becoming sinners, just as Christ's obedience leads to righteousness. In neither case, however, does he describe how this transpires. Just as he leaves unanswered the question as to how we participate in the righteousness made available by Christ, so also he does not declare how we are implicated in the results of Adam's transgression. In fact, if we were to understand Paul as declaring that we all suffer Adam's guilt apart from our own personal involvement in his sin, then parallelism would demand that we also see his reference to Christ's work as including all humankind in the acquittal he makes operative in the human realm. If Adam's guilt is imputed to all, then fairness demands that Christ's righteousness be as well.

What is not addressed here, however, finds answer elsewhere in the epistle. The essence of the Pauline gospel, which is articulated especially in the second section of the epistle, is the declaration that God bestows righteousness on the one who is united to Christ in faith. Similarly, in the opening chapters of the Book of Romans Paul explains how we participate in the death that has its genesis in Adam: We come under the power of death and condemnation through personal sin.

We conclude, then, that Romans 5:12-21, like Ephesians 2:3, does not clearly and unequivocally declare that all persons inherit guilt directly because of Adam's sin. The biblical case for original guilt is not strong.

The Reality of Original Sin

Our human experience is clear: Although we on occasion do what is right and indeed live in accordance with certain aspects of God's law, our human nature has been corrupted. The source of our sinful attitudes and actions is not merely the external environment; rather, they issue forth from the inner core of our being, from the human heart.

Original sin is the theological answer to this question. Since the first sin in the Garden, we find ourselves involved in a radical failure that encompasses our very nature. What is the source of the corrupt nature? Our experience confirms what Christian theology has declared for centuries: this corruption is not our doing, but comes to us. We inherit the depraved nature from our ancestors and ultimately from our first parents. Hence, the depraved nature comes to us in the same way that other basic traits do. We may say that it lies in our human gene pool. At the same time, however, we must add that our sinfulness is also derived in part socially: We teach each other to sin.

With this in view, we must include under the category of original sin the corruption in human nature as derived from Adam, that is, from our common inherited humanity. Our failure to measure up to God's design is not merely an external force but also an inherited part of each person. Each of us will and does sin, once we are in a position to reflect moral choices in action and thereby to act out what is present within our nature by heredity and socialization.

Original sin, however, does not directly entail guilt. The possession of this fallen nature alone does not bring condemnation. Rather than declaring that guilt is directly due to original sin, the biblical writers teach that God judges us according to our works (Jer. 17:9-10; Rom. 2:6). The great Judge renders his verdict not on the basis of our fallen nature, but because of our deeds, which we do as our depraved nature expresses itself in thought or overt action.

This understanding of original sin returns us to the concept of "openness to the world." As we have noted throughout our study of anthropology, humans are characterized by the restless quest to move beyond every specific form of the world. This quest points toward both our ultimate dependence on God and our special God-given destiny. As participants in the common human failure that began with Adam, we all miss the mark; wilfully or passively, we do not live in accordance with the goal of community that God has set before us. This failure is not merely one of our own doing, for it is a dimension of our common human inheritance.

Original sin raises the question: When do we begin to participate in the common human failure? The best response acknowledges that the potential for our involvement in the break-down of community is present in us already in infancy. Specifically, we find its roots in the ego-centricity and focus on the concern for self-survival which characterizes that stage of human life. Infants are largely unaware of anything outside of their own little world. They are ego-centric and self-absorbed, although at this stage egocentrism does not entail guilt.

What begins in innocency, however, can become malicious. Left unchecked it will prevent the development of healthy, God-honoring attitudes that balance personal independence and a sense of self-worth with a full awareness of our dependence on creation, each other, and ultimately the Creator. Hence, the self-absorption of infancy has the potential to develop into a community-destructive force within each of us—a depraved nature. Eventually this depraved nature expresses itself in moral choices that are either overly egotistical or overly self-abasing, and hence are displeasing to God. In this way, what ought to drive us to a quest for God and the fulfillment of our destiny to participate in the community of God degenerates into a search for a humanly devised substitute. We thereby miss the mark and suffer the consequences.

The Results of Sin: Our Human Situation

We, of course, have no direct contact with original sin. We have no experience of the first sin, nor are we cognizant of our own initial entry into its realm. Yet we are aware of our personal participation in sin as an outworking of our choices, attitudes, and actions. Consequently, we have some inkling of the terrible results of sin.

Our study of sin, therefore, concludes with an exploration of this experientially real dimension of our human situation. The presence of sin carries results for life now—results for our standing before God and for our existence in the world. We may use four metaphors—interpersonal relations (alienation), legal standing (condemnation), cosmic forces (enslavement), and personal ability (depravity)—to view the human situation before God and in the world as a consequence of sin.

Alienation

As our use of "community" as an integrative motif for systematic theology suggests, the fundamental metaphor by means of which we may understand the results of sin is interpersonal relations. God designed us to enter into relations with others—to participate in the community of God. The divine intention is that we live in harmony with creation, that we enjoy fellowship with one another, and that we participate in the divine life. Through community, we in turn find our identity as children of God.

Sin, however, is the failure to live according to this design. In fact, the fundamental result of sin is the loss of community. This loss occurs in all the dimensions of harmonious existence God intends for us.

The destruction of community occurs on the level of our relationship to creation. As we noted earlier, sin means that we no longer live in harmony with the "garden" in which the Creator placed us. Designed to enjoy fellowship with the rest of God's good creation, we now live in alienation from the natural world around us. Rather than seeing ourselves as creative beings under God, we seek to be the creator, to control nature and enslave it to serve us. We no longer see the earth as an organic whole which we serve on God's behalf. Rather, in our insatiable but misguided quest for a "home," we view the earth as the raw material for our transforming activity.

Furthermore, our sin has destructive influences on our surroundings. Persons placed in creation to reflect the character of God no longer show forth the image of the Creator. Consequently, creation suffers. As Paul declares, creation itself now exists—yea, groans—under the bondage caused by human sin, awaiting the new creation that will mark the consummation of God's program (Rom. 8:19-22).

The loss of community likewise operates on the interpersonal level, for sin severs relationships to others. Although we are designed to enjoy wholesome, enriching fellowship with each other, we now find ourselves exploiting and being exploited. Our loss of community expresses itself as we jostle with each other for power, influence, and prominence, or as we allow ourselves to be robbed of our dignity and sense of worth. In short, sin alienates us from each other.

Above all, sin functions at the level of our relationship to God. Being the destroyer of community, sin gives birth to alienation from God. Designed to be God's friends, even God's children, our sin leads us to live as enemies of God (e.g., Romans 5:10a). Rather than enjoying the presence of God, we flee. We live in fear, presuming that God is hostile toward us, although we are in fact the hostile ones and project our hostility on God. Despite our infinite dependence, we run from the only one who can overcome our fear, brokenness, and hostility, the one who can fulfill our deepest needs.

Sin, therefore, destroys the community God intends for his creation. And we are the responsible persons. Because of the unmistakable loss of community, we do not fulfill God's design for us. Consequently, we are alienated from our own true selves. We simply are not who we are meant to be.

Condemnation

We may also describe the reality of sin in our lives by appeal to a legal metaphor. Because of sin we stand condemned before a righteous God. Condemnation refers to the sentence or judgment which hangs over us in our sin. Designed by God to be righteous—to mirror his own holy character—we live in sin. As our fallen nature works its way in our actions, we commit sins. Therefore, we stand guilty before our Creator (John 3:18).

We do not experience the full legal outworking of sin in this life. The sentence that hovers over us remains unexecuted, except for the downward spiral which sin inaugurates in our lives (Rom. 1:18-32). One day, however, this will change. At the final judgment the righteous Judge will pronounce his verdict, and all guilty human beings will be banished from his presence (Rev. 20:11-15; 40). Despite appearances to the contrary, we are, therefore, headed for hell, which is but the natural outworking of our current failure to live in accordance with God's intention. In this sense, we may affirm that even now sin leads to condemnation.

The use of the term "condemnation" to refer to the awful results of sin raises the question of possible exceptions. Are all humans without exception (save those redeemed by Christ) condemned? Or are there special cases, certain persons who do not stand under this general declaration? Specifically, given that concepts such as condemnation apply to persons who follow the normal course of human development, do those who have not so developed—such as infants and the severely mentally-retarded—stand apart from this verdict?

In seeking a response to this question, we must recall that the eschatological judgment will bring to light primarily our deeds. Insofar as the Holy Spirit will root out our depravity, our nature comes under divine judgment. But only our works will form the basis for the final verdict. Consequently, although all persons inherit a sinful disposition, only those who have given expression to the fallen nature through wrong moral choices stand under condemnation. The sentence falls only on those whose deeds mark them as guilty. On this basis, we conclude that persons who do not develop the moral potential do not fall under the eternal condemnation of the righteous God.

Our conclusion concerning those who have not yet developed to the point of making moral choices is in keeping with Jesus' declaration that the kingdom of God belongs to children (Matt. 18:1-14; 19:14).

This thesis is confirmed by indications in the Bible that normal human development includes a transition from innocency to responsibility and hence to potential judgment. Somewhere in childhood we move from a stage in which our actions are not deemed morally accountable to the responsibility of acting as moral agents. In short, we cross a point which some refer to as the "age of accountability."

For example, upon arriving at the borders of Canaan, the Israelites concluded that they could not conquer the land. God declared that those responsible for this rebellious decision would not enter into the promised land. However, persons under twenty years of age did not fall under this condemnation. Thus, God judged competent adults for the action of the people, whereas he deemed their children innocent (See Deut. 1:39; Num. 14:29-31). Isaiah's prophecy of the sign of Immanuel carries a similar implication. In speaking about the child who will be born to the young woman the prophet says,

> He will eat curds and honey when he knows enough to reject the wrong and choose the right. But before the boy knows enough to reject the wrong and choose the right, the land of the two kings you dread will be laid waste (Isa. 7:15-16).

One proponent of the concept of an age of accountability was the Baptist theologian Augustus Hopkins Strong. He acknowledged that infants are in a state of sin and therefore need to be regenerated. At the same time, they are guilty of no actual sin. Consequently, Strong concluded that those who die in infancy "are the object of special divine compassion and care, and through the grace of Christ are certain of salvation."[47]

---

47. Strong, *Systematic Theology*, 2:661.

Enslavement

We may also express the biblical message concerning the effects of sin as a struggle of cosmic forces. Viewed in this context, sin is an alien, evil force that holds us in its grasp. It is a cosmic power that enslaves its prey.

The biblical term "enslavement" harkens back to the first century practice of slavery. Just as conquering armies enslaved subjected peoples, so also we find ourselves slaves to a hostile, foreign force called sin. No longer able to exercise choice, we discover that we must obey sin, for it exercises power over us.

Closely connected with this cosmic metaphor of sin is the Reformation idea of the "bondage of the will." To understand what Luther and Calvin meant when they argued that the will is in bondage, we must differentiate between two viewpoints concerning the nature of moral freedom.

Generally we use as our model of moral freedom the experience of choosing that comes from everyday, mundane decision-making. In keeping with this model, we think of freedom as the ability to decide whether we will act and how we will act. Consequently, we picture ourselves as disinterested decision-makers, standing before decisions unencumbered by any overpowering inclination to decide in one direction or the other: "Should I wear my blue shirt or my brown one?" From this experience we extrapolate to the area of morality and use the same model of the disinterested decision-maker. Just as we decide as an uncoerced decision-maker which clothes to wear from among the various possibilities, so also we make free moral choices from among the alternatives.

As important as this model has been to the modern way of thinking, it is not the Reformers' concept of freedom.

An alternative understanding defines moral freedom as the ability to live in accordance with our destiny. The ideal of freedom, therefore, is not to become a neutral decision-maker, choosing from among the possibilities that confront us in the moment of decision. Rather, that model is but one specific instance of the modern myth of the autonomous self. Indeed, in the face of moral decisions, the choosing individual is never a neutral, autonomous self with respect to decisions. The choosing individual faces moral choice already predisposed. When the dynamic of moral decision is so understood, "freedom" means the release from the predisposition toward evil in order to be able choose the good.

The first model has some merit. It is indeed true that we stand before moral decisions with some degree of neutrality and objectivity. We do make choices, which are in some sense "free," that is, they are uncoerced decisions from among seemingly equally possible alternatives. There is, therefore, value in seeing decision-making in terms of the model of the "free" individual standing before alternatives and choosing as a neutral moral agent.

Yet we must also conclude that our supposedly neutral choices are limited. Our options are limited by outward influences and circumstances which narrow the range of possible actions or responses to a situation. In addition, our free actions are also limited by the inward disharmony—the propensity to sin—lying within our hearts. Only within these boundaries is choice even conceivable.

This limitation of choice is in part what the Reformers meant by the concept of the bondage of the will. But we may more readily understand this seemingly difficult concept when we consider its relationship to our fulfillment of the divine design. The opposite of the bondage of the will is the freedom of the will. In the context of the human destiny, this term means not merely the ability to choose from among options, but the ability to live in accordance with our design as given by God. Such freedom is exactly what we lack. As a result of sin, we are in bondage, for by our own strength we simply cannot live according to God's design (Isa. 64:6). All our lives we live under bondage to the power of sin which holds us in its grasp, even though we—like the Pharisees—might think we are free (John 8:333-34). Consequently, we must be set free from bondage in order to live out our God-given destiny.

Freedom, therefore, is God's gift bestowed on us though participation in community with Christ. As Jesus said, "If you hold to my teaching, you are really my disciples. Then you will know the truth, and the truth will set you free" (John 8:31-32).

Depravity

The final metaphor arises from human ability. In this context, sin results in depravity. Depravity is our human inability or powerlessness to remedy our dire situation.

The problem of sin is radical; it extends to the core of our being. It requires a radical cure, a cure that comes from outside us and goes to the core of our problem. If our human condition is to be altered, we require a power no less than God himself.

Critics often misunderstand the evangelical emphasis on depravity. The historical source of the concept was the Reformers' rejection of the teachings of the Roman Catholic Church concerning the effects of the fall. As we noted in the previous chapter, the medieval scholastics had concluded that the fall resulted in the loss of the likeness of God (the superadded gift which Adam enjoyed in the Garden), but not the marring of the image of God (our natural human powers, especially the power of reason). On the basis of the assumption that despite the fall our natural powers are fully operative, Thomas Aquinas argued that reason is capable of attaining a certain knowledge about God. Through unaided reason humans can come to understand that there is a creator and they can know various truths concerning what God as creator must be like. Nevertheless for Thomas the supernatural knowledge of God necessary for salvation lies beyond the ability of unaided reason, for it is known only by supernatural revelation.

The Reformers rejected the viewpoint of the scholastics, which they saw as based on the mistaken disjuncture between the likeness and the image of God. The Reformers asserted that the fall marred the divine image, that is, that the effects of sin extend to all dimensions of human existence. The natural human powers are operative, but they are darkened by sin. Even reason falls under sin's power, and consequently it can lead us astray. Because all our powers are subjected to sin, the fall leaves us unable to attain knowledge of God by unaided human effort. This predicament is what the Reformers meant by "total depravity." If knowledge of God and salvation from sin is to come, it must come from God.

This then is our predicament. Created by God, we are good. We are designed for community and intended to reflect the character of the triune Creator. But we are caught in a failure that has characterized human existence from the beginning. Our failure to reflect the community of God is a radical problem, for it infects even the core of our being. Only the radical activity of God can overcome our alienation, condemnation, enslavement, and depravity. Before exploring God's radical intervention, we must turn our attention to a final dimension of our human existence in the world, namely, to our experience of the presence of other moral agents, a topic discussed under the theological heading of angelology.

Our Spiritual Co-Creatures

Are not all angels ministering spirits sent to serve those who will inherit salvation? (Heb. 1:14)

Outline

Biblical faith asserts that we are not alone in the universe. Our world is populated by other life forms, of course. In addition to the physical creatures, the biblical authors indicate that spiritual realities also participate in God's created realm. Like humans, these realities are moral agents, responsible to God to fulfill a divinely given mandate.

Traditionally, Christian theologians speak of these spiritual realities under the broader rubric of angelology. Some thinkers add demonology as a separate category. In that both classes share certain common characteristics, we will not completely separate the two. Rather, we will view angels and demons under the broader concept of "spiritual realities," or angelology. At the same time, we acknowledge the important moral difference between the two: Angels are the good servants of God, whereas demons have set themselves against the Creator.

Classical theologies tend to separate the discussion of angels and demons from the doctrine of humanity. However, the connection between these spiritual realities and human affairs is so great that angelology can be best delineated as we find its proper context within anthropology. For this reason, we place our discussion of angelology as the final chapter in the doctrine of humanity.

Traditional treatments of angelology focus on the nature of these realities viewed as actual beings. Our discussion therefore must begin here. But a contemporary angelology cannot merely assert that angels and demons form a class of beings who seek to affect us as individuals. Rather, the doctrine must speak as well about the more corporate connection between the spirit world and human existence. We accomplish this through a discussion of "structures of existence." The chapter then concludes by employing the findings of these sections as a foundation for dealing with the important matter of superstition.

The Nature of the Spiritual Realities

The Scriptures, especially the post-exilic books of the Old Testament and the New Testament writings, simply assume the existence of spiritual beings. This is not surprising. During the era of history in which these documents were written such beings were an accepted part of the world view of the Near East. Angels and demons, therefore, play an integral role in the biblical drama. Thus mediated by the Bible, angelology came to be a topic within Christian theology. Exactly what are these spiritual realities? How are we to understand the nature and place of angels and demons within the world God has made?

We begin by looking at the changing fate of angelology in theological history. From that vantage we then can look back to the biblical theology that formed the original impetus for the systematic theological treatment of the topic.

Angelology in Christian Theology

Theologians have not been consistent in their interest in angelology. Nor have they afforded this study a consistent place in the systematic study of Christian doctrine.

The Middle Ages: speculative angelology. Although the church fathers occasionally spoke about spiritual beings, theological reflection on angels and demons reached its high point in the Middle Ages. In addition to the presence of supernatural, spiritual beings in the biblical writings, the interest of medieval theologians in these realities was sparked by popular religious convictions in which the spirit world played an important role. Medieval Christians firmly believed in the reality of spiritual beings, especially demons. These Christians feared demons whom they saw as powerful agents present everywhere in the world. They were concerned with incantations and other rituals that could render them ineffective. Even church buildings could not provide total sanctuary unencumbered by the demonic. Hence, the great gothic cathedrals housed carvings of demons, which haunted the seats in the choir and served as gargoyles on the roofs.

The medieval scholastics probed the intricacies of angelic and demonic life. Although the questions they raised appear strange today, their queries cloaked important considerations concerning the relationship of this class of beings to the space-time continuum which is a part of human existence.

The schoolmen asked whether angels could be in two places at the same time.[1] Thereby they raised the issue concerning the nature of angels as created, yet non-material realities. As created beings are they limited with respect to space and time—localized in the manner that humans are? Or as spiritual beings, do they share in the omnipresence of God?

The medieval theologians also supposedly speculated as to how many angels can stand on the point of a needle. Lying behind this seemingly nonsensical question was an important issue concerning the relationship of pure spiritual creatures to space: Are such beings spacial creatures—beings who despite their non-material substance displace space as humans do? Or are they more like God, who as a spiritual being does not have spacial dimensions?[2]

---

1. Thomas Aquinas answered this question in the negative. See, Thomas Aquinas, *Summa Theologica* 1.52.3, trans. Fathers of the English Dominican Province, revised Daniel J. Sullivan, volume 19 of the *Great Books of the Western World,* ed. Robert Maynard Hutchins (Chicago: Encyclopedia Britannica, 1952), 19:280.

2. See, ibid. 1.52.1-2 [278-80].

The theologians also inquired concerning the length of the interval between the creation of the angels and the fall of some of them into sin.[3] (Thomas Aquinas favored the opinion that the devil sinned "at once after the first instant of his creation."[4]) This question asks about the goodness of these beings as created by God. It also raises the matter of their deliberative powers: Do their thinking and willing transpire in time? That is, do these activities require a length of time, as do ours? Or like God, do they transpire in eternity apart from the passing of time?

By debating these issues, the scholastics developed a highly sophisticated angelology, which they gave a specific role and place in the wider medieval theology.

The Reformation: biblical angelology. The Reformers continued the medieval inclusion of angelology within the corpus of systematic theology. However, their outlook toward this topic differed greatly from that evidenced by the probings of their scholastic forebears. Reformation theologians tended to eschew the more philosophically inclined speculations of the Middle Ages and to confine their work to systematizing the biblical material concerning angels and demons.

John Calvin stands as an example of the Scripture-centered approach of Protestant thinkers. In his *Institutes* he offered a simple, biblically oriented definition of angels. They are "'ministering spirits' [Heb. 1:14], whose service God uses for the protection of his own, and through whom he both dispenses his benefits among men and also carries out his remaining works."[5] The Geneva reformer clearly placed Satan and the demons under divine control.[6] Consequently, they serve God's good purposes, and we are assured of victory over them "because God bends the unclean spirit hither and thither at will, he so governs their activity that they exercise believers in combat...yet they never vanquish or crush them."[7] In this

---

3. See, ibid. 1.62.5, 1.63.4-6 [321, 328-31].

4. Ibid. 1.63.6 [331].

5. John Calvin, *Institutes of the Christian Religion* 1.14.9, in *Library of Christian Classics* volumes 20-21, trans. Ford Lewis Battles, ed. John T. McNeill (Philadelphia: Westminster, 1960), 20:169.

6. Ibid. 1.14.17 [175-76].

7. Ibid. 1.14.18 [176].

manner, Calvin avoided the medieval interest in the demonic. The hosts of darkness, he asserted, act only with the consent of God and only within the broader context of God's program. In fact, they exist for our sakes. They serve as the tools of God to assist believers in the process of sanctification, helping us to become strong and mature.

The Enlightenment: rejection of angelology. Beginning with the Enlightenment, both the ornate philosophical speculation of the Middle Ages and the unadorned biblical summarization of the Reformers collapsed. The inclusion of angelology in the systematic-theological corpus characteristic of the older thinkers gave way to its rejection. Angels became an embarrassment to Christian theologians who sought to articulate the faith in an age of science and rationalism. The idea that the universe was populated by spiritual entities seemed out of place in a world in which what was real was defined solely by the scientific method. As Bernard Ramm aptly summarized, in such a climate angels "seem to intrude upon the scene like the unexpected visit of the country relatives to their rich city kinsfolk."[8]

Enlightenment thinkers and scientists, therefore, worked together to eliminate spiritual beings from the Western cosmology. In this task they had at their disposal a powerful tool, Ockham's razor. Attributed to the medieval thinker William of Ockham, although never quite stated in his writings, this methodological dictum asserted that "entities are not to be multiplied beyond necessity."[9] According to this approach, in explaining phenomena we should employ no more principles than are necessary, accepting the simplest hypothesis which can explain the data. With Ockham's razor in hand, Enlightenment rationalists shaved off the embarrassing whiskers of supernatural beings from the modern cosmology.

Friedrich Schleiermacher encapsulated the dilemma which angelology posed for the modern theologian. The belief in angels was undeniably part of the Christian tradition; yet in the modern world it

---

8. Bernard Ramm, "Angels," in *Basic Christian Doctrines*, ed. Carl F. H. Henry (New York: Holt, Rinehart and Winston, 1962), 65.

9. "Ockham's Razor," in the *Dictionary of Philosophy and Religion*, ed. William L. Reese (Atlantic Highlands, N.J.: Humanities Press, 1980), 399. Erickson offers this definition of the concept: "no more concepts ought to be introduced than are necessary to account for the phenomena." Millard J. Erickson, *Christian Theology*, three volumes (Grand Rapids: Baker, 1983), 1:167.

was humiliatingly "medieval." As a way of resolving the impasse, the nineteenth century German thinker asserted that while angels may possibly exist, they are dispensable, for the question of their existence "ought to have no influence upon our conduct.[10] Consequently, he concluded: "for the actual province of Dogmatics the subject remains wholly problematic, and none but a private and liturgical use of this conception is to be recognized."[11]

The Enlightenment undermining of angelology was, of course, paralleled by the loss of place for demons. Jeffry Russell summarizes the situation: "Generations of socially oriented theologians dismissed the Devil and the demons as superstitious relics of little importance to the Christian message."[12]

Contemporary theology: a renewed interest. The mid- to late-twentieth century, however, brought an unexpected reemergence of angelology. Theologians who had simply passed over the discussion of spiritual realities as no longer significant suddenly discovered that they must take this forgotten aspect of the Christian tradition with renewed seriousness.

One important source fueling the renewal of the doctrine of angels and demons has been increased *contact with non-Western societies* which have never discarded concepts pertaining to the spirit world. But not to be overlooked is the importance in this regard of popular culture in our society, which has witnessed a rebirth of interest in spiritual realities.

The popular curiosity was sparked in part by speculation beginning in the 1960s concerning the possibility of other intelligent life in the universe. Popularizers such as Erich von Daniken built on the burgeoning phenomenon of unidentified flying objects, advancing the postulate that the ancient myths and stories of angels were the residue of human encounters with "God's from outer space," that is, with visitations from extra-terrestrial intelligent life.[13]

---

10. Friedrich Schleiermacher, *The Christian Faith*, ed. H. R. MacKintosh and J. S. Stewart (Edinburgh: T. & T. Clark, n.d.), 159.

11. Ibid., 160.

12. Jeffry B. Russell, *The Devil: Perceptions of Evil from Antiquity to Primitive Christianity* (Ithaca, NY/London: Cornell University Press, 1977), 222.

13. See, Erich von Daniken, *Chariots of the Gods?*, trans. Michael Heron (New York: Bantam Books, 1971); *Gods from Outer Space*, trans. Michael Heron (New York: Bantam, 1972); *The Gold of the Gods*, trans. Michael Heron (New York: G. P. Putnam's Sons, 1973).

Whereas von Daniken and his colleagues were convinced of the presence among us of angelic beings, others in popular culture focused on the reality of the demonic. Important in this context has been the rapid increase of practices which are either explicitly occult or which merely find their genesis in non-rationalistic beliefs but which nevertheless mark the reemergence of the demonic into our vocabulary. Whether by reading their daily horoscope or by more consequential practices such as participation in seances, fortune-telling, witchcraft, or satanic worship, people who might otherwise appear to have no religious orientation give evidence to belief in the power of supernatural realities.

Just when it seemed that rationalism and science had exorcised cosmic powers from the Western world view, therefore, spiritual beings have returned through the back door. They have been reincarnated by the *contemporary quest for supernatural experiences* and for supernatural power among the children of the scientific revolution. Contemporary theologians are discovering that we cannot ignore these developments. Rather, we must become mindful of the importance of categories we thought were discarded in the Enlightenment.

In addition to pressure from popular culture, angelology has reemerged in our theological vocabulary by means of another route, namely, through *existentialist theology*. Especially important for existentialism is the concept of the demonic. The use of this category dates to the "father of modern existentialism," the nineteenth-century thinker Søren Kierkegaard. The melancholy Dane appealed to the idea of the demonic as a means whereby to interpret the existential situation of the human person.[14]

Perhaps no theologian in the twentieth century has explored angelology in general and the concept of the demonic in particular in greater depth than has Paul Tillich. In his *Systematic Theology* this heir of Kierkegaard describes angels as "powers of being":

---

14. See, Søren Kierkegaard, *The Concept of Dread*, trans. Walter Lowrie (Princeton, N.J.: Princeton University Press, 1957), 105-21.

> In our terminology we can say that the angels are concrete-poetic symbols of the structures or powers of being. They are not beings but participate in everything that is.[15]

The demonic, in turn, refers to those structures both in individual and social life that claim for themselves an ultimacy they do not possess. Reminiscent of the thinking of Kierkegaard, Tillich asserts that in making such a claim to ultimacy, these structures cause human beings to confuse natural self-affirmation with destructive self-elevation.[16]

Recent developments in popular culture and theology invite us to read with a new openness the references to spiritual realities we find in the pages of the Bible.

A Biblical Theology of Angels

The world view of antiquity—including that of the biblical writers—had no difficulty making room in the universe for the presence of immaterial or spiritual beings. The various references to these realities in the Bible provide a picture.

Like other inhabitants of the universe, spiritual beings are God's creatures. Therefore, they are not equal to God. Although they differ from humans in that they are not material beings, they nevertheless have the powers of will and reason. In addition, they are moral beings who engage in actions which are either right or wrong. The basic purpose of the spiritual beings is rendering service to God, whether in praising him or in ministering on his behalf in the realm of human affairs.

Some spiritual beings fulfill their God-given role; these are the angels of God. The biblical authors suggest that their number is great (Matt. 26:53 and Rev. 5:11) and even that they are grouped into classes such as cherubim, seraphim, and archangels. Other spiritual beings, however, have chosen not to act in accordance with the divine purpose. These are the demons, whose chief is Satan.

---

15. Paul Tillich, *Systematic Theology*, three volumes (Chicago: University of Chicago Press, 1951), 1:260.
16. Ibid., 1:49,222; 2:51.

With this brief overview in mind, we may now look more closely at what the biblical authors say about angels.

Definition. References to angels pervade the Bible. The English word "angel" is actually a transliteration of the Greek *angelos*, which the Septuagint employs to translate the Hebrew *mal<ak*. Yet we must be cautious not to assume that every occurrence of these words marks a reference to spiritual beings. On the contrary, both *angelos* and *mal<ak* are broader in meaning. Rather than referring inherently to spiritual beings, these terms mean simply "messenger." Consequently, they can refer to human messengers as sent by another— whether by a human or God—with a special commission to fulfill.

The Old Testament writers occasionally refer to both prophets (Haggai 1:13; Isa. 44:26; 2 Chron. 36:15) and priests (Mal. 2:7; Eccl. 5:6) as *mal'akim*. Similarly, in the New Testament John the Baptist as the one who fulfilled Old Testament prophecy (Mark 1:2; Matt. 11:10), the envoys John sent to Jesus (Luke 7:24), the messengers Jesus dispatched to Samaria (Luke 9:52), and the Israelite spies harbored by Rahab (James 2:25) are all *angeloi*. Despite this broader meaning, however, most occurrences of each term have in view a heavenly being charged by God with some commission.

Angels in the Old Testament. Spiritual beings are present and play a role throughout the Scriptures. Yet, the documents suggest that the understanding of the biblical community concerning angels underwent a definite development from one era to the next during the time the Bible was written.

The foundations for an emerging angelology lie early in Hebrew history. This is evidenced by the presence—albeit subdued—of references to angels in the pre-exilic Hebrew writings. The original model for the idea of angelic hosts may have been the ranks of an imperial army or more likely the attendants belonging to a great royal court.[17] In Hebrew understanding, the courts of earthly monarchs pointed toward the heavenly court of the divine Sovereign. Therefore, just as an entourage of servants surrounded earthly rulers, so also the divine Ruler must have his consort of heavenly beings.

---

17. Elaine Pagels, "The Social History of Satan, the 'Intimate Enemy': A Preliminary Sketch," *Harvard Theological Review* 84/2 (1991): 106.

As the entourage of God the heavenly beings fulfilled various functions. Their duties included offering praise and rendering service to their Monarch (Isa. 6:1-8). But they also assisted God in doing his bidding in governing the world (1 Kings 22:19). Hence, they stood ready to be dispatched to protect God's earthly people (2 Kings 6:17) or to carry out his judgments.

Also important to the development of Old Testament angelology was the Hebrew struggle against polytheism. One means the ancient people of God utilized in their attempt to set forth the single sovereignty of Yahweh in the context of competing tribal gods was to add the gods of the nations to the entourage of the one and only God. Thus, the Hebrews viewed the foreign gods as subordinate to Yahweh and accountable to him.[18] And Yahweh, in turn, was unique among the gods which were simply his heavenly beings:

> For who in the skies above can compare with the LORD?
> Who is like the LORD among the heavenly beings?
> In the council of the holy ones God is greatly feared;
> he is more awesome than all who surround him
> (Ps. 89:6-7).

Specially noteworthy in the historical pre-exilic literature is a specific figure—the angel of Yahweh. This being is generally mentioned in distinction from other angels. The angel of Yahweh is the divine messenger par excellence, for he is the one supremely sent by God with a commission to fulfill. At the same time, the angel of Yahweh is not just a messenger, but embodies or personifies Yahweh's assistance to Israel. In fact, the texts often tie the angel of Yahweh closely to Yahweh—even being God as he enters into human apperception.[19] As a result of this association, humans who witness the appearance of the angel of Yahweh often cry out, "I have seen God and still live." This phenomenon led certain theologians, especially Protestant scholastics, to construct a bridge between the angel of

---

18. G. B. Caird, *Principalities and Powers* (Oxford: Clarendon, 1956), 2, 6; D. S. Russell, *The Method and Message of Jewish Apocalyptic* (Philadelphia: Westminster, 1964), 236.

19. Gerhard von Rad, "Angelos," in the *Theological Dictionary of the New Testament*, ed. Gerhard Kittel, trans. Geoffery W. Bromiley (Grand Rapids: Eerdmans, 1964), 1:77.

Yahweh and Christ, even concluding that references to this angel were Christophanies, appearances of the pre-incarnate Logos.[20]

Beginning with the exile and climaxing in the intertestamental period, the subdued recounting of encounters with heavenly messengers gave way to a developing Hebrew angelology. Heavenly beings now mediate divine communications to God's servants—the prophets and apocalyptic seers (Ezek. 40:3; Dan. 7:16; 10:14)—who in turn write down the messages. Further, these heavenly beings have personal names, such as Gabriel (Dan. 8:16) and Michael (Dan. 12:1). Not all of these beings are good. Rather, they are divided into opposing heavenly forces—good angels and evil demons—who engage in cosmic battle (Dan. 10:12-13;10:20-11:1). And these beings play a significant role in the unfolding of world history climaxing in the eschatological events (Dan. 12:1-4).

Angels in the New Testament. These late Old Testament and intertestamental themes concerning angels undergo further enhancement in the New Testament era. Crucial in this development are the synoptic gospels, which account for 51 of the 175 New Testament occurrences of the term *angelos.*[21]

The gospels portray angels as active participants in the story of Jesus. This is, of course, theologically understandable. As the Son incarnate, Jesus is the presence of God and the mediator of God's lordship. Wherever the divine Son is, we would expect to find present as well representatives of the heavenly court praising to God the Son (Rev. 5:11-12). For this reason, angels naturally are involved in heralding Jesus' birth (Luke 1:11-20, 26-38; 2:9-15), in ministering to him in his need at crucial points in his ministry (Luke 22:43), and in announcing his triumph over death at his resurrection (Matt. 28:5-7).

Angelic involvement in eschatological events is also a dominant theme of New Testament angelology. The synoptic gospels develop the apocalyptic theme that angels will accompany the Son of Man at

---

20. E.g., G. W. Hengstenberg, *The Christology of the Old Testament*, two volumes, reprint edition (Mac Dill AFB, FL: MacDonald, n.d.), 1:80-91.

21. Ingo Broer, "Angelos," in the *Exegetical Dictionary of the New Testament*, ed. Horst Balz and Gerhard Schneider, English translation (Grand Rapids: Eerdmans, 1990), 1:14.

his coming (Matt. 13:39; 25:31; Mark 8:38; 13:37; Luke 12:8; 2 Thess. 1:7). And the seer of Revelation describes the participation of angels in the events surrounding the great eschatological day, especially the judgments of God (Rev. 7:1; 8:1-9:21; 16:5).

Connected to this theme is the idea subtly presented in several New Testament texts that the angels are interested in the unfolding drama of salvation. Perhaps angelic interest in the conduct of the church lies behind Paul's warning that women wear head coverings "because of the angels" (1 Cor. 11:10).[22] Less controverted is Peter's indication that angels are curious concerning the time of grace proclaimed by the Old Testament prophets (1 Pet. 1:12). Stronger still is the Pauline theme that the salvation process has cosmic ramifications, that is, implications for the angels (1 Cor. 4:9) and for "the rulers and authorities in the heavenly realms" (Eph. 3:10).

The continuity between the New Testament angelology and its foundation in the Old Testament is evident finally in the strict prohibition against the worship of angels and involvement in angel cults. This prohibition sets the New Testament apart from a variety of popular first century religious practices. The apostolic witness proclaims that Christ is not an angel but is above the angels, for they worship him (Heb. 1:5-14). As a consequence, in Christ believers are likewise above the angels (Heb. 2:5-9), for we will one day judge the heavenly beings (1 Cor. 6:3). Until that day, however, the angels minister to the people of God in ways that are largely unknowable to us.

The most pervasive theme of angelology which the New Testament authors inherited from the Old Testament and ancient Judaism is that of the cosmic drama which divides the spiritual beings into two opposing forces—the good angels of God and the demonic hosts under the leadership of Satan. To this dark side of biblical angelology, we must now turn.

---

22. Thus, for example, Werner Foerster, "Exousia," in *TDNT*, 2:574. Others, however, suggest that it is actually demons who are in view in this text. See Broer, "Angelos," in *EDNT*, 1:15.

A Biblical Theology of Demons

Among the larger group of spiritual realities, the biblical writers speak of a specific group of evil entities called "demons." Consequently, this too has become a category for theological reflection. Like the good angels, they are generally seen as spiritual beings. In fact, they are sometimes termed "fallen angels." For these reasons, many theologians discuss demons under the broader topic of angelology.

Definitions. The Greek language of the first Christian century had two words for the darker spiritual beings, *daimon* and *daimonion*. *Daimon* predated *daimonion*, for it was the usual term for these realities in classical Greek. More specifically, it originally denoted the gods or the lesser deities. Similar to the traditional religious outlook of certain other societies *daimon* carried associations with the dead. Hence, Werner Foerster, writing in the *Theological Dictionary of the New Testament*, declares that in popular belief a *daimon* was

> a being, often thought of as the spirit of the dead, endowed with supernatural powers, capricious, and incalculable, present in unusual places at particular times and at work in terrifying events in nature and human life, but placated, controlled or at least held off by magical means.[23]

Partially due to the positive religious associations *daimon* connoted in classical Greek, the Jews who translated the Hebrew Bible into Greek (the Septuagint) and the New Testament authors who followed their lead avoided using the term. In its place they introduced *daimonion*, originally a neuter adjective which became a substantive. This word occurs 63 times in the New Testament.[24]

The New Testament sets forth a conscious awareness of demons as an organized opposition to God and to God's good intention for his creation. Yet this heightened awareness of the demonic developed first during the intertestamental period, partly through contact of Jewish exiles with Iranian-Chaldean thinking during the Babylonian captivity.[25]

---

23. Foerster, "Daimon," in *TDNT*, 2:9.
24. Otto Boecher, "Daimonion," in the *EDNT*, 1:271.
25. Ibid., 1:271.

Demons in the Old Testament. In contrast to the New Testament and to the world of ancient Greece, the Old Testament gives little place to the concept of the demonic. This suggests that the ancient Hebrews were largely unaware of such beings. In his treatment of the topic, Foerster concludes, "the whole sphere of demonology appears only on the margin in the OT." More specifically, in contrast to the beliefs of other cultures, "the OT knows no demons with whom one may have dealings in magic even for the purpose of warding them off."[26]

Despite the general reticence to speak of the demonic, there appear to be a few references in the Old Testament to evil spirits. Two Hebrew terms are often viewed as likely referring to demonic beings—*shed* and *sayer*, both of which, interestingly, offer a connection between idolatry and the demonic. For example, the song with which Moses ended his farewell address contains a reference to Israel's idolatry described in terms of sacrificing to *shedim*: "They sacrificed to demons which are not God—gods they had not known, gods that recently appeared, gods your fathers did not fear" (Deut. 32:17). Similarly, the psalmist refers to Israel's sin of sacrificing sons and daughters to *shedim* (Ps. 106:37).

Sayer was originally an adjective meaning "hairy," but it came to be a noun indicating a "buck" or "goat" (i.e., "the hairy one"). From this meaning arose its reference to a goat-shaped idol found at one of the ancient shrines (Lev. 17:7). According to the chronicler, the first king of the northern kingdom (Jeroboam) "appointed his own priests for the high places and for the goat and calf idols he had made" (2 Chron. 11:15).

Despite the acknowledgment of malevolent supernatural beings, the ancient Hebrews focused on the uniqueness of Yahweh as the one true God. The writers occasionally depict "gods of the nations" as hostile powers. But so all-pervasive was the divine sovereignty in the understanding of the early Hebrews that they ascribed to Yahweh evil events which the Greeks would attribute to a *daimon* (Isa. 45:7; Amos 3:6). Whatever agents did act in a seemingly harmful manner could be pictured only as somehow connected with God (1 Sam.

---

26. Foerster, "Daimon," in *TDNT*, 2:11.

16:14-23; 19:9), as one of his emissaries (as one of the *malakim*). As we will observe, the strict Hebrew concern for the status of Yahweh as the only God meant that even Satan himself belonged to the court of God (Job 1:6).

One lucid example of the contrast between the pre- and post-exilic views lies in a comparison of the two narratives describing King David's numbering the people. The pre-exilic author accounts for this fateful event by declaring that God "incited" David to command that the census be taken, because the divine anger burned against his people (2 Sam. 24:1). In his account of this event, the post-exilic chronicler, in contrast, cites Satan (actually, "an adversary") as the instigator (1 Chron. 21:1).

The crucial development of a Jewish demonology did not occur, therefore, until the exile and especially in the intertestamental period. The demons came to be seen as envious spirits which attack, harm, and even seek to destroy human beings. Chief among them was God's enemy, Satan. In addition, the literature of the intertestamental period incorporated the idea of two aeons. The present order with its suffering lies under the domain of Satan and his hosts. As a consequence, the present aeon is in conflict with God's plan which will be revealed in the coming aeon.

Demons in the New Testament. As in the case of angelology in general, the New Testament writers accepted the several developing themes concerning the demons and Satan. At the heart of the apocalyptic world view of the New Testament is the concept of two kingdoms or two ages—the conflict between God and his spiritual opponents. In the struggle of the ages, demons are significant agents. They form a unified kingdom of evil under the leadership of their chief, Satan. As such they are the agents of Satan's will and are locked in mortal conflict with God's kingdom.

The New Testament writers view demons as "fallen angels" (2 Pet. 2:4; Jude 6). They are those spiritual beings who are not fulfilling God's intent for them. In that they fail to fulfill their design, these beings participate in sin. Under the direction of their chief, they also seek to advance sin in the world by means of their interaction with humans, working to blind unbelievers to the truth of the gospel, to tempt believers to sin, and to incite persecution of Christians. Demons always exercise a detrimental influence, seeking to harm the well-being of God's creation and to destroy community. Hence, they desire to compel human agents to injure the natural environment, God's creatures, other humans, and even themselves. If given opportunity, demons can take possession of a human person and thereby impair or distort the personality.

The good news of the New Testament, however, is that Jesus has been victorious over the powers of evil. In this age, he shares this victory with all who are part of his community. On the great eschatological day he will completely destroy all demonic forces.

A Biblical Theology of Satan

Of greatest interest in the biblical demonology is the figure of the chief of the demons, generally known in the New Testament and Christian theology as Satan. Yet, Satan is not the only personage who is of interest in this context.

Names related to Satan. Although seldom used in the Old Testament, *Leviathan* is nevertheless important as a representation of the archenemy of God. Originally the name referred to a mythical sea monster who was a creature of God (Job 41:1; Ps. 104:26). But Leviathan also came to carry evil overtones (Job 3:8), ultimately serving as the personification of Chaos against whom God does battle in bringing about creation (e.g., Ps. 74:14). In his prophecy, Isaiah offers an interesting twist to this figure who originally arises in the wisdom literature. The prophet transfers Yahweh's battle against this mythical archenemy to the eschatological future, to the day in which God delivers Israel (Isa. 27:1).

More significant than Leviathan in the history of Christian thought is the figure of *Lucifer*. The name itself arises from only one text in the Bible (Isa. 14:12) and is related to the Hebrew phrase *helel ben shachar*. The Latin Vulgate (an early translation of the Bible into Latin) employed the Latin derivative, "Lucifer," meaning "light bearer" to translate the Hebrew *helel*, which is either a verb meaning "to wail" or a noun meaning "shining one." Many Christians throughout church history, including Tertullian, Origen, most medieval thinkers, and John Milton's literary masterpiece *Paradise Lost*, have equated the "light bearer" (Lucifer) with Satan. Careful exegesis, however, leads to the conclusion that Isaiah did not have the chief of the demons in view, but rather the king of Babylon.[27]

Satan in the Old Testament. Despite the presence of other figures in the Bible, without a doubt the most significant biblical figure representing God's chief opponent is "Satan" or the devil. Whereas the English term "devil" gives evidence to a Greek background, "Satan," which is commonly used as the actual name for God's rival, has Hebrew origins. This English name is a transliteration of the Hebrew noun *Satan*, which in turn is derived from the verb *saten*, "to accuse." As a derivative of the verb, *satan* means basically "accuser" or "adversary." In the Old Testament the word occurs without the article ten times, all in Numbers, Samuel, Kings, Chronicles, and Psalms. Theologically more important are the seventeen occurrences of the noun with the article, all of which are in two books—Job and Zechariah.

As the meaning of the term suggests—"the one who accuses" or "the adversary"—*satan* denotes function. Hence, its significance probably arose out of the judicial life of Israel. Just as in any earthly court, the function of accuser—similar to our prosecuting attorney— is also important to the heavenly court. In functioning in this manner, the accuser acts in the interest of justice and, therefore, in the interest of God. Hence, Neil Forsyth concludes, "In the collection of documents…known to Christians as the Old Testament, the word [Satan] never appears as the name of the adversary…rather, when the satan appears in the Old Testament, he is a member of the heavenly court, albeit with unusual tasks."[28]

---

27. For a defense of this position, see Robert Alden, "Lucifer, Who or What?" (unpublished essay, Denver Conservative Baptist Seminary). Not all modern theologians have rejected the traditional view, however. For an example, see Reinhold Niebuhr, *The Nature and Destiny of Man* (New York: Charles Scribner's Sons, 1941), 1:180.

For a discussion of the mythological background of this text, see John D. W. Watts, *Isaiah 1-33*, volume 24 of the *Word Biblical Commentary*, ed. David A. Hubbard, et al. (Waco, Tex.: Word, 1985), 24:209-12. See also Otto Kaiser, *Isaiah 13-39: A Commentary*, trans. R. A. Wilson, in *The Old Testament Library*, ed. Peter Ackroyd, et al. (Philadelphia: Westminster, 1974), 23-43.

28. Neil Forsyth, *The Old Enemy: Satan and the Combat Myth* (Princeton, N.J.: Princeton University Press, 1987), 107.

The function of the accuser ("the satan") is set forth in the drama of Job. Satan is a member of the heavenly court (Job 1:6; 2:1) who functions in accordance with this title; he is the accuser—the prosecutor—who acts in the interest of God by raising questions concerning the righteous. In the prologue, God approaches Satan with the name of Job. He asks the accuser if he has looked into the situation of this man, who apparently stands as an example of the righteous person. To this the accuser suggests that Job's righteousness is merely superficial (hence the dialogues in Job 1:6-12; 2:1-5). Then the drama begins.

Somewhere in his story, however, the accuser in the court of God develops a hostile intent. Rather than simply acting as the one who tests the righteous on God's behalf, he becomes the one who maliciously tempts them to sin. The satan—the accuser—becomes Satan, the "accuser of the saints," the one who is hostile toward humans. In so doing, he becomes hostile toward God's intentions as well. Hence, in Zechariah's prophetic vision, Yahweh rebukes "the satan" who stands ready to accuse Joshua the high priest (Zech. 3:1-2). It is but a small step from hostility toward God's program to Satan's final position as God's archenemy.

Satan in the New Testament. As the curtain rises on the New Testament narrative, Satan retains the Old Testament function of the accuser in the divine court, who as such has access to God (Luke 22:31; Rev. 12:1-6). The coming of Jesus marks a new stage in the story of the accuser: Satan has "fallen from heaven" (Rev. 12:5-12; Luke 10:18; John 12:31; 16:11), which means that Satan has lost his function in the court of God.

We may best understand this apocalyptic event theologically in the context of the work of Christ. In the Old Testament era Satan could justly function as the accuser of the people of God. Because God had not yet provided atonement for human sin, even the saints were unrighteous, unable to stand in God's presence. But Christ's work has altered this situation. Having endured the cross on our behalf, Jesus now intercedes for the saints "at the right hand of the Father." Consequently, Satan no longer is able to gain the hearing of God. Because of the intercession of our "defense attorney," the accuser has lost his position of being our prosecutor. Consequently, "Satan has fallen from heaven" means that he is no longer able to bring accusation against the people of God (Rom. 8:31-39, esp. vv. 33-34).

The Book of Revelation adds an additional aspect of Satan's fall from heaven. Having been deprived of his position in the heavenly court, the accuser now functions on the earth, where he seeks to disrupt God's program. Having become the archenemy of God, he acts as the head of a unified kingdom of evil (Mark 3:22–26). And he holds undisputed sway outside the church, except when his rule is challenged by the gospel (1 Cor. 5:5,13). This understanding of Satan's position in the world lies behind the early Christian practice of "delivering over to Satan," that is, putting a person outside the church fellowship.

In his attempt to thwart God's program, Satan steers his activities in two directions, toward unbelievers and toward the church. The enemy seeks to hold unbelievers in his grasp by blinding their eyes to the truth of the gospel. He also attempts to undermine the work of God's people, launching an attack against the Christian community which includes both external persecution (1 Pet. 5:9; Rev. 12:17) and internal temptation, deceit, and seduction (2 Cor. 11:14).

Indeed, Satan prowls about like a roaring lion. Yet even now he is a defeated foe whose end is sure. On the basis of the triumph over Satan won by Jesus in his life, death, and resurrection, the New Testament anticipates the final, future chapter of the history of Satan. At Christ's return, Satan will be consigned to "the lake of fire." Thus, how great is the fall of Satan. The one who began as God's servant, the accuser in the court of God, in the end is completely banished from God's realm.

Satan ranks as perhaps the most fascinating figure within angelology. The story of Satan's fall leads us to wonder how a creature of such prominence within God's own court could defect and became the evil one par excellence. But the power in the story lies in its grave implications. As Elaine Pagels insightfully notes, "Satan is no alien enemy; on the contrary, he is the intimate enemy."[29] This theme, the

---

29. Pagels, "The Social History of Satan," 114.

saga of how a member of God's own court became his enemy, lies at the heart of the biblical drama itself. It points to the heart of evil, which is ultimately the violation of community: One of *us* breaks fellowship and becomes one of *them.*

Angelology and Structures of Existence

Many evangelicals see angels and demons as spiritual beings who seek to influence individual humans. There is, of course, biblical foundation for such a focus. Unfortunately, such thinking readily leads to the conclusion that the activity of these beings is limited to protection by guardian angels or demonic possession. Christians who have never encountered either readily assume that they stand outside the realm of angelic or demonic activity.

The Bible provides the foundation for a broader understanding of the activity of the cosmic spiritual forces. These beings continuously and universally affect humans. The spiritual realities function in connection with what we may call "structures of human existence." The concept of structures of existence, therefore, provides a fruitful basis for developing a further dimension for a contemporary angelology, for this idea offers a point of connection between the biblical world of spiritual beings and the realm of ongoing human life.

To develop the connection between the structures and angelology, we must look first at the concept itself, then search out the link between the idea of structures and certain biblical concepts, before finally drawing together a theology of the structures or a structural angelology.

The Structures of Existence

Simply stated, structures of existence are those larger, suprahuman aspects or dimensions of reality which form the inescapable context for human life and which therefore condition individual and corporate human existence. The structures are related to human social interaction in all its dimensions and on all levels. As such they form the core of what facilitates that interaction. The structures penetrate daily life, often even imperceptibly. In fact, they are so much a part of life that their presence repeatedly goes unrecognized.

The function of the structures. Hendrikus Berkhof in his monumental little treatise on the subject describes the crucial function of the structures. They undergird human life and society so as to preserve them from disintegration and chaos.[30] The structures give cohesion to life, he notes, "fixing the path for the individual as well as for society." Berkhof then cites several specific examples:

> We may think of the place of the clan or tribe among primitive peoples, or of the respect for ancestors and the family which for centuries gave form and content to Chinese life. We may point to Shintoism in Japan, to the Hindu social order in India, to the astrological unity of ancient Babel, to the deep significance of the *polis* or city-state for the Greeks, or to the Roman state.[31]

As Berkhof suggests, the concept of structures of existence is ancient. In the intertestamental and New Testament era, for example, expression of the idea among the nations of the Near East took several forms. One was astrology. Proponents asserted that the stars and other heavenly bodies form the context for human life and thereby influence individual existence. Similarly, evidence to the concept of structures of existence lies in the ancient gnostic religions, which developed an intricate hierarchy of heavenly beings who they believed held the keys to human destiny. These ideas, it appears, lay behind Paul's polemic against the *stoicheia*, "the powers in the heavenly realm" (Gal. 4:3,9; Col.2:8,20). As we will see, the apostle's polemic offers a biblical foundation for a theology of the structures.

Although the idea that we live within structures of existence is ancient, it has gained a more nuanced articulation in the modern world. In describing the structures, James F. Cobble, Jr., for example, speaks about "a power complex" in the context of which modern life transpires:

> A power complex composed of an entangled network of forces now conditions human existence. No one escapes the influence "it"

---

30. Hendrik Berkhof, *Christ and the Powers*, trans. John H. Yoder (Scottdale, Penn.: Herald, 1962), 30,33.
31. Ibid., 34.

transmits through every available medium—every institution, whether political, industrial, commercial, economic, medical, educational, or religious. Every source of communication and power, whether personal or impersonal, is an integral part of the life-shaping system we have created, but which now largely functions beyond both our control and welfare.[32]

According to Cobble, this "power complex" consists of the multitude of inextricable structures of existence within which we live today.

The Mennonite thinker John Howard Yoder also builds from the seminal work of Hendrickus Berkhof. In *The Politics of Jesus*, he elaborates on the structures influencing human existence. Yoder describes them as organizational principles for human existence in society and divides them into several types: religious, intellectual, moral, and political. Religious structures constitute the religious undergirding of stable societies. Intellectual structures include the various ideologies by means of which human beings perceive the nature of reality. Moral structures are the codes and customs which various societies employ in order to organize the moral life of the people. Political structures are the systems of politics by means of which civil governments operate.[33]

The existence of structures. Human life is bound with structures of existence. Any link between the structures and angelology, however, must pass through the prior question concerning their actual existence. In what sense can we say that such structures exist?

We note immediately that the structures of existence are structures of *human* existence. They do not have independent reality apart from humankind but are, in a sense, constructs that human society has created. Religious, intellectual, moral, and political structures are indeed the product of human beings. They are developed and shaped by human social interaction. For example, human beings are involved in government, both in determining the system of government and in actually governing human political affairs. Whatever reality the structures possess, therefore, their existence is of a special

32. James F. Cobble, Jr., *The Church and the Powers* (Peabody, Mass.: Hendrickson, 1988), 5.
33. John Howard Yoder, *The Politics of Jesus* (Grand Rapids: Eerdmans, 1972), 145.

type, different from the existence of beings such as humans or perhaps even angels.

At the same time, however, to say that structures are merely human constructs is to oversimplify their reality. Although developed and employed by human beings, in some sense the structures lie beyond human control. This is so, for we cannot live in the world apart from the structures. They form the context for individual human life within the human community and for human social interaction. Thus, for example, political structures may change but humans always live under some type of government; the economic system may be altered but commerce in some form will continue; moral codes and customs change but our sense of morality is always conditioned by larger mores.

The structures lie beyond our control in another manner as well. Specific structures are independent of persons who live under them. No specific group of individuals has the ability to alter greatly the structures in the context of which we live.

Ultimately, therefore, the structures of existence exist independently of us. They may not be agents who act totally apart from humans, but they nevertheless enjoy a degree of independent existence. Perhaps we can best term their status as quasi-independent existence. They exist as well in that they exercise power, for there is a link between exerting influence and being real.

Structures are not only quasi-independent, they are quasi-personal. In our discussion of God as person, we noted that the concept of personhood is connected with the idea of existing beyond the control of another, or being mysterious or incomprehensible at one's core. In this sense, the structures of existence are personal. Ultimately they lie beyond human control. And there always remains a dimension of the mysterious about them. The depths of their reality, as it were, are never subject to human scrutiny and probings. In fact, the structures seem to take on personalities, wills, and even histories of their own.

An example is the United States government. Despite repeated attempts by many presidents and congressional leaders to control it, the federal government seems to have a life of its own. There are dynamics at work in this political structure which simply are no longer subject to the American public or even to the attempts by elected officials to "rein in the ropes."

Structures of Existence and the Bible

How does angelology connect to this discussion of the structures of existence? Our path returns us to the Bible and the search for a biblical context in which to understand this idea. We ask, therefore, Is there a connection between structures and the biblical understanding of spiritual realities?

Structures and spiritual beings. In pursuing this connection we must be careful not simply to equate structures of human existence with the spiritual beings. The apocalyptic and rabbinic writings of the intertestamental period apparently made such a connection, for they viewed the powers as personal, spiritual beings which influence earthly events.[34] Yet Paul did not.[35] And rightly so. The structures always remain structures of *human* existence. While they come to have a quasi-independent and quasi-personal existence, they remain tied to human life.

Despite this difference between the biblical portrayal of spiritual beings and the concept of structures of human existence, we dare not separate them totally either. Rather, a common aspect links the two.

Structures and the "powers." Perhaps the most direct link between spiritual beings and structures of existence lies in the Pauline concept of the "powers." The background to Paul's understanding lies both in the Hebrew and intertestamental writings and in the popular astrological ideas of the Greco-Roman world.

To describe the powers, the apostle uses several terms almost synonymously. The most significant of these is the word *stoicheion*. For the Greeks, the *stoicheia* ("elemental principles") were the primary building blocks of the universe (hence, 2 Pet. 3:10, 12). But from their primary relationship to the physical world, the *stoicheia* also had influence over human affairs. Like the contemporary concept of structures, the Greeks looked to the *stoicheia* as the powers which af-

---

34. H. Berkhof, *Christ and the Powers*, 17.
35. Ibid., 23-26.

fect human existence through precepts, doctrines, and human traditions (e.g., Col. 2:20-22).

The apostle presents an ambivalent or double-sided evaluation of the powers. They were created by God and created through and for the benefit of Christ (Col. 1:16). Hence, they are good. Yet they now stand in opposition to God and Christ, and consequently to us (Col 2:8). And they enslave those who obey them (Gal. 4:8-11). As a result, we battle against them (Eph. 6:12). Paul, however, is convinced that Christ has gained the victory over the powers. On the cross our Lord disarmed the powers (Col. 2:14-15), so that we need no longer serve them (Col. 2:16).

Structures and governance. The Pauline concept of the elementary principles points in the direction of the deeper relationship between structures of human existence and the spiritual realities. This link lies in the idea of governance. We have already noted that the structures participate in the broader governing of human life. By providing the context in which human interaction can occur, they facilitate and to some degree determine that interaction.

The Bible sets forth as one central dimension of the function of the heavenly beings that of serving as agents of God's governing of the world. The pages of Scripture offer several points of connection between spiritual beings and government. The most obvious is the apocalyptic theme of spiritual forces as standing at the head of earthly, human governments (Dan. 10:12-13,20). Another theme is that of involvement of angels in moral and religious structures. This is evident in the tradition that angels mediated the law to Moses.

How did the biblical faith community come to view the spiritual beings as involved in God's governing of human affairs? Although their reality was a natural extension to the heavenly court of the entourage of human monarchs, it seems that the place of the spiritual beings in the cosmos came to be augmented as the biblical writers sensed more keenly the transcendence of God. Awareness of the divine otherness brought a corresponding heightening of awareness of the role of angels as governing intermediaries between God and the world.

A Theology of the Structures

The idea of governance provides a key to understanding the role of both angels and demons in human structures. This in turn facilitates the delineation of a theology of the structures under the rubric of angelology. Setting forth of this doctrine depends on a clearer understanding of the original intent of God for the structures as well as the actual involvement of angels and demons with these structures.

God's intent for the structures. Because they are part of God's benevolence—God's ordering of his good creation for the benefit of humankind and all creatures—the structures of human existence as intended by God are good. God desires that human interaction lead to the development of dynamics of human social life that are conducive to the establishment of community. In fact, community can only emerge in the context of structures. To the extent that God designed them to foster community, therefore, structures are positive, even life-giving.

The governing role of the structures returns us to our conclusions about the spiritual beings. God designed the angelic hosts with the purpose that they serve God's governing of the world, especially in the realm of human life. To this end they are to work through the structures of human existence, which structures naturally arise as the product of human interaction. These beings are to guide the structures for our benefit, so that they might facilitate the establishment of a truly human community.

To offer one example, God intends that religious structures such as the moral law orient our existence toward God-honoring actions. To this end, the moral codes of our society should show the parameters in which truly loving relationships can emerge. The task of angels is to enhance the governance of human affairs by establishing wholesome social morality.

God established the structures with a good intent directed toward building community. God likewise designed the spiritual realities connected to these structures in order that they exercise a positive influence through structures of human existence, employing them in the task of fostering community among the inhabitants of God's good universe.

The evil manipulation of structures. Despite God's good intention for the structures, however, they can be manipulated for evil purposes. The structures can be pressed into service against God, humankind, and creation. In this manner, what God intends as a means to promoting community can actually weaken it. When this occurs, the structures have fallen under the influence of dark powers, or the demonic.

The possibility that the structures can be manipulated for evil lies already within their foundational role as providing cohesion to life. As Berkhof notes, "by holding the world together, they hold it away from God, not close to Him."[36] Whenever they become the means whereby direction is turned away from God and to life apart from God, the structures hinder community with God. Given their cohesive role in human life, structures also risk demanding for themselves a loyalty due only to God. Whenever this occurs, the structures become vehicles for idolatry.

Through the diabolical misuse of structures, evil realities bring humans into structural bondage. Rather than aiding people in building community, the powers enslave them, demanding rigid obedience to traditions and forms that, in themselves, cannot be the objects of our loyalty. Structures likewise become a channel for evil whenever they are pressed into the service of promoting evil ends—whenever they are co-opted into advancing the will of Satan rather than the will of God. The legal and policing agencies of civil government may be exploited for the purposes of Satan's attack on the people of God. Or legislative structures may be subverted for the sake of encoding laws which are destructive of the community God intends for his creation.

Finally, structures become a channel for evil when they fail to advance God's rule. God desires that the structures of existence foster the kind of human interaction that embodies the principles of the kingdom of God. However, whenever the hallmarks of the divine reign, which is the rule of justice, righteousness, and love, are lacking in human social life, the structures have failed to conform to the divine intent.

36. Ibid., 30.

In these various ways, evil spiritual realities attempt to manipulate the structures. Their goal is that of thwarting God's program—preventing, undermining, and destroying community. In all such cases, rather than fulfilling their purpose of fostering fellowship with God, harmony within creation, and rich interpersonal relations, the structures degenerate into the very forces which pull creation apart. The rigid attempt to obey the decrees of human structures becomes a source of guilt and frustration that drive us away from God. The same rigidity causes division among humans, as we divide into mutually excommunicating factions in our quest to construct, interpret, defend, and compel compliance with precepts, ideologies, and other focal points of our competing loyalties. And through our battles with each other, we not only fail to reflect the image of God to creation, but we also disrupt and destroy the world around us.

The structures, therefore, have the potential not only to be the instrument of angels; they can also become the tool of demons. The New Testament presents human government as a case in point. Paul speaks of the civil sphere—and specifically of the Roman magistrate—as God's servant, for it provides for the punishment of the wicked and the rewarding of the good (Rom. 13:1-7). The Book of Revelation, in contrast, presents the same Roman civil structure as demonic, manipulated by Satan himself in his attempt to injure the church through persecution.

The religious dimension of life offers another biblical example. Paul declares that despite appearances to the contrary demonic influence is exercised through religious or moral codes. This influence seeks to bring Christians into bondage through legalism (Col. 2:20–23). And demonic involvement introduces false teaching supported by human traditions. According to Paul, the source of such teaching is "seducing spirits" (1 Tim. 4:1).

Even the Old Testament law falls victim to this manipulation and misuse. According to Paul, the law which is God's good instrument intended to bring us to Christ, readily becomes an imprisoning power over us (Gal. 3:23-24). Just like the grip of astrological beliefs over the Gentiles, the apostle warns, the slavish attempt to obey the law can enslave believers. This occurs as persons seek stability and structure for their lives through a scaffolding of laws,[37] which rather than drawing us to community with God, actually becomes a false god— that is, the source of a false sense of meaning, security, and identity.

Structures and Christ. One further point begs to be asserted, however. The structures can be manipulated by demonic forces. Nevertheless, because Christ has punctured Satan's power, structures of human existence ultimately lie under the Christ's lordship. They belong to his kingdom not only in the order of creation (that is, because they are God's good creation) but also in the order of redemption. This means that the structures will one day conform to the reign of God. Hence, on the basis of Paul's lofty statement to the Colossians (Col. 1:19), Hendrickus Berkhof offers this insightful conclusion:

> God reconciles the Powers—and not only men—with Himself through Christ's death. This thought is strange to us; we usually think of reconciliation as an act relating only to persons. Here Paul uses it in a broader sense, as meaning a restoration of proper relationships. In this sense the Powers as well are object of God's plan of redemption. By virtue of this purpose they will no longer lie between man and God as a barrier, but can and shall return to their original function, as instruments of God's fellowship with His creation.[38]

Because we have this eschatological hope that the structures of existence will be freed from their current susceptibility to manipulation, even now we can anticipate the in-breaking of the reign of Christ into the realm of the structures. Even in this era of transition, we can find evidences of the proper functioning of the structures. Under the leadership of his Spirit, we can seek to bring the structures into closer conformity with the will of God. At least partially, therefore, the structures of human existence can be agents for fostering the community that is the intent and purpose of our God.

The Demonic and Superstition

One final dimension of angelology remains, the connection between the activity of spiritual beings and the superstitious practices of humans, involvement dating back to the most ancient times. How

---

37. Ibid., 22,37.
38. Ibid., 41.

are we to understand the varied and manifold beliefs and practices found in nearly all societies? Are they merely unfortunate, but virtually harmless traditions? Or do they bring the participant into contact with actual spiritual realities?

Superstition and the Old Testament

Like other ancient cultures, the people of the Near East were imbued with ideas about supernatural realities. Given the widespread involvement in superstitious practices among the surrounding nations, it is not surprising that such activities allured the people of Israel. As an evidence of the temptation that the religious attitudes of the nations must have exerted on Israel, the Old Testament literature contains abundant warnings against such activities. The Hebrew community of faith knew about mediums, soothsayers, magicians, practitioners of witchcraft, and sorcerers. How were the ancient people of God to respond?

The Old Testament opposition to superstition. Simply stated, the Old Testament writers were unconditionally opposed to superstition. The Torah contains strictures against superstitious practices, involvement in which was to be punished by death (Lev. 19:26; 20:27). Some of the prohibitions in the Torah are succinct and stated quite matter-of-factly, couched for example within the context of laws concerning diet and hair (Lev. 19:26; 20:27) or sexual purity (Ex. 22:18). Others offer a more extended condemnation drawing together a variety of related practices.

The intensity of the Old Testament condemnation of superstition is evident in Moses' command to the children of Israel as they prepared to move into the land of promise:

> When you enter the land the LORD your God is giving you, do not learn to imitate the detestable ways of the nations there. Let no one be found among you who sacrifices his son or daughter in the fire, who practices divination or sorcery, interprets omens, engages in witchcraft, or casts spells, or who is a medium or spiritist or who consults the dead. Anyone who does these things is detestable to the LORD, and because of these detestable practices the LORD your God will drive out those nations before you. You must be blameless before the LORD your God (Deut. 18:9-13).

This text sets forth the important Old Testament theme that abstention from all superstitious practices was to be a mark separating Israel from her neighbors. As the text indicates, in this matter the Canaanites whom they dispossessed were to stand as a warning to Israel, for the practice of superstition by these peoples was one of the chief sins for which God was severely judging them. Later in Israel's history the prophets would look for a day when God would similarly judge Israel's enemies—specifically Assyria and Babylon which carried Israel into captivity. Divine judgment would fall in part because of the superstitions of these nations (Mic. 5:12; Isa. 47:9,12).

The presence of superstition in Israel. Despite strong divine prohibitions, however, Israel did engage in superstitious activities. Involvement reached to the highest level of political leadership. Although Saul drove the soothsayers out of the land, in his time of trouble Israel's first king sought out "the witch of Endor" in order to contact the spirit of the departed prophet Samuel (1 Sam. 28). The chronicler asserts that this was one factor contributing to Saul's own untimely death (1 Chron. 10:13).

Involvement in superstitious activities continued into the time of the exile. In fact, the prophetic historians claim that superstition was among the sins that led to the defeat of both Israel and Judah at the hand of their powerful enemies.

According to the compiler of 2 Kings, the invasion of the northern kingdom by the Assyrians was God's punishment on Israel for the involvement of the people in such activities (2 Kings 17:17-18). In the same manner, the chroniclers harshly evaluated the reigns of kings such as Manasseh, who engaged in these practices (2 Chron. 16:6; 2 Kings 21:1-16). Although perhaps not as widespread, superstition was present in the more godly southern kingdom of Judah as well (Ezek. 13:18).

Superstition and idolatry. Why were the Old Testament writers so adamant in opposing superstitious beliefs and practices? According to the prophets, Israel's involvement in superstition was an evidence of a deeper, grave religious sin. Second Kings, for example, cites the sorcery of the people as an expression of a more fundamental abomination:

> They worshiped other gods and followed the practices of the nations the LORD had driven out before them.... They worshipped idols.... They forsook all the commands of the LORD their God and made for themselves two idols cast in the shape of calves, and an Asherah pole. They bowed down to all the starry hosts, and they worshiped Baal. (2 Kings 17:7-16)

Similarly, of the wicked king Manasseh, the chronicler declares,

> He did evil in the eyes of the LORD, following the detestable practices of the nations the LORD had driven out before the Israelites. He rebuilt the high places his father Hezekiah had demolished; he also erected altars to the Baals and make Asherah poles. He bowed down to all the starry hosts and worshiped them. He built altars in the temple of the LORD and said, "My Name will remain in Jerusalem forever." In both courts of the temple of the LORD he built altars to all the starry hosts. (2 Chron. 33:2-5)

As these texts indicate, involvement in superstition was one dimension of that great evil plaguing the ancient people of God and against which the prophets of Yahweh contended—the sin of idolatry. For this reason, the struggle against idolatry forms the theological background for the repeated Old Testament strictures against superstition. In the eyes of God's prophets, all superstitious practices were idolatrous. But wherein did the connection between superstition and idolatry lie?

The biblical era was an age of tribal deities and of conflict among the gods. In Israel, the question of the strong God led to the problem of idolatry. The biblical authors knew that if one God is stronger than any rival, he alone is worthy of worship. As a result, their claim concerning the exalted status of Yahweh led the prophets to speak out relentlessly against idolatry in Israel. For Israel to be involved in idolatry was not only an affront to their particular tribal deity, but more significantly a violation against the one and only God, who sovereignly rules over all spiritual realities and powers.

Because they understood superstition as idolatry, the Old Testament writers uncompromisingly rejected such practices. All these activities explicitly acknowledge and pay homage to lesser powers, to claimants of deity that are not the one God Almighty. This is especially evident in what has always been one central dimension of superstition, namely, the practice of consulting a medium or sooth-sayer for guidance concerning the future, which in turn is perhaps the epitome of idolatry. Divination entails looking to lesser powers for guidance rather than to the one true God, who alone is sovereign over the future and the fountainhead of all wisdom.

Therein lay the tragedy of Saul's visit to the witch of Endor. As the chronicler explains, the king "consulted a medium for guidance, and did not inquire of the LORD" (1 Chron. 10:13-14). Rather than beseeching the God of Israel, he turned to a creature. Later the proph-et Isaiah asked a rhetorical question to declare the folly of such ac-tions:

> When men tell you to consult mediums and spiritists, who whisper and mutter, should not a people inquire of their God? Why consult the dead on behalf of the living? (Isa. 8:19).

God's people cannot dabble in superstition. To do so is to offer au-thority and obedience to powers other than the sovereign God of the universe.

The Status of the Powers Lying Behind Superstition

The Old Testament condemns superstition because it is irrevoca-bly connected to idolatry. Involvement in superstitious practices constitutes acknowledging in lesser powers what belongs solely to the one God. But what is the actual status of the powers to which people erroneously pay homage through such activities? Are they real or merely imagined? The Bible contains two basic responses to this question.

The reality of the powers. First and most obvious, the biblical writers acknowledge the reality of the powers. These claimants to deity are real. The authors of Scripture link idolatry and, as a conse-quence, superstition not with God and the good, but with the demon-ic. The powers are real, but they are evil and malicious. Consequently, involvement with idolatrous superstitious practices places one in contact with demons—not with God. Superstition can only bring a person into the domain of realities that are hostile both to God and to humankind.

As we have noted, the Old Testament use of *shed* and *sayer* suggests a connection between idolatry and demons. And it forms a background for the New Testament strictures against involvement in superstition. Such practices are idolatry and consequently place practitioners in contact with demons. Hence, Paul warns the Corinthian believers that they cannot both eat at the Lord's table and participate in idolatry:

> Do I mean then that a sacrifice offered to an idol is anything, or that an idol is anything? No, but the sacrifices of pagans are offered to demons, not to God, and I do not want you to be participants with demons (1 Cor. 10:19-20).

Because of the lure of superstitious beliefs, the New Testament writers repeatedly spoke against the common first century practice of worshipping and serving the powers connected with such activities. Hence, Paul lists among the acts of the sinful nature "idolatry and witchcraft" (Gal. 5:20). The seer in Revelation warns that God will judge such practices and banish idolaters from his eternal kingdom (Rev. 9:21; 21:8; 22:15). Paul cautions his associates against those who "abandon the faith and follow deceiving spirits and things taught by demons" (1 Tim. 4:1; cf. 2 Tim. 4: 4), against those who are devoted to godless myths and old wives' tales (1 Tim. 4:7; 1:4), and even against those who pay attention to Jewish myths (Titus 1:14).

According to the biblical authors, the powers that lie behind idols and superstition are real. In some sense they actually exist. They are not good powers, however, but evil, for they are linked with demons. Consequently, idolatry, and with it superstition, must be avoided because it mediates contact with the demonic, never with God.

The powers as unreal. There is, however, a second biblical response to the question of the status of the realities lying behind superstition. These powers, the Bible asserts, have no objective existence whatsoever.

The non-acknowledgment of the reality of other supposedly divine beings is evident in the Old Testament. As we have noted, at least until the time of the exile the Hebrews attributed to the rule of God events—even tragic experiences—that other peoples would have relegated to the lesser deities, such as a *daimon* (2 Sam. 24:16).[39] According to the Old Testament, God alone is sovereign; ultimately he controls the events in his world. Consequently, the gods of the nations are nothing, except perhaps members of the heavenly court of Yahweh.

Perhaps the most lucid statement of the denial of the objective reality of other deities is found in Paul's conclusion to his discussion of the pressing issue of idolatry. He writes,

> So, then, about eating food sacrificed to idols: We know that an idol is nothing at all in the world and that there is no God but one. For even if there are so-called gods, whether in heaven or on earth (as indeed there are many "gods" and many "lords"), yet for us there is but one God, the Father, from whom all things came and for whom we live; and there is but one Lord, Jesus Christ, through whom all things came and through whom we live. But not everyone knows this. (1 Cor. 8:4-7).

Hence, idols are not objectively real, for there is only one God, not many gods.

How can we bring together these seemingly contrary interpretations of the status of idols? Perhaps the clue lies in Paul's statement, "But not everyone knows this." He suggests that the power of idols—and hence of demons—lies in the ignorance of humans apart from Christ. In their ignorance about the truth of the one God, people acknowledge the realm of demonic idols. As they pay homage to these spirits, they allow them to exercise power over their lives. In so doing such realities gain for those who acknowledge them actual, objective existence.

A Christian Stance Toward Superstition

Having surveyed the biblical declarations concerning idols and the demonic, we are now in a position to draw certain conclusions concerning the matter of superstition.

Our primary conclusion must be negative. *The Bible is unambiguous in warning us that all such practices carry a grave danger.*

---

39. Foerster, "Daimon," in *TDNT*, 2:11.

Hence, we must caution ourselves against any involvement in superstition. We must acknowledge that in some important sense we are indeed surrounded by spiritual realities. But the activities of sorcerers, mediums, soothsayers, and practitioners of witchcraft can only serve to put us into contact with malevolent, not benevolent powers—powers of darkness not of light. We dabble in these matters only to our own detriment and harm.

Contrary to the teaching of human religious traditions, the source of our well-being does not lie in attempts to tap into the powers of the spirit world. Rather than looking to astrology or to a spirit which might appear to be an emissary of light, we must realize that "[e]very good and perfect gift is from above, coming down from the Father of the heavenly lights, who does not change like shifting shadows" (James 1:17). To the eternal God alone we should direct our prayers, our requests for guidance and help. We can do so confident that he alone can and does supply what we need, and that he alone is the sovereign who dispatches the good powers of the spirit realm to minister to us (Heb. 1:14).

Our next conclusion arises from the relationship of the powers to Christ. As we have noted, the New Testament declares categorically that *whatever principalities and powers there are in the spiritual realm are under the authority of the Risen Christ.* Because he has freed us from servitude to, and fear of the hosts in the spirit realm, we would be foolish even to consider embracing beggarly superstitions, whether this bondage be subservience to the "elementary principles" of the superstitious religions (Col. 2:20-22) or to the rules and rituals of the Jewish legal structures (Gal. 4:3,9). On the contrary, as the liberated children of the one God, we are to proclaim the good news of freedom to those held captive to superstitious beliefs.

But Christ's relationship to the powers lies even deeper, which leads to our most important conclusion. *Christ has exposed the powers for the non-realities that they are.* As Paul declares, "having disarmed the powers and authorities, he made a public spectacle of them, triumphing over them by the cross" (Col. 2:15). By so doing he has shown that the elemental principles were in actuality created through and for Christ (Col. 1:16). God's intention is that they serve him and by extension that they serve believers. The good news that the powers were created through and for Christ and for us means that we can now appropriate whatever truth is present in what for others are religious practices, but which in fact are not, pressing them into the good service for which they were intended.

To what extent, then, are we at liberty to affirm, even to engage in certain practices that others view as superstitious? To answer this question, we must divide superstitious activities into two categories based on their relationship to idolatrous beliefs. On the one hand, certain practices are inextricably tied to idolatry and therefore are thoroughly pagan. Perhaps the most obvious example is soothsaying or necromancy—that is, the attempt to gain contact with the dead or with spirits for the purpose of obtaining guidance concerning the future. As we have seen, the Bible views these practices as abominations. Indeed, they constitute direct denials of faith in the one true God who alone is sovereign over the future and to whom alone we are to look for guidance for living.

In a similar manner, dabbling in any form of astrology or divination is inadmissible. Like consulting the spirits, these practices mark a turn away from the only God of the future in a vain attempt to gain access to the future. Astrology mistakenly postulates that the heavenly bodies, which are actually only creatures of the one true God, can affect our lives. And divination assumes that through certain acts we can get in touch with powers that know the unknown. In neither case, however, do the participants seek guidance from the only source of wisdom. Instead they ascribe to lesser powers what belongs to God alone. For this reason, therefore, all such practices are at their core idolatry.

On the other hand, some superstitions are not essentially tied to idolatry. An example can be the use of traditional medicine. Lying beneath certain apparently superstitious practices in the healing arts of traditional religions may be insights into the relationship between human wholeness and the realm of nature. The shamans of traditional African religions may know of effective herbs and medicines. Unfortunately, these insights are often enclosed within religious practices that pay homage to idols and spirits. Because Christ has freed his people from all superstitions and because the powers were created through and for him and his followers, we can look for the liberation of whatever truths are found in the superstitions from their bondage to the false religious husk in which that kernel of truth lies hidden.

How then should we approach superstitious beliefs and practices. Simply stated—with great caution and with vigilant discernment. On the one hand, we understand that as religious beliefs and practices, all superstitions are idolatry, even demonic. Therefore, we are cautious; we resolutely refuse to become involved in any idolatrous superstition.

At the same time, we know that ultimately there is only one God and that Christ is the one through whom and for whom all things are created. Consequently, we unwaveringly refuse to acknowledge the power the so-called realities behind superstitions claim over the lives of practitioners. We seek to be discerning. We look for whatever wholesome truth designed for the benefit of human well-being may have become entrapped within the husk of the superstitious practices of the traditional belief systems of the world's peoples. By reuniting people with the one God who is their Creator, we may employ such helpful insights for the furtherance of human well-being and community. This belongs to the advancement of the benevolent reign of the one true God and the establishment of the divine community throughout the entire world.

Part 3
Christology
The Doctrine of Christ

The Bible presents salvation history in narrative form. It recounts of the acts of the triune God in accomplishing his intention for creation. From beginning to end God's intent is the establishment of community. Throughout history the Creator who noted the solitariness of the first human in the Garden of Eden is actively bringing into being the community he envisions for the world.

One day God's activity in history will climax with the coming of the new heaven and new earth, as anticipated by the Old Testament prophets and developed more fully by the closing chapters of the Book of Revelation. This future new order will be characterized by community in the fullest sense. The peoples of the new earth will live together in peace. Nature will again fulfill its purpose of providing nourishment for all earthly inhabitants (Rev. 22:1-4). Most glorious of all, however, God will dwell with humans on the new earth, bringing to completion the ultimate divine design for creation (Rev. 21:3; 22:3-5).

The establishment of community as the overarching purpose of God forms the integrative motif or ordering principle for systematic theology. We have already explored the implications of this theme for the doctrines of God and of humankind. When viewed in terms of the theme of community, theology proper (the doctrine of God) becomes the explication of the nature of the God whose goal is that of establishing community. This God is the Triune One, the community of the three persons. The Christian understanding of God as the Trinity sets forth God as the foundation for establishing the eschatological community. God is throughout eternity the community of the Father, Son, and Spirit. In history, therefore, the triune God is at work seeking to bring creation into participation in this eternal fellowship. The God presented in Christian theology is likewise the Creator God. In keeping with this theme, the doctrine of creation presents the triune God at work in bringing the world into existence and shaping the universe in accordance with the divine eternal purposes. This doctrine sets the context for discussing God's activity in bringing about reconciliation—community—within the creation which is the product of his hand.

The theme of community forms the basis for constructing a Christian anthropology (doctrine of humankind) as well. Understood in this manner, anthropology is the explication of the nature of humankind as the object of the divine action in bringing about community. Christian anthropology sets forth the glorious truth that humans are created in the divine image, a concept best understood in a corporate or community sense. Although created for community, because of the fall humans are estranged from themselves, from each other, from their environment, and—most tragically of all—from God. Yet the Christian story does not end on the negative note. Humans are also the objects of God's reconciling work.

In this way, the doctrine of humankind is the bridge to the remaining doctrines of systematic theology. God is at work effecting our reconciliation and thereby completing the divine goal of creation, the establishment of the eschatological community. The remainder of our systematic theology is the explication of this gracious activity of God, especially as it is carried forth by the Son and the Spirit.

In Christology we reflect on the role of Jesus of Nazareth—whom Christians acknowledge as the Christ—in the reconciling, community-building work of the triune God. The doctrine of Christ is the systematic-theological reflection on two central questions: Who is Jesus? And what does Jesus accomplish? That is to say, Christology focuses on the Christian affirmation concerning the identity and mission of Christ.

In articulating our beliefs about Christ's person and work—Christology explores the central affirmations of the Christian faith. These form the focus of the four chapters in this third part of our systematic theology. Jesus is divine, God in human form (chapter 9). Jesus is human, one with us (chapter 10). Jesus is both divine and human in one undivided person (chapter 11). Jesus is our Savior, the one who makes salvation available for sinful humankind (chapter 12).

The Fellowship
of Jesus the Christ
with God

Therefore let all Israel be assured of
this: God has made this Jesus whom
you crucified, both Lord and Christ.
(Acts 2:36)

Outline

Jesus' Lordship
   The cosmic Lord
   Our personal Lord
   The Lord of history

Christology is the study of the identity and mission of the Christ whom Christians proclaim is Jesus of Nazareth. In Jesus Christians find the self-revelation of God—God incarnate—and God acting definitively for the salvation of humankind. In Jesus they find as well the disclosure of the divine intention for humankind, which is life in community. Christology, therefore, is the believing community reflecting on our confession of faith in Jesus as "God with us." In Christology we declare that God has acted in this specific human life—Jesus of Nazareth, who is the Christ—to effect our salvation.

The doctrine of Christ lies at the heart of the Christian faith. At the heart of Christology, in turn, is the confession that God is present in Jesus. But what do we mean when we affirm the presence of God in Jesus who is the Christ? And can we continue to state this confession in the changing context in which we live? With these questions in view we turn to the development of the first dimension of our Christology, the exploration of Jesus' fellowship with God. In what sense can we affirm that Jesus participates in the divine community?

Foundations: Jesus, the Divine One

The Christian church was born out of the acknowledgment that Jesus is Immanuel, "God with us." His early Jewish followers believed that in Jesus they had encountered Yahweh himself. As the writers of the New Testament reflected on the implications of this experience for Jesus' identity, they concluded that he is both God and Savior (2 Pet. 1:1). Jesus of Nazareth, they asserted, is divine. This confession lies at the foundation of the Christian faith and therefore of our Christology.

How are we to understand this Christian affirmation? Are we confessing that Jesus is God, and if so, in what sense is this true? As a prelude to tackling these weighty questions, we must inquire concerning the foundation for this affirmation. On what basis do we affirm that Jesus is the divine One?

The place to begin our inquiry is with theological history. Only after seeing how the theologians of the church came to express their understanding of the divine dimension of the person of Jesus can we seek a proper foundation for this Christian faith assertion.

Development of the Affirmation of Jesus' Deity

Who is Jesus? The identity of the man from Nazareth has been the most perplexing question of all history. Already during Jesus' ministry speculation abounded as to his true identity (Matt. 16:13-16). The discussion did not cease with the writing of the New Testament books. On the contrary, one of the challenges that motivated the church fathers was the clarification in the context of the Roman world exactly who Jesus is. The central dispute that engulfed the church in its first centuries centered on the question, Who is Jesus in relation to God?

Christological controversy in the second century. In the years from about 100 until about 200, the church was wracked by a fundamental christological difference of opinion, the genesis of which lay already in the apostolic age. As the gospel spread beyond its original cradle in Palestine into the wider Roman world, a tension arose between the Jewish and Greek mentalities.[1]

Because of their background in strict monotheism and moralism, believers with a Jewish heritage tended to find the key to Jesus' identity in his role as the new Moses; he was a man sent from God to uphold the divine law. In contrast, Gentile believers were imbued with the more rationalistic approach to religious questions which characterized the Greek heritage and with the typically Greek philosophical interest in questions of metaphysics, being, and substance. Consequently, they tended to emphasize Jesus' ontological deity as the heavenly messenger of truth.

These quite different emphases spawned two early heretical understandings of the person of Christ. The *adoptionist* Christology of

---

1. For this characterization of the situation, see J.W.C. Wand, *The Four Great Heresies* (London: Mowbray, 1955), 21-27.

the Ebionites embodied the Jewish orientation.[2] Advocates understood Jesus as a mere man who by scrupulous observance of the law was justified and thereby became the Messiah. Hence, Jesus was adopted by God for the purpose of carrying out the divine program.

Followers of various *docetic* heresies, including the gnostics, in contrast, reflected Greek concerns.[3] As the underlying Greek term *dokeo* ("to seem" or "to appear") suggests, proponents asserted that the divine Christ did not have an actual human body; his body was only a spectral appearance, a phantasm, so that the suffering and death of Christ were merely an appearance. The docetics argued that if Christ suffered he was not God; if he was God he did not suffer.

The church theologians attempted to clarify the Christian affirmation of Jesus as the divine One in the face of the misunderstanding of the Ebionites and the gnostics. The second-century apologists devised the *Logos* Christology. Their proposal brought together ideas from Philo, Stoicism, and the Johannine prologue. The personal *logos*—the rationale principle of the universe—was with God unexpressed in eternity. Twice the *Logos* came to expression, at creation and more recently in the form of Jesus of Nazareth. Jesus, therefore, is the divine One insofar as he is the incarnation of the divine *Logos*.

The use of the *Logos* concept to resolve the christological problem concerning the relationship of Jesus to God was a novel idea. Nevertheless, the proponents of the *Logos* Christology left an unanswered question: Granted that the mystery of Christ's identity lies with the divine *Logos* becoming linked with the human man Jesus, what is the exact nature of this relationship? In fact, the *Logos* Christology left open the possibility of conceiving the link between the *Logos* and the human Jesus in either an adoptionistic or a docetic manner.

The *monarchians* perceived this unresolved tension. They accused the proponents of the *Logos* Christology of bitheism—of envisioning two Gods, the eternal God and the divine *Logos*. Against what they perceived as the heresy of the apologists, the monarchians set out to preserve the heritage of monotheism. Their concern took

---

2. Ibid., 24. See also, J.N.D. Kelly, *Early Christian Doctrines*, revised edition (San Francisco: Harper and Row, 1978), 139.

3. Wand, *The Four Great Heresies*, 24-26; Kelly, *Early Christian Doctrines*, 141-42.

the form of two distinct Christologies. Proponents of dynamistic monarchianism pursued the adoptionism of the Ebionites. They postulated that at some point in Jesus' life the *Logos* descended on the man Jesus, although there was much disagreement as to exactly when this occurred.[4] The modalistic monarchians, in contrast, followed the docetic Christology of the gnostics.

The Arian controversy. The second century ended without the ascendancy of one dominant Christology. Consequently, the next two-hundred fifty years marked a time of christological conflict within the church. J. W. C. Wand characterizes this period as the era of the "four great heresies."[5] At the heart of the controversies was a struggle between two basic methods in Christology, one centering in Antioch, Syria, and the other in Alexandria, Egypt. Influenced by the Jewish mentality, the Antiochians emphasized the humanity of Jesus to the point of overshadowing Jesus' deity or destroying the unity of Jesus' person. As residents of the center of Greek learning, the Alexandrians emphasized Jesus' deity, but risked overshadowing his humanity or obliterating the distinction between deity and humanity.

The first christological controversy led the church past a milestone in the development of orthodoxy, the affirmation of the deity of Jesus. The kindling that sparked the debate was the teaching of Arius. His understanding of Jesus' person displayed one of the dangers inherent in the Antiochian christological method, the overshadowing of Jesus' divinity by his humanity. At the heart of Arius's concern was the premise that God is an undifferentiated whole. On this basis he argued that the *Logos* or Son is a creature and therefore must have had a beginning: "the Son is not unbegotten, nor part of the unbegotten in any way...before he was begotten or created or appointed or established, he did not exist; for he was not unbegotten."[6] Arius's opponents offered this summary of his argument: "If the Fa-

---

4. Theodotus of Byzantium, for example, suggested that the descent of the *Logos* happened at the baptism of Jesus, whereas Paul of Samosota apparently maintained that the presence of the Word was somehow connected with the moral development of Jesus. Kelly, *Early Christian Doctrines*, 116, 118

5. Hence the title, Wand, *The Four Great Heresies.*

6. "The Letter of Arius to Eusebius," in *Documents of the Christian Church*, ed. Henry Bettenson, second edition (London: Oxford University Press, 1963), 39.

ther begat the Son, he that was begotten had a point of existence, hence it is clear that there was a time when the Son was not."[7] Therefore, Arius did not view the terms "Son" and "Logos." as ontological, but as titles of courtesy connected to Jesus' final glory.

Against Arius, the church father Athanasius argued on the basis of soteriology that Jesus must be fully divine. Salvation, which Athanasius understood as partaking of the nature of God, can be brought to humankind only by one who is truly God. In Christ, Athanasius maintained, "The Word was made man in order that we might be made divine."[8]

The church rejected the position of Arius at the First Ecumenical Council held in Nicea in A.D. 325 . The council formulated a confession which declared that Jesus was "begotten of the Father...of the substance of the Father...begotten not made, of one substance with the Father." The creed then concluded with an unmistakable rejection of the Arian Christology:

> But to those who say, Once he was not, or he was not before his generation, or he came to be out of nothing, or who assert that he, the Son of God, is of a different *hypostasis* or *ousia*, or that he is a creature, or changeable, or mutable, the Catholic and Apostolic Church anathematizes them.[9]

In this way the Council of Nicea affirmed the deity of Jesus, conceived of in largely Greek philosophical categories, as the first tenet of orthodox Christology.

The Basis of Christology

Orthodox Christians since Nicea have agreed that the First Ecumenical Council merely expressed in the Greek philosophical categories of ontology what is present already in embryonic form in the Scriptures, namely, that Jesus is divine. But on what basis can believers make such an assertion? More specifically, is there a histori-

---

7. Socrates, "The Arian Syllogism," in *Documents of the Christian Church*, 40.

8. Athanasius, *De Incarnatione*, 54, in *The Early Christian Fathers*, ed. and trans. Henry Bettenson (New York: Oxford University Press, 1969), 293.

9. "The Creed of Nicaea," in *The Creeds of the Churches*, ed. John H. Leith, third edition (Atlanta: John Knox, 1982), 31.

cal foundation—a basis in Jesus' own life—to which we can appeal for this central christological statement? Or is the affirmation of Jesus' deity a faith construct without any historical foundation?

From the first century to the modern era, Christian thinkers were convinced that faith statements find their proper foundation in actual events in history. Consequently, despite their general acceptance of the method often called "Christology from above" with its emphasis on the eternal Sonship of Jesus, theologians from Augustine to Luther declared that we base our affirmation of Jesus' deity on the witness of the gospel narratives concerning the historical life of Jesus of Nazareth.

The pietistic movement within Protestantism, however, brought a subtle shift, which in turn marked the advent of a new direction. The pietists differentiated between "head knowledge" and "heart knowledge," thereby opening the way for the "heart" to validate what the "head" might find uncertain. In the 1900s this innovation bore grievous theological fruit, as many thinkers sought to disconnect christological assertions from their moorings in the history of Jesus of Nazareth.

The specific question that occasioned the modern controversy was that of the relationship of the Jesus of history (Jesus of Nazareth as he actually lived) to the Christ of faith (the living Christ proclaimed by, and continually present in the church). As a reaction to the nineteenth century "quest of the historical Jesus"—the attempt to get back to Jesus himself in order to build theology on his person and teaching—many twentieth-century theologians, following the lead of the German thinker Martin Kähler,[10] tended to focus attention on the Christ of the *kerygma*.

Some of these thinkers recoiled at the suggestion that the faith assertion concerning the deity of Jesus must rest on a historical foundation.[11] In their estimation, any attempt to ground the affirmation of Jesus' deity on the history of the Nazarene leads to an damaging meshing of faith and history. If our confession requires a historical foundation, they argued, faith is subjected to the shifting sands of

---

10. For his position, see Martin Kähler, *The So-called Historical Jesus and the Historic, Biblical Christ* [German edition: 1896], trans. Carl E. Braaten (Philadelphia: Fortress, 1964).

historical research. How can the certainty of faith ever be established by the uncertainties of historical scholarship? they cried.[12]

If the certainty of faith is not to be based on the uncertainties of history, what can form the foundation of the confession of Jesus' deity? One proposal declares that the christological assertion is ultimately based on our contemporary encounter with the living Christ, the Christ from beyond who comes to us in the present.

The roots of this proposal lie in the thinking of the philosopher Søren Kierkegaard (1813-1855). In his book *Philosophical Fragments* (1844),[13] for example, the "melancholy Dane" outlined two types of religion. The religion of Socrates, which he viewed as the religion of immanence, suggests that truth is present within each human being. Therefore what is required is only a midwife, one who assists the individual in giving birth to that immanent truth, but who is incidental to the process. Hence, in the end, self-knowledge is likewise knowledge of God. In contrast, the religion of Jesus—and of otherness—asserts that each person is destitute of truth. Thus, we require a teacher who brings both the truth and the conditions necessary for understanding it. In this outlook the teacher is not merely midwife, but Savior and Redeemer. This teacher, according to Kierkegaard, is Jesus Christ, whose identity ultimately is paradoxical—an object of faith and not merely of reason.

The thinking of Martin Kähler and Søren Kierkegaard had an immense impact on several leading theologians in the early twentieth century, including Emil Brunner, Karl Barth, and Rudolph Bultmann. Their emphasis on the Christ who comes from beyond marked a renewal of the older "Christology from above," which challenged the ascendancy the "Christology from below" gained in the previous

---

11. Perhaps the most influential twentieth-century critic of a history-based Christology was Rudolf Bultmann. For his position, see Rudolf Bultmann, *Jesus Christ and Mythology* (New York: Charles Scribner's Sons, 1958), 84. See also Rudolf Bultmann, "Bultmann Replies to His Critics," in *Kerygma and Myth: A Theological Debate*, ed. Hans Werner Bartsch (New York: Harper and Row, 1961), 211.

12. This position builds from the differentiation between the ground of faith and the reflection on (or content of) faith, which Wolfhart Pannenberg claims was first proposed by the nineteenth century theologian, Wilhelm Herrmann. See Stanley J. Grenz, *Reason for Hope: The Systematic Theology of Wolfhart Pannenberg* (New York: Oxford University Press, 1990), 160.

13. Søren Kierkegaard, *Philosophical Fragments*, trans. David F. Swenson, revised Howard V. Hong (Princeton, N.J.: Princeton University Press, 1962), 11-27.

century. Nineteenth century thinkers sought to answer questions concerning Jesus' identity by looking first to the historical person of Jesus, thereby moving from Jesus' life as a human to the confession that Jesus is the Son. Barth and others reversed the order. They now moved from the confession of Jesus' Sonship to an understanding of his historical human life, and hence started the christological quest with an affirmation of Jesus' deity.

"Christology from above" suggests that our confession of Jesus' deity arises from our present experience of the Christ who confronts us in the present. Advocates of this position may be found among theologians of otherwise quite different theological orientations. The well-known black theologian James Cone, for example, declares that the black church bears witness that the meaning of Christ lies in the encounter with the crucified and risen Lord who is present today in the struggle for freedom.[14]

While not necessarily agreeing with Cone's liberation perspective, many evangelicals follow a similar route when they claim to know that Jesus is the divine One on the basis of an experience of the Lord's presence among us today. Evangelicals emphasize, however, that the Holy Spirit causes us to see the truth about Jesus. Indeed as Paul writes, "No one can say 'Jesus is Lord,' except by the Holy Spirit" (1 Cor. 12:3).

We readily acknowledge the truth asserted by those who emphasize the importance of the contemporary experience of the living Lord or the role of the Holy Spirit in bringing us to see the identity of Jesus. Yet we must demur whenever anyone suggests that our search for the foundation of our affirmation of Jesus' deity simply ends here. We simply cannot agree with the implication that Christology can bypass the history of Jesus of Nazareth. Our discussion of why this is the case must wait, however, until we have set forth exactly what aspect of Jesus' history is foundational to our Christology.

---

14. James Cone, *God of the Oppressed* (New York: Seabury, 1975), 121-22.

The Foundation of Our Christological Affirmation

Separating the Christ of faith from the Jesus of history would allow us to lift our affirmation of Jesus' deity above the "shifting sands" of historical research. But this gain comes at great cost. For this reason, many contemporary thinkers have reaffirmed the wisdom of acknowledging that there must be some historical foundation for the Christian assertion that Jesus is divine. Yet, what aspect of Jesus' life forms this foundation? Several proposals are the most plausible.

Jesus' sinlessness. One possibility is that our affirmation of Jesus' divinity rests on his perfect life. This proposal is attractive largely because of its relationship to the traditional theological assertion of Jesus' sinlessness.

Evangelicals readily affirm the sinlessness of our Lord. In addition, however, Jesus' perfect life was of special interest to nineteenth-century Protestant liberalism. Although eschewing all attempts to prove that Jesus was without sin,[15] Friedrich Schleiermacher, for example, nevertheless put the affirmation of the perfection of Jesus to theological use. The "father of modern theology" linked Jesus' sinlessness to "the constant potency of His God-consciousness," which in turn was "a veritable existence of God in Him."[16]

The New Testament authors were convinced that Jesus lived a sinless life, that is, that he committed no action which could be called sin (Heb. 4:15). The Fourth Gospel suggests that the claim to sinlessness finds its source in Jesus' own self-consciousness, which was a point of contention between the Master and his pious Jewish opponents (John 8:46). In contrast to Barth's contention that Jesus participated in our sinful condition,[17] several biblical texts suggest that Jesus was free from even the disposition to sin that characterizes fallen humanity (1 John 3:5; Heb. 9:14; 2 Cor. 5:21), as many Reformed theologians have postulated.[18] In any case, the New Testament writ-

---

15. Friedrich Schleiermacher, *The Christian Faith*, ed. H. R. MacKintosh and J. S. Stewart (Edinburgh: T. & T. Clark, n.d.), 362.

16. Ibid., 385.

17. See Karl Barth, *Church Dogmatics*, trans. Geoffrey W. Bromiley, (Edinburgh: T. & T. Clark, 1958), 4/2:92-93.

18. For a recent statement, see Gordon R. Lewis and Bruce A. Demarest, *Integrative Theology*, three volumes (Grand Rapids: Zondervan, 1990), 2:336-38.

ers hold up the life of Jesus as the model for believers to emulate (1 Pet. 2:21-23).

Yet all appeals to Jesus' sinlessness promise more than they can deliver. They lack an objective historical foundation, as is evident by the fact that the claim that Jesus was sinlessness was contested during his earthly sojourn. The religious leaders of his day were convinced that he was a great sinner. He readily associated with the most unpious of people. He openly flaunted the traditions of the Jewish community and even of Moses himself. Worst of all, he was guilty of blasphemy. The controversial nature of Jesus' own conduct suggests that our affirmation of the Master's sinlessness is ultimately a faith statement and not an immediately obvious historical conclusion. In fact, it gains credence only in the light of Easter, only in the light of God's vindication of Jesus' earthly life in the face of the opinions of Jesus' opponents. Rather than being a foundation for faith, therefore, our declaration that Jesus was sinless is dependent on faith.

Appeals to Jesus life pose a logical difficulty as well. Even if Jesus' sinlessness had been uncontested, the link from a perfect human life to our confession of deity is tenuous. Would sinlessness provide sufficient grounds for affirming that a human being is divine? Would a perfect human being necessarily be God? All believers will enjoy a perfect, sinless existence in the eschatological community of God. Because perfection is the destiny of all members of God's family, the sinlessness of Jesus cannot function as a foundation for the assertion of his deity.

To anticipate a conclusion of chapter 11, rather than being a basis for asserting Jesus' deity his sinlessness is an indication of his perfect humanity. Jesus' perfection means that he is a model for us to follow, not that he is God in human form.

At the same time, the perfect life of Jesus has significance for the assertion of his deity. Jesus' sinlessness stands as an attractive feature of his person. As we read the gospel accounts of Jesus' conduct, we are drawn to him—led to wonder who he might be. Jesus' unique life, therefore, invites us to consider further the question of his identity.

Jesus' teaching. Many evangelicals look to Jesus' teaching as providing the historical foundation for the assertion of his deity. As in the case of the appeal to his sinlessness, this proposal can claim strong interest among nineteenth-century liberal thinkers, who argued that we derive our declarations concerning Jesus' identity from his grand moral teaching. The great liberal scholar Adolf von Harnack summarized the Master's teaching as three interrelated truths: the kingdom of God and its coming, God the Father and the infinite value of the human soul, and the higher righteousness associated with the commandment of love.[19]

Although attractive, this proposal suffers from the same shortcomings as the appeal to our Lord's sinlessness. Jesus' teaching evoked a mixed reaction from his original hearers, even triggering the charge of blasphemy from the religious leaders of his day. Consequently, only when we have first come to confess his deity can we conclude that his teaching is the authoritative word of God.

Further, authoritative moral teaching alone does not provide a sufficient foundation for the declaration that a teacher is divine. For this reason, even if his original audience and people throughout history would have hailed his teaching as morally superior to that of all other religious leaders, this would not demand the further confession that Jesus is divine. Rather than being a basis for the affirmation of Jesus' deity, we acknowledge the authority of his moral teaching on the basis of this confession.

Jesus' death. Jesus' crucifixion is another candidate for the historical basis of our confession of his deity: The death of Jesus displays his true identity. The Gospels themselves stand at the genesis of this proposal. According to Matthew, observation of the events preceding Jesus' death led the Roman soldiers to conclude, "Surely he was the Son of God" (Matt. 27:54). What is found in embryonic form in the New Testament comes to full flowering in popular evangelical piety, as we sing, "He could have called ten thousand angels. But he died alone for you and me."

---

19. Adolf von Harnack, *What Is Christianity?* trans. Thomas Bailey Saunders (New York: G. P. Putnam's Sons, 1901), 55.

Viewed in isolation, however, Jesus' death is a highly problematic event. Unless understood within the context of a prior faith-commitment, we could readily dismiss it as at best the sacrifice of a well-intended popular hero and martyr or the self-induced demise of a deluded idealist. The seemingly paradoxical nature of Jesus' death finds expression even among the accounts of the evangelists. One unmistaken intent of Mark and Matthew in including Jesus' entreaty, "My God, my God, why have you forsaken me?" (Mark 15:34; Matt. 27:46) is that the Savior experienced estrangement from God. Rather than marking Jesus as divine, therefore, the cross stands as the point at which God abandoned him.

The death of Jesus derives its lofty theological significance from the truth of the assertion that Jesus is divine. The godforsakenness of his death becomes significant only because Jesus is divine. Only if he is Immanuel, God with us, does his death have value for sinful humankind.

In his provocative book *The Crucified God* Jürgen Moltmann offers one of the most creative reconceptions of the theological implications of the cross. Moltmann's treatment underscores the foundational importance of a prior faith-commitment for our understanding of the significance of Jesus' death. Building on the godforsakenness of Jesus in his death, the German theologian argues that the cross is a trinitarian occurrence, "an event between God and God."[20] On the cross, the "Fatherlessness of the Son is matched by the Sonlessness of the Father."[21] But even Moltmann's highly provocative treatment presupposes the deity of Jesus as the Second Person of the Trinity and therefore does not succeed in grounding the confession of Jesus' deity on his sacrifice.

The declaration of Jesus' deity does not arise obviously from the historical event of his death. On the contrary, if we are to make sense out of the cross, we must presuppose that Jesus is divine.

Jesus' claim. Many evangelicals find the historical foundation for the deity of our Lord in Jesus' own claim concerning his person. The

---

20. Jürgen Moltmann, *The Crucified God*, trans. R. A. Wilson and John Bowden (New York: SCM, 1974), 244.
21. Ibid., 243.

widely read *Systematic Theology* of the revered early twentieth-century Baptist scholar, Augustus Hopkins Strong, offers a case in point. Strong argues that during his earthly ministry Jesus both possessed a knowledge of his own deity and exercised divine powers and prerogatives.[22] More recently, Millard Erickson reflected a similar approach. He built his case from "the biblical evidence for the deity of Christ," the foremost of which is Jesus' own self-consciousness, which for Erickson is clearly delineated in the various claims Jesus made about himself.[23]

The Jesus depicted in the four Gospels did set forth a fantastic claim concerning his own person. In his little primer on the faith *Basic Christianity*,[24] John Stott summarizes the materials under four headings. (1) Jesus' claim came through his self-centered teaching. Although demanding humility in others, the Master repeatedly pointed to himself—declaring that he was the bread of life, the light of the world, the resurrection and the life, the fulfillment of the Old Testament, and the one who would draw all persons to himself (John 12:32). (2) The signs Jesus performed entailed an implicit declaration that he enjoyed a unique, divine status. By changing water into wine, feeding multitudes, restoring sight to the blind, and raising the dead, our Lord asserted that he was inaugurating God's new order. (3) By exercising functions belonging wholly to God, Jesus was articulating an indirect claim to deity. He forgave sin, which the Jews interpreted as blasphemous, and he claimed divine prerogatives as the one who could bestow life, teach truth, and even judge the world. (4) Finally, Jesus occasionally issued a direct divine claim. This claim included assertions of a unique relationship with the Father, for he is the Son, is "in the Father," and knows the Father. He declared that he is the "I Am," which the Jews immediately understood as an appeal to the divine name (John 8:51-59). Jesus asserted that he is one with the Father (John 10:30-33). And the resurrected Lord accepted worship (John 20:26-29).

---

22. Augustus Hopkins Strong, *Systematic Theology*, three volumes (Philadelphia: Griffith & Rowland, 1907), 2:681-82.

23. Millard Erickson, *Christian Theology*, three volumes (Grand Rapids: Baker, 1984), 2:684-88.

24. John R.W. Stott, *Basic Christianity*, second edition (London: InterVarsity, 1971), 21-34.

Modern biblical criticism has called into question the historical factualness of much of the Gospel material cited by evangelical apologists such as Stott. These findings weaken considerably all appeals to Jesus' lofty self-consciousness. We cannot counter the claims of critical scholars by simply arguing from the doctrine of biblical inspiration to the total trustworthiness of the Gospel writings. Our assertions concerning the Bible's inspiration and complete trustworthiness are themselves faith declarations which as such must be set aside during the search for the historical basis of the Christian assertion of Jesus' deity.

Modern higher criticism, therefore, demands that we not be overly quick in assuming that the New Testament narratives present straightforward historical facts. Nevertheless, the Gospel materials are significant for the question of Jesus' self-consciousness. New Testament scholars have discovered that a claim to uniqueness pervades every strata of the process that led to the development of the four Gospels. The only plausible conclusion we can draw from this finding is that the source of this claim lies in Jesus himself, that is, in his understanding of his identity and in his teaching concerning his mission. Jesus did indeed assert that he enjoyed a unique relationship to the Father.

The conclusion that Jesus claimed to be unique narrows the options concerning our evaluation of him.[25] Of course, Jesus' claim may have been true, in which case we are called to acknowledge him as divine. However, if his claim was false, then we must question either Jesus' integrity as one who knowingly sought to delude others, or his veracity, for he had deluded himself. In either case, the falsehood lodged in his claim undercuts the possibility that he is either an authoritative teacher or an exemplary human whose life is worthy of emulation. In short, it seems that Jesus is either divine or we ought to dismiss him.

Our knowledge of Jesus' claim may narrow the possible conclusions we can draw concerning his identity, but it cannot guide us as to which opinion is ultimately correct. His claim cannot form the de-

---

25. For an outline of this, see Josh McDowell, *Evidence that Demands a Verdict* (Campus Crusade for Christ, 1972), 107-13.

finitive historical foundation for the declaration that Jesus is divine. The difficulty lies in the tenuous connection between a personal claim and the truth of such an assertion. Jesus is not alone in claiming a unique relationship with God. Other religious figures of his day and since then have made similar professions. As the proliferation of first-century messiahs and the multitude of contemporary religious movements and personality cults indicate, religious teachers or their disciples can make outlandish claims and thereby gain a following. We must never mistake lofty personal claims for an actual substantiated foundation for acknowledging the claimant's uniqueness.

What is noteworthy about Jesus, however, is that his claim looked for, and even demanded a future vindication. Jesus' declarations concerning his identity and mission entailed a challenge, as it were, to the one he called "Father" to confirm the truth of his self-consciousness. Jesus' self-awareness pointed to the future, to the day when God would act on his behalf to exonerate him and his ministry.

Jesus' resurrection. The future orientation of Jesus' claim to uniqueness leads us to another possible historical foundation on which to ground the Christian affirmation of Jesus' deity, namely, his resurrection. Before evaluating this suggestion, we must probe concerning the propriety in calling the resurrection historical. Can we say that Jesus' resurrection is a historical event?

The tendency among theologians since the Enlightenment has been to deny the historicity of the resurrection. Such denials range from the dismissal of the theological importance of the idea to the radical reinterpretation of its meaning. Schleiermacher follows the former route. In his estimation, "The facts of the Resurrection and the Ascension of Christ...cannot be laid down as properly constituent parts of the doctrine of His Person."[26] The German theologian's argument is instructive:

> For if the redeeming efficacy of Christ depends upon the being of God in Him, and faith in Him is grounded on the impression that such a being of God indwells Him, then it is impossible to prove any immediate connection between these facts [i.e., the resurrection and ascension] and that doctrine. The disciples recognized in Him the Son

---

26. Schleiermacher, *The Christian Faith*, 417.

of God without having the faintest premonition of His resurrection and ascension, and we too may say the same of ourselves; moreover neither the spiritual presence which He promised nor all that He said about His enduring influence upon those who remained behind is mediated through either of these two facts.[27]

In contrast to Schleiermacher's simple dismissal of the idea as theologically irrelevant, many twentieth-century critics of the historicity of Jesus' resurrection reinterpret the concept. Typical is the assertion that the biblical stories, when correctly interpreted, describe the resurrection of the crucified Jesus in the hearts of his disciples. Rudolf Bultmann, for example, refused to speak of the resurrection as an event of past history.[28] To him, the resurrection is neither the return of a dead man to life in this world nor the translation of Jesus to a life beyond;[29] rather, it is the elevation of the Crucified One to the status of Lord. As a result, "faith in the resurrection is really the same thing as faith in the saving efficacy of the cross."[30]

Despite the predominance of the rejection of the idea among modern theologians, several prominent and powerful voices have defended the historical nature of Jesus' resurrection.[31] Thinkers who assert that the resurrection of Jesus is a historical event appeal to a several considerations. The foundational evidence, of course, is that of the New Testament writings themselves. All four evangelists and Paul (1 Cor. 15:3-7) bear witness to the resurrection of Jesus as a historical fact. But at the heart of the evidence are two traditions that predate the writing of the Gospels—the traditions of the empty tomb and the post-resurrection appearances.[32]

The Gospels report that the tomb was empty on Easter and assert that the empty tomb stands as a sign that Jesus triumphed over death.

---

27. Ibid., 418.
28. Bultmann, "New Testament and Mythology," in *Kerygma and Myth*, 39, 42.
29. Walter Schmithals, *An Introduction to the Theology of Rudolf Bultmann* (Minneapolis: Augsburg, 1968), 145.
30. Bultmann, "New Testament and Mythology," in *Kerygma and Myth*, 41.
31. In the late 1960s North American evangelicals hailed the work of Wolfhart Pannenberg, because he employed the resurrection of Jesus, viewed as an event of history, as the linchpin of his entire Christology. See Wolfhart Pannenberg, *Jesus—God and Man*, trans. Lewis L. Wilkins and Duane A. Priebe, second edition (Philadelphia: Westminster, 1977), 53-114.
32. For an extensive discussion of these traditions, see Pannenberg, *Jesus—God and Man*, 88-106.

As we would expect, the appeal to the empty tomb is controversial. Critics offer several other explanations for this phenomenon. Some suggest that the women, being strangers in the city, went to the wrong tomb. In response, however, we note that many other persons, including the disciples, viewed the same tomb; it seems unlikely that so many would make the same mistake concerning where Jesus' body had been laid. An ancient explanation is that the disciples of Jesus stole his body (Matt. 28:11-15). This alternative seems unlikely insofar as the persons who purportedly perpetrated such a hoax were subsequently willing to die as martyrs for their declaration that Jesus was risen. The suggestion that the Jerusalem authorities took the body is even less plausible, for these same authorities could then have squelched the entire Christian movement by merely producing the body when the story of Jesus' resurrection began to circulate in the city. Since the Enlightenment the theory that Jesus did not actually die but merely went into a swoon has repeatedly gained adherents.[33] However, the unlikelihood that Jesus could even have survived the ordeal of the final hours of Passion Week, let alone have given the impression that he had conquered death, makes the "swoon theory" border on the incredulous.

Standing in importance with the empty tomb tradition is the witness to post-resurrection appearances of Jesus. This testimony is important, in that it suggests that the resurrection is a historical event because many people saw Jesus alive after Easter. Again, critics have been quick, but unsuccessful, in discounting the significance of this evidence. Some suggest that the supposed appearances were fabrications. But the strength of this proposal is diminished by the appeal to living witnesses found in what may be the earliest assertion of the resurrection, that of Paul (1 Cor. 15:3-8). Equally unsatisfying is the suggestion that the appearances were hallucinations or subjective visions. The appearances of Jesus as described by the witnesses do not occur in the kinds of situations that are conducive to halluci-

---

33. For a twentieth-century popularization of this thesis, see Hugh J. Schonfield, *The Passover Plot*, Bantam Book edition (New York: Bantam Books, 1967), 151-62. However, as late as 1991 this theory continued to gain defenders. See the newspaper report, "Christ could have faked death on cross, article purports," *Vancouver Sun* (April 27, 1991): A3.

nation, namely, a strong inward desire or a predisposing outward set-ting. On the contrary, the followers of Jesus saw no hope of seeing Jesus again after his crushing death, and the settings of the appear-ances were varied in location and in time of day. Nor were these ex-periences merely subjective visions, for they were apprehended by several persons at the same time.

Confirming evidence for the historicity of the resurrection arises from two further sources. Easter resulted in a change in the day of worship among the disciples of Jesus. Although they had been steeped in the strict Jewish heritage concerning the Sabbath, soon af-ter the events of Holy Week the early believers began to gather on the first day of the week—"the Lord's day"—to celebrate the resur-rection of Jesus (1 Cor. 16:1-2; Rev. 1:10). Easter also sparked the phenomenal growth of the infant church. A company of believers in the Resurrected One immediately developed among pious Jews (Acts 2:41,47), and in a few years the message concerning Jesus' res-urrection had become a potent force in the entire Roman world (Acts 17:6; Col. 1:6).

The resurrection formed the foundation for the early Christian un-derstanding of the identity of Jesus. The testimony to Jesus' resur-rection was central to all apostolic preaching. His resurrection was also the one event in Jesus' life that repeatedly served as the primary apologetic for the early believers' assertion that he is the Messiah (Acts 2:32-36; 17:18; 13:32-39; 1 Cor. 15:14-17). The New Testa-ment documents even put forth the resurrection as lying at the heart of Christian faith itself (Rom. 10:9).

The New Testament indicates that the early believers viewed the resurrection as God's confirmation of Jesus' understanding of him-self and his mission. Through this act, God himself confirmed Jesus' claim concerning his own uniqueness—which claim looked for and demanded a future confirmation. As a consequence, Jesus' resurrec-tion stands as the sign of his divine identity (Rom. 1:4).

Despite the decisive role played by the resurrection in the New Testament witness to Jesus' deity, we must temper our positive eval-uation of this event as central to the historical foundation for that christological affirmation. We dare not understand the resurrection in an adoptionistic manner. This event does not constitute Jesus' deity. Jesus did not become divine when he came forth from the dead. Rather, in the resurrection God sounded the verdict concerning Jesus' life: Jesus is divine, and insofar as from the resurrection onward he is who he claimed to be, he always has been the Son.

Our evaluation of the resurrection must be tempered in another manner as well. Just as we discovered with the other proposals, the resurrection as an isolated event that happened to Jesus is incapable of forming the foundation for our affirmation of Jesus' deity. The Bible knows of others who returned from the dead, indicating that there is no obvious connection between the survival of death and being divine. Even an event as unique as Jesus' resurrection does not carry within itself its own significance. Viewed from a purely historical perspective, his resurrection might mean only that at this stage in the evolutionary process natural forces "coughed up" a human being who was able to overcome death.

Jesus' claim and his resurrection. Given these considerations, our quest does not terminate with our knowledge of the resurrection of Jesus. Rather it lies in a combination of the last two alternatives. We propose, therefore, that the historical foundation for our assertion of Jesus' deity rests on his personal claim as confirmed by the resurrection.

As we have seen, through his teaching and actions Jesus did indeed set forth a claim to his own uniqueness. This claim called forth a future confirmation. The claim of Jesus, with its view toward a future confirmation, forms the immediate context in which to understand the resurrection. In fact, it is only within this context that Jesus' resurrection takes on the meaning that the New Testament community saw in it: In response to the plea of Jesus, "God raised him from the dead" (Acts 13:30). The resurrection, therefore, is nothing less than God's confirmation of Jesus' understanding of his identity and mission.

There is yet a wider context for understanding the resurrection as the exoneration of Jesus' claim, namely, the apocalyptic expectation of the end of the age. The Master asserted through his teaching and deeds that in him the new age was arriving—that the kingdom of

God had come near (Mark 1:15). According to the apocalyptic seers, the dawning of the new age would be marked by the general resurrection. Given this context, raising Jesus from the dead was the only possible way that God could confirm the activities of one who issued such a unique claim to fellowship with himself. Through the resurrection the one Jesus called "Father" gave ultimate and final acknowledgment to the work of his messenger. The resurrection is God's declaration that through his ministry, Jesus had indeed inaugurated the divine reign. In him God is truly at work enacting his eschatological purpose, which is the establishment of the community of God.

On the basis of the historical foundation of Jesus' claim and its confirmation through the resurrection, we assert Jesus' deity. From this affirmation the other lofty features of his life gain their significance. If Jesus is divine, he is indeed perfectly sinless and thus worthy of emulation. If he is God's messenger, Jesus' teaching is truly the authoritative word of God. And if Jesus is God with us, then his crucifixion is in truth the suffering of God on our behalf for our salvation.

The Historical Foundation and Faith

We affirm that Jesus is divine on the basis of his history. More specifically, our christological assertion arises out of Jesus' claim to a special relation to his Father, which claim God confirmed through the resurrection. This specific historical appeal indicates why a foundation for faith is crucial.

Earlier we concurred that our experience of the presence of the living Christ provides a crucial confirmation of Jesus' deity. However, this experience is itself dependent on the history of Jesus of Nazareth. Jesus' history guarantees that our present experience is nothing less than the experience of the living Lord. If God was not present in the mission of Jesus and if God did not raise this same Jesus from the dead, we could no longer claim to experience the presence of the Resurrected One now. Unless it is true on historical grounds that Jesus came forth from the grave, we have no certainty that there is a living Christ who encounters us in the present.

From this consideration follows an important soteriological corollary. Our christological assertion requires this specific historical basis because the encounter that mediates salvation to us is the encounter with Jesus the Savior. But if our faith has no foundation in God's historical act confirming Jesus' claim, we have no assurance that Jesus is alive and consequently that we have encountered the divine Savior himself. On the contrary, our hope for salvation may only rest on an encounter with a lofty idea or a philosophical system, such as the ideal of self-giving love. Paul aptly summarizes our situation:

> And if Christ has not been raised, your faith is futile; you are still in your sins. Then those also who have fallen asleep in Christ are lost. If only for this life we have hope in Christ, we are to be pitied more than all men. (1 Cor. 15:17-19)

Similarly, we concurred earlier that the Holy Spirit testifies to Jesus' deity. Here as well the historical foundation is nonnegotiable. The historical reality of Jesus' claim and its confirmation in the resurrection are crucial for the contemporary testimony of the Holy Spirit to Jesus' deity. Our question is simple: If the claim of Jesus was not confirmed in the resurrection, on what basis does the Holy Spirit now testify to the deity of the Nazarene?

This question can be viewed from two perspectives. If Jesus never claimed a special relationship to his Father, the Holy Spirit would appear to be witnessing to something that Jesus himself never knew. And if the Father had not confirmed Jesus' claim, the Spirit would appear to be witnessing to a truth that the Father himself had never declared. In either case, we could rightly question whether it was indeed the Spirit of the Father and the Son who was bearing witness to the deity of Jesus. Indeed, the Spirit would thereby be showing himself to be an alien spirit who was adding a new testimony beyond that borne by Jesus to himself and by God to his Son. And if he is an alien spirit, we have not encountered the triune God—the Father, Son, and Spirit who together are one God.

We conclude, then, that the foundation for our faith assertion that Jesus is divine consists in the historical truths that Jesus did indeed claim a unique relation to his Father and that the Father confirmed this claim in the most appropriate manner, by raising Jesus from the dead. These dimensions of the history of Jesus form the historical givens that make faith credible.

The threefold conception of faith set forth in the Reformation is helpful in this context. Faith begins with *notitia*, the knowledge of the history of Jesus. This historical knowledge brings *assensus*—assent, spiritual acknowledgment or agreement that Jesus is divine. As we will see in the pneumatology section, *assensus* must translate into *fiducia*, what Richard Muller calls "the crown of faith"[34]—trust in Jesus as "God with Us."

Implications: Jesus as One with God

Central to the Christology of the church is the affirmation that Jesus is divine. In the man from Nazareth, God himself encounters us. This kerygmatic affirmation is not simply the product of the theologizing of the church, for its foundations lie in the history of Jesus himself. He claimed to be uniquely related to his Father. And God confirmed this claim through the resurrection, which in the apocalyptic context in which it occurred marked the beginning of the end of the age. Consequently, the affirmation of Jesus' deity is motivated by reflection on the history of Jesus, specifically his claim as confirmed in his resurrection.

Our appraisal of Jesus' history, leading as it does to the assertion of his deity, carries a crucial, non-negotiable theological implication for Jesus' relationship to God. Jesus is one with God.

The conclusion that Jesus is one with God arises out of the apocalyptic context which conveys meaning to both his message and his resurrection. Occurring this context, Jesus' message concerning the inauguration of God's reign and its confirmation by God mean that in Jesus, God has initiated his eschatological reign. Because the inaugurator of the kingdom can only be the king himself, Jesus' claim as confirmed through the resurrection indicates that Jesus is one with God.

---

34. Richard A. Muller, "fiducia," in the *Dictionary of Latin and Greek Theological Terms* (Grand Rapids: Baker, 1985), 118.

In what sense are we to understand this declaration? To this thorny problem we must now turn.

Jesus' Unity with God

From the history of Jesus we arrived at the conclusion that this historical person is divine. From this assertion we can only conclude that Jesus is one with God. But how ought we to understand this affirmation?

Function versus ontology. Recent theological history has been dominated by two basic ways of understanding the fundamental Christian assertion, "Jesus is one with God." Some theologians advocate a functional Christology, whereas others argue for an ontological approach.

(1) The most readily evident interpretation of Jesus' unity with God understands the affirmation functionally. The functional approach yields the conclusion that by asserting Jesus' deity we are declaring that he functioned in a divine manner. We could view this in the context of Jesus' activity: he acted in accordance with a divine function. As Jesus fulfilled the lofty task assigned to him on God's behalf, we find God at work in him (2 Cor. 5:19; John 4:34; 9:4). We could likewise characterize Jesus' functional unity with God volitionally: In Jesus we find the will of God fully actualized, for Jesus willed only the will of God.

An important modern advocate of functional Christology was the nineteenth-century German liberal theologian Albrecht Ritschl. He theorized that Jesus fully completed his divinely given vocation, and as a consequence Jesus carries the value of deity for the church. Perhaps the most celebrated recent presentation of functional Christology was articulated by the lesser-known colleague of Karl Barth, Oscar Cullmann. The functional thrust of Cullmann's approach is evident in his assertion, "When it is asked in the New Testament, 'Who is Christ?', the question never means exclusively, or even primarily, 'What is his nature?', but first of all, 'What is his function?'"[35] Cullmann maintained that the key to unlocking the mystery

---

35. Oscar Cullmann, *Christology of the New Testament*, trans. Shirlie C. Guthrie and Charles A. M. Hall, revised edition (Philadelphia: Westminster, 1963), 3.

of Jesus' relationship to God lies in our Lord's role in "salvation history," that is, in God's acting in human history to bring about his eschatological purposes. The early church, in turn, described this role through the various christological titles they bestowed on Jesus.

The advocates of functional Christology correctly declare that Jesus is functionally one with God. In fact, the functional approach is the proper place to begin in the search to understand Jesus' unity with God.[36] But can we say more? Can we move beyond function to talk about ontology?

The answer voiced by many modern thinkers is "no." Although from the patristic era to the Reformation theologians were readily willing to speak about Jesus' deity in ontological terms, the traditional viewpoint became suspect in the modern era. One important cause of the radical change in approach was the popularity of the thesis that ontological terminology is solely a reflection of the Greek philosophical outlook and is totally foreign to the Hebrew soil on which Jesus walked. Thus, it was theologically fashionable in the first half of the twentieth-century not only to articulate a purely functional understanding of the unity Jesus enjoys with God but also to disclaim any attempt to move beyond the supposedly functional categories of the New Testament to the ontological concerns of the later creeds.

(2) Despite the lure of the anti-Greek sentiment with its dismissal of ontological categories, contemporary theologians are once again returning to the quest for an ontological, as well as a functional, Christology. The renewed interest in ontology has been fuelled by several important critiques of the purely functional approaches that had their day in the 1940s and 1950s.[37]

Recent studies acknowledge that the attempt to speak ontologically about Jesus' identity is visible already among certain New Testament writers. As the Christian message moved into the Greek world, the early believers grappled with the task of expressing the message about Jesus in a way that would communicate his identity to the wid-

---

36. E.g., Emil Brunner, *The Christian Doctrine of Creation and Redemption*, trans. Olive Wyon (Philadelphia: Westminster, 1952), 271-72.

37. E.g., James Barr, *Semantics of Biblical Language* (New York: Oxford, 1961); Brevard Childs, *Biblical Theology in Crisis* (Philadelphia: Westminster, 1970).

er gentile world. The renewed interest in ontological categories is fuelled as well by the growing realization that in contrast to the claims of the proponents of functional Christology, we cannot avoid the ontological dimension of contemporary questions concerning identity and personhood.

For reasons such as these, we must move beyond functional Christology to ask the difficult but crucial question concerning the ontological relationship between Jesus and God. In so doing, we must look more closely at the traditional theological declaration that Jesus is ontologically one with God. We ask, therefore, In what sense is Jesus not only one in function, but also one in essence with the Father? To what extent and on what basis can we affirm the words of the creed of Nicea?

> We believe…in one Lord Jesus Christ, the Son of God, begotten of the Father as only begotten, that is, from the essence of the Father, God from God, Light from Light, true God from true God, begotten not created, of the same essence as the Father.[38]

Jesus as the revealer of God. At the heart of the movement from a functional to an ontological understanding of Jesus' unity with God is the Christian affirmation of his revelatory role (John 14:9-10)— Jesus is the revealer of God. This affirmation facilitates the transition from functional to ontological Christology, because the statement, Jesus is the revealer of God, transcends the demarcation between function and ontology.

Revelation, of course, marks a functional connection between Jesus and God. The task of revealing God is a divine activity which Jesus carries out, for he is revealing the essence of God. But the task of revelation also carries ontological implications, insofar as the revealer cannot be separated from what is revealed. As a consequence of this connection, Jesus participates by necessity in the essential nature of the one he reveals. He must be ontologically one God and share in the divine essence which he exemplifies.

The declaration, Jesus is the Revealer of God, can actually carry two meanings. We may interpret it objectively. Hence, "Jesus is the

---

38. "The Creed of Nicaea," in *Creeds of the Churches*, 30-31.

revealer of God" means that in Jesus we find the essence of God pictured before us. In him we see God. Even if the picture is partial, it is nevertheless an accurate portrayal of God's essence. Jesus, then, is the embodiment of the divine essence, and therefore he is ontologically one with God.

As the Revealer of God, Jesus mediates an objective picture of God throughout his entire earthly life and ministry. Each dimension of Jesus' sojourn is revelatory. His teaching informs us about God; his character shows forth the qualities of God; his death reveals the suffering of God; and his resurrection vividly declares the creative power of God.

The central content of the picture Jesus mediates is that God is love. Through his life, teaching, death, and resurrection, Jesus shows us this dimension of the divine essence. Further, his life describes the qualities of that love. Above all, the divine love is salvific: It seeks the lost, suffers with the afflicted, and redeems the fallen. God's love is likewise jealous, as is evident in the picture of Jesus as the righteous judge.

Not only may we interpret the declaration, Jesus is the Revealer of God, objectively, it also has a subjective aspect. It means that Jesus is the one who seeks to introduce us to God (Matt. 11:27; Luke 10:22). He desires that the divine character or godliness become a vital reality within and among us. This forms a link between the work of the Son and the Spirit. The activity of the Holy Spirit makes evident in our lives the qualities or character which Jesus vividly revealed to us as constituting the character of God. In this sense, Christ—the Revealer of God—must be "formed" in us (Gal. 4:19). As this transpires, we truly become the image of God.

The declaration that Jesus is the Revealer of God carries an important implication concerning God's relationship to creation. It suggests that God is now the revealed God. Jesus' coming inaugurated a qualitatively new state of affairs. Because Jesus has come, the veil has been pulled aside and the hidden God is forever manifested for all to see. Hence, he brought about the era of the revealed God.

This is not to deny the testimony to the divine reality proclaimed by creation itself (general revelation) nor the importance of Old Testament history in the process of revelation. Rather, we claim that in contrast to the fragmentary nature of the revelation found in creation's witness and even in the Old Testament, in Jesus we find a surpassing revelation—the complete and final self-disclosure of God. Jesus is the divine revelation toward whom creation and the Old Testament both point. And in the light of Jesus both the witness of creation and all history gain their meaning, for he discloses publicly the true significance of the Old Testament and of the witness found in creation. The self-disclosure of God in Jesus, therefore, is unique.

Nor is this to suggest that all persons readily perceive the revelation of God on the face of Jesus. This is obviously not the case. Nevertheless, one day the entire world will acknowledge fully Jesus' revelatory function. The grand eschatological event will inaugurate a glorious state of affairs, for it will constitute God's ultimate self-disclosure. Yet even this unveiling will be the revelation of Jesus. The same Jesus who in his life, death, and resurrection is the revelation sent by the Father to humankind will be revealed in his complete glory and majesty as truly the Son of the Father.

Because as the revelation of God Jesus is one with God, he is the mediator of genuine knowledge of God. This means that Jesus is the focus for our understanding who God is and what God is like. In the final analysis, therefore, we must measure all theological statements concerning the divine character and essence by Jesus' life and teaching. In addition, as the revealer of God Jesus is the mediator of our knowing God. The way to God comes solely through Jesus of Nazareth.

On this basis, we can affirm in this context an important category of evangelical theology, "special revelation." The revelatory unity of Jesus with God means that we are the recipients of a revelation from God which goes far beyond the general testimony concerning the divine reality present to all humankind. In Jesus we find God's "special" revelation, for in and through Christ God makes himself understandable. As we noted in chapter 2, history is the vehicle for God's self-revelation. But this historical revelation becomes visible in the light of Jesus, for he is the meaning of history and the one who provides the unity to history.

Jesus' Fellowship with the Father

The key in our search for an understanding of Jesus' relationship to God lies in the statement, "Jesus is the Revealer of God." In this affirmation we declare that Jesus participates in the eternal reality of God—that he is the embodiment of the divine essence. But this declaration raises a question: What characterizes the divine essence that Jesus revealed to us?

As we will see, this question is crucial because it forges the link between Christology and theology. In posing it, we find ourselves face to face with the connection between the historical life of Jesus and the divine Trinity. The key to understanding this connection lies in the fellowship Jesus enjoyed with the one he called "Father." We must now explore how this is the case.

Jesus' compassion. We begin our exploration by reminding ourselves of the central New Testament description of what Jesus, as the Revealer of God, came to show us concerning God. At the center of the Gospels is Jesus' revelation of the compassionate heart of the loving God. They bear witness that Jesus understood his mission as the expression of the self-giving, compassionate love of God.

We cite several examples. John explains that Jesus' primary mission was to save, not to judge and condemn (John 3:17). Using the imagery of the good shepherd, Christ emphasized that he came to give himself completely, even to the point of sacrificing his own life for the sake of others (John 10:10-11; see also Matt. 20:28; Mark 10:45). Luke reports that at the synagogue in Capernaum Jesus appealed to Isaiah in order to explain that his purpose included the practical goals of bringing freedom, healing, and release to people in distress (Luke 4:18-19).

As the one who knew that his task was to reveal the compassionate love of God, Jesus was himself characterized by compassion. The Master was gripped by compassion when he saw the aimlessness of the common people who were as "sheep without a shepherd" (Matt. 9:36; Mark 6:34). His heart was moved when he saw the sick (Matt. 14:14). His compassion was kindled by the plight of specific individuals, such as the two blind men he met outside the city of Jericho (Matt. 20:34). The crowds who grew hungry as they intently listened to his teaching evoked from him the same response (Matt. 15:32; Mark 8:2). Above all, Jesus was filled with compassion in response to the sorrow people experienced at the loss of loved ones. When he saw a woman weeping over the death of her son, Jesus' "heart went out to her" (Luke 7:13), and at the tomb of Jesus' friend Lazarus the Master wept (John 11:35).

Jesus' compassion expressed itself in ministry. As he observed the needs of people around him, needs which sparked his emotion, he engaged in action in order to alleviate the misery of others and minister to their needs. To those who had lost loved ones Jesus responded by raising the dead (John 11; Luke 7:14). To people lacking guidance Jesus offered instruction and teaching (Mark 6:34). To the sick Jesus administered healing (Matt. 14:14; 4:23; 9:35; 19:2).

Jesus' compassion was all-encompassing. It extended beyond his friends to include the multitudes. It encircled his enemies and those who rejected him. Even when his arrest and death were imminent, Jesus' heart still went out to others. Anticipating the final rejection he would experience from the nation he loved, Jesus wept over the city of Jerusalem (Matt. 23:37). Then, during his arrest Jesus offered his healing touch to the soldier whose ear had been injured in the scuffle (Luke 22:51). In his hour of death, our Lord's thoughts were directed toward the needs of those who rejected him. Jesus prayed that the forgiving mercy of his Father be extended even to the soldiers who were crucifying him: "Father, forgive them, for they do not know what they are doing" (Luke 23:34). Jesus' own actions, therefore, stand as apt illustrations of his teaching.

The loving compassion Jesus displays reveals the essence of the God who is love. This conclusion takes us to the threshold of the relation of Jesus to the Father. To cross this threshold, however, we must probe yet deeper into the revelatory life of Jesus.

Jesus' special fellowship with God. The compassion that characterized Jesus' life and death finds its source in a more foundational dimension of his existence. It was an outgrowth of the relationship—the special fellowship—the Master enjoyed with his God. Jesus was conscious of a special vocation. He had come to display the compassionate heart of the loving God. But his awareness of this special vocation was connected to a prior consciousness, namely, that he shared a special relationship to the God who had sent him into the world. This consciousness of fellowship with God offers us the ultimate entry into the ontological relationship between Jesus and God.

Perhaps his sense of a special fellowship was most vividly evident in Jesus' means of address to God. His preferred address, given in the Gospels by the Aramaic word "Abba," is actually a term of endearment expressing close familial ties, somewhat similar to the English "Dad." Jesus, therefore, related to God as Father, and he was conscious of a special filial relation to God.

How significant is this tangible expression of Jesus' consciousness? Scholars have debated the extent to which Jesus' understanding of his relationship to God marks a new phenomenon in Hebrew religious history. Gauthier Adalbert Hamman, reflecting the conclusion of many scholars, asserts that the reference to God as Father was a part of Hebrew religious life as early as the Exodus.[39] This acknowledgment of God's paternity emphasized Israel's status as a people chosen with a special mission in the world. Later in the exile, the Hebrews came to see God as the Father not merely of the corporate nation but also of the individual righteous person.

In contrast to Hamman's view, Joachim Jeremias argues that the specific use of "Abba," which he sees as a colloquialism derived from the speech of children, finds no parallel in Judaism:

> It definitely represents Jesus' own most characteristic mode of speech and it is the profoundest expression of his authority and of his consciousness of his mission (Matt. 11:27)....A new way of praying is born. Jesus talks to his Father as naturally, as intimately and with the same sense of security as a child talks to his father."[40]

Whether or not Jeremias has overstated the case, Jesus' understanding of his relationship to God as evidenced in his addressing God as "Abba" constitutes a development beyond the Old Testament Hebrew mindset. This address gives evidence to a profound filial

---

39. Hamman writes, "The first evidence dates back to the Exodus from Egypt when God himself stated: 'Israel is my first-born son' (Ex. 4, 22)." Gauthier Adalbert Hamman, *Prayer—the New Testament* (Chicago: Franciscan Herald Press, 1971), 90.

40. Joachim Jeremias, *The Prayers of Jesus* (Naperville, Ill.: Alec R. Allenson, 1967), 78.

consciousness in Jesus. He sensed a special relationship to God and a special task in God's program. As Hamman rightly concludes,

> Christ's use of the word Father acquires a new meaning, because it actually fulfils the eschatological promise made by Yahweh to his people. The Son of the Father has been sent to carry out the work of salvation.[41]

With this conclusion Jeremias is in agreement:

> In this term *abba* the ultimate mystery of his mission and his authority is expressed. He, to whom the Father had granted full knowledge of God, has the messianic prerogative of addressing him with the familiar address of a son.[42]

The unparalleled closeness Jesus sensed with the Father produced in him a certainty of being heard whenever he addressed "Abba." An example of this is found in Jesus' prayer prior to raising Lazarus: "Father, I thank you that you have heard me. I knew that you always hear me, but I said this for the benefit of the people standing here, that they may believe that you sent me" (John 11:41b-42). Similarly, there is close connection evidenced between Jesus' profound sense of mission as sent by God and his filial relationship to God. Hamman has correctly observed:

> Every situation, every petition always brought Jesus back to the object of his mission, the divine will, the work his Father had entrusted to him. Jesus desired nothing else. Prayer enabled him to discern and bless the plan of his Father whom he had come to serve. His petitions had no objects other than the good will of the Father and the will to act in his service....
>
> Therefore he could give thanks before a miracle; since his Father always granted what he asked, his will being entirely in accord with that of God. This submission motivated his filial and absolute trust.[43]

Jesus' sense of a special filial relationship to, or fellowship with the one he called "Abba" is not simply an indication of the self-consciousness of a historical human. Rather, it carries grave theological

---

41. Hamman, *Prayer—The New Testament*, 92

42. Jeremias, *The Prayers of Jesus*, 97. See also John H. Wright, *A Theology of Christian Prayer* (New York: Pueblo, 1979), 26.

43. Hamman, *Prayer—The New Testament*, 182.

implications. Because this Jesus is the revelation of God, his filial self-consciousness discloses not only an isolated historical self-consciousness, but also an eternal relationship. Jesus displays the relationship of the Son of the Father. As a result, the one who referred to God as his own Father is none other than the eternal Son of the Father.

By extension, the special love shared between Jesus and Abba also carries far-reaching theological implications. The Jesus who dedicated himself to God as the loving, obedient servant who reveals the compassionate heart of God and who in turn was beloved by God is the one who also in all eternity is the only begotten, beloved Son of the Father who gives back to the Father the love he receives. Hence, the voice from heaven at Jesus' baptism, "This is my Son, whom I love; with him I am well-pleased" (Matt. 3:17), declared not only a temporal but also an eternal affirmation concerning Jesus' identity. The earthly Jesus is the eternal Son, who is well-pleasing to the Father.

On the basis of his earthly life, therefore, we conclude that this historical person, Jesus of Nazareth, is the eternal Son of the Father. The relationship Jesus enjoyed with Abba is the fellowship that characterizes the interaction between the Father and the Son in the eternal divine life. As the divine Son, Jesus lives in intimate community with the Father. Hence, this historical person is none other than the one who throughout all eternity belongs to the triune God as the eternal Son in community of love with the Father, which love is the Holy Spirit.

Jesus, therefore, reveals to us the fellowship—the community—of the triune God. Jesus discloses in his relationship to his Father the divine dynamic of love that characterizes the eternal relationship between the Father and the Son, which dynamic is the Holy Spirit. Thereby, Jesus shows us what God is like: God is the community of the Father, Son, and Spirit. In this sense, Jesus is indeed deity, for he shares with the Father who sent him the divine essence—love—which is the Spirit of the Father and the Son.

Jesus' Lordship

Having affirmed Jesus' ontological unity with God, we must return again to the functional unity they share. The bridge from ontology back to function lies in the christological title, "Lord," which is both ontological and functional in significance. Because Jesus is one with God, he functions as God present in the world. But God is ultimately present to the world as its sovereign Creator, that is, as its lord. It comes therefore as no surprise that the New Testament authors repeatedly speak of Jesus as Lord. What does this designation entail?

The cosmic Lord. Basically, through the confession "Jesus is Lord" we affirm a fundamental truth concerning the relationship between Jesus and the cosmos: Jesus is the Lord of the universe. Our initial understanding of this statement generally focuses on rulership and power. Ultimately, Jesus is the powerful ruler of the cosmos, and this, we must add, by virtue of his identity as the divine Son.

The cosmic dimension of the concept of lordship finds echo throughout the New Testament. In his great christological hymn, Paul moves from Jesus' deity to his universal lordship. This Jesus, he says, stands above every power, so that to him everyone in the universe will pay homage (Phil. 2:9-11).

Our personal Lord. Although Jesus' lordship will not be completely actualized or displayed until the eschaton, the biblical vision of that great day ought to affect our attitudes and actions in the present. Consequently, we readily speak of his lordship not only in cosmic but also in existential terms. "Jesus is Lord" means "Jesus is the ruler of my own life." We have granted him this status by virtue of our personal commitment to Jesus.

Paul brings together the cosmic and existential aspects of our affirmation and draws out one of its many far-reaching practical implications:

> The weapons we fight with are not the weapons of the world. On the contrary, they have divine power to demolish strongholds. We demolish arguments and every pretension that sets itself up against the knowledge of God, and we take captive every thought to make it obedient to Christ. (2 Cor. 10:4-5)

In other words, because he is both Lord of the cosmos and Lord of my life, Jesus must reign over all, including over every thought.

The Lord of history. Mention of his reign over all thoughts leads us to a related dimension of Jesus' lordship. As Lord he is the revelation of the meaning of the history of the entire universe, as well as of my personal life. Because Jesus is Lord of all, all creation—and within it each human life—ultimately can find true unity in him alone. Herein lies a great scandal of the Christian faith: The universal history of all creation and the histories of every person who has ever lived ultimately find their significance in, and take their meaning from one brief historical life—Jesus of Nazareth.

Because of its scandalous nature, the affirmation "Jesus is Lord" by means of which we confess both the existential and the cosmic lordship of Jesus of Nazareth, is both divisive and unitive. It is undeniably divisive in that it sets those persons who make this confession apart from those who do not. Thereby, this confession marks a great dividing line that runs through humankind. But this confession also unites. The affirmation, "Jesus is Lord," brings together into one fellowship which transcends the ages all of those who acknowledge his lordship.

10

The Fellowship of Jesus the Christ with Humankind

For he has set a day when he will judge the world with justice by the man he has appointed. (Acts 17:31)

Outline

Central to our faith as Christians is the confession, Jesus of Nazareth is the Christ. By this declaration we are asserting that in Jesus we find both God's self-revelation and God himself acting definitively for our salvation. Consequently, we affirm that Jesus is divine, the Son who participates in eternal fellowship with the Father within the triune God.

In confessing that Jesus is the Christ we are also declaring another dimension of the reality of Jesus of Nazareth. We are saying that in this historical life we find not only true deity, but also essential humanity. Not only is he the embodiment of God, Jesus is also the embodiment of God's intention for us, which we may capsulize as "life in community." Consequently, Jesus is not only the one who participates in the eternal community of the triune God, he is also the exemplar of creaturely fellowship. Therefore, he is both truly God and truly human.

What do we mean when we affirm that we find creaturely fellowship displayed in Jesus who is the Christ? In this second segment of our Christology we seek to explicate the Christian confession of Jesus' oneness with God's creatures. We now seek to answer the question, What does it mean to affirm the humanity of Jesus?

Jesus as a Human

The confession of Jesus' deity has engendered heated controversy among modern theologians. The parallel declaration, Jesus was a human being, in contrast, now enjoys nearly universal affirmation. As the Scottish theologian D. M. Baillie stated,

> It may safely be said that practically all schools of theological thought today take the full humanity of our Lord more seriously than has ever been done before by Christian theologians.[1]

While the universal acknowledgment of Jesus' humanity may mean that this basic christological affirmation is uncontested, its significance and implications are not for that reason immediately obvi-

---

1. D. M. Baillie, *God Was in Christ*, second edition (New York: Charles Scribner's Sons, 1948), 11.

ous. In this chapter, therefore, we tackle the construction of a contemporary understanding of the christological confession of Jesus' humanity in its various dimensions. Our first task is to ask concerning the nature of the humanness in which Jesus participated. En route to the development of such an understanding we must remind ourselves of the process in the patristic era that led to the canonizing of the assertion of the full humanness of our Lord.

Development of the Affirmation of Jesus' Humanity

In chapter 9, we sketched the process that climaxed in the First Ecumenical Council in Nicea. The council affirmed Jesus' deity in the face of the Arian challenge to that aspect of the New Testament witness to Jesus' identity. The controversy that surrounded the second of the "four great heresies"[2] formed the impetus for the church to affirm the parallel aspect of Jesus' identity—his complete humanity.

Arianism overemphasized certain concerns endemical of the thinkers of Antioch. To counter the threat to the affirmation of Jesus' complete deity which it perceived in the Arian Christology, the council invoked the metaphysical language of Greek philosophy, affirming that Jesus shared the essence of the Father. But the Nicean appeal to Greek philosophical categories opened the door to an equally dangerous tendency that moved in the direction exactly opposite from that traveled by Arius. The second great heresy, Apollinarianism, therefore, came as an outworking of the Alexandrian christological concerns.

Apollinarianism. The Apollinarian heresy arose out of concern to maintain the unity of the person of Christ, while taking seriously the Nicean assertion that Jesus is "consubstantial" ("of the same substance" or "one in essence") with the Father. In keeping with this concern, Apollinarius described Jesus as being "one nature com-

---

2. This characterization is put forward in J.W.C. Wand, *The Four Great Heresies* (London: Mowbrays, 1955).

posed of impassible divinity and passible flesh."[3] For Apollinarius, therefore, Jesus was "the flesh-bearing God."[4]

Underlying this Christology was a specific anthropology, without which its proponent never could have devised his conception of the unique nature of Christ. Apollinarius understood the human person as consisting of a plurality of substantial entities. He conceived of a Jesus in which the divine aspect—the *Logos*—replaced one of the human substantial entities.

At first, Apollinarius's position reflected a dichotomist anthropology.[5] (The human being is a composite of the material and the immaterial aspects.) Jesus, he postulated, was unique in that in the incarnation the divine *Logos* joined himself with a human body, replacing the immaterial substance otherwise present in each human person. Perhaps seeing that such a Christology had no hope of gaining acceptance, Apollinarius subtly altered his position to build upon a trichotomist anthropological foundation. (The human person consists of three substantial entities—body, soul, and spirit.) He postulated that in the incarnation the *Logos* took to himself human nature (body and soul) but not a human person (body, soul, and spirit). In Jesus of Nazareth the body and soul (the vital principle of the body) were indeed human. Jesus' spirit, however, was not that of a human person but the divine *Logos*.

Although initially welcomed by many as an ingenious solution to the question of Jesus' identity, Apollinarius's position soon engendered opposition. Critics perceived that his Christology was incompatible with the Christian assertion that Jesus is the bearer of salvation. If the earthly Jesus did not possess a human spirit, the divine *Logos* did not take to himself that crucial aspect of human nature. Consequently, in his incarnation the Son did not redeem our spirit. This critique was motivated by an important theological assumption: What the *Logos* did not assume in the incarnation, the *Logos* could not redeem. In examining Apollinarius's views, Grego-

---

3. Cited in J.N.D. Kelly, *Early Christian Doctrines*, revised edition (San Francisco: Harper and Row, 1978), 291.

4. Ibid.

5. Wand, *The Four Great Heresies*, 74-75.

ry of Nazianzus, archbishop of Constantinople put the matter poignantly: "If any one has put his trust in him as a man without a human mind, he is himself devoid of mind and unworthy of salvation. For what he has not assumed he has not healed; it is united to his Deity that is saved."[6]

In addition to the soteriological problem, opponents of Apollinarius claimed that he was virtually a docetist. If the *Logos* functioned as the spirit of Jesus, the divine dimension of Jesus' person functioned as the controlling principle of the incarnate life. In such a case, Jesus could not have been fully human.[7] The physical body as animated by the soul was but the vehicle through which the divine *Logos*, "hidden" within, worked.

The Council of Constantinople. The church leaders officially settled the Apollinarian controversy at the Second Ecumenical Council held in Constantinople in 381. This council both reaffirmed the christological decision of Nicea and anathematized the position of Apollinarius. Against the challenge posed by his heretical proposal, they declared that orthodox Christology included the affirmation of the full humanity of Jesus of Nazareth.

Jesus as Sharing in True Humanness

The Council of Constantinople concluded that the affirmation of Jesus' full humanity lies at the heart of orthodox Christology. But what does it mean to assert that Jesus is fully human?

The obvious place to begin in our quest to understand the christological affirmation, "Jesus is truly human," is with the actual nature of the humanity he bore. In what sense was he an actual human being? Concerning his human nature, the confession of Jesus' humanity leads to the assertion that the humanness which characterized his existence was true humanness. As the writer to the Hebrews declares, "Since the children have flesh and blood, he too shared in their humanity" (Heb. 2:14). We must, however, describe further the

---

6. Gregory of Nazianzus, "An Examination of Apollinarianism," in *Documents of the Christian Church*, ed. Henry Bettennson, second edition (London: Oxford University Press, 1963), 45. See also, Kelly, *Early Christian Doctrines*, 297.

7. Kelly, *Early Christian Doctrines*, 296.

humanness in which Jesus participated and which he shares with all the children of Adam.

To discover what characterized the humanness of Jesus we must take a cursory look at his earthly life as described in the Gospels. By traversing this route, we actually follow the lead of the New Testament writers themselves. For them, Jesus' historical life forms the foundation from which they draw conclusions concerning his fundamental humanness.

Jesus and the conditions of human existence. Observation of the life of Jesus of Nazareth as depicted in the Gospels leads us to conclude that he was truly human, in the sense that Jesus lived under the conditions of earthly existence as humans do. He participated in our existential humanness. As our own experience suggests, the conditions of human existence include such common dimensions of life as knowing human needs, undergoing times of trial and temptation, and being subjected to a variety of limitations. According to the Gospels, all of these aspects of human life characterized Jesus' existence.

The Gospels suggest that Jesus experienced the range of needs common to all humans. He knew physical needs. For example, when Jesus arrived in the village in Samaria after a long journey, he was tired and thirsty (John 4:6-7). Jesus experienced psychological needs, including the necessity of companionship. When faced with the prospect of betrayal and death, Jesus requested that his three closest friends support him in his hour of despair (Matt. 26:36-38). Jesus experienced spiritual needs. He knew the importance of communing with his Father in prayer. The Gospels picture him as repeatedly withdrawing from his task of ministering to the throngs of destitute people in order that he might be refreshed through periods of solitude and prayer (Mark 1:35).[8]

To say that Jesus lived under the conditions of human existence means likewise that he underwent trials and faced temptations. The synoptic Gospels narrate three crucial occasions in Jesus' life during which he endured the onslaught of Satan. He encountered the devil directly subsequently to the Master's baptism (Matt. 4:1-11). He ex-

---

8. For a concise discussion of the prayer life of Jesus, see Stanley J. Grenz, *Prayer: The Cry for the Kingdom* (Peabody, Mass.: Hendrickson, 1988), 11-18.

perienced an indirect satanic confrontation through Peter's suggestion that Jesus need not die (Matt. 16:22-23). And he wrestled with Satan as he anticipated the agony of the cross in Gethsemane (Matt. 26:36-39). The author of Hebrews draws from Jesus' experience of temptation a crucial soteriological implication: "For we do not have a high priest who is not able to sympathize with our weaknesses though we have one who has been tempted in every way just as we are yet was without sin" (Heb. 4:15).

This conclusion—that Jesus survived temptation unscathed—leads us to ask, Were the temptations he faced real? Classically, the question was posed in terms of the possibility of Jesus falling in the face of temptation: Could Jesus have sinned? Of course queries such as this are highly theoretical, for Jesus in fact did not sin. Yet it does raise the matter of the sense in which Jesus was free from sin: Did Jesus feel the pull of temptation as we do? Our response must be carefully nuanced.

It appears from the New Testament that Jesus' relationship to temptation differed from ours in one important way: He did not experience its enticement in the manner that we do. James declares concerning us: "but each one is tempted when, by his own evil desire, he is dragged away and enticed" (James 1:14). We know from the Gospels that Jesus was not pulled onto sin in this manner. In this sense, we can affirm the classical Reformed position that Jesus was free from the taint of original sin, that is, from the propensity to sin all humans inherit from Adam.[9] In distinction from what we readily experience, Jesus was not drawn into sin by an evil desire inherent within his humanness.

At the same time, however, in another sense Jesus' experience did resemble ours. He knew actual temptation. In fact, he bore the full weight of temptation to a degree that surpasses our battle against evil.[10]

---

9. For a discussion, see Gordon R. Lewis and Bruce A. Demarest, *Integrative Theology*, three volumes (Grand Rapids: Zondervan, 1990), 2:336-38.

10. See the helpful discussion in Millard J. Erickson, *Christian Theology*, three volumes (Grand Rapids: Baker, 1984), 2: 718-21. Erickson cites Leon Morris, *The Lord from Heaven: A Study of the New Testament Teaching on the Deity and Humanity of Jesus* (Grand Rapids: Eerdmans, 1958), 51-52.

To understand this, we can take a cue from our own experience. We repeatedly discover that the intensity to which we sense the force of the onslaught of temptation corresponds to the degree to which we are resisting it. In those areas where we are especially vulnerable, we know little of the power of temptation. In such situations we yield to the evil impulse without a struggle, sometimes even without perceiving our own defeat. In other areas—areas where we are gaining victory over the tempter—we have a greater sense of its power. Our knowledge of the difference between resisting and yielding places us in a position to become more completely aware of the depth of the enticement being offered to us. It is in these areas that the struggle against temptation is most intense, and consequently where we must withstand the greater weight of temptation.

In a heightened manner, Jesus knew the full fury of temptation. He was keenly aware of the alternatives Satan offered to him. He was completely cognizant of what was at stake in the choices placed before him. And he was entirely conscious of the cosmic implications of the decisions he needed to make. In this sense, then, he shared in the most intense manner the human experience of undergoing trial and temptation. Indeed, the temptations which confronted Jesus were real.

Living under the conditions of human existence also meant that Jesus was subject to the limitations common to humans.

The Master lived with the temporal limitations we face. His days were limited to twenty-four hours and his weeks to seven days. The length of Jesus' earthly sojourn was also finite. In fact, he lived less than half the average North American lifespan, for his life was cut short after some thirty years. Further, Jesus was limited in location. He simply could not be everywhere at once; for just as we are, Jesus was localized. In addition, our Lord was limited in strength. He could not accomplish everything he might have wanted to do. Nor could he push himself beyond his capacities. Like all humans, he required the renewal brought through sleep, relaxation, and solitude. Finally, Jesus was even limited in knowledge, for he did not know the exact time of the eschatological arrival of the Son of Man (Matt. 24:36).

Living under these limitations carried an important implication for Jesus' life, just as it does for ours. Similar to our situation, in order to accomplish his overall mission Jesus was restrained to make choices in his ministry. Because he simply could not do everything, be everywhere, or accomplish everything, the Master needed to order his activities. He too engaged in the business of choosing from among the many good engagements that vied for his attention and time, selecting from among them in accordance with how they fit with the priorities of his mission.

Jesus and human growth. The true humanness of Jesus means not only that he lived under the conditions of human existence that we all experience; he developed and grew as a human, just as we do. Need we say that Jesus did not emerge from the womb perfectly mature? Indeed the Third Evangelist reminds us that Jesus was once a boy. During his childhood he grew physically, intellectually, spiritually, and socially (Luke 2:52). Even as an adult, Jesus continued to learn through experience the realities of living. As the author of the Epistle to the Hebrews so vividly concludes from the earthly life of Jesus, "Although he was a son, he learned obedience from what he suffered" (Heb. 5:8).

In short, Jesus of Nazareth had no predisposing advantages. He traveled no shortcut to maturity, transcended none of the limiting aspects of embodied existence, was spared no difficulty in living in this fallen world. On the contrary, he was truly one with us; he experienced fully our humanness.

Implications of Jesus' humanness. The New Testament writers find the reality that Jesus was fully human crucial to his role in the program of God. Specifically, his sharing in existential humanness carries soteriological implications. The writer to the Hebrews offers this summary statement:

> Since the children have flesh and blood, he too shared in their humanity so that by his death he might destroy him who holds the power of death...For this reason he had to be made like his brothers in every way, in order that he might become a merciful and faithful high priest in service to God, and that he might make atonement for the sins of the people. (Heb. 2:14, 17)

His participation in our existential nature, the writer argues, makes possible Jesus' work in saving us from sin and in sharing with us his victory over death. Unless Jesus is human—unless he participated on our existential situation—we are still in sin and subject to death. Indeed as the orthodox theologians argued against Apollinarius, what the eternal *Logos* did not take to himself he could not redeem.

Jesus' experience of humanness also carries an implication for our practical, day-to-day living. Jesus can sympathize with us as we struggle with the situations of life in a fallen world. This theme is likewise articulated by the writer of the Epistle to the Hebrews. He reminds us that because Jesus lived the fully human life, our great high priest understands our situation (Heb. 4:15). But his sympathy is not merely a passive emotion. On the contrary, "Because he himself suffered when he was tempted, he is able to help those who are being tempted" (Heb. 2:18). In short, Jesus knows, Jesus cares, and Jesus provides for us.

Jesus as the True Human

The christological assertion, "Jesus is fully human," carries the idea that Jesus participated in our existential humanness. But we must take our confession concerning the humanity of the Master a step farther. The humanity of Jesus does not only mean that he was one human being among many. Rather, our affirmation claims as well that Jesus is unique among humans. He is uniquely human—truly human.

The Foundation for Affirming Jesus as the True Human

The idea that Jesus is the true human has typically formed the linchpin of the christological proposals of modern theology. Yet we must look more closely at the foundation they offer for this affirmation.

The foundation in Jesus' earthly life. The theme, Jesus is the true human, was particularly prominent among thinkers in the 1800s.

They tended to move from some aspect of Jesus' existence to the conclusion that he is the ideal or paradigmatic human person.

For example, in keeping with his understanding of the moral focus of theology, the post-Enlightenment German philosopher and Lutheran churchman Immanuel Kant set forth an understanding of Jesus oriented toward his life as a moral example. Foundational to Kant's Christology is the thesis that the "Son of God" refers to the archetype of the morally perfect human person, an archetype which existed eternally in the mind of God and which is the true object of human faith. Jesus, in turn, is the historical exemplar of the divine archetype who therefore serves as the pattern for living.[11]

In a similar manner, Schleiermacher spoke of Jesus Christ as the ideal human, insofar as our Lord is the one in whom developed a perfect God-consciousness in its full historical realization. As such, Christ is both the mirror in which we may see our own sin and the redeemer, the one who implants in us the God-consciousness which characterized his own life.[12]

The thinking of Kant and Schleiermacher sparked a renewed interest in Jesus as a human person which led to the nineteenth century quest of the historical Jesus.[13] At the apex of this interest, Albrecht Ritschl (1822-1889) proposed an ingenious approach to Christology which synthesized the major strands of the thought of the century. Ritschl built from the historical life of the Nazarene to the church's confession of his deity, the key to which lay in the concept of Jesus' value for the Christian community.[14]

From Jesus' historical life, Ritschl concluded that our Lord was the man who perfectly lived out his divinely given vocation. This vo-

---

11. Immanuel Kant, *Religion within the Limits of Reason Alone*, trans. Theodore M. Greene and Hoyt H. Hudson, Harper Torchbooks/ The Cloister Library edition (New York: Harper and Row, 1960), 54-59.

12. Friedrich Schleiermacher, *The Christian Faith*, ed. H. R. MacKintosh and J. S. Stewart (Edinburgh: T. & T. Clark, n.d.), 367, 379, 385, 424-25.

13. For an account of this movement, see Albrecht Schweitzer, *The Quest of the Historical Jesus*, trans. W. Montgomery [first German edition: 1906] Macmillan Paperbacks edition (New York: Macmillan, 1964). See also Charles C. Anderson, *Critical Quests of Jesus* (Grand Rapids: Eerdmans, 1969), 9-86.

14. For this understanding of Ritschl, see Stanley J. Grenz and Roger E. Olson, *Twentieth Century Theology: God and the World in a Transitional Age* (Downers Grove, Ill.: InterVarsity, 1992), 56-58.

cation was directed toward the realization of God's kingdom, which the German theologian defined as God's moral will actualized in human life. Not only did Jesus live in perfect obedience to the divine will, however, he also influenced others to embrace the same moral imperative, thereby giving birth to the community of Christ. The central importance of Jesus' influence leads his community to confess his deity, which confession reflects the value Jesus has for them. In other words, in the estimation of his followers Jesus' value is nothing less than deity.

The nineteenth-century theme of Jesus as the ideal human spilled over into twentieth-century thought. It found echo, for example, in Paul Tillich, who postulated that Jesus is the Christ insofar as he is the bearer of the New Being.[15] Reminiscent of Schleiermacher, Tillich honored Jesus both as the one who was transparent to the divine Ground of Being at the foundation of his existence and as the one who brings the new being to others. Jesus mediates the new being in that he enables each of us to follow his example and become transparent to the Ground of Being at the basis of our own personal existence.

The theme that Jesus is the ideal human was also prevalent in the Christologies of the radical theologians of the 1960s. They built from Tillich and from Dietrich Bonhoeffer's idea of Jesus as "the man for others." In their turn away from God to the human figure of Jesus, these thinkers explored the implications of his life for our contemporary context, proposing that in this secular age we must willingly serve the needs of people in the world.[16]

These and other more recent proposals, including liberation theology, construct a Christology of Jesus as the ideal human on the foundation of some universally significant dimension of his reality that in some way or another finds its basis in Jesus' earthly life. In our discussion of Jesus' humanness, however, we did not employ to the general Gospel description of his earthly life as the foundation for

---

15. Paul Tillich, *Systematic Theology*, three volumes (Chicago: University of Chicago Press, 1957), 2:97.
16. For a discussion of this movement, see Grenz and Olson, *Twentieth Century Theology*, 145-69.

the conclusion that he is our ideal. Rather, from that description we concluded that Jesus participated in our existential humanness. In drawing this conclusion from the history of Jesus, we followed the path of the New Testament writers themselves, for whom the basic outline of his historical life forms the foundation for affirming Jesus' oneness with humans.

The foundational importance of the resurrection. In contrast to the method employed in modern liberal Christologies, we maintain that the declaration of the unique humanness of Jesus does not arise from Jesus' earthly life. His life indicates only that he was one human among others. Instead, we can come to assert that Jesus is uniquely human only through reflection on the significance of the resurrection as God's confirmation of Jesus' self-consciousness. Only the resurrection can substantiate the Christian claim that Jesus is the paradigm for all human existence.

In chapter 9, we noted the foundational importance of Jesus' resurrection for our understanding of the christological assertion that Jesus is divine. The resurrection was the appropriate manner by which God acknowledged Jesus' claim to a unique relationship with the Father. Consequently, this event led us to conclude that Jesus is the eternal Son of the Father and that as the Son he participates in the eternal fellowship of the triune God.

In a similar manner, the resurrection, understood as God's confirmation of Jesus' self-consciousness as the truly human one, leads us to affirm the unique, exemplary humanity of our Lord. Hence, as in the confession of his deity, our affirmation of Jesus' status as the ideal human is based on his claim concerning his own identity as confirmed by God in raising him from the dead.

Jesus' claim to uniqueness. In his earthly life Jesus did claim to be the unique human—to be the truly human one. The Master proclaimed that he was the one who had come to show us how to live. He asserted that he, and not the religious leaders of his day, knew God's intention for humankind (Matt. 19:1-9). This claim was evident in his teaching. Jesus repeatedly took upon himself the prerogative of interpreting the divine will for God's people as it had been set forth in the Old Testament. He professed to know the true meaning of the Torah (Matt. 5:21-48). He chastised his opponents for their misunderstanding of Scripture (Mark 12:24). And he boldly declared that the religious leaders had substituted humanly devised precepts for God's own will (Mark 7:9).

Jesus' claim to be the unique human, the one who had come to show us how to live, was evident as well in his call to discipleship. He enjoined his hearers to follow him—to become his disciples. In Jesus' day, the role of disciple entailed learning from the manner in which one's master lived, patterning one's life after the example of the teacher. Jesus explicitly called his hearers to enter into this kind of relationship with him: "Take my yoke upon you and learn from me" (Matt. 11:29).

Taken by itself, Jesus' claim to be the unique human would have been audacious. We could view his declaration "I am the way and the truth and the life" (John 14:6) as vain and prideful. For this reason, Jesus' self-consciousness as the teacher of the truth concerning the way to life, just as his parallel claim to enjoy a special relation to the Father, called for a response from God. God must either confirm the opinion of his opponents who considered him a great sinner or acknowledge that Jesus is in truth the embodiment of true humanity. God's response came in the resurrection. By raising Jesus from the dead, God declared that this man is indeed the paradigmatic human he claimed to be. This event, therefore, marks God's declaration of the correctness of Jesus' unique claim concerning his humanity.

The Content of Our Affirming Jesus as the True Human

The foundation for our affirmation that Jesus is the true human lies in his claim as confirmed by the resurrection. This occurrence in the history of the Nazarene signifies that Jesus himself is the true human person and therefore the paradigm for all human beings. Jesus, in other words, is the revelation of humanness as intended by God. What each of us is designed to be—and what God intends, even destines us to become—has already been revealed in the man Jesus of Nazareth.

Jesus and the resurrection. The revelation of true humanity we find in Jesus focuses on God's ultimate purposes for us as his creatures. God's purposes, however, stand in stark contrast to our present human experience: God did not create us for estrangement but for fellowship; not for death, but for life; not for bondage but for freedom.

Yet one might object that the history of Jesus paints an opposite picture, for Jesus' life ended in tragedy—he was crucified as a common criminal. Indeed, viewed in isolation the cross would mark the disastrous end to his earthly life, calling into question any sense in which Jesus could be the revelation of God's intention for us. Or alternatively the cross may indicate that God's intentions for us are evil, for he purposes our death and therefore our lives are ultimately meaningless.

According to the writers of the New Testament, however, the cross is not revelatory apart from the resurrection; Good Friday makes sense only from the perspective of Easter. Jesus' resurrection dispels the darkness of his cross, bringing it into the light of the new day. God did not abandon Jesus to the godforsakenness and separation he experienced through his death. On the contrary, God gloriously raised him to new life.

When seen through the eyes of the Easter proclamation, the cross takes on a totally new and wonderful meaning. It is not the tragic end to the life of a miracleworker and healer whose ministry met with stiff opposition. Rather, the cross is the glorious climax to the self-giving of the one who stands as a model of the pathway to life. Jesus died in accordance with the principles that he espoused in his own teachings and actions, namely, that greatness in God's kingdom comes through servanthood, suffering, and self-denial (Mark 8:34-38; 10:35-45). He shows that even death itself can be the route to life and blessing for many (John 12:24).

As God's confirmation of Jesus' entire life, teaching, and death, therefore, the resurrection leads us to view Jesus as the true human. This event provides insight into the paradigmatic humanity as revealed by Jesus, for his resurrection sets forth the risen Christ as the ultimate pattern for full humanness as intended by God.

We must understand the paradigmatic nature of Jesus' humanness in an ontological sense. Through the resurrection, Jesus reveals the transformed ontological reality that we will one day become. In raising him from the dead, God transformed Jesus' earthly, bodily existence into the glorious, incorruptible state to which the early witnesses to the risen Christ gave testimony. But this transformed humanness is precisely God's design for us. As Paul reminds his readers, "And just as we have borne the likeness of the earthly man, so shall we bear the likeness of the man from heaven" (1 Cor. 15:49). In fact, the witness of the New Testament is that we will undergo transformation at Jesus' glorious return: "For the trumpet will sound, the dead will be raised imperishable, and we will be changed" (v. 52). Then we will reflect the reality that is now displayed in Jesus the resurrected one. Indeed, "when he appears, we shall be like him, for we shall see him as he is" (1 John 3:2). The transformed humanness which now characterizes the resurrected Jesus reveals that God intends that we too live eternally as spiritual-physical beings.

Jesus and community. We must also understand the paradigmatic humanness of Jesus in a broader sense. The confirmatory understanding of the resurrection means that God has acknowledged Jesus as the revelation of the nature of God's reign and of life within that realm. The eternal, kingdom life in which God intends for us to participate does not focus on the isolated individual saint. Rather, kingdom living is life-in-community. The resurrection confirms that Jesus is the pattern as to what life-in-community entails.

For Jesus, foundational to life-in-community was life in community with his Father. The fellowship he shared with God included both communing with him in solitude and humbly acting in perfect obedience to the Father's will in all areas of life, even to the point of death (Phil. 2:8). Jesus' was continually conscious of living in the presence of his Father.

His obedience to the Father's will meant that Jesus also lived in fellowship with others. He was no self-sufficient recluse, no isolated individual. Rather, life-in-human-community included both mutuality of friendships and compassionate ministry to the needy. Jesus was both the "man for others" and the one who received the gift of friendship from others. And Jesus showed that community ought to know no boundaries; it reaches from friends to the outcast and hurting, and even encompasses one's enemies.

For Jesus, life in community included appreciation for nature and fellowship with other creatures. In his teaching Jesus repeatedly appealed to God's care for the natural world—for plants and animals, for the grasses and the sparrows. His spiritual life led him to embrace the wilderness and enjoy the beauty of creation. And he gave evidence to his identity by calming the sea.

Jesus revealed that God's ideal for humans entails life-in-community. From Jesus, we learn that we only come to participate fully in our humanity as we live in fellowship with God, with others, and with creation around us.

Jesus and the upward fall. The affirmation of Jesus as the true human carries an important anthropological implication. It calls into question the concept of the "upward fall," which has gained a widespread hearing since being advocated by George Hegel in the nineteenth century.[17]

This idea asserts that the fall of humanity was not ultimately a negative occurrence. On the contrary, it was beneficial, in that the fall facilitated our human independence from God which is an indispensable aspect of the process from infancy to maturity. Interpreted in classical theological categories, the fall is integral to the divine design for the world. It was a necessary step between innocency and reconciliation. In this sense, then, as the movement "upward" from the immaturity of innocency to the maturity of reconciliation—the fall into estrangement, to borrow Tillich's concept[18]—is a positive aspect of our human condition.

The paradigmatic life of Jesus, however, stands as the devastating critique of the concept of the upward fall. Jesus reveals that the human ideal is the seemingly paradoxical life of independence through obedience, rather than through disobedience. As he willingly lived in total dedication to the Father's will, Jesus showed himself to be the

---

17. For a recent statement of this idea, see Dorothy Soelle, *To Work and to Love: A Theology of Creation* (Philadelphia: Westminster, 1984), 74-75.

18. Tillich, *Systematic Theology*, 2:44.

eternal Son who is independent from the Father but who also draws his life from the Father.

We noted earlier that our confession that Jesus is truly human carries the implication that he can save us in all dimensions of our human existence and that he can sympathize with us as we struggle with the situations of life in a fallen world. Now we add that our confession "Jesus is the true human" implies that he is our model. As his disciples, we are to pattern our lives after him. That is, we too are to seek life-in-community, just as Jesus revealed to us that this is God's design for human existence.

Jesus as the New Human

Jesus is the true human, for he is our ideal, the paradigm for human life. There is yet a further dimension of Jesus' unique humanity. As the true human, Jesus is also the New Human, or to employ the biblical imagery, the New Adam.

In drawing this conclusion, however, we have moved from the implications both of the events of Jesus' life and of his confirmatory resurrection. We now build from the conclusions of the early church. Thus, we have traversed the ground from the Jesus of history to the Christ of faith. Whereas we derive the confession, Jesus is the paradigm human, from the event of Jesus' resurrection as the confirmation of his own self-consciousness, the affirmation that Jesus is the New Adam flows from the experience of the early believers.

Basically, the "New Adam" Christology developed by the early church focuses on the ongoing function of the risen Lord as the founder of a new humanity, the fountainhead of a new order of human beings. Although implicit elsewhere, this early Christology is especially evident in Paul's Epistles. In two passages, he sets forth an extended comparison between the first Adam and Jesus Christ as the second Adam (Rom. 5:12-21; 1 Cor. 15:21-22, 45-49). Whereas the first Adam brought disobedience, sin, and death to his descendants, Christ has mediated obedience, grace, and righteousness leading to life (Rom. 5:19, 21; 1 Cor. 15:22). The theme of Jesus as the head of a new humanity is also evident in Paul's grand declaration of the unity of Jew and Gentile in Christ:

> For he himself is our peace, what has made the two one and has destroyed the barrier, the dividing wall of hostility....His purpose was to create in himself one new man out of the two....(Eph. 2:14-15)

Paul speaks of this new company as the church, which is metaphorically Christ's body (Col. 1:18).

Viewed biblically, then, "Jesus is the New Human" means that he is the head of the new company, who in turn comprise the new humankind. Our participation in the new humanity is based on the headship of Jesus the Christ. We are this new company only in so far as we are drawn together through our union with him (Rom. 6:3-5; 2 Cor. 5:17). According to the New Testament, the new humankind consists of those who through Christ have been made righteous (Rom. 5:19). Consequently, they are destined to share in the resurrection which Jesus has already experienced (1 Cor. 15:22).

As these texts indicate, the glorious hope we share as participants in Christ's new humanity is directed toward the future, toward our participation in the eschatological community of God. Yet we already participate in the new humanity. As the new people of God, we have been given the task of living in the present in accordance with the principles of the eschatological community which we already are (at least proleptically). Even now we seek to be the disciples of the Lord and thereby to point the world to the grand community in which God intends that we all share. In this way, then, the theme of Jesus as the New Human forms a bridge between Christology and ecclesiology (the doctrine of the church), which is the subject matter of part 5.

Just as the affirmations "Jesus is truly human" and "Jesus is the true human," the confession "Jesus is the New Human" carries practical importance for life in the present. Fundamentally, it means that Jesus is our trailblazer. He is, to employ the words of Hebrews, "the author and perfecter of our faith" (Heb. 12:2). As our trailblazer, he travels before us, bidding us to follow his lead. As our leader, he takes responsibility for bringing his people to the goal the Father sets before us. Thus, as the fountainhead of our existence as the new humanity he provides the resources for the life of his people.

Therefore, the key to living in the present does not lie with our abilities, but with the provision we derive from the Risen Lord, the

New Human. Jesus Christ provides these resources ultimately by sending us his Spirit. In this sense, the concept of Jesus as the New Human provides a bridge to pneumatology, which forms the fourth focus of our systematic theology.

Jesus as the Universal Human

The confession of Jesus' humanity takes us beyond the declaration that Jesus was truly human—that he participated in existential humanness just as we do. Our affirmation also means that Jesus is the true or unique human. He reveals God's design for us, which is life-in-community. As such he is the paradigm for us. He is also the New Human, the fountainhead of a new company, the new humanity.

These conclusions, however, raise a grave question. In what sense can Jesus function as the paradigm and trailblazer for all humankind? In what sense can we affirm that Jesus is the universal human? In exploring our answer to this question, we must approach the topic from three standpoints, querying it from the standpoint first of the marginalized of the world, then of women, and finally from the general perspective of discipleship.

Jesus and the Marginalized

At first glance, the truth of the affirmation, "Jesus is the universal human," appears to be incompatible with the experience of the underprivileged or disadvantaged of the world. In fact, insofar as the marginalized form the majority of the world's people, how can we even dare continue to articulate our lofty christological assertions concerning Jesus' humanity?

It is sadly true that the gospel proclaimed by the contemporary church often appears as good news only for the privileged, the economically well-off, or the powerful. To all such persons Jesus seems to offer a comfortable existence here and the promise of heaven in the hereafter. More specifically, Jesus appears to be the paradigm for wealthy, gifted, and upwardly mobile. Evangelical church life readily gives the impression that Jesus wants us respectable, successful, and happy. And our typical evangelical prayer concerns suggest that to this end, he intervenes to help us through the minor setbacks of life.

Most people in the world, however, do not fit the image often modeled by evangelical churches. How can this Jesus be the paradigm for the great multitude who do not enjoy, nor ever can hope to experience the "North American dream"? In finding a response to this query, we must turn again to the Jesus of history.

Scholars agree that Jesus himself was not wealthy. He was born into a typical lower-middle-class family,[19] perhaps even into poverty. His earthly father, Joseph, was a common tradesman, a carpenter, who may have died before Jesus commenced his own ministry. The possible poverty of Jesus' family may lie behind parts of the Magnificat of Mary narrated by Luke. Upon hearing that she would bear the Messiah, she gloried in the God who "has been mindful of the humble state of his servant" (Luke 1:48). Mary declared the nature of God's action in socioeconomic terms: "He has brought down rulers from their thrones but has lifted up the humble. He has filled the hungry with good things but has sent the rich away empty" (vv. 52-53).

The primary focus of Jesus' ministry and the primary audience for his message were not the privileged few of his day but the disadvantaged, the outcast, the "sinners." He directed his compassionate ministry and teaching toward them, so much so that he gained the reputation of being a friend of sinners (Matt. 11:19).

For the masses of needy people, his message was good news. He spoke about a God who was acting for their salvation, who offered them participation in his kingdom, and who would accept them unconditionally, so long as they came to him in humble faith. His message marked a stark contrast to the teaching of the religious leaders of his day, who placed unbearable demands on the people (Luke 11:46). No wonder the common people heard him gladly!

Jesus did welcome the rich and the privileged into his band of followers. But by and large, they found his message hard. To the self-righteous religious leaders he sternly pronounced impending judgment, and to the self-sufficient rich he predicted impending ruin

---

19. Philip L. Culbertson, "What Is Left to Believe in Jesus after the Scholars Have Done with Him?" *Journal of Ecumenical Studies* 28/1 (Winter 1991): 5.

(Luke 12:16-21). He challenged the proud to humble servanthood, and he admonished the advantaged of society to solidarity with the poor and outcasts (Luke 11:41). Jesus proclaimed that God is no respecter of persons; his Father is not impressed by wealth and social standing, nor even by outwardly pious prayers and acts. Rather than marking them as privileged, wealth actually hinders a person from entering the kingdom. And Jesus exposed the hypocrisy of the privileged of his day, calling them to lay aside the trappings of their stature for the sake of true repentance and a changed lifestyle. Consequently, he declared that even teachers of Israel must be born again, the great needed to become like little children, and the social elite must become servants of all, in order to be counted great in the kingdom.

Jesus' message of unmerited grace has not changed. Just as he accepted unconditionally the outcasts of his day who came to him empty-handed, so also he does not demand that the marginalized of our world attempt to make themselves respectable through some act of self-reformation. He welcomes into his discipleship band all who cry out to him in their need and who desire to follow him. The privileged today can expect from him no gospel of cheap grace. As in the first century, he offers only the message of costly grace which demands that we set aside all pretension to self-merit. We can receive the salvation he offers only as we come to see ourselves as the spiritually impoverished persons that we actually are—indeed, as before God standing on the same plane with the most destitute and the most wicked in our world.

Jesus' message, therefore, remains the great leveler. The God he reveals acknowledges no socioeconomic distinctions. Just as our Lord spoke against the self-righteous Pharisees of his day, so also he exposes all failure to reflect the principles of the eschatological community. The message of the New Testament, therefore, is that all share the failure to live in accordance to God's will to community. In fact, this failure lies at the foundation of the humanly contrived inequalities that permeate life in our fallen world. Consequently, Jesus' message of salvation for the repentant and his paradigm of life-in-community apply to all humans regardless of social class or economic status. He invites all persons to put aside worldly standards of appraisal and see themselves as members together of the one humanity standing in need of the salvation available only in Christ. As the one who exposes our failure and offers the means to overcoming it, Jesus is indeed the universal human.

Jesus and Women

Equally difficult today, and perhaps theologically even more problematic, is the maleness of Jesus. Does the fact that the our Lord lived as a male constitute an indispensable dimension of his status as the ideal human? How ought women to understand themselves in the light of a male Savior? Indeed it would seem that Jesus' maleness weighs against the possibility that he can function as the universal human.

At certain periods in Christian history, theologians interpreted Jesus' maleness to mean that being male constitutes essential humanness. They viewed women, in turn, as in some sense deficient humans. Although similar attitudes can still be found today, thinkers have almost universally rejected this outlook. Yet the rejection of the older idea, while correct, has not answered the question of the significance of the maleness of the Master. Consequently, theologians are engaged in a search for ways to overcome this problem.

Contemporary radical feminists have concluded that there can be no means of salvaging either Jesus' maleness or Jesus himself. Mary Daly spoke for many in concluding, "A patriarchal divinity or his son is exactly *not* in a position to save us from the horrors of a patriarchal world."[20] Others, however, have been less despairing. Some propose that although the earthly Jesus was male, the resurrected Lord is neuter. A foundation for this view lies in Jesus' description of the purportedly asexual nature of the participants in the kingdom of God: "At the resurrection people will neither marry nor be given in marriage; they will be like the angels in heaven" (Matt. 22:30).

---

20. Mary Daly, *Beyond God the Father: Toward a Philosophy of Women's Liberation* (Boston: Beacon, 1973), 96.

A variation on this theme views the essence of the resurrected Lord inclusively. Specifically, it incorporates the now often repeated idea that Jesus was resurrected into the fellowship of the church. Paul Avis, for example, draws the two themes together:

> The citizens of heaven will be like the angels "in immortality and felicity, not in body." Correspondingly, the body of Christ after the resurrection and ascension is no longer the individual physical male body of Jesus of Nazareth but the corporate spiritual body of the Church, the Body of Christ.[21]

This second alternative falls prey to an obvious christological problem. The idea that Jesus was resurrected into the body of his church does carry certain merit. But if it is interpreted to mean that this is the sole focus of the resurrection, it dismisses the individual dimension of that event. The New Testament authors obviously viewed the resurrection as an event in the life of Jesus himself, the transformation of his embodied person into the realm of eternal life.

In addition to this christological problem, both of these alternatives suffer from a central anthropological difficulty. They fail to take our sexuality seriously. Sexuality—our fundamental maleness and femaleness—is an indispensable dimension of our existence as humans, as embodied creatures. If Jesus' resurrection is the transformation of the historical embodied person, this event cannot constitute the elimination of his fundamental maleness. Jesus' declaration that participants in the kingdom will not marry temporalizes the marital bond. But his statement does not mean that life in the kingdom will be devoid of the deeper dimensions of our sexuality which function apart from genital sexual activity and lie at the foundation of such activity.[22]

Another proposed way of dealing with the difficulty of Jesus' fundamental sexuality is through feminization—transforming Jesus Christ into Jesa Christa. Apart from the obvious violation of the historical foundation for christological affirmations it entails, to feminize Jesus is to minimize his particularity. It denies his existence as

---

21. Paul Avis, *Eros and the Sacred* (London: SPCK, 1989), 44.
22. See Stanley J. Grenz, *Sexual Ethics* (Irving, Tex.: Word, 1990), 13-14.

the particular historical person, for whom masculinity was integral to the completion of his task.

This observation points us in the direction of the answer to the dilemma. Our answer begins with an understanding of the precise reason why Jesus' maleness was indispensable. Rather than enthroning the male as God's ideal for humankind, the maleness of Jesus provides the vehicle whereby his earthly life could reveal the radical difference between God's ideal and the orders and structures that characterize human social interaction. Given the context in which he lived (and the context of most of human history) Jesus' maleness was an indispensable dimension of his vocation. Only a male Jesus could have offered the radical critique of the power systems of his day which we find prevalent in his message.

To see this, we need only look at the alternative. Had the Savior of humankind come as a woman, she would have been immediately dismissed solely on the basis of her sex. Nor could her actions have been interpreted as countercultural, for her self-sacrificial ministry would have been interpreted as merely the living out of her socialized ideal role.[23]

Thus, to be the liberator of both male and female, Jesus needed to be male. His liberating work which encompasses both male and female marks Jesus as the New Human.

We can best understand the liberating work of the male Jesus as we place it in the context of the biblical description of the male-female roles within the orders of human society. The thesis of the Genesis creation narratives is that in the beginning God created male and female to live in supplementary relationships and thereby to reflect the image of the triune God. In the fall, however, supplementarity was replaced by hierarchy. God described this fallen order to Eve after the disobedience of the first human pair: "Your desire will be for your husband, and he will rule over you" (Gen. 3:16).

Into this situation Jesus brought a new paradigm. Our Lord liberated men and women from their bondage to the social orders that have characterized the world since the fall but which violate God's

---

23. Suzanne Heine, *Matriarchs, Goddesses and Images of God*, trans. John Bowden (Minneapolis: Augsburg, 1989), 137-45.

intention for human life-in-community. Jesus liberated males from the role of domination that belongs to the fallen world, in order that they can be truly male. He provided this liberation as the true human—our model. As a male, Jesus revealed that the way to life does not lie in acting the part of the strong, dominating, and self-sufficient male. As the New Human—our trailblazer—he gave us the Spirit by whose power males can live after the pattern of the Master.

The male Jesus liberated women as well, however. On their behalf he acted as the paradigm human standing against the male system. He brought them to participate in the new order where sex distinctions no longer determine rank and worth. As the author of their faith, the New Human, he provided resources to leave the past behind—to forgive and to be forgiven—and to seek the new order in which supplementarity is the rule.

Jesus' action on behalf of the liberation of women began in his earthly life. To accomplish his mission to women, the male Jesus transgressed the social norms of his day which prescribed the proper manner of treating women. In contrast to the rabbis and the Romans, he always related to women with highest respect. He not only defied social mores, he also destroyed religious custom, for he encouraged women to participate in areas reserved solely for men.

Jesus liberated women likewise in the unique message he addressed to them. As his encouragement of Mary who desired to sit at his feet against the wishes of Martha indicates, Jesus called women away from their daily chores as servants to the task of nurturing their relationship to God. Similarly, Jesus engaged the Samaritan woman he met at the well in a discussion of worship and the identity of the Messiah. In response to the woman who blessed Jesus mother for her act in giving him birth, Jesus contradicted the traditional way of blessing women, namely, for their role in childbearing; he declared that hearing and keeping the word of God is the source of blessing (Luke 11:27).

There is a further aspect to the manner in Jesus serves as the universal human which is raised by the question of his maleness. Contrary to the modern way of reading the Gospels, Jesus is not our paradigm as an isolated individual. He is not the hero of the myth of the autonomous individual, which so permeates the modern mentality. Instead, Jesus is our paradigm as an individual-in-community. The community focus encompassed the various directions of his life.

Jesus is the paradigm of the individual in community with God. It is instructive to note that Jesus fulfilled his entire vocation in conscious dependence on the Father and with the empowerment of the Spirit. Even his resurrection was not a feat accomplished by the independent Jesus. On the contrary, the witness of the New Testament is that God raised him from the dead through the power of the Holy Spirit (Rom. 8:11). As we noted earlier, Jesus is also the paradigm of the individual in community with others and even with nature.

The confession "Jesus is the true human" means that Jesus reveals to us God's design for our lives. It would be erroneous, however, to conclude from Jesus' maleness that God's intention is that we all be male. Rather, the paradigm that Jesus offers is that we all—whether male or female—find our identity by following his example, that is, through life-in-community. This divine pathway to life is often more readily understood by women. Our Lord reinforces this understanding and empowers them to live it out. Jesus' maleness stands as a reminder to men that they must follow the same path, if they would discover the nature of their fundamental maleness; to be truly male they must rely on the strength God gives through the Spirit.

Our discussion leads to the conclusion that Jesus is the universal human. He is not merely the Savior of the privileged or the male. On the contrary, he is the paradigmatic human and the New Human. For this reason, in Christ we are indeed all one, for in him "there is neither Jew nor Greek, slave nor free, male nor female" (Gal. 2:28).

Jesus and the Individual

As Christians we claim that Jesus is the universal human. His message is for all, regardless of sex or socioeconomic distinctions. Our confession that he is the true human and the New Human is applicable for all people, even if its articulation and implications will vary from context to context and situation to situation. Yet we must ask, How does Jesus function today in our personal lives as the universal human?

The basic answer to the question of the universality of Jesus lies with the applicability of his own personal story. Jesus becomes the universal human in our experience as his story is related to our story in the life of discipleship. As we become his disciples, Jesus' life becomes for us both the paradigm human life and the empowering life. His life is paradigmatic insofar as we view our lives in accordance with the fundamental pattern that characterized his, namely, that of self-sacrificial life-in-community.

Patterning our lives after his ought not to be taken in a simplistic, moralistic fashion, however. We do not engage in every task in exactly the same manner Jesus did. Indeed, how could we, given the great changes of intervening centuries that separate our context from his? Nor does this mean simply asking in every situation, What would Jesus do? Although beneficial, such an approach to life leads to a truncated understanding of discipleship, limiting our task in following Jesus to the realm of outward conduct.

Discipleship as patterning our lives after Jesus means that Jesus' model and teaching become the standard by comparison to which we evaluate our innermost attitudes and our outward actions. Like Jesus, we live conscious of our presence before God who is our Abba. As a consequence, we continually seek to follow after the life of community with God, others, and creation which he pioneered among us and which he seeks to empower us to do. Conversely, we become conscious of our own sinfulness as we see how we fail to measure up to the standard of his life and teachings. As a result, we seek to live before God and others in humble repentance and faith in the faithful, forgiving God about whom Jesus spoke and to whom he pointed.

Jesus' story becomes our story in the life of discipleship in another way as well. He becomes the universal human in our experience as we derive our identity from his, which he shares with us. After his pattern, we too see ourselves as the children of the God he called "Abba." He affirms us as his brothers and sisters. We now ourselves as heirs with him of great future that God has for his creation, which we even now proleptically enjoy.

The new identity we have in Jesus, who is the universal human, leads to the incisive dimension of discipleship. Jesus' story becomes our story as it forms the focal point for the integration of our own lives. We no longer seek to understand our narrative in the old manner, as revolving around the former "ultimate concern" that shaped our existence. Indeed, our encounter with the story of Jesus calls into question our former attempts to make sense out of our lives. In destroying the old identity, Jesus replaces it with a new paradigm, a new center around which we can draw the fragmented strands of our lives into a single narrative. Now our lives make sense as we see that our sinful, alienated past has given way to the present enjoyment of fellowship and the anticipation of the fullness of life-in-community awaiting us in the future.

This life of discipleship after the paradigmatic life of Jesus takes us out of our separate and separated existence. Jesus becomes the universal human in our experience as we enter the fellowship he offers, the life-in-community to which he directs us. This fellowship is from beginning to end a corporate reality, the community of his disciples. Because these themes lead us beyond Christology into pneumatology and ecclesiology, their explication must wait until we have explored the remaining two affirmations of our doctrine of Christ.

11

The Fellowship of Deity and Humanity in Jesus

regarding his Son, who as to his human nature was a descendant of David, and who through the Spirit of holiness was declared with power to be the Son of God by his resurrection from the dead: Jesus Christ our Lord. (Rom. 1:3-4)

Outline

As Christians we affirm that Jesus of Nazareth is at the same time both truly divine and truly human. Disclosed together in this historical life we find essential deity and humanity. He embodies both God's own nature and God's intention for us, namely, "life in community." Jesus, in other words, participates in the eternal community of the triune God while being the exemplar of creaturely fellowship.

How is this possible? How can we affirm that Jesus is both one with God and one with us? How can we find deity and humanity present in one historical life? To these questions we now turn, as we take up the challenge of speaking about the relationship between the two central dimensions of Jesus' personhood. In this chapter we reflect on the personal unity of our Lord.

Our discussion begins with a delineation of the Christological affirmation itself, that in Jesus we find both deity and humanity. Our intent is first to probe the unity of the two dimensions in Jesus. Then we turn our attention to the incarnation, a concept which has played such an important role in theological history as a description of the unity of Jesus' person. Finally, the chapter concludes with a look at the virgin birth of Jesus and its significance for the unity of his person.

Jesus as Divine and Human

Although perhaps controversial, taken by themselves neither foundational christological affirmation—Jesus is fully divine; Jesus is fully human—is inherently paradoxical. But when the two are combined into a third—Jesus is both divine and human—the situation is greatly altered. We must, therefore, explore this seemingly paradoxical christological declaration which combines what otherwise appears to be disjunctive—deity and humanity.

Our exploration begins with a sketch of the historical developments after Nicea and Constantinople. We ask, In what sense did the church affirm that deity and humanity are united in the one person of Jesus? This historical discussion, in turn, forms the context for our perusal of the biblical materials. Specifically, we will interact with two central Christological titles which provide insight as to how the one person of Jesus the Christ is both divine and human. Only then can we draw our conclusions concerning the linchpin of the unity of deity and humanity in Jesus.

The Historical Debate Concerning Jesus' Person

As we have noted, the councils at Nicea and Constantinople settled the thorny theological questions concerning Jesus' deity and humanity. The church leaders concluded that the orthodox faith rests on the affirmation that Jesus is truly divine and truly human. Rather than bringing all christological debate to an end, however, these decisions merely opened the way for the next round of controversy.

Given that Jesus is both divine and human, the question now arose as to how orthodox Christians should understand the unity of his person. What is the exact relationship of these two dimensions within the one Jesus? Are deity and humanity totally distinct? Do they merge into one nature? With these questions the church struggled for nearly a century.

In taking up these issues, the christological debates after Nicea and Constantinople continued the dialectic between the concerns of the two great intellectual centers of the ancient church, Alexandria and Antioch.[1]

The Alexandrians suggested that the two natures, humanity and divinity, are not so contradictory so as to make impossible their union in one person. The Antiochians, on the other hand, maintained that these two substances are so distinct that no essential unity could be possible between them. If the union of the human and divine cannot be in substance, it must lie in some other area, such as in the volitional dimension.

The Nestorian controversy. Antiochian considerations lay behind the third of the "four great heresies," Nestorianism, named for Nestorius, a student of Theodore of Mopsuestia.[2] The christological controversy, however, was not sparked by a theological disagreement, but by a debate concerning piety, specifically, whether it is proper to call Mary "the bearer of God," as was being demanded by the heightened Mariology developing in the church. Nestorius argued that such a designation was inappropriate. Although Jesus' humanity came through Mary, his divine element came solely from God. Mary bore a man, who was the vehicle of deity, but not God.[3]

Nestorius sought to counteract what he perceived to be a fusion of Jesus' humanity and deity in the teaching of Alexandria. In its place he posited a voluntary union of persons in Jesus.[4] The *Logos* united with a perfect human, a union developed and maintained by the exercise of a good will.[5]

At the foundation of the Nestorian position lay another heresy, the anthropology developed by Pelagius.[6] According to Augustine's theological antagonist, a human person is endowed at birth with sufficient grace to reinforce the human will in its battle against sin. Sin,

---

1. This thesis is propounded in J.W.C. Wand, *The Four Great Heresies* (London: Mowbrays, 1955), 33-37, 89, 110.

2. For a discussion of Theodore's position, see J.N.D. Kelly, *Early Christian Doctrines*, revised edition (San Francisco: Harper and Row, 1978), 303.

3. Ibid., 311.

4. Ibid., 314.

5. Wand, *The Four Great Heresies*, 94, 98.

6. Ibid., 99-101.

in turn, is not a state of being but lies entirely in human action. Because of this endowment, an individual could theoretically attain perfection. Nestorius saw this perfectible human substance revealed in Jesus. The man Jesus employed the natural endowment of grace without fail. This exercise of his good will effected the voluntary union between Jesus and the *Logos*. For Nestorius, therefore, Jesus was the "God-bearing man."[7]

What appeared to many to be an ingenious Christology had an Achilles' heel. Nestorius's keen opponent, Cyril of Alexandria, pinpointed the problem.[8] Theodore's teaching as reformulated by his student implied that each nature (deity and humanity) was capable of standing alone. Thereby he risked dividing Jesus into two separate persons. The unity between two such disjunctive dimensions could only be conceived of as a volitional, rather than an ontological union. But if divinity and humanity are united only through Jesus' will, there is no genuine incarnation. Jesus is not God incarnate; in him we do not find the essence of God.

The Third Ecumenical Council, meeting in Ephesus in A.D. 431, agreed with Cyril. In ruling against Nestorius, the assembly declared that Jesus is one person, not two.[9] But the council did not determine the actual nature of the one person of Jesus. It took yet a fourth skirmish with heresy—with Eutychianism or monophysitism—to bring the orthodox position to completion.

The Eutychian controversy. During the Nestorian conflict, Eutyches accused Nestorius of dividing Jesus into two natures. In setting forth his alternative, he interpreted the church's confession that Jesus was "one person" with the idea that our Lord possessed only "one nature" (hence, "monophysitism"). As a result, Eutyches conceived Jesus as one in whom divinity and humanity mingled to form a new nature. When questioned by official church representatives, he confessed, "after the birth of our Lord Jesus Christ I worship one nature, viz, that of God made flesh and become man."[10] Eutyches termed

---

7. Specifically, Nestorius declared that "the man" was the temple in which "the God" dwelt. As cited in Kelly, *Early Christian Doctrines*, 314.

8. Ibid., 317-18.

9. Wand, *The Four Great Heresies*, 108.

10. As cited in Kelly, *Early Christian Doctrines*, 332.

Christ's incarnate substance "the one incarnate nature of God the Word."[11]

In seeking to avoid the danger which had plagued Nestorianism—dividing Jesus into two persons—Eutyches fell into the opposite error. He conceived of the incarnate life as a third substance which was neither divine nor human, but in which divinity clearly overshadowed humanity.[12]

In the face of the monophysite heresy church leaders met once again. At the Fourth Ecumenical Council, held at Chalcedon in 451,[13] they built from a lengthy treatise on the nature of Christ written by Leo, the Bishop of Rome. The deliberations of the council led to the drafting of the well-known Chalcedonian formulation, which became the watershed for all subsequent Christology. At the heart of the declaration are several phrases crafted with the goal of explicitly rejecting each of the four great heresies: "acknowledged in two natures without confusion, without change, without division, without separation."[14] The church leaders were convinced that within these four words lay the mystery of deity and humanity in Jesus and therefore that these terms mark the boundaries of orthodox Christology.

Christology after Chalcedon. The Chalcedonian formulation became the standard for orthodox Christianity. Yet it did not bring to an end all Christological argument. Perhaps the most consequential subsequent debate was the monothelite controversy. At issue were the implications of the Chalcedonian Christology under the rubric of the volitional dimension of the incarnate life. How many "wills" were present in Jesus Christ?

The monothelites (from a Greek construct meaning "one will") drew their position from the Chalcedonian Christology. Because Jesus is one person, they concluded, our Lord had only one will, namely, the will of the *Logos*. The *Logos* was the moving force in the person of Jesus and directed his obedient human nature. The orthodox thinkers, however, were convinced otherwise. Central to their

---

11. Wand, *The Four Great Heresies*, 111.

12. Kelly, *Early Christian Doctrines*, 333.

13. For a helpful description of the Council of Chalcedon, see Philip Schaff, *History of the Christian Church*, fifth edition (New York: Charles Scribner's Sons, 1899), 3:740-47.

14. "The Chalcedonian Definition" as cited in Wand, *The Four Great Heresies*, 118.

conclusion was the reasoning that had led their forebears to reject Apollinarius's Christology years before: Complete redemption demands a complete incarnation, including the assumption of a human will. In A.D. 680, the Sixth Ecumenical Council declared as orthodox the affirmation that Jesus Christ possessed two wills.[15]

The Reformation debate. During the Reformation, Protestant thinkers reopened the ancient question of the proper way of conceiving Christ's person. The Reformers were divided in their understanding of the patristic doctrine of *communicatio idiomatum*[16] (that the properties of both natures—deity and humanity—are communicated to, or interchanged in the one person of Jesus Christ[17]).

Luther had appealed to an analogy of iron and heat in order to understanding the divine and human in Christ: Just as heat pervades an iron bar so also in the incarnation Jesus' divinity extends throughout his humanity. On this basis, Luther's followers supposed that the unity of the two natures in Jesus' person requires a genuine communicating of the divine attributes to his human nature. The human nature participates in the divine attributes, especially in the glory and majesty of deity. Yet Jesus' humanity is not thereby lost, nor are human attributes transferred to his divine nature.

One important implication of the Lutheran teaching relates to the reality of the risen Lord. The human nature of the resurrected Jesus participates in the omnipresence of his divine nature. As a consequence, Christ's body and blood are actually present in the Eucharist. In chapter 20, we will look more closely at the debate about the Lord's Supper which divided the Protestant movement.

Furthermore, Lutherans maintained that nothing is accomplished by either of Jesus' two natures without the cooperation of the other. This includes acts that may appear to be unique to either his deity or

---

15. For a discussion of the monothelite position and the Council decision, see Schaff, *History of the Christian Church*, 4:490-500. See also, Kenneth Scott Latourette, *A History of Christianity* (New York: Harper and Brothers, 1953), 284-86.

16. For a synopsis of the Lutheran-Reformed debate, see Richard A. Muller, *Dictionary of Latin and Greek Theological Terms* (Grand Rapids: Baker, 1985), 72-75. See also Justo L. Gonzales, *A History of Christian Thought*, three volumes (Nashville: Abingdon, 1975), 3: 116-18.

17. Kelly describes the term in this manner: "that in view of the unity of Christ's person, His human and divine attributes, experiences, etc. might properly be interchanged." Kelly, *Early Christian Doctrines*, 143.

his humanity. For example, in his sufferings during the crucifixion, Christ's divine nature remains in communion with his human nature. This principle means that we ought never to view the two natures in isolation from each other. Rather, Jesus Christ functions at all times as both divine and human.

Calvinists, in contrast, rejected the Lutheran suppositions. They rejected the realist view of the *communicatio idiomatum* proposed by the Lutherans, which postulates that the one person bears the attributes of both natures. Reformed thinkers thought of the two natures as remaining separate even within the unity of Jesus' person. The communication of attributes was merely a verbal predication, they claimed. As a result of their view, the Calvinists spoke of Jesus as sometimes operating from the human nature and at other times from his divine nature.

Because of their differing perspectives, Calvinists and Lutherans had lingering doubts about the orthodoxy of the other party. Calvinists were worried that their Lutheran colaborers came dangerously close to the Eutychian heresy. If the divine characteristics are transferred to the human nature, as Luther's analogy suggested, was not Jesus' humanity engulfed by his divinity? Lutherans, in turn, wondered if the Calvinists were not somewhat Nestorian in their thinking. Was not any suggestion that Jesus sometimes acted from his human nature and other times from his deity an example of the error of separating the two natures?

The fundamental difference in perspective that arose in the patristic era between Antioch and Alexandria and which flared up again in the sixteenth century in the debate between the Lutheran and Reformed traditions has never been fully and satisfactorily resolved. The patristic church bequeathed to us the legacy of affirming that Jesus is at the same time fully divine and fully human, and that he is one person in whom the two natures are neither fully separable nor fused. But the church—perhaps as a wise acknowledgment of our human limitations—has never set forth an orthodox understanding which penetrates the heart of the mystery of the person of our Lord.

The Foundation for Affirming the Unity

Although never articulated to the satisfaction of all thinkers, the controversies led the church to conclude that in Jesus we find two complete natures in one person. Yet thinkers have not been able to explain the exact relationship between deity and humanity in the one person of Jesus. We must therefore explore the New Testament documents for insight into this question.

The problem as to how Christians should conceive of Jesus did not arise first in the patristic era through the dialectic of Antioch and Alexandria. On the contrary, the issue was raised already within the infant church. In their attempt to speak to the apparent contradiction of Jesus' divine-human person, the early Christians employed several christological titles. These lay at their disposal because of the Hebrew (and possibly Greek) context in which the incarnate life occurred. The New Testament documents indicate that Jesus' followers used two specific titles to affirm their belief that as this human being, Jesus is truly divine.

Jesus as the Word. The first important Christological term that links humanity and deity is the title "Word." The underlying Greek term, *Logos*, occurs repeatedly in the New Testament (some 330 times). It carries special significance, however, when used as a theological conclusion about the historical appearance of Jesus. John, for example, declared that Jesus is "the Word" in the prologue to the Fourth Gospel and later in the introduction to his first epistle. This use of the term is pregnant with theological significance. In the words of Hubert Ritt, it "stands out sharply from all the others."[18]

"Word" was especially well suited to function as a central christological title in the early church, because the term has rootage in both the Greek term *logos* and the corresponding Hebrew concept *davar.*

Originally, the term *logos* was related to counting, reckoning, or explaining. *Logos* later accrued a deeper significance, as H. Kleinknecht, writing in the *Theological Dictionary of the New Testament*, notes:

---

18. Hubert Ritt, "logos," in the *Exegetical Dictionary of the New Testament*, ed. Horst Balz and Gerhard Schneider, English translation (Grand Rapids: Eerdmans, 1991), 2:359.

we have in view the use of *logos* for word, speech, utterance, revelation, not in the sense of something proclaimed and heard, but rather in that of something displayed, clarified, recognized, and understood; *logos* as the rational power of calculation in virtue of which man can see himself and his place in the cosmos; *logos* as the indication of an existing and significant content which is assumed to be intelligible; *logos* as the content itself in terms of its meaning and law, its basis and structure.[19]

The *logos*, therefore, was connected to the rationality and understandability of the world:

It is presupposed as self-evident by the Greek that there is in things, in the world and its course, a primary *logos*, an intelligible and recognizable law, which then makes possible knowledge and understanding in the human *logos*. But this *logos* is not taken to be something which is merely grasped theoretically. It claims a man. It determines his true life and conduct. The *logos* is thus the norm. For the Greek, knowledge is always recognition of a law. Therewith it is also fulfillment of this law.[20]

In short, the Greeks viewed the *logos* as "the principle of the universe," the perceivable inner law of reality by which humans ought to orient themselves.

The biblical context for the christological affirmation, "Jesus is the Word," lies in the Old Testament concept of "the word of God." This in turn arises out of the Hebrew term *davar*, which is generally translated either "word" or "thing." Basically, *davar* means "the background of a matter." Kleinknecht explains that as such it carries a noetic and a dynamic aspect. Noetically, *davar* refers to the exhibiting of the meaning of a thing, so that through this display the thing is known and subject to thought, because its nature is brought to light. In its dynamic aspect, *davar* is what contains the power of something, whether that power is felt by the one who receives the word or is present in the effect that this word has in history.

As a consequence of this double-sided meaning of *davar*, the phrase "word of God" carries a double significance. Noetically, it refers to what is revelatory, to what reveals the significance of an event

---

19. H. Kleinknecht, "logos," in the *Theological Dictionary of the New Testament*, ed. Gerhard Kittel, trans. Geoffery W. Bromiley (Grand Rapids: Eerdmans, 1967), 4:80-81.
20. Kleinknecht, "logos," in the TDNT, 4:81.

or even reveals the nature of God. Dynamically, the "word of God" stands for the creative power of God, such as God's wisdom in creation (Prov. 8:22-31), or even God's utterance as carrying power. (Hence, in the first creation narrative God speaks, and it was so.)

The two aspects of the Old Testament concept of the "word of God" are blended in the christological title "Word" which the New Testament predicates of Jesus. This is evident in the paradigmatic text, the Johannine prologue, which brings together the creative role of the Word ("Through him all things were made without him nothing was made that has been made"—v.3—"He was in the world and though the world was made through him the world did not recognize him"—v.10) with its revelatory significance ("The word became flesh and lived for a while among us. We have seen his glory, the glory of the one and only Son who came from the Father full of grace and truth"—v.14).

Although Paul does not explicitly use the term, the hymn to the Christ found in the first chapter of Colossians displays the same blending of the revelatory and creative aspects indicative of the Old Testament concept of *davar*:

> He is the image of the invisible God, the first born over all creation. For by him all things were created: things in heaven and on earth, visible and invisible, whether thrones of powers or rulers or authorities, all things were created by him and for him. (Col. 1:15-16)

The declaration, "Jesus is the Word," therefore, constitutes a theological statement concerning the significance of this historical life. In him, God's revelation is disclosed and God's power is operative. As a result, the title asserts that in Jesus of Nazareth the power of God is at work revealing the meaning of all reality—even the nature of God. To refer to Jesus as the Word is to affirm that as this human being, he is the revelation of God.

Jesus as the Son. The other significant Christological title is "Son," which is related to the designation "Son of God." This title played a central role in the church's description of Jesus' identity. Its use, however, predates the New Testament era.

In the ancient Near East "son" was predicated of those persons who were thought to be the offspring of the gods. Recipients of the title included the king, who was begotten of the gods, or persons who possessed extraordinary and hence "divine" powers.

More important for its New Testament use is the Old Testament background of the title. To the ancient Hebrews "son" indicated election to participation in God's work. The "Son of God" was God's special agent, chosen to carry out God's mission in the world or elected to obedience to the electing God. Consequently, the Old Testament authors employed the designation "Son of God" with reference to Israel as a people. On other occasions it designated kings or specific persons with special commissions (Ex. 4:22; Hos. 11:1; Isa. 1:2; 2 Sam. 7:14).

In the Gospels, the title "Son" focuses on the historical life of Jesus. At times it appears to be merely a commonplace designation without great christological significance, being merely Jesus' own way of referring to himself or one manner in which others refer to him. At other times, it carries loftier connotations, referring to Jesus' unique relationship to God or his unique role in God's work. Most significant of all, however, is the use of the term to declare Jesus' unique obedience to the Father's will. In keeping with the Old Testament context of the term, as the totally obedient one he is truly the Son, the one God chose for a mission to which he is obedient.

The epistles set forth the final conclusion of the early community about the significance of Jesus as the Son. On the basis of his unique sonship, his followers inferred Jesus' status as divine: As this man, he is deity. The Book of Hebrews offers a lucid example of this heightened Son-Christology: "The Son is the radiance of God's glory and the exact representation of his being, sustaining all things by his powerful word" (Heb. 1:3). A similar lofty Christology is evident in Paul's declaration, "For in Christ all the fullness of the Deity lives in bodily form" (Col. 2:9).

The declaration that as this man Jesus is divine—the use of the title "Son" to assert the deity of the man Jesus—did not arise *sui generis*. Rather, the early believers drew this conclusion from Jesus' earthly life, which when viewed in the context of the Old Testament was indeed the life of the Son. The affirmation "Jesus is the divine

Son of God" was for them an obvious deduction from his unique obedience to the unique mission God gave to him.

The movement from the observation of Jesus' faithfulness in his mission to the affirmation of his deity as the Son is evident in John's declaration,

> And we have seen and testify that the Father has sent his Son to be the Savior of the world. If anyone acknowledges that Jesus is the Son of God, God lives in him and he in God. (1 John 4:14-15)

In the same way, the author of Hebrews based his Son-Christology on the earthly life of Jesus. The one who is the "radiance of God's glory" is he who "made purification for sins." For this reason, he is the Son, the one who is begotten by the Father (Heb. 1:3-5; see also 4:14-15; 5:4-5).

In short, the divine connotation of the title Son is an extension of its Old Testament foundation warranted by the unique life of Jesus of Nazareth. Jesus lived as the uniquely obedient one. He came with a unique mission within the purposes of God, and he fulfilled that unique mission perfectly, being obedient to the Father's will to the end. As such, Jesus is the unique Son of God, the one who enjoyed a unique relationship to the Father. As the unique Son, the "one and only Son" or the "Only Begotten" (John 1:14), he is the divine Son of the Father.

The title "Son," therefore, came to carry similar exalted aspects as the designation "Word." The connection between "Son" and "Word" is evident in the opening verses of the Epistle to the Hebrews:

> In the past God spoke to our forefathers through the prophets at many times and in various ways but in these last days he has spoken to us by his Son, whom he appointed heir of all things and through whom he made the universe. The Son is the radiance of God's glory and the exact representation of his being sustaining all things by his powerful word. (Heb. 1:3-4)

Although the term *Logos* does not occur here, the text blends the revelatory and creative aspects inherent in the idea of the "word of God." As "the radiance of God's glory and the exact representation of his being" and the one through whom God made the universe, the Son is the revelation of the meaning of all reality and of God's essence. As this revelation, he is the powerful "word of God" that sustains the universe and through whom God has spoken.

The Relationship Between Deity and Humanity in Jesus

Through the biblical titles "Word" and "Son" we confess that in Jesus we find both deity and humanity together in one person. More specifically, the declarations "Jesus is the Word" and "Jesus is the Son" are two vehicles for confessing the great christological truth that this particular man, Jesus of Nazareth, is divine. By so doing, these scriptural titles point the way to a resolution of the mystery of Jesus' person. They suggest how Jesus is both divine and human.

Jesus and revelation. The christological titles "Word" and "Son" offer the basis for probing into the mystery of Jesus' person through their common connection with the idea of revelation. The two titles capsulize the Christian confession that Jesus is the one who reveals both essential deity and humanity to us. As this revelation, Jesus brings the two together in his one person.

To see this, we must return to the fundamental confessions voiced by the early church at Nicea and Constantinople: Jesus is "truly divine and truly human." In chapter 9, we concluded that the affirmation "Jesus is divine" means that he is the revelation of God's nature, the one who shares in the triune community. As we saw in chapter 10, the declaration of Jesus' humanity means that he is the revelation of essential human nature, the exemplar of human fellowship or life in community. The common element in both confessions is the assertion of Jesus' revelatory significance. From this we may conclude that the unity of deity and humanity in Jesus is a revelatory unity. Hence, his status as revelation is the linchpin that brings together in one person these two seemingly discontinuous dimensions.

Although critics suggest that all appeals to revelation as the focus of the unity of Jesus' person entail a merely functional, and hence a truncated Christology, the opposite is actually the case. Because Jesus' significance as revelation brings together the deity and the humanity we confess concerning his person, it provides the link from function to ontology, thereby overcoming the problem of functional verses ontological Christology. Revelation constructs this bridge in that it arises as a conclusion from Jesus' earthly life but then leads to a conclusion about his eternal reality. Let us follow this christological method more closely.

If our faith is to be more than private speculation—if it is to carry a public dimension—we must base our christological assertions on historical considerations. That is, our conclusions must arise from observing Jesus' life, death, and resurrection. Our conclusions about Jesus' revelatory significance fit this requirement. In chapters 9 and 10, we concluded on the basis of our observation of Jesus' personal claim (including his teachings and his actions) that he functions as deity and humanity. Jesus claimed to enjoy a unique relation to God and to be the exemplary human, claims which God confirmed in raising Jesus from the dead. On the basis of the function he fulfilled (both that he enjoyed a unique relationship to God and lived as the paradigm human) we affirm his revelatory significance. Because he functions as the truly divine and the truly human one, we conclude that Jesus reveals the nature of God and of humanity.

But our christological method demands that we take a further step. Inherent in revelation is participation. To the extent that a revelatory agent truly discloses the essence of something, the vehicle of disclosure must participate in the reality it discloses. In other words, "revelation of" implies a certain "participation in." insofar as Jesus discloses both essential deity and essential humanity, he must participate in the divine and the human realities. Jesus' revelatory unity, therefore, leads explicitly to his ontological unity with God and humankind.

As this historical life, then, Jesus of Nazareth is both divine and human. He is both essential deity and essential humanity. The unity of his person lies in his revelatory significance. Because of the connection between disclosure and ontological participation, Jesus' revelatory unity means that in his person he brings together the truly divine and the genuinely human.

Jesus and community. With this conclusion we are not yet at our final destination, however. There is yet another point that our two fundamental confessions share in common, namely, the concept of community.

As the revelation of God, Jesus participates in the divine life. He shares in the community of the triune God, for he is the eternal Son, the Second Person of the Trinity. Similarly, as the revelation of essential humanity, he also participates in true human life.

Community reminds us that the divine life and human life are not totally disjunctive. At the heart of both is life-in-community. In chapter 2 we concluded that God is characterized by community, for he is the social Trinity. Furthermore, we saw in chapter 6, that God intends that human living likewise be characterized by community, for the image of God is a community concept. In addition, true human life is the enjoyment of community with God.

In his earthly life as well as through his resurrection and exaltation, Jesus brings together the two dimensions of community. He participates in the eternal triune reality as the Son, the Second Person of the Trinity. This is evident in his claim to a unique relation to the Father, which God confirmed in the resurrection. At the same time, Jesus is the trailblazer of the new human community. He is the New Human, the head of a new humanity. Hence, he shares true community with all who are his disciples. As our trailblazer, he is the one who mediates to us the fellowship of the new humanity, which he shares with all who are united in him through the Holy Spirit.

As the previous statement indicates, these christological themes spill over into pneumatology. Consequently, the final affirmation of Jesus' personal unity rests with the Holy Spirit. As we noted in chapter 2, the Spirit is the spirit of the eternal love relationship between the Father and the Son. He brings us, in turn, to share in that great love relationship as those who are in fellowship with the Father because of the Son. In this manner, the Holy Spirit confirms the unity of Jesus' person.

The Incarnation

The titles "Word" and "Son" represent two crucial early Christian responses to the christological mystery as to how Jesus was both divine and human. Through these titles the church declared that this human, Jesus of Nazareth, is divine. Closely related to the titles is the assertion that Jesus is the incarnate one, the *Logos* in human form. Since the formulation of the Chalcedonian Christology, which climaxed the work of the first five centuries of theological reflection, orthodox thinkers have appealed to this idea as the key to the christological mystery.

How are we to understand the incarnation? In what sense can we say that Jesus is the incarnation of the *Logos* or the Second Person of the Trinity? To this issue we must now turn. In so doing, we glance again at the story of theological history in order to gain a context in which to develop a contemporary incarnational Christology.

The Incarnation in Theological History

The Chalcedonian formulation incorporated the central features of late patristic incarnational Christology.[21] That Christology focused on the condescension and self-humiliation of the divine *Logos*, the Son, in taking to himself human nature. It included as well the exaltation of human nature to inseparable communion with the divine *Logos* because of that act. Hence, the Chalcedonian Christology viewed the incarnation as the act of the divine *Logos*. In the incarnation, the Son did not unite with a human person, but with human nature, which gained existence in its connection with the *Logos* (*enhypostasis*). As a consequence of the incarnation, the one person Jesus Christ enjoys the properties of the two natures (*communicatio idiomatum*).

Chalcedon claimed foundational importance for orthodox Christology. As a result, the incarnation became the focus of theologizing after the fifth century. The centrality of the incarnation is especially evident in Protestant theology, as thinkers delved into the question of the actual dynamics of the incarnate life.

The kenosis theory. During the era of Protestant scholasticism, the dynamics of the incarnation formed the topic for intense discussion among Lutherans. They engaged at great length with the question as to exactly what the incarnation of the *Logos* meant for the divine and

---

21. For a summary of the Chalecdonian theology, see Schaff, *History of the Christian Church*, 3:750-72.

human attributes. We have already noted one dimension lying behind this interest, namely, the tension the doctrine of *communication idiomatum* caused between the Lutherans and the Calvinists.

One important suggestion came in the form of what has been known as the *kenosis* theory.[22] Taking their cue from the great christological hymn of Philippians (especially Phil. 2:7), proponents theorized that at the incarnation the *Logos* divested himself of those divine attributes which are incompatible with existence as a human being, particularly omnipotence, omnipresence, and omniscience. The divine moral attributes, in contrast, are compatible with human existence. Hence, the *Logos* retained love, mercy, and justice. Other theorists went even farther. In the incarnation, they suggested, the Son laid aside all the divine attributes.

Despite its initial popularity, the flaw in the *kenosis* theory soon appeared. If in the incarnation the Son divested himself of certain divine attributes, the incarnate Christ is less than God. Therefore, Jesus does not reveal to us essential deity. The *kenosis* theorists, therefore, were on the verge of violating the decision of the first ecumenical council and of placing themselves at odds with the Nicene formulation. The confession of Jesus' true deity demands that in the incarnate life the *Logos* must possess all the essential attributes of God.[23]

Modifications to the kenosis theory. Other thinkers moved to salvage what they saw as the truth within the *kenosis* understanding. To this end they proposed a modified thesis.

The reformulated theory postulates that in the incarnation the *Logos* did not lay aside the divine attributes themselves, not those powers inherent to deity. Rather, the Son gave up the independent exercise of these powers. In other words, although he retained all the attributes, powers, or prerogatives of God, the earthly Jesus refused to draw on his divine abilities merely at his own whim. Rather, he willingly submitted his prerogative to use his divine capabilities to his Father's will as directed by the Spirit.

---

22. For a summary of this theory, see Gordon R. Lewis and Bruce A. Demarest, *Integrative Theology*, three volumes (Grand Rapids: Zondervan, 1990), 2: 252-53; G. C. Berkouwer, *The Person of Christ*, trans. John Vriend (Grand Rapids: Eerdmans, 1955), 27-29.

23. See, Berkouwer, *The Person of Christ*, 30-31.

For example, Jesus readily exercised omniscience when doing so fit with his Father's intentions, such as when he encountered Nathaniel. Yet he refused to call upon this attribute when it meant going beyond what his Father desired. Thus, he admitted that even he not know the time of the coming of the Son of Man, for this prerogative belonged solely to the Father.

This modified *kenosis* theory has gained prominence, especially among evangelical theologians.[24] Other evangelicals, however, gravitate toward a further modification. The propose that in the incarnation the Son voluntarily set aside the continuous use of his divine powers, in order that he might grow as a human.[25]

The incarnation as the paradox of grace. Lutheran thinkers have not been the only ones to reflect on the nature of the incarnate life. Indeed the Reformed emphasis on volition sparked one of the most creative christological reformulations of the twentieth century. In his book *God Was in Christ*, the Scottish thinker, Donald M. Baillie, proposed a new vantage point from which to view the dynamics of the incarnation.[26] Baillie argued that the key to understanding the union of the human and the divine in Jesus of Nazareth lies in the paradox of grace articulated by Paul to the Galatians:

> I am crucified with Christ nevertheless I live. Yet not I, but Christ lives in me. And the life I now live I live by the grace of the Son of God who loved me and gave himself up for me. (Gal. 2:20)

In this text, Paul suggests that the task of Christian living is fulfilled in a paradoxical way. It is totally the work of the individual; at the same time, it is totally the work of God. So also Jesus was a man who himself carried out a divine mission; at the same time this mission was fulfilled through him totally by God.

The Critique of Incarnational Christology

Despite the genuine differences evidenced in the above sketch, thinkers that have been chiefly concerned to remain orthodox in their

---

24. It was preferred by Strong, for example. Augustus Hopkins Strong, *Systematic Theology*, three volumes (Philadelphia: Griffith and Rowland, 1907), 2:703-704.

25. This position is espoused in Lewis and Demarest, *Integrative Theology*, 2:284-85.

26. D. M. Baillie, *God Was in Christ*, second edition (New York: Charles Scribner's Sons, 1948).

christological presentations have generally tended to follow a similar approach. At the heart of this basic Christology are several assertions:[27] Jesus combines in one person a divine and a human nature. The incarnation, understood as a historical event (perhaps occurring through the virginal conception), was the means whereby the union of these two natures was effected. This act was the work of the Second Person of the Trinity, the *Logos*. This act resulted in a "hypostatic union" of deity and humanity in Jesus, that is, one in which the personal center of the earthly life was the eternal Son, with the human nature existing only through its union with the *Logos* (*enhypostasis*). Finally, the historical act of incarnation occurred in the womb of Mary.

How should we evaluate this widely held post-Chalcedonian Christology? At the onset, we must acknowledge that its central intent is correct. The traditional view has as its goal the preservation of both the deity and the humanity of Jesus, in accordance with the decisions of the church councils and the testimony of the New Testament. While correct in its intent, we must add that the incarnational Christology is beset with grave problems. Consequently, it has been the recipient of a variety of criticisms in the modern era.

Criticisms of the traditional understanding. Some thinkers reject the traditional Christology on the basis of its apparent mythological tone. The idea of the Son assuming human nature in the womb of Mary parallels too closely the ancient stories of descents of gods into our world for a time and their subsequent ascent again into the heavenly realm. In a similar manner, critics chide proponents of incarnational Christologies for using Greek philosophical categories. They argue that Greek concepts, such as "substance" or "essence," and fixed ontological categories, such as a "human nature" and a "divine nature," are foreign both to the Hebrew and to the contemporary mindset. We now know, as did the ancient Hebrews, that there are no such fixed essences that precede actual historical life.

Perhaps weightier than either of these, however, is a further objection. Implicit in the traditional position is an incipit Docetism, or at

---

27. See, for example, Schaff's exposition of the Chalcedonian theology. Schaff, *History of the Christian Church*, 3:750-58. See also, Lewis and Demarest, *Integrative Theology*, 2:271-87.

least overtones of Apollinarianism. Although proponents of incarnational Christologies generally have no desire to deny Jesus' full humanity, in practice they often picture the incarnate life in terms of the eternal Son hidden in a human body. In this manner, Jesus becomes a divine being who functioned during his earthly sojourn through a human exterior.

Finally, traditional Christologies sometimes exemplify a faulty christological method. By envisioning the incarnation as the act of the eternal *Logos* in taking to himself a human nature in the womb of Mary, this approach readily falls into the dangerous trap of conceiving of the *Logos* apart from Jesus. Indeed, if we understand the incarnation as an act that occurred at a specific moment in history (somewhere around 4-6 B.C.), our inquisitive minds naturally ask, What was the *Logos*, the active agent of the act of incarnation, doing before the incarnation? Thereby we separate what for the New Testament cannot be divided; we objectify what in the New Testament is a Christological title describing significance of Jesus. Because *Logos* is a title for Jesus, there is no other *Logos* or Son except Jesus of Nazareth. When we speculate about the *Logos* apart from Jesus' historical life, we lose the significance of the term as a christological title.

Significance of the incarnation. The problems inherent in many incarnational Christologies lead us to question whether we have correctly understood the biblical concept of incarnation. Perhaps the difficulty lies in the attempt to follow the well-worn christological pathway that views this concept as the story of the historical descent of a preexisting, wholly divine being (the *Logos*).

Our surmising is confirmed when we look at the central New Testament texts from which theologians build the concept of incarnation. Especially important are the Pauline hymn to the self-abasing Jesus (Phil. 2:5-11) and the Johannine prologue (John 1:1-14). Texts such as these do not follow a narrative pattern. They do not depict the incarnation as the historical movement of a preexistent *Logos*. Paul does not mention the *Logos* at all; rather, he writes about Christ Jesus. The historical person Jesus refused to clutch his divine prerogatives but was God's humble, obedient servant even to the point of death, and as a consequence he possesses the highest name. The confession of Jesus as Lord, therefore, is a conclusion Paul drew from the life of Jesus of Nazareth who is therefore the Christ.

The meaning of the incarnation in the Johannine prologue is more complex. John does speak about the divine *Logos* who was with God in the beginning and who became flesh. However, the apostle's intent is hardly that we understand the incarnation as an act of the eternal *Logos* who assumes human nature in the womb of Mary. In contrast to much incarnational Christology, John does not pinpoint an exact historical moment (such as Jesus' conception) at which time the incarnation occurred. Nor does he cite the virgin birth as the vehicle that facilitated the beginning of the incarnate state of the eternal *Logos*. In fact, the Johannine prologue does not even mention Jesus' birth.

Rather than focusing on Jesus' miraculous birth, John appeals to eyewitnesses who observed our Lord's earthly life. On the basis of personal observations of Jesus' life (not his birth), these persons bear testimony to the incarnation:

> The Word became flesh and lived for a while among us. We have seen his glory, the glory of the one and only Son, who came from the Father, full of grace and truth. (John 1:14)

In Jesus, the early witness have seen the divine glory, a glory evidenced throughout the earthly life of Jesus.

For John, then, "the Word became flesh" (the incarnation) does not focus on how Jesus came into existence. More importantly, it is a theological declaration of the significance of the Master's earthly life. When he confesses Jesus as the incarnate Word, John is claiming that as this human being, Jesus is divine; he is God's revelation.

With this in view, how are we to understand the incarnation? Our task can be expedited as we embark on the route traversed by Paul and John. We must take our position with the eyewitnesses. This means, however, that we cannot follow those theologians who understand "incarnation" as a specific occurrence in history and who therefore define it as the beginning point of Christology. We cannot articulate the great christological mystery by explaining how it was possible for the eternal *Logos* to assume human nature.

With the early witnesses, we must employ a Christology "from below." We search for the answer to the identity of Jesus by looking at his historical life. Rather than being the presupposition of Christology, the confession of the incarnation—"the Word became flesh"—can only be the conclusion of our reflections on Jesus' person.

When we look first at Jesus of Nazareth, we arrive at the conclusion we explored in this chapter and which the apostles confessed: In this one historical, personal life we find revealed who God is and who we are to be—true deity and true humanity. As this human being, Jesus is divine. In this affirmation, which is a confession about the entire life of Jesus, lies the significance of the confession of the incarnation. Rather than a description of some purported activity of the eternal *Logos*, "incarnation" is a christological confession. It capsulizes what we find in Jesus of Nazareth, namely, that he is the "word"—the dynamic, revelatory word of God—in human form.

The foundation for this confession, Jesus is the incarnate one, is not limited to Jesus' birth. All of his life, including his resurrection as the confirmation of his claims concerning himself, indicates that in Jesus the Word has come in the flesh. In short, we do not celebrate the incarnation merely at Christmas, but throughout the church year climaxing at Easter.

Jesus' Preexistence

Closely related to the incarnation and consequently to the christological title "Word" (*Logos*) is the preexistence of Christ. As we have seen, because of the connection in Hebrew thought between the "word of God" and the divine reality, the title "Word" unites Jesus with God himself. This unity, in turn, leads to preexistence. The dynamic revelation of God (the Word) must always be present with God, and therefore it is eternally existent by necessity. If Jesus is the Word, there must be a sense in which he is an eternal reality.

How are we to understand the concept of preexistence in the light of the conclusions about the title "Word" and the incarnation we delineated in this chapter?

The problem of preexistence. The previous discussion cautions us against conceptions that link preexistence directly to the *Logos*, rather than to Jesus. Indeed, many Christians see preexistence as a natural conclusion from the incarnation, understood as the narrative of the Son. Predicating the attribute to the *Logos*, they conceive of preexistence as referring to the existence—even the activity—of the *Logos* prior to his assuming human form in Mary's womb.

On this basis, some theologians investigate the activity of the Christ in the Old Testament era, concluding for example that the appearances of the Angel of Yahweh were preincarnation "Christophanies."[28] Others speculate concerning the role of Christ in "original creation," even asserting that the one who became a baby in Bethlehem called the worlds into existence.[29]

Although christologically illegitimate, these seemingly impudent questions have some credence. They couch a deeper christological issue, namely, whether the eternal Son is active apart from the historical person, Jesus of Nazareth. We could pose this question in a somewhat restricted manner: In what sense is Jesus of Nazareth active in the world since his death, resurrection, and ascension? So viewed, the question moves us beyond Christology proper into pneumatology and ecclesiology.

The question, however, can also be broadened: In what sense is the *Logos* active beyond the action of Jesus? When placed in the context of world religions, the question becomes: Are there other historical figures in whom the Son has been or is operative? Or we could pose it exegetically: What does John mean by "the light that gives light to everyone (John 1:9)? These have become weighty issues in our day.

The meaning of preexistence. Enroute to our delineation of the concept of preexistence, we must set forth several principles which will guide our thoughts. One such principle is the observation that whatever it may mean, according to the New Testament, preexis-

---

28. See, for example, E. W. Hengstenberg, *Christology of the Old Testament and a Commentary on the Messianic Predictions*, two volumes, English translation, reprint edition (Grand Rapids: Kregel, 1970).

29. For an example, see Jerry Falwell, "The Revelation of the Incarnation," *Fundamentalist Journal* 7/11 (December 1988), 10.

tence is an attribute describing Jesus of Nazareth. We are concerned, therefore, to understand the preexistence of *Jesus*, and not that of some purported eternal being—whether the *Logos* or the Son— viewed apart from him.

This observation cautions us against a temptation inherent in certain incarnational theologies. We must never use preexistence as a means of separating the Son from Jesus of Nazareth, in order to speculate about the activities of the *Logos* apart from the historical person. As we noted above, such speculation destroys the central importance of the title *Logos*, by which the New Testament writers confess the meaning of the historical person Jesus. Like the title to which it is related, we would suspect that "preexistence" is a theological statement about the identity of Jesus of Nazareth.

Our conclusions must also be guided by a proper understanding of the original intent of the preexistence doctrine in the early church. This teaching served as a polemic against all forms of adoptionism.[30] Although we may not agree with modern suggestions that the early Christology evolved through a lengthy process, we must acknowledge the basic correctness of the widely held theory explaining the development of Christology in the New Testament era.[31] Important among the first believers was the question, When did Jesus become the Son? The New Testament gives evidence to several potential answers to this question: his future coming, his ascension, his resurrection, his baptism, his conception. Seeing all these options as potentially adoptionistic, the church quickly came to a final, far-reaching conclusion: Jesus is the Son "from eternity." Hence, they attributed preexistence to him.

Jesus and preexistence. With the early church we readily confess that Jesus is the preexistent one. But what does this mean? In what sense can we predicate preexistence to a historical person. At its heart, the doctrine of preexistence speaks about the uniqueness and

---

30. Wolfhart Pannenberg, *Jesus—God and Man*, trans. Lewis L. Wilkins and Duane A. Priebe, second edition (Philadelphia: Westminster, 1977), 149-50.

31. For a summary of this theory, see Raymond E. Brown, *The Virginal Conception and Bodily Resurrection of Jesus* (New York: Paulist, 1973), 43-44.

finality of Jesus of Nazareth. There are three senses in which we should understand this assertion.

(1) Preexistence asserts the theological truth that Jesus belongs to God's eternity. Similar to the christological title "Word," the confession of Jesus' preexistence speaks about his relationship to God.

By confessing his preexistence, we declare that this human being, as this specific human person, is eternal deity. Contrary to the opinion of many, his brief historical life is more than a blip in time. Instead Jesus discloses the very heart of eternity, for that short life is nothing less than the revelation of God. As Paul writes, "God was pleased to have all his fullness to dwell in him" (Col. 1:19). Because in Jesus we find eternity, this historical life belongs to the eternal realm, the realm of God himself.

By confessing Jesus' preexistence—that Jesus belongs to God's eternity—we affirm the uniqueness and finality of his earthly life. Thereby, our affirmation of preexistence carries far-reaching implications for human beliefs and religion. We declare through our confession that Jesus is the embodiment of truth. His life is the truly religious life. And his teachings are true teachings, revealing the eternal truth of God himself. As a result, Jesus is the standard for measuring all religious truth. All other truth claims must be weighed in accordance with this one historical person.

(2) Preexistence declares likewise that the historical life of Jesus carries significance beyond the boundaries of his brief life. He gives meaning to all history. Jesus is the divine principle of creation from whom all of reality takes its meaning. Jesus' earthly life is the meaning of all history. It clarifies events of the Old Testament, which point to him. And it is the foundation for events of the New Testament era, that is, the time between his advent and his second advent.

This is the point of John's declaration, "The true light that gives light to every person was coming into the world" (John 1:9). A similar idea is present in the Colossian hymn. After declaring that Jesus reveals the fullness of deity ("For God was pleased to have all his fullness dwell in him"), the apostle adds, "and through him to reconcile to himself all things, whether things on earth or things in heaven, by making peace through his blood shed on the cross" (Col. 1:20).

Jesus is the focal point of history, for the human story receives its meaning from its relationship to Jesus of Nazareth.

(3) Preexistence means that Jesus' life is the story of history itself. That is, his life narrative includes more than the thirty-three years of his earthly sojourn. All history—whether the time of preparation for his coming or the outworking of his coming, including the preparation for his second coming—is his story, the story of the one Jesus Christ.

The Virgin Birth

Often connected with the incarnation as the means of explaining the unity of deity and humanity in Jesus is the virgin birth. Since as early as the fourth century, theologians have proposed that his special birth forms the link between Jesus' eternal sonship and his historical earthly life as a human being. In this event God and woman join to form the genesis of a historical life. Consequently, theologians have been attracted to the virgin birth as providing the historical vehicle whereby the incarnation took place. Because of its traditional theological importance, we include in our chapter on the unity of Jesus' person a discussion of this important question: Does the virgin birth provide the linchpin for an incarnational Christology?

The virgin birth has belonged to the confession of the church throughout its entire history. It is embedded in the second article of the Apostles' Creed as one of the central aspects of the church's confession: "I believe…in Jesus Christ…Who was conceived by the Holy Spirit, born of the Virgin Mary, suffered under Pontius Pilate, was crucified, dead and buried."[32]

Despite its nearly universal acceptance in the church since the early third century, perhaps no christological affirmation has been more problematic in modern times than the declaration "born of the Virgin Mary." In Protestant circles since the Enlightenment and among Roman Catholic scholars since Vatican II, this traditional affirmation

---

32. "The Apostles' Creed," in *Creeds of the Churches*, ed. John H. Leith, third edition (Atlanta: John Knox, 1982), 24.

has generated much controversy. At issue in the present discussion is the assertion that, in the words of Raymond Brown, "Jesus was conceived in the womb of a virgin without the intervention of a human father, i.e., without male seed."[33]

Because of the modern debate over this doctrine, en route to an examination of the virgin birth as the means of the incarnation, we must raise the more fundamental question about the historicity of this event. A historical perspective[34] provides the context for our discussion. We then turn our attention to an appraisal of the modern discussion. Finally we draw several conclusions about the doctrine itself as a prelude to the broader question of the nature of the incarnation.

The Historical Context of the Modern Debate

In the creeds which the church has recited since the patristic era, the faithful have continually affirmed that Jesus was born of a virgin. Although the church has not wavered in its confession of Jesus' virgin birth, its theologians are not in agreement about its meaning. This ebb and flow of theological understanding forms the context for the modern debate over the propriety of the traditional confession.

Affirmations of the virgin birth. Perhaps the first of the church fathers to refer to the virgin birth in his writings was the second century martyr Ignatius of Antioch. Yet he mentioned it in the context of the atonement rather than the incarnation.[35] More important for the development of the classical christological understanding of the virgin birth was the work of Irenaeus. However, he did not appeal to this event in order to highlight Jesus' deity, as became common practice later, but to combat the gnostic heretics who denied Jesus' full humanity.[36]

The theologians of the 300s and 400s set forth the principles that were to govern the more complete theology of the virgin birth that came to predominate in the medieval church. Lactantius postulated

33. Brown, *The Virginal Conception*, 27.

34. For a concise overview of the history, see Thomas Boslooper, *The Virgin Birth* (London: SCM, 1962).

35. Ignatius, *To the Ephesians*, xix, in *Documents of the Christian Church*, ed. Henry Bettenson (London: Oxford University Press, 1969), 41.

36. Boslooper, *The Virgin Birth*, 33-34.

the theory of the two origins of Christ as corresponding to his two natures.[37] Jesus' first nativity was spiritual and motherless, for he was begotten from all eternity by the Father. His second nativity in Bethlehem marked a birth in the flesh without a father. Consequently, he is Son of God through the Spirit and Son of Man through the flesh. Eusebius and Jerome were responsible for shifting the theological gaze from the virgin birth of Jesus to the virginity of his mother, thereby opening the way for the subsequent concept of Mary's perpetual virginity.[38] It was Augustine, however, who endowed the virgin birth with its great christological significance. The great church father suggested that Jesus' conception apart from "carnal lust" (normal sexual relations) was the foundation for his sinlessness.[39]

The confession that the virgin birth was a miracle that marked the beginning of Jesus' life reigned throughout the medieval and Reformation eras. Thinkers in the Enlightenment, however, called it into question. Because of its perceived connection to the miraculous, a category that was suspect to the critical minds of the age of reason, many of them cast the doctrine aside on naturalistic and rationalistic grounds.[40]

Reinterpretations of the virgin birth. What the Enlightenment rationalists cast out the window, theologians in the 1800s brought in through the back door. Yet they did not advocate a simple return to the precritical miraculous understanding of the doctrine. These thinkers were armed with the view that a biblical story is not to be judged solely on the basis of its rational credibility but rather for its religious meaning. Applying this principle to the story of the virgin birth, they concluded that the event may be historically suspect yet nevertheless meaningful for faith.

Schleiermacher, for example, rejected the claim that the exclusion of the male sexual contribution to Jesus' conception formed the basis for either Jesus' sinlessness or the implanting of the divine in his hu-

---

37. Ibid., 42.
38. Ibid.
39. Augustine, *Enchiridion* 41, and *On the Holy Trinity* 13.18, in *A Select Library of the Nicene and Post-Nicene Fathers of the Christian Church*, ed. Philip Schaff (Grand Rapids: Eerdmans, 1956), 180, 251.
40. Boslooper, *The Virgin Birth*, 87.

man nature.[41] Yet he did not simply throw out the idea of a miraculous birth as inconsequential. On the contrary, he concluded that the "general idea of a supernatural conception remains...essential and necessary, if the specific pre-eminence of the Redeemer is to remain undiminished."[42]

The most important innovation came from David Friedrich Strauss. The German New Testament scholar sought to overcome the impasse between the two reigning interpretations of sacred histories. He rejected both the supernaturalistic explanation, which claimed that all such events are historical and thus indispensable to Christianity, and the naturalistic alternative, which countered that these events are unhistorical and therefore unimportant.

Against both, he appealed to the category of evangelical myth: "We distinguish by the name *evangelical mythus* a narrative relating to directly or indirectly to Jesus, which may be considered not as the expression of a fact, but as the product of an idea of his earliest followers."[43] On the basis of its analogy to the myths about the births of great persons found in other religious traditions, Strauss concluded that the virgin birth story is a declaration in narrative form of the importance of Jesus.[44]

Strauss's theories aroused a storm of criticism. In response, some theologians continued to defend the supernatural character of the virgin birth.[45] They argued that the miraculous conception of Jesus was in keeping with his status as God's highest revelation. And it formed the supernatural beginning point for God's salvific action in Christ. Those who marched together under the banner of fundamentalism to fight modernist ideas elevated the virgin birth to one of the "five fundamentals," the foundational doctrines essential to the integrity of the Christian faith.[46]

---

41. Friedrich Schleiermacher, *The Christian Faith*, English translation, ed. H. R. MacKintosh and J. S. Stewart (Edinburgh: T. & T. Clark, n.d.), 404.

42. Ibid., 405.

43. David Friedrich Strauss, *The Life of Jesus, Critically Examined* [fourth German edition: 1840] trans. Marian Evans, two volumes (New York: Calvin Blanchard, 1860), 1:69.

44. Strauss, *Life of Jesus*, 1:130-34.

45. An important example is J. Gresham Machen, *The Virgin Birth of Christ*, reprint edition (1930; Grand Rapids: Baker, 1965).

46. For an early discussion of the five fundamentals, see Stewart Grant Cole, *The History of Fundamentalism* (New York: R. R. Smith, 1931), 34.

Other thinkers pursued further the pathway Strauss had blazed. Certain scholars postulated that the story is an early Christian attempt to speak about the significance of Jesus. Working from this principle, they sought to discover the origin of the idea. Some searched for its genesis in the stories found in other ancient religions.[47] Others subjected the narratives to historical and literary criticism, hoping to discover its roots in Hellenistic Judaism or in the Christological thinking of Hellenized Jewish Christians.[48]

The contemporary debate arose out of this impasse between conservative supernaturalists and proponents of higher critical scholarship.

Current Debate about the Virgin Birth

Given the territory that scholarly opinion has covered over the past centuries, it comes as no surprise that theologians today do not speak with one voice concerning the virgin birth. The contemporary debate is not limited to Protestants, however. Rather, it is now engulfing Roman Catholic theologians as well.

Protestants and the virgin birth. Protestant theologians form "a divided house." Some continue to find christological significance in the virgin birth as a historical event. Others reject it out of hand.

Perhaps the most significant positive assessment of the virgin birth in the twentieth century came from the great Swiss thinker, Karl Barth. In his monumental *Church Dogmatics* Barth sounds a ringing affirmation of the miracle of this event.[49] The virgin birth at the beginning of Jesus' earthly life and the resurrection at its end constitute for the Swiss theologian "a single sign that this life is marked off from all the rest of human life."[50] More specifically, the virgin birth denotes the mystery of revelation, namely, that God stands at the start where genuine revelation transpires.[51]

---

47. For a detailed discussion of the literature of the German history of religions school, see Boslooper, *The Virgin Birth*, 135-86.

48. For a discussion of this approach, see Boslooper, *The Virgin Birth*, 189-223.

49. The section carries the appropriate title, "The Miracle of Christmas," Karl Barth, *Church Dogmatics*, trans. G. T. Thomson and Harold Knight, ed. G. W. Bromiley and T. F. Torrance (Edinburgh: T. & T. Clark, 1956), 1/2:172-202.

50. Ibid., 182.

51. Ibid.

Barth offers a creative, albeit highly controversial, exposition of the significance of the virgin birth. Not only does Jesus' birth from a virgin signify the miraculous nature of the human existence of the one who reveals God, it also pronounces a judgment on humankind. This event embodies a denial of any power, attribute, or capacity for God in humanity, for Jesus' miraculous birth occurred apart from human sexual union. Lying behind Barth's argument is his understanding of the roles of male and female in the sex act: The male represents humanity in our innate ability, whereas the female presents humanity in our passivity and receptivity. In bringing Jesus into the world apart from human father yet through a human mother, God set aside our activity and used only our passivity. Barth explains that in Jesus' birth humankind is involved only in a non-willing, nonachieving, nonsovereign form, hence in a form that can only receive.[52]

Arrayed against Barth are many of the major modern Protestant thinkers. His colleague Emil Brunner, for example, rejected the virgin birth for theological reasons lying at the core of Christology. Brunner found a subtle incompatibility between the virgin birth and both the incarnation and Jesus' humanity. The birth accounts, he argued, preclude a pretemporal existence of a Son of God who at a definite point in time became human.[53] Furthermore, if Jesus had no human father, he lacked the most essential ingredient in being human, namely, being born exactly in the manner that we all are.[54]

More recently, the prominent German theologian Wolfhart Pannenberg followed Brunner's lead in rejecting the virgin birth as incompatible with what for him is the higher christological affirmation of Jesus' preexistence. On the basis of the New Testament texts that describe Jesus' origin, he concluded that "in the virgin birth we have to do with legend." Through the virgin birth stories the narrators intended to give a new interpretation of Jesus' divine sonship, namely, that he was the Son of God from the beginning of his life.[55]

---

52. Ibid., 188-92.

53. Emil Brunner, *The Christian Doctrine of Creation and Redemption*, trans. Olive Wyon (Philadelphia: Westminster, 1952) 352-56.

54. Ibid., 353.

55. Wolfhart Pannenberg, *The Apostles' Creed*, trans. Margaret Kohl (Philadelphia: Westminster, 1972), 73, 75. See also Pannenberg, *Jesus—God and Man*, 141-50.

Even as conservative a thinker as the post-World War II German Lutheran theologian Helmut Thielicke expressed doubts concerning the historicity of the virgin birth. Consequently, he relegated this doctrine to optional status, claiming that it is not an obligatory christological confession.[56]

Roman Catholics and the virgin birth. Whereas Protestant theologians have been divided on this issue since the Enlightenment, their Roman Catholic counterparts appeared to be united in affirming the traditional view. This united front began to crack, however, shortly after Vatican II.

Beginning in the 1960s the reticence to reject an article of doctrine so crucial to the Mariology of the Church began to wane. The first public questioning of the dogma may have occurred in Holland.[57] In 1965, J. van Kilsdonk shocked his colleagues by declaring the biological understanding of the virgin birth to be a barrier to genuine Christology. Shortly afterward, the authors of the new Dutch Catechism omitted any explicit mention of the biological virginity of Mary in its treatment of Jesus as "born of God." The work explains only that Matthew and Luke were expressing the theological truth that Jesus was born "wholly of grace, wholly of promise," that he "was *the* gift of God to mankind." Through these stories the evangelists "proclaim that this birth, does not depend on what men can do of themselves—infinitely less so than in other human births."[58]

Ambiguity about the virgin birth quickly became the norm among progressive Roman Catholic theologians. In his overview of systematic theology, *Foundations of the Christian Faith*, Karl Rahner, one of the chief architects of the theology of the Second Vatican Council, only incidentally mentioned the virgin birth.[59] Rahner presented the doctrine as an example of his seminal distinction between an object of faith and a ground of faith. Because it cannot be historically verified, Jesus' virgin birth can only be the former, never the latter. Sim-

---

56. Helmut Thielicke, *The Evangelical Faith*, trans. Geoffrey W. Bromiley, three volumes (Grand Rapids: Eerdmans), 2:414.

57. Brown, *The Virginal Conception*, 22-24.

58. *A New Catechism*, trans. Kevin Smith (New York: Herder and Herder, 1967), 74-75.

59. Karl Rahner, *Foundations of Christian Faith: An Introduction to the Idea of Christianity*, trans. William V. Dych (New York: Crossroad, 1984), 235-50, especially 243.

ilarly, in his monumental study *Jesus*, the Dutch scholar Edward Schillebeeckx concluded that the virgin birth stories do not intend "to impart any empirically apprehensible truth or secret information about the family history. On the contrary, they encapsule a truth of revelation: "this Jesus is holy and Son of God from the very first moment of his human existence."[60]

Yet not all recent Roman Catholic statements have been cautious about the importance of the virgin birth. Other voices are returning to the importance of the traditional teaching.[61]

Points of Debate Concerning the Virgin Birth

Many evangelicals may wonder why modern theologians find the virgin birth so controversial. For them the situation is quite simple: Matthew and Luke teach that Jesus was born of the virgin Mary, just as the church has always confessed. Why, then, does the virgin birth stand at the center of such controversy?

In seeking an answer to this question, we must note what is at issue in the modern discussion. Scholars who put forth arguments against the traditional interpretation of the birth narratives do not generally reject the doctrine of the virgin birth outright, nor do they advocate that the church cease to confess this statement of the creed. What they do reject is the traditional claim that the virgin birth must be understood as a historical event. Following the lead of D. F. Strauss, they suggest that the narrators never intended that the stories be understood as historical. Rather they are theology couched in narrative form, "evangelical myths" (Strauss) or "aetiological legends" (Pannenberg). At issue, then, is the historical understanding versus the theological interpretation of Matthew and Luke's inclusion of the virgin birth narratives.

But why is the historical character of the virgin birth questioned? And what lends support to the traditional understanding of this event as history? The considerations that either favor or mitigate against a

---

60. Edward Schillebeeckx, *Jesus: An Experiment in Christology*, trans. Hubert Hoskins (New York: Crossroad, 1981), 555.

61. For an example, see Philip A. Mellor, "The Virgin Birth and the Theology of Beauty," *Irish Theological Quarterly* 57/3 (!991): 196-208.

historical understanding of the narratives may be organized into theological (or doctrinal), historical, and textual arguments.[62]

Theological arguments. Both critics and proponents of the historical interpretation of the virgin birth appeal to doctrinal considerations in stating their case.

(1) Critics claim that the virgin birth raises insuperable difficulties for two other christological affirmations. As we noted earlier, theologians such as Brunner and Pannenberg claim that Jesus' preexistence and his virgin birth are incompatible. They base this conclusion on a widely held scenario concerning the development of Christology in the early church.[63] Adherents theorize that the earliest believers were concerned with the question as to what event in the history of Jesus marked the point at which he became the Son.[64] Some declared that Jesus will be the Son at his future return. Others pointed to his ascension, his resurrection, and finally his baptism as the occasion at which time he became the Son. The infancy narratives arose in this context. They were told and retold with the intent of explaining that Jesus was the Son from conception. In the end, however, the church came to the conclusion that Jesus always was the Son and settled on the affirmation of his preexistence as the highest christological declaration.

Although it carries a certain plausibility, this argument may not be as forceful as it appears. It postulates a highly contestable theory explaining the development of New Testament Christology. And it assumes the existence of a fundamental incompatibility between preexistence and birth from a virgin. This too has met stiff criticism recently.[65]

Critics also argue that a historical virgin birth raises difficulties for the confession of Jesus' full humanity. Ironically, Jesus' humanity was precisely what the early church fathers thought had been confirmed in his historical birth by a virgin (after Gal. 4:4?).[66] Modern

---

62. This schema is found in Brown, *The Virginal Conception*, 38-68.

63. Brunner, *The Christian Doctrine of Creation and Redemption*, 352; Pannenberg, *Jesus—God and Man*, 141-50.

64. Schillebeeckx argues for a quite different theory. He claims that Christology arose out of Jewish ideas, especially the belief that Jesus is the eschatological prophet. See *Jesus*, 514.

65. See Brown, *The Virginal Conception*, 43 note 58.

66. Ibid., 33. That this was the case with Ignatius of Antioch is suggested in Robert S. Paul, *The Atonement and the Sacraments* (New York: Abingdon, 1960), 43.

critics, however, complain that the lack of normal human parentage by necessity results in a docetic Jesus (hence Brunner's argument cited earlier). In addition, they aver that Jesus' knowledge of his miraculous birth would have given our Lord an awareness of his uniqueness from the beginning, thereby exempting him from the struggle of coming to self-awareness that typifies all human life.

Despite the frequency by which it appears in critical works, the purported incompatibility of the virgin birth with Jesus' full humanity is not persuasive. The first variation on this argument depends on the assumption that "normal" birth is constitutive of being human. We have argued, however, that humanness is ultimately linked to our fulfillment of the divine design, which is life in community.

The second argument erroneously assumes that Jesus would have concluded solely from knowledge of his virgin birth that he was the divine Son. Although the cultural milieu in which Jesus grew to maturity did employ stories of miraculous births, such extraordinary conceptions were viewed simply as marking a person as potentially great or wise, and not necessarily as constituting ontological deity. More important in first-century Palestine was the widespread apocalyptic expectancy which pointed to the general resurrection, and not a virgin birth, as the event that would mark the advent of the kingdom and hence of the coming of the messianic king.

(2) Proponents also appeal to theological considerations in arguing that the virgin birth must be historical. They maintain that the historicity of this event is necessitated by certain doctrines of the faith.

One such doctrine is the Roman Catholic dogma of the sanctity of Mary. Traditional Catholic piety, which celebrates the perpetual virginity of Mary, looks to Jesus' mother as the model of celibacy. Lying behind this piety, of course, are the assumptions that a virginal conception is nobler than conception through marital intercourse and that celibacy is a higher form of Christian life than marriage.

Prominent among conservatives of various confessional traditions is the suggestion that Jesus' sinlessness—specifically, his freedom from the sinful nature that is ours through original sin—requires that he be born of a virgin.[67] Generally presupposed in this thesis is the

---

67. For a contemporary statement of this thesis, see C. S. Lewis, "Miracles," in *God in the Dock: Essays on Theology and Ethics*, ed. Walter Hooper (Grand Rapids: Eerdmans, 1970), 31.

assumption that original sin is propagated through sexual intercourse itself, perhaps because of the arousal of sensual appetites that occurs in the act, as Augustine proposed. This argument, however, is questionable. In contrast to the Bible, it presents a highly negative evaluation of marital sexual relations. An alternative approach asserts that the taint of original sin is somehow propagated through the male sperm, an idea that fails to find either biblical or scientific support.

Perhaps the strongest theological argument supporting the historicity of the virgin birth moves from Jesus' divine sonship. Proponents maintain that the denial of the virgin birth necessitates the denial of the incarnation and of Jesus' deity. We acknowledge that Jesus' deity and his virgin birth appear compatible; they even seem to be related somehow. Yet there is no necessary movement from the latter to the former. As we established in chapter 9, the historical foundation for our affirmation of Jesus' deity rests on the Master's claim as confirmed by the resurrection. The virgin birth may add additional credence to what is established on the grounds of these historical events. But the early apostolic proclamation never appealed to the virgin birth as providing the necessary foundation for the declaration that Jesus is divine.

In a similar manner, the incarnation of Jesus as set forth in the New Testament is not dependent on his virgin birth. Because this lies at the crux of our discussion in this chapter, the support for this conclusion depends on the conclusions of our subsequent delineation of the incarnation.

Historical arguments. Not only are theological considerations important, proponents and critics of the historicity of the virgin birth appeal likewise to historical arguments. They draw conclusions from the earliest evidence to the role that the declaration, "Jesus was born of a virgin," played in the post-apostolic church.

Critics find support in evidence that points to a rejection of the virgin birth in the second century and which therefore indicates the presence of a tradition claiming Jesus was born through natural conception. One possible source was the gnostic Christian sects. The gnostics, however, opposed the virgin birth on philosophical rather than historical grounds.[68]

---

68. Brown, *The Virginal Conception*, 48.

More significant are the indications by Justin and Origen that certain Jewish Christians declared that Jesus was solely of human origin. This, however, is outweighed by evidence to widespread knowledge of the virgin birth in the second century. This evidence indicates that Christians of various origins and in many places—Palestine, Antioch, Asia Minor, and Rome—accepted its historicity.[69]

Textual arguments. In addition to theological and historical considerations, the modern debate focuses on textual arguments. Scholars of both persuasions seek to determine whether or not the tradition of the virgin birth that predates and was inscripturated in Matthew and Luke is historical.

(1) The chief thesis critics propound is that the story of the virgin birth does not go back to the earliest apostolic traditions. Rather it was a later invention, introduced by the Evangelists as a symbolic representation intended to carry strictly theological meaning. To this end, they point out the implied "high" Christology of the stories, which they claim is incompatible with what they purport to have been the slower, developmental manner in which the early church came to its christological conclusions.

Stronger is the argument from the undeniable silence of most of the New Testament.[70] This suggests that the virgin birth tradition was unknown by the earliest believers and hence may indeed have been subsequently invented for symbolic, theological purposes.

In addition, critics question the historicity of the material within the narratives of the virgin birth. They assert that the two Gospel accounts are irreconcilable, as is indicated by the presence of problems such as the two genealogies (also compare Matt. 2:14 and Luke 2:39). Therefore, both narratives cannot be accurate. Critics also point out the nonhistorical structuring of the accounts. They argue that Matthew is highly folkloric (with angels, a star, treasures), and Luke is obviously stylized (as is evidenced by two annunciations, two births). Critics find certain details to be historically questionable, such as the family connection between Jesus and John the Baptist (especially in the light of John 1:31), the census in Palestine, and

---

69. For a summary of the evidence, see Brown, *The Virginal Conception*, 48-52.
70. E.g., Thielicke, *The Evangelical Faith*, 2:408-409.

the claim of Davidic descent, which they claim is better understood as a theologoumenon (theological hypothesis) based on the title Son of David.

While these arguments are not to be lightly dismissed, they are also not conclusive. Even those who assume that certain of the details of the narratives are not historically accurate, need not abandon the basic historicity of the entire story. Although the silence of the New Testament may suggest that the virgin birth was unknown to certain of the early witnesses, it does not necessarily follow that it was unknown by all (It may simply not have fit their purposes.) or that it is therefore not historical. And we have no conclusive evidence to suggest that the "high" Christology was a late development. On the contrary it seems to have been at the heart of the Christian proclamation from the beginning.

(2) Proponents also appeal to textual considerations in defense of the claim that the virgin birth was a historical event.

They note that although ideas of miraculous births were widespread, the search for parallels in other religious traditions yields the conclusion that the Gospel stories are unique.[71] The evangelists' depiction of Jesus' divine conception and human birth without anthropomorphism, sensuality, or suggestions of moral irregularity are found nowhere in the literature of other religions.[72] On the basis of the scholarly consensus that the canonical virgin birth stories are unique, proponents ask how critics who deny that the narratives are historical can account for the coming into being of such creative thinking.

Proponents appeal as well to evidence that the rumor of Jesus' irregular birth, which was prevalent at least by the time of Origen in the late second century, may have dogged Jesus himself and the early church. This evidence includes the description of Jesus as the son of Mary, which deviates from the cultural norm of identifying a person by the father's name, unless the paternity was uncertain (Mark 6:3).[73] Likewise, there may be a sarcastic innuendo of illegitimacy in the

---

71. This is the conclusion reached in Brown, *The Virginal Conception*, 62.

72. For this conclusion, see Boslooper, *The Virgin Birth*, 185.

73. Ethelbert Stauffer, "Jeschu ben Mirjam," *Neotestamentica et Semitica: Studies in Honour of Matthew Black*, ed. E. Earle Ellis and Max Wilcox (Edinburgh: T. & T. Clark, 1969), 119-28.

comment of the Jews who emphatically underline their own legitimate parentage (John 8:41; note the emphatic Greek construction of pronoun plus verb). The birth narratives, especially Matthew's, seem to be responds to such charges. But rather than treading the obvious route—claiming that Jesus was born at the proper interval after the union of Mary and Joseph—the evangelist tells the fantastic story of a virgin birth. If this was not a historical event, we are left wondering why our author utilized such an unlikely and inopportune tactic.

The Virgin Birth and Christology

The state of the discussion to date suggests that we do well to accept the majority opinion of the church throughout its history. We affirm that the virgin birth was indeed a historical event.

Several factors support this conclusion. An important consideration is the inconclusiveness of the arguments of those who deny the historicity of the event. Unless there is overriding reason to chart a separate path, we may entrust our judgment to the nearly unanimous conclusions of the church as a whole. The debate over the virgin birth has provided no such overriding considerations.

Although not conclusive, the arguments in favor of the historical nature of Jesus' virgin birth also tip the scales in the affirmative direction. Our earlier discussion left us with the impression that the link between the virgin birth and other doctrines is not strong. At the same time, the historical and textual considerations provided a more conclusive case.

The weakness of the connection between the virgin birth and other doctrines leads to an important theological conclusion. While being an important doctrine, the virgin birth is not christologically indispensable. Christology does not rise or fall with the historicity of the virgin birth in the way that it is dependent on Jesus' historical resurrection. The confession that Jesus was born of a virgin coheres well with the twin christological affirmations that Jesus is fully divine and fully human. But rather than confirming these assertions, it provides an additional substantiation for what we have already concluded on other historical grounds, namely, on the basis of Jesus' claim concerning his identity as confirmed in his resurrection.

With this in view, we see the wisdom in Rahner's distinction between a ground of faith and an object of faith. The virgin birth does not function as the ground of faith; it is not the historical foundation of our christological confession. Instead, it is an object of faith—an article of the faith we confess. In short, we are not Christians because Jesus was born of a virgin. Rather, because we are Christians we affirm with the church, "I believe...in Jesus Christ...Who was conceived by the Holy Spirit, Born of the Virgin Mary."

To conclude: The virgin birth cannot support the entire weight of our incarnational Christology. We do not affirm with John that "the Word became flesh and lived of awhile among us," because Jesus was born of a virgin. Rather, we confess the incarnation because of the entirety of Jesus' life, including his claim concerning his person and God's confirmation of that claim in the resurrection. Because Jesus is Immanuel, God-with-Us, the incarnate Word of God, the Son, we gladly affirm with the Evangelists and the church throughout its history that he was born of the virgin Mary.

12

The Mission of Jesus

For this reason I was born, and for this I came into the world, to testify to the truth. (John 18:37)

Outline

At the heart of the Christian faith is the confession that God is present in Jesus of Nazareth. In the previous three chapters, we explored the meaning of this confession for Jesus' identity. We asserted that he reveals both true deity (chapter 9) and true humanity (chapter 10) in one personal life (chapter 11).

Jesus' ministry is inherent in his identity. Theologians generally divide Christology into the related topics of "Christ's person" and "Christ's work." When so divided, which theme ought to precede the other? Reformed thinkers traditionally move from the person of Christ to his work in salvation, whereas Lutherans often begin with Christ's work as forming the foundation from which to understand his person.

In our Christology we have followed the basic Reformed approach, albeit with a major difference. Rather than the older nomenclature ("person" and "work"), we prefer the designation "identity" and "mission" as lying closer to the Hebrew way of thinking that pervades the Bible. Although we move from Jesus' identity to his mission, we acknowledge a fluidity between these two topics. We cannot understand the identity of our Lord in isolation from his mission in the world. Nor does his action on our behalf make sense apart from understanding who he is.

Because of the close connection between Christ's identity and mission, we ought not to see this fourth chapter of our Christology as marking a transition beyond "the person of Christ" to "the work of Christ." On the contrary, our description of Jesus' mission is the final statement about his identity, just as the previous three chapters comprise the necessary context for our understanding of the topics which follow here.

Theologians in the classical Western theological tradition tend to delineate Jesus' mission primarily as God's antidote for our sinful human situation. More narrowly, many look to the fall of Adam for the context in which to describe the work accomplished by Christ. Regardless of its theological propriety, placing the work of Christ in the context of the fall invites inquisitive minds to pose the speculative question: If Adam had not sinned, would Christ have come? Although itself purely hypothetical and consequently unanswerable, lurking behind this query lies an important theological issue that draws our attention to the purpose of Jesus' coming: What was the mission of the earthly Jesus? In what context are we to understand Jesus' vocation? Finally, is the work that Jesus accomplished primarily restorative or elevative? Did he reinstate humankind to the pristine reality of the primeval Garden, or does he lift us to a realm beyond what the first humans enjoyed in their innocency?

We now grapple with the purpose of Jesus' coming. In the following pages, we seek to express in what sense Jesus the Christ not only restores what we lost in the fall but also takes us beyond Adam to the eschatological community at the center of God's purposes.

Our construction of a contemporary understanding of the mission of Jesus comes in three parts. We begin somewhat broadly, looking at the general task in terms of which the early church understood Jesus. We ask: How did Jesus view his vocation? And how did the community of faith interpret the life of the Nazarene? Next we focus on the more specific issue of the atoning work of our Savior. In what sense did Jesus' life and death alter our relationship to God? Finally, we capsulize his ongoing work on our behalf. What aspects of the work of the triune God in the world may we attribute to our resurrected and ascended Lord?

The Vocation of the Earthly Jesus

The question of the mission of Jesus has been a central aspect of Christology throughout theological history. It was raised already in his lifetime by his followers. After his resurrection the community of faith diligently sought to make sense out of Jesus' life. The response of early church to the question, What did Jesus come to accomplish? took the form of images, designations, and even certain christological titles that depict the vocation he so wondrously fulfilled.

The community of faith drew their interpretation of the vocation of our Lord primarily from the Hebrew context in which Jesus lived and died. Yet they were not totally reticent to borrow from the Greek setting to which the gospel quickly spread. In all of this, they claimed precedence in the self-understanding of Jesus himself.

The early Christians saw in the life of the Nazarene a threefold vocation: Jesus came to fulfill the Old Testament hope; he was the herald of the kingdom of God; and he resolved to die in obedience to his Father's will.

Fulfilling the Old Testament hope

Our understanding of Jesus' mission must begin with the Old Testament context in which it originally transpired. Indeed, during his earthly sojourn the man from Nazareth first sparked the interest of his contemporaries because they sensed that he might be the fulfillment of the promises God had given to his people as written in the books of the Hebrew Bible. As was indicated by the speculation that surrounded him wherever he went, paramount on the lips of the people of Palestine was the question: Could this man be the one whom generations of pious Jews had awaited? Because of the importance of this context, we must begin our description of the vocation of the Nazarene by asking, In what manner is Jesus the fulfillment of the hope of the Old Testament?

Viewing Jesus within the context of the Old Testament hope demands that we determine the actual content of the expectations which the late Hebrew writers fostered. What were the faithful people of God awaiting? In what sense did Jesus fulfill their hopes? Above all, two dimensions of that anticipation are crucial. These in turn are related to two christological titles which the early church employed to describe the significance of Jesus—"prophet" and "Messiah."

Jesus as the prophet. Despite years of apparent divine silence, the people of first-century Palestine were imbued with the expectation that God would again send a prophet among them. Hope abounded that the lengthy hiatus—the "silent era" during which God had not spoken—would come to an end. God would once again raise up a prophet. And this act would mark the end of the age.

The popular hope for national revival came to be focused in the anticipation of a great prophet who would arise "in the spirit and power of Elijah" (Luke 1:17), just as Malachi at the end of the Hebrew prophetic canon had predicted (Mal. 4:5). The task of this eschatological prophet would be twofold. He would announce the end of the age, together with God's final offer of salvation to his covenant people. And he would act as eschatological forerunner (Isa. 40:3-5), preparing the way for the arrival of another, whether the Messiah sent by God or Yahweh himself (Mal. 3:1). How does Jesus stand in relationship to the prophet his contemporaries anticipated?

The Gospel texts plainly indicate that many people hailed the Nazarene as a prophet (Matt. 21:11). On at least one occasion, Jesus himself inquired about the talk that buzzed throughout Palestine (Matt. 16:14-15; Mark 8:27-28). In response to his query, his disciples summarized the opinions of others. Some held the general view that Jesus was one of the prophets. Others, however, were more specific: He was John the Baptist reincarnated or even Elijah, that is, the eschatological prophet.

Jesus' understanding of his vocation, however, was more complicated. On the one hand, he did not simply equate his role with that of the anticipated prophetic figure. Rather, he relegated the status of eschatological prophet to another—to John the Baptist—whose coming marked the appearance of Elijah and the climax of the prophetic era (Matt. 11:7-15; Mark 9:13). On the other hand, as Jesus came to grips with his impending death and the complicity of his contemporaries in that event, he linked himself with the long line of prophets that had preceded him and whose fate he would soon share (Matt. 23:29-39). The early believers, in turn, ascribed prophetic significance to Jesus (Acts 3:22; 7:37). Following their example, theologians have traditionally listed "prophet" among the three offices of Christ.

How are we to reconcile the prophet-Christology of the church with Jesus' description of John the Baptist as the last prophet? During his ministry, Jesus avoided overt use of the designation "prophet." The reason for his reticence probably lay in his understanding of the contrast between his own vocation and certain accepted expectations about the awaited eschatological figure. He did not come to serve as the forerunner of another; in this sense he was not the anticipated prophet. Rather, his mission was more intimately bound to the eschatological in-breaking of God into history.

When his followers reflected on his life from the post-Easter vantage point, they rightly concluded that Jesus had fulfilled the other aspect of the prophetic hope. He announced the end of the age and God's final offer of salvation. Yet even in this dimension, he was more than a prophet. Jesus did not merely proclaim the divine message; rather, he embodied God's complete, eschatological salvation.

In this manner, the arrival of the eschatological prophet was more complicated than the people had anticipated. The grand renewal of the prophetic office came through the combined ministries of John the Baptist and Jesus. All four evangelists assert that John was the great forerunner, the fulfillment of the prophecy of Isaiah (Matt. 3:1-3; Mark 1:1-4; Luke 3:1-6; John 1:22-23). Through his proclamation of the coming end of the age and his call to repentance and baptism, the Baptist set the stage for the eschatological events. But John left the completion of the process to another (Luke 3:15-17). Jesus' ministry marked the heightening of what John had begun. The Nazarene was the one for whom the Baptist had prepared the way. As the embodiment of the eschatological action of God, Jesus came as the great fulfillment of the Old Testament hope, the climax of the renewal of the prophetic office.

Jesus as the Messiah. Jesus' role as the embodiment of God's eschatological action leads to another aspect of his vocation in fulfillment of the Old Testament hope. He came as the one to whom John the Baptist pointed. But the person for whom John acted as forerunner was the Messiah of God.

In invoking the title "Messiah" to characterize the vocation of Jesus, we are immediately faced with a difficult problem. Central to the proclamation of the church throughout its history has been the confession of the messiahship of Jesus—that Jesus is the Christ. Yet during his earthly sojourn our Lord avoided the term. If Jesus is the Messiah as the church proclaims, why was the Nazarene so hesitant to use the title with respect to himself? Before tackling this question, we must look more closely at the Gospel texts which suggest otherwise, those in which Jesus appears to make explicit claim to be the Christ.

One such occasion occurs during his trial before the Sanhedrin. In Mark's narrative, the climax of the ordeal came when the high priest raised the question of Jesus' understanding of his own identity and mission: "Are you the Christ the Son of the Blessed One?" (Mark 14:61). Mark's rendering of Jesus' response into the Greek *ego eimi* ("I myself am") indicates an emphatic affirmation of his messiahship. It would appear that on this occasion Jesus asserted unequivocally that he is the Messiah.

Comparing the Mark narrative to those of Luke and especially Matthew, however, leaves us with some uncertainty about details of this crucial point in the trial. Above all, Jesus' response to the query of his opponents may have been more ambiguous than we would conclude from Mark.

Luke divides what Mark presents as a single question of the chief priest into two queries pressed upon our Lord by the assembled council. First they demanded, "If you are the Christ, tell us" (Luke 22:67). Paralleling a feature of Mark's narrative, Luke notes that in his answer our Lord directed attention away from the title Messiah: "But from now on, the Son of Man will be seated on the right hand of the mighty God" (vv. 68-69; compare Mark 14:62). On the basis of this response, the council posed the second question, "Are you then the Son of God?" Luke renders Jesus' reply with the Greek *humeis legete hoti ego eimi*. Unfortunately, many modern English translations give definiteness to what in the original is indefinite. Rather than the positive claim, "You are right in saying that I am"

(NIV), a literal rendering of the Greek text is more ambiguous: "You yourselves say that I am" (v. 70, cf. KJV).

Matthew's narrative includes an additional element. The hearing reaches its climax with the high priest's solemn adjuration which, as in Mark's account, brings together the two christological titles separated in Luke's Gospel: "I charge you under oath by the living God: Tell us if you are the Christ, the Son of God" (Matt. 26:63). To this unusual query Jesus offered an equally unusual reply, which Matthew renders "Su *eipas*" (v. 64). Again many modern English translations fail to reflect the ambiguity of these words. Rather than the unequivocal claim—"Yes, it is as you say" (NIV)—Matthew's Greek is more vague: "You yourself say so." Hence, Jesus uttered no straightforward answer to the high priest's question. To this noncommittal response, however, Jesus added an assertion similar to that found in both Mark and Luke: "But I say to all of you: In the future you will see the Son of Man sitting at the right hand of the Mighty One and coming on the clouds of heaven." In Matthew's account, therefore, our Lord deliberately corrected the high priest's question by changing the reference from "Messiah" to "Son of Man."

Despite differences over details, according to all three evangelists, Jesus sought to turn the attention of the council from the Messiah to the figure of the Son of Man, which designation our Lord seems to have preferred. In addition, in all three narratives the council reached its verdict on the heels of Jesus' reference to the Son of Man. Matthew is the most unequivocal in indicating that Jesus' linking of himself to the Son of Man was the basis on which the high priest concluded that the Nazarene was guilty of blasphemy (Matt. 26:65). Luke is somewhat less definite, inserting between Jesus' Son of Man claim and the council's verdict our Lord's evasive answer to the additional question as to whether he was the Son of God (Luke 22:70-71). Mark is the least clear about the source of the high priest's cry of blasphemy, for it follows both Jesus' acknowledgment of his messiahship and his reference to the Son of man. In any case, we cannot definitively conclude from any of the narratives that Jesus was charged with blasphemy for claiming to be the Messiah (which claim would not be inherently blasphemous). The fuller details of the event offered by Matthew lead to the conclusion that Jesus likely did not voice an overt, explicit claim to messiahship on this occasion.

In contrast to the varying accounts of the hearing before the Sanhedrin, the three synoptic Gospels closely parallel each other in their description of Jesus' interaction with Pilate. Reminiscent of the high priest's query, the Roman governor asked Jesus, "Are you the King of the Jews?" (Mark 15:2; Matt. 27:11; Luke 23:3), a designation which carries clear messianic overtones. All three, Gospels render Jesus' response in a manner that corresponds with Matthew's depiction of his reply to the high priest: *"Su legeis"* ("You yourself say so"). Those present seemed to interpret his statement as being too ambiguous to constitute self-incrimination, for the chief priests then proceeded to accuse him of "many things" (Mark 15:3-5; cf. Matt. 27:12-13), and Pilate concluded, "I find no basis for a charge against this man" (Luke 23:4).

Perhaps the strongest intimation of acceptance of the messianic title came during the important incident at Caesarea Philippi, the midpoint in Jesus' ministry. All three synoptic narratives cite Peter's grand confession, "You are the Christ" (Matt. 16:16; Mark 8: 29; Luke 9:20). Although Matthew's longer version depicts Jesus as praising Peter for his insight, in none of the accounts did our Lord himself voice the claim to be Messiah. On the contrary, he strictly warned them to keep the matter silent, then immediately turned the discussion away from the messiahship to his own impending suffering. In the narratives of Mark and Luke, Jesus linked suffering to the Son of man.

Rather than documenting an explicit claim to be the Messiah, therefore, these incidents confirm that Jesus was reticent to appeal to this title as designating his mission. According to Luke, however, the situation changed radically after Easter. In contrast to his earlier hesitancy, the risen Lord readily applied the term "Messiah" to himself. For example, the lament of the Emmaus disciples led to the mild rebuke: "Did not the Christ have to suffer these things and then enter his glory?" (Luke 24:26). Later that day he explained to the disciples in the upper room, "This is what is written: The Christ will suffer and rise from the dead on the third day" (v. 46).

In other words, after experiencing the cross and the resurrection, the Lord linked himself to this figure. The christological significance of this change is astounding. Now that through his passion he has suffered and entered into his anticipated glory (Phil. 2:9; Heb. 1:3-4), the risen Lord can claim his rightful status as the Messiah of God.

The Book of Acts and the Epistles provide ample evidence that the early church emulated the risen Lord in this designation. The believers routinely spoke of Jesus as the Christ. In fact, this title became so common as the favorite identification for the Lord that it fuses with his earthly name. "Jesus the Christ" was shortened to "Jesus Christ." The proclamation of the early church also followed the lead of the resurrected Lord, linking Jesus' messiahship to the Easter experience. In the Pentecost sermon, for example, Peter's declaration, "Therefore let all Israel be assured of this: God has made this Jesus, whom you crucified, both Lord and Christ" (Acts 2:36), is predicated upon the apostle's claim that the Christ is resurrected and exalted to the right hand of the Father (vv. 31,33).

In the light of the centrality of the messiahship of Jesus for the life and proclamation of the early believing community, how should we understand Jesus' hesitancy to accept the designation prior to his resurrection? Perhaps the same dynamic is at work here that we noted in the case of Jesus' ambiguous relationship to the title "prophet." Just as he did not see his vocation as corresponding to the expectations concerning the coming of the prophet, so also Jesus rejected the widely held understanding of the task of the Messiah. In fact, his struggle with, and rejection of first century messianic anticipations provide a helpful context in which to understand the temptation accounts in Matthew and Luke. These narratives suggest that such popular expectations lay at the heart of Satan's attack on our Lord.

In one sense of the term, therefore, Jesus was not the Messiah. He did not come to fulfill the expectations of the people.

Although Jesus was not the Messiah many of his contemporaries had envisioned, in the light of the Easter event the title is a suitable designation. As a foretaste of the grand eschatological revelation of his identity, the resurrection confirmed Jesus' role in the program of God. He was indeed elected by, and sent from God with a vocation. For the fulfillment of his unique task he was endowed with the fullness of the Holy Spirit. Consequently, when viewed from the vantage point of the anticipatory event of Easter, Jesus is the Messiah of God—"the anointed one"—the true fulfillment of the Old Testament hope.

Heralding the Divine Reign

Jesus' mission occurred in the context of the promises inscripturated in the Hebrew Bible. He came as the fulfillment of the Old Testament hope. As a result, we speak of our Lord as prophet and God's Messiah. Jesus' mission occurred likewise in the context of the apocalyptic movement, which developed during the late Old Testament and intertestamental periods.[1] Seen in the light of apocalyptic expectations, Jesus came as the herald of the kingdom of God.

The centrality of the kingdom. According to the synoptic gospels, God's eschatological rule stood at the heart of Jesus' entire ministry. This theme was the central message of his preaching. The nearness of the divine reign, he declared, entails a command to repent and believe the gospel (Mark 1:15). Those who respond enter the kingdom, which for them is not only future but also present. His awareness of the divine reign also motivated Jesus' deeds. His mighty acts were not simply miracles, but signs which confirmed the nearness of God's rule: "But if I drive out demons by the finger of God, then the kingdom of God has come to you" (Luke 11:20).

Above all, however, the apocalyptic expectation of the reign of God was definitive for Jesus' self-understanding. Our Lord was conscious of the presence of the in-breaking reign of God in his own person and mission. In fact, he saw his vocation as mediating God's rule. As his opponents who charged him with blasphemy readily perceived, this self-awareness entailed an implicit claim to unity with God (John 10:31-33). Jesus' only response to his critics was to assert that he was not the source of this astounding claim. Rather, it came

---

1. For a discussion of the apocalyptic movement, see Paul D. Hanson, ed. *Visionaries and Their Apocalypses* (Philadelphia: Fortress, 1983).

from the Father himself, who had sent him and who was now working through him (hence, vv. 34-38).

As the one through whom the Father worked, Jesus embodied the divine reign. Because he embodies the kingdom, wherever Jesus is, the rule of God is present. Consequently, God's reign is both a present and a future reality. In his earthly ministry Jesus brought the dynamic of the kingdom of God into our world; as a result, the kingdom is here. The story of Jesus, however, is not yet complete. One day the glory of Christ will be publicly revealed. That grand eschatological event will bring the fullness of the reign of our God.

Jesus as the Son of man. On the basis of the close connection between Jesus and the kingdom of God, theologians have traditionally seen in Christ's work a second office. Not only is he "prophet," he is also "king." These theologians generally link the kingship of Jesus to the Messiah, understood in quasi-political terms. As the son of David, our Lord is king Messiah. The role of Jesus within the apocalyptic expectations of the reign of God, however, suggests another figure as the appropriate christological designation for his mission as the herald of the kingdom. Jesus is the Son of man.

The genesis of the Son of man title may lie in the use of the phrase in the Book of Ezekiel as a designation of the visionary himself (see also Dan. 8:17).[2] On over ninety occasions, God addresses the prophet as "son of man," perhaps to remind him of his own mortality, but more likely to picture him as representing Israel or even humanity as a whole.

More important as the context for any explicitly christological use of the phrase in the New Testament is its presence in the Book of Daniel and its development in the apocalyptic literature of the intertestamental period. In his night vision, Daniel saw a figure "like a son of man coming with the clouds of heaven." Being led into the presence of the Ancient of Days, "he was given authority, glory and sovereign power"—an everlasting kingdom. Consequently, "all peoples, nations and men of every language worshipped him" (Dan. 7:13-14).

---

2. See, for example, E. M. Sidebottom, *The Christ of the Fourth Gospel: In the Light of First Century Thought* (London: SPCK, 1961), 74-78.

The Jewish apocalypticists may have been influenced by (or at least drew from a common source as) an oriental and Hellenistic conception, the Primordial Man or the myth of Anthropos. This figure was a heavenly, preexistent being, often thought of as the ideal, prototype human and the redeemer of humankind.[3] Whatever its origin, the Jewish apocalypticists understood the Son of man as a heavenly being who is now hidden from view but who will appear at the end of the age to judge the peoples of the world and to establish the nation of saints.

The Gospels indicate that Jesus repeatedly used the designation "Son of man." However, there is much scholarly discussion as to the significance of his use of this expression.

On occasion, our Lord may have spoken the phrase in a more general, non-Christological sense to refer to human beings as such. Perhaps his declaration, "The Sabbath was made for man not man for the Sabbath, so the Son of man is Lord even of the Sabbath" (Mark 2:27), is one example. The parallelism in Jesus' words and the context in which he spoke them suggest that here "son of man" is not a christological title. Rather, in keeping with a common Hebraic way of talking and reminiscent of such texts as Psalm 8:4, the phrase designates humans as humans. Jesus, then, is teaching that because God instituted the seventh day for our benefit, God's original intention—and not a set of humanly devised laws—should govern our use of the sabbath.

Bible scholars commonly divide Jesus' other "Son of man" sayings into three categories: those referring to himself in his present situation, those referring to his passion, and those speaking of a future coming of the Son of man.[4] More helpful, however, is an alternative differentiation. On some occasions, Jesus seems to have used the phrase "Son of man" as a self-designation, a substitute for "I" (compare Matt. 16:13 with Mark 8:27), with the purpose of drawing attention to his words or actions. Reminiscent of the similar use in Ezekiel, Jesus' practice of referring to himself in this way may have

---

3. Sigmund Mowinckel, *He That Cometh*, trans. G. W. Anderson (New York: Abingdon, 1954), 420-31.

4. J. Ramsey Michaels, *Servant and Son* (Atlanta: John Knox, 1981), 285.

arisen from his profound awareness of being addressed by his Father and therefore of acting under the authority of God.[5] If this is the case, this seemingly simple self-designation carries implicit Christological implications.

What may be implicit in Jesus' designation of himself as "Son of man" gains explicit christological importance on those occasions when Jesus speaks of the coming eschatological judge. Here the apocalyptic world view in which the figure of the Son of man plays a central role and the specific vision of Daniel emerge in their fullness. Like Daniel, Jesus pierces the veil of the world as it now appears and sees the hidden, eschatological realm where the Son of man is seated "on the right hand of power and coming in the clouds" (Mark 14:62). He calls his followers to catch the same vision.

The question remains, however: Who is the Son of man? Some scholars, most notably Rudolf Bultmann, argue that Jesus was not referring to himself but to some transcendent, supernatural figure yet to come.[6] Nevertheless, a growing number of other scholars acknowledge that Jesus linked himself with this important apocalyptic figure. J. Ramsey Michaels spoke for many when he concluded, "There is little doubt that in the Son of man of the Jewish apocalyptic tradition...Jesus came to see his own role and destiny.[7] In any case, the Jesus of the Gospel narratives clearly made such a connection. He promised his disciples that they would participate in the glorious reign of the Son of man (Matt. 16:27-28; 19:28), for the Son of man will acknowledge at his coming those who already confess his name (Luke 12:8; 9:26; Mark 8:38).

As we will see, Jesus' talk of the imminent suffering of the Son of man gains added significance in the light of our Lord's identification of himself with the eschatological judge.

---

5. Ibid., 286-87.

6. Rudolf Bultmann, *Theology of the New Testament*, trans. Kendrick Grobel, two volumes (New York: Charles Scribner's Sons, 1951), 2:9.

7. Michaels, *Servant and Son*, 289.

The One Sent to Die

Old Testament promises of the coming of the Messiah and a revival of prophecy formed the context for Jesus' fulfillment of the hope of generations of pious Hebrews. Daniel's vision of the eschatological Son of man and the apocalyptic anticipation of the inbreaking of the divine reign formed the context for Jesus' heralding of the kingdom of God. Less obvious to the contemporaries of our Lord but no less central to his vocation was a third aspect. Jesus came as the one sent to die.

Jesus' consciousness of his death. That Jesus did die on the cross is an unassailable historical fact. But was the Nazarene aware of his impending fate so as knowingly and willingly to face death? Or was the cross a tragedy that befell our Savior? In the modern era it has been fashionable to deny that Jesus anticipated his own death. Critical scholars tend to discount his various predictions found in the Gospel narratives as *vox post eventu*, sayings put into Jesus' mouth by the church after the event. Contemporary thinkers, however, are more likely to credit Jesus with greater foresight. They acknowledge that he saw suffering and death as the probable end of his ministry, perhaps even as an essential part of his mission.

The likelihood of his demise at the hands of his opponents would come as no surprise to our Lord. He knew that Israel boasted a long history of rejecting God's messengers. As his conflict with the Jewish leaders intensified, Jesus became increasingly vocal in declaring what would mark its climax, even incorporating this theme into his parables (Mark 12:1-8). Just as the prophets had suffered at the hands of God's enemies, so they would also put him to death. As a prophet, he would die in Jerusalem (Luke 13:33).

Yet Jesus' attitude toward his death went beyond mere cognition of its imminence. More than passively acquiescing to the inevitable, Jesus saw this event as the focal point and climax of his mission. He had come in order to die. He, therefore, would willingly give his life.

Above all, however, Jesus sensed that his dying marked the highest obedience to the will of his Father. He sensed the confirmation of the obedient nature of this act repeatedly throughout his sojourn and again near the end of his life, as our Savior struggled for the final time in the Garden of Gethsemane on the night of his arrest. Through his prayer, "Yet not what I will, but what you will" (Mark 14:36), he gained assurance that his death was indeed the pathway that obedience demanded. Jesus resolutely faced death, therefore, because he believed that through this act, he would glorify his Father—or actually the Father would glorify his own name (John 12:28).

Jesus as the Suffering Servant. Suffering at the hands of God's enemies on behalf of God and God's covenantal purposes was a typical theme within the prophetic tradition. Yet as his struggle in Gethsemane suggests, Jesus' understanding of his death as his ordained means of glorifying his Father through perfect obedience went beyond the general prophetic motif. Rather, its context lay in a specific prophecy which Jesus undoubtedly knew well. His was a special role in the program of God, for he was to be the Suffering Servant of Yahweh.

The background of this designation lies in the servant poems of Isaiah (Isa. 42:1-4; 49:1-6; 50:4-11; 52:13—53:12).[8] We no longer can discern who the author saw as the Suffering Servant. This figure may refer to the nation of Israel as a whole, to the prophetic community in general who suffer in their mission, or to one specific prophet, perhaps even Isaiah himself.[9] Nor did Jesus ever explicitly use the title for himself. Nevertheless, these poems provide a fruitful context in which to understand the vocation of Jesus.

Primarily, the Suffering Servant of Isaiah's poems is the servant of God. God acknowledges him as "my servant, whom I uphold, my chosen one in whom I delight" (Isa. 42:1). Through him God himself will display his splendor (Isa. 49:3). At the same time, as he acts in obedience to God's will this figure is also the servant of the people, suffering on their behalf: "We all, like sheep, have gone astray, each of us has turned to his own way; and the Lord has laid on him the iniquity of us all" (Isa. 53:6).

In this way the suffering servant motif appropriately describes Jesus' own mission. Our Lord clearly interpreted his vocation as radical servanthood. He would so live in complete obedience to the will

---

8. Mowinckel, *He That Cometh*, 187.
9. See, for example, the discussion of Mowinckel, *He That Cometh*, 213-57.

of his Father that in the end he would die at the hands of God's enemies. As the servant who humbly obeys his Father's will and thereby glorifies the Father, Jesus serves a crucial role as God's agent on behalf of others. Through his own example he models the pathway to life—the manner of living that his disciples are to follow (John 13:12-15). But his obedience to the point of death does more than show the way to true living, it makes that life available.

In John's narrative, Jesus draws a principle from nature to illustrate the life-giving provision of his death on behalf of others: "I tell you the truth, unless a kernel of wheat falls to the ground and dies, it remains only a single seed. But if it dies, it produces many seeds" (John 12:24). In the same manner, he must give his life, in order that new life can spring forth for his followers. The synoptic Gospels incorporate this theme in their account of Jesus' greatest object lesson, the Last Supper. Bread symbolizes his life, which he would soon give in death for them. The fruit of the vine represents the new covenant, which will soon be ratified through his sacrifice on their behalf. Through his self-giving act, they will be able to participate with him in the eschatological kingdom of God.

The early community made explicit the servant-Christology implicit in Jesus' self-understanding. They interpreted Jesus' actions (Matt. 8:16-17) and above all his death (Acts 8:32-35) by appeal to Isaiah's Suffering Servant. As a consequence, in capsulizing the work of Christ traditional theology rightly adds to the designations "prophet" and "king" that of "priest."

Jesus' Self-consciousness

Our survey leads to the conclusion that the Jesus of the four Gospels exhibited a unique self-consciousness. He perceived his task as that of fulfilling the Old Testament hope, of being the herald of the kingdom, and of dying on behalf of the people. The juxtapositioning of these three dimensions provides a vantage point from which to perceive the self-understanding of the Nazarene. Jesus drew together these three themes, which he found in the Jewish tradition. He saw his vocation as being Messiah, Son of Man, and Suffering Servant.

In fact, his unique self-consciousness lies in his singular blending of the three traditional figures.[10]

At the heart of Jesus' conception of his task lay his unparalleled employment of Isaiah's motif of Suffering Servant in order to redefine the vocation of the kingly Messiah of the Old Testament hope and the Son of man, the righteous judge so important to the apocalypticists. In his earthly ministry, servanthood predominated. Jesus understood his task as that of suffering in obedience to his Father and on behalf of the people. He must experience rejection, even death, in fulfillment of his vocation. Only then would the eschatological glory follow.

Jesus' conception of a suffering and dying Liberator may not have been completely new to the Jewish tradition. Nevertheless, it ran counter to the widely held ideas of his day. For this reason, Jesus found himself compelled to reject popular expectations about such eschatological figures as the Messiah and the Son of man. For this reason Jesus sought so intensely to reorient the thinking of his disciples as to the nature of God's eschatological activity in the world.

From Jesus' teaching and actions we conclude that, as the Suffering Servant, Jesus is both the Son of man and the Messiah. Our Lord drew together the motif of suffering and his self-designation as the Son of man, which in turn had implicit messianic overtones. Mark's Gospel declares unequivocally that in predicting his imminent suffering Jesus repeatedly referred to the Son of man and to a future messianic glory. The Evangelist points out that, beginning with the incident at Caesarea Philippi, Jesus emphasized how the Son of man must first suffer before entering into his glory:

> He then began to teach them that the Son of man must suffer many things and be rejected by the elders, chief priests and teachers of the law, and that he must be killed and after three days rise again. He spoke plainly about this. (Mark 8:31; see also 9:31; 10:33-34)

Jesus' awareness that as the Suffering Servant he is the Son of man carries far-reaching significance for our understanding of this figure. According to the apocalyptic tradition, the Son of man is the

---

10. This conclusion is reminiscent of the thesis of Mowinckel in *He That Cometh*.

coming eschatological judge, the one who will mete out justice and before whom all peoples will stand. Because he is the Son of man, Jesus is that eschatological judge. As the primordial man, however, he is not only the one who will pronounce judgment, but also the standard by whom and against whom we will be measured. In this manner, the title Son of man returns us to the conclusion of chapter 11. Jesus is the true human, the revelation of the essence of humanity as designed by God. But we may now add a further dimension to our earlier assertion: In his vocation as the Suffering Servant we discover the character of Jesus, which is our standard. In his life and death, Jesus reveals that God's design for us is that we live as obedient servants of our heavenly Father and minister—even suffer—for the sake of others.

In keeping with this emphasis on Jesus' servanthood as the model for his followers, Paul spoke of our participation in the sufferings of Christ. Jesus' sufferings "flow over into our lives," he declares (2 Cor. 1:5). In fact, the apostle welcomes this "fellowship of sharing in his sufferings." Thereby we become like Christ in his death so that we may also hope to participate in his resurrection (Phil. 3:10-11). Paul even rejoiced in his sufferings on behalf of other believers. In this manner, he testified, "I fill up in my flesh what is still lacking in regard to Christ's afflictions, for the sake of his body, which is the church" (Col. 1:24).

As the Pauline theology of suffering suggests, Jesus' unique blending of the Suffering Servant with the Son of man is implicitly carried forth in the New Testament Epistles. Especially significant is the implied use of this motif in texts that speak about sanctification. Whenever the authors urge us to grow to maturity in our Christian life, the standard they invoke is Christ (Eph. 4:13). This pattern often focuses on Jesus' mission of suffering for our sakes, whether by direct appeal to his own example (1 Pet. 2:18-25) or by elaboration of the character traits which he himself demonstrated (Gal. 5:22-24).

To summarize: The innovation at the heart of Jesus' self-consciousness was the reinterpretation of the mission of Messiah and Son of man in accordance with the figure of the Suffering Servant. As a consequence, the development of Christologies that use these designations does not mark a violation but a continuation of Jesus' own awareness of his task. Jesus' understanding of his mission forms the foundation for his universal significance. He is the revelation of God's design for human life. Consequently he is the judge, the standard against whom we are measured and into whose likeness we will be conformed. Indeed, "even the Son of Man did not come to be served, but to serve, and to give his life as a ransom for many" (Mark 10:45).

The Atonement and the Mission of Jesus

Jesus integrated into his self-consciousness themes which he drew from the context in which he ministered. He came as the fulfillment of the Old Testament hope that God would again act salvifically on behalf of his people, even on behalf of the entire world. He appeared as the herald of the reign of God, proclaiming and embodying the good news that God's eschatological rule is already inaugurated. And he came die, to suffer on behalf of the cause of God. Hence, he who is the Suffering Servant of God is also Messiah and Son of man.

Jesus' self-consciousness as the one sent to die confronts us with the central mystery of the vocation of Christ, namely, his calling to be obedient to his divine mandate to the point of death. Out of Jesus' own self-awareness, therefore, arose the early Christian proclamation that Jesus is the atonement for human sin. How are we to understand this central declaration of our faith? What is the significance of his death? And how does Jesus' sacrifice affect us?

We cannot understand the full meaning of the cross of Christ. We can only stand in silence before it, acknowledge its wonder, and submit to its power. At the same time, the theological task requires that we reflect on this grand confession of our faith in order that we might understand its significance. Our attempt to make sense out of this divine mystery leads us first to theological history, as we search out the meanings others have seen in this event. Then we return to the biblical images themselves. These in turn provide the foundation for a contemporary grappling with the atoning mission of Jesus of Nazareth.

The Atonement in Theological History

In contrast to the grave issues surrounding Jesus' person, no ecumenical council has determined the boundaries for christological reflection on the atoning work of our Lord. Nevertheless, the matter has generated spirited discussion throughout theological history. Of the many ideas that thinkers have proposed, three continue to exert the greatest power in the church—the dynamic, the objective, and the subjective conceptions.[11]

Dynamic imagery. A first way of speaking of Jesus' atoning work employs dynamic imagery. Jesus has overcome the powers that enslaved humankind. This conception was prominent in the early church, died out in the Middle Ages, was revived briefly in the Reformation, and has gained a following in the modern era.[12]

Although not the first to reflect on the nature of the atonement, Irenaeus (about 140-202) may have been the first to attempt to arrive at an explanation of its workings,[13] viewing Christ's work in dynamic terms. Irenaeus's understanding built from the representative character of Christ's work as the second Adam. According to the early church father, Jesus "recapitulated"—retraced and carried to a higher level—the theological history of humankind.

Central to Irenaeus' thought was his consideration for what is fitting for God to do. God acts only in conformity with his own nature even in dealing with the devil. Thus, even though Satan had tyrannized humans unjustly, in Christ God acted in accordance with his own just nature: "He who was powerful Word and also truly man redeemed us by his own blood by a rational transaction, and gave himself as a ransom for these who had been taken into captivity...attaining his purpose not by force...but by way of persuasion."[14] In addition, Irenaeus viewed the atonement as cosmic or all-inclusive in its intention. Jesus not only redeems individuals but also

---

11. For a helpful survey of the atonement in theological history, see Robert S. Paul, *The Atonement and the Sacraments* (Nashville: Abingdon, 1960), 35-281.

12. For a twentieth century explication of this theme, see Gustaf Aulen, *Christus Victor*, trans. A. G. Hebert, paperback edition (New York: Macmillan, 1969).

13. Paul, *The Atonement and the Sacraments*, 47.

14. Irenaeus, *Adversus Haereses*, 5.1.1, in *The Early Christian Fathers*, ed. Henry Bettenson, second edition (London: Oxford University Press, 1969), 79.

humankind; he came not only for individual creatures but for creation.

From these considerations emerged Irenaeus's conception of the atonement, commonly known as the ransom theory. Humankind was in bondage through sin to the devil, who exercised actual power over us. Our bondage required that we be bought back by a ransom to which the devil would also consent. At the same time, this provision depended solely on the nature of God who was both just in his actions toward Satan and loving in his resolve to intervene on our behalf.

Irenaeus, like many who followed him, probably never intended that his theory be viewed as a description of a transaction in the history of creation. It was merely a picture of the meaning of the victory of Christ.[15] Subsequent thinkers, however, obscured the bishop's emphasis on God's justice and love as the undergirding principle for the divine act of ransom.

Gregory of Nyssa (335-395), for example, theorized that the devil, jealous over human happiness, seduced Adam. The power which he exercised over his victim fed his pride, so that when Satan saw the goodness of Jesus he wanted to destroy him. But failing to see the deity that was veiled in Jesus' humanity, "Satan swallowed the hook, the Godhead, with the bait, the humanity of Jesus."[16] In defense of God's strategy, Gregory appealed to the "beneficent deception" that a physician may employ to ensure the cure of a patient. Ultimately, the divine redemption would serve even Satan's best interests.

The dynamic conception of the atonement drew likewise from the work of Athanasius. Rather than Jesus' death as the focal point of the atonement, this church father spoke of Christ's work as an outworking of the incarnation. In this sense, his view of the atonement paralleled his understanding of salvation as deification, capsulized in his famous dictum, "The Word was made man in order that we might be made divine."[17] Seeing us under the penalty of death, the eternal

---

15. Paul, *The Atonement and the Sacraments*, 52.

16. Origen, "An Address on Religious Instruction" [*Oratio Catechetica*] 24, in *The Christology of the Later Fathers*, volume 3 of the *Library of Christian Classics*, ed. Edward Rochie Hardy and Cyril C. Richardson (Philadelphia: Westminster, 1954), 300-302.

17. Athanasius, *De Incarnatione*, 54, in *The Early Christian Fathers*, 293.

word of God entered the human situation in order to turn creation from this awful fate. But Athanasius struggled with the question as to why it was necessary for Jesus to die on the cross. How is human salvation related to his death?

Augustine addressed Athanasius's problematic question. The death of Jesus was necessary in order to give human beings hope in the face of despair, for the cross demonstrates the infinite price that God was prepared to pay in order to save lost humankind.[18] At this point, however, the bishop of Hippo appealed to the ransom idea, for he viewed the death of Jesus as freeing us from the power of the devil. Because Satan conquered humankind through an act of justice, not power, we fell justly under his grasp. However, the devil overextended himself when he slew the sinless Jesus Christ, thereby taking something which did not belong to him. Therefore, justice demanded that he also release those who were in bondage to him.[19]

Objective imagery. The church fathers spoke of the atonement in dynamic imagery rather than technical theory. Beginning with the musings of Anselm, Archbishop of Canterbury (1093-1109), theologians gravitated to objective conceptions of the atonement, to explanations which treat Christ's sacrifice and its effects as actual happenings in history.

As the title of his famous book *Cur Deus homo?* (Why God Became Man) suggests, Anselm struggled with the question posed by Athanasius. Drawing from themes set forth earlier by Tertullian and Cyprian,[20] Anselm articulated his influential satisfaction theory.

Anselm's goal was both apologetic and didactic. He intended to convince unbelievers through reason that they stand indicted by God and therefore in need of the help available in Christ. He also desired to support faith by giving believers a logical reason for their trust in Jesus Christ. Hence, Anselm sought to demonstrate the rationality of the atonement[21]—how the plan of redemption arises out of God's

---

18. For this characterization of Augustine's position, see Paul, *The Atonement and the Sacraments*, 60.
19. Ibid.
20. For this interpretation, see Aulen, *Christus Victor*, 81-84.
21. Ibid., 91.

own nature—by showing there was no other way for God to save humankind except through Christ's sacrifice.

Foundational to Anselm's position was his rejection of an idea central to the ransom theory, the concept of double allegiance.[22] This idea no longer fit the feudal society into which Western Europe had moved since the days of Irenaeus. According to feudal law, the devil depicted in the patristic imagery actually exercises legal right over human beings, because he had become *de facto* monarch over humankind. For this reason, we have legitimate cause for serving Satan until God reasserts his own claim over us. Anselm wanted to guard against this misunderstanding and thereby to protect the biblical teaching that all creatures, including the devil himself, have only one rightful allegiance. To this end, he envisioned our seduction by Satan as that of a mutinous slave persuading others to join in a rebellion. Consequently, the atonement of Christ cannot be directed to the devil, only to God.

In keeping with feudal categories, the archbishop defined sin as the refusal of God's vassals to give their Sovereign what is due him. This refusal is an outrage which demands recompense to God's honor. Through sin each person is a rebel, an outlaw, who has forfeited all legal rights, and therefore is under the just condemnation of God. The divine King cannot allow the rebellion to go unpunished, but must maintain kingly honor in the face of human sin. Nor can satisfaction be merely the pledge of absolute obedience in the future, for ongoing obedience is what we rightfully owe our Sovereign.

In short, we are unable to settle our account with God by our own efforts. If satisfaction is to be rendered, it must be given by one who is both human, in order to recompense God for the honor humans owe him, and divine, in order to live completely without sin. This was the reason why "God became man."

Yet the question remained, Why did Jesus need to die? According to Anselm, the satisfaction our Savior rendered could not consist in his holy life. Perfect obedience to God was also Jesus' human duty. The point of atonement lay in Jesus' voluntary death as the sinless one, which brought infinite honor to God. Thereby our Savior won

---

22. For this understanding of Anselm, see Paul, *The Atonement and the Sacraments*, 74.

merit which he can share with others and which forms the basis for the forgiveness of sin. For Anselm in contrast to Athanasius the incarnation was merely the means that made possible the atonement, which in turn focuses not on the life, but solely on the death of Jesus.[23]

Subjective imagery. No sooner had the satisfaction theory, which has characterized the Latin church, received its classic formulation than it engendered its paradigmatic criticism. Anselm's younger colleague, Abelard (1079-1142),[24] rejected the satisfaction theory because of what he saw as the false view of God which it presupposed: What kind of a God could be pleased by the blood of an innocent person?[25] In so doing he had raised an objection that Anselm himself had voiced in his own work. But in contrast to the great proponent of the satisfaction theory, Abelard concluded that the death of Jesus cannot satisfy God's honor.

In the place of Anselm's objective theory, Abelard offered the beginnings of what has become the classic subjectivist alternative, the "exemplarist" theory. Rather than placating God, Jesus' death is directed toward us. As the grand exhibition of God's great love for humankind, the death of Jesus frees us from our fear of God's wrath and kindles in us a desire to love God.[26] This desire fulfills all that God demands and allows him to forgive our sin.

The exemplary nature of Christ's death, central to Abelard's proposal, was not a new idea. In contrast to Anselm who introduced a new set of categories into the discussion, Abelard's importance lies in his elevation of one previously articulated understanding of the atonement to the central meaning of Christ's work.[27]

---

23. See Aulen's characterization of Anselm's theory. Aulen, *Christus Victor*, 84-92.

24. Many interpreters set Abelard's interpretation of the atonement against that of Anselm. See, for example, Paul, *The Atonement and the Sacraments*, 80. See also, Kenneth Scott Latourette, *A History of Christianity* (New York: Harper and Brothers, 1953), 504.

25. Peter Abelard, "Exposition of the Epistle to the Romans" 2, in *A Scholastic Miscellany: Anselm to Ockham*, volume 10 in the *Library of Christian Classics*, trans. Eugene R. Fairweather (Philadelphia: Westminster, 1956), 283.

26. Ibid.

27. Paul, *The Atonement and the Sacraments*, 81.

From the twelfth century to the twentieth, thinkers who found the dominant objective theories theologically suspect generally gravitated to variations on Abelard's subjectivist alternative.[28]

Modifications to Anselm's theory. Despite the critique of thinkers such as Abelard, the objective approach to the atonement indicative of Anselm's theory continued its dominance into the era of the Protestant Reformation. Although the Reformers themselves employed various concepts to understand the atonement, including the patristic idea of Christ's victory over the devil,[29] they set the stage for the ascendancy of an innovative alteration of the medieval understanding, called the penal theory.

Calvin, following one of Luther's images, suggested that the satisfaction Christ paid was not directed to God's honor, as in Anselm's view, but to God's wrath with its sentence against sin. Just as a judge condemns a convicted felon, so also God justly condemns us for sin. In this context the Geneva reformer spoke about Christ's work as our substitute.[30] At the same time, Calvin attempted to soften the apparent harshness of the penal conception[31] by placing it within the context of sacrifice,[32] thereby seeking to emphasize that there is no hostile division between the Father and the Son. Out of love, he declared, God sent Christ to be a sacrifice to turn aside the punishment which the Judge of the world must require of all lawbreakers.

Although the decades that followed the Reformation witnessed the introduction of several additional theories, none was able to compete with the penal theory. It became the quasi-orthodox doctrine of the atonement from the mid-sixteenth until well into the nineteenth century.[33] And it remains perhaps the most widely accepted understanding among evangelicals today.[34]

---

28. For a discussion of the renewal of the subjectivist approach, see Paul, *The Atonement and the Sacraments*, 135-61.

29. In his book *Christus Victor*, Aulen proposes this thesis.

30. John Calvin, *Institutes of the Christian Religion*, 2.12.3, trans. Ford Lewis Battles, volumes 20 and 21 of the *Library of Christian Classics*, ed. John T. McNeill, two volumes (Philadelphia: Westminster, 1960), 466-67.

31. This is the judgment of Paul, *The Atonement and the Sacraments*, 102-103.

32. Calvin, *Institutes of the Christian Religion*, 2.15.6, *Library of Christian Classics*, 1:501-503.

33. Paul, *The Atonement and the Sacraments*, 109.

34. See, for example, Millard J. Erickson, *Christian Theology*, three volumes (Grand Rapids: Baker, 1984), 2:815.

The predominance of the penal conception may be connected historically with the demise of the feudal system and the rise of nations. The law of the state replaced the honor of the ruler as the foundation for social order. In response, theologians came to view sin as the transgression of the codified law of civil government and to understand government as the upholder and the avenger of the civil law.

The Significance of Jesus' Death in the New Testament

Jesus knew that his vocation included faithfulness to the will of God to the point of death. He came as the Suffering Servant, the one sent to die. But what does his death mean? The New Testament writers themselves sought to make sense of the cross of the innocent Jesus. Their musings yielded several themes concerning the theological significance of this awe-inspiring event.

Jesus' death as our example. Certain New Testament authors depict Jesus' death in subjective terms—as our example. As the revelation of God's intention for human living, in death as in life Jesus stands as our example, the one whose ways ought to influence the conduct and attitudes of his followers. Specifically, he exemplifies such godly traits as humility (Phil. 2:3-8), patient suffering (1 Pet. 2:21-23), and love (Eph. 5:2). For this reason, the New Testament writers admonish us to emulate the qualities we see displayed in Jesus' life and death.

Jesus's death as our ransom. The biblical texts also employ dynamic imagery to describe the accomplishment of our Savior.[35] Certain verses state explicitly that Jesus is our ransom (Eph. 1:7; Heb. 9:12; 1 Tim. 2:6). On other occasions, the biblical authors also note the direction of Christ's redeeming work. Hence, his action frees us from all wickedness" (Titus 2:14) or from the "empty way of life" handed down to us from our ancestors (1 Pet. 1:18).

Although the devil is sometimes mentioned (John 12:31; Heb. 2:14; 1 John 3:8), he figures less prominently in the biblical ransom texts than in the dynamic imagery that predominated in the patristic

---

35. For an overview, see Aulen, *Christus Victor*, 61-80.

era.[36] More central in the Pauline literature is the motif of the victory of Christ over the principalities and powers which hold us in bondage (e.g., Col. 2:15) including the law (Gal. 3:13), or over death with its connection to sin (Rom. 8:2). Rather than focusing on Jesus' death as a ransom paid to any creaturely power, the apocalyptic seer speaks for the general New Testament community in proclaiming the goal of Jesus' death as purchasing *for God* a people from every nation (Rev. 5:9).

Jesus' death as our expiation. Just as certain New Testament texts provide the foundation for the development of dynamic imagery, so also other statements lead to theories which suggest that Jesus' work is somehow objective. It is a "propitiation" directed toward God. While biblical scholars generally agree that the New Testament contains such language, they disagree concerning its meaning. Is Jesus' death a propitiation in the strict sense of placating God's wrath or in the wider sense of "expiation" (as covering human sin)? The exegetical debate centers largely around a group of Greek words that share a common root.[37]

Originally meaning "cheerful" or "happy," the adjective *hileos* came to connote "friendly," "gracious," or favorable." In the Septuagint (the Greek translation of the Old Testament), *hileos* is predicated only of God, and when added to the verb "to be" its meanings include "to forgive," "to accept hurt," "to have pity on." The term occurs only twice in the New Testament, as a negative protestation (Matt. 16:22) and in a citation of the prophet Jeremiah (Heb. 8:12), where it means "merciful" or "forgiving."

In the pagan Hellenistic world, the verb *hilaskomai* originally meant "to make gracious" or "to placate." In the Septuagint, however, it signifies "to become merciful." The related term *exilaskomai* denotes the action of the priest who sacrifices for the sins of the people. *Hilaskomai* occurs only twice in the New Testament. In Jesus' story of the Pharisee and the publican, the term takes its standard

---

36. Even Aulen acknowledges this, at least in the case of Paul. Aulen, *Christus Victor*, 67.

37. See, for example, Friedrich Buechsel, "hileos," in the *Theological Dictionary of the New Testament*, ed. Gerhard Kittel, trans. Geoffrey W. Bromiley (Grand Rapids: Eerdmans, 1965), 3:300-301.

Septuagint meaning, as the repentant sinner cries to God for mercy (Luke 18:13).

The isolated use of *hilaskomai* to speak of Christ's work as high priest is theologically more important. Christ was made like us in order that "he might make atonement for the sins of the people" (Heb. 2:17). In this text, the author employs the present infinitive of the verb (*hilaskesthai*) together with a noun in the accusative case (*hamartias* ["sin"]). This construction, known as the accusative of reference,[38] suggests that Christ's work is directed toward human sin, not God's wrath.

The words *hilasterion* and *hilasmos* each occur only twice in the New Testament. The epistle to the Hebrews uses *hilasterion* to refer to the mercy seat in the tabernacle where sacrifices were offered (Heb. 9:5). Although Christ's work is not in view here, this occurrence of the term suggests that New Testament references to Christ as our "propitiation" are probably allusions to the Old Testament provision for the covering of sins.

Of more direct Christological significance is Paul's statement that God put forth Christ as a *hilasterion*, thereby vindicating his righteousness in passing over former sins and in justifying all who express faith in Jesus (Rom. 3:25-26). The force of the typological imagery is that Christ's death is the new focus of atonement, replacing the mercy seat of the tabernacle.[39] The Pauline reference offers the context for the parallel Johannine declaration that Christ is the *hilasmos* for the sins of the world (1 John 2:2; 4:10).

What can we conclude from these observations? Taken as a whole, the primary emphasis of the word group is the activity resulting in God's mercy or forgiveness. As the imagery of the mercy-seat in the tabernacle suggests, this occurs because Jesus' death covers our sins. Christ's work, therefore, is primarily directed toward human sin and not God's wrath. Nevertheless, the effects of his action do not stop there. Indeed, because Christ's atoning sacrifice covers

---

38. H. E. Dana and Julius R. Mantey, *A Manual Grammar of the Greek New Testament* (New York: Macmillan, 1927), 93.

39. See Jürgen Roloff, "hilasterion," in the *Exegetical Dictionary of the New Testament*, ed. Horst Balz and Gerhard Schneider, English translation (Grand Rapids: Eerdmans, 1990), 2:186.

sin, God is now able righteously to forgive our sins and to declare us righteous, resulting in a restored relationship.[40]

Jesus is our reconciliation. The idea that Jesus' death serves as the covering for human sin leads naturally to an additional theme, which is especially evident in the Pauline literature. Christ has become our reconciliation.

Many evangelicals look to Paul's use of this imagery in Romans as the paradigmatic statement:

> For if, when we were God's enemies, we were reconciled to him through the death of his Son, how much more, having been reconciled, shall we be saved through his life! Not only is this so, but we also rejoice in God through our Lord Jesus Christ, through whom we have now received reconciliation. (Rom. 5:10-11)

The apostle's point is clear: Jesus' death effects a new relationship between us and God. Through Christ, we who were God's enemies now enjoy fellowship with him.

The focus on reconciliation between sinful humans and the righteous God must always remain central in our theological reflections. Nevertheless, elsewhere Paul provides the foundation for widening the scope entailed in the idea. The reconciling work of Jesus extends to human relationships. On the cross, he destroyed the barriers dividing human beings (Eph. 2:11-22).

Even this observation does not bring us to the boundary of the effects of Jesus' death, however, for Christ's work has cosmic implications. To the Colossians, Paul writes,

> For God was pleased...through him to reconcile to himself all things, whether things on earth or things in heaven, by making peace through his blood, shed on the cross. (Col. 1:19-20)

The immediate focus of this statement may well be the heavenly powers, which the apostle earlier declares were created through and for Christ (v. 16). His statement implies, therefore, that as the structures of existence once again find their center in the Lord, their hostility toward us can give way to harmony.

---

40. Ibid.

There remains a further dimension of the universality of Christ's reconciling work. The biblical writers also envision the reconciliation of humankind with the entire creation, including our physical environment which will experience the cessation of hostilities and the advent of peace. One day the animals will live in harmony with each other (Isa. 65:25), and the leaves of the trees will bring healing to the nations (Rev. 22:2). The christological center of the Bible leads us to conclude that this reconciliation will come as the effect of the work of Christ on behalf of the entire cosmos.

Paul presents a final aspect of the imagery of reconciliation. It is God himself who effects this restored relationship through the death of Jesus: "God was reconciling the world to himself in Christ, not counting men's sins against them" (2 Cor. 5:18). Objective descriptions of the atonement readily give the impression that Jesus stepped forward in order to placate the anger of God. This Pauline theme, however, allows for no such split between the Father and the Son. Jesus' sacrifice is the means that God planned to bring us to himself. In accordance with this understanding, the apostle concludes his great declaration by imploring his audience as the voice of God himself, "Be reconciled to God" (v. 20).

Jesus' Death and Us

On the basis of these biblical and theological materials, we may now develop more explicitly our conception of the atonement. In what sense is Jesus God's provision for the crucial needs of humanity bound in sin?

The atonement and the human predicament. We begin with a general answer. In chapter 8, we concluded our discussion of sin by summarizing the human condition through a series of metaphors. Given the biblical motifs mentioned above, these anthropological images provide a helpful context in which to set forth the multifaceted significance of Jesus' atonement on our behalf. Christ is God's provision for our fallen condition.

When viewed from the realm of interpersonal relationships, Jesus died in order that we who were God's enemies might enjoy reconciliation. Seen from the forensic (legal) perspective, Christ's death is an atoning sacrifice which covers human sin so that God can forgive us and the verdict of condemnation need no longer fall. The cosmic metaphor suggests that in the face of our bondage to an alien slave-master—whether the principalities and powers, sin, the devil, or death—Jesus died to purchase our redemption. Understood within the ethical realm, Jesus is God's provision of an example to guide us in the midst of the moral disorientation that plagues us. In short, to counteract our human depravity—our hopeless inability to remedy our situation or to please God—Christ came as our substitute, accomplishing for us what we were powerless to do for ourselves.

Our reception of Christ's atonement. Given these pictures of the benefits of Christ's death, how do we become the recipients of his act on our behalf? This question—the application of Jesus' atoning sacrifice to our sinful situation—returns us to the issue of the atonement that has been central throughout theological history. Are we to understand the work of Jesus as objective or subjective in intent? Is it an event of history that fundamentally alters reality, or is it primarily directed toward evoking a response from sinful humans?

The New Testament declares that the atoning work of Jesus is an objective, completed fact (1 Pet. 3:18). Our Savior died once for all. This act effected a fundamental alteration in the relationship between God and humankind, and it sealed his authority over the cosmic powers. The New Testament also indicates that Jesus' provision is intended to move us to appropriate its benefits. In fact, Christ's death is of no value unless we respond in faith to the God who in Jesus purchased reconciliation.

How can we bring together these seemingly diverse ideas? Perhaps an analogy suggests the answer: Suppose the leader of a country announces a total amnesty for all jailed persons. That provision is in effect for the individual languishing in prison only if the prisoner personally appropriates the offer and walks out of the jail. So also Jesus' death has altered the relationship between God and humanity and has freed us from the dominance of hostile powers. Yet until we appropriate the new status he offers us, our Savior's death is of no salvific effect. For this reason, the New Testament writers declare that despite Jesus' sacrifice the one who does not believe "stands condemned already" (John 3:18).

As our expiation, Jesus' sacrifice covers all sin, so that God is able to forgive any and all. Hence, Christ's death radically altered the relationship between God and humankind. At first glance, this declaration appears to lead inevitably to universalism, the teaching that in the end all will be saved. But is this indeed the case?

Although fuller treatment of this complex topic must await the eschatology section, here we can offer a preliminary answer related to the present context. If the atonement were directed only toward God's set disposition against sin, we could gladly affirm that all humans will eventually enjoy fellowship in the eschatological community of God. However, our wretched human situation consists not only of the sin that evokes God's displeasure, but also our own enmity against God. Through Christ, God is reconciled to us. But in our sin we remain at odds with him. From God's side, therefore, the atoning sacrifice of Jesus is universal; from the human side, however, its efficacy requires our response, namely, that we be reconciled to the God who has reconciled the world to himself (2 Cor. 5:19-20). This means that all may not be saved. Some may hold on to their set enmity against God despite Christ's provision.

The application of this principle to the reality of hell follows naturally. Were the problem that required Christ's death only with God, hell would be a fleeting phantom. However, our enmity against our Maker and Savior means that hell remains a real possibility, for it is ultimately our own doing. Stubborn human hostility necessitates it.

The atonement and community. With these considerations, however, we have still not pierced to the core of the atonement. As in other dimensions of our theology, our understanding of the atoning work of Christ must arise out of the biblical vision of God's overall purpose. We declare repeatedly in this volume that God intends to establish the eschatological community which marks his reign. The anticipated fellowship encompasses a redeemed humankind, dwelling within a redeemed creation, and enjoying the presence of our Redeemer—the triune God. Christology delineates Jesus' role in this program. Through his atoning work, our Savior is Revealer, Effector, and Originator of God's eschatological community.

Jesus' atoning work arises within his role as the Revealer. We concluded in our studies of his divinity and humanity that our Lord reveals both God's essence and his design for human life. He reveals the God who is the eternal community (the social Trinity), and he discloses God's intention for human existence, namely, life-in-community.

We noted earlier as well that Jesus unveils God's essence and intent through his life and teaching. The Nazarene embodies the divine principle of life, that living in obedience to the Father and for the sake of others is the true pathway to the community which constitutes the divine reign. But Jesus' revelatory role also extends to his death. In fact, viewed from the perspective of the resurrection, the cross marks the climactic moment of his entire life, for it stands as the grandest object lesson of his teaching. What our Lord proclaimed in his teaching and modeled in his life—that the fullness of community lies in the giving of one's life—his death gloriously displays.

Not only is he the Revealer of life-in-community, Jesus is also the Effector of that community. As the one who opens the way for us to participate in true fellowship, our Savior authors among us the divine design for human life.

As in his work of revelation, our Lord engaged in this role through his life and teaching. In calling his disciples and appointing the twelve apostles, for example, the Nazarene gathered the symbolic new community of God. In entering into table fellowship with "tax collectors and sinners" and supremely in the Last Supper, Jesus set forth the expanding nature of the eschatological community which God had already begun to establish through our Lord's ministry. In calling his hearers to enter the kingdom by repenting and believing the gospel (Mark 1:15), Jesus established the foundation for participation in the community of God.

What was implicit in these acts became explicit in Jesus' death. Supremely through the cross he is the Effector of the community of God. To understand the role of Jesus' death in establishing community, we must view the results of the cross both negatively and positively.

Seen from the negative perspective, Jesus' death fosters community in that through this self-giving act he dismantled whatever hinders our participation in God's purpose for human existence. Specifically, Jesus' sacrifice covers the sin which evokes God's condemnatory verdict against us. As a result, the wall of guilt can no longer bar us from enjoying reconciliation with God. Further, Jesus dethroned the alien powers that reign over us. Stripped of their actual power, these forces need no longer bind us; they cannot stop us from returning to our heavenly Father. For example, the power of sin and the devil can no longer demand our loyalty and thereby keep us at enmity against God. Neither the terror of death's consequences nor any other hostile, fear-inducing force now bodes separation from God and his love (Rom. 8:38-39).

In addition to eliminating what prevents us from coming to God, Jesus' death facilitates the community God purposes to establish. Our Savior opened the way to fellowship with God by bearing the cost of transforming from God's enemies to his friends.

The cessation of hostilities never comes without costs. Among these is the price of taking the first step to end the conflict. In Christ, God took the initiative to terminate the hostilities within creation and to renew the fellowship he intends for all to enjoy. As the herald of the reign of God and the proclaimer of his offer of salvation for which he died, our Savior took upon himself the cost God incurred in seeking reconciliation.

In his life climaxing in death, Jesus likewise bore the cost of pointing us to the way to life. In the incarnate life, God himself was living out in human history the divine principle of life and the principle of divine life, so that we might know about and willingly share in that life.

Above all, the cost of reconciliation includes bearing the pain and hostility the broken relationship produced. In the case of our enmity with God, our sin and failure caused great harm to God's creation and great pain to God the Creator. In Jesus, God himself willingly bore that hurt in order to make reconciliation possible. But how does this great bearing of pain transpire?

Theologians often remark that through his experience of godforsakenness on the cross, Christ tasted alienation so that we might enjoy reconciliation.[41] In the incarnate life of the Word-made-flesh, we see God the Son taking upon himself the consequences of human sin. As a result, all the pain that has ensued from the fall—whether pain that we inflict or pain that we experience—need no longer bar the way to true fellowship between the creature and the Creator, and by extension, true fellowship among us. However, this observation does not explicate the full mystery of the dynamic of the cross. The godforsakenness Jesus bore affected the Father as well as the Son. The Fatherlessness of the Son entailed the Sonlessness of the Father. In this manner, the cross marked the entrance of the pain of human sin into the heart of the triune God. The consequences of our hostility toward God interrupted the relationship between Jesus and his Father, so that we in turn might share in the eternal fellowship between the Father and the Son. As we will see in part 4, the Holy Spirit establishes this fellowship in us. He is therefore the Spirit both of that relationship and of our relationship with the triune God. How great is the love of our God and Savior!

Finally, in the divine program of establishing community, Jesus is not only Revealer and Effector, he is also Originator. Our Lord stands at the beginning of a new fellowship of humans, forming its foundation and fountainhead. The new corporate reality Jesus inaugurates is the church, the company who pioneer the eschatological community of God (which is the topic of part 5). Jesus' entire life, death, and resurrection mark his work in originating the proleptic community, the foretaste of the eternal fellowship in the kingdom of God. At his glorious return he will complete his role as Originator, as he establishes the fullness of the eschatological community (which is a topic of part 6). Until that great day, the risen Lord continues to function as the originator of community life through his on-

---

41. See, for example, Jürgen Moltmann, *The Crucified God*, trans. R. A. Wilson and John Bowden, second edition (New York: Harper and Row, 1974), 145-53.

going presence in the church, a presence mediated by his Spirit (which theme leads us to pneumatology).

Christ's substitution. This understanding of the dynamic of the atonement provides the context to view a final issue, namely, the nature of Christ's substitution. The New Testament teaches that Jesus' death is vicarious; he died *for us* (Gal. 1:4; 2 Cor. 5:21; Eph. 5:2; Heb. 9:28). But in what sense is he our substitute? In seeking to understand this dimension of Jesus' work, we must differentiate between his acting as the substitute for our sins and his dying our death.

The New Testament teaches that Jesus is the vicarious sacrifice for our sins. As we noted above, the Savior bore our iniquities—became our substitute—so that the dire results of sin need no longer come upon us. This act does not mean that all negative results of human failure are suddenly rendered inoperative. Indeed, each of us, we together, and even creation itself continue to suffer many of the consequences of our personal and corporate iniquity. The atonement means rather that we need no longer bear the ultimate consequences of sin. Because Jesus is our expiation, the eternal alienation that sin threatens—separation from the eschatological community of God—can be rendered ineffective. In addition, from the perspective of our participation in the eschatological community, Jesus' sacrifice both relativizes and temporalizes our present experiences of sin's effects.

According to Paul, sin's awful, abiding product is death (Rom. 6:23). Therefore, the claim that Jesus bore the eternal results of human iniquity leads naturally to the way his death is our substitute. In what sense does Jesus taste death for us, so that we need not die? Recently several theologians, including Wolfhart Pannenberg and Dorothy Soelle, have introduced a helpful differentiation between "exclusive" and "inclusive substitution."[42] Does Jesus' death on our behalf exclude our participation, so that we no longer need to die (exclusive substitution)? Or does his death mean that although we will die our experience is transformed by his participation in it (inclusive substitution)?

---

42. For a discussion of Pannenberg's use of this term, see Stanley J. Grenz, *Reason for Hope: The Systematic Theology of Wolfhart Pannenberg* (New York: Oxford University Press, 1990), 121-22, 127-28.

Both aspects of substitution are correct, but each in its own proper context. With respect to eternal death—alienation from the eschatological community of God—Jesus' sacrifice means that we need not undergo what he bore on our behalf (exclusive substitution). On the cross he experienced Godforsakenness for us, so that we might enjoy eternal fellowship with God. With respect to the more immediate, albeit temporal reality—physical death—the work of our Savior does not mean that we will never die. Nevertheless, even here he remains our substitute. He went through death on our behalf, in order to transform the experience for us (inclusive substitution). We may die. But because Christ has died for us we are convinced that even this evil foe cannot "separate us from the love of God that is in Christ Jesus our Lord" (Rom. 8:38-39).

The Ongoing Work of Christ

We have looked at the vocation Jesus fulfilled and the atonement our Savior provided. Our Christology concludes with a brief summary of his ongoing work as the risen Lord.

The Exaltation

The foundation for our conclusions concerning Jesus' present ministry lies with yet another event in his narrative, namely, the exaltation. Many modern biblical scholars have treated the Lukan depiction of the Lord's ascension into heaven with benign neglect, if not hostility. Nevertheless, we cannot relegate the affirmation that Jesus is exalted to the right hand of the Father to the fringe of New Testament Christology. In the early church, the proclamation of the exalted Christ clearly served an apologetic and didactic function (Acts 2:33; Heb. 1:3-4). This event carries theological significance, for it marks the transition from Jesus' completed work to his ongoing ministry.

The exaltation derives its transitional function from the open-endedness of Jesus' narrative. Because his life, death, and resurrection are events of human history, we properly speak of them as past. But as we observed in our discussion of Christ's preexistence, the story of the Nazarene does not end with Holy Week. Rather, as the risen Lord, Jesus is alive now, and as the returning Son of Man his story will continue into the eschaton. Consequently, in addition to his completed task, the New Testament leads us to speak of both Jesus' present ministry and his future work.

Jesus' Present and Future Ministry

The ascension marks the beginning of Jesus' present ministry. And it sets the stage for his future work on our behalf.

Jesus' present ministry. Central to Jesus' present ministry is his intercession on behalf of his people (Rom. 8:34; Heb. 7:25; 1 John 2:1). As the Exalted One, Christ is our Advocate, the one who pleads our cause with our heavenly Father.

We ought not view intercession as a new dimension of Jesus' activity first inaugurated on Ascension Day. Rather, his ongoing advocacy role is the direct result and outworking of his completed work. Jesus intercedes for us because his sacrifice on the cross covered human sin. The ministry of our Advocate is also the outworking of the prayer life of the earthly Jesus. During his sojourn on earth, the Master petitioned his Father not only on behalf of the twelve disciples but also for "those who will believe in me through their message" (John 17:20). Our exalted Lord continues that ministry as he now pleads for us in heaven.

Our experience of prayer as the people of God is tied to the intercession of our Advocate. As we imitate the example of the earthly Jesus, including the pattern he left to us (Matt. 6:9-13), our prayer becomes the extension of his historical praying. As we consciously seek to pray in his name and are prompted by his Spirit to approach God as "Abba"—as our loving heavenly Father—our prayer becomes the extension of his presence as our advocate with his Father.[43]

In addition to acting as our advocate, the exalted Lord directs his church. The ascension did not inaugurate the absence of Jesus. On the contrary, in accordance with the promise he gave to his original followers (Matt. 28:16-20), this event made possible the continuing

---

43. See Stanley J. Grenz, *Prayer: The Cry for the Kingdom*, (Peabody, Mass.: Hendrickson, 1988), 15-18.

presence of the risen Lord with his people everywhere, a presence mediated by the Holy Spirit.

The exalted one also functions as the Lord of the cosmos. Like his presence with the church, Jesus' present lordship is mediated by the Spirit, who now works toward expanding God's reign. In the present age, Christ's lordship is a hidden reality, albeit a reality perceived through the eyes of faith.

Jesus' ongoing ministry. One day the present task of our Lord will climax in what from our perspective is his yet future ministry. At the consummation of history, the one who at the ascension was installed as Lord of the cosmos will visibly act as the universal Lord. On that great eschatological day, the Son will complete his work on behalf of the reign of the triune God. He will then return the kingship to the Father, and God will be "all in all" (1 Cor. 15:24, 28).

Implication of Jesus Ongoing Ministry for Prayer

The differentiation between the completed and ongoing ministry of Jesus provides the framework by means of which we can understand in what sense we may properly direct adoration, confession, thanksgiving, and petition to Jesus the Christ.

Our theological concern is that we always pray in accordance with our Lord's functions within the divine program. On this basis, we conclude that it is always appropriate to adore Jesus in prayer as we call to mind who he is, just as we bring adoration to the Father. Such prayers are not dependent on the work of Christ, for they focus on his eternal reality as the divine Son and on the qualities which are his because he shares in full deity. Likewise, we can direct prayers of thanksgiving to Jesus. We can express gratitude for what he has done, is doing, or will do. It is also important that we thank our heavenly Father for sending the Son to us.

Less obvious is whether we can confess sins to Jesus in prayer. When we recall that our Lord acts as our advocate with the Father, we may at times be drawn to confess sin to him. At the same time, sin is always against God our Father and destroys the fellowship he desires that we enjoy, and he is the one who forgives sin. Therefore, it is generally preferable to confess our sins to him.

Our primary theological difficulty lies with petition. Again here, our concern is that our address in prayer be in keeping with the function of each trinitarian person. This principle suggests that we should direct to Jesus only such requests as pertain to his ongoing work. We may beseech him to act as our advocate, or we may groan for the day when he will return in glory. In general, however, we should cultivate the practice of directing our petitions to "the Father of the heavenly lights," the source of "every good and perfect gift" (Jas. 1:17), just as Jesus himself instructed us in the Lord's prayer.

Jesus' ascension opens the way for his ongoing work. Our contemplation of his presence in the world as the exalted Lord and his future return lead us to consider the Holy Spirit. The Spirit mediates Christ's presence with us and one day will bring God's program to completion in our Lord's return. Therefore, the ascension directs us beyond Christology to pneumatology.

Part 4
Pneumatology
The Doctrine
of the Holy Spirit

The Bible narrates the activity of the triune God in accomplishing the divine intention for creation. This narrative focuses on God's activity in bringing salvation to sinful humankind. Our systematic-theological reflection on the biblical drama began with God the Father, the foundation for creation and salvation. Our attention then shifted to God the Son incarnate in Jesus the Christ, as we spoke of his role in the reconciling, community-building work of the triune God. In the life, death, and resurrection of the Nazarene we find God reconciling the world to himself. Jesus, therefore, reveals God's essence and intention for us.

We now turn our attention to the third person of the Trinity, the Holy Spirit. As in the Christology section, we are interested in the Spirit's identity and mission. However, we must reverse the proportion of discussion devoted to each topic. Whereas in Christology Jesus' person was paramount, in pneumatology the work of the Spirit predominates.

In one succinct chapter we set forth the identity of the Holy Spirit (chapter 13), before launching into his mission. The Spirit's work encompasses two basic dimensions. We explore the traditional doctrine of the Bible (bibliology) under the theme of the Spirit's work in Scripture (chapter 14). The second dimension of the Spirit's mission, his work in salvation (soteriology), encompasses the remainder of our systematic theology. Within the pneumatology section, we articulate only one aspect of soteriology, the Spirit's mission in the salvation of the individual human. Our discussion comes in two parts, first the inauguration of personal salvation, or conversion (chapter 15), and then the ongoing process of salvation, or sanctification (chapter 16).

13

The Identity
of the Holy Spirit

But the Counsellor, the Holy Spirit,
whom the Father will send in my
name, will teach you all things and
will remind you of everything I
have said to you. (John 14:26)

Outline

Aspects of the Spirit's identity as the power of God
His identity as the eschatological Creator Spirit

In the past, the Holy Spirit was the unknown trinitarian person. George S. Hendry pinpointed the situation: "It has become almost a convention that those who undertake to write about the Holy Spirit should begin by deploring the neglect of this doctrine in the thought and life of the Church today." The chief reason for this neglect, according to Hendry, lies with the doctrine of the Holy Spirit itself, for it "is beset with difficulties and obscurities, which baffle the mind, and which no book has yet been able to dispel."[1]

Since Hendry penned these words in the 1950s the church has witnessed an unparalleled explosion of interest in the Holy Spirit. Interest in the Spirit was once the domain of fringe groups such as the Montanists of Tertullian's day, the "enthusiasts" of the Radical Reformation, or the Pentecostals of the early 1900s. Today, however, Christians of many denominations want to know and appropriate the Holy Spirit. Believers within nearly all Protestant traditions churches and even the Roman Catholic Church claim to have received the "baptism of the Spirit."

The surge in interest in the Holy Spirit has infected theologians as well. Reminiscent of Hegel's emphasis on God as the Absolute Spirit, Paul Tillich set a new theological agenda in the third volume of his *Systematic Theology* by elevating the importance of the Spirit to our understanding of life.[2] Soon thinkers such as Jürgen Moltmann[3] and Wolfhart Pannenberg[4] took up Tillich's challenge, seeking new and creative, new ways to grasp the Spirit's identity. The definitive treatise on pneumatology that many thinkers await has yet to appear. Yet theologians no longer avoid speaking about the Holy Spirit. Once slighted in theological presentations, pneumatology has re-

---

1. George S. Hendry, *The Holy Spirit in Christian Theology*, revised and enlarged edition (Philadelphia: Westminster, 1965), 11.

2. Paul Tillich, *Systematic Theology*, three volumes (Chicago: University of Chicago Press, 1963), 3:11-282.

3. See for example, Jürgen Moltmann, *The Spirit of Life: A Universal Affirmation* (Minneapolis: Fortress, 1992).

4. Wolfhart Pannenberg, "The Spirit of Life," in Wolfhart Pannenberg, *Faith and Reality*, trans. John Maxwell (Philadelphia: Westminster, 1977).

emerged as a central topic of systematic theology, as many thinkers now grapple with the Spirit's identity.

Exactly who (or what) is the Holy Spirit? Evangelicals often use a simple approach in delineating their understanding of the Holy Spirit. They set forth their pneumatology in the context of two questions: Is the Spirit fully divine, or a reality less than God the Father? Is the Spirit fully person, or merely an impersonal force? Proponents of the classic method respond to these questions with a biblical proof of the Spirit's deity followed by a similar argument for his personhood. When added together, these two proofs lead to the theological conclusion that the Spirit is the third person of the Trinity.[5]

Our attempt to describe the identity of the Holy Spirit diverges from this approach. We too will develop an understanding of the Spirit's identity as both a distinct person and a participant with the Father and the Son in the one divine reality. But foundational to our endeavor will be a study of the Spirit's functions within salvation history, which led to the doctrine of the Trinity. From this vantage point we will then draw together an understanding of the Spirit within the context of the triune God.

The Spirit in Salvation History

The simple words of the third article of the Apostles' Creed capsulize the church's confession of the third person of the Trinity: "I believe...in the Holy Spirit." Like the Father and the Son, the Spirit is fully personal and fully divine. In addition, he is coequal with the Father and the Son in the divine work in history and in the life of the believing community.

We noted in chapter 2 how the work of many thinkers climaxing with the Cappadocian fathers brought the church to conclude that our God is three persons in one divine essence. Implicit in the doctrine of the Trinity is the belief that the Holy Spirit is fully divine and personal. Yet the high pneumatology of the church was the conclusion of a long struggle which began with the biblical people of God them-

---

5. For an example of this method, see Millard J. Erickson, *Christian Theology*, three volumes (Grand Rapids: Baker, 1985), 3:857-62. See also the shorter work, Bruce Milne, *Know the Truth* (Downers Grove, Ill.: InterVarsity, 1982), 176-77.

selves. The Christian confession of the Spirit's deity and personhood was the product of centuries of God's encounter with his people in Israel and in the early church. In short, the developing experience of the Spirit in salvation history led to the maturation in the awareness of the Spirit's identity.

Our reflections on the Spirit's identity must follow the progressive revelational approach that characterized the biblical era itself. Consequently, we begin our search for the identity of the Spirit by retracing his footsteps through the scriptural narrative. Only then can we understand the Spirit's place within the triune God.

The Holy Spirit and the Old Testament Era

The Hebrews were not trinitarians as we are. The Old Testament does not explicate the intricate pneumatology presupposed by the doctrine of the Trinity. Nevertheless, the ancient writings give evidence to the presence in Israel of a profound awareness of God's Spirit.

The Spirit of God in the Old Testament. As we noted in our discussion of the doctrine of God (chapter 3), the Hebrew word for spirit, *ruach*, carries theological importance.

At its foundation is the idea of "wind" (Gen. 8:1; Ex. 10:13) and hence "breath" (Ezek. 37:1-10).[6] The ancients we aware of the close connection between breath and life. Breathing indicated the presence of life, whereas its cessation meant that life had come to an end. Consequently, from its basic meaning grew the use of *ruach* to refer to the life principle in living creatures (Gen. 6:17; 7:15,22). Because the Hebrews believed that all creaturely life found its source in God, *ruach* also denoted the divine power which creates and sustains life. In this sense the term became closely linked to the divine life and God's bestowal of life.

The concept of the divine life-giving power led the Old Testament writers to speak of the Spirit of God whom God sends to accomplish his goals. In this sense, the Spirit is the divine power at work in the

---

6. See, for example, Friedrich Baumgaertel, "pneuma...: Spirit in the OT," in the *Theological Dictionary of the New Testament* ed. Gerhard Kittel and Gerhard Friedrich, trans. Geoffrey W. Bromiley (Grand Rapids: Eerdmans, 1968), 6:359-62.

world. Although the presence of God's Spirit in nature suggested the idea of God's immanence, the concept of God sending his Spirit reminded them of the parallel idea of the divine transcendence. They sensed that as Spirit the transcendent God entered the natural order unpredictably. Similarly, God could revoke the gracious gift of his Spirit. Consequently, as Eichrodt pointed out, the Hebrews were conscious of an unbridgeable gulf separating humans from the eternal God (Gen. 6:1-4).[7]

Spirit, therefore, referred ultimately to God. Isaiah, for example, expressed this connection when he contrasted human armies with God, who is the sole source of protection: "But the Egyptians are men and not God; their horses are flesh and not spirit" (Isa. 31:3). God alone is spirit, the prophet asserted.

Because of the connection between Spirit and God, the Old Testament writers linked God's Spirit closely to God. Isaiah asked his audience, "Who has understood the mind [literally, Spirit] of the Lord, or instructed him as his counsellor?" (Isa. 40:13). The Spirit is God as the incomprehensible one (beyond human understanding). Therefore, the Old Testament writers thought of the Spirit as God's knowledge of himself (see also 1 Cor. 2:10-12). Likewise, in praise to God the psalmist asked the rhetorical question, "Where can I go from your Spirit? Where can I flee from your presence?" (Ps. 139:7). In this text, God's Spirit denotes God in his omnipresence; the divine Spirit mediates the universal presence of God to his creatures. Elsewhere, the psalmist declared that the Spirit of God was the one against whom Israel rebelled in the wilderness (Ps. 106:33).

The idea of sinning against God introduces our common designation for the third person of the Trinity, the *Holy* Spirit. The phrase occurs only rarely in the Old Testament, however, and always in connection with human sin (Ps. 51:11, Isa. 63:10–11). In these texts, the term "holy" is likely an adjective, rather than the first part of a two-word noun. Holy Spirit connotes God's Spirit in his moral holiness in contrast to human sinfulness.

---

7. Walther Eichrodt, *Theology of the Old Testament*, trans. J. A. Baker, two volumes (Philadelphia: Westminster, 1967), 2:49.

After committing adultery with Bathsheba, David cried, "Do not cast me from your presence or take your Holy Spirit from me" (Ps. 51:11). Aware of Saul's earlier loss of the Spirit, David was concerned that his transgression not result in a similar fate. He feared that because God's Spirit is holy (morally upright), his sin would result in the withdrawal of God's presence as mediated by the Spirit.

Texts which speak of the Spirit of God indicate that the ancient Hebrews differentiated between God and his Spirit. The Old Testament concept of God's Spirit, therefore, forms the first step in the progressive revelation that leads to the full biblical pneumatology and eventually to the doctrine of the Trinity.

Functions of the Spirit of God in the Old Testament. The ancient Hebrews were cognizant of God's Spirit, though they were not fully aware of the triune divine reality. They understood that the Spirit fulfilled certain important functions both in creation and within the life of the people of God.

Old Testament writers placed the Spirit's role in creation at the foundation of all dimensions of his activity. They knew God's Spirit above all as the Creator Spirit. He is the agent of God's creative action and the one by whom God sustains the world.

The first creation narrative gave evidence to the link between the Spirit and creation. Before God spoke his creative words, the Spirit of God "was hovering [or 'brooded'] over the waters" (Gen. 1:2). Alluding to the connection between "breath" and "Spirit," the psalmist described the breath of God's nostrils as carrying a creative effect (Ps. 18:15). According to the second creation narrative, God's act of breathing gave life to the first human (Gen. 2:7). In this text the narrator used terms related to *nephesh* rather than *ruach*. Yet we must read it in the light of other passages which clearly indicate that the presence of the Spirit is indispensable for human life (Gen. 6:3; Eccl. 12:7).

On several occasions, the Old Testament writers spoke of the Spirit as the sustainer of life. They were aware of his upholding activity in nature. When God removes the Spirit creatures die, but when he sends his Spirit the earth is renewed (Ps. 104:29-30; Isa. 32:15). Above all, they knew that the Spirit's presence sustains human life (Gen. 6:3; Job 27:3; 34:14-15). All living creatures, therefore, owe their existence to the work of God's Spirit.

As we will see, the role of the Spirit in creation carries crucial theological implications.

Not only does the Spirit function as God's agent in creation, according to the Old Testament writers he also acts in special ways in the lives of certain persons. The Spirit was God's supernatural power coming on specific individuals for specific tasks. His coming might simply enhance the potential that a person already had. The Spirit's endowment mediated creativity in the use of personal skills, such as the practice of crafts and the making of artistic designs (Ex. 31:1-5; 35:31). Or his presence might facilitate the exercise of leadership abilities (Judg. 3:10; 6:34).

The Spirit could also mediate an actual supernatural endowment. This provision sometimes took the form of great power. Sampson exercised superhuman physical strength whenever the Spirit came upon him (Judg. 14:6,19; 15:14). For others, especially the prophets, the Spirit mediated an ecstatic experience. Overwhelmed by the Spirit, they came under direct supernatural control (1 Sam. 10:6,10; 19:19-24). But most generally, the Spirit's presence meant that a prophet sensed the compulsion to speak on behalf of God (Num. 24:2-3; 2 Chron. 15:1-2).

Whatever form it took, the Spirit's presence provided the recipient with the resources necessary to complete a divinely-ordained task. God's Spirit, and not human ability, was the indispensable provision for accomplishing God's program (Zech 4:6). Therefore, the Spirit's presence dispelled fear and fostered strong, courageous action (Hag. 2:4-5).

The era of the monarchy reflected a more institutionalized understanding of the Spirit's endowment. Israel looked to their political and religious leaders, especially kings, priests, and prophets, for his presence among them. In this context, certain rites gained added significance. Anointing with oil symbolized the Spirit's coming (1 Sam. 16:13). The laying on of hands represented the transference of the Spirit from one person to another (Num. 27:23; Deut. 34:9).

Throughout the Old Testament era the Spirit's coming and empowerment always remained transient. No one—not even office holders—could presume to possess the Spirit permanently. Even the rite of anointing provided no guarantee that the divine endowment would continue indefinitely. Saul was a tragic example. Because of his disobedience, the Spirit departed from the hapless monarch (1 Sam. 16:14).

By means of his Spirit, God was present with his covenant nation. Yet not everyone enjoyed a direct experience of God. Instead most Israelites knew only the corporate dimension of God's presence. Being the bearers of the Spirit, the officers functioned as the mediators of the divine presence with his people. The representative nature of his office and the problem it caused when on one occasion God shared the Spirit with the elders (Num. 11:25) led Moses to cry out, "I wish that all the Lord's people were prophets and that the LORD would put his Spirit on them!" (v. 29).

Eschatological direction of Old Testament pneumatology. In the end, the Old Testament people of God knew only an unsatisfying experience of the Spirit. His presence was transitory, not permanent. It was selective—enjoyed by only a few—not universal. And it was largely corporate, possessed by the people as a whole rather than as individuals.

Their unsatisfactory experience of the Spirit kindled within the people a hope for a better day in the future. The prophets looked to a coming era which would be characterized by the fullness of the Spirit. The prophetic hope included the expectation that the unique bearer of the Spirit would come. They anticipated the Anointed One, on whom the fullness of the Spirit would rest (Isa. 42:2). This future endowment with the Spirit would not be solely the possession of the Coming One. On the contrary, the Messiah would pour out the Spirit on all God's people.

The prophets declared that one day God would pour out his Spirit on the house of Israel (Ezek. 39:29). No longer would the Spirit's presence be selective or merely corporate, mediated to the people by their officers. Instead, that event would inaugurate the universal experience of the divine presence (Joel 2:28-29). Each person would now have immediate access to God's Spirit. Likewise, the Spirit would no longer be merely an external reality. Rather, God would inaugurate a new covenant with his people marked by the permanent presence of the Spirit within each one. Teachers would no longer be needed in Israel, for God would write his laws on the hearts of all (Jer. 31:31-34; Ezek. 36:25-38).

During the Old Testament era, therefore, the Spirit functioned in an eschatological manner. The partial, unsatisfying experience of his presence led God's people to direct their attention to the future. They eagerly hoped for a new, grand day, when the present foretaste would give way to the full reality—God dwelling permanently among them through his Spirit.

The Holy Spirit and the Christ

Old Testament pneumatology was implicitly eschatological, focusing in God's future action on behalf of his people. This eschatological pneumatology provided the context in which Jesus of Nazareth carried out his ministry. The New Testament indicates that both Jesus and the early church understood his identity and mission as the fulfillment of the Hebrew pneumatological hope. The first century believers testified that in Jesus of Nazareth the eschatological expectations of the ancient Hebrews had come to fruition. He was, therefore, the fulfillment of the Old Testament pneumatology.

Jesus—the bearer of the Spirit. The Old Testament people anticipated the coming of a singularly Anointed One and the subsequent outpouring of the Spirit. According to the New Testament, Jesus of Nazareth embodied both dimensions.

The early church clearly believed that Jesus was the one uniquely endowed by the Spirit awaited by the prophets. According to the Fourth Gospel, John the Baptist proclaimed this understanding, for he spoke of Jesus as the one to whom "God gives the Spirit without measure" (John 3:34). More importantly, the evangelists claimed that our Lord himself was the source of their view. In Luke's narrative, Jesus launched his ministry in Nazareth by announcing in the synagogue the fulfillment of Isaiah's prophecy of the Anointed One:

> The Spirit of the Lord is on me, because he has anointed me to preach good news to the poor. He has sent me to proclaim freedom for the prisoners and recovery of sight for the blind, to release the oppressed, to proclaim the year of the Lord's favour. (Luke 4:18-19, quoting Isa. 61:1-2)

Jesus was energized by a unique anointing of the Spirit. New Testament writers emphasized this dimension of our Lord's ministry by indicating the role the Spirit played at certain crucial points in Jesus' earthly life. Matthew and Luke connected the Spirit with the birth of Jesus. In announcing God's intention to Mary, the angel declared, "The Holy Spirit will come upon you, and the power of the Most High will overshadow you" (Luke 1:35). Likewise, all four Gospels noted the Spirit's involvement at Jesus' baptism, specifically his descent upon Jesus like a dove, which may be a symbol of the Spirit's endowment of our Lord for his mission. Reflecting on the Christ event, Paul focused on the role of the Spirit in Jesus' resurrection. He testified that through the power of the Holy Spirit God raised Jesus from the dead (Rom. 8:11; see also 1:4).

Jesus knew the Spirit's endowment throughout his ministry. The Gospels indicate that the Spirit provided Jesus with guidance, even leading him into the wilderness to be tempted (Matt. 4:1). The Spirit also provided our Lord with power, for Jesus claimed to drive out demons by the Spirit of God (Matt. 12:28).

The early church believed that Jesus fulfilled the other aspect of Old Testament pneumatology as well. As the one uniquely endowed by the Spirit, he was also the one through whom the outpouring of the Spirit would come. According to the Gospels, Jesus' earthly ministry marked the nearness of the fulfillment of the Old Testament hope for the Spirit's outpouring. The evangelists presented the mission of John the Baptist in this context. He was the forerunner, who prepared the way for the one who would baptize in the Spirit (John 1:29-34). Jesus echoed John's message concerning the nearness of the day of the Spirit. Luke noted Jesus' promise that the Spirit was among the good gifts the Father would give to those who ask (Luke 11:13; compare with Matt. 7:11).

The Gospel writers asserted further that because Jesus was the mediator of the Spirit, the Spirit's outpouring was dependent on him.

He was the one who will give the water which becomes "a spring of water welling up to eternal life" (John 4:14). Before this could happen, however, Jesus needed to complete his own mission. He must first "go away"—that is, be glorified—so that the "Counsellor" could come (John 16:7).

John brought these themes together in an incident that occurred during one celebration of the feast of tabernacles. He reported that on this occasion Jesus cried out, "If anyone is thirsty let him come to me and drink. Whoever believes in me, as the Scripture has said, streams of living water will flow from him" (John 7:37-38). The narrator then explained: "By this he meant the Spirit, whom those who believed in him were later to receive. Up to that time the Spirit had not been given, since Jesus had not yet been glorified" (John 7:39). According to John, Jesus' declaration was a prediction of the future outpouring of the Spirit, which could only occur with the completion of his own task.

In the book of Acts, Luke presented a similar interpretation. In his Pentecost sermon, Peter declared that Jesus' exaltation bestowed on the risen Lord the privilege of pouring out the Spirit in accordance with Old Testament prophecy (Acts 2:33).

Jesus' promise concerning the coming Spirit. The early church was convinced that Jesus was the fulfillment of the Old Testament pneumatological hope. He was the one who was both uniquely endowed with the Spirit and through whom the outpouring of the Spirit would come. In addition, however, his disciples found in Jesus' message a specific promise concerning the Spirit's imminent coming.

The Fourth Gospel located the occasion of Jesus' delivering this promise within his farewell discourse in the upper room just before his betrayal (John 14:16). John identified the promised figure as "another Counsellor" or "helper" (Greek: *allon parakleton*). The noun "helper" is a somewhat technical word that refers to one who is called along side to assist (*parakletos*).[8] To it John adds the adjective "another" (*allos*), which implies a similarity[9] between the Coming One and the Lord himself. Jesus' promise, then, was that the Father

---

8. Johannes Behm, "parakletos," in TDNT, 6:804.

9. See Ray Summers, *Essentials of New Testament Greek* (Nashville: Broadman, 1950), 27.

would send another one, similar to the Lord, who would stand with the disciples to assist them in their mission.

Jesus' ensuing description indicated that the coming helper would fulfil certain tasks. He would mediate the ongoing presence of the Lord with his people (John 14:16-19), reminiscent of Jesus' promise, "I am with you always even to the end of the age" (Matt. 28:20). Likewise, this helper would be the disciples' teacher, reminding them of the Lord's instructions (vv. 25-27) and guiding them into truth (John 16:12-15). Finally, the coming Spirit would testify concerning Jesus and form the foundation for the disciples' own testimony (John 15:26-27). His testimonial task, however, would not be directed primarily to the followers of Jesus but to the world (John 16:7-11).

Other New Testament writers described Jesus' promise of the Spirit's imminent coming as that of a personal power present with his followers. The power of the Spirit would facilitate the completion of their assigned task as his witnesses (Acts 1:8). Consequently, whenever called on to give a reason for the hope within them (1 Pet. 3:15), his messengers could rely on the Spirit for the appropriate words (Mark 13:11). The Spirit would also empower them to work signs. In fact, because of the Spirit, Jesus' followers would do even greater acts that what they observed during his earthly ministry (John 14:12).

Pentecost—the fulfillment of Jesus' promise. During his earthly ministry, the bearer of the Spirit proclaimed the coming day of the Spirit, the glorious outpouring of God's Spirit on his people. Did our Lord's promise come to fulfillment in a specific event? And in what sense do his followers share in that fulfillment? The New Testament writers offered two possible occasions for the fulfillment of Jesus' promise.

The first comes from the pen of John. The author of the Fourth Gospel included an incident of Spirit endowment during Jesus' postresurrection ministry. John's narrative is brief and subjective in orientation, focusing the experience on the recipients of the Spirit. On Easter, while the disciples are in hiding "for fear of the Jews" (John 20:19), the risen Lord appeared. After commissioning those present, "he breathed on them and said, Receive the Holy Spirit" (v. 22). Then he entrusted to his followers the power of binding and loosing.

John's connection between "breath" and "Spirit" is unmistakable. Through this image, the author of the Fourth Gospel invoked the Genesis creation account, in which God breathed into the newly formed human being. The Evangelist thereby conveyed the point that Jesus is now creating the new humanity among his disciples. For John, therefore, the coming of the Spirit marked the climax of Jesus' mission.

In the Book of Acts, in contrast, Luke placed the reception of the Spirit after Jesus' ascension, specifically, on Pentecost (Acts 2:1). Luke's narrative incorporated both objective and subjective elements. The coming of the Spirit marked an objective, historical event in history. The narrator reported that "a sound like the blowing of a violent wind came from heaven" (v. 2) Reminiscent of the Old Testament connection between "wind" and "Spirit" (see also John 3:8), this image symbolizes the supernatural in-breaking of God's Spirit into the world from the transcendent realm. For Luke, this was an objective event, for it resulted in a new state of affairs in the world: The Spirit had come.

In addition to being an objective event, the Spirit's coming at Pentecost was also subjectively experienced. Each person present was "filled with the Spirit" (v. 4). This resulted in the inauguration of a new corporate reality, a fellowship of all who were given "the one Spirit to drink" (1 Cor. 12:13). The sense of community resulting from the inward experience of the Spirit formed the basis for the subsequent sharing of goods within the Jerusalem church. Because they all participated in the same spiritual reality, they wanted to share with one another the material goods they possessed (Acts 2:44-45).

In the Book of Acts, the coming of the Spirit marked the inauguration of a new era, the age of the mission of the church. The phenomenal growth of the new community of faith began already on Pentecost (Acts 2:41). The central goal of the Book of Acts is to narrate the expansion of the church from Jerusalem and ultimately throughout the Roman world.

The presence of two different accounts of the outpouring of the Spirit—John's narrative of Easter evening and Luke's chronicle of Pentecost—raises the question of authenticity. Which, if either of the two narratives, is historically accurate? Or if they are both correct, how can they be harmonized?

One suggested means of harmonizing the two texts views them as narrating two completely different experiences.[10] Proponents note that John's account of Jesus' statement used what is known as the anarthrous construction (the noun is not introduced by the definite article), which they see as allowing the translation, "Receive a holy spirit." This text, therefore, does not describe the outpouring of the Holy Spirit but the conversion of the disciples, their reception of a new human spirit. Acts 2, in turn, describes their subsequent, post-conversion "baptism of the Spirit." While plausible, this solution seems highly contrived, and therefore has failed to gain a wide following.

Many scholars conclude that at best only one of the narratives—probably John's—is likely to have a historical base.[11] They theorize that in contrast to John, Luke invented his own chronological scheme for theological reasons. Because of the Old Testament significance of Pentecost, he wanted to present the coming of the Spirit coincidental with this important feast. Of course, anyone who regards all biblical narratives as having high historical integrity would find this proposal problematic.

Perhaps the best suggestion is to look at both accounts as referring to the same spiritual experience while allowing each of them to stand on its own.

The significance of John's story lies in its purpose in his particular portrait of Jesus. Through this short narrative the Fourth Evangelist desired to emphasize that the outpouring of the Spirit is dependent on the mission of Jesus and marked its completion. The Spirit's coming was no new thing, independent of the gospel of Jesus the Christ.

---

10. For a discussion of this possibility, see H. R. Reynolds, *The Gospel of St. John*, in the *Pulpit Commentary*, ed. H.D.M. Spence and Joseph S. Exell (New York: Funk and Wagnalls, n.d.), 2:474.

11. Alan Richardson, *Introduction to the Theology of the New Testament* (London: SCM, 1958), 116-19.

Rather, the work of the Spirit is the extension of what Jesus accomplished.

This does not yet answer the historical question: Does John 20:19-23 narrate an actual event of history? Or is it merely a shortened treatment of what actually occurred on Pentecost, but which John transposed to Easter?

The idea of prolepsis, which draws from the work of earlier exegetes such as H. B. Swete, is helpful in this context. A proleptic event is an occurrence that forms a preexperience of what happens in its fullness only later. The event in the upper room on Easter was just such a proleptic occurrence.[12] In order to clarify the close link between the Spirit and Jesus, John reminded his readers of a proleptic event that occurred prior to Pentecost: Jesus breathed on them, thereby symbolizing the future outpouring of the Spirit that he would soon effect as the exalted Lord.

Building from the work of Swete, Lindsay Dewar drew a helpful comparison between John 20:22 and the Last Supper:

> As we have already seen, the evangelist says (John 7:39) that the Holy Spirit was not yet (given) because Jesus was not yet glorified. By this it is clearly implied that he *could* not be given until then...We should probably understand the whole action proleptically. In doing so, indeed, we have a parallel in the Last Supper. This could not be a Eucharist, in the full sense, before our Lord had passed through death and risen again. Until then the bread and the wine could only proleptically be called His Body and His Blood. Likewise here our Lord bestows the authority of the Spirit upon the Apostles for binding and loosing, an authority which could not, so to say, "come to life" until after Pentecost. Nor is there any evidence that it did so.[13]

In short, both events occurred. However, the disciples' encounter with Jesus on Easter marked a prolepsis of what would happen in its fullness on Pentecost.

---

12. For Swete's suggestion, see Henry Barclay Swete, *The Holy Spirit in the New Testament: A Study of Primitive Christian Teaching*, reprint edition (London: Macmillan, 1921), 167-68.

13. Lindsay Dewar, *The Holy Spirit and Modern Thought* (New York: Harper and Brothers, 1959), 40.

The Spirit and the Community of Christ

As bearer of the Spirit, Jesus embodied the fulfillment of the Old Testament pneumatology. He came as the uniquely Anointed One. As the result of the completion of his earthly ministry he poured out the Spirit on his followers. Through this event the Spirit assumed a new role. Now his identity focuses on the church, the community of Christ. To understand this, we must look once again at Pentecost.

The significance of Pentecost. Luke's account of Pentecost indicates that this event marked the fulfillment of a grand prophetic tradition. The terminology the narrator used in describing the experience of the disciples—"All of them were filled with the Holy Spirit and began to speak with other tongues as the Spirit enabled them" (Acts 2:4)—is reminiscent of the Baptist's proclamation of a coming baptism with the Spirit (Luke 3:16). Peter's specific use of Joel's prophecy to describe the miraculous phenomena (vv. 16-22) affirmed that the Old Testament hope for a universal presence of God's Spirit had now been inaugurated. By linking Jesus' exaltation with the sending of the Spirit (v. 33), Peter's sermon affirmed that the ascended Lord had fulfilled his promise.

As the grand fulfillment of prophecy, Pentecost was a nonrepeatable event. Its singularity arises from its importance as a milestone in the history of God's activity marking the inauguration of a new age. The Spirit entered the world in a unique way at Pentecost. This entrance can occur only once. The significance of the Spirit's filling of the upper room disciples lies in this context. The coming of the Spirit on the group signified the creation of the Spirit-endowed, Spirit-empowered, Spirit-led community. This event, the birth of the church, can occur only once.

Pentecost was nonrepeatable. But it was not merely a passing occasion of prophetic fulfillment. Nor do the effects of this event end in the upper room and with the disciples who were gathered there. On the contrary, the coming of the Spirit marked the inauguration of the age of fulfillment (1 Pet. 1:10-12). And the reality of Pentecost embraces all believers. All now enjoy the presence of the Spirit, who forms us into one fellowship. Hence, Paul declared, "For we were all baptized by one Spirit into one body...and we were all given the one

Spirit to drink" (1 Cor. 12:13). Insofar as we are joined to the community of Christ, we all participate in the Pentecost experience, which is the reception of the endowment and the empowerment of the Spirit. In fact, Paul declared that if we do not "have" the Spirit we do not even belong to Christ (Rom. 8:9). Pentecost, then, was an event of the church.

Because of this connection between our inclusion in Christ's community and our participation in the Spirit, we need not expect to follow the chain of events that occurred in the upper room. Prior to the coming of the Spirit, the disciples waited, prayed, and prepared for this event in obedience to our Lord's command (Acts 1:4). But now the church lives in the post-Pentecost era. The waiting is over! The Spirit is come! Rather than praying for the Spirit's coming, our task is to "walk in the Spirit," that is, to appropriate the Spirit's dynamic.

The Holy Spirit and the risen Lord. In so far as the Spirit mediates the presence of the risen Lord within his community, Pentecost likewise inaugurated the fulfillment of the promise of the Lord to be with his disciples until the end of the age (Matt. 16:20). This raises the question as to the relationship between the Holy Spirit and Jesus. Who is the Spirit vis-à-vis our Lord? The New Testament writers responded to this issue by speaking of both affinity and distinction.

The New Testament suggests a close affinity between the Spirit and the risen Lord. For John, the coming of the Spirit constituted the coming of the Lord himself (John 14:15-18). Similarly, Paul closely associated the two in the lives of Christians. For the believer to be "in Christ" (Rom. 8:1) and to be "in the Spirit" were one and the same reality (Phil. 2:1). For this reason he could equate possession of the Spirit and belonging to Christ (Rom. 8:9).

At the same time, the risen Lord and the Holy Spirit are not simply interchangeable.[14] As we have noted, both John and Luke clearly emphasized that the Spirit does not come until Jesus' work was completed, whether through the resurrection (John 20:19-23) or the ascension (Acts 2:33). The Spirit's function, therefore, is subsequent and instrumental to that of Jesus, whom he glorifies (John 16:14) and to whom he bears testimony (John 15:26). In keeping with this un-

---

14. C.F.D. Moule, *The Holy Spirit* (Grand Rapids: Eerdmans, 1978), 26.

derstanding, Paul referred to the Holy Spirit as "the Spirit of Christ" (Rom. 8:9; Phil 1:19) or "the Spirit of the Son" (Gal. 4:6). In fact, to cite the conclusion of George S. Hendry, "There is no reference in the New Testament to any work of the Spirit apart from Christ. The Spirit is, in an exclusive sense, the Spirit of Christ."[15]

The instrumental nature of the Spirit carries far-reaching theological significance. It means that viewed salvation-historically, the Western church was correct in adding the *filioque* clause to the ancient creed.[16] This clause emphasizes the normative significance of the work of Christ for the Christian understanding of the Spirit's activity.

The themes of affinity and distinction combine in one important Pauline text: "Now the Lord is the Spirit, and where the Spirit of the Lord is, there is freedom. And we, who with unveiled faces all reflect the Lord's glory, are being transformed into his likeness with ever-increasing glory, which comes from the Lord, who is the Spirit" (2 Cor. 3:17-18). According to Paul, the risen Lord is present and active among his community as the Spirit, for "the Lord is the Spirit." Yet the two remain distinct, for the Spirit is always "the Spirit of the Lord," and it is the Lord's likeness into which the Spirit transforms us.

Since Pentecost, therefore, the Spirit enjoys a new identity. He is the "vicar of Christ," the mediator of the presence of the risen and exalted Jesus within his community. The Spirit teaches, leads, and empowers the church on the Lord's behalf. In so doing, he is the Lord at work in the believing community.

The Spirit's present representational function does not exhaust his place in the life of the community of Christ, however. On the contrary, the biblical writers know of a future aspect of his activity, indicating a further dimension of his identity. He is God's dynamic effecting the consummation of history. Paul saw the primary dimension of the Spirit's eschatological work toward the community in the transformation of believers' bodies. Hence, he declared that through

---

15. Hendry, *The Holy Spirit in Christian Theology*, 26.

16. This conclusion is increasingly coming under attack. For examples of recent scholars who reject Barth's defense of the *filioque*, see Hendry, *The Holy Spirit in Christian Theology*, 42-52.

the Spirit the God who raised Jesus will "give life" to our mortal bodies (Rom. 8:11). This future event also carries cosmic significance. It will mark the liberation of creation from its bondage and its participation in "the glorious freedom of the children of God" (v. 21).

In the meantime, the indwelling Spirit acts as the "down payment" or the guarantee of our future salvation (2 Cor. 1:22; 5:5; Eph. 1:13-14). For Paul, the connection of the Spirit to Jesus' resurrection meant that the Spirit within us—the one who even now is transforming our inner person into Christ's likeness (Rom. 8:10; 2 Cor. 3:18)—is also the promise of our own future bodily transformation (Rom. 8:11).

The Spirit in the Trinitarian Life

In the preceding section, we observed the development of pneumatology through the stages of salvation history. From the anticipatory understanding of the Spirit among the ancient Hebrews we moved to the christocentric pneumatology that characterized Jesus' earthly life. Then our study concluded with the post-Pentecost focus on the presence of the Spirit himself in the Spirit-endowed church enroute to the eschatological consummation of God's program.

To this point, we have sought to express the identity of the Spirit within the context of salvation history, that is, through appeal to the progressive revelation found in the Bible. Our conception of the Spirit, however, cannot be derived solely from his role within God's program for the world. Rather, to determine who he is we must also look to his presence within the Trinity. To this end, our discussion now shifts from salvation history to the triune God of history. Yet, as we will see, even this perspective will quickly bring us once again to view the work of God in the world.

Our discussion begins with the eternal, triune God apart from the world, as we view the Holy Spirit in the context of the immanent Trinity. Then we must take another sweep through salvation history, this time viewing the Holy Spirit as a participant in the work of the triune God in the world (the economic Trinity).

The Foundation of Pneumatology in the Immanent Trinity

Throughout Christian theological history, the confessions of faith devised by the people of God have been trinitarian. They link the Holy Spirit with the Father and the Son in the one divine reality. Consequently, the identity of the Spirit finds its primary reference point in the eternal, triune God. But who is the Spirit within the one God?

The basic identity of the Spirit. To answer this question, we must remind ourselves of the conclusions we reached in our discussion of the Trinity (chapter 2). We discovered that the Spirit is the Spirit of the relationship between the Father and the Son. Let us briefly retrace the background and implications of this understanding.

The primary movement in the eternal God, we argued, is what the fathers called "the eternal generation of the Son." Throughout all eternity the Son draws his life from the Father, and the Father shares his life with the Son. This eternal dynamic forms the identity of both the Father and the Son. The first person of the Trinity is the Father of the Son, and the second person is the Son of the Father.

The differentiated first and second persons are also bonded together. This bond is the mutual love they share. Consequently, the secondary movement in God is the eternal "spiration" or "procession" of the Spirit. He is the Spirit of the love between the Father and the Son.

Our basic postulate—the Spirit is the reciprocal love of the Father and the Son—describes the Spirit's fundamental identity within the triune God. As the Spirit of that eternal relationship he is both fully deity and person.

The deity and personhood of the Spirit. As we noted in chapter 2, in the theological struggles of the fourth century the affirmation of the Spirit's deity was even more problematic than the confession of the deity of Jesus. The chief opponent of the orthodox position was Arius of Alexandria. The church soundly rejected his first postulate—the Son was the first creature of the Father—at the Council of Nicea (325 A.D.). Yet many otherwise orthodox thinkers, including Macedonius of Constantinople, retained doubts about the status of the Holy Spirit.[17] Perhaps Arius's additional thesis—the Spirit was the first creature of the Son—was correct.

During the ensuing debate, Athanasius pinpointed the crucial dimension of the question. If the Spirit who enters our hearts is not in fact the Spirit of God, then we have no true community with God.[18] In the wake of the Macedonian controversy, the church agreed with Athanasius, finally dogmatizing the personhood of the Spirit at the Council of Constantinople (A.D. 381).[19]

The ancient church correctly pinpointed the indispensable importance of the Spirit's deity. We would argue that the affirmation of the full deity of the Spirit arises out of an understanding of the Spirit's primary identity within the immanent Trinity. Because the bond of the Father and the Son is a relationship between eternal persons it is an eternal bond. The Father loves the Son with an eternal love, and the Son reciprocates that love eternally. This observation forms the theological context for the biblical declaration, "God is love," understood to mean that love characterizes the essence of God. The relationship between the Father and the Son—the eternal love they share—is the Spirit. This means that the Spirit is himself both the essence of God—namely, love (the eternal love of the Father and the Son)—and eternal. Together with the Father and the Son he is fully deity. For this reason, "Spirit" as "love" is both the third person of the triune God and the characterization of the one divine essence (John 4:24; 1 John 4:8).

As the relationship of the Father and the Son, the Spirit is also personal. Although perhaps self-evident to us, this assertion has repeatedly engendered doubts and even outright denial from many thinkers throughout theological history. The personhood of the Father and of Jesus the Son are readily conceivable. But to affirm that the Spirit is person is quite another matter. Some people find it easier to think of the Spirit in impersonal terms. In their minds, he is more like a

---

17. See J.W.C. Wand, *The Four Great Heresies* (London: Mowbray, 1955), 67-69; J.N.D. Kelly, *Early Christian Doctrines*, revised edition (San Francisco: Harper and Row, 1978), 243.

18. Kelly, *Early Christian Doctrines*, 257-58.

19. Wand, *The Four Great Heresies*, 78.

force—a mysterious divine force—than a person alongside the Father and the Son.

The affirmation that the Spirit is person arises from his foundational identity within the triune God, following from the personal nature of the first two trinitarian members. Because the Father and the Son are persons, the relationship they share is intimate, personal love. The Spirit of that relationship cannot be otherwise than person, just as the Father and the Son are.

The personhood of the Spirit arises from the personal character of God as well. The love that binds the Father and the Son is the essence of the one God, for "God is love." God is also personal. Therefore his essential nature—love—is likewise personal. This essence is also the third person of the Trinity, the Holy Spirit, who as the "concretization" of that essential divine character must be person.

The personhood of the Spirit is not merely an abstract theological idea. Rather, it carries importance for faith. In fact, in the realm of faith it is crucial that the Spirit is person in relation to us.[20] Only if the Spirit is person, does the living, personal God unite us with Christ, for the Spirit mediates our union with the Lord.

The Holy Spirit and the Economic Trinity

As we noted in chapter 4, although the dynamic of the triune God is self-sufficient within the eternity of the divine life, it overflows into the act of creation. In the context of his program for the world, the one God is the economic Trinity—Father, Son, and Spirit active in effecting the divine design for creation. Consequently, our understanding of the Holy Spirit must encompass his identity within this context as well. For this reason, we now view the Spirit as the third member of the economic Trinity.

A basic understanding. Succinctly stated, within the context of the economic Trinity the Spirit is the power of God at work in the world bringing to completion the divine program.

---

20. Hendry, *The Holy Spirit in Christian Theology*, 42. For the genesis of this idea, Hendry cites Martin Kähler, "Das schrifmaessige Bekenntnis zum Geiste Christi," in *Dogmatische Zeitfragen* (Leipzig: Deichertsche Verlagsbuchhandlung, 1908), 1:137-76.

As we noted in the doctrine of God, each of the trinitarian persons has a specific role within the one economy of the one God. The Father functions as the source or originator. As such, he sends the Son and the Spirit. The Son, in turn, bears the claim of the Father into the world, in order that the Spirit may be sent. The Spirit's role is that of completing the divine task, so that the eschatological community of the triune God may indeed come in its fullness.

The specific role of the Spirit within the economic Trinity—as the Completer of the divine design—arises from his fundamental identity within the immanent Trinity. To see this, we must remind ourselves that God's program in the world is itself an overflow of the dynamic within the eternity of the triune God.

As we noted in chapter 4, the entire drama of creation and redemption, climaxing in the eschatological new community, is the outflow of the eternal relationship between the Father and the Son. God is self-giving love, namely, the love shared by the Father and the Son which is the Holy Spirit. Being love, God willingly creates the world. Because the Son desires that others share in the eternal relationship he enjoys with the Father (John 17:24), he willingly acts on behalf of the Father to make salvation available to the world. Because he is the Spirit of that divine relationship, God sends his Spirit to bring us into fellowship with himself, that is, into the fellowship of the Son and the Father.

The Spirit, in other words, is the dynamic of God at work completing the divine program of effecting the eschatological community. He is the one who brings us into participation in the eternal love relationship between the Father and the Son. The essence of this divine power is love, which is the character of the Father-Son relationship and consequently of the one God. The Spirit, therefore, is the love of God at work in the world.

Aspects of the Spirit's identity as the power of God. The identity of the Spirit as the power of the triune God in the world follows a significant theological movement from creation to redemption and then back to creation.

Lying at the basis of the whole is the Spirit's identity as the foundation of life. As the Creator Spirit, he is integrally involved in the divine act of creation.

The Spirit is the pervasive power of God immanent within all life. But he is also the transcendent, inbreaking dynamic who facilitates the supernatural endowment of life and mediates the divine presence within the people of God. With the addition of this dimension of his role, we see the Spirit's identity beginning to encompass a redemptive dimension.

In the coming of the Messiah, the Spirit assumes his identity as the endowment who energizes the ministry of Jesus. The exalted Lord in turn endows his people with the Spirit. Here the aspect of the Spirit's identity in redemption is clearly prominent.

After Pentecost, we see the Spirit as the dynamic power of God in the community of Christ. But this role includes mediating life—life now to our inner person with the promise of future life to our bodies. Consequently, this marks the beginning of the movement of the Spirit's identity from the realm of redemption to that of creation.

One day the Spirit will again be the Creator of life in the complete sense. In the eschatological renewal, he is the power of God effecting the fullness of life.

His identity as the eschatological Creator Spirit. The identity of the Spirit within salvation history displays an interplay of the themes of creation and redemption. As we have seen, this interesting interplay climaxes in the Spirit's role in the eschatological new creation. From this observation we conclude that his ultimate identity within the economic Trinity is that of "the eschatological Creator Spirit." Therefore, we draw our deliberations to a close with a closer look at this designation. What does it mean to identify the third member of the Trinity as the eschatological Creator Spirit?

To see more clearly the propriety of identifying the third trinitarian person as the eschatological Creator Spirit, we must look first at the significance of the term "eschatological" within that designation. Simply stated, within the economic Trinity the Spirit is "eschatological" because he is the Completer. Ultimately, the goal of the Spirit is to glorify the Father through the Son by bringing God's reign to completion, and this by consummating the establishment of the eschatological community. As the one who completes the task of the triune God in the world, therefore, the Spirit is implicitly eschatological. His task is to effect the ultimate goal of God's program for creation. Thereby, he also effects the completion of the work of the economic Trinity.

The eschatological dimension of the Spirit's identity lies at the heart of the biblical narrative. The Old Testament prophets anticipated the inauguration of the eschatological era of the Spirit. They awaited the time when God would give the Spirit to all. This outpouring of the Spirit would inaugurate the redeemed community and mark the inbreaking of God's reign.

Within this Old Testament prophetic context, the New Testament proclaims the dawn of the time of the end. Jesus of Nazareth has completed his work, and as the exalted Lord he has poured out the Spirit into the world. The long-anticipated era is now here, and the community of Christ enjoys the Spirit's presence. The New Testament adds, however, that the consummation of the age remains yet future. One day the Spirit who is the "down payment" and promise of salvation will effect our complete fellowship with the Father through the Son.

The eschatological nature of the Spirit's identity leads to its "creative" dimension. As the agent of God's activity in completing the divine program for creation, the Spirit is the Creator Spirit. Primarily he is creative in that he effects the new creation—salvation—among humankind. Viewed in its fullness, salvation is an eschatological event, for salvation means that we reflect the design God intends for humanity. But en route to that event, the Spirit remains operative. As the one who indwells each believer, he is at work in our lives increasingly conforming us to the likeness of Christ. As the mediator of the presence of the risen Lord, the Spirit indwells the community, transforming us to become the foretaste and forebear of the new humanity.

The Spirit is creative likewise in his role in the world as a whole. As the power of God completing the divine plan, the Spirit effects the new creation in the universe. Ultimately, the Spirit acts as the Completer of God's intent for the world only at the eschaton, when he establishes the new heaven and the new earth. Nevertheless, in the meantime he remains active in the world. And he seeks to bring us to experience a foretaste of the eschatological community which will be characterized by harmonious human existence on the new earth.

The eschatological Spirit, therefore, is the Creator Spirit.

In chapter 5 we declared that all three members of the Trinity are involved in the one act of creation. The Father is its source and ground, and therefore he is the Creator in the ultimate sense. As the *Logos* (the principle of creation), the Son is the intermediated agent of creation, the one through whom God creates all things. The Spirit in turn is the power of God operative in creation, the dynamic by whom God brings creation into existence.

We noted as well that "creation" is not merely a statement about the distant past. Rather the one creative act is also future, being the consummation of the work of the triune God. This one act of God is essentially trinitarian. All three trinitarian persons participate in the effecting of the eschatological new creation. The Father is the Creator in the ultimate sense. He is the one who makes all things new (Rev. 21:5). As the *Logos*, the Son is the pattern to whom all participants in the new order will be conformed (1 John 3:2). And the Spirit is the power of God at work that brings about the new creation, including our resurrection (Rom. 8:11). Consequently, the triune God brings about the eschatological event of creation: The Father creates through the Son by the Spirit.

In the meantime the Spirit is the pledge or guarantee of the new creation. As the eschatological Creator Spirit he is already at work giving life to believers. In so doing, he promises that we will participate in the eschatological community of God (Rom. 8:16-17; Eph. 1:13-14). This eschatological Creator Spirit is active within the community of Christ, the church. His presence among us guarantees the consummation of the new society of humankind in the eschatological reign of God. Finally, the eschatological Creator Spirit is the source of life in creation. As he continually renews the natural world, he guarantees the eschatological renewal of the cosmos in the new heaven and new earth.

The identity of the third trinitarian person as the eschatological Creator Spirit provides the link from the economic Trinity to immanent Trinity. The Spirit is God at work drawing creation into God's fellowship, into true community. As the Spirit brings us into community, he mediates our participation in the eternal relationship between the Father and the Son.

The work of the economic Trinity which the Spirit completes, therefore, has as its goal the participation of God's creation in the life of the immanent Trinity. The actual tasks which the Spirit fulfills within this one work of the triune God are the specific topics of the following three chapters and, by extension, of the remainder of our systematic theology.

14 The Spirit and the Scriptures

We have not received the spirit of the world but the Spirit who is from God, that we may understand what God has freely given us. This is what we speak, not in words taught us by human wisdom but in words taught by the Spirit, expressing spiritual truths in spiritual words. (1 Cor. 2:12-13)

Outline

The Spirit's mission is to complete the program of the triune God in the world. To this end, he is the Creator Spirit. Not only is he the source of life, the Spirit is the power of the eschatological renewal of life. He is the agent who brings into being the new creation (2 Cor. 5:17). He effects the union of believers with Christ and Christ's community, the reconciled people of God. At the consummation, the Spirit's mission will reach its ultimate goal as he establishes the glorious fellowship of the redeemed people living in a redeemed world and enjoying the presence of their redeemer God. En route to that day, the Spirit nourishes the spiritual life he creates.

Scripture is one aspect of the Spirit's mission of creating and sustaining spiritual life. He both authors and speaks through the Bible, which is ultimately the Spirit's book. By means of Scripture he bears witness to Jesus Christ, guides the lives of believers, and exercises authority in the church.

Because the Bible is the Spirit's book, its purpose is instrumental to his mission. For this reason, we construct our doctrine of the Bible within the context of pneumatology, treating the Spirit's activity in Scripture as one dimension of his overall mission. Our pneumatological bibliology begins by delineating the integral relationship of the Spirit to Scripture. We then describe the specific task in which the Spirit engages. On this foundation, we set forth in what sense the Bible is revelation. Finally, we draw the chapter to a close with a reaffirmation of biblical authority.

The Spirit as the Foundation of Scripture

As Christians we are a "people of the Book." We declare that the Bible is the foundation of our faith and the source of guidance for our lives. This declaration, however, requires a theological formulation which articulates the intimate relationship between Scripture and the Spirit. In acknowledging the Bible, we are actually looking to the Holy Spirit who addresses us through its pages.

The close connection between the Spirit and the Bible as his instrumentality is explicitly stated in what Bernard Ramm calls the "Protestant principle of authority." According to Ramm, "The proper principle of authority within the Christian church must be...the Holy Spirit speaking in the Scriptures, which are the product of the Spirit's revelatory and inspiring action."[1]

This principle is not the sole possession of Protestants, for it belongs to the common heritage shared by Christians. Nevertheless, it is especially indicative of the Reformed tradition, and it received its definitive articulation in the Westminster Confession of Faith:

> The Supreme Judge, by which all controversies of religion are to be determined, and all decrees of counsels, opinions of ancient writers, doctrines of men, and private spirits, are to be examined, and in whose sentence we are to rest, can be no other than the Holy Spirit speaking in the Scripture.[2]

This "classic" Reformed confession declares that the final source to which we look is neither Scripture in itself nor any private "word from the Spirit." Rather, our authority consists in what some theologians call an external principle (the Bible) combined with an internal principle (the witness of the Holy Spirit). In short, Scripture is authoritative in that it is the vehicle through which the Spirit chooses to speak. Our first task in developing a pneumatological bibliology,

---

1. Bernard Ramm, *The Pattern of Religious Authority* (Grand Rapids: Eerdmans, 1959), 28.
2. The Westminster Confession of Faith, 1.10, in *Creeds of the Churches*, ed. John H. Leith, third edition (Atlanta: John Knox, 1982), 196.

therefore, is to look more closely at the relationship between the Spirit and Scripture.

Inspiration and Illumination

The Christian tradition propounds a vital connection between the Bible and the Spirit. Classical Protestant theologians articulated this relationship in a twofold work of the Spirit in Scripture. A decision of the early church concerning the canon paved the way for this bibliological approach.

A council meeting in Carthage in A.D. 397 asserted that nothing should be read in the church as divine Scripture except the twenty-seven books of our New Testament (in addition to the Old Testament writings).[3] In effect the council declared that the Bible is complete. Since then, Christians have agreed that the canon is closed. We do not, nor will we at any future time deem any other documents to be on par with the books in our Bible.

The conclusion that the process of Scripture formation has been completed facilitates theologians in distinguishing between two aspects of the Spirit's work: inspiration and illumination. Because the canon is closed, we differentiate between the Spirit's completed activity as the agent in the original composition of the biblical documents (inspiration) and his ongoing action in bringing people to understand the truth in those documents (illumination).

We must therefore begin our study by looking at the meaning of each of these two terms. Only then can we view them together as forming the one act of the Spirit.

The concept of inspiration. Inspiration has played a central role in bibliology. Theologians do not agree, however, as to what the term means.

Some theologians understand the word as referring to the Spirit's activity in the lives of the authors of Scripture. They define inspiration as his activity in "superintending" the lives of prophets, apostles, and other authors so that what they came to write is Scripture. For the foundation of this understanding, proponents appeal to texts

---

3. J. R. McRay, "Bible, Canon of," in the *Evangelical Dictionary of Theology*, ed. Walter A. Elwell (Grand Rapids: Baker, 1984), 141.

which speak of God's prophets receiving messages from the Lord which they subsequently wrote down (Jer. 36:1,2; Ezek. 11:5; Mic. 3:8; 2 Pet. 1:21). Consequently, this view is often known as the prophetic model. Augustus Hopkins Strong offered a classic articulation: "Inspiration is that influence of the Spirit of God upon the minds of the Scripture writers which made their writing the record of a progressive revelation."[4]

Other theologians build from the Pauline declaration, "All Scripture is God-breathed" (2 Tim. 3:16). On this basis, they assert that "inspiration" refers to a quality of the biblical writings themselves. C. H. Dodd, for example, declared,

> When people today speak of inspiration...they are...thinking of...a quality in the product...if the term "inspiration" is to retain any place in our vocabulary, then it is certain that the Bible contains inspired writings.[5]

These two positions are not mutually exclusive. We could construct a mediating position by simply affirming the central element in each alternative. Indeed, some thinkers distinguish within the one act of "inspiration" an active sense (the action of the Spirit), a passive sense (the effect of the Spirit's action on the human author), and a terminal sense (the biblical writings as the deposit of the Spirit's influence).[6] In keeping with this distinction we may define "inspiration" as primarily an activity and secondarily a deposit. It is that work of the Holy Spirit in influencing the authors and compilers of Scripture to produce writings which adequately reflect what God desired to communicate to us.

The biblical documents suggest that the Spirit used a wide range of means in influencing the writers of Scripture. Certain texts imply that humans were the passive recipients of material given through di-

---

4. Augustus Hopkins Strong, *Systematic Theology*, three volumes (Philadelphia: Griffith and Rowland, 1909), 1:196.

5. C. H. Dodd, *The Authority of the Bible*, Harper Torchbook edition (1929; New York: Harper and Brothers, 1958), 36.

6. See the characterization of the traditional understanding by Thomas A. Hoffman, "Inspiration, Normativeness, Canonicity, and the Unique Sacred Character of the Bible," *Catholic Biblical Quarterly* 44 (1982): 453. For a recent reaffirmation of the classical view in an updated form, see, James M. Reese, "Inspiration: Toward a Sociosemiotic Definition," *Biblical Theology Bulletin* 21/1 (Spring 1991): 10.

vine dictation (Ex. 19:3-6; Lev. 1:1; Num. 7:89; 12:8; 1 Sam. 9:15; Isa. 6:8-9; Rev. 14:13). Other passages indicate that godly people were active agents in the process (Mark 12:36; Acts 1:16; 28:25; 1 Cor. 14:37). Hence, we find in the Bible differing writing styles, varying accounts of the same events, and even outbursts of human emotion (2 Cor. 11:1). Certain sections of the Bible purport to be based in eye witness accounts or to report the encounters certain persons had with God (Ex. 24:1-11; 1 Kings 22:19; Isa. 6:1-5; 2 Cor. 12:1-4).

Because of this variety, we ought not to apply any one theory to the entire Bible. We can offer only a broad statement as an attempt to summarize what the texts themselves suggest: By direct command, a sense of urgency, or simply a personal desire or compulsion, God's Spirit moved spiritual persons within the faith community to write or compile from dictation, experience, tradition, or wisdom those documents which reflect what God desired to have recorded in order that his purposes might be served.

The concept of illumination. The Spirit's work within Scripture did not end in the distant past. Throughout history he continues to act, speaking to people through the Bible. Theologians commonly refer to this dimension of his activity as illumination.

The theological idea of illumination arises from several biblical texts. An oblique reference to the idea may lie in Elihu's comment to Job, "But it is the spirit in a man, the breath of the Almighty, that gives him understanding" (Job 32:8). Three references in the New Testament are more important. Both John (1 John 5:7,11) and Paul (1 Cor. 2:6-16; 2 Cor. 3:14-17) emphasize the crucial importance of divine action if we are to perceive spiritual truth. According to Paul, our depraved condition lies behind the necessity of divine illumination. Because of sin, our hearts are darkened so that we no longer acknowledge the truth about God (Rom. 1:18-23). God himself, therefore, must illumine our minds if we are to come to know him. John reports that in his farewell discourse Jesus described more plainly in what form God's provision would come. Our Lord promised to send the Holy Spirit, who would guide his disciples into truth (John 14:26).

Illumination, therefore, belongs to the mission of the Spirit. He makes the Bible "come alive," as he causes the people of God to understand the significance of the biblical texts for life in the present.

The emphasis on illumination within Reformed bibliology led certain Puritans to develop a corollary doctrine, the concept of "further light." John Robinson articulated this idea in his parting words to the Pilgrims as they set out from Holland for the New World. The pastor admonished his flock to look for the further light which the Spirit of God would yet pour forth from the Scriptures.

The early Baptists took Robinson's advice to heart. They appealed to his challenge to be open to further light in arguing that the Holy Spirit was leading them to forsake church tradition in favor of the radical, albeit biblical practice of believers' baptism. The Spirit speaking through the Scriptures had caused them to see that rediscovering the proper biblical baptism was yet another step in the reformation of Christ's church.[7]

The One Act of the Spirit

The theological distinction between inspiration and illumination carries a certain validity. Yet it also poses an unfortunate risk. This distinction can too rigidly separate what is in fact a close relationship between the two dimensions of the Spirit's one activity in Scripture.

Contrary to what seems to be a clear historical and logical progression from inspiration to illumination, the two are actually intertwined. This connection lies not only in our theological confession concerning the Bible, but also in the historical process of Scripture formation itself. In both cases, the inspiration of Scripture is connected to the phenomenon of illumination. But exactly how are the two related?

Functional and canonical approaches. In recent years, many scholars have attempted to delineate the nature of the relationship between inspiration and illumination.[8]

---

7. This was the position of the eighteenth century American Baptist leader, Isaac Backus. See Stanley J. Grenz, *Isaac Backus—Puritan and Baptist*, NABPR dissertation series #4 (Macon, Ga.: Mercer University Press, 1983), 230.

8. For a summary of the contemporary alternatives, see Francis Schlüssler Fiorenza, "The Crisis of Scriptural Authority: Interpretation and Reception," *Interpretation* 44/4 (October 1990): 353-68.

One proposal starts with the role of Scripture within the Christian community and then draws conclusions concerning the Bible's normative value.[9] This functional understanding is reflected in the various attempts to speak of the Bible as the Christian "classic," including proposals of such luminaries as James Barr and David Tracy. It surfaces as well in the recent emphasis on narrative as a focal point for the theological enterprise. David Kelsey, for example, argued that the Bible is normative in the church because it shapes new human identities and transforms individual and community life.[10]

Perhaps more influential than the functional approach is a proposal which moves in a somewhat opposite direction. Proponents of the canonical method seek insight into the normativeness of the Bible for us today by looking to the historical process of the formation of Scripture.[11] To this end they study the origin, redaction, and canonization of the biblical writings, in order to uncover the paradigmatic pattern of interpretation and reinterpretation displayed in that process.

One important architect of the canonical approach is Brevard Childs. He explored the ongoing authority that the traditions exercised in the life of the ancient community which in turn led to the fixation of the biblical texts in their canonized form. For example, Israel recognized that the words of a prophet within a specific historical situation had authority apart from their original use. The community transmitted this authoritative tradition in a form compatible with its function as Scripture, and subsequent editors in turn built this form and use into the structure of the text.

---

9. The report to the 1971 Louvain meeting of the World Conference on Faith and Order, entitled "The Authority of Scripture," offers a case in point. The document breaks with the older dogmatic tradition by not deducing the authority of the Bible from its inspiration. Instead, according to the characterization of Avery Dulles, "it establishes the authority of the Bible on the ground of its religious value for the church, and then proceeds to postulate inspiration as the source of that authority." Avery Dulles, "Scripture: Recent Protestant and Catholic Views," in *The Authoritative Word*, ed. Donald K. McKim (Grand Rapids: Eerdmans, 1983), 246.

10. David Kelsey, *The Uses of Scripture in Recent Theology* (Philadelphia: Westminster, 1975). For a subsequent statement, see David Kelsey, "The Bible and Christian Theology," *Journal of the American Academy of Religion* 48 (1980): 385-402.

11. For a statement of this approach by an evangelical, see Stephen Reid, "An Evangelical Approach to Scripture," *TSF Bulletin* 8/4 (March-April 1985): 2-10.

According to Childs, this historical process has important herme-neutical implications.[12] We must always interpret a text in its canon-ized form and in relation to the ancient community of faith.[13] In his words: "When seen from the context of the canon both the question of what the text meant and what it means are inseparably linked and both belong to the task of the interpretation of the Bible as Scrip-ture."[14]

The canonical approach implies that our affirmation of biblical in-spiration is a statement of faith, a claim that the Holy Spirit works through "the canonical context of the church."[15] Hence, the develop-ment of the concept of canon was no arbitrary act, for thereby the church "bore witness to the effect that certain writings had on its faith and life."[16] In other words, for the early communities—just as for us today—the affirmation of the inspiration of Scripture was in-tertwined with the experience of illumination.

Despite the differences between the canonical and the functional approaches, both bring inspiration and illumination together within the context of the believing community. Throughout history the peo-ple of God have confessed the inspiration of those texts which are now lodged in the biblical documents, because believers have heard in them the Spirit's voice as they struggled with the issues they faced in their unique and ever-changing contexts. The Baptist scholar Edgar V. McKnight draws the implications of this assertion:

> The Bible is seen, then, not as a finished and static fact or collec-tion of facts to be analyzed by increasingly sophisticated methods, but as a potentiality of meaning which is actualized by succeeding generations in light of their needs and by means of approaches sup-plied and authenticated by their world views.[17]

---

12. Brevard Childs, *Introduction to the Old Testament as Scripture* (Philadelphia: Fortress, 1979), 60.

13. Ibid., 74.

14. Brevard Childs, *Biblical Theology in Crisis* (Philadelphia: Westminster, 1970), 141.

15. Childs, *Biblical Theology in Crisis*, 104.

16. Ibid., 105.

17. Edgar V. McKnight, "Errantry and Inerrancy: Baptists and the Bible," *Perspectives in Religious Studies* 12/2 (Summer 1985): 146.

The connection between the Spirit's enlivening of the texts and the community's confession of their authority as the product of his inspiring activity may actually be the point of the *locus classicus* for the traditional doctrine of inspiration, 2 Timothy 3:16-17.[18] Through the rare use of *theopneustos*, which may intend an allusion to God's breathing into the nostrils of Adam making him spring to life, Paul declared that "God breathes into the Scripture" thereby making it useful.[19] As the evangelical Greek scholar Edward Goodrick concludes, rather than supporting "the pristine character of the autographs,"[20] the text focuses on how valuable the Spirit-energized Scriptures are. The church, in short, came to confess the inspiration of Scripture because the early believers experienced the power and truth of the Spirit of God through these writings. They knew these documents were "animated with the Spirit of Christ."[21]

As in the past so also today the Spirit chooses to speak through this human instrumentality. Consequently, we gladly join with the one church of all ages in affirming that the Bible is the deposit of divine revelation. Like they, we readily acknowledge that these human words are the Word of God.

The development of Scripture in the community. This discussion suggests that the Spirit's work in inspiration and illumination is closely linked with the integral relationship between Scripture and the believing community. Because the connection between the Bible and the community of faith is both historical and ongoing, it encompasses illumination and inspiration. This connection, in turn, provides the context in which to understand the Spirit's role in the process which led to the compiling of Scripture.

Until recently, the classical prophetic paradigm reigned as the accepted theory of the composition of the Bible. This model is helpful, for some of the canonical books were indeed written by individual

---

18. Edward W. Goodrick, "Let's Put 2 Timothy 3:16 Back into the Bible," *Journal of the Evangelical Theological Society* 25/4 (December 1982): 479-87.

19. The Greek term *theopneustos* ("inspiration") occurs only here in the New Testament. Many expositors find the clue to its meaning in its etymology (*theos* [God] + *pneuma* [breath or spirit]), which yields the idea "God-breathed" or "expired by God." But the declaration itself does not spell out clearly what this means for the activity of the Spirit in Scripture.

20. Goodrick, "Let's Put 2 Timothy 3:16 Back into the Bible," 486-87.

21. Hoffman, "Inspiration, Normativeness, Canonicity," 457.

authors as the Holy Spirit moved them to compose their respective works (2 Pet. 1:20-21). Nevertheless, it would be inaccurate to extend the idea of single authorship—and with it the prophetic model—to the composition of the Bible as a whole. This paradigm simply does not fit all the canonical materials.[22] Rather than being the collection of the writings of individual authors, our Bible is the product of the community of faith that cradled it. The compiling of Scripture occurred within the context of the community, and the writings represent the self-understanding of the community in which they developed.[23]

The Scriptures witness to the fact that they are the final written deposit of a trajectory that incorporates a variety of elements, including oral traditions and other source documents. Within the community these took on a life of their own, as it were, forming part of the authoritative materials that the community under the Spirit's direction interpreted and reapplied to new situations. Though the moving of that Spirit, the Old and New Testament peoples brought together these materials at different stages in community life in response to perceived needs. We may subsume all such needs, however, under their Spirit-produced sensed responsibility to preserve for the sake of the continuity of the community the testimony to the historical events that shaped it, as well as the interpretation of these events and certain applications of them to community life.

As Paul Achtemeier rightly concludes:

> the major significance of the Bible is not that it is a book, but rather that it reflects the life of the community of Israel and the primitive church, as those communities sought to come to terms with the central reality that God was present with them in ways that regularly outran their ability to understand or cope.[24]

With this in view, we must expand our understanding of the Spirit's activity in the Scripture-forming process. His work encompasses

---

22. For a critique of the extension of the "prophetic model" to all of Scripture, see Paul J. Achtemeier, *The Inspiration of Scripture* (Philadelphia: Westminster, 1980), 99-104.

23. Or better stated, the Bible represents the understanding of those persons that came to form the enduring trajectory of that community, for at times the biblical writings offer a sharp critique of the attitudes and actions of the wider people.

24. Achtemeier, *The Inspiration of Scripture*, 92.

the original authors of those several biblical books that came from the pens of single individuals. But it also extends to the workings of the Spirit among the Hebrew and early Christian communities, insofar as these people participated in the process of bringing Scripture into being. In fact, we may say that the directing activity of the Spirit blanketed the entire trajectory that climaxed with the coming together of the canon as the book of the people of God.

This expanded understanding means that we cannot describe the Spirit's work in the canonization process solely by appeal to the classical idea of inspiration. Critical to, and lying behind the production of the canon was the Spirit's illuminating work. The community forged the documents into one Bible, because they found these writings to be the vehicle through which God addressed them. Hence, the recognition of the Spirit's inspiration was always inseparable from the phenomenon of his illumination.

We need only reflect on our contemporary experience of illumination for a clue to this historical process. The Spirit attunes us today to understand and apply Scripture to our present situation. So also he spoke to the ancient people of God through the oral traditions and writings which they brought together in the Bible. In fact, certain texts reflect the manner in which people in the ancient communities appropriated the earlier materials. Yet we must acknowledge one far-reaching difference. Israel and the early Christian community engaged in the interpretive task within the context of the process of the formation of the canon. We now enjoy the Spirit's illumination as he speaks to us through the completed Bible. They participated in the process of Scripture formation; we do not.

The risk of subjectivism. The position outlined above may appear to be beset with one potential danger. We might wonder if the close connection between the affirmation of inspiration and the phenomenon of illumination could expose us to the risk of subjectivism. Might we not be tempted to make the inspiration of the Bible dependent upon our hearing the voice of the Spirit in its pages, losing thereby the objective reality of inspiration in a manner reminiscent of the older neoorthodoxy?

The danger of subjectivism is real. Therefore we must be cautious. Yet a lapse into this error is not inevitable. We avoid subjectivism as we remember that our declaration of the inspiration of the Bible asserts that this book is objectively divine Scripture; the Bible is Scripture regardless of whether or not we subjectively acknowledge this status. It is Scripture because it is the book of the church. Further, we affirm the Bible as Scripture because we participate in the one church of Jesus Christ. We confess that the Bible is inspired not primarily because we ourselves hear the Spirit's voice in its pages, as important as our personal experience of illumination is. Rather we articulate this confession because we are the contemporary manifestation of the one people of God who have always been the people of the book.

Our attempt to avoid the danger of subjectivism ought not to blind us to the opposite danger. We cannot follow the lead of those theologians who set forth the inspiration of the Bible as the first thesis of the doctrine of Scripture. On the contrary, we must acknowledge that our affirmation of the divine character of the Bible is linked with the Spirit's work in illumination. Because throughout its history the community of faith has heard the voice of the Holy Spirit in the pages of the Bible, we now confess that the Scriptures are the product of the inspiration of that same Spirit.

The Task of the Spirit
Speaking Through Scripture

As the instrumentality of the Spirit, the Bible is the book of the community. How does the Spirit-illumined Bible function among the people of God? What does the Holy Spirit accomplish through Scripture, which is his instrumentality?

Scripture as the Source of Spiritual Sustenance

The beginning point for understanding the task of the Spirit working through Scripture lies within our divinely-given tendency as Christians to view the Bible as the place—ultimately the only place—where we find the message of everlasting life. We believe this book is, in the words of Clark Pinnock, "the God-given documentation which preserves for all time the gospel of our salvation."[25] Consequently, we readily look to Scripture in order to be nourished in our faith.

The attitude toward the Bible which sees it as the source of spiritual sustenance is but the contemporary expression of a pietistic tradition dating at least to the 1600s and 1700s. Thinkers such as Philip Jakob Spener (1635-1705)—the "father of Pietism"[26]—and August Hermann Francke (1663-1727) focused on the importance of the Bible reader's spiritual condition: Only the regenerate understand Scripture correctly, they asserted.[27] For the Pietists, talk about the truth-claims of the Bible was less important than the fact that "truth claims," that Scripture lays hold of the life of the reader and calls that life into divine service.[28] For them, the ultimate goal of Bible study is spiritual formation. Consequently, the Pietist way of reading the Bible included both diligence in bringing of all our hermeneutical skills to bear on a passage and patience in listening for God's voice speaking through that text.[29]

In a sense, the Pietist tradition was merely embodying emphases of the biblical documents themselves. The writers of Scripture repeatedly bear witness that their primary purpose was that of fostering in the reader a relationship with God—of advancing the reign of God which is the establishment of the redeemed community. The Bible intends to proclaim the good news of salvation to sinful humans and to mediate to believers spiritual nourishment. But how does the Spirit accomplish this through Scripture?

---

25. Clark Pinnock, "What Is Biblical Inerrancy?" in *The Proceedings of the Conference on Biblical Inerrancy 1987* (Nashville: Broadman, 1987), 75.

26. "Spener, Philip Jakob," in William R. Reese, *Dictionary of Philosophy and Religion* (Atlantic Highlands, N.J.: Humanities, 1980), 544.

27. C. John Weborg, "Pietism: Theology in Service of Living Toward God," in *The Variety of American Evangelicalism*, ed. Robert K. Johnston and Donald W. Dayton (Downers Grove, Ill.: InterVarsity, 1991), 170-71, 176.

28. Weborg, "Pietism," 176.

29. Michael Hardin, "The Authority of Scripture: A Pietist Perspective," *Covenant Quarterly* 49/1 (February 1991):9.

The Constitutional Role of Scripture

A clue to an understanding of the ongoing activity of the Spirit in Scripture is what Francis Fiorenza calls its constitutional role: The Bible functions as "the constitution of an ongoing community."[30] These writings provide the foundation for the life we share as believers, that is, for our identity as the Christian community.

Yet we ask, What about the Bible gives it this lofty role? Simply stated, the biblical writings are constitutional in that they are the product of the foundational stage in the history of the faith community, first in Israel and then in the church. Because they set forth what constituted our identity as the people of God at the beginning, they hold primary status at all stages in the life of the community of believers. These documents act in this manner not only because they came first, but because everything that follows is built on them.[31]

Still we are left with the question, How do the Scriptures become constitutional for us today? Here we appeal to the idea of interpretative framework. The Bible is foundational for believers in every generation in that it provides the interpretive framework for the Christian community.

Scripture mediates to each generation a set of categories that define and facilitate entrance into the faith community. The Bible narrates the story of God's work in the world, which begins at creation and climaxes in the future eschaton. The central purpose of this story is to be the Spirit's instrumentality in bringing sinful humans to change direction. This change occurs as they reinterpret their own life narratives in terms of the categories of that story and to link their personal stories with the story of God through connection with the story of the people of God. As we proclaim the "old, old story," the Holy Spirit calls its hearers into the family of God and assists them in viewing all of life from the perspective of that story.

This interpretive framework not only establishes the identity of the community, it also preserves it.[32] The categories Scripture medi-

---

30. Fiorenza, "The Crisis of Scriptural Authority," 363.

31. See, John Howard Yoder, "The Use of the Bible in Theology," in *The Use of the Bible in Theology*, ed. Robert K. Johnston (Atlanta: John Knox, 1985), 103-20.

32. Kelsey, *The Uses of Scripture in Recent Theology*, 89.

ates to us provide the paradigm for life within the believing community. Through Scripture the Spirit shapes our identity as the community of Christ and as individual members of that community. Within the common life of the church the Holy Spirit uses the Bible, in the words of David Kelsey, "to nurture and reform the self-identity both of the community and of the individual persons who comprise it."[33] Hence, this book is the bearer of a life-changing message, the good news of available power for newness of life. It is given to us by God in order that our hearts may be open to receive the gift of the Spirit's energizing presence.

To this end, the Spirit speaking through the Bible orients our present both on the basis of the past and in accordance with a vision of the future. The past orientation transposes the contemporary hearer of the biblical narrative back to those primal events that originally constituted the community of God. For the ancient Hebrews, the Exodus was the central primal event. For the church the life, passion, and resurrection of Jesus and the subsequent sending of the Holy Spirit are constitutive. But the goal of the narrative does not lie simply in recounting the story. Rather, through the retelling of the narrative, the Spirit recreates the past within the present life of the community. In so doing the texts provide paradigms and categories—an interpretive framework—by means of which the community under the direction of the Spirit can come to understand and respond to the challenges of life in the present.[34]

William Herzog II summarizes the integration of past and present in this manner:

> The living Word lures us into the world of the patriarchs and prophets or the times of the apostles and disciples not to leave us with their solutions but to model the perpetual task of the people of God who were called to interrogate their traditions and texts in the light of the living presence and activity of God so that we might catch a glimpse of *how* they entered faithfully into the creative work given to them. Seen in this light, Scripture reveals the task to which we are called, the fulfillment of which requires our creative participation.[35]

33. Ibid., 214.

34. For a somewhat similar idea, see James Barr, *The Scope and Authority of the Bible* (Philadelphia: Westminster, 1980), 126-27.

35. William R. Herzog II, "Interpretation as Discovery and Creation: Sociological Dimensions of Biblical Hermeneutics," *American Baptist Quarterly* 2/2 (June 1983): 116.

In addition to constructing our present from the past, the Spirit speaking through the biblical story mediates a future orientation. The Bible declares God's intention for the world. It presents a vision of an ideal order in which human beings live in harmony with each other, with God, and with all creation. His generalization may be to sweeping, but James Barr is surely moving in the right direction when he notes,

> Narratives are not necessarily written because of a primary interest in the past. They can be written to provide pictures of the promises of God which will come to pass in the future. Even if their literal purport concerns the past, their theological function and purpose may be directed towards the future.[36]

Like the orientation to the past, the future direction of the biblical materials seeks to affect our present existence. The Spirit uses the biblical vision to spur us to view our situation in the light of God's future and to open ourselves and our present to the power of that future already at work among us and in our world.

The illumining work of the Spirit speaking through the Scriptures always occurs within a specific historical-cultural context. His activity during the biblical era, which brought about the formation of the canon, occurred within the changing contexts of the ancient Hebrew people and the early church. In the same way the Spirit's illumination in the life of the church occurs within the various contexts in which the community of Christ lives.

The acknowledgment that the Spirit's illuminating activity occurs within the changing historical-cultural context of the people of God heightens our appreciation for the theological importance of cultural context in the hermeneutical task. We seek to listen to the voice of the Spirit through Scripture, who speaks to us in the thought-forms, categories, and conditions of the world in which we live.

The Bible and Revelation

The Bible is a vehicle the Spirit uses in orienting our present on the basis of the past and in accordance with a vision of the future.

---

36. Barr, *The Scope and Authority of the Bible*, 36.

With this conclusion, however, we have not yet pierced to the heart of the church's affirmation concerning Scripture. The people of God have always confessed that the Bible itself is somehow connected with revelation and consequently in some sense is the actual Word of God. Our bibliology, therefore, must also set forth our understanding of the relationship between Scripture and God's self-disclosure.

The Concept of Revelation

The beginning point in this effort lies in what we have established thus far concerning the Bible as the Spirit's book. Scripture is ultimately a function of the Spirit. It finds both its source and its abiding importance in the activity of the one who breathes it (2 Tim. 3:16), that is, who breathes life into the community through the message proclaimed in its pages. The Spirit's central role in the formation of Scripture and in the application of the biblical message in the life of the faith community suggests that pneumatology is the bridge between the revelation and the Bible as the instrument in our coming to know God. We must develop the relationship between revelation and Spirit-breathed Scripture.

Barth's proposal. Karl Barth pioneered a pneumatic doctrine of Scripture.[37] At the heart of the lasting vitality of his position are two theses Barth developed in the opening volume of his *Church Dogmatics*.[38] In the first, the Swiss theologian set forth a threefold conception of revelation. Revelation is primarily the Word of God disclosed, which is essentially Jesus the Christ, the Word incarnate. Secondarily, revelation is the Bible as "the word of God written." In a tertiary manner revelation is human proclamation of the word of God.

In his second thesis, Barth posited an intimate relationship among the three aspects of revelation. The word written and the word proclaimed are revelation in a dependent manner, namely, in so far as

37. Bernard Ramm has offered a service in raising Barth's banner within evangelicalism. See, for example, his *After Fundamentalism: The Future of Evangelical Theology* (San Francisco: Harper and Row, 1983).
38. Karl Barth, *Church Dogmatics*, second edition, trans. G. W. Bromiley (Edinburgh: T. & T. Clark, 1975), I/1:88-124.

they are witnesses to God's self-disclosure. In short, for Barth the revelatory nature of the Bible is dependent on its function as a witness to the revelation of God in Jesus Christ.

Although we may resist his inordinate emphasis on the event character of revelation, Barth was surely correct in his delineation of the relationship between Scripture and Christ. As G. C. Berkouwer asserted, "Every word about the God-breathed character of Scripture is meaningless if Holy Scripture is not understood as the witness concerning Christ."[39]

Revelation in the Bible. The dependent relationship between the inscripturated word and the Word incarnate comes into focus through the biblical concept of revelation. In Scripture, the term "revelation" occurs primarily in the verb form and generally refers to the act of uncovering or unveiling what is hidden.[40] Only secondarily does it mean what is uncovered in the act—the static deposit produced by the revelatory action. Consequently, the revelation of God is the divine act of self-disclosure which reveals ultimate truth, namely, the triune God himself.

Divine revelation, therefore, can be nothing less than God disclosing himself to us. In this sense, God's revelation is the theological antidote to his hiddenness. Because of human depravity God is veiled to us, and we can do nothing to pierce that veil. God remains hidden unless and until he takes the initiative in disclosing himself to us. But this is precisely what occurs in the act of revelation!

Revelation is God disclosing himself and not merely cognitive truths or propositional statements. At the same time, however, God's revelation is connected to statements about God. Such assertions serve to aid in the epistemological process of coming to know God, in that we learn of God in part by hearing about who he is and what he is like. Likewise, statements about God arise as the natural outworking of our coming to know him, as we reflect on the experience of knowing God and on the one who has encountered us.

---

39. G. C. Berkouwer, *Holy Scripture*, trans. and ed. Jack B. Rogers (Grand Rapids: Eerdmans, 1975), 166.

40. Dewey M. Beegle, *Scripture, Tradition and Infallibility* (Grand Rapids: Eerdmans, 1973), 19-21.

The fullness of the divine self-disclosure lies in the future—at the eschaton. This assertion follows from the declaration that history is God's chosen medium of revelation, for only at the eschaton is the meaning of history ultimately disclosed. At that time, God's *de jure* reign will also be *de facto*. Then it will be plainly evident how all of history takes its meaning from the consummation of the reign of God, that is, from the establishment of the eschatological community of God.

Despite its eschatological orientation, revelation is nevertheless a present reality. The eschatological unveiling of God has appeared proleptically in history. Central to the Christian faith is the confession that the focal point of this revelation is Jesus of Nazareth, "the word made flesh." In relationship to Jesus and because of him all history has revelatory significance, in so far as it derives its meaning from this historical life. When understood from the perspective of the divine self-disclosure in Jesus, the events of history also provide insight into the nature of the God revealed in Christ.

Many theologians agree that God's historical revelation is mediated to us through act plus interpretation.[41] This understanding implies that the focus of divine revelation is not what we may call "brute historical facts" (*historie*), but rather "interpreted facts" (*geschichte*). Revelatory does not come through an unexplained occurrence but the interpreted event and its place in the flow of history. We encounter God through the interpreted story as it is retold and applied to life. In this encounter the Spirit is present, for he empowers the interpreted story for the sake of our salvation.

This connection suggests that we may approach the concept of revelation by appeal to the idea of "paradigmatic events."[42] A paradigmatic event is an occurrence that captures the imagination of a community. It shapes and forms the community's way of looking at

---

41. See, for example, John Goldingay, *Approaches to Old Testament Interpretation* (Downers Grove, Ill.: InterVarsity, 1981), 74-77. See also, James I. Packer, *"Fundamentalism" and the Word of God* (Grand Rapids: Eerdmans, 1958), 92; George Eldon Ladd, "Revelation, History, and the Bible," *Christianity Today* 1/25 (September 30, 1957): 7; Daniel B. Stevick, *Beyond Fundamentalism* (Richmond, Va.: John Knox), 104-6. For the neoorthodox position, see John Baillie, *The Idea of Revelation in Recent Thought* (New York: Columbia University Press, 1956), 62-65.

42. See, for example, Richard J. Coleman, *Issues of Theological Conflict* (Grand Rapids: Eerdmans, 1980), 109-10.

the whole of reality and the community's understanding of its experience of reality. For this reason, the community preserves the memory of the event, it reinterprets the occurrence in the light of the subsequent historical situations in which the community finds itself, and it discovers in the happening the source of an ongoing hope for the future. In this way paradigmatic events become a continual source of revelation. Each succeeding generation understands itself in terms of the experiences of the past history of the community.

Revelation and Scripture. As Christians, we acknowledge that the human words of the Bible are God's Word to us. Yet how this is the case is complex. We cannot simply equate the revelation of God with the Bible.[43] Donald Bloesch confirmed the historical precedence for such a differentiation: "A careful examination of early Protestant orthodoxy as well as of Puritanism and Pietism reveals that the distinction between the word of God and the words of the Bible was quite common."[44] More importantly, this distinction arises from the Bible itself.

New Testament authors preclude us from making a simple one-to-one correspondence between the words of Scripture and the word of God. They used the phrase "the word of God" in a more complicated fashion. The Baptist scholar Paul Rainbow concluded from his textual study[45] that these writers never used the phrase "the word of God" to refer to the Jewish Scriptures. Rather, they reserved the term for messages actually spoken by God to, or through, prophets and which center above all on the person and work of Jesus. Consequently, according to the New Testament community, "the word of God" is the Holy Spirit announcing the good news about Jesus, which word the church speaks in the Spirit's power and by the Spirit's authority.

How does Scripture fit into this picture? Rainbow adds that the Bible is a trustworthy record of God's speaking in the past. Therefore,

---

43. The tendency to make such an equation has been criticized by William J. Abraham, *The Divine Inspiration of Holy Scripture* (Oxford: Oxford, 1981).

44. Donald G. Bloesch, *The Future of Evangelical Christianity* (Garden City, N.Y.: Doubleday, 1983), 118.

45. Paul Rainbow, "On Hearing the Word of God," unpublished convocation address, North American Baptist Seminary, 1990.

it provides "an absolutely sure criterion by which we can test the church's proclamation of the word of God in the present."[46]

As Rainbow's thesis suggests, in an important sense the "word of God"—and hence revelation—precedes Scripture. This is obviously true historically, for the divine initiation of communication from God to humankind occurred before the inscripturation process. In addition, revelation carries logical priority, for Scripture presupposes the reality of revelation.[47] As Bloesch observed, "The Bible is a divinely appointed channel, a mirror, or a visible sign of revelation."[48]

In another sense, however, revelation and Scripture are interrelated. The divine self-disclosure in the past did not occur at a single point of history, which was then followed by its inscripturation. Rather, revelation arose together with the process of the development of canonical Scripture. In part God's revelatory work came in and through the formation of Scripture. Under the guiding hand of the Spirit the community of faith sought to understand the ongoing work of God in the world in the light of the earlier divine self-disclosure and the oral and written traditions that the earlier events had called forth.

For example, the early Christians groped with the significance for the heritage of monotheism posed by their foundational confession of Jesus' lordship and the undeniable experience of the Spirit's presence among them. The final outworking was the doctrine of the Trinity.

God's revelatory work included as well the community's attempts to determine the implications of the divine self-disclosure for life. God had entered into covenant with them, and because he is a holy God they were to be holy as well. The biblical documents reflect the presence of a process by which the ancient people of God, under the guidance of the Spirit, came to discover the practical implications of

---

46. Ibid., 14.

47. Barr, *The Scope and Authority of the Bible*, 16; Beegle, *Scripture, Tradition and Infallibility*, 307-308.

48. Bloesch, *The Future of Evangelical Christianity*, 118. Bloesch claims that this was the position of the church from the patristic era through the Reformation.

the divine holiness for their own vocation as God's covenant partners.

God's ultimate self-disclosure, however, lies yet in the future. Consequently, even after the closing of the canon the church participates in the ongoing challenge of exploring the outworking for faith and life of our calling as the community of Christ. Yet, intervening events have introduced one crucial difference. We now seek to be the faithful people of God with completed canon in hand. We do not share in the task of Scripture formation. Rather, we seek to be the contemporary expression of the one people of God whose identity and existence are bound to the God who has disclosed himself in history and consequently are informed by the Bible.

The Bible as Revelation

On the basis of this understanding of revelation, we may speak of the Spirit-illumined Bible as "the revelation of God." The Bible is God's Word to us. The connection between Scripture and revelation is threefold.

The Bible as derivative revelation. Primarily, the Bible is revelation in a derivative sense. It is the witness to the historical self-disclosure of God and the record of that revelation. It testifies that God has indeed revealed himself. God has, as it were, lifted the veil. No longer is God hidden; he now stands for all time as the Revealed One.

God has revealed himself and his intentions for creation in the proleptic historical events as the biblical authors prophetically interpreted them and applied them to life. The Bible is the written testimony to, and the deposit of this divine self-disclosure. In the Bible we read the historical events and their interpretation, for the Scriptures faithfully transmit interpreted salvation history to the contemporary reader.

In this sense, the Bible is divine truth. In fact, there is no other book to which we can go in order to learn about God's action in history in disclosing himself to humankind. There is no other valid message about God, but the biblical message. In this sense, the Bible is God's word to us.

The Bible as functional revelation. The Bible is also revelation in a functional sense: It is revelatory. Scripture points beyond itself, directing the reader's attention to the revealed God and informing the reader as to how God can be known. In fact, the message of the Bible is the Spirit's instrumentality in authoring in us salvation and sanctification. As the Spirit illumines our hearts to understand and respond to the scriptural texts which he brought into existence, these human words—which always remain objectively the word of God—become the word of God in our subjective experience.

Consequently, we do not idolize the Bible as an end in itself.[49] With the Psalmist we confess, "Your word is a lamp to my feet and a light for my path" (Ps. 119:105). As our spiritual lamp, it is the means to see the pathway.[50] We honor the Bible as the Spirit-inspired and Spirit-illumined means to knowing God and walking with our Lord. There is no other way of learning about the divine reality except through an encounter with the living God. This encounter is facilitated by the biblical message. In this sense, the Bible is God's word to us.

Bible as mediate revelation. Finally, the Bible is revelation in the sense of an intermediator. It mediates to us the proper understanding of God's essence. It is God's word to us insofar as it is the word about God.

Ultimately, the topic of Scripture is the triune God. His essence is portrayed therein as love, and he is described in its pages as the Savior God. The Bible presents the outworking of God's essence through the story of God's activity in history in bringing about salvation. As the Spirit illumines our hearts to grasp the biblical message, we come to understand God as our loving Savior. As it mediates this awareness to us, the Bible is God's revelation. In fact, there is no other source to which we can turn in order to read about the character of God. In this sense, the Bible is God's word to humankind.

---

49. The charge of idolizing the Bible dies hard. It was repeated as late as 1982. See Sallie McFague, *Metaphorical Theology* (Philadelphia: Fortress, 1982), 4.

50. See, Justo Gonzales, *Manana: Christian Theology from a Hispanic Perspective* (Nashville: Abingdon, 1990), 86.

Biblical Authority

As the book of the Spirit the Bible is his instrumentality. Through it the Spirit speaks to us, and thereby he leads us to know God himself. For this reason, Christians honor the Bible as their authority. What is the basis for the affirmation that the Bible is our authority? And to what extent is Scripture authoritative for our life as the community of believers?

The Trustworthiness of Scripture

Many Christians recognize a close connection between the authority of the Bible and its veracity. Consequently, some theologians construct the affirmation of biblical authority on the foundation of the Bible's total trustworthiness. They build this, in turn, from the doctrine of inspiration. The Spirit's inspiring activity leads to "infallible" and "inerrant" documents, they argue, which therefore are trustworthy and authoritative. Further, the Bible is authoritative in each of its parts because the Spirit's inspiration extends to all aspects of Scripture. It is both "verbal" and "plenary." We must look at these four great words more closely, before drawing our conclusions concerning the veracity of Scripture.

Verbal, plenary inspiration. The words *verbal* and *plenary* capsulize the traditional understanding of the extent of inspiration.

"Plenary inspiration" means that the Holy Spirit's activity in superintending the writing of Scripture extends to the entire Bible. All that is found within the canon is Scripture, the product of the oversight of the Holy Spirit.

Proponents find the concept of plenary inspiration in the Bible itself: *All* Scripture is God-breathed, the biblical author declared (2 Tim. 3:16). Although the apostle had only our Old Testament in view when he penned these words, advocates assert that the principle may be extended to the New Testament as well.

"Verbal inspiration" is more difficult to define. Basically this term declares that the activity of the Holy Spirit extends to the very words of Scripture. We must be careful, however, not to equate the idea with the theory of divine dictation. Rather than asserting that God dictated every word, we ought to understand verbal inspiration as only claiming that the Spirit superintended the process of word selection and word order to the extent that they are capable of communicating the intended meaning of the text. Insofar as words and syntax are the primary carriers of meaning, the concept of verbal inspiration emphasizes divine involvement in the writing of Scripture so that the words employed in the documents convey God's intended message.

An infallible, inerrant Bible. Some theologians employ the terms "infallible" and "inerrant" to describe the veracity of the Bible that arises from its inspiration by the Spirit.

Simply stated, the declaration, "the Bible is infallible," means that these writings are "not liable to deceive." Because the Spirit moved in the lives of the authors, the product can be trusted. The writers do not intend to lead their readers astray.

In contrast to infallibility, the word *inerrant* has been a topic of debate during the last several decades. At the height of the discussion, theologians gravitated to three basic positions. These may be termed the "strict inerrantist," the "limited inerrantist," and the "non-inerrantist" views.[51] To these three we would offer a fourth.

(1) "Full" or "strict" inerrantists claim that the Bible is without error whenever it speaks to any subject—history, geography, astronomy, measurement, science—even when the details included are incidental to the central intent of the text. Such precision, they add, can only be predicated of the original manuscripts of the Bible[52] and not the versions and translations we possess. Further, they approach the matter of alleged problems in the Bible deductively. Earlier in his career Clark Pinnock spoke for the whole: "In our approach to biblical difficulties then we do *not* give equal weight to the phenomena

---

51. This delineation is similar to that in Clark H. Pinnock, "Evangelicals and Inerrancy: The Current Debate," *Theology Today* 35/1 (April 1978): 66-67. Other observers of the debate enumerate a greater number of positions. See, Robert M. Price, "Inerrant the Wind: The Troubled House of North American Evangelicals," *The Evangelical Quarterly* 55/3 (July 1983):129-44. Dockery distinguishes nine positions. David S. Dockery, "Variations on Inerrancy," *SBC Today* (May 1986): 10-11.

52. See, for example, Paul D. Feinberg, "The Meaning of Inerrancy," in *Inerrancy*, ed. Norman L. Geisler (Grand Rapids: Zondervan, 1979), 296.

and to the doctrine of inspiration."[53] He then explained, "Because of our confidence in Jesus Christ, and in the light of the doctrine of inspiration which he taught, we accept the high doctrine of the inerrancy of Scripture *before* we are able to adjust all the phenomena of Scripture to it."[54]

Because the Scriptures are inerrant, proponents claim that ultimately there can be no actual discrepancies in the biblical texts, only apparent problems. In fact, one demonstrable, actual error could call into question the entire strict inerrantist doctrine of biblical authority.[55]

Strict inerrantists derive inerrancy primarily from the teachings of the Bible or from inferences drawn from them, rather than from the phenomena of the Bible. Nevertheless, they generally seek to correlate the doctrine with the data of the texts.[56] This has led some of them to engage in harmonizations of seemingly varying accounts of historical events or to qualify what the term inerrancy guarantees.

(2) "Moderate," "partial," or "limited" inerrantists assert that the Bible is without error whenever it speaks concerning matters of faith and practice. They leave open the possibility that Scripture may contain minor errors in topics lying outside the area of its major purpose—salvation—or in details incidental to the central intent of a text. Hence, they reject the emphasis on perfect historical and scientific accuracy they find in the strict inerrantist position. Instead, they prefer to view inerrancy in terms of "fidelity to the truth that God intends to teach us in and through the biblical text."[57]

Because its trustworthiness lies in its central meaning, which may be correctly reflected by copies or even translations which contain errors, moderates do not limit inerrancy to the original manuscripts.

---

53. Clark Pinnock, "Limited Inerrancy: A Critical Appraisal and Constructive Alternative," in *God's Inerrant Word: An International Symposium on the Trustworthiness of Scripture*, ed. John W. Montgomery (Minneapolis: Bethany, 1974), 151.

54. Ibid., 153.

55. Alexander A. Hodge and Benjamin B. Warfield, "Inspiration," *Presbyterian Review* 2 (1881):245.

56. This approach is stated matter-of-factly by Millard J. Erickson, "Problem Areas Related to Biblical Inerrancy," in *The Proceedings of the Conference on Biblical Inerrancy 1987*, 176.

57. Donald Bloesch, "In Defense of Biblical Authority," *Reformed Journal* 34/9 (Sep. 1984): 29-30.

The crucial question for them is always the central intent of a text and its significance for faith and Christian living.

Limited inerrantists tend to construct their doctrine of Scripture inductively, that is, based on the texts themselves and on an awareness of the presence in the Scriptures of possible problems.[58] In contrast to many strict inerrantists, they are not committed to the task of harmonizing or eliminating all apparent problems.

(3) Moderate inerrantists pose the issue of biblical reliability in accordance with the question, "In what areas?" And they answer: "in religion and ethics." Advocates of a third position, in contrast, raise the matter of biblical truth and reliability by asking, "For what purpose?" They are concerned, in other words, with the intention of the biblical documents.[59] Proponents of this alternative reject the term "inerrancy" as simply inadequate.

Proponents of this position prefer the word *infallible* as a description of biblical authority. The Bible is infallible, in that it makes no false or misleading statements on any matter of faith and practice,[60] or in the sense that it is "entirely trustworthy."[61] This infallibility is not limited to the original manuscripts but extends as well to translations. Despite the errors they encompass, these documents are likewise able to fulfill God's intention for Scripture.

Advocates of the infallibility position suggest that biblical authority cannot be demonstrated by reasoned arguments. Rather, it is accepted by faith through the illumination of the Spirit.[62] The Scriptures do not claim to be inerrant, they argue. In fact, they conclude that inerrancy is a recent innovation of "scholastic" theologians and not the historic position of the church.

As the academic debate unfolded, the distance separating the discussion partners began to narrow. Inerrantists found themselves qualifying and nuancing their understanding of what it means to con-

---

58. For an early sounding of this note, see Robert H. Mounce, "Clues to Understanding Biblical Accuracy," *Eternity* 17 (June, 1966): 16-18.

59. R. T. France, "Evangelical Disagreements about the Bible," *Churchman* 96/3 (1982): 232.

60. Stephen T. Davis, *The Debate about the Bible* (Philadelphia: Westminster, 1977), 23.

61. I. Howard Marshall, *Biblical Inspiration* (Grand Rapids: Eerdmans, 1982), 72.

62. In the words of one proponent, "It can only be believed, experienced, known through one's acceptance of the gospel of Christ." Harry R. Boer, *Above the Battle?* (Grand Rapids: Eerdmans, 1975), 87.

fess the total veracity of the Bible. At the same time, those who questioned the validity of that term found themselves confronted with the need to affirm in no uncertain terms their allegiance to the Bible and their full confidence in the Scriptures.[63] As I. Howard Marshall, who favors the term "infallibility," concluded from his reading of the Chicago Statement penned by the International Council on Biblical Inerrancy,

> If inerrantists are standing for the truth of Scripture, understood in scriptural terms, then their position is no different in principle from that of the other school of evangelical Christians who also affirm the entire trustworthiness of Scripture.[64]

(4) The debate about biblical inerrancy was not merely an exercise in semantics. Rather, it has yielded several important conclusions, which form a fourth position to which some scholars are now gravitating.

First, in developing our conception of biblical inerrancy, we must see the place of both deductive and inductive reasoning. The deductive method moves from theological premises to conclusions concerning the Bible: Because God cannot lie and because Scripture is inspired by God, the Bible must be wholly true. This syllogism may be valid in establishing inerrancy, but it cannot define the concept.

We must determine the meaning of inerrancy inductively, not deductively. To do so, we must begin with the phenomena of the biblical texts themselves, including the apparent difficulties present in the documents.[65] The inductive method yields the conclusion that adequacy for the purpose of the author is of paramount significance for any useful concept of inerrancy. The biblical writers were not concerned with the modern preoccupation with precision of detail. The authors of the documents expressed God's truth in the concepts and understandings of the period in which they wrote. They likewise used phenomenological language and described events from the viewpoint of the observer and not necessarily in keeping with the modern scientific understanding of truth. Viewed from this perspec-

---

63. E.g., Pinnock, *The Scripture Principle*, 225.
64. Marshall, *Biblical Inspiration*, 71.
65. See Mounce, "Clues to Understanding Biblical Accuracy," 17.

tive, inerrancy refers to the statements of the Bible within their own context. These contexts vary, for they include genre—poetry, prophecy, narrative, wisdom sayings, etc. We approach each text with the assumption of its truthfulness, looking to its context and genre to understand how it truthfully functions in its own setting.

Second, we must understand inerrancy in the light of the Bible's own stated purpose. After declaring that Scripture is God breathed and therefore profitable, the author of 2 Timothy 3:16 discloses the purpose for which the Bible has been given. It instructs unto salvation and is profitable for teaching, reproof, correction, and training in righteousness (see also Rom. 15:4; 1 Cor. 10:6,11). When taken as a whole the Bible intends to narrate the story of the coming of the Messiah so that lost, sinful humans might have life through him (Luke 24:25-27, 44; John 20:30-31; Acts 3:21-24; 10:43; 28:23-25). The Biblical writers include whatever details they deem necessary to accomplish this purpose.

Likewise we must understand inerrancy according to the Bible's own concept of what constitutes error. Most generally the biblical writers spoke of error as mistaken theological conceptions and moral wrong-doing (Ps. 95:10; Jas. 5:20), rather than in the modern sense of precision in factual details. The purpose of the Bible is to provide guidance so that we might avoid moral and theological error, as well as think and live properly. In accordance with this, John cautioned against the spirit of error, which for him was the refusal to give heed to true apostolic direction (1 John 4:6).

Third, however important inerrancy may appear to be, a person need not affirm that the Bible is without error in all areas in order to acknowledge it as authoritative. Indeed, most persons find translations of the Scriptures, which are definitely not inerrant, to be authoritative and profitable. Even the author of 2 Timothy 3:16 was probably not referring to the Hebrew original of the Old Testament but rather to the Greek Septuagint (the Bible of the people) when he declared all Scripture to be "God-breathed."

With these considerations in view, we conclude that properly understood, "inerrancy" can be a valuable term. It provides a vehicle for expressing our high regard for the Bible as the Spirit's instrumentality. As Clark Pinnock declared, the term is a reminder of the demand to take "the whole of Scripture seriously as the word of God."[66] Hence, inerrancy is a theological affirmation of the Bible as totally trustworthy. It demands that we approach the text humbly, open to being taught by the Spirit as to how we can be God's people.

Biblical authority and the authority of the Spirit. In the final analysis, no theory about the Bible itself accounts for its trustworthiness and hence its authority. Instead, to understand the authoritative function of the Bible, we must return to the pneumatological context in which all aspects of our discussion concerning Scripture properly lie.

We noted above that the Bible presupposes revelation. This discovery indicates that at least from our perspective Scripture is the servant of revelation.[67] In the same manner, as the Spirit's instrumentality it is servant to the work of the Spirit. Consequently, the Spirit-energized revelatory message presented through Scripture takes primacy over the vehicle by means of which it is transmitted. Whatever authority the Bible carries as a trustworthy book, it derives from the trustworthiness of the divine revelation it discloses and ultimately from the Spirit who infallibly speaks through it.

In declaring the trustworthiness of the Bible, therefore, we must keep in mind that it is ultimately not the book itself which we are affirming. Rather, we are confessing our faith in the Spirit who speaks his revelatory message to us through the pages of Scripture. In declaring its infallibility and inerrancy, we are actually affirming the trustworthiness of the Spirit whose vehicle the Bible is.[68]

The Extent of Biblical Authority

The Bible is authoritative because it is the trustworthy instrumentality of the Spirit. It is the bearer of the Word of God disclosing revelation to the reader. To what extent is Scripture our authority?

Our sole authority. An unequivocal affirmation of biblical authority follows logically from what we said concerning the revelatory significance of the Bible. Because this book is revelation in the

---

66. Pinnock, "The Inerrancy Debate," *Theology News and Notes* (special issue, 1976): 12.
67. This theme is developed in Berkouwer, *Holy Scripture*, 195-212.
68. See, for example, Bloesch, "In Defense of Biblical Authority," 30.

threefold sense described earlier, the Spirit speaking through its pages is our sole authority. Only the Bible is so intimately related to the historical revelation of God so as itself to be termed "revelation." Only the Bible constitutes the written record of the revelatory historical occurrences, together with the prophetic interpretation and application of these events. Only the Bible directs our attention to God in Christ, thereby bringing us face-to-face with the loving, Savior God.

As John Baillie declared, "The Scriptures are holy because they are the vehicle through which the Gospel is communicated to us."[69]

Our authority in all of life. Yet in making these lofty assertions about the Bible we risk saying too little. We cannot stop short of an unequivocal affirmation that biblical authority encompasses every dimension of our lives as believers.

Traditionally, Baptists and certain other traditions have declared that the Bible is our authority for faith and practice.[70] Some thinkers have interpreted this dictum narrowly, suggesting that it constitutes a limitation on the scope of biblical authority. Such an interpretation, however, fails to reflect the implication, if not the intent, of the traditional maxim.

The Bible's authoritative status radiates outward from any narrow conception of "faith and practice," until it encompasses all of life. This phenomenon is a function of the all-encompassing nature of human religious convictions. Try as we will, we cannot successfully marginalize our religious orientation to the fringes of life. Such commitments ultimately affect all areas of personal and corporate existence. This means, however, that whatever is determina-

---

69. Baillie, *Idea of Revelation in Recent Thought*, 117.

70. The early English Baptists expressed their understanding in chapter 1 ("Of the Holy Scriptures") of the London Confession (1677): "The Holy Scripture is the only sufficient, certain, and infallible (a) rule of all saving Knowledge, Faith, and Obedience;" reprinted in *Baptist Life and Thought: 1600-1980*, ed. William H. Brackney (Valley Forge, Pa.: Judson, 1983), 64. Two hundred thirty year later, in responding to the establishment of the Federal Council of Churches, a Baptist writer used the typical terminology about the authority of the Bible: "the New Testament ONLY is our authoritative and absolute rule of faith and practice." James W. Willmarth, "The Federal Council, Part 1," *Watchman* 90 (December 17, 1908): 20, reprinted in *Baptist Life and Thought*, 344.

tive of these convictions will exercise ultimate authority over our entire being.

Consequently, to confess that the Bible is authoritative for "faith and practice" means that Scripture must saturate all of life. Placing ourselves under the teaching of the Bible commits us to confessing a biblical world view. A biblically-informed outlook, in turn, will eventually permeate our attitudes and actions in every facet of life.

The Bible may not intend to function as the kind of precise authority on the various branches of modern learning that some believers want to maintain. Nevertheless, in a more profound sense its authority extends to every dimension of the Christian's outlook. H. N. Ridderbos articulates the point well:

> Scripture is not concerned only with persons' *religious* needs in a pietistic or existentialistic sense of that word. On the contrary, its purpose and authority is that it teaches us to understand everything *sub specie Dei*—humanity, the world, nature, history, their origin and their destination, their past and their future. Therefore the Bible is not only the book of conversion, but also the book of history and the book of creation. But it is the book of history of salvation; and it is this point of view that represents and defines the authority of Scripture.[71]

Our acknowledgment that the Bible is authoritative in faith and practice demands, therefore, that we apply to every area of life what the Spirit is speaking through the Scriptures. Jesus himself provided the foundation for this conclusion. He admonished his hearers to put into practice his sayings (Matt. 7:24-27), an admonition echoed by James' entreatment that we be "doers" and not only "hearers" of the word (James 1:22-25).

This takes us back to our foundational point. Our commitment to the Bible is crucial, for Scripture forms the foundation for our Christian ethos. At the heart of the community of faith lies a vision that arises out of our common experience with the Lord. As a result, the Bible is significant. Scripture provides the categories by means of

---

71. H. N. Ridderbos, "The Inspiration and Authority of Holy Scripture," in *The Authoritative Word*, 186.

which we understand ourselves and organize the stories of our lives. In addition, it determines what constitutes presence within the community of the faithful followers of the God who is revealed in Jesus Christ. In short, from the message of the Bible we gain our identity as the people of God. And through Scripture we learn what it means to be the community of faith in the world.

15 The Dynamic of Conversion

Jesus answered, "I tell you the truth, unless a man is born of water and the Spirit, he cannot enter the kingdom of God. Flesh gives birth to flesh, but the Spirit gives birth to spirit." (John 3:5-6)

Outline

Incorporation into a new community
Conversion and Church Initiation Rites
Historical and contemporary positions
The New Testament teaching
Conversion as faith expressed through baptism

The Holy Spirit, the Third Person of the Trinity, completes the program of the one God. As the Creator Spirit, he is the author of life and the facilitator of new life, bringing to fruition God's salvation in the world. God's activity encompasses all creation, but humankind is its focus. The Spirit applies Christ's work to humans, effecting our union with the Lord and with each other in Christ's community.

The Spirit's special saving activity in an individual begins with conversion. We may define conversion as that life-changing encounter with the triune God which inaugurates a radical break with our old, fallen existence and a new life in fellowship with God. This transforming encounter with God lies at the foundation of our Christian experience. Despite its centrality to our faith, however, conversion remains a mystery. Exactly how the "great transaction" transpires—how God brings us to know him—is beyond our comprehension. Nevertheless, as Christians we desire to understand more fully this dynamic: What exactly inaugurates the Christian walk? What occurs in the wonderful encounter which lies at the basis of our faith?

In this chapter we explore our initiation into the life of faith. To this end, we view three aspects comprising one dynamic of conversion: our personal response to the gospel, the divine working which underlies that response, and the participation of the faith community in this event.

The Individual Aspect of Conversion

According to Mark's Gospel, Jesus called his hearers to respond individually to his announcement of the nearness of the divine reign: "After John was put in prison, Jesus went into Galilee, proclaiming the good news of God. 'The time has come,' he said. 'The kingdom of God is near. Repent and believe the good news!'" (Mark 1:14-15).

In this short admonition, our Lord set forth what constitutes the essential personal response to the divine message—repentance and faith—which therefore mark the individual dimension of the encounter with God.

Repentance

Repentance lies at the heart of the gospel. Repentance was central to the proclamation of John the Baptist (Matt. 3:5-12; Luke 3:7-14), Jesus (Matt. 4:17; 11:20-21; Luke 5:32; 13:3-5; 15:7,10; 16:30; 24:45-47), and the early church (Acts 2:38; 3:19; 8:22; 17:30; 26:19-20). Repentance was likewise a focal topic of apostolic teaching (Rom. 2:4; 2 Peter 3:9).

The Old Testament provided the background for the call to repentance sounded by Jesus and the early Christians. Over one thousand times[1] the ancient writers (especially the prophets) made theological use of the Hebrew word *shub*, which means "turn" or "return."[2] In such contexts, it refers either to the turning away from evil to God in repentance or the turning from God to evil in apostasy. In the former instances, the term carries volitional overtones, bearing the ideas of turning around, being converted, and returning to the one true God with a resulting change in behavior.[3] The related Hebrew word, *naham*, which reflects the idea of displaying emotion,[4] suggests the radical, heartfelt nature of repentance (Job 42:6).

The New Testament understanding of repentance centers on two Greek terms, *epistrepho* and *metanoeo*. Although the two are sometimes used interchangeably (compare Acts 3:19 and 26:20), scholars also detect nuanced differences between them. *Metanoeo* emphasizes the negative impulse of turning away from sin.[5] *Estrepho* is broader, sometimes including the idea of faith and hence referring to

---

1. For this conclusion, see the standard study of this Hebrew word. William Lee Holladay, *The Root "Subh" in the Old Testament* (Leiden: Brill, 1958), 6.

2. See V. P. Hamilton, "shub," in the *Theological Wordbook of the Old Testament* [TWOT], ed. R. Laird Harris, Gleason L. Archer, Jr., and Bruce K. Waltke (Chicago: Moody, 1980), 2:909-10.

3. F. Laubach, "epistrepho, *metamelomai,*" in "Conversion, Penitence, Repentance, Proselyte," *The New International Dictionary of New Testament Theology*, ed. Colin Brown (Grand Rapids: Zondervan, 1981), 1:353-57.

4. Marvin R. Wilson, "naham," in TWOT, 2:570-71.

the entire conversion process. In the words of Laubach, it means "a fundamentally new turning of the human will to God, a returning home from blindness and error to the Savior of all."[6]

Both *epistrepho* and *metanoeo* imply that repentance is a radical matter, a turning within the human heart (Luke 1:16-17; 2 Cor. 3:16-17). This is especially evident in the use of *metanoeo*. According to William D. Chamberlain this word refers primarily to the "springs of action" or "the source of our motives" and not to either the actions or the motives themselves.[7]

Metanoeo underwent an interesting development in meaning.[8] Etymologically the word arises from the verb *noeo* (to know) and the preposition *meta* (after). Thus, basically repentance means "to know after," that is, to have knowledge about something after it happens. However, the term also entails an expanded meaning. *Metanoeo* includes the change of opinion resulting from such knowledge. Indeed, as we come to know the effects of our actions, we often change our estimation concerning their correctness. Added as well is the emotional dimension, that is, regret. People who change their opinion often also regret the course of action previously pursued. They sense displeasure, even sorrow, for having acted as they did. Finally, *metanoeo* includes the idea of "resolve." Regret concerning a previous course of action readily leads to the desire to alter one's future conduct in response to the sorrow arising from the changed opinion.

Repentance, then, involves a total, radical alteration within the core of our personal being. It includes a mental change, as we gain a new attitude toward our actions, even toward our state of existence. It means admitting our spiritual poverty, as in the beatitude: "Blessed are those who know that they are spiritually poor" (Matt. 5:3). Repentance likewise entails an emotional change. We feel regret, sorrow, even hatred for our conduct and for our pathetic spiritual

---

5. See Walter Bauer, *A Greek-English Lexicon of the New Testament and Other Early Christian Literature* [BAGD], second edition, ed. William F. Arndt, F. Wilbur Gingrich, and Fredrick W. Danker (Chicago: University of Chicago Press, 1979), 512; Laubach, "estrepho, *metamelomai,*" NIDNTT, 353-57.

6. Laubach, "estrepho, *metamelomai,*" in NIDNTT, 355.

7. William D. Chamberlain, *The Meaning of Repentance* (Philadelphia: Westminster, 1943), 41.

8. On this see J. Goetzmann, "metanoia," in "Conversion, Penitence, Repentance, Proselyte," NIDNTT, 1:357-59.

situation. Paul reflected this emotion in an autobiographical note in his Epistle to the Romans: "For what I want to do I do not do, but what I hate I do" (Rom. 7:15). Repentance also marks a volitional change. Repentant persons desire to alter their future course of action. As Paul cried, "For what I do is not the good I want to do" (Rom. 7:19; see also Matt. 5:6).

Radical repentance is intricately related to conversion. Without a recognition of personal need we cannot receive the provision God has made in Christ. Although heartfelt repentance is necessary for conversion, alone it is insufficient. Our sense of sorrow for sin cannot make amends for the past; nor can our desire for change alter the future. Because we are under condemnation for sin and are held fast by sin's grasp, we stand in need of the atonement gained by Jesus and the indwelling power of the Spirit if we are to experience true liberation from the effects of our miserable situation. To repentance must be added faith.

Faith

Faith is the second aspect of the human response to the gospel. Jesus emphasized the importance of faith (John 6:35, 47). The early believers called their hearers to respond in faith to the gospel (Acts 6:43; 16:31). And faith was central to apostolic teaching. This is especially evident in Paul's theology with its focus on *sola fides*—justification by faith alone.

Since as early as the Reformation, theologians have generally viewed saving faith as encompassing three components—*notitia, assensus*, and *fiducia*.[9] These three form a progression. Faith begins with *notitia* (knowledge). This entails becoming aware of the actual content of God's promises contained in the gospel, including the historical narrative of Jesus' passion and resurrection. *Notitia* leads to *assensus* (assent), the intellect acknowledgment of the truth of the gospel message. Faith first comes to completion, however, in *fiducia* (trust). By an act of the will a person appropriates the intellectual knowledge gained (*notitia*) and acknowledged (*assensus*).

---

9. See *Fides*, in Richard A. Muller, *Dictionary of Latin and Greek Theological Terms* (Grand Rapids: Baker, 1985), 115-16.

These distinctions are more than mere scholastic distinctions. They provide a helpful schematization of the New Testament idea of faith. The biblical authors understand our response to the gospel in a manner that resembles *notitia, assensus,* and *fiducia.*

Paul declared that faith begins with hearing the gospel message (Rom. 10:12-17) which facilitates our obtaining knowledge of its contents (*notitia*). Then follows the intellectual act of assenting to truth claims contained in the gospel message (*assensus*). These two dimensions are evident in the repeated use of phrases such as "believe that" or "have faith that." To "believe that" entails an intellectual act, acknowledging certain statements as being true representations of specific aspects of reality.

According to the New Testament, in faith a believer gives assent to the truth of statements which comprise the heart of the gospel. John set forth certain declarations concerning Jesus' identity as "the holy one of God" (John 6:69; 8:24; 20:30-31). Paul cited among the foundational truths of the Christian proclamation assertions about our Lord's passion: Jesus died, was buried, rose again, and appeared to witnesses, all in accordance with the Old Testament (1 Cor. 15:1-8). Elsewhere the apostle brought together Jesus' identity and history as the "word of faith we are proclaiming": "That if you confess with your mouth, 'Jesus is Lord,' [identity] and believe in your heart that God raised him from the dead [history], you will be saved" (Rom. 10:8-9).

New Testament faith, however, does not end with either *notitia* or *assensus.* Rather, saving faith involves commitment. This is evidenced in the repeatedly employed phrase, "believe in," or literally "believe into." Like *fiducia,* "believing in" entails personal trust. Specifically, the early church called others to "believe in Jesus," that is, to entrust themselves to Christ for salvation (John 3:16).

We may illustrate the movement from *notitia* and *assensus* to *fiducia* by means of an analogy. Suppose that desiring to relax after a day of activity, we set out on a quest for a suitable place to sit. Our search directs us to an apparently useful easy chair in the living room. After some reflection on reports concerning the chair—including statements about its weight-bearing capabilities (*notitia*)—we acknowledge that the piece of furniture is sturdy enough for our purposes (*assensus*). Yet in order for the chair to be of any practical value to us we must take a further step. Knowledge and assent must lead to commitment. We must actually sit down—appropriate the message of available relaxation and commit our well-being to the chair for good or ill (*fiducia*). It is only in sitting in the chair that our quest, which has moved through knowledge and assent, comes to its ultimate goal, namely, trust.

So also with saving faith. Foundational to faith is knowledge of the message about the God who has acted in Jesus. It also includes acknowledgment of the truths contained in the gospel. But faith remains incomplete without trust; we must entrust ourselves to Jesus as Savior and commit our lives to him as Lord.

Our Response: Repentance and Faith

Conversion occurs as an individual responds to the gospel. In repentance we see ourselves as sinners: as alienated from God, justly condemned, and enslaved by sin. We acknowledge that our life's direction is misguided, we feel remorse for this condition, and we desire to follow a new direction. But we know that we are ultimately helpless. We are unable to begin anew and powerless to remedy our situation.

Faith works hand in hand with repentance. We become aware of the good news of God's action in Christ: Jesus, God's Son, died for human sin and rose again by God's power. We acknowledge this gospel message as true, not only in some general sense but also as applicable to our situation. Finally, we appropriate the work of God in Christ, trusting Jesus alone for salvation and confessing him as Lord.

In the above discussion, we separated the personal response to the gospel into the constituent parts of repentance and faith. While this is conceptually possible, in our encounter with God, the two are actually intertwined. True repentance presupposes and includes faith, and vital faith carries repentance within it.

The inseparable experiential connection between the two is borne out by the tendency of the New Testament to include faith within repentance. Joachim Jeremias found this proclivity in Jesus' parables. In the story of the prodigal son, for example, his assurance of his father's love motivates the young man to return home in repentance. Although grace is not the only theme, our Lord presented God's grace as the primary motive for repentance (Luke 13:6-9; see also Rom. 2:4). Jeremias concluded:

> Repentance means learning to say Abba again, putting one's whole trust in the heavenly Father, returning to the Father's house and the Father's arms.... In the last resort, repentance is simply trusting in the grace of God.[10]

What Jesus inaugurated, the apostles advanced. In their proclamation, the early church coupled repentance with faith (Acts 20:21).[11] Occasionally the texts use the terms interchangeably or employ one to mean both (Acts 2:38; 17:30; 26:20; cf. Acts 3:19; 10:43; 13:38). Repentance and faith are inseparable—each includes the other—as the instrumentality of receiving God's gift of salvation.

As the working together of repentance and faith, conversion marks a great turning point. It is our personal break with the old life and our entrance into the new. Above all, conversion consists in a turning to God. In this great transaction God draws our face toward the one who in Christ has loved us and has made salvation available. Through repentance and faith we dedicate ourselves to a new Master, the Lord Jesus Christ.

Linked to this turn toward God is a turning to others. In repentance and faith we leave behind the old self-centered way of living and dedicate ourselves to follow the example of Jesus, the man for others. We seek the good of all persons, knowing that acts which minister to people in their need are acts of service to Christ (Matt. 25:40). The Bible repeatedly reminds us that conversion to God is inseparable from a turning to others. John, for example, is clear: "If anyone says, 'I love God,' yet hates his brother, he is a liar. For anyone who does not love his brother, whom he has seen, cannot love God, whom he has not seen" (1 John 4:20). The apostle was echoing the words of Jesus himself, who linked love for God and for neighbor as first and second among the great commandments (Mark 12:28-34).

---

10. Joachim Jeremias, *New Testament Theology* (London: SCM, 1971), 156.
11. See Maximilian Zerwick, *Biblical Greek* (Rome: Editrice Pontificio Instituto Biblico, 1990), 60.

Conversion constitutes a turning to creation as well. Implicit in repentance from our living strictly for ourselves is a new concern for everything God has made. We now desire to imitate God, including sharing his concern for creation. In this manner we seek to mirror for all creatures the character of the Creator himself.

In all these aspects, conversion also means a turn toward oneself, that is, toward one's true self as intended by God. Through repentance and faith, we commit ourselves to live out in our own lives the divinely-given design for us as humans. In this sense, salvation is the completion of creation. What God intended from the beginning, he brings into being through our new life in Christ. Conversion marks our turning toward the eternal purpose for our existence that God has willed from the beginning.

The Divine Aspect of Conversion

The individual dimension of conversion has been the special emphasis of the revivalist tradition, which has been characterized by some historians call "convertive piety."[12] Evangelical groups such as the Baptists offer the church of Jesus Christ an indispensable service by keeping conversion at the forefront. Evangelicals are convinced that people must respond personally and individually to the gospel with repentance and faith.

We must not allow our emphasis on the individual response to the gospel, however, to overshadow the divine dynamic in the conversion process. The Reformed tradition has contributed to soteriology by reminding us of the primacy of God's activity in salvation. Calvinists have especially elevated the divine aspect of the dynamic of salvation. In their understanding, regeneration is solely the work of God in the life of a sinner, from which flows conversion as our human response to God's effectual call.[13]

---

12. Donald W. Dayton, "The Limits of Evangelicalism," in *The Variety of Evangelicalism*, ed. Donald W. Dayton and Robert K. Johnston (Downers Grove, Ill.: InterVarsity, 1991), 48.

13. See for example, John Gill, *A Body of Doctrinal Divinity*, 6.13, reprint edition (Atlanta: Turner Lassetter, 1965), 545. Not all Calvinists agree, however. Erickson argues, "the biblical evidence favors the position that conversion is prior to regeneration." Millard Erickson, *Christian Theology*, three volumes (Grand Rapids: Baker, 1985), 3:932.

Viewed from the perspective of its divine aspect, conversion is the work of the Holy Spirit. We must now explore the thesis that repentance and faith, while being our own willed response to the gospel, is at the same time the product of God's Spirit ministering to us.

The Spirit's Activity in the Conversion Process

A central theme of the New Testament is the good news that God is effecting the conversion of people who hear the gospel proclamation. In fact, the writers clearly assert that God's grace is indispensable to the transformation that inaugurates the Christian walk. The authors of the New Testament constantly remind us that salvation can never be attained through human effort alone. All our attempts to earn salvation by obeying the law are inadequate. As Paul stated, "no one will be declared righteous in his sight by observing the law; rather, through the law we become conscious of sin" (Rom. 3:20; see also Gal. 2:16,21).

In the anthropology section, we discovered the theological foundation for this conclusion: Humans are totally depraved. Sin has spread to every aspect of our existence, leaving no nook or cranny of our being untouched, no capability unaffected which otherwise might have enabled us to facilitate our own salvation. Because all human effort is ultimately insufficient, if we are to be saved the initiative must come from God and by his grace.

The biblical message, however, declares that God has indeed graciously acted on our behalf. In the midst of our spiritual deadness he saves us (Eph.2:1; Col. 2:13), and he saves us by grace (Eph. 2:8-9; Titus 3:4-6). Salvation comes as the Spirit authors new, spiritual life in us (John 3:5-8).

In a sense, the Spirit is the mysterious person of the divine Trinity. He works quietly without drawing attention to himself. Further, his workings are often simultaneous with human action, as he empowers us to do what God wills. Therefore, his activities occur undetected and unnoticed, sometimes even being mistaken for our own efforts. In addition, the Spirit's work itself often appears to be mysterious. What he does seems to lie beyond the realm of the everyday, the normal, the natural.

Nowhere does the Spirit's activity seem more mysterious than in conversion. Yet the New Testament points to several specific, vital functions that belong to the mission of the third trinitarian person. In the conversion process, he acts in conviction, call, illumination, and enablement.

Conviction. The Holy Spirit works in the conversion experience as the agent who fosters conviction of sin. It is his task to bring us to an awareness of our own personal sin and our involvement in sinful structures. According to John's narrative, in his upper room discourse Jesus promised that the Spirit would engage in this crucial activity: "When he comes, he will convict the world of guilt in regard to sin and righteousness and judgment" (John 16:8). In this statement our Lord indicated that the Spirit's workings in a person's life would lead to a consciousness of one's own sinful status, a realization of God's standard of righteousness, and an awareness of a coming day of judgment.

The convicting activity of the Spirit is indispensable to the dynamic of conversion. His work fosters the acknowledgment of sinfulness without which our personal response to the gospel is precluded. How can we sense regret and sorrow for our failure and our acts of unrighteousness unless we are conscious that we are displeasing to God? How can we turn from sin to God if we are not aware that we at enmity with him? How can we cast ourselves on the merciful God revealed in Christ if we do not sense that we need mercy? The good news of the Bible is the message of available forgiveness: "If we confess our sins, he is faithful and just and will forgive us our sins and purify us from all unrighteousness" (1 John 1:9). But our confession is dependent on the consciousness of our desperate situation and great need. The Holy Spirit seeks to foster in us the awareness of this need.

Call. In addition to convicting people of sin, the Spirit is at work in conversion as the agent of God's call directed toward sinful humans.

To understand this aspect of the Spirit's work, we must differentiate between two dimensions of the biblical concept of "call." One dimension is the calling which believers enjoy. The New Testament refers to Christians as the recipients of a special status as the uniquely called of God. Peter reminded his hearers that God "called you out of darkness into his wonderful light" (1 Peter 2:9; see also Rom. 9:24; 1 Cor. 1:9-24; 2 Tim. 1:9).

The context for this special calling is a call of a more general nature, the Spirit's summons to humans inviting us to share in the salvation God offers. Jesus portrayed this call in the parable of the wedding feast (Matt. 22:1-14). In the story, the king's servants proclaim his invitation to many people. However, some refuse to come, others pay no attention to them, and one arrives in improper attire. Consequently, our Lord concluded his story with the terse comment: "For many are invited, but few are chosen" (v. 14).

Jesus' story suggests wherein lies the focal point of the Spirit's activity in calling persons to salvation. Just as in the parable the king sends his servants to summons the people to the banquet (Matt.22:10), so also the divine invitation to salvation is announced by the servants of the King, the human messengers of the good news. The Spirit's call comes through the proclamation of the gospel. As God's heralds declare the message, the Holy Spirit speaks. He energizes their words, calling those who hear to repentance and faith.

This idea of the coworking of the Spirit with human messengers is implicit throughout the Bible. Paul, for example, outlined in reverse order the process that leads to conversion (Rom. 10:13-15): personal response, belief, hearing, preaching, sending of messengers. Thus, indispensable for the saving encounter with God is the hearing of the gospel from human messengers serving as God's chosen instruments. Within their message comes the divine call: "…God chose you to be saved through the sanctifying work of the Spirit and through belief in the truth. He called you to this through our gospel" (2 Thess. 2:14). For this reason, Paul could claim that the triune God himself was speaking through his message: "We are therefore Christ's ambassadors, as though God were making his appeal through us. We implore you on Christ's behalf: Be reconciled to God" (2 Cor. 5:20). The agent of this divine speaking through human messengers is the Holy Spirit.

The foundation for the New Testament conception of the energizing presence of God in the words of God's messengers lies in the Old Testament. The prophets were especially conscious of their role as the mouthpiece for God's Spirit. Yahweh spoke through them to the recipients of their message. Isaiah depicted the proclaimed word as the vehicle for the divine power which energizes it. Through him God compared the potency of his word with the life-giving force of water:

> As the rain and the snow come down from heaven, and do not return to it without watering the earth and making it bud and flourish, so that it yields seed for the sower and bread for the eater, so is my word that goes out from my mouth: It will not return to me empty, but will accomplish what I desire and achieve the purpose for which I sent it. (Isa. 55:10-11)

Through the proclamation of the gospel, therefore, the Holy Spirit issues God's gracious call to its hearers, summoning them to share in God's salvation. Those who answer this general call, who respond to the good news in repentance and faith, discover that they are the uniquely called of God.

Illumination. The Spirit's work in conversion likewise encompasses illumination. The Spirit enlightens the minds of the hearers of the gospel to see the divine truth disclosed therein.

The importance of illumination in the process of conversion becomes evident when we remind ourselves of the blinding effects of sin. In our state of bondage, we simply cannot grasp spiritual truth. As Paul explained, "The God of this age has blinded the minds of unbelievers, so that they cannot see the light of the gospel of the glory of Christ" (2 Cor. 4:4). If clear understanding is to come, it must be given by God. This, Paul added, alluding to God's act in the original creation of the world, is exactly what happens in conversion: "For God, who said, 'Let light shine out of darkness,' made his light shine in our hearts to give us the light of the knowledge of the glory of God in the face of Christ" (v. 6)

As the instrumentality of the risen Lord's activity in the world, the Spirit is the agent of the triune God in opening our hearts to perceive the truth of the gospel (1 Cor. 2:10). Only as a consequence of his work can we respond to the proclaimed message in repentance and faith. Luke noted this dynamic in the conversion of Lydia, for "The Lord opened her heart to respond to Paul's message" (Acts 16:14).

Enablement. In the process of conversion the Holy Spirit also enables an individual to respond to the gospel. He is the power making repentance and faith possible.

Paul spoke of the presence of the Spirit's power within his own proclamation of the gospel. He reminded the Corinthian believers that he did not come to them with eloquence or superior wisdom, but in weakness and fear. Nevertheless his message of the cross was accompanied by "a demonstration of the Spirit's power." As a consequence, their faith rested on divine power, not human wisdom (1 Cor. 2:4-5).

Whereas the primary focus of the Spirit's illuminating work is the mind, he directs enablement toward the human will. The task of the Spirit is to woo and strengthen the will, in order that the individual both desires and is able to respond to God's call. Like the other aspects of the Spirit's work, this activity is necessitated by our woeful situation. Because we are enslaved by sin, our will is in bondage. We lack the power necessary to overcome sin and freely obey the Spirit's call. If we are willingly to embrace the reconciliation our loving Father offers, we must be enabled. This is what the Spirit does, offering to us the power to say no to sin and yes to the gospel summons.

As in the other dimensions of the Spirit's work, the focal point of his enabling action is the proclamation of the good news (Rom. 10:17). As human agents declare the gospel, the Spirit acts through the message to strengthen the hearer to respond. Hence, Paul correctly extolled the gospel as "the power of God for the salvation of everyone who believes" (Rom. 1:16). The good news is God's powerful word simply because the Spirit chooses to act through human proclamation of the saving message.

Conversion and the Baptism of the Spirit

Nearly all evangelical thinkers agree that the Spirit works in the dynamic of conversion. But theologians differ concerning some of the details of that involvement. Perhaps none has been more divisive in recent decades than the disagreement over the relationship of the encounter with God we call "conversion" and the experience which the New Testament terms "the baptism of the Spirit."

The discussion of the connection between conversion and Spirit baptism which has caused so much ferment in churches of many traditions is a relatively recent phenomenon. It came on the heels of the phenomenal growth of Pentecostal churches in the twentieth century, together with the inroads of Pentecostal thinking into more mainline bodies.

Modern Pentecostalism. Although the term "pentecostal" encompasses a variety of religious expressions, all Pentecostals share one conviction, virtually by definition: Conversion must be followed by a second life-transforming event generally called "the baptism in the Spirit."[14] What forms the foundation of this conviction?

The theological roots of modern Pentecostalism lie in the ferment within evangelicalism in the nineteenth century.[15] Although not the only influence, scholars agree that the holiness movement of that era was "the cradle in which the Pentecostal revival was rocked."[16] America had become fertile soil for the teachings of John Wesley, the founder of the Methodists. Wesleyans drew from their leader the idea of a "second blessing," a definable moment of grace after conversion which decisively breaks the stranglehold that sin otherwise exercises even over a believer's life. Others, however, looking to American revivalist thinkers such as Charles G. Finney, came to view the postconversion experience less in terms of the sanctification process—as the eradication of sinful desires—and more as an enduement of power, whether for witness, service, or Christian living. The approach of the turn of the twentieth century sparked a great expectation among certain participants in the holiness movement that the "former rain," the miraculous power demonstrated in the New Testament church, would be restored in the form of the "latter

---

14. Grant Wacker, "'Wild Theories and Mad Excitement,'" in *Pentecostals from the Inside Out,* ed. Harold B. Smith (Wheaton, Ill.: Victor, 1990), 21.

15. For a full discussion, see Donald W. Dayton, *Theological Roots of Pentecostalism* (Grand Rapids: Zondervan, 1987).

16. William W. Menzies, "The Non-Wesleyan Origins of the Pentecostal Movement," in *Aspects of Pentecostal-Charismatic Origins,* ed. Vinson Synan (Plainfield, N.J.: Logos, 1975), 97.

rain," a final outpouring of the Spirit which would bring history to a close.

Many historians place the actual beginnings of the movement, however, in two events which brought these various strands together and then connected speaking in tongues to the second work of grace. The first event occurred in Topeka, Kansas. Students at a small Bible school led by Charles Fox Parham concluded that the Bible teaches a baptism of the Spirit subsequent to conversion with speaking in tongues as its sign. On January 1, 1901, at her request Parham laid hands on Agnes Ozman, and as a consequence she prayed in tongues.[17] The second event followed five years later in Los Angeles. A black Holiness preacher, William J. Seymour, who had been influenced by Parham in Houston, Texas, organized a series of meetings in a former Methodist church on Azusa Street. The three-and-one-half-year revival that ensued included the phenomenon of tongues speaking.[18] The Azusa Street revival of 1906-1909 marked the beginning of the worldwide Pentecostal movement.

These events constitute the genesis of the *first wave* of the modern Pentecostal phenomenon. We may term this original expression as "doctrinal pentecostalism," though the movement was more experiential than doctrinal. The first wave led to the formation of a host of new church bodies, in part due to the opposition Pentecostals received in the mainline churches.[19] Many of these new groups eventually formed their own denominational structures, institutionalized the Pentecostal experience, and devised doctrinal standards which included the necessity of the post-conversion baptism of the Spirit and speaking in tongues as its sign.[20]

In the 1960s a *second wave* of Pentecostalism lapped on the shores of the church in the form of what is called "the charismatic movement." Its origin probably lies in the ministry of Dennis Bennett, who while rector of St. Mark's Episcopal Church in Van Nuys, Cal-

---

17. John Thomas Nichol, *The Pentecostals* (Plainfield, N.J.: Logos, 1966), 27-28.

18. Vinson Synan, "Frank Bartleman and Azusa Street," in Frank Bartleman, *Azusa Street,* reprinted edition, (South Plainfield, N.J.: Bridge, 1980), xvi-xx.

19. Richard Quebedeaux, *The New Charismatics* (Garden City, N.Y.: Doubleday, 1976), 36-37.

20. See, for example, the "Statement of Truth" of the Pentecostal Fellowship of North America as printed in Nichol, *The Pentecostals*, 4.

ifornia, received the baptism of the Spirit in 1959.[21] The movement marked an expansion of the Pentecostal experience beyond the classical Pentecostal churches into older mainline churches.

The first wave sparked the founding of many new denominations, but those involved in the second wave did not leave their churches. Rather, they often sought to work within the structures. Further, the new charismatics were less adamant that speaking in tongues was the necessary sign of the Spirit's fullness. As the ranks of the charismatics came to encompass not only adherents of various Protestant traditions but also Roman Catholics, they were also more tolerant of differing doctrinal persuasions.[22] What united the new charismatics, therefore, was not adherence to a specific pneumatology but a common experience of the Spirit. We may therefore, term this second wave "experiential Pentecostalism."

The charismatic movement was followed by yet a *third wave*.[23] Participants did not discount speaking in tongues, which had been the hallmark of the previous two waves. Nevertheless they shifted the interest to other outward manifestations of the Spirit among the people of God. These miraculous phenomena had always been a part of Pentecostalism, but they had been overshadowed by the emphasis on speaking in tongues. Of special significance were the gift of prophecy and demonstrations of power, such as physical healing, exorcism, and even raising the dead.

An initial impetus to the third wave came with the renewed interest in "signs and wonders" associated with Professor C. Peter Wagner of the Fuller Seminary School of World Missions. As the movement continued, however, the mantle of leadership fell to John Wimber, who led renewal seminars throughout the world and gave inspiration for the founding of an informal association of new third-wave churches called the Vineyard Fellowship. Wimber's name, more than that of any other, became synonymous with third-wave Pentecostalism.

---

21. Quebedeaux, *The New Charismatics*, 54-56.
22. Ibid., 152-54.
23. Hence, Robert P. Menzies, "The Distinctive Character of Luke's Pneumatology," *Paraclete* 25/4 (fall 1991), 17.

Pentecostal view of Spirit baptism and tongues. As this historical sketch indicates, the label "Pentecostal" encompasses a large spectrum of similar and yet somewhat divergent opinion. Unfortunately, recent discussions of Pentecostalism readily fuse and confuse a variety of issues that must be kept separate. Important to our discussion here are two questions that touch the relationship between conversion and the baptism of the Spirit: What do the New Testament writers mean when they speak of this event? Is the phenomenon of speaking in tongues the sign of the baptism?

Pentecostals, especially participants in the first and second waves, generally adhere to a common understanding of Spirit baptism and the relationship of tongues speaking to it. According to the standard Pentecostal pneumatology, conversion does not necessarily put us in touch with all the spiritual power God desires to bestow on his children. Rather, full contact with the Holy Spirit comes through a subsequent experience, generally called "the baptism of the Spirit," but sometimes also known as "the filling of the Spirit." Assemblies of God New Testament scholar Robert P. Menzies summarized the Pentecostal understanding:

> Pentecostals generally describe Spirit-baptism as an experience (at least logically if not chronologically) distinct from conversion which unleashes a new dimension of the Spirit's power: It is an enduement of power for service.[24]

This deeper encounter with the Spirit, Pentecostals maintain, is God's will for each Christian. It constitutes an individual Pentecost, for it is the fulfillment of the biblical promise that Christ would baptize his followers in the Holy Spirit. Pentecostals interpret this promise as intended for individuals, rather than for the believing community as a corporate unit. John Thomas Nichol noted, "Every Pentecostal believes in the reality of a present-day experience for believers such as was received by the early disciples on the Day of Pentecost (Acts 2:4)."[25] For them Pentecost is "a relevant and recurring phenomenon."[26]

---

24. Menzies, "Luke's Pneumatology," 18.
25. Nichol, *The Pentecostals*, 8.
26. Ibid., 9.

Finally, many Pentecostals view speaking in tongues as the definitive sign of this glorious event. For its biblical foundation advocates appeal mainly to the experience of the early church as described in Acts. Luke's narrative, they claim, indicates that the early Christians experienced a baptism of the Spirit subsequent to water baptism. Proponents find this primarily in the account of Pentecost itself. On that day, the upper room disciples—who as the faithful followers of Jesus had already been converted—were the recipients of a postconversion Spirit baptism (Acts 2:1-4). Advocates see the pattern of Pentecost confirmed in the narrative of the early Samaritan converts (8:14-17). Although they believed and had even been baptized, these new converts did not receive the Holy Spirit until Peter and John came from Jerusalem and laid hands on them.

Pentecostals also appeal to experiences recounted in Acts in setting forth the thesis that speaking in tongues is the sign of the presence of the Spirit. Here again the primary evidence is the account of Pentecost. The coming of the Spirit resulted in the miraculous speaking in tongues by all who had assembled in the upper room (2:4). The same phenomenon confirmed the Spirit's presence on two subsequent occasions as well: the conversion of Cornelius and his household (10:44-47) and Paul's encounter with the Ephesian disciples of John the Baptist (19:6).[27]

An evaluation of the Pentecostal position. These examples are noteworthy and important. However, they do not offer conclusive support for the Pentecostal pneumatology. Three considerations lead to this conclusion.

(1) The first arises from the understanding of Pentecost we reached in chapter 14. We noted that Pentecost was a unique, nonrepeatable event in the history of salvation. Prior to his outpouring on that day, the Spirit had not yet come into the world in this significant way, nor had the church as such been born. Consequently, Pentecost was a singly significant occasion, designed to signal both the dawning of the new age of prophetic fulfilment and the beginning of the expansion of the church.

---

27. Ibid., 10.

For this reason, Pentecost was a corporate event. It was an occurrence in life of the community of Christ in which we all share through our inclusion in that community. The corporate nature of this historical event indicates that we ought not to await our own private "Pentecost," for the Spirit has already fallen on God's people. The sequence of events recorded in Acts 2, therefore, does not comprise a paradigm for us to follow. Rather, we enjoy the fullness of Pentecost when we become members of the one church which dates its beginnings to that glorious day. Their Pentecost was the one Pentecost and therefore ours as well.

The nonrepeatable nature of that event calls into question the emphasis on personal experiences of Pentecost. A second consideration raises doubts about the normative significance of the Acts narratives. Contrary to the claim implicit in the pentecostal pneumatology, the Book of Acts displays no single pattern of God's activity with respect to either the baptism of the Spirit or speaking in tongues.

Pentecostals correctly note that the Samaritans received the Spirit sometime after conversion and water baptism (Acts 8:12, 14-17). For Cornelius and his household, however, the baptism of the Spirit apparently occurred simultaneously with conversion and prior to water baptism. While Peter was proclaiming the gospel to them, the Spirit was "poured out" and they spoke in tongues (10:44-48).

Taken as a whole, the experience of the early church suggests that the conversion of Cornelius's household, and not that of the Samaritans, follows the more typical pattern. Indeed, it is easier to understand how the Samarian situation could be an exception to the normal scenario than to fit the conversion of Cornelius into a pattern derived from Acts 8. Either of two factors may account for the uniqueness of the Samaritan experience.

Luke seems to have been motivated by a desire to demonstrate a salvation-historical dependency of the Samaritan Christians on the Jerusalem leadership.[28] This is understandable given the religious hostility between the Jews and the Samaritans. God's withholding

---

28. This suggestion has been defended by many exegetes. See, for example, G. W. H. Lampe, *The Seal of the Spirit* (London: Longmans, Green, and Co., 1951), 70. For a critique of this position, see, Manzies, "Luke's Pneumatology," 22.

the Spirit from the Samaritan converts until the arrival of Peter and John may have been a way of overcoming the historical division between the two groups by bringing them together in the one community of Christ under the leadership of the apostles.

Then again the delay may be related to our Lord's entrusting to Peter and the apostles the keys to the kingdom. The scattering of believers from Jerusalem into Samaria marked the first occurrence of evangelization beyond the boundaries of the Jews. But the gospel was not carried to this new people-group by the apostles, for they had remained in Jerusalem. Therefore, God may have withheld the Spirit until his designated emissaries arrived. In this manner, Luke documented Peter's role in unlocking the kingdom for the Samaritans (just as he later unlocked it for the Gentiles through his role in the conversion of Cornelius) in accordance with the Lord's promise.

The same lack of a single pattern appears in the manner of the confirmation of the reception of the Spirit. Pentecostals correctly cite situations in Acts in which speaking in tongues confirmed the Spirit's presence. Other accounts, however, do not report the presence of this phenomenon. For example, we find no suggestion that Paul spoke in tongues when he was initially "filled with the Spirit" (9:17-19). Similarly, the conversion of the jailer's household in Philippi seems to have resulted in the fullness of the Spirit. But his presence was marked by their being "filled with joy"—which Paul declares belongs to the fruit of the Spirit—and not by speaking in tongues (16:31-34).

As in the case of the delay in the reception of the Spirit, we may find a ready explanation as to why on occasion speaking in tongues accompanied the Spirit's coming. In each case, Luke seems to be indicating that God employed this phenomenon as a confirming sign in situations where the Spirit's presence may have otherwise been questioned. That this was the case on Pentecost seems obvious from Peter's apologetic use of the phenomenon as the sign of the fulfilment of Joel's prophecy. The case of Cornelius yields a similar conclusion. The Jerusalem believers were not yet convinced that salvation in Christ was for the Gentiles. Therefore, they questioned Peter's activity, until the apostle recounted how the bestowal of the

Spirit had been confirmed through the very sign that the early believers received at Pentecost (11:15-18). We may likewise surmise that John's disciples may have lacked assurance of the truth of what for them was a new teaching about the Holy Spirit had it not been confirmed by this miraculous sign (19:6). Perhaps these episodes are examples of Paul's explanation of the significance of the tongues phenomenon written to the Corinthians: "Tongues, then, are a sign, not for believers but for unbelievers" (1 Cor. 14:22).

(2) The Pentecostal argument from Acts is further weakened by an observation of a more general nature. Although we ought not to discount his theological interest,[29] Luke's account remains primarily a historical narrative, a recounting of the progress of the gospel from Jerusalem to Rome. He described how God was at work in the first century, in order to encourage his readers in their belief that God has disclosed salvation in Christ, not to give detailed instructions as to how God must work in believers' lives. Consequently, even if we did find in the book a single pattern of God's activity, that discovery in itself would not demand that the pattern be explicitly reproduced today, unless, of course, it were central to Luke's theological interest and confirmed by the Epistles. While important, historical narrative alone is not necessarily a sure foundation for doctrine.[30]

(3) This comment suggests a third consideration. We must not appraise the Pentecostal position merely by appeal to what we might construct to be Luke's own pneumatology, but more importantly in the light of the explicit teaching of Paul. In so doing, we discover disquieting difficulties with Pentecostalism.

Paul considers the Holy Spirit to be universally present among Christians. In the only reference to the baptism of the Spirit in all the New Testament Epistles, the apostle predicates this reality to every member of the body of Christ: "For we were all baptized by [in] one Spirit into one body—whether Jews of Greeks, slave or free—and we were all given the one Spirit to drink" (1 Cor. 12:13). Paul never

---

29. On this, see I. Howard Marshall, *Luke: Historian and Theologian* (Grand Rapids: Zondervan, 1970).

30. For a contrary position, see Roger Stronstad, *The Charismatic Theology of St. Luke* (Peabody, Mass.: Hendrickson, 1984), 11.

suggested that there are actual believers on whom the fullness of the Spirit had not yet fallen. On the contrary, for the apostle not having the Spirit is paramount to not belonging to Christ (Rom 8:9).

Paul looked to lifestyle, rather than tongues speaking, for the confirmation of the Spirit's presence. The "fruit of the Spirit" consists in Christlikeness in character (Gal. 5:22-23), he declared. In the midst of his discussion of spiritual gifts, Paul directed the Corinthians to the "most excellent way"—life centered on love (1 Cor. 13)—rather than to the use of charismatic endowments and ecstatic experiences.

Although the apostle counseled his readers in many dimensions of Christian living, nowhere did he command us to be baptized with the Spirit. Rather, he seems to assume that all believers already share in this experience. This does not mean, however, that he issued no injunctions governing our relationship to the Spirit. On the contrary, he counseled all believers to be filled continually with the Spirit (Eph. 5:18), to live by the Spirit (Gal. 5:16), to keep in step with the Spirit (Gal. 5:25), and to avoid extinguishing the Spirit's fire (1 Thess. 5:19). These commands are applicable to all Christians, indicating that neither conversion or any second work of grace takes us beyond the need to give continual heed to the Spirit's presence within us.

Spirit baptism, conversion, and Spirit filling. These considerations suggest that in the New Testament the phrase "the baptism of the Spirit" expresses a dimension of the miracle that occurs at conversion. This encounter with the Holy Spirit is so radical that we can speak of it as immersion in the Spirit. Through our participation in the bestowal of the Spirit we participate together with all believers in the new age and the blessings of the new covenant.[31]

The baptism of the Spirit is a finished and unalterable reality accomplished at conversion when we participate in the one Pentecost of the church. Consequently, we need not await or expect any subsequent experience of the Spirit which could mediate to us a greater relationship to him or a deeper experience of his power. Rather than entering on a quest for yet another spiritual encounter, we should concentrate on appropriating and enjoying the provision of the Spirit given to us in conversion.

---

31. James Dunn, *Baptism in the Holy Spirit* (London: SCM, 1970), 38-54.

The baptism of the Spirit is a finished reality which we accept by faith. Nevertheless, we ought never to ignore or take for granted our relationship to the Spirit. Paul's commands, such as the injunction that we be continually filled with the Spirit, remind us of the importance of the Spirit's controlling influence at each moment and in every situation of life. This ongoing experience of yielding to the Spirit's control is the key to power for witness and service, and for victorious, godly living (Acts 4:31; Eph. 5:19-21). Although we can celebrate with those in whose lives God has chosen to work in such a manner, we dare neither universalize nor elevate their experience of a supposedly postconversion encounter with the Spirit into the norm. Rather than seeking a second blessing—a life changing enduement of the fullness of the divine power—we ought to concentrate our attention on the constant filling of the Spirit. The attempt to be transparent to the Spirit in the moment by moment living of the Christian life may seem less "miraculous" than an additional extraordinary experience with God. Yet it is ultimately the true pathway to joy, fruitfulness, and victory.

The Community Aspect of Conversion

We have noted that conversion occurs as we respond obediently to Jesus' command to "repent and believe the gospel." At work in this grand encounter is the power of God himself, the Holy Spirit. He acts in and through the gospel proclamation to convict us of sin, call us to salvation, illumine our minds to see divine truth, and strengthen our wills to regret sin and turn to God. So vital is his working that through this encounter we are immersed in the Spirit.

There is, however, yet another perspective from which we must view the dynamic of conversion. The individual response to the gospel as facilitated by the working of the Spirit occurs within a specific context, namely, that of the community of faith.

In the past, the community dimension of conversion has been the unique focus of advocates of "high church" ecclesiologies, theologians who emphasize the role of the church in begetting and fostering spiritual life in believers. High church traditions have a great regard for church rites and for act of incorporation into the visible body of believers. Although in part 5 we will delineate a "low church" ecclesiology, we must nevertheless retain the awareness of the importance of the believing community in the process of conversion, which high church thinkers emphasize.

The Role of the Community in Conversion

Conversion is not *sui generis*. It never occurs in isolation. We do not experience a saving encounter with God on our own. Rather, the faith community serves as the context for personal repentance and faith. But what role does the community play?

Proclamation of the gospel. An obvious dimension is the crucial role of the faith community is in the proclamation of the gospel. Our personal response to God's saving action in Christ occurs within the context a believing community who remembers and heralds that divine activity. The community recounts in word, ritual, and practice the story of Jesus and its significance for all humankind. As a corporate body and through its individual members the church announces the message, in response to which people become believers.

The idea that the task of announcing the good news of salvation belongs to the corporate people of God is implicit in the Bible. Paul, for example, concluded that a person does not call on the name of the Lord in isolation. Rather, personal saving faith is facilitated by the hearing of the gospel as proclaimed by messengers who have been sent (Rom. 10:13-15). God, of course, is ultimately the one who sends forth emissaries of the word, but in this venture he uses the community of faith.

The role of the church as God's agent in the sending of messengers is especially evident in the calling of missionaries. The commissioning of Paul provides an example from the life of the early church:

> While they [the church in Antioch] were worshipping the Lord and fasting, the Holy Spirit said, "Set apart for me Barnabas and Saul for the work to which I have called them." So after they had fasted and prayed, they placed their hands on them and sent them off. (Acts 13:2-3)

So began the great advance of the gospel into wider Roman world. This incident reminds us that the believing company encourages, dedicates, commissions, and supports those who carry the good news to the unevangelized. Perhaps we would witness the beginnings of a new era of missions if we were to follow the example of the Antiochian believers and revive the practice of corporately seeking the will of the Spirit.

The church's role includes not only sending messengers to the unevangelized but also reiterating the message in its own locale. Both as a corporate body and as individual members we are to set forth an ongoing witness within the context in which the Lord has placed us. Our witness includes even our actions toward each other, for if we become a genuine community of love and care others will note that we are Jesus' disciples (John 13:35). As we continually proclaim the good news to those around us, we water the seed of the gospel which others have sown (1 Cor. 3:6-7). This process is not limited to the church's specifically evangelistic activities. It occurs likewise within the context of corporate worship and nurture. Through these activities, people associated with the congregation who have not as yet come to a full profession of faith repeatedly encounter the gospel message in spoken, enacted, and lived proclamation.

Even when people come to faith simply by reading the Bible, the community remains present. Through the Scriptures they encounter the proclamation of the one faith community which spans the centuries from the first to the present.

Incorporation into a new community. The church's proclamation forms the context for conversion in that the proclaimed, enacted, or lived word forms the vehicle through which the Spirit works to bring an individual to repentance and faith. In this sense, through its involvement in proclamation the church plays an indirect role in that great transaction. In these various ways, the church is indeed "the pillar and foundation of the truth" (1 Tim. 3:15). There is, however, another sense in which the church is more directly involved in conversion. The community incorporates those who respond to the gospel.

Contemporary thinkers are rediscovering the importance of the social unit—the community—for human living. In contrast to the central postulate of modern radical individualism, no one exists simply as an isolated individual, as an autonomous, self-sufficient, unencumbered self. On the contrary, to be human means to be a social being. Our existence is always embedded in some wider social reality.

In the same way, conversion occurs in the context of a specific community. This event marks one's incorporation into the church, the community of Christ. Our response to the gospel entails not only turning from sin to God, but also turning from an old to a new community of participation.

The incorporation into the community of Christ in conversion involves the reception of a new cognitive framework. Contemporary thinkers have observed that the community in which we participate mediates to us a set of foundational categories through which we view and experience ourselves and the world.[32] In the conversion process, the new believer appropriates the cognitive framework of the Christian community. This new set of categories becomes the vehicle for a reorientation of one's perspective, facilitating the formation of a new identity and the construction of a new value system.

As an agent of the reorientation of a person's perspective, the church acts as a community of memory and hope. It retells its own history as arising out of the biblical story, which is the constitutive narrative of the Christian community. In so doing, the church mediates the message of God's past saving action with its promise of available salvation in the present. At the same time, the church directs our attention toward the future, to the goal of God's actions in history. By anchoring us in its past and drawing our gaze to God's future, the church provides a transcendent vantage point for life in the present. It offers people a new context of meaning and invites them to connect their personal aspirations with the community of those who seek to embody God's own purposes.

The connection between conversion and incorporation into the community is evident in the process of identity formation. Our sense of personal identity develops as we tell our narrative, that story in which the various threads of our lives come together in a unified,

---

32. This opinion was recently articulated by George A. Lindbeck, "Confession and Community: An Israel-like View of the Church," *Christian Century* 107/16 (May 9, 1990): 495.

meaningful whole. The personal narrative lies at the basis of a person's sense of who he or she is. Consequently, finding ourselves means, among other things, finding the story in the context of which our lives make sense.[33] But our personal stories are never isolated units. They are touched by the stories of other persons and ultimately the story of a larger people of which we are a part. Our narratives, therefore, are always embedded in the story of the community in which we participate.[34] The community mediates to us a larger, transcending story which transmits to us our ideas of ultimate meaning.[35]

In conversion the story of the Christian community becomes the context for reorientation of our personal story. In this event, we encounter the narrative of God's action in history as told by the community of faith. This encounter leads to a personal crisis in identity, as the seeker accepts the categories of the new community as the valid framework for his or her own personal narrative. These new categories demand a radical reinterpretation of the convert's life story along the pattern of the biblical story. At its heart, the framework we derive from that biblical narrative follows the dialectic of disorientation and reorientation: We speak of "old" and "new," "being lost" but "having been found." Ultimately we draw from the framework of "sin" and "grace."

A lucid example is the reorientation that occurred as Saul the persecuter of the church became Paul the apostle of Christ. Reflecting on his former life as a zealous Jew, Paul concluded to the Philippians, "But whatever was to my profit I now consider loss for the sake of Christ" (Phil. 3:7). He admitted to the Corinthians, "For I am the least of the apostles and do not even deserve to be called an apostle, because I persecuted the church of God (1 Cor. 15:11), With this in view, he later termed himself "the worst of sinners" (1 Tim. 1:15-16). How often has Paul's reflection become the paradigm for subsequent converts!

---

33. Robert N. Bellah, et al., *Habits of the Heart: Individualism and Commitment in American Life*, Perennial Library edition (New York: Harper and Row, 1986), 81.

34. See, for example, Alisdair MacIntyre, *After Virtue*, second edition (Notre Dame: University of Notre Dame Press, 1984), 221.

35. E.g., Lindbeck, "Confession and Community," 495.

Not only do we derive the cognitive framework by means of which to reformulate our personal narrative, in conversion we also accept the story of the Christian community as our own. Through this act we become a part of this particular people who have this specific history. Because they are now my people—or I have become one of them—their history is also mine.

In addition to identity formation, the link between conversion and incorporation into the community of Christ is evident in the process of constructing a system of values. According to the New Testament our union with Christ, which the Spirit works in conversion, entails not only mental assent to a set of doctrines, but also commitment to embodying in our beliefs, attitudes, and actions the meanings and values that characterized Jesus' own life. In this process the church is crucial.

Contemporary thinkers recognize the important role of the community in developing character, virtue, and values. Simply stated, we are imbued with the basic outlook of the community in which we participate. Conversion occurs as we encounter a new community which has a distinctive value system and through that encounter we come to accept their understanding as our own. As it confronts us with the redemptive story and its own history and traditions, the believing community mediates to us the framework for the formation of a new set of values or a new world view. As the church becomes the community in which we live and in whose life we participate, its values begin to shape our own.

Finally, conversion and incorporation are connected, because the encounter with God marks at the same time participation in a new fellowship of allegiance and a new confessional community. Implicit in our presence in a community of participation is personal loyalty to the principles for which the community stands. We worship the "gods" of the people from whom we derive our sense of the transcendent, and we confess with them our common faith in these "gods."

The act of repentance and faith constitutes a grand reorientation of our community of participation. We lay aside whatever old allegiances formerly demanded our loyalty and turn to the God revealed in Jesus Christ. In conversion we forsake the loyalties of our former community of participation and accept as our own the allegiance to Christ embodied by his community. We disassociate ourselves from the faith confession of all other communities; with the community of Christ we confess faith in Jesus as Lord. As a result, we are now one in confession and loyalty with a new community, the followers of Christ.

As we will explore in greater length in chapter 20, baptism serves as the sign of the new identity in Christ which the Spirit mediates to us in conversion. Baptism, however, is not merely an act of the individual believer. It is a symbolic act of the church. This is why we do not baptize ourselves. By means of this act, the church through its representatives initiates a new believer into the community. Beginning with conversion as expressed through baptism and then subsequently formalized through church membership, we declare that we have moved into a new community of participation, the people who name Jesus as Lord.

Conversion and Church Initiation Rites

Our mention of baptism in the context of conversion confronts us with a thorny theological issue: What is the relationship of the rites of the church, especially baptism, to the reception of the Spirit at conversion?

Historical and contemporary positions. Perhaps the dominant position in the church since the Middle Ages has been what we may call "baptismal regeneration." Many theologians declare that the Spirit is mediated to the individual through the church initiation rites, especially baptism. At least until the changes made at the Second Vatican Council in the 1960s the Roman Catholic Church provided the most obvious example of a faith tradition that espoused baptismal regeneration. However, this understanding also draws adherents from Protestant ranks, especially among high church Anglicans[36] (Episcopalians) and Lutherans.[37] Recently, several Anglican thinkers

---

36. See, for example, Lampe, *The Seal of the Spirit.*

37. See, for example, Mark Ellingsen, *Word and Spirit: Theology in the Pulpit* (Atlanta: John Knox, 1983), 141-45. See also, Carl E. Braaten, "Baptism," in *Christian Dogmatics*, ed. Carl E. Braaten and Robert W. Jenson (Philadelphia: Fortress, 1984), 2:315-33.

have proposed a variation of this general view, arguing that the Spirit is given subsequently to baptism through confirmation and the laying on of hands.

Adherence to baptismal regeneration has not been limited to groups that practice infant baptism (pedobaptists), however. In the 1800s, the followers of Alexander Campbell combined this teaching with the Baptist emphases on believers' baptism and immersion. Even today many of Campbell's followers teach that to be saved a person must be immersed as a believer because the Spirit is given through this act.

Nearly all contemporary evangelicals eschew the doctrine of baptismal regeneration. In so doing, however, some have moved far in the opposite direction. They deny that the reception of the Spirit is connected in any way to church rites. We receive the Holy Spirit at conversion, they argue, that is, at the point of our personal decision for Christ. Advocates of this view espouse what we may call a "weak" theology of baptism, one which recognizes no actual link between the church's initiation rites and the miracle of conversion. Hence, baptism may carry some significance, but it neither regenerates the sinner nor mediates the Spirit. A weak baptismal theology is ecumenically advantageous, in that it allows persons who practice baptism differently to affirm one another as Christians sharing the same Spirit.

The New Testament teaching. When we take our query concerning baptism and conversion to the New Testament, we discover an array of seemingly inconclusive data.

(1) Proponents of weak theologies of baptism can point to certain texts to substantiate their position. The early church, they claim, readily separated conversion and the initiation rite, indicating that the grand transaction occurs apart from baptism. Jesus, for example, promised salvation to the thief on the cross, even though the repentant convict was clearly not baptized prior to his death (Luke 23:42-43). The conversion of Cornelius's household offers a more typical situation, for these believers received the Spirit and then Peter baptized them (Acts 10:44-48).

What is implicit in these incidents appears to be confirmed by Paul. In his own ministry, he seems to have deemphasized baptism. The apostle noted, for example, that he baptized few of the Corinthian converts, citing as rationale: "For Christ did not send me to baptize but to preach the gospel" (1 Cor. 1:14-17). Indeed Paul's emphasis on salvation by faith alone (Rom. 10:9-10) seems to leave little room for baptism, which in comparison to faith appears to be a human work.

(2) Other texts seem to favor a "strong" theology of baptism. Despite his remark in 1 Corinthians, Paul himself may have seen a close connection between this act and conversion. In his more systematic treatment of Christian doctrine in Romans, the apostle drew a connection between baptism and our union with Christ's death and resurrection (Rom 6:3-5).

According to John's Gospel, Jesus forged a similar link between baptism and the reception of the Spirit. In his dialogue with Nicodemus our Lord declared, "Unless you are born of water [understood as a reference to this rite[38] and the Spirit, you cannot see the kingdom of God" (John 3:5).

Peter also saw baptism as integral to conversion. After his Pentecost sermon, the early leader instructed the inquirers, "Repent and be baptized" (Acts 2:38). In his first Epistle, the apostle compared the role of baptism in salvation to that of the ark, asserting that baptism "now saves you also" (1 Pet. 3:21).

(3) Our inquiry into conversion and the rites of the church is further complicated by a third group of New Testament texts which introduce another rite, the laying on of hands, into the process. Luke reported that this act was instrumental in conveying the Spirit to the first Samaritan believers (Acts 8:14-17) and to the disciples of John the Baptist whom Paul encountered (19:1-7).

These incidents gain added significance in the light of the apostle's reference to Timothy's confirmation. Paul suggested that the gift of the Spirit was conferred through this rite (2 Tim. 1:6-7).

---

38. G. R. Beasley-Murray, *Baptism in the New Testament* (Grand Rapids: Eerdmans, 1962), 226-32.

Conversion as faith expressed through baptism. Our overview of the New Testament appears to lead to no consensus. How, then, can we bring together these seemingly disjointed texts into a unified doctrine?

In constructing our understanding of the relationship of conversion to the rites of the church we must pay heed to the approach to Acts which we outlined in our discussion of the baptism of the Spirit. Although Luke is a theologian as well as a historian, his primary emphasis on history cautions us against using his narrative as our sole appeal in matters of what God intends to be the experience of all Christians. Further, the accounts in Acts suggest no one clear pattern universally present in the early decades of the church which we could therefore conclude is normative for all. Within these limitations, however, the Acts narratives are significant as a informative refection of the thinking of the early church.

The Book of Acts indicates that the early Christians saw a clear link between the bestowal of the Spirit and water baptism. This close association arose, in so far as the normal conversion experience entailed inward, personal commitment expressed through the outward, communal act of baptism. The assumed connection between water baptism and Spirit baptism illumines what otherwise appears to be Peter's strange urgency to baptize Cornelius's household. The apostle's understanding of the close connection between the two dimensions of conversion motivated him to administer baptism immediately when he was convinced that the Spirit had fallen on the new believers.

The documents indicate as well that the early church did not separate conversion and baptism temporally or theologically as is commonplace today. On the contrary, first-century believers brought together personal faith and baptism as its public declaration into one undifferentiated reality both in practice and in their understanding of conversion. This composite view of conversion explains the otherwise difficult statements that seem to make baptism essential for salvation (Mark 16:16; 1 Peter 3:21).

The Book of Acts suggests finally that the laying on of hands following baptism may have been a common, if not usual, practice in the early church. The believers did not see it as a rite separate from baptism, however, but as part of a single act of initiation. They may have employed baptism (the outward declaration of inward faith), and the laying on of hands (the sign of the reception of the Spirit and of the oneness of God's people) in one symbolic expression of the mystery of conversion.

With these observations, however, we have not yet answered the difficult question with which we began. Is any rite of the church, such as baptism, essential to the conversion experience? Let us now forge a concise response.

Conversion is an intricate dynamic. At its heart is our personal response to the gospel as facilitated by the Spirit and transpiring within the context of the faith community. This response encompasses our inward personal commitment (repentance and faith) and its outward testimony administered by the church (baptism). Our query, therefore, actually raises the question concerning the relationship of the inward, personal dimension to the outward, public, and more communal.

If one aspect of this dynamic must be singled out as the *sine qua non* of conversion, then our answer can only be: repentance and faith. Personal commitment is the central dimension of saving faith. Whoever comes to God in repentance and by faith claims the work of Jesus Christ will be saved.

Although ultimately inward commitment constitutes the essence of our response to the gospel, such commitment never stands alone. True inward faith always expresses itself in outward signs (James 2:14-26). For this reason, we dare not disengage the inward dimension of repentance and faith from its public sign, which according to the New Testament is baptism. Indeed the early Christian community clearly drew together inward, personal faith and baptism as its outward, communal expression. To a lesser extent, the early believers also emphasized the laying on of hands as a sign of the Spirit's presence. Therefore, we today do well to view these outward expressions, especially baptism, both in theory and in practice as significant aspects of the process of conversion. We ought never to allow our belief that a person may be saved without baptism to give license to the separation of what God intended in normal circumstances to be joined together.

We have observed that the dynamic of conversion consists in three aspects: our personal response of repentance and faith; the divine work of the Spirit of God in conviction, call, illumination, and enablement; and the community's activity in proclaiming the good news and initiating new believers into the fellowship of Christ through water baptism. Although divisible into these three components, the experience of conversion is one, unified dynamic which we must hold together both in thought and practice.

Likewise, a reciprocal relationship exists among the three aspects of conversion. The personal response of repentance and faith is not possible without the divine work of the Spirit and normally ought to come to fruition in baptism and church membership. The work of the Spirit in conversion is mediated through the proclamation of the gospel and in some sense the rite of baptism. The goal of his activity is personal inward commitment coupled with the public confession of faith expressed in baptism. Finally, as a rite of the church, baptism is meaningless unless it serves as the Spirit-energized sign of personal commitment to Christ. But this observation anticipates what we will discuss in greater depth in part 5.

16

Individual Salvation: The Wider Perspective

For those God foreknew he also predestined to be conformed to the likeness of his Son, that he might be the firstborn of many brothers. And those he called, he also justified; those he justified, he also glorified. (Rom. 8:29-30)

Outline

Representative positions
The order of salvation and the future community

As the facilitator of new life, the Creator Spirit completes the saving activity of the triune God. Although it encompasses all creation, the focus of God's salvation is fallen humankind. A central aspect of this endeavour is the Spirit's action in applying Christ's work to individual humans. He brings us into union with the Lord and with each other in Christ's community.

In chapter 15 we looked at the dynamic that marks the beginning of salvation in us. Now we turn our gaze to the broader context, the entire transaction of God's salvation of individual humans, in the context of which the Spirit's inauguration of our life in Christ occurs. The discussion comes in two parts. We look first at our human experience of salvation. From our perspective, salvation begins with repentance and faith, continues throughout life, and comes to completion at our Lord's return. Second, we view the entire process as a unified whole within the context of eternity in order to draw conclusions concerning election and the ordering of the Spirit's saving work within God's purposes.

Contemplation of the grand sweep of salvation ought to lift our hearts to praise the triune God whose saving activity arises out of his immense love for us.

The Process of Salvation

Viewed from the perspective of God's ultimate intention for us, salvation is one divine act, the work of the Spirit in bringing us into full conformity with the likeness of Christ. From our human perspective, however, salvation moves through stages. In this sense, the old evangelical response to the question "Are you saved?" correctly reflects our experience: I have been saved; I am being saved; I will be saved.

When seen from our vantage point, therefore, the experience of salvation occurs in three stages. "Conversion" marks the inauguration of personal salvation. The transformation the Spirit effects in us is a lifelong process which we label "sanctification." We anticipate at the end of the age our "glorification," the completion of the Spirit's work of renewal.

Conversion

As we pointed out in chapter 16, our experience of the Spirit's activity in salvation begins with conversion. Conversion is that life-changing encounter with the triune God which inaugurates the process of forsaking our old ways as fallen creatures and living in accordance with God's design for human existence.

In our previous discussion we saw that the glorious transaction occurs when an individual responds to the gospel as enabled by the Spirit and within the context of Christ's community. Now we view conversion from the perspective of what the Spirit accomplishes in us through this event. We inquire concerning the Spirit's deposit, mediated to us in conversion, which forms the foundation for the process of salvation as a whole.

Conversion and the human predicament. One helpful way of looking at the Spirit's accomplishment in conversion is by understanding it as God's antidote for the predicament caused by sin. Through the grand transaction, the Spirit applies to the repentant sinner the provision Jesus Christ has made available to us. We may view the Spirit's application of Christ's provision in accordance with the metaphors we employed in our discussions of human sin (chapter 7) and Jesus' mission (chapter 12).

(1) We may understand the Spirit's application of the work of Christ in the context of a metaphor drawn from interpersonal relations. Seen from this perspective, in conversion the Spirit effects *regeneration*. In the miraculous transaction that marks the beginning of our Christian experience, he authors in us new spiritual life. In this manner, we become members of the family of God and enjoy restored fellowship with our Creator.

The Greek term translated "regeneration" in the King James Version of the Bible, *palingenesis*, occurs only twice in the New Testament. In one instance, it refers to the "renewal of all things" which will occur when the Son of man comes in judgment (Matt. 19:28) More important for our purposes is Paul's declaration that God "saved us through the washing of rebirth and renewal [*palingenesis*] by the Holy Spirit" (Titus 3:5). This verse sets forth the foundation for the theological meaning of the concept. "Regeneration" is important means to understand personal salvation because it is related to the biblical concept of the new birth and it is produced by the Holy Spirit.

The connection between regeneration and the new birth is immediately obvious in the Greek word. *Palingenesis* ("regeneration") is derived from the verb *gennao* (active: "give birth to"; passive: "be born") and the adverb *palin* ("again, once more"). Consequently, the term "regeneration" is etymologically related to the idea of rebirth. The theological significance of the word, therefore, arises from the metaphor contained within it. Regeneration refers to our spiritual birth, the transaction that brings us into intimate relationship with God as his children. Just as physical birth endows the newborn with a special relationship with his or her parents, so also our spiritual birth means that we are sons or daughters of God and members of his family. Through regeneration, we now participate in the divine family as God's spiritual children.

Paul also indicated that regeneration occurs by means of the work of the Holy Spirit. At conversion the Spirit authors new, spiritual life in us.

With this background in view, we may place the Spirit's act of regeneration within the context of human sin. Because of sin, we are alienated from God who by virtue of creation is our Father. Designed to be his friends, we have made ourselves enemies of the Creator. Into this situation, Jesus Christ came to provide reconciliation. In him, God opened the way to bring our hostility to an end. In conversion, the Spirit applies this provision to an individual. He is the agent of the new birth, creating new divine life in us. Consequently, we are born into God's family (John 1:12-13); that is, through the Spirit we share in divine life as the spiritual offspring of God. We who once were God's enemies are now members of God's own family. Consequently, we enjoy fellowship with him.

In short, regeneration occurs as the Spirit applies Christ's work of reconciliation to us in order thereby to transform our hostility toward

God into fellowship with him. Regeneration is God's ultimate response to our problem of alienation. It is the work of the Spirit, made possible by the work of the Son, in accordance with the will of the Father.

(2) We may also draw from a legal metaphor in seeking to comprehend the Spirit's work of applying the provision of Christ. Viewed in this manner, through conversion the Spirit effects *justification*. The grand transaction is the Spirit's work in granting us a new standing before God. We are now treated as righteous in God's sight.

Historically, Protestant theologians have tended to define salvation primarily in terms of this metaphor. This interest dates to the father of the Reformation himself, Martin Luther. As an Augustinian monk Luther set out on a personal quest to find a gracious God. Luther's discovery of the God who in Christ freely forgives sin and justifies the sinner gave shape to his theological orientation. At the heart of Luther's theology is the Pauline theme of justification by grace through faith alone. This emphasis, which he bequeathed to his followers, constitutes one of Luther's lasting legacy in the church.

The biblical background for the theological term "justification" lies in the concept of righteousness. Although this connection is not so obvious in the English words, it is readily evident in their Greek counterparts. To justify (*dikaioo*) means to make righteous (*dikaios*), resulting in a state of righteousness (*dikaiosune*). In classical Greek, the terms in the word group were associated with civil virtue. A righteous person was "one who conforms, who is civilised, who observes custom," one who fulfils personal obligations, or one who observes legal norms.[1] Thus, righteousness entailed a set disposition leading to obedience to the civil law and fulfillment of one's civil duty. Because of its importance to civil life, the Greeks included righteousness among the four cardinal virtues and elevated it as a basic legislative principle.[2]

The Old Testament writers understood righteousness (related to the Hebrew terms *tsaddiq, tsedeq,* and *tsedaqah*) primarily in the

---

1. Gottlob Schrenk, "dikaios," in the *Theological Dictionary of the New Testament,* ed. Gerhard Kittel, trans. Geoffery W. Bromiley (Grand Rapids: Eerdmans, 1964), 2:182
2. Gottlob Schrenk, "dikaiosune," in TDNT, 2:193.

context of God's judgments. Above all, God is the righteous judge. Consequently, the Greek focus on virtue pales in importance to the Hebrew concern for how a person can stand in this judgment as expressed in the law, which is its standard. The righteous person, the Old Testament writers concluded, is the one "who fulfils his duties towards God and the theocratic society, meeting God's claim in this relationship."[3] And righteousness is "the observance of the will of God," as is well-pleasing to him.[4]

The ninety-one occurrences of *dikaiosune* in the New Testament reflect a broad understanding of its meaning influenced sometimes by the Greek but more readily by the Hebrew background. Occasionally the term refers to God's just judgment exercised by Christ at his return (Acts 17:31; Rev. 19:11). More often its use continues the Old Testament tradition, meaning right conduct in accordance with the will of God or uprightness in the face of divine judgment.[5]

The majority of occurrences of *dikaiosune* are in the Pauline letters. Paul too declared that only the righteous can enjoy true fellowship with God. But he emphasized the great theological truth that this righteousness does not arise from the law. Rather than being the result of our own work, fellowship comes only through God's sovereign, gracious, and decisive intervention in Christ,[6] through whom he is abidingly faithful to himself and to his people.[7]

God's act in bestowing righteousness on us as a gift is what Paul termed "justification." God can graciously justify the sinner because of Christ's work on our behalf. In justification, God does not create right conduct in us. Rather, he imparts righteousness to us as a new standing before him. The divine Judge views us as righteous. God can justify the ungodly who believe because of his justifying action in the death and resurrection of Christ.[8]

---

3. See Schrenk, "dikaios," 185.

4. Schlenk, "dikaiosune," 196.

5. Ibid., 198.

6. Ibid., 202-3.

7. Karl Kertelge, "dikaiosune," in the *Exegetical Dictionary of the New Testament*, ed. Horst Balz and Gerhard Schneider, English translation (Grand Rapids: Eerdmans, 1990), 2:328.

8. Schlenk, "dikaioo," in TDNT, 2:215.

Justification, then, is a forensic term, referring to a change in our legal standing before God.[9] Like regeneration, we may view it in the context of God's response to our human predicament. Because of sin, we stand condemned before the holy God. In love, however, God sent Christ to make provision for our sin. Through his death, Jesus covered our sin so that the just sentence of condemnation need not fall on us. The task of the Holy Spirit is to apply Christ's expiation to individuals. This occurs in conversion, which inaugurates a new standing before God. We are justified—declared righteous in God's sight.

Justification, therefore, is God's ultimate answer to the condemnation that stands over us because of sin. The Father sent the Son to die for us, and now the Spirit applies the fruit of his death to our lives. As a result, we can enjoy a new standing before God. Reformed theologians often describe justification as God's act of imputing to a sinful person the righteousness of Christ.[10] Hence, the concept carries a picture. God strips off our "filthy rags" of sin and replaces them with the "coat" of Christ's righteousness.

(3) The third metaphor we use in understanding the work of the Spirit arises from the cosmic drama of the conflict between God and the powers of evil. In conversion the Spirit effects our *liberation* from enslavement to hostile forces. His presence mediates to us freedom—the ability to reject sin and choose God's will.

Freedom is an important New Testament theme. Paradigmatic is the promise of true freedom which Jesus voiced in a discussion with Jews who had believed in him. He declared, "if the Son sets you free, you will be free indeed" (John 8:36). Hence, as Niederwimmer observes, in the New Testament the concept "represents the unsurpassed freedom that Christ gives to the believer, the citizen of the eschatological world."[11]

The New Testament writers placed this freedom in the context of a cosmic drama. As we noted in chapter 8, the human predicament does not consist only in the sentence of condemnation brought upon

---

9. Kertelge notes that in the New Testament *dikaioo* always carries a forensic or judicial stamp. "Dikaioo," in EDNT, 2:331.

10. E.g., Louis Berkhof, *Systematic Theology* (Grand Rapids: Eerdmans, 1953), 517.

11. Kurt Niederwimmer, "eleutheros," in EDNT, 1:432.

us by our acts of failure. In addition, hostile alien powers exercise control over our lives. Above all, we are enslaved to sin. This bondage means that we lack the freedom to live in accordance with God's design. Rather than obeying God, we willingly and necessarily find ourselves ruled by an evil taskmaster—sin. With this situation in view Jesus replied to the Jews, "I tell you the truth, everyone who sins is a slave to sin" (John 8:34).

Our bondage to sin places us under the grip of another hostile force—death. Indeed "the wages of sin is death" (Rom. 6:23). Consequently, our slavery to sin has both a present and a future dimension. We are spiritually dead now. One day we will die physically. And in all eternity we will be separated from fellowship with God.

The good news of the gospel, however, is that Jesus Christ has been victorious over the forces of evil. By conquering sin, death, and Satan, he provided redemption for us, effecting the release of those who were in bondage. Through conversion, the Spirit applies Christ's victory to our lives. One day he will mediate to us full liberty from the power of sin and death through the resurrection (Rom 8:11). Even now, however, he indwells us thereby counteracting the enslaving control of sin.

The Spirit's presence brings freedom. As Paul noted, "where the Spirit of the Lord is there is freedom" (2 Cor. 3:17). Paul's autobiographical remark to the Romans is the testimony of countless believers: "through Christ Jesus the law of the Spirit of life set me free from the law of sin and death" (Rom. 8:2). Because of the Spirit, we are indeed free. Because we are no longer slaves to sin (6:14), as we "walk in the Spirit" we are able to obey God.

This freedom is ours as a gift of God. We cannot gain it through our attempts to live in obedience to the law (Rom. 3:20). On the contrary, Paul noted that sin actually misuses the law, twisting it to become a vehicle for sin's own evil ends. He wrote autobiographically, "But sin, seizing the opportunity afforded by the commandment, produced in me every kind of covetous desire...and through the commandment put me to death" (7:8,11). For this reason, Paul was so adamant in warning believers not to return to bondage through a relapse into legalism (Gal. 2:4; 5:1).

We must be careful not to confuse the freedom promised by Christ and facilitated by the Spirit with the everyday experience of choosing from among options. In the New Testament, freedom does not mean the ability to be a disinterested decision-maker, to stand before choices unencumbered by any overpowering inclination to decide in one direction or the other. Indeed, in the face of moral decisions the choosing individual is never a neutral, autonomous self, but faces moral choice already predisposed. New Testament freedom is the ability to live in accordance with our destiny. It entails the release from the predisposition toward evil in order to be able choose the good.

Living in freedom, however, does not mean living without restraint. On the contrary, freedom is God's gift bestowed on us though participation in community with Christ. It entails discipleship. As Jesus said, "If you hold to my teaching you are really my disciples. Then you will know the truth and the truth will set you free" (John 8:31-32). Hence, we are liberated from bondage to sin in order to be "slaves to righteousness" (Rom. 6:18) or "slaves of God" (v. 22). Genuine freedom, therefore, is life in community. As such it includes the capacity for service to others (Gal. 5:13), even the capacity to renounce one's own freedom for the sake of others (1 Cor. 9:19; 10:23-24).

(4) The final motif through which we may view the Spirit's application of Christ's provision in salvation is that of *empowerment*. In conversion the Spirit bestows on us power for service.

Human sin is a radical reality. It touches every dimension of life thereby leaving us in a depraved (that is, helpless) state of existence. Specifically, sin leaves us powerless to serve God and others in the way God intends. Into this hopeless situation Jesus came as our substitute. He accomplished for us what we cannot do for ourselves.

As the one who applies Christ's provision to us, the Holy Spirit endows us with divine power. Specifically, his presence is the power we need for a lifetime of service to God and for God's kingdom (Acts 1:8).

Conversion and the establishment of community. In conversion, the Spirit applies to us the provision made available by Jesus. In so doing, he mediates to us God's regeneration, justification, freedom, and power. But the saving work of the Spirit is not intended to overcome the problem of sin as an end in itself. Rather, these grand effects of the Spirit's activity in conversion are all directed toward a higher, more glorious goal, which is nothing less than the central focus of the saving action of the triune God. We are rescued from sin in order that we may participate in the fellowship of the redeemed humanity living in a redeemed world and enjoying the presence of the redeemer God.

Conversion, therefore, is the event which marks our entry into the ongoing activity of God in bringing his creation to this grand *telos*, the establishment of community. In conversion, the Spirit initiates us into the present experience of community. It, in turn, is the foretaste of the full fellowship that God will bring to pass at the culmination of history. With this in view, we must look more closely at the community the Spirit authors through conversion.

(1) Above all, through this grand transaction the Spirit brings us into community with God. The Spirit's work in effecting such fellowship is the outworking of his identity within the eternal Trinity. He is the Spirit of the relationship between the Father and the Son. Consequently, when the Spirit indwells us, present within is the very community of the triune God himself. In other words, in effecting salvation in our lives, the Spirit brings us to participate in the eternal relationship the Son enjoys with the Father, which relationship he in fact is. His presence elevates us beyond our seemingly insignificant human existence and causes us to taste the fellowship present within the eternity of God. Although we remain forever distinct from God, through the Spirit we share in the dynamic life of the Trinity.

For this reason, the great biblical metaphors of salvation focus on fellowship with the Father through the Son. "Regeneration" refers to the relational dimension of fellowship. We who were God's enemies now experience community with him, because the Spirit has effected our new birth into the Father's family as the brothers and sisters of the Son. Similarly, "justification" signifies the legal aspect of fellowship. The Spirit has caused us to exchange our unrighteousness, which formerly barred the way to community, with the righteousness of the Son himself, thereby bringing us to enjoy fellowship with the Father. Through the term "freedom" we view fellowship in terms of the cosmic drama. Once we were slaves to an alien evil force acting against the plan of the Father and consequently took part in the conspiracy against our Creator. But now as the Spirit applies to us the work of Christ, we are liberated to participate in the same freedom that the Son enjoys before the Father. Finally, the Spirit provides us who were powerless with the power to live according to the pattern that characterizes the Son's response to the Father.

(2) In mediating to us fellowship with God, the Spirit also brings us into community with one another and with all creation. We are not saved in isolation, nor in order to enjoy an exclusivistic relationship with the triune God. Rather, through conversion the Spirit brings us to participation within a community, the disciples of Jesus and the new creation of God.

The motifs of salvation imply this dimension. Regeneration speaks of the new family into which the Spirit causes us to be born. Consequently, we do not experience our new relationship with God in isolation. Rather, the Spirit's application of the Son's provision of reconciliation is ours as we becomes members of the one new humankind among whom the old hostilities have been erased (Eph. 2:14-18).

In the same manner, righteousness carries implications not only for our relationship to God, but also for our conduct toward each other and by extension to all God's creation. We are justified in God's presence not so that we can exist in isolation, but in order that we may act righteously toward each other and toward all creatures. Indeed, as Jesus repeatedly taught, our reception of the gift of forgiveness and right standing before God ought to issue forth in right social conduct (Matt. 18:21-35). Because we know we are all only sinners saved by grace, we give careful attention to the special bond of unity and peace that the Spirit produces among us (Eph. 4:3).

The concepts of freedom and power point in the same direction. We are freed from sin and empowered by the Spirit in order to serve one another and together to show forth to all creation the character of God (to live as the image of God). It is only as we demonstrate through our actions that the Spirit of love is among us that we show to the world that we are a people in fellowship with God.

Although for purposes of discussion we readily separate the individual and corporate aspects of salvation, we must remember that in fact they are only facets of a single whole. We cannot participate in God's salvation apart from our incorporation into the redeemed people. But neither can we be truly members of Christ's community unless we are also united individually to him. Individual salvation, therefore, is a community phenomenon. This theme leads us to ecclesiology, which is the topic of part 5.

Sanctification

The saving work of the Holy Spirit in an individual does not end at conversion. This event is only the beginning of a process of transformation into Christlikeness which extends throughout our days. We speak of this ongoing process as "sanctification." In the strict theological sense sanctification is the Holy Spirit accomplishing God's purpose in us as Christian life proceeds.[12] Or viewed from the human perspective, it is our cooperation with the Spirit in living out in daily life the regeneration, justification, freedom, and power which is ours through conversion, so that we grow in Christlikeness and service to God.

The concept of sanctification in the Bible. Although the English words do not betray such a connection, the term "sanctification" in the original biblical languages is closely related to the idea of holiness, understood as meaning "being separated" and hence "sacred." In fact, both the Hebrew and Greek words indicate that "to sanctify" means "to make holy," that is, "to set apart." In its widest use, therefore, sanctification is the act or process of making something holy by setting it apart.[13]

This aspect of sanctification reflects one of the most universal dimensions of human culture. Nearly all societies give place to the idea of the sacred, the set apart, the holy. All religious traditions include

---

12. See R. E. O. White, "Sanctification," in *Evangelical Dictionary of Theology*, ed. Walter A. Elwell (Grand Rapids: Baker, 1984), 970.

13. Otto Procksch, "hagiazo," in TDNT, 1:111.

rituals designed to facilitate the act of setting things apart and thereby making them holy.

The Old Testament documents repeatedly refer to what is holy, to holiness, or to the act of making holy. These references cluster around a family of Hebrew terms sharing a common root—the verb *qadash*, the noun *qodesh*, and the adjective *qadosh*—which represents the idea of setting apart, especially for the work of God.[14]

In ancient Israel the act of sanctification could encompass a wide variety of objects—places (Ex. 3:5; Deut 23:14; Ps. 2:6; Neh.11:1), animals or inanimate objects (Deut. 15:19; Ex. 29:43-44; 27-28; 2 Cor. 7:1-2; Lev. 27:14-17), points in time (Gen 2:3; Joel 1:14; Lev. 25:10), and human beings (Ex. 13:2; 28:41; 19:10; Jer. 1:5). Above all, however, the Hebrews knew that God is holy or sacred (Lev. 11:44). Therefore his worshipers were to set him apart from, and to revere him above all other gods. God's exalted status, in turn, formed the basis for setting apart persons, things, and even the nation itself. Because God is holy, Israel was to be holy—separate from the world and the things of the world (Lev. 11:44; 19:2; 20:7,26; 21:8). The Old Testament texts likewise reveal a broad understanding of the agency of sanctification. A person may sanctify oneself (2 Chr. 29:5) or be sanctified by another (Ex. 19:10-11). The act may entail rituals, such as sacrifices (29:10-11), washings (29:4), or anointings (29:7).

We tend to think of sanctification (the act of making holy) as bound up with the moral or spiritual qualities of what is holy. The Old Testament concept, however, focuses more on position, specifically the relationship between God and what is consecrated to him.[15] The act of sanctifying sets something or someone apart from the ordinary for use in God's service (28:41). The sacred may also refer to what has fulfilled the requirements for entrance into God's presence (19:10-11). However, such an enabling act does not necessarily produce the inward or moral quality of detachment from sin. More generally, the term implies a forensic understanding of holiness. To

---

14. Robert B. Girdlestone, *Synonyms of the Old Testament*, second edition reprint (1897; Grand Rapids: Eerdmans, 1973), 175.

15. Girdlestone, *Synonyms of the OT*, 175.

sanctify, therefore, entails a legal declaration of a new relationship to God.

The New Testament authors used a family of Greek terms to speak about sanctification. The family includes the verb *hagiazo* (20 occurrences), the adjective *hagios* (230 occurrences), and the nouns *hagiosmos* (10 occurrences), *hagiotas* (only in Heb. 12:10; 2 Cor. 1:12), and *hagiosune* (only in Rom. 1:4; 2 Cor. 7:1; 1 Thess. 3:13).[16] *Hagiasmos* properly refers to sanctification itself, for the word denotes the act of sanctifying or consecrating.

The concept of sanctification in the New Testament resembles its Old Testament counterpart. It too embraces a variety of objects: material things (Matt. 23:17,19; 2 Tim. 4:15), God's people (1 Cor. 6:11; 1:2; Acts 20:32; 26:18; Heb. 10:10, 14), and God (John 17:11; 1 John 2:20; Rev. 6:10), whose name is to be hallowed (Matt. 6:9). The New Testament authors also include Christ, who like God is to be set apart (1 Pet. 3:15; John 10:36; 17:19a), and above all the Spirit, who is the *Holy* Spirit.

Various texts include each of the trinitarian persons as the agency of the sanctifying act: the Father (1 Thess. 5:23-24; Heb 10:10; John 17:17; Eph. 4:1), the Son (1 Cor. 1:2; Eph. 5:26-27; John 17:19; 1 Cor. 1:30; Col. 1:22; Heb 2:11; 10:10-14; 13:12), and the Holy Spirit (Rom. 15:16; 2 Thess. 2:13; 1 Pet. 1:2). The New Testament also suggests that we are involved in this process (Rom. 6:19; 2 Tim 2:21; 1 Tim. 2:15; Heb 12:14; Rom 12:1), specifically as we exercise faith in Christ (Acts 26:18) and yield to God (Rom. 6:19, 22; 12:1).

The act of sanctification entails a new status before God (2 Thess. 2:13). Stronger than its Old Testament counterpart, *hagiasmos* can also carry reference to moral qualities (Eph 5:27; Col. 1:22; 1 Pet. 1:15-16; 2 Pet. 3:11). Further, sanctification is tied to obedience (1 Pet. 1:2), for it is intended to lead to holiness in lifestyle (Rom. 6:22; Heb. 12:14).

Taken as a whole, the biblical idea of sanctification carries several related meanings. It includes the human act of regarding God as holy, that is, as unique among, exalted over, and separated from the gods or from everything in creation (Matt. 6:9; Luke 11:2; 1 Pet.

---

16. Horst Balz, "hagios," in EDNT, 1:16.

3:15). To sanctify God, therefore, means to ascribe holiness to him or to acknowledge his holiness by word or deed. Sanctification refers likewise to the human act of separating someone or something from the realm of the ordinary (Matt. 23:17,19; John 10:36; 2 Tim. 2:21). In this act, which may include a ritual or a commissioning, we dedicate what is sanctified to God for his special use. Finally, sanctification is that activity of God through the Holy Spirit by which he makes the individual believer holy (John 17:17; Acts 20:32; 26:18; 1 Cor. 1:2; 1 Thess. 5:23). It is to this third meaning that we now turn our attention.

The theological concept of sanctification. The Hebrew and Greek terms for sanctification (*qadash, hagiazo*) are connected to the idea of the holy. This connection indicates that the foundation for the theological concept of sanctification lies in the holiness of God.

We noted in the discussion of the divine attributes that God's holiness entails both his uniqueness (God is set apart from all creation) and his moral uprightness (God is untainted by sin in all he does). Because God is the standard for humans who are to be his image, the divine holiness forms the foundation for the biblical emphasis on God's activity in fostering holiness in us (sanctification). Because God is holy, he commands us to be holy. The task of the Holy Spirit is to effect in us what God commands.

God's activity in our sanctification arises not only out of his holiness, but also from his purpose in calling out a people to be his own. We find this purpose evident in the choosing of Israel in the Old Testament and in the calling of the worldwide church of Jesus Christ in the present age. In keeping with the divine purpose, the sanctified people of God are to view themselves as God's own possession. We belong to the God who has chosen us, and we exist in order to honor him and to serve his purposes in the world (Eph. 1:11-12).

God's sanctifying activity consists in two dimensions, which we may refer to as "positional" and "conditional." *Positional sanctification* reflects the dominant relational aspect depicted by the Hebrew and Greek terms. It refers to our "position" before God which we enjoy by virtue of our new status in Christ. Through our relationship with Christ, God has declared us to be set apart and holy; we belong to him. Paul gave expression to this dimension in his greeting to the sinful Corinthian Christians: "To the church of God in Corinth, to those sanctified in Christ Jesus and called to be holy" (1 Cor. 1:2; [the infinitive verb "to be" is not in the original text]).

Positional sanctification, therefore, is an objective reality, a standing in righteousness which is ours solely by virtue of the grace God extended to us in Christ and which the Holy Spirit applies to our lives. We receive this reality solely by faith.

The new status which God has freely bestowed on us is crucial. It not only fixes our relationship with him, it also serves as the fountainhead out of which the Christian life emerges. As Procksch notes in the *Theological Dictionary of the New Testament*, "Christian morality does not arise on the basis of a new action but on that of a new state which is best expressed as *hagiasmos.*"[17]

The actual transformation of our lifestyle, the morality that arises out of our new position and progressively comes to characterize our lives, we may call *conditional sanctification*. In contrast to positional sanctification, it refers to our present spiritual condition, specifically, to the extent to which we measure up to God's ideal in our current attitudes and actions. Hence, conditional sanctification entails our current level of spirituality, including the morality of the life we are living. In short, it refers to our character and conduct.

As this sketch suggests, the two dimensions of sanctification differ immensely. Rather than a fixed, objective position granted us by God (positional sanctification), conditional sanctification is subjective, experiential, and consequently variable. It is our movement from imperfection and immaturity to increasing conformity to the standard, which is Jesus Christ. Rather than being the product of God's gracious fiat which we can only accept by faith, conditional sanctification arises as we cooperate with the Holy Spirit in his goal of transforming our lives. Although in the end it is the Spirit's work, we must diligently apply ourselves to the task of being brought into conformity with Jesus Christ. We must: "Make every effort...to be holy; without holiness no one will see the Lord" (Heb. 12:14).

---

17. Procksch, "hagios," 108.

The sanctification process. Understood in its conditional sense, sanctification is a process. Paul testified to his own experience of a continual movement toward the final goal: "Not that I have attained all this, or have already been made perfect, but I press on to take hold of that for which Christ Jesus took hold of me" (Phil 3:12-14; see also 2 Cor. 3:18; Eph. 4:14). In addition to such explicit references, the various commands to grow in holiness or to become holy provide implicit witness to the progressive nature of conditional sanctification. Peter drew an admonition from the Old Testament: "But just as he who called you is holy, so be holy in all you do; for it is written: 'Be holy, because I am holy'" (1 Peter 1:15-16).

Of utmost significance in the process of sanctification, of course, is the working of God's Spirit. Paul reminded his readers that the Spirit carries on a war with the old sinful nature (Gal. 5:17). Likewise, this Spirit provides the necessary power for overcoming temptation (1 Cor. 10:13) and sin (Rom. 8:12-14).

While the ultimate agent of sanctification is the Holy Spirit, in this process he requires our personal cooperation. In fact, we must diligently apply ourselves to the task (2 Peter 1:5-11). Foundational to our involvement in the battle against our opponent is the utilization of the provision God has given us (2 Pet. 1:3), including our spiritual weaponry (Eph. 6:10-17). Important as well is fervent prayer (Eph. 6:18; Matt. 26:41). But above all, we must love one another (1 Pet. 4:8).

Perfectionism. The goal of the Holy Spirit in sanctification is to foster Christlikeness in us—that we eventually attain "the full measure of the stature of Christ" (Eph. 4:14). When do we attain the goal of our efforts? This question brings us to one of the divisive debates about sanctification in theological history. Does the sanctification process culminate in this life, bringing us to attain some type of perfection here ("perfectionism")? Or do we remain imperfect and fallen in all aspects of our existence until the eschatological renewal?

Although there are several varieties of perfectionism in theological history, modern perfectionism began with Wesley's doctrine of "entire sanctification." The founder of the Methodists believed that

579

God had promised to save us from all willful sin, and to do so before death.[18]

Wesley's followers drew from their leader the idea of a "second blessing," a definable moment of grace which breaks decisively the stranglehold that sin otherwise continues to exercise over a believer's life. Wesleyan perfectionism, therefore, anticipates a moment in our experience—which we lay hold of through faith—when our former sinful desires are eradicated. The cessation of the inner war against sin means that the heart is "fully released from rebellion into wholehearted love for God and others."[19] We are set free "to love with the love of God Himself shed abroad in the heart by the indwelling Spirit."[20]

Wesley saw God's promise of entire sanctification in a variety of biblical passages (Deut. 30:6; Ps. 130:8; Ezek. 36:25,29; Matt. 5:48; 6:13; 22:37; John 3:8; 17:20-21, 23; Rom. 8:3-4; 2 Cor. 7:1; Eph. 3:14-19; 5:25,27; 1 Thess. 5:23).[21] Yet the Wesleyan doctrine is not based so much on specific texts as an attempt to see Scripture holistically. Melvin Dieter explains:

> Wesleyans believe that lying behind the biblical and theological themes outlined above—the meaning of creation, the fall of men and women, the understanding of law and grace, and the ministry and work of the Holy Spirit—is the most prominent of all biblical themes, namely, the call to sanctification, or holiness, itself, with its ultimate end an ongoing relationship in love with God and all others.[22]

Nevertheless, one biblical text stands above all others as providing explicit support for the idea of perfectionism:

> No one who lives in him keeps on sinning. No one who continues to sin has either seen him or known him.... No one who is born of God will continue to sin, because God's seed remains in him, he cannot go on sinning, because he has been born of God." (1 John 3:6,9; see also Luke 1:69-75; Titus 2:11-14; 1 John 4:17)

---

18. Melvin E. Dieter, "The Wesleyan Perspective," in *Five Views on Sanctification* (Grand Rapids: Zondervan, 1987), 15.

19. Ibid., 17.

20. Ibid., 27-28.

21. Ibid., 15.

22. Ibid., 30.

These verses may not be the strong affirmation of this doctrine that they at first appear to be. Earlier in the same epistle, John seemed to assert the exact opposite teaching, namely, that sin is continuously with us. He wrote, "If we claim to be without sin, we deceive ourselves and the truth is not in us" (1 John 1:8). In fact, John placed the desire that his readers live perfect lives together with the anticipation that they will in fact continue to fall: "My dear children, I write this to you so that you will not sin. But if anybody does sin, we have one who speaks to the Father in our defense—Jesus Christ the Righteous One" (1 John 2:1). It seems therefore, that John did not anticipate "entire sanctification" in this lifetime. Only when Christ returns will we enjoy perfection: "But we know that when he appears, we shall be like him, for we shall see him as he is" (1 John 3:2).

How, then, are we to understand John's declaration that the believer does not sin (1 John 3:6,9)? For the answer, opponents of the doctrine of perfection point to John's use of present tense verbs, which in the Greek language regularly refer to continuous action. The apostle's point was that believers do not make sin a continuous, habitual action. True believers do not *habitually* sin, even though they continue to commit specific acts which displease God.

This understanding of John's comment places him in continuity with other New Testament writers. Even adherents of perfectionism acknowledge that the New Testament contains no explicit exhortation to seek an experience of total sanctification.[23] On the contrary, as we noted earlier Paul emphasized continual growth in holiness. Throughout his life, he denied that he had reached perfection (Phil. 3:12,14). Only as he faced imminent death, did he claim to have "finished the race" and "kept the faith" (2 Tim. 4:7).

Despite this critique, we must applaud the Wesleyan perspective for rightly highlighting the importance of the biblical theme of sanctification. And as Melvin Dieter points out, the ultimate goal of this process is living in love.[24] Ultimately, therefore, the Wesleyan vision is an anticipation of community. It reminds us that the Spirit's

---

23. Ibid., 32.
24. Ibid., 30.

work in salvation leads to the establishment of community—our enjoyment of fellowship with God, with one another, and with all creation.

The goal of community, however, is never fully attained in this life. It will be ours only at the eschatological renewal. Consequently, so long as we live on this earth we never move beyond the need for the prodding of the Spirit. The process of sanctification, we conclude, remains with us until we have "finished the race"—that is, until our final glorification.

Glorification

The lifelong nature of the sanctification process leads us to anticipate a final aspect of our experience of the Holy Spirit's work in personal salvation. We call this final experience glorification. Simply stated, glorification refers to the Spirit's eschatological completion of our salvation, when he brings us to reflect perfectly the goal of our conversion and sanctification.

The biblical writers rarely spoke of the glorification of human beings. Rather, God is the one worthy of being glorified. However, in one key text Paul did mention our glorification by God: "those he justified he also glorified" (Rom. 8:29-30). Later we will look more closely at Paul's recounting of the various stages in the divine program. In this context we need note only that glorification stands at the end of the sequence the apostle enumerates. Although Paul's certainty of the fact led him to use the past tense, he undoubtedly had in mind here the eschatological completion of our salvation.[25]

The idea of our future glorification is implicit throughout the New Testament. Peter offers a clear example. He declared that our inheritance—full salvation—is being kept for us until that eschatological event (1 Peter 1:3-5).

---

25. For Paul's use of the aorist tense to refer to the certainty of the future event, see, Charles R. Erdman, *The Epistle of Paul to the Romans* (Philadelphia: Westminster, 1925, 1946), 103-104; W. Robertson Nicoll, ed., *The Expositor's Bible*, six volumes (Rahway, N.J.: Expositor's Bible Company, n.d.), 5:575; William Sanday and Arthur C. Headlam, *A Critical and Exegetical Commentary on the Epistle to the Romans*, in the *International Critical Commentary*, fifth edition (Edinburgh: T. & T. Clark, 1902), 218.

The agent at work in this dimension of our salvation is the same Holy Spirit who facilitates every step of the divine project. Hence, Paul claimed that believers have already received the guarantee or pledge of the final salvation, namely, the indwelling Holy Spirit (2 Cor. 5:5; Eph. 1:13; 4:30). The Spirit who is now present within Christians will accomplish the final transformation of God's people at Jesus' return (Rom. 8:11, 13-17).

The experience of glorification will encompass our entire existence, for at that time the Spirit will transform us into complete Christlikeness. John wrote, "But we know that when he appears, we will be like him, for we shall see him as he is" (1 John 3:2).

The Spirit's transformation will include, or course, our character. We will be Christlike insofar as we come to mirror perfectly the fruit of the Spirit (Gal. 5:22-23), which Jesus Christ exemplified. Hence, we will be characterized by righteousness not only in our standing before God through Christ, but also in our actual living. To facilitate this renewal of virtue, we can anticipate that the Spirit will root out our fallen sinful nature. Because we will no longer be susceptible to temptation and sin, we will be totally free to obey God perfectly.

The effects of glorification will not be limited to the so-called spiritual dimension of our existence, however. Rather, the Christlikeness which the Spirit will cause us to share will extend to our physical bodies as well. Paul declared that "he who raised Christ from the dead will also give life to your mortal bodies through his Spirit who lives in you" (Rom. 8:11). Hence, we can take quite literally John's vision of the new order: "There will be no more death or mourning or crying or pain, for the old order of things has passed away" (Rev. 21:4). Our bodies will no longer be subject to decay, sickness, disease, or death. They will be made perfect, in accordance with the pattern of the glorified body of our risen Lord. Indeed he is the first fruits of those who will attain to the resurrection (1 Cor. 15:20,23).

Although it occurs as the culmination of the salvation of the individual believer, glorification is a corporate reality. Rather than happening to each of us alone, the resurrection which facilitates our glorification occurs only as we are participants in the one body of

Christ. Likewise, this event does not usher us into a life of autonomous isolation, but brings us to the enjoyment of an eternal fellowship in community with God, each other, and the new creation. In short, glorification mediates our participation in the final purpose of God, that is, the eschatological community toward which God directs all his saving activity.

The Eternal Context of Salvation

Viewed from our perspective, salvation is the process that begins with conversion, moves through sanctification, and leads to glorification. If we look behind our experience, however, we discover that salvation is one unified act of the triune God within which the Spirit is at work bringing us into full conformity with the likeness of Christ. The Spirit's work, therefore, occurs within a wider context, namely, God's eternal purpose.

Divine Election

At the heart of the eternal context in which the Spirit's work in salvation lies is the electing nature of God. We experience salvation because the triune God, who is relational in his own nature, chooses to enter into relationship with us his creatures. He calls sinful humans to share in the divine fellowship (2 Pet. 1:4). This central dimension of God's eternal intention leads us to the concept of election.

Election has been one of the central themes of the Reformed theological tradition. Above all, Reformed theologians look to the electing God for the key to the mystery of salvation.[26] Despite their shared interest in election, however, they have not come to agreement concerning the exact nature and significance of the divine choice. On the contrary, the mention of the doctrine of election leads us to the ever-smouldering Calvinist-Arminian controversy.

---

26. Erickson, for example, begins his discussion of the doctrine of salvation by introducing the concept of predestination, which he defines as "God's choice of individuals for eternal life or eternal death." Election, in turn, is the positive side of predestination, namely, God's "selection of some for eternal life." Millard Erickson, *Christian Theology*, three volumes (Grand Rapids: Baker, 1985), 3:908.

The controversy over the five points of Calvinism. "Calvinism" is the term we use to designate the theological system which came to dominate the Reformed wing of Protestantism. Although explicitly invoking the legacy of the great Geneva reformer, John Calvin (1509-1564), Calvinism in its classical form actually took shape in heated debate surrounding the teachings of James Arminius (1560-1609).[27] The center of the controversy occurred in Holland and was officially resolved at the Synod of Dort (1618-19), which approved the well-known "five points of Calvinism."

(1) The five points embody the central motivation of the Calvinist theological system, namely, the desire to uphold the sovereignty of God in all his dealings with his creatures, but above all in the matter of the salvation of individuals. We may enumerate the Calvinist focus on the sovereignty of God in individual election using the famous "tulip" acrostic.

Total depravity ("t") declares that the effects of the fall extend to every aspect of human existence; no human person possesses the ability to gain access to God by personal merit. *Unconditional election* ("u") means that God selects individuals for salvation solely according to his grace and by his own will; it is not based on personal merit nor even on any prior conditions that humans fulfill, such as a positive response to the gospel. *Limited atonement* ("l"), which has been a point of controversy among Calvinists themselves, asserts that Jesus' death is solely for the elect, not for the lost. The doctrine of *irresistible grace* ("i") points out that the workings of the Holy Spirit in the life of an individual always triumph. Because the Spirit will eventually be successful in wooing the human will, the elected person will not ultimately resist the grace of God.[28] The *perseverance of the saints* ("p") capsulizes the assurance that the elect person will continue in faith in Jesus Christ throughout life. Despite times of backsliding, in the end the true believer will not falter so as to lose one's elect status.

---

27. For a summary of Arminius's teachings in comparison with the "five points of Calvinism," see Charles M. Cameron, "Arminius—Hero or Heretic?" *Evangelical Quarterly* 64/3 (1992): 213-27.

28. Louis Berkhof, *Systematic Theology*, revised and enlarged edition (Grand Rapids: Eerdmans, 1953), 115.

(2) Since their defeat at the Synod of Dort, Arminians have been placed on the defensive. As a consequence, many Christians now view Arminianism more as a reaction to the perceived difficulties with Calvinism than as a positive theological system in its own right. Arminianism has become a blanket term for those who reject the five points of Calvinism together with the corresponding Calvinist understanding of election.

Arminians reject the Calvinist conception of election because they see in it a God who is partial and unjust. A God who arbitrarily chooses some to eternal life and either forsakes the rest or capriciously damns them is not the righteous, morally upright God of the Bible who does not show favoritism (Acts 10:34). The critique voiced by the Baptist theologian William Newton Clarke is typical: "it is quite impossible to think that God draws lines among men by his determinative will, and independently marks off a certain part of mankind to whom alone the gift [i.e., the impartation of divine life] shall be available."[29]

Critics likewise fault the Calvinist doctrine of election for its apparent determinism. In Calvinism history loses its contingency. What appear to be the non-necessary events of history are nothing more than the unfolding of the determinations made by God prior to creation. This is especially evident in matters pertaining to individual salvation, for God's eternal electing decision, and not free human action, determines who will be saved. Such determinism seems to contradict our common understanding of history and our experience of decisionmaking.

Arminians also fault the Calvinist doctrine of election because of its connection to what they see as the faulty idea of perseverance. If it is indeed foreordained that the elect will persevere, they ask, why is it that the Bible repeatedly commands the believer to hold fast (Heb. 6:4-12)?

Finally, critics find the Calvinist doctrine of election problematic because of its link to irresistible grace. Irresistible grace poses difficulties in several areas. For example, it is theologically problematic,

---

29. William Newton Clark, *An Outline of Christian Theology*, twentieth edition (New York: Charles Scribner's Sons, 1912), 391.

for it implies that God alone is responsible for thwarting his own will. If grace is irresistible, the God who "is not willing that any should perish" (2 Pet. 3:9) denies to a large segment of humankind the grace apart from which no one can come to "the knowledge of the truth." God's saving hand is held out to those to whom he arbitrarily refuses the power needed to respond. This makes a sham of the imagery of God as a loving Father waiting with open arms for the wayward son (Luke 15:11-24; Rom 10:21).

Arminians also claim that irresistible grace is difficult to reconcile with the biblical understanding of grace. The New Testament indicates that God's grace is available even to those who perish (Titus 2:11; 2 Cor. 6:1), and the ministry of grace is to be present universally in the world (John 12:32; 16:8-11; 2 Cor. 5:19). Consequently, the overarching tone of the entire New Testament is one of "whosoever will may come" (Rev. 22:17). This seemingly universally available grace cannot be the irresistible variety so important to Calvinism.

Critics also see irresistible grace as philosophically problematic, when viewed in terms of the old question of the relationship between "ought" and "can": Does a moral command entail the ability to obey? Arminians declare that an actual moral choice—such as that of accepting or rejecting God's salvation—requires the presence of bonafide options. In philosophical terms, moral decisions require not only an "ought" but a "can." According to Calvinism, although all persons ought to come to Christ, not all can, for not all are the objects of God's irresistible grace. All are challenged by the divine "ought," but many lack the "can."

(3) Despite attacks such as these, Arminianism has not been able to displace Calvinism within the Reformed tradition, at least among conservative theologians. The preeminence of Calvinism may be due to certain strengths which overshadow whatever weaknesses it may encompass.

The Calvinist emphasis on election is helpful in so far as it highlights the role of the triune God, and especially the Holy Spirit, in salvation. It forthrightly asserts the inescapable necessity of the working of the Holy Spirit, if our human sinfulness is to be overcome in the experience of salvation. Calvinism not only emphasizes the role of the Spirit as the active agent in conversion, but also as the power of God mediating victory over sin and producing Christlikeness in us. This emphasis should encourage us to stand fast and be courageous.

The Calvinist understanding of election is likewise helpful in so far as it highlights the profound mystery of personal salvation. After we have come to the end of all our statements as to how and why conversion occurs, we are still left with the central existential question: How is it that I am a Christian? Why was I privileged to hear the gospel message and to respond to it, when so many others have not? Calvinism reminds us that at this point we stand before an unfathomable mystery, for the final answer does not lie in ourselves nor with anything we have done. We have not merited salvation. We cannot even point to our beggarly acceptance of the gospel as the basis for God's acceptance of us. In the end, all is of God.

The decrees of God. Their commitment to divine sovereignty and individual election has led traditional Calvinists to move beyond the "five points" and delve deeper into the mystery of God's electing activity. They typically have framed salvation in the context of God's decision before the creation of the world, with history being the outworking of God's eternal decrees. Calvinist theologians, therefore, seek to rise above the flux of time and perceive the plan present to the divine mind from eternity past. They find that the one eternal divine decision consists of a series of decrees. However, Calvinists are not in agreement concerning the exact order of the four central elements within the eternal divine decision.[30]

One major proposal begins with the decree of election, that is, God's decision to glorify himself by magnifying his grace and justice in the salvation of some creatures and the perdition of others. Next comes the decree to create the elected and the reprobated rational creatures. The decree to permit the fall follows. The divine decision climaxes in the decree to justify the elect and to condemn the nonelect. We may term this order "supralapsarian" (from the Latin

---

30. Rather than the two basic positions outlined below, Erickson divides Calvinists into three positions. Erickson, *Christian Theology*, 3:918.

lapse, "fall," and *supra* "above"), because it places the decree of election prior to the decision to permit the fall.

More popular among Calvinists today is the position which places the decree to create humanity in holiness and blessedness first. Then follows the decree to permit humankind to fall by human self-determination. Next comes the decree of election, i.e, God's decision to save a certain number out of this guilty, aggregate whole. The last of the four is the decree to leave the remainder of humankind in their sin and subject them to just punishment. This position is called "infra-" or "sublapsarian Calvinism," because the decree of election follows after the decree to allow the fall.

A move from supralapsarianism to infralapsarianism is not without theological significance. By shifting the decree of election from first place (before the fall) to third (after the fall) in the order of the divine decree, infralapsarian Calvinists soften what they perceive to be the harshness of the "double predestination" explicitly taught in the stricter alternative. In contrast to supralapsarianism which views God as predestining both the elect to salvation and the lost to perdition, infralapsarian predestination moves in only one direction. It refers to God's choice of some to be favored by grace. For the cause of the condemnation of the lost, infralapsarian Calvinists look to human sin, rather than God's explicit determination.

Beyond this difference between the two varieties of Calvinism lies a broader consensus in theological method which encompasses even many of their Arminian discussion partners. As a whole, Reformed theology tends to view salvation from the perspective of God's decision prior to the creation of the world. The central issue between Calvinists and Arminians focuses on the relationship between God's eternal decision and the historical personal response to the gospel: Does the act of repentance and faith happen because God foreordains it (Calvinism), or does God foreordain this event because it happens in history and as a consequence he foreknows it (Arminianism)? Stated more theologically, is the divine foreknowledge (understood as God's cognition of events before they occur) dependent on divine foreordination (understood as determining that these events will happen)? Or is foreordination dependent on foreknowledge?

As we noted above, Arminians generally believe the Calvinist concept of election violates human free will. If our response to the gospel is foreordained in the sense that God determined it for no reason except his own mysterious, sovereign will, then "free choice" is a mirage. Calvinists in turn accuse Arminians of deprecating God's ultimate sovereignty. If foreordination is based on God's foreknowledge, then his decision to save is dependent on human action (that is, our response in time) and not solely on his own free, unmerited grace.

So stated, we can readily see that both discussion partners are seeking to defend an important theological conviction. Is there any way to move beyond the apparent dilemma? Need we choose between divine sovereignty and human freedom?

Election to Community

The impasse to which the debate between Calvinism and Arminianism leads suggests that the difficulty may lie with the context in which theologians have traditionally posed the question.

As we noted above, Reformed theologies, whether Calvinist or Arminian, frame election within the context of the eternal past, for they inquire about the decree concerning the final salvation of individuals present in the mind of God prior to creation. These theologians set forth what we may call the classical doctrine of election. According to Wolfhart Pannenberg this classical doctrine of election is characterized by "the timelessness of the divine decision in regard to its subject, the restriction of its objects to individuals (in most cases to unrelated individuals), and finally the predominance of a transcendent salvation as constituting the purpose decided upon in the act of election."[31]

The proper orientation point for theology, however, is not the unfathomable eternity past. Instead we must look to the revealed intention of God for his creation in which his work in history will culminate. Although it is not chronologically first in the historical flow, the final goal of history is logically first in the order of being.

---

31. Wolfhart Pannenberg, *Human Nature, Election and History* (Philadelphia: Westminster, 1977), 46.

Only the end of the process determines ultimately "what is." We are, therefore, what we will be. The doctrine of salvation reminds us that "what we will be" is the community of the people of God.

(1) Viewed from the perspective of the divine intention, election is fundamentally corporate. God's eternal purpose, which forms the foundation for our understanding of his historical saving work, is that through the Spirit we participate in the glorious relationship that the Son enjoys with the Father. To this end, the Spirit unites us as one body with Jesus Christ. Election, therefore, is bound with community; we are elected to community and for community. Being elect means being "in Christ," and hence participating in a corporate reality. As Paul declared, "in him [i.e., Christ] we were also chosen" (Eph. 1:11). Our election occurs only in Christ, and therefore only as we are in Christ can we speak of participation in election.

Further, the biblical concept of election includes being chosen as a people in history for participation in the ongoing sweep of God's activity in the world. In the Old Testament, the primary electing event was the Exodus, and its goal was that Israel belong to God (Deut. 7:6-8) as a people through whom God could bless all the nations of the earth (Gen. 12:3). God elected Israel in order that they might fulfil a mission to the Gentiles (Isa. 2:3; 42:1), thereby serving God's historical purposes. This forms the context for the inauguration of the New Testament church as the new expression of the elected people of God. The great electing event was the coming of Jesus Christ and the pouring out of the Spirit. By virtue of our incorporation into Christ's body, God has elected us and mandated us to proclaim the gospel in all the world (Matt. 28:16-20). Consequently, we invite people everywhere to join us in serving the grand purpose of God in history which will culminate in the coming of the eschatological community.

The primary emphasis of our election, therefore, is the chosenness we enjoy as a people in Christ to participate in God's program in history. We have the wonderful privilege of serving God among the nations. Nevertheless several divisive questions remain: Who is in Christ? What is the significance of the biblical concept of predestination? And do those in Christ persevere?

(2) By our first query we are moving beyond the matter of who participates in the sweep of God's activity in history (which is an issue of ecclesiology). We are asking as well, Who in the end will be saved? This question moves us beyond pneumatology to eschatology, to the issue of the final judgment, the discussion of which comes in Part 6. We may anticipate our conclusion, however. The unfolding of history climaxing in the final harvest marks the determination of who is ultimately in Christ and consequently who will participate in the eternal community (Matt. 13:24-30).

This observation, in turn, forms the context for a proper understanding of predestination. The paradigm biblical text that describes this concept comes from Paul:

> For those God foreknew he also predestined to be conformed to the likeness of his Son that he might be the first born among many brothers. And those he predestined he also called, those he called he also justified, those he justified he also glorified. (Rom. 8:29-30)

Contrary to our expectations, in these verses the apostle did not give attention to the question of who will be saved. Rather, he used the idea of predestination to give us assurance that God's purpose will be served, which purpose is nothing less than the eschatological glorification of believers. For Paul, therefore, predestination is eschatological in orientation.

The Pauline declaration suggests that neither traditional position concerning foreknowledge and predestination is strictly correct: Divine foreknowledge is neither the basis for predestination, nor the result of it. In fact, foreknowledge as understood in Reformed theologies has little to do with Paul's idea of predestination. The apostle cited as the basis of predestination God's purpose to glorify those who belong to Christ, that is, who are in Christ and therefore are elect. Foreknowledge as referring to God's cognizance of events before they occur, in contrast, is a function of God's omniscience. All events are present to the mind of God as themselves, and consequently God is immediately cognizant of all historical occurrences, even those which from our perspective are yet future.

(3) Finally, we must look at the implications of the corporate conception of election for the question of perseverance. Does conver-

sion guarantee participation in the eschatological people of God, or can we lose our saved status?

In seeking an answer, we must clarify the fifth point of Calvinism. The *perseverance of the saints* implies that the presence of the Spirit guarantees that the one who is truly converted will remain in faith to the end. Hence, Louis Berkhof defines perseverance as "that continuous operation of the Holy Spirit in the believer, by which the work of divine grace that is begun in the heart, is continued and brought to completion."[32]

The Calvinist doctrine of the perseverance of the saints, therefore, is not to be confused with the modern doctrine of "eternal security." Proponents of this doctrine, which they often capsulize in the cliche "once saved, always saved," assert that a decision for Christ fixes our eternal destiny no matter what may be our subsequent conduct.[33] In this sense, then, eternal security teaches an unhistorical salvation: our eternal status is unaffected by historical events, having been fixed by our decision for Christ. The doctrine of the perseverance of the saints, in contrast, is a statement about history: True conversion will be demonstrated through subsequent events.

Seen as a statement about history, perseverance reflects the concept of election outlined above. This doctrine asserts that the historical process itself, leading to its final culmination, reveals who are actually in Christ. Those in whom the Spirit is truly operative will in the end be faithful to their calling and "finish the race." Those who forsake the faith may someday return to faith, because the indwelling Spirit will complete his saving mission. Or they may never repent from their apostasy, revealing thereby that they were never genuinely converted. As John declared concerning those who departed from the community to which he wrote,

> They went out from us, but they did not really belong to us. For if they had belonged to us, they would have remained with us; but their going showed that none of them belonged to us. (1 John 2:19)

---

32. L. Berkhof, *Systematic Theology*, 546.

33. For a sketch of the rise of this position, see Dale Moody, *The Word of Truth* (Grand Rapids: Eerdmans, 1981), 361-63.

In any case, the future unfolding of history culminating in the eschaton reveals who are in Christ—those in whom the Spirit is now at work.

Within this context the biblical references to "abiding in Christ" are significant. The one who is truly in Christ will heed such admonitions and consequently remain faithful, for the empowering Spirit dwells within. The presence of the Spirit is made evident as they "finish the race" and consequently receive the crown of righteousness from the righteous Judge (2 Tim. 4:8).

The *Ordo Salutis*

We are now in a position to bring together our understanding of salvation within the context of God's eternity. Doing so, however, demands that we tackle one final issue, the order of the aspects of personal salvation within the one divine salvific program. We must now inquire concerning the *ordo salutis* (order of salvation).

Historical perspective. Although the human experience of salvation has been present among the people of God throughout the centuries, the theological concern for the order of the events of salvation is a relatively recent phenomenon. Specifically, it is a fruit of the Reformation.[34] Prior to the sixteenth century, Christian thinkers placed little emphasis on, nor made clear distinctions among the various aspects of personal salvation. Beginning with the Reformation and especially in the Puritan era, theologians sought to set forth the correct *ordo salutis*. The goal of their reflections was the delineation of the logical flow of the necessary elements in the salvation process. Reformed theologian Louis Berkhof offered this description:

> The *ordo salutis* describes the process by which the work of salvation, wrought in Christ, is subjectively realized in the hearts and lives of sinners. It aims at describing in their logical order, and also in their interrelations, the various movements of the Holy Spirit in the application of the work of redemption.[35]

34. L. Berkhof, *Systematic Theology*, 419.
35. Ibid., 415-16.

After the Reformation era thinkers within the major confessional groups—Lutheran, Reformed, and Roman Catholic—set forth their representative understandings of salvation. These formation remain the classical positions of their respective traditions, but they have not fared well in contemporary theology. Modern heirs of the era of Protestant scholasticism and the counter-Reformation have either freely altered older models in accordance with the perceived needs of the day or rejected the inquiry into the *ordo salutis* as theologically inappropriate. The Dutch Reformed scholar Hendrikus Berkhof, for example, complained that such categorization turns "the way of salvation into a psychological process."[36] Similarly, Lutheran theologian Gerhard O. Forde faulted the enterprise because "it led to a fundamental distinction between the means of salvation on the part of God (word and sacraments) and the means of salvation on the part of humans (faith and good works)."[37]

While questioned by many theologians today, evangelical thinkers have retained a keen interest in the exact order of the Spirit's working and our human response.[38] This interest is not without foundation, for the inquiry into the *ordo salutis* raises crucial questions concerning the nature of salvation. For this reason, we must look more closely at the matter.

Representative positions. We may classify the major proposals in accordance with the major branches of the Western church—Lutheran, Reformed, and Roman Catholic.

(1) In *Lutheran* theology, justification through faith stands at the forefront. Consequently, for the foundation of salvation the Formula of Concord and the early Lutheran thinkers looked to "objective reconciliation," the reality that in Christ God has been reconciled to humankind.[39] In the gospel God announces this to us and offers us the subjective reception of justification. The gospel mediates to us the

---

36. Hendrikus Berkhof, *Christian Faith*, trans. Sierd Woudstra (Grand Rapids: Eerdmans, 1979), 478.

37. Gerhard O. Forde, "Christian Life," in *Christian Dogmatics*, ed. Carl E. Braaten and Robert W. Jenson, two volumes (Philadelphia: Fortress, 1984), 2:428-29.

38. See, for example, the discussion of the "logical order" of salvation in Erickson, *Christian Theology*, 3:932-46.

39. Francis Pieper, *Christian Dogmatics*, ed. John Theodore Mueller, English translation, three volumes (1934; St. Louis: Concordia, 1951), 2:419.

power not to resist the Spirit's saving operation. Our repentance leads to regeneration or saving grace, which occurs quickly or gradually according to the strength of our resistance to the Spirit's working.[40] Regeneration endows us with saving faith by means of which we appropriate the forgiveness given by Christ. We are then adopted into God's family, united with Christ, and receive the means for obedient living. Our possession of these blessings is not permanent, however, but dependent on our continuing in faith.

Building on Luther, the systematicians summarized the Spirit's work in salvation. His one activity is divisible into a logical order. He "calls, illumines, convicts, justifies, renovates, unites with Christ, and sanctifies."[41]

(2) Unlike their Lutheran counterparts, *Reformed* theologians do not find the foundation for salvation in the fact of God's reconciliation to humankind but in the prior purposes of God that form its context. In spite of their common starting point, representatives of this tradition differ widely concerning the proper formulation of the *ordo salutis*. The sketches they offer tend to be detailed and complex. Nevertheless, theologians who claim the legacy of Calvin are in general agreement concerning the sequence of four elements which they see as lying at the heart of the order of salvation: God's general call, God's effectual call, regeneration, and the personal response of repentance and faith. After these follow the less controversial elements such as justification, sanctification, perseverance, and glorification.[42]

The order of the four central elements is crucial, because it reflects the fundamental Calvinist approach to individual salvation. Although God calls all persons through the gospel (general call), the announcement which brings results comes only to the elect (effectual call). The effect of this call is regeneration, which is wholly the work of the Spirit. It occurs imperceptibly and prior to any human response; hence, regeneration is "subconscious." The response of re-

---

40. See, for example, Heinrich Schmid, *The Doctrinal Theology of the Evangelical Lutheran Church*, trans. Charles Hay and Henry E. Jacobs, third edition (Philadelphia: United Lutheran Publication House, 1899 [reprint: Minneapolis: Augsburg, n.d.]), 460-80.

41. Robert W. Jenson, "The Holy Spirit," in *Christian Dogmatics*, 2:129.

42. L. Berkhof, *Systematic Theology*, 418.

pentance and faith, in turn, constitutes the first sign that God has already brought about regeneration and given the Holy Spirit to the elect person. It marks the penetration of the Spirit's work in regeneration to the conscious life of the sinner.[43]

(3) In part as a reaction to Protestantism, *Roman Catholic* theologians meeting at the Council of Trent (1545-1563) set forth the orthodox Catholic view concerning salvation, which focuses on cooperation between the individual and the Holy Spirit. For those not baptized in infancy the process begins when a person hears the gospel announcement of God's justice and is aroused and aided by divine grace. The recipient who does not resist this grace joins with the Spirit in preparing for justification. According to the Council, this preparation occurs

> when, understanding themselves to be sinners, they, by turning themselves from the fear of divine justice, by which they are salutarily aroused to consider the mercy of God, are raised to hope, trusting that God will be propitious to them for Christ's sake; and they begin to love Him as the fountain of all justice, and on that account are moved against sin by a certain hatred and detestation, that is, by that repentance that must be performed before baptism; finally, when they resolve to receive baptism, to begin a new life and to keep the commandments of God.[44]

Baptism, the instrumental cause of justification, effects the remission of sins and the infusion of the supernatural virtues (faith, hope, and love).[45] Holy living must follow, as believers "through the observance of the commandments of God and of the Church, faith cooperating with good works, increase in that justice received through the grace of Christ and are further justified."[46] This is crucial because a baptized Christian can lose the grace of justification through either unbelief or a mortal sin. Nevertheless, such a person can be restored through the sacraments, especially penance.[47]

---

43. Ibid.

44. "The Canons and Decrees of the Council of Trent" 6.6, in *The Creeds of the Churches*, ed. John H. Leith, third edition (Atlanta: John Knox, 1982), 410-11.

45. "The Canons of Trent" 6.7, in *The Creeds of the Churches*, 412.

46. "The Canons of Trent" 6.10, in *The Creeds of the Churches*, 414.

47. "The Canons of Trent," 6.14, in *The Creeds of the Churches*, 417-18.

The order of salvation and the future community. Although dissimilar in many respects, the traditional perspectives on the order of salvation share a fundamental characteristic. They move from the past through the present and into the future. Thereby the past becomes the perspective from which theologians describe the elements within the order of salvation.

The biblical text which above all others provides the foundation for the theological interest in describing the order of salvation suggests a different approach. Again we cite Paul's words,

> For those God foreknew he also predestined to be conformed to the likeness of his Son that he might be the first born among many brothers. And those he predestined he also called, those he called he also justified, those he justified he also glorified. (Rom. 8:29-30)

In these verses the apostle ordered the elements of salvation with a view toward God's final goal. Foundational to the *ordo salutis*, therefore, is the eschatological consummation of salvation or glorification.

The eschatological orientation of salvation means that the only proper starting point for the *ordo salutis* is the divine intention, God's salvific purpose. As we have noted, his intent is to glorify himself by bringing us to participation in the eternal community that he has planned for those who belong to him. Hence, the Spirit's work, which is foundational to the process of salvation from start to finish, is the eschatological transformation that we will share with all other believers and with all creation. All other dimensions of the Spirit's activity find their significance in the certainty of our final glorification. In fact, so certain is Paul that this will transpire that he treats what is from the human perspective a future event as if it had already occurred: "those he justified [a past event] he also glorified [a future event spoken of as if it were already in the past]."

Glorification, the primary goal of God's saving activity, leads naturally to the other aspects, which are directed toward it and subservient to it. Enroute to the eschatological transformation, the Spirit is conforming us in an increasing manner to the standard, which is Christ (conditional sanctification). The process of sanctification, however, has a definite genesis, namely, the Spirit's entrance into a person's life, providing regeneration, justification, freedom, and power (positional sanctification). This beginning point has no ultimate significance in itself, however, but carries meaning only as the first step in the process that leads to God's final goal.

The entrance of the Spirit into the life of a sinner happens in conjunction with conversion. From the personal perspective conversion occurs when an individual responds to the gospel in repentance and faith. For this to happen, however, a person must be confronted with the message, whether through human proclaimers or through Bible reading. As the word of God goes forth, the Spirit is present seeking to convict, call, illumine, and enable.

As the text in Romans indicates, the entire experience of salvation is surrounded by God's own purposefulness. Consequently, the strictly theological elements of the *ordo salutis* follow. We speak of the divine purposefulness as "predestination." As we noted earlier, predestination is not "God's choice of individuals for eternal life or eternal death,"[48] but his resolute intention to bring believers to the final goal of his saving work (glorification). Indeed, we are "predestined to be conformed to the likeness of his Son." God's intention to effect glorification, in turn, arises out of his foreknowledge, his eternal cognition of us as those who are in Christ. Foreknowledge is a function of God's omniscience, his eternal cognition of the entire sequence of creaturely time, for God is the meaning of the whole.

To summarize: The order of salvation entails glorification, sanctification, conversion, application of the word, predestination, foreknowledge, omniscience. In this manner, our salvation, which is effected by the work of the Spirit, is surrounded by the eternity of the triune God, whom we will praise throughout all eternity as participants of the great community of the redeemed.

Our discussion of salvation leads to the community of faith, which exists in the world as the foretaste of the great eschatological choir of praise to our Savior God. In this manner, pneumatology forges the link from Christology—the doctrine of Christ—to ecclesiology—the doctrine of Christ's church. To this doctrine, therefore, we must now turn.

---

48. Erickson, *Christian Theology*, 3:908.

Part 5
Ecclesiology
The Doctrine of the Church

The Bible is the narrative of the activity of the triune God in seeking the salvation of humankind. In the pneumatology section, we explored the role of the Holy Spirit in effecting the salvation of individual humans. Salvation, however, never occurs in isolation. Rather, we receive divine grace in order to be members of a community. Indeed, God's purpose is to establish "one new humanity" consisting of a reconciled people (Eph. 2:14-19), and in this manner to overcome the horizontal effects of the estrangement we experience due to sin. Because sin brings alienation between humans, God directs his saving action toward the healing of interpersonal relationships. According to the New Testament the focal point of God's new reconciled society is the church of Jesus Christ.

The systematic articulation of the Spirit's work among the corporate people of God is ecclesiology or the doctrine of the church. Our ecclesiology moves through four topics. We begin by exploring the nature of the church as the eschatological covenant community (chapter 17). As the fellowship of believers we enter into relationship with God and with one another. This covenantal relationship is a foretaste of the future community we will share in the new creation and a sign of the eternal community of the triune God himself. With this understanding of the lofty nature of the church in view, we examine the community in the world. Our examination opens with the church's ministry as a community that glorifies God through worship, edification, and outreach (chapter 18). We then move to the practices of commitment—baptism and the Lord's supper—that initiate and perpetuate loyalty to Christ within the community (chapter 19). Our ecclesiology concludes with the organization of the community, including membership in the body, its governmental structures, the Spirit's provision of leaders for the ministry, and the act of ordination (chapter 20).

17

The Church—
the Eschatological
Covenant Community

*For he has rescued us from the
dominion of darkness and brought
us into the kingdom of the Son he
loves. (Col.1:13)*

Outline

The Church as Community
  The Basis in the Covenant and the Kingdom
    The community of the covenant
    Community and the divine purpose
  Community and the Divine Nature
    The church as the image of God
    The church and the Spirit

Although not all North Americans would claim to be Christians, nearly all have some acquaintance with the church. As an institution, the church has played an influential role in our society. Despite this widespread contact, misconceptions abound concerning the nature of the church. Some people think of it primarily as a building, an edifice in which believers worship God. Others consider the church to be one of the many organizations competing for the loyalties of contemporary people. Hence, it is a group in which people may choose to hold membership according to personal preference.

Ideas such as these, as prevalent as they may be, simply do not go to the essence of the church. They do not reflect the understanding set forth by the New Testament and articulated by theologians throughout church history. How, then, ought we to view the church? What is the nature of the fellowship which the New Testament writers claimed was inaugurated by Christ himself?

In recent years many theologians have begun their ecclesiology by focusing on the church's mission,[1] thereby speaking of the church in dynamic terms.[2] Traditionally, however, Christian thinkers have emphasized its static, theoretical essence. This chapter explores the foundational question of ecclesiology—that of the nature of the church. We set forth our understanding by appeal to three concepts which describe its fundamental nature: covenant, kingdom sign, and community. The church, we assert, is a people standing in covenant, who are a sign of the divine reign and constitute a special community. In short, the church is the eschatological covenant community.

---

1. E.g., Dale Moody, *The Word of Truth* (Grand Rapids: Eerdmans, 1981), 427-33.
2. E.g., Colin Williams, *The Church*, volume 4 of *New Directions in Theology Today*, general ed. William Hordern (Philadelphia: Westminster, 1968), 20.

The Church as a Convenant People

Fundamentally, the church of Jesus Christ is neither a building nor an organization. Rather, it is a people, a special people, a people who see themselves as standing in relationship to the God who saves them and to each other as those who share in this salvation. As the early church father Hippolytus declared, "It is not a place that is called church, not a house made of stones and earth....It is the holy assembly of those who live in righteousness."[3] Stated theologically, the church is a people in covenant.

Several biblical and historical themes flow together to form our conclusion that the church is a covenant people.

Ekklesia

One fountainhead for the conclusion that the church is a covenant people lies with the Greek word, *ekklesia*, which the New Testament writers commonly used to designate the church.[4] This term arises from a verb *kaleo* ("to call") plus the preposition *ek* ("out of"). On this etymological basis, many theologians conclude that the idea of "the called out ones" inheres in the resulting noun *ekklesia*.[5]

The New Testament employment of *ekklesia* provides an important link between the church of Jesus Christ and the Old Testament nation of Israel. The Jewish scholars who translated the Hebrew Scriptures into Greek (the Septuagint) chose *ekklesia* to render the Hebrew word *qahal* ("assembly"), which the historical writers used to refer to Israel as the "congregation" or "assembly of the Lord" (Deut. 23:1ff; 1 Chron. 28:8).

These Old Testament references may have formed the background for Jesus' promise that he would build his congregation (Matt. 16:18; 18:17). Regardless of the genesis of the dominical declaration, the early Christians clearly believed that our Lord himself had instituted the church. Their fellowship, therefore, was the con-

---

3. Hippolytus, *Daniel*, 1.17.6-7, as cited in J. G. Davies, *The Secular Use of Church Buildings* (London: SCM, 1968), 4.

4. E.g., Millard J. Erickson, *Christian Theology* (Grand Rapids: Baker, 1983-85) 3:1031.

5. See, for example, Lewis Sperry Chafer, *Systematic Theology*, seven volumes (Dallas: Dallas Seminary Press, 1948), 4:39.

tinuation of the movement Jesus began when he called the recipients of his message to be his disciples. In addition, however, given its presence in the Septuagint, their choice of *ekklesia* as their self-designation suggests that the early Christians linked themselves as the followers of Jesus to what God had begun in the wilderness with the nation of Israel.

Although the Old Testament formed the theological context, the linguistic significance of the New Testament use of *ekklesia* arises out of its common use in the first century Roman world. *Ekklesia* connoted an "assembly," the citizens of a given community called together to tend to city affairs (Acts 19:32,39,41).[6] The early Christians found in this term a helpful means for expressing their self-consciousness. They saw themselves as a people called together by the proclamation of the gospel for the purpose of belonging to God through Christ.[7]

The choice of *ekklesia* as the designation of the Christian community suggests that the New Testament believers viewed the church as neither an edifice nor an organization. They were a people—a people brought together by the Holy Spirit—a people bound to each other through Christ—hence, a people standing in covenant with God. Above all, they were God's people (2 Cor. 6:16).

The conception of the church as the *ekklesia*, God's covenant people, has played an important role in Baptist ecclesiology throughout its history. Hence, the Baptist systematic theologian Dale Moody concluded, "The priority of the spiritual organism over the institutional organization is obvious in all this great theological stream."[8] In recent years, however, the focus on the church as people has also generated broad consensus in the church as a whole, as is evident, for example, in the important ecumenical document, *Baptism, Eucharist and Ministry.*[9]

---

6. Jürgen Roloff, "ekklesia," in the *Exegetical Dictionary of the New Testament,* ed. Horst Balz and Gerhard Schneider, English translation (Grand Rapids: Eerdmans, 1990), 1:411; Karl L. Schmidt, "ekklesia," in the *Theological Dictionary of the New Testament,* ed. Gerhard Kittel and Gerhard Friedrich, trans. Geoffrey W. Bromiley, ten volumes (Grand Rapids: Eerdmans, 1964-76), 3:513

7. For a discussion of the adoption of the term by the early community, see Roloff, "ekklesia," in EDNT, 1:412.

8. Moody, *The Word of Truth,* 441.

9. *Baptism, Eucharist and Ministry,* Faith and Order Paper #111 (Geneva: World Council of Churches, 1982), 20.

The Nation, the Body, and the Temple

The use of the term *ekklesia* in the New Testament indicates that the early believers conceived of the church as a covenanting people. This conclusion is confirmed by several of the metaphors used by the New Testament writers to provide insight into the nature of their fellowship. Three are especially important, each of which is related to a member of the Trinity.[10]

The nation of God. The New Testament speaks of the church as a nation and a holy priesthood belonging to God (1 Pet. 2:9). This metaphor is readily connected with the Old Testament rootage of *ekklesia*. Just as Israel had been chosen to be the people of God—God's nation—so now the New Testament church enjoys this relationship. Despite the profound similarity between the two, there is also one important difference. No longer is status as God's nation based on membership within a specific ethnic group. Now people from the entire world are called together to belong to God; the church is an international fellowship comprising persons "from every tribe and language and people and nation" (Rev. 5:9).

Whereas "nation" focuses on status, "priesthood" connotes function. It too is rooted in, while forming a contrast to the Old Testament. In ancient Israel certain persons carried out prescribed priestly functions. Whereas in Israel only a few were selected from among the people to act as priests, in the church all the people of God belong to the priestly order, and the ministry of the priesthood is shared by all.[11]

The body of Christ. The New Testament also speaks of the church as the body of Christ (Eph. 1:22-23; 1 Cor. 12:27) of which he is the

---

10. According to Kenneth Cauthen [*Systematic Theology* (Lewiston, N.Y.: Edwin Mellon, 1986), 296], the implicit trinitarianism of the choice of these metaphors and their significance as the three major motifs in the history of Christian thought dates to Leslie Newbigin's book *The Household of Faith* (New York: Friendship, 1954). Millard Erickson, who employs them in his ecclesiology [*Christian Theology*, 3:1034-41] cites as the source of the idea, Arthur W. Wainwright, *The Trinity in the New Testament* (London: S.P.C.K., 1962).

11. For a short discussion of the idea of priesthood, see Alex T.M. Cheung, "The Priest as the Redeemed Man: A Biblical-Theological Study of the Priesthood," *Journal of the Evangelical Theological Society* 29/3 (September 1986):265-75. For the ecumenical convergence on this matter, see *Baptism, Eucharist and Ministry*, 23. See also, Walter Marshal Horton, *Christian Theology: An Ecumenical Approach* (New York: Harper & Brothers, 1958), 202-43.

head (Col. 1:18).[12] The background for this picture does not lie so much in the Old Testament as in human anatomy. Both the relationship of the physical body to its head and the organic unity of the human body signify what is to be true of the church.[13] As his "body," the church exists solely to do the will of Christ and in this way be his presence in the world. Like the human body, the church is also a unity made up of diversity (1 Cor. 12:1-31). Not all members have the same function, but all have the same goal; all are to be concerned for the others and to use their gifts in service to the whole.

The temple of the Spirit. According to the New Testament, the church is likewise the temple of the Holy Spirit (Eph. 2:19-22; 1 Pet. 2:5). Like the first image, the wellspring for this metaphor lies in the Old Testament. In Israel the temple was in some special way God's earthly dwelling place (2 Chron. 6:1-2). Now, however, the focal point of God's presence is no longer a special building but a fellowship of his people. The presence of the Spirit among us carries grave ethical implications. Because we are the temple of the Spirit, we must live holy lives (1 Cor. 6:19-20).

The Church as Mystical, Universal, and Local

Our understanding of the church as a covenanting people arises likewise out of the diversity of manifestations of this body as indicated by the New Testament. Some thinkers find within the Scriptures the classical differentiation between the universal (or invisible) and the local (or visible) church.[14] Perhaps more appropriate, however, is a three-part delineation: mystical, universal, and local.

The broadest manifestation is the "mystical church," the one body composed of all believers of all ages (Heb. 12:22-23), the one cosmic

---

12. There is some discussion as to whether this biblical image is to be understood merely metaphorically or actually. Some thinkers argue that since the ascension the church is the actual body of the resurrected Lord. See, for example, Raimon Panikkar, "A Christophany for Our Times," *Theology Digest* 39/1 (1992): 3-21.

13. For the recent discussion, see, Andrew Perriman, "'His body which is the church...' Coming to Terms with Metaphor," *Evangelical Quarterly* 62/2 (1990): 123-42. See also Barbara Field, "The Discourses Behind the Metaphor 'the Church is The Body of Christ' as Used by S. Paul and the 'Post-Paulines,'" *Asia Journal of Theology* 6/1 (April 1992): 88-107.

14. E.g., Augustus Hopkins Strong, *Systematic Theology* (Philadelphia: Griffith & Rowland, 1909), 3:887-91.

fellowship that transcends time. The "universal church" is composed of all believers on earth at any given time, the one worldwide fellowship that transcends spatial boundaries. If frequency of use is the chief indication, however, the New Testament places greatest emphasis on the local manifestation of the church, an emphasis continued in the literature of at least the first three centuries.[15]

As the visible fellowship of believers gathered in a specific location, the local church is the most concrete expression of the covenanting people. At the same time, the gathered congregation derives its significance from its participation in, and as the representation of the common whole.[16] Each congregation is nothing less than the local reality of the one church. Therefore, each local church is the church of Jesus Christ in miniature. Because the local expression is the church of Jesus of Christ in miniature, all the lofty phrases used in the New Testament of "the church" are to be true of each congregation of believers.

The Marks of the Church

More widely employed in theological history to provide the foundation for ecclesiology than the distinction between the invisible and the visible church has been the delineation of the marks of the church. Since the destruction of the organizational unity in the West, this approach has been closely connected with the question concerning the essence of the true church. As Paul Avis noted, "Reformation theology is largely dominated by two questions: 'How can I obtain a gracious God?' and 'Where can I find the true Church?' The two questions are inseparably related..."[17] The post-Reformation discussion of the *vera ecclesia* formed the historical context for the emergence of the covenant idea as the focal understanding of the nature of the church.

---

15. John D. Zizioulas, *Being and Community: Studies in Personhood and the Church* (Crestwood, N.Y.: St. Vladimir's Seminary Press, 1985), 148.

16. Schmidt, "ekklesia," in TDNT, 3:504,535.

17. Paul D. L. Avis, *The Church in the Theology of the Reformers* in *New Foundations in Theology Library* (Atlanta: John Knox, 1981), 1.

The classical alternatives. Building from the wording of the Apostles' Creed, theologians of a variety of traditions have denoted the essence of the church in terms of its four marks—apostolicity, catholicity, unity, and holiness. Although historically Protestants and Catholics have enjoyed basic agreement concerning the four, the major church traditions view these marks differently. Nevertheless, the dominant tradition has favored what we might classify as a "high church" ecclesiology (represented by the Roman Catholic, Orthodox, and to some extent Anglican traditions).

High church theologians tend to elevate the first mark, apostolicity, above the other three and to endow it with a special significance. They understand the apostolicity which guarantees the perpetuity of the church primarily by appeal to the idea of apostolic succession. Participants in the Western traditions[18] have often understood apostolic succession as a historical link from the present to the first century. Consequently, the true universal church is that body whose bishops trace their ordination from one generation to the previous generation, eventually to the first century.[19] Because of their concern that a church could outwardly conform to the four marks but lack a vital relationship with Christ, the Reformers shifted the focus to Word and Sacrament. In so doing they offered an alternative to the high church ecclesiology of the medieval thinkers. Hendrikus Berkhof described the Protestant position in this manner: "the pure preaching of the word and the right administration of the sacraments, in accordance with the Bible...would guarantee the bond with Christ, unobstructed by human devices."[20]

During the ferment that followed the Reformation, certain of the free churches, including the Baptists, took yet a further step. The radical reformers developed an ecclesiology which followed neither of the prior two alternatives. They opted for what we know as congre-

---

18. For the more eschatological perspective of the Eastern tradition, see Zizioulas, *Being as Community*, 166-208.

19. Joseph Cardinal Ratzinger, *Principles of Catholic Theology*, trans. Sister Mary Frances McCarthy (San Francisco: Ignatius, 1987).

20. Hendrickus Berkhof, *Christian Faith*, trans. Sierd Woudstra (Grand Rapids: Eerdmans, 1979), 409.

gationalism.[21] This view asserts that the true church is essentially people standing in voluntary covenant with God.

Both of the older models could be, and in fact were construed as allowing for a parish or territorial church. The bounds of such a church were determined merely by the political boundaries of the civil order, with all citizens within that boundary being members of the parish church. The congregationalists, in contrast, advocated a vision of the church which saw it as a spiritual people gathered out from the wider society.[22] According to Robert T. Handy, our forebears argued that the church "was not parochial, diocesan, provincial, or national, but was congregational, gathered by an act of mutual confederation ... expressed in a covenant."[23] Hence, in their opinion the church exists as believers join together with the purpose of walking with one another as God's people under Christ.

Historically, the move to the idea of a covenant as forming the foundation of the church brought several innovations, which sharply separated congregationalism from the older conceptions. By asserting that the church is formed through the covenanting of its members, congregationalists reversed the order of priority. No longer did the corporate whole take precedence over the individual as in the medieval model. On the contrary, the congregationalists viewed the church as the product of the coming together of individual Christians rather than the individual Christian being the product of the church. As a result, in the order of salvation the believer—and not the church—stands first in priority.

Further, the covenant idea developed out of the teaching of Martin Bucer (1491-1551) and the English Puritan movement which added

---

21. For a discussion on the rise of congregationalism, see Stanley Grenz, *Isaac Backus - Puritan and Baptist,* NABPR Dissertation Series, # 4, (Macon, Ga.: Mercer University Press, 1983) 11-33, 37-40.

22. For example, in 1572 John Field defined a church as "a company or congregation of the faithful called and gathered out of the world by the preaching of the gospel." Quoted in Edmund S. Morgan, *Visible Saints: The History of a Puritan Idea* (New York: 1963), 14.

23. Robert Theodore Handy, "The Philadelphia Tradition," in *Baptist Concepts of the Church,* ed. Winthrop Still Hudson (Philadelphia: Judson, 1959), 36.

"discipline" to "word and sacrament" as essential to the true church.[24] This move launched a quest for church purity.[25]

Of most significance, however, the move to covenant came to imply that the church exists only in local congregations.[26] Where there is no covenanting community, there is no church. And the covenant is by its very nature local, being the agreement among a particular, visible group of believers.

The specifically Baptist ecclesiology with its advocacy of believer's baptism developed within this broader free-church conception. The early English Baptists came to differ with their congregationalist coreligionists concerning the exact act that constituted the covenant. They concluded that the covenant which joins believers in the church of Jesus Christ is sealed in baptism. This understanding logically entailed the rejection of infant baptism, for that practice simply could not express the believer's personal covenant with God and with the baptizing community.[27]

Biblical consideration. The New Testament does not explicitly address the question of the marks of the church. Nevertheless, the documents do present several pertinent themes.

As we have seen, the early Christians asserted that believers themselves constitute the church. This understanding is evident in the term they chose to express their self-identity (*ekklesia*), and it is prominent in much of the New Testament imagery of the church (1 Pet. 2:5; 1 Cor. 12:12,27).[28]

---

24. Avis cites Bucer as the genesis for this idea, although showing that its seeds were already present in Luther and especially Calvin. Avis, *The Church in the Theology of the Reformers*, 45-50. On Calvin, see also 30-31.

25. See Grenz, *Isaac Backus*, 16, 20.

26. The *New Hampshire Confession of Faith* omitted any reference to the concept of the universal church. For the significance of this, see Winthrop S. Hudson, "By Way of Perspective," in *Baptist Concepts of the Church*, 27.

27. Grenz, *Isaac Backus*, 25-28

28. The New Testament emphasis on people as constituting the church must not be confused with the modern individualism that apparently gained strength in Baptist circles with the teachings of Francis Wayland, who conceived of the church as an aggregate of saved individuals (see Norman H. Maring, "The Individualism of Francis Wayland," in *Baptist Concepts of the Church*, 147). The first-century Christians, in contrast, understood themselves as individually members of the corporate whole. Hence, their ecclesiology exhibited a healthy balance between the individual and the group.

The New Testament balances this emphasis on the corporate people with an acknowledgment of the foundational role of church leaders. Matthew and Acts explicitly emphasized the primacy of Peter and the significance of the twelve apostles. We need not embrace papalism to acknowledge that Jesus anticipated Peter's future role in the initial establishment of the infant church. Peter would give leadership to the Jerusalem community and spearhead the proclamation of the gospel in the regions beyond the city (Matt. 16:15-19).[29]

Similarly, Paul set forth the crucial role of leaders in the church. He put apostles and prophets at the head of the list of those God has appointed in the church (1 Cor. 12:27-28), although he was careful to balance this teaching with a parallel emphasis on the giftedness of all within the community (v. 7). Elsewhere, the apostle declared that Christ has given leaders to the church for the purpose of edifying the whole body (Eph. 4:11ff). Because of its importance, leadership is a worthy goal to which believers should aspire (1 Tim. 3:1), but all would-be office holders must pass stringent spiritual requirements (vv. 2-13).

The New Testament, however, places the primacy of leaders within the context of an equal emphasis on servanthood and humility as the marks of true leadership. Leaders ought never to see their positions as a source of pride or an excuse for dominating others. They are to serve the people (Mark 10:41-45), ministering as shepherds and examples—never as overlords (1 Pet. 5:1-5).

Balanced congregationalism. The covenant ecclesiology of congregationalism returns us to the emphasis we noted in our discussion of *ekklesia*. Congregationalism asserts that ultimately the essence of the true church lies with its people. Yet the *ekklesia* is no ordinary collection of persons. Rather, because the church has been called out of the world by the preaching of the gospel in order to live in covenant, it is constituted by people with a special consciousness. Because they all confess allegiance to Christ, participants in the church are conscious that they stand as a body under his lordship; they comprise a people in covenant with God through Christ. At the same

---

29. See, for example, Raymond Brown, Karl P. Donfried, and John Reumann, ed., *Peter in the New Testament* (Minneapolis: Augsburg, 1973).

time, their mutual confession of Jesus as the Christ means that the members are conscious of their special standing in fellowship with each other; their shared commitment to be disciples of the Lord entails a commitment to one another. The church-constituting covenant is a mutual agreement to walk together as the people of God. Because of this mutual covenant, each member senses a responsibility not only to belong to God but also to nurture the confession of Christ in all others. In short, because of Christ the church is a company of believers in covenant with God and each other.

Although the early congregationalists were correct in affirming that the church is constituted by people who enter into covenant, we must remember that the church transcends the totality of its members at any given time. We participate in a fellowship that has already enjoyed a covenantal history. This realization balances the older congregationalist assertion that the believer is logically prior to the church. Rather than focusing on the primacy of either, we must balance the individual and the corporate aspects of Christian identity. Specifically, the church and the believer are mutually interdependent. Because the coming together of believers in mutual covenant constitutes the church, it is the covenant community of individuals. At the same time, the church possesses a history and tradition that transcends its present membership. Therefore, through the proclamation of the gospel it gives birth to the faith of those who enter the covenant people.

The Church as the Sign of the Kingdom

The church is a covenanting people. It consists of those whom the Spirit has called out of the world through the gospel proclamation to walk together as God's people. This covenanting people, however, are not an end in themselves. Rather, the church as a people-in-covenant is related to God's larger intention.

If we were to point to one topic that above all others has been the recipient of the labors of biblical scholars and theologians in the twentieth century it would no doubt be the kingdom of God. Indeed the idea of the divine reign as depicting God's overall intention lies at the heart of much of the Bible. It is not surprising, therefore, that the appearance of the church in the New Testament era occurred within the context of the biblical teaching of the broader reality of God's rule. Consequently, our ecclesiology must set forth our understanding of the church within the context of God's reign.[30]

The Biblical Conception of the Kingdom

To lay the foundation for our understanding of the church within the context of divine reign, we must look more closely at the biblical teaching about the kingdom of God. In what sense is God "king"? And what constitutes his reign?

Old Testament teaching about the kingdom. The concept of the kingdom of God is widely present in the Hebrew Scriptures. To gain an overview of the Old Testament teaching we must take a cursory look at the Hebrew verb *malak* ("to be king," "to rule").[31] Of the several cognates of this term, three are most important.

Melukah generally refers to "kingship" or "royalty," that is, a quality of rulership. On several occasions, however, it carries a second meaning, the aspect of a physical "realm." *Melukah* occurs in conjunction with "Yahweh" twice: The psalmist declares that God possesses a universal right to rule (Ps. 22:28), whereas the prophet Obadiah looked for a future day when God would reign in Israel (Obad. 21).

A second cognate, *malcuth,* means primarily "royal honor," "power," "dominion," or "dignity." It is also used to refer to a king's reign, or even to the realm ruled. In fact, *malcuth* undergoes an interesting development from the early to the late Old Testament books. In the earlier works the term refers to the kingship of a monarch. In the late books, in which most of the occurrences are found, this usage is sometimes maintained, but to it is added the concept of "realm." The term is used in conjunction with "Yahweh" to declare that God's dominion is universal (Ps. 103:19) and everlasting (145:13).

---

30. Erickson, for example, lists the relationship between the church and the kingdom as the first of four special problems. *Christian Theology,* 3:1041.

31. For the definitions of these terms, see Samuel Prideaux Tregelles, *Gesenius' Hebrew and Chaldee Lexicon to the Old Testament Scriptures* (Grand Rapids: Eerdmans, 1949), 476-80.

By far the most frequently used cognate of *malak* is *mamlakah*. Like the others, it carries two basic meanings, "kingdom" (or "realm ruled") and "sovereignty" (that is, "right to rule"). It is also used with reference to God. David acknowledged that God's right to rule is universal (1 Chron. 29:11). Elsewhere, Abijah claimed that even the rebellious northern tribes lay under God's kingship (2 Chron. 13:8).

These observations suggest that the Old Testament authors make no great distinction between a monarch's right to rule and the physical realm of the king's dominion; they are two poles of one basic concept. Further, the Old Testament writers declares that Israel is God's kingdom in a special way, in that Israel acknowledges his kingship. At the same time, God's right to rule properly extends over the entire world, even though many humans disregard it. One day, however, all nations will follow Israel in this confession (Zech. 14:9,16).

The Greek term that the New Testament writers used follows this basic Old Testament pattern. Karl Ludwig Schmidt, writing in the *Theological Dictionary of the New Testament*, declares: "In relation to the general usage of *basileia*, usually translated 'kingdom,' it is to be noted first that it signifies the 'being,' 'nature' and 'state' of the king. Since the reference is to a king, we do best to speak first of his 'dignity' or 'power.'"[32]

The kingdom and Jesus. Although the Old Testament heritage is important as its context, the major source for the Christian conception of the divine kingdom lies in the teaching of Jesus himself. The conception of our Lord is especially indicated by the Synoptic Gospels (which contain about 80 percent of the New Testament occurrences of the Greek word *basileia*[33]). In fact, according to Mark, Jesus' message centered around the proclamation of God's rule (Mark 1:15).

A cursory reading of the first three gospels suggests that Jesus' teaching followed the basic pattern set forth in the Old Testament. Our Lord sometimes suggested that the kingdom is a present reality

---

32. Karl Ludwig Schmidt, "basileia," in TDNT, 1:579.
33. Luz writes, "Most of the 162 uses of *basileia* in the NT employ the word in the phrase *basileia tou theou* (or *basileia ton ouranon* or *tou patros*) and are found in the Synoptic Gospels." Ulrich Luz, "basileia," in EDNT, 1:210.

(Luke 17:20), present because the prophetic time is fulfilled (Matt. 11:2-26; Mark 1:14-15; Luke 4:21) and Satan has been defeated (Matt. 12:28-29; Luke 10:9,18,20). But Jesus also declared the kingdom to be future (Luke 21:31), albeit a reality that is at hand (Mark 1:14-15). He spoke of the kingdom as both a realm over which God rules and God's reign, rulership, or right to rule.

Twentieth-century New Testament scholars have disagreed as to what Jesus actually meant by these seemingly immensely different statements. The modern discussion of this issue was launched by Johannes Weiss's little book, *Jesus' Proclamation of the Kingdom of God* (1892).[34]

From his study of the authentic sayings of Jesus, Weiss concluded that Jesus taught that the kingdom is wholly future (hence, the designation of Weiss' position as consistent eschatology). Further, Jesus' concept of the kingdom was not that of a society which he would establish but an eschatological in-breaking of God into history. Jesus never equated the kingdom with the society of his disciples and thus with the fellowship of his followers. Consequently, Jesus stood in the ancient apocalyptic tradition and not in the tradition of the liberal ethical moralists of nineteenth-century Europe. Instead of the liberal view, Weiss argued that Jesus saw himself as the bearer of the Spirit of God against the kingdom of Satan, the one entrusted with the task of driving the present world ruler from his position of lordship. Jesus also understood his mission as proclaimer of the gospel message of the kingdom: God would establish his kingdom; therefore, people must prepare themselves for its arrival. When Jesus' hearers failed to show fruits of repentance and when their leaders blasphemed the Spirit, Jesus concluded that he must also die in order to remove the guilt of the people. At death he would be installed in heaven, and his disciples would continue his proclamation of the kingdom message, resulting in repentance on the part of their generation. Consequently, Jesus refocused his immediate task toward the gathering of a band of followers who would await the kingdom of God.

---

34. Johannes Weiss, *Jesus' Proclamation of the Kingdom of God*, (1892) trans. Richard H. Hiers and David L. Holland (Philadelphia: Fortress, 1971).

An alternative to Weiss' understanding, realized eschatology, was championed by the British scholar, C. H. Dodd.[35] Dodd denied that Jesus was merely the herald of the kingdom of God who waited for its coming. Rather, he was the inaugurator of the kingdom, who saw in the events surrounding his mission indication that "the sovereign power of God has come into effective operation."[36] Therefore, Jesus' message was not that a kingdom would come in the future, but that through his ministry the eschatological events were now transpiring. Consequently, the biblical authors were convinced that the eschatological hopes of the Old Testament had all been fulfilled in Jesus. God's formerly hidden rule was now revealed. Evil had been overthrown, sin had been judged, and new life was available for God's people.

By the middle of the century, the debate between Weiss and Dodd was resolved through a third, mediating position. Although differences of opinion remained as to how the two dimensions fit together,[37] New Testament scholars came to agree that in Jesus' mind the kingdom of God was both present and future—already and not yet—and it was both an event and a sphere of existence.

In recent years, the older consensus has begun to give way to a newer understanding that has deepened the insights of the already/not yet view.[38] Many scholars are now convinced that the kingdom of God points to the self-disclosure of God, "God in strength,"[39] or

---

35. Charles Harold Dodd, *The Parables of the Kingdom* (London: Nisbet & Company, 1935); C.H. Dodd, *The Apostolic Preaching* (New York: Harper & Brothers, 1951).

36. Dodd, *Parables of the Kingdom*, 44.

37. Jeremias spoke of eschatology in the process of realization, in that the present and future aspects of the kingdom are related as the beginning of a process is related to the end. Joachim Jeremias, *New Testament Theology*, trans. John Bowden (New York: Charles Scribner's Sons, 1971). Kümmel focused on promise and fulfillment, arguing that in Jesus the future is related to the present as a promise is related to its fulfillment in the coming kingdom. Werner Kümmel, *Promise & Fulfillment*, trans. Dorothea M. Barton (Naperville, Ill.: A.R. Allenson, 1957). Cullmann invoked the imagery of D-day and V-Day. Christ has won the battle, but the consummation of his victory is future. Oscar Cullmann, *Christ and Time*, trans. Floyd V. Filson, rev. ed. (Philadelphia: Westminster, 1964). Finally Ladd spoke the presence of the future. In Christ the future is present in power, but its consummation is still to come. George Eldon Ladd, *A Theology of the New Testament* (Grand Rapids: Eerdmans, 1974).

38. Marcus J. Berg, "Jesus and the Kingdom of God," *Christian Century* 102/13 (April 22,1987):378-80.

39. Bruce D. Chilton, *God in Strength: Jesus' Announcement of the Kingdom*, reprinted edition (Sheffield, England: JSOT, 1987 (1978), 287-88.

the sovereign activity of God.[40] God's rule is his ultimate intervention in human affairs. The coming of the kingdom, consequently, creates a new way of life in the present.

The biblical drama of the kingdom. Our survey of the biblical materials and the contemporary debate places us in a position to offer a systematic description of the divine reign. Helpful to our theological understanding is a differentiation between *de jure* (in principle) and *de facto* (in fact) rulership. By means of this distinction we may recast the biblical drama in terms of the kingdom idea.

Lying behind the Bible narrative is the idea that as creator, God is *de jure* monarch; the kingship belongs to God by right. Because God created everything, God possesses the right to rule over all creation. Consequently, the entire universe is the kingdom of God or the realm of God's dominion *de jure*. In principle the entire universe constitutes the realm over which God exercises kingship. According to the biblical drama, however, what is true *de jure* is not yet fully true *de facto*. God has given humans the privilege and responsibility of acknowledging his rule. In our sin, however, we have rejected the kingship of the Creator. Thereby we have erected an enclave of rebellion in which another—Satan—appears to reign. As a creature, this *de facto* ruler is a usurper, for he does not possess the right to rule that is God's alone.

The biblical story focuses on Jesus who came as the bearer of the claim of God to rulership and the one who embodies the kingdom of God. Jesus' life, death, resurrection demonstrate God's claim to rulership. Through his exaltation, Jesus has been installed as Lord of the universe. This demonstration of God's rulership entails the demand that all persons acknowledge God as sovereign. Some obey that demand—confess Jesus as Lord—and thereby enter the kingdom of God. Similarly, as the principles of the kingdom permeate human society, the kingdom of God is also present.

The biblical drama of the kingdom climaxes by moving from the past and present to the future. Although the kingdom is here, this presence is partial and not yet consummated. For this reason there re-

---

40. Bruce D. Chilton, "Introduction," in The Kingdom of God in the Teachings of Jesus, ed. Bruce Chilton, *Issues in Religion and Theology 5* (Philadelphia: Fortress, 1984); 25.

mains a future, eschatological aspect of the kingdom. One day all persons will acknowledge the lordship of Jesus (Phil. 2:10-11). Likewise one day the principles of God's kingdom will be universally actualized in the new human society that God will inaugurate. At that time, what is God's by right (*de jure*) will also be true in fact (*de facto*). The entire universe will be the realm of God's rule.

In short, the kingdom of God is both present and future. On the one hand, the divine reign is related to Christ's first advent. It is a reality that people can enter (Mark 9:47; Matt. 21:31-32), for it is the kingly power of God.[41] Hence, the kingdom is a "sphere of existence" in which people are called to live. It is an incorporation into God's powerful invasion of our world. As such it consists in doing the will of God (Matt. 6:10; 7:21-23), and it demands a radical decision (13:44-46). To enter the kingdom means to participate in "the already inaugurated explosion of God's power into the world," to cite the description of Joel Marcus.[42]

On the other hand, the consummation of the divine reign awaits the glory surrounding Christ's second advent. One day all creation will be brought into conformity with the divine intent. Only then will the kingdoms of this world truly become the kingdom of God and God's will truly be done on earth as it is in heaven.

The Kingdom and the Church

The kingdom of God comes as that order of peace, righteousness, justice, and love that God gives to the world. This gift arrives in an ultimate way only at the eschaton, at the renewal of the world brought by Jesus' return. Nevertheless, the power of the kingdom is already at work, for it breaks into the present from the future. As a result, we can experience the divine reign in a partial, yet real sense prior to the great eschatological day. The already/not yet character of the kingdom provides the context in which we may raise the question of the kingdom and the church.

---

41. See Joel Marcus, "Entering into the Kingly Power of God," *Journal of Biblical Literature* 107/4 (1988):663-675.
42. Ibid., 674

Church and kingdom in Christian thought. Although the rediscovery of the kingdom concept is a twentieth century phenomenon, the relationship between the church and the kingdom is an old theme. Augustine wrestled with it,[43] and his position—or perhaps a misunderstanding of it—formed the basis for the virtual equating of the earthly reality of the divine kingdom with the visible church that came to characterize ecclesiology in the Middle Ages. The claim of medieval Roman Catholicism that presence in the visible church is tantamount to being in the kingdom of God, coupled with the sacramental system and excommunication, invested great power in the clergy.

Many Protestants followed a somewhat similar path insofar as they equated the kingdom with the invisible church, the spiritual body of Christ. Even in nineteenth-century liberal thinking the idea persisted, as theologians closely linked the kingdom of God with the society of people of goodwill. Hence, the Baptist thinker Hezekiah Harvey of Hamilton Theological Seminary could write: "The church is the visible, earthly form of the kingdom of Christ, and is the divine organization appointed for its advancement and triumph."[44]

In evangelical circles a quite opposite response to the question of the relationship between the church and the kingdom took root through the influence of classical dispensationalism. This system introduced a rigid, even metaphysical dichotomy between the church and the kingdom. Israel is God's earthly people, whereas the church constitutes his spiritual, heavenly people. Older dispensationalists defined the kingdom as the future, temporal (one thousandyear) rule of Messiah over the earth.[45] During the millennium, Israel and not the church will enjoy prominence.[46]

The church in the kingdom. By reintroducing the eschatological dimension to ecclesiology dispensationalism has served an important purpose. Yet from our sketch of the biblical drama we conclude

---

43. See, for example, Augustine, *The City of God*, 20.9, trans. Marcus Dods, Modern Library edition (New York: Random House, 1950), 725.

44. Hezekiah Harvey, *The Church: Its Polity and Ordinances* (Philadelphia: Judson, 1879), 24-25.

45. Chafer, *Systematic Theology*, 4: 385-86.

46. See for example Chafer, *Systematic Theology*, 4:10-13

that we dare neither equate nor radically separate the church and the kingdom. Rather, we must understand the church in the context of the kingdom.

A proper ecclesiology understands the church within the context of the kingdom because the biblical concept of the kingdom of God is broader than the church. The reign of God includes His inherent right to rulership. Because this right is connected with God's status as creator, it is not dependent on any one earthly manifestation of the divine reign, such as the coming of the church.

Even in its manifestation in creation, the kingdom remains broader than the church. The kingdom concept encompasses God's domain in all of its aspects, which when viewed eschatologically includes the entire created universe as well as the heavenly court. The church, in contrast, arises from God's program in calling out a people to belong to him through Christ.

We must understand the church in the context of the kingdom not only because the kingdom is broader in scope than the church, but also because the church is dependent on the kingdom. God's right to rule declared and demonstrated by Jesus produces the church. As the message of Jesus' lordship is proclaimed, the Holy Spirit creates an obedient human response, which includes building the corporate fellowship of the people of faith. The church, therefore, is called forth by the proclamation of the kingdom of God. It is the *product* of the kingdom,[47] produced by the obedient response to the announcement of the divine reign.

The church is the product of the kingdom in another way as well. It derives its purpose from God's activity in the world. The Holy Spirit calls the community of faith into being, in order that it might proclaim Jesus' kingdom message and live in the world as the company of those who acknowledge in the present the coming reign of God. In this sense, the church is the "eschatological company," the body of those who bear testimony by word and deed to the divine reign, which Christ will consummate at his return and hence will be present throughout the cosmos.

---

47. E.g., C. Rene Padilla, "The Mission of the Church in the Light of the Kingdom of God," *Transformation* 1/2 (April-June, 1984): 17.

Ecclesiological implications. The understanding of the relationship between the church and the kingdom we have outlined has far-reaching implications for our understanding of the church. The link of the church to the reign of God means that ecclesiology has an unavoidable future reference. This eschatological orientation leads to a dynamic ecclesiology.

God's kingdom is eschatological. It marks the goal of God's work in history, the fullness of which lies in the yet unconsummated future. This future—the eschatological reality—and not the past or even the present constitutes our corporate life, just as it determines our individual identity. What the church is, in short, is determined by what the church is destined to become. And the church is directed toward the destiny God intends for humankind—participation in the consummated reign of God.

This outlook stands in contrast to more platonic conceptions which regard the church in the world as the manifestation of some pure Form or Idea.[48] Reformed theologians who follow this approach tend to view the church as constituted by the heavenly archetype existing in God's mind prior to creation. The ideal church is the eternal reality; the purpose of the church in history, in turn, is that of approximating as closely as possible its archetype. The older Calvinists conceived of the true, invisible church as the elect company.[49] Before the creation of the world God determined who would be the elect—whom he would effectually call out of the world into salvation.[50] They viewed the mission of the church in the world (the visible church), in turn, as bringing within its boundaries all the elect, all those who were chosen by God in eternity past.

In contrast to all platonic conceptions which look to the eternal past, the dynamic understanding suggests that the church is constituted by its future destiny as related to God's reign. Believers enter

---

48. Erickson, for example, defends this idea as present already in the New Testament. See, Erickson, *Christian Theology*, 3:1033.

49. Hence, the Westminster Confession: "The catholic or universal Church, which is invisible, consists of the whole number of the elect, that have been, are, or shall be gathered into one, under Christ." *The Westminster Confession*, 25.1, in *Creeds of the Churches*, ed. John Leith, third edition (Atlanta: John Knox, 1982), 222.

50. *Westminster Confession*, 10.1, in Leith, *Creeds of the Churches*, 206.

into covenant with God and each other so that they might be an eschatological community, the fellowship that pioneers in the present the principles that characterize the reign of God. Hence, they point the way toward the kingdom.

Consequently, the identity of the church in the world does not focus merely on bringing into the fold those whom God elected before the creation of the world. Rather, at its heart is the goal of modelling in the present the glorious human fellowship that will come at the consummation of history. The church, therefore, is a foretaste of the eschatological reality that God will one day graciously give to his creation. In short, it is a sign of the kingdom.

The Church as Community

The church is the covenant people of God and the sign of the eschatological kingdom. As helpful as these perspectives are, however, they do not completely describe the eschatological covenantal people that God is seeking to create. To these two, therefore, we must add yet a third perspective: The church is a community.

The Basis in the Covenant and the Kingdom

The introduction of the idea of community immediately raises the question concerning its foundation. On what basis can we assert that the church is a community? And what does this declaration mean? The beginning point in our search for the foundation of the idea of community lies in what we have concluded thus far concerning the nature of the church: The church is both a people in covenant and a sign of the kingdom.

The community of the covenant. Insofar as it is the covenanting people, the church is a community. This conclusion arises from the biblical descriptions of the church, for these are couched in community terminology. The early believers saw themselves as a special people, a people united together because they had been called out of the world by the gospel to belong to God. The New Testament writers referred to the church as a new nation, a body, a temple. And although this people transcends spatial and temporal boundaries, according to the Scriptures it is chiefly manifested in a visible, local group of believers who covenant to be the local expression of the church. All of these images point to the same fundamental idea: The church is a community.

The community focus indicative of the New Testament images is sharpened by the reciprocal relationship between the individual believer and the corporate fellowship indicative of the church as a covenant people. As we noted earlier, the church is formed through the coming together of those who have entered into covenant with God in Christ and thus with each other. At the same time, the corporate fellowship fosters the faith of those who come to participate in it. As a body of people in covenantal relationship with each other and as the faith-facilitating people, the church is a community.

The covenant enhances the community dimension of the church. Indeed, the presence of the covenant is what transforms a loosely related group of people into a community. To see how this is the case, we must look again at the twofold direction of the covenant that believers share.

The covenant which stands at the foundation of the church as a community is primarily vertical. It focuses on the triune God whose people we are. The church consists of those persons who declare individually their loyalty to God through Christ. The basis of the church covenant, therefore, is our personal confession, "Jesus is Lord." We are a people—a community—in that we all share this fundamental faith commitment. In fact, because we all confess Jesus' lordship, the bond between us is greater than all other human bonds.[51] This elevation of the covenantal bond above all other human relationships lay at the heart of Jesus' call to discipleship: "Anyone who loves his father or mother more than me is not worthy of me; anyone who loves his son or daughter more than me is not worthy of me" (Matt. 10:37).

Because we share a common allegiance to Jesus which is our highest loyalty, we also share a commitment to join together to be the people of God. The covenant which inheres in the church, therefore,

---

51. For a discussion of this point, see Stanley J. Grenz, *Sexual Ethics* (Waco, Tex.: Word, 1990), 21-23.

is our agreement to walk together, to be a people in relationship with one another. We who name Jesus as Lord, therefore, are one body—a community. This realization led the early Jerusalem believers to hold even their material possessions in common (Acts 4:32-35).

Viewed theologically, the Holy Spirit is the facilitator of the covenant that forms the foundation of Christ's community. He is the one who brings us to confess Jesus' lordship, which confession lies at the foundation of the covenant we share (1 Cor. 12:3). He is likewise the bond which links us as one unified people. As Paul indicated, among us is a oneness which is nothing less than a unity produced by the Spirit himself (Eph. 4:3).

The crucial role of the Holy Spirit leads us to conclude that although Christ institutes the church, the Spirit constitutes it.[52] The church as Christ' institution confronts us as a historical reality. The Spirit's constitution of the church as a community, however, involves us. He brings us together to be the contemporary expression of the one church of Jesus Christ.

Community and the divine purpose. Our search for the foundation of the idea of church as community is enhanced likewise by the connection between the church and the kingdom outlined above. This connection suggests an additional foundation for the idea that the church is a community: God's program in history leading to the consummation of his reign. Therefore, we must also look to the ultimate purpose of God.

Classical theology rightly affirms that God's program in the world is directed to individuals in the midst of human sin and need. Unfortunately, this emphasis—correct as it is—all too often settles for a truncated soteriology resulting in an inadequate ecclesiology. The program of God includes the salvation of the individual, of course, but it overflows the human person in solitary aloneness. Our salvation occurs in relationships, not in isolation. Hence, God's purpose includes human social interaction. And it moves beyond the isolated human realm to encompass all creation. God's concern does not end with the redeemed individual as an individual. Rather he de-

---

52. Zizioulas, *Being as Communion*, 140.

sires a reconciled humankind (Eph. 2:14-19) living on the renewed new creation and enjoying his own presence (Rev. 21:1-5a).

In short, God's program is directed toward, and is experienced in community. For this reason, the church is far more than a collection of saved individuals who band together for the task of winning the lost. The church is the community of salvation.

The corporate-cosmic dimension of God's program arises from a wider soteriology related to the fuller biblical picture of the nature of guilt and estrangement. We are alienated from God, of course. But estrangement also taints our relationships with one another, with ourselves, and with creation. Consequently, the divine program leads not only toward establishing individual peace with God in isolation; it extends as well to the healing of all relationships—to ourselves, to one another, and to nature.

With a view toward the transformation of estrangement into community, the Father sent the Son and poured out the Holy Spirit. God sent the Spirit at Pentecost as the outworking of Christ's completed work. His intent was to establish the corporate body of Christ to be the one new people composed of Jews and Gentiles reconciled to each other (Eph. 2:11-22). Although the final experience of this community comes only at the consummation of history, the Holy Spirit is even now bringing together into one body a people that transcends every human division. The community of faith represents every nation and every socio-economic status, and it consists of both male and female (Gal. 3:28).

The Spirit's ongoing work, therefore, means that the eschatological community which arrives in its fullness only at the consummation of human history is already present among us in a partial, yet genuine manner. God intends for us to enjoy this present reality in many ways (including family relationships, friends, and even society). But its focal point is the community of the followers of Christ. The Christian church is a distinctive fellowship formed by God through the life, death, and resurrection of Jesus.[53] It is a community

---

53. See, for example, James William McClendon, *Ethics: Systematic Theology Volume One* (Nashville: Abingdon, 1986), 158-239.

of shared commitment to Christ transcending spatial, temporal, social, and gender boundaries.

Community and the Divine Nature

The description of the church as the covenanting people focuses our attention on its actual manifestation in human history. The link between the church and the kingdom purposes of God places it in the larger context of God's program for history, especially the consummation of that program in the eschatological reign when God's purposes will be fully realized. The third description—the church as community—lifts our conception beyond the activity of God in history to the life of the triune God himself, which provides the foundation for that activity.

The ultimate basis for our understanding of the church lies in its relationship to the nature of the triune God himself. Hence, our ecclesiology, like the other foci of systematic theology, finds its point of departure in the doctrine of God.

The church as the image of God. As we have noted, God's purposes are directed toward bringing his highest creation—humankind—to reflect the eternal divine nature, that is, toward bringing us to be the image of God.

In chapters 3 and 4 we set forth the thesis that the character of God is best described by the term "love." Love characterizes God even apart from the world. Throughout eternity God is Father, Son, and Holy Spirit—the community of love. More specifically, the dynamic of the Trinity is the love shared between the Father and the Son, which is the Holy Spirit. God's purpose is to bring glory to his own triune nature by establishing a reconciled creation in which humans reflect the reality of the Creator. The triune God desires that human beings be brought together into a fellowship of reconciliation, which not only reflects God's own eternal essence, but actually participates in his nature (2 Pet. 1:4).

The understanding of God as the social Trinity, the community of love, carries far-reaching ecclesiological implications. From Pentecost to the end of the age the focal point of the reconciled society in history is the church of Jesus Christ, the covenant people. The church is a people who covenant together to belong to God—that is, to be holy, to be set apart from the world for God's special use. As this holy people, we are to proclaim in word and action the principles of the kingdom, showing others what it means to live under the divine reign. But more importantly, as Christ's people we are to show forth the divine reality—to be the image of God. To be the people in covenant with God who serve as the sign of the kingdom means to reflect the very character of God. The church reflects God's character in that it lives as a genuine community—lives in love—for as the community of love the church shows the nature of the triune God.[54] Enroute to the consummation of his purpose, therefore, God calls the church to mirror as far as possible in the midst of the brokenness of the present that eschatological ideal community of love which derives its meaning from the divine essence.

The church and the Spirit. Viewed within the context of the triune God himself, the church is a community. This assertion, like the understanding of the church as the covenant people and as the sign of the kingdom, returns us to the role of the Holy Spirit as the completer of the program of the triune God. Ultimately, the community which is to characterize the church results from our communion with the Spirit. To understand this, we must review the grand sweep of God's eternal purpose as it relates to his own triune nature.

The Father sent the Son in order to realize God's eternal design to draw humankind and creation to participate in his own life. In conversion, the Son gives us the Spirit, who causes us to be the children of God. But this filial status is exactly the relationship the Son enjoys with the Father. Through conversion, therefore, the Spirit—who is the Spirit of the relationship between the Father and the Son—constitutes us the brothers and sisters of Christ. Thereby he brings us to share in the love the Son enjoys with the Father. Through the Spirit,

---

54. This theme has been the subject of a few preliminary explorations. For an example of a discussion from a free church perspective, see Miroslav Volf, "Kirche als Gemeinschaft: Ekklesiologische Ueberlegungen aus freikirchlicher Perspective," *Evangelische Theologie* 49/1 (1989): 70-76. For developments within Roman Catholic ecclesiology, see Kilian McDonnell, "Vatican II (1962-1964), Puebla (1979), Synod (1985): *Koinonia/Communio* as an Integral Ecclesiology," *Journal of Ecumenical Studies* 25/3 (Summer 1988): 414.

we participate in the love that lies at the heart of the triune God himself.

Participation in the dynamic of trinitarian love, however, is not ours merely as individuals in isolation. Rather, it is a privilege we share with all other believers. Because of Christ's work on our behalf and the Spirit's activity within us, we are coadoptees into the family of God, coparticipants in the relationship enjoyed between the Father and the Son, which is the Holy Spirit. In mediating this relationship to us the Spirit draws us together as one family. Only in our Spirit-produced corporateness do we truly reflect to all creation the grand dynamic that lies at the heart of the triune God. As we share together in the Holy Spirit, therefore, we participate in relationship with the living God and become the community of Christ our Lord.

Consequently, the community of love which the church is called to be is no ordinary reality. The fellowship we share with each other is not merely that of a common experience or a common narrative, as important as these are. Our fellowship is nothing less than our common participation in the divine communion between the Father and the Son mediated by the Holy Spirit. As Tillard rightly declares,

> the ecclesial *koinonia* can be defined as the passing of the Trinitarian Communion into the fraternal relations of the disciples of Christ....Seen from the human side, the ecclesial *koinonia* is none other than the fraternity of the disciples of Christ Jesus but in so far as it is caught up, seized by the Spirit who inserts it in the relation of the Father and the Son.[55]

We are one people, therefore, because we are the company of those who the Spirit has already brought to share in the love between the Father and the Son. We truly are the community of love, a people bound together by the love present among us through the power of God's Spirit. As this people, we are called to reflect in the present the eternal dynamic of the triune God, that community which we will enjoy in the great eschatological fellowship on the renewed earth.

Only our primary identity as coparticipants in the fellowship of the triune God forms the ultimate foundation for the various other

---

55. J.M.R. Tillard, "What Is the Church of God?" *Mid-stream* 23 (October 1984): 372-73.

facets of our doctrine of the church. Our coparticipation in the divine life provides the basis for the ministry of the church in the world (chapter 18). This coparticipation supplies the context for understanding the rites of the community (chapter 19). And it constitutes the link between the church as a whole and its local, visible expressions, thereby offering a vision out of which to construct a facilitating church structure (chapter 20).

Since his exaltation, the risen Lord continues his program at the behest of the Father through the Holy Spirit who was poured out at Pentecost. This Spirit constitutes the church as the body of Christ, whose ministry is the continuation of Christ's ministry. To this ministry we now turn.

18 The Ministry of the Community

But you are a chosen people, a royal priesthood, a holy nation, a people belonging to God, that you may declare the praises of him who called you out of darkness into his wonderful light. (1 Pet. 2:9)

Outline

The church is a dynamic reality. It consists of a people in covenant. This covenant people pioneer in the present the principles that characterize the future kingdom of God, thereby constituting a sign of the divine reign. As the covenant people who anticipate the future consummation of God's intention for humankind, the church is a community. The fellowship of believers seeks to reflect for all creation the nature of the triune God himself, namely, the love between the Father and the Son which is the Holy Spirit. In short, the church is the eschatological covenant community of love.

As a special community existing in the world, the church possesses a divinely given ministry. Its ministry arises from the church's nature as a people in covenant with God and one another, a sign of God's reign, and a reflection of the divine love. We now explore the great ministry we share as the people of God. We look first at the fundamental purpose of the church's existence. This in turn forms the context for delineating the specific mandate Christ has given to his church.

The Purpose of the Church

The proper starting point for describing the ministry of the church lies with God's ultimate purpose for his people. Why did Christ initially institute the church? And for what end does the Spirit continue to constitute the church today? Our final answer to this question can only be: "for God's glory." The church in all its expressions exists ultimately for the sake of the glory of the triune God.

The Church in God's Purposes

To set forth a proper ecclesiology, we must view the church from the perspective of God's wider purposes. Doing so brings us immediately to the conclusion that the church exists for God's glory. Crucial to the fulfillment of the wider purposes of God is his activity in history from creation to consummation. In history God is at work in bringing to pass his intention for all creation. His calling the church into existence is one central moment in the accomplishment of this wider purpose. What is this grand purpose of God?

The church and the purpose of creation. The biblical authors repeatedly suggest that the fundamental purpose of all creation is to glorify God. The psalmist indicates that God's glory is the divinely given task of nature: "The heavens declare the glory of God; the skies proclaim the work of his hands" (Ps. 19:1). As God's special creation and the recipients of God's special concern, humans likewise are to praise their Creator: "How good it is to sing praises to our God, how pleasant and fitting to praise him!" (147:1).

Although God made all creation in order to praise his name, something has gone wrong. In our sinfulness we fail in our task of living for the divine glory. Our failure has affected the universe, which, as Paul describes it, "was subjected to frustration...in hope that the creation itself will be liberated from its bondage to decay and brought into the glorious freedom of the children of God" (Rom. 8:20-21). As a consequence, God directs his saving action toward bringing us to participate with all creation in glorifying God.

Christ came with this purpose in view. In his high priestly prayer on the eve of his death, Jesus placed his impending sacrifice in the context of glorification: "Father, the time has come. Glorify your Son, that your Son may glorify you... I have brought you glory on earth by completing the work you gave me to do" (John 17:1,4).

As the recipients of God's grace in Christ, we are the people whom Christ purchased for the sake of God's glory. Paul clarified that this was the goal of God's action in extending grace to sinful humans: God predestined us to be adopted into his family "to the praise of his glorious grace, which he has freely given us in the One he loves" (Eph. 1:5-6). God has included us "in Christ" so that we might live "for the praise of his glory" (1:11-14). But our status as trophies of grace has ramifications beyond this life. Throughout eternity we will bear witness to the amazing grace of God and in this manner bring glory to him (2:6-7).

The church and the glory of God. The fundamental purpose of the church, therefore, is to bring glory to God. Christ instituted the church in accordance with his mission to glorify God in the world. Similarly, the Holy Spirit constitutes us as the fellowship of God's people in order that through us God might be glorified in the present.

Our conclusion that the existence of the church is to glorify God has far-reaching significance for the life of the church in the world, both in its universal and its local expressions. It means that the ultimate motivation for all church planning, goals, and actions must center solely on our desire to bring glory to God. We must direct all that we say and do as the eschatological covenant community toward this ultimate purpose, namely, that God be glorified through us. Because this is our ultimate goal, we must carefully monitor the various dimensions of church life, seeking to bring everything under this one priority. In this manner we can follow the spirit of Paul's admonition: "So whether you eat or drink or whatever you do, do it all for the glory of God" (1 Cor. 10:31; see also Rom. 15:6).

God's Purpose in Glorification

The emphasis we have outlined above has been a part of theological reflection on the church from the first century to the present. The Reformed theological tradition has focused particularly on God's glory as the final rationale and goal for the divine work in both creation and salvation.

Despite the long pedigree enjoyed by this proposal, it has not always been articulated in a manner consistent with what theology teaches concerning the character of God. Some presentations of the divine will to glorification leave the impression that God reserves all praise and honor for himself in a manner that sets God's own character in direct opposition to the biblical ideal. The Bible sets forth humility as God's intention for humans. Paul, for example, admonished his readers, "Do nothing out of selfish ambition or vain conceit, but in humility consider others better than yourselves" (Phil. 2:3). According to the apostle, the kind of humility that ought to characterize us was exemplified by Jesus Christ himself (vv. 5-8).

How different from the example of Christ and the ideal for humankind appears the attitude of a God who directs all his activities toward his own exaltation, demanding that all creation glorify him alone. In what sense could we model ourselves after the divine character so understood? If God seeks only his own glory, how could we live as the divine image?

God's glory is indeed the final goal of all God's actions. But in order to make sense out of this assertion, we must understand it in its proper context. In our reflection on the divine purpose we ought not to think of God as a solitary subject. Such reflection would lead us inevitably to view God as so enamored with his own surpassing greatness that he relishes the acclamations of his creatures. That God is more akin to Aristotle's Unmoved Mover, who as the only reality worthy of his own contemplation sets himself only to be cognizant of himself.[1] Rather, we must approach this theme from the perspective of God as triune.

As we set forth in chapter 2, God is eternally triune. The inner dynamic of the triune God is love—the relationship shared between Father and Son which is the Holy Spirit. We have likewise noted that God's intention in history is an outworking of his own eternal nature. His goal for humankind is that we be the image of God, that is, the reflection of the very nature of the Creator. But the Creator is none other than the triune God—Father, Son, and Holy Spirit—the divine community of love. Consequently, God's work in history is ultimately corporate; God intends to bring to pass a reconciled creation in which humans reflect in relationship to each other and to the universe around us the reality of the triune Creator. Hence, God's actions are aimed at establishing the reconciled community of love as the human reflection of the social Trinity—the divine nature—which is love.

In this manner, God's soteriological purposes arise out of the glorification of his own triune nature. By establishing the eschatological community of love, the covenant people, God brings into being a new humankind, a people who mirror for all creation the divine character and essence. As his essential nature is made manifest in creation, the triune God is glorified. Rather than a cosmic egotist who demands the opposite quality in his creatures, therefore, he is the triune God who desires that humans mirror his own holy character,

---

1. Aristotle, *Metaphysics*, 12:1-10 (1069a18-1076a4), in *Great Books of the Western World*, ed. Rubert Maynard Hutchins (Chicago: William Berton, Publishers, Encyclopedia Britannica, Inc., 1952), 598-606.

which is love. As we live in fellowship, we bring honor to the One who is himself the divine community of love.

As the example of Christ indicates, true community requires that its participants relate to each other with humble servanthood motivated by love. For this reason, the Bible elevates humility, exemplified by Jesus' humble obedience to the will of his Father, as the human ideal.

En route to the consummation of God's purposes, the church is the primary vehicle for mirroring the divine image. As the people united together, God calls us to exemplify in the midst of the brokenness of the present the eschatological ideal community of love, which is the divine essence. The church is to be the fellowship of individuals who are bound together by the love present among them through the power of God's Spirit which is exemplified by humble service to each other and the world. Indeed, as we exist in love, we reflect what God is like. Thereby, we bring glory to him, for we exemplify the love that lies at the heart of the dynamic of the triune God, which Christ himself has revealed to us.

The Mandate of the Church

The ministry of the church lies within the context of our existence as the community of God's people who bring glory to him. The Bible links the glorification of God with love-motivated obedience to an entrusted vocation. The greatest example, of course, is Jesus himself. He was obedient to God's will to the point of death. Hence, immediately prior to his passion, he prayed, "I have brought you glory on earth by completing the work you gave me to do" (John 17:4; see also Phil. 2:5-11). Jesus' obedient fulfillment of his vocation expresses the eternal love of the Son for the Father.

In the same manner, our obedient acceptance of the vocation God has given us brings glory to Christ and through him to the Father. Jesus himself spoke of this glory. In his great prayer, our Lord rejoiced in the glory he had received through his disciples (John 17:10). Earlier, he told his friends that their fruitfulness brings glory to the Father: "This is to my Father's glory, that you bear much fruit, showing yourselves to be my disciples" (John 15:8).

The link between obedience to a vocation and God's glory indicates that the church glorifies God as it is obedient to its Lord, that is, as it fulfils its divinely-given mandate to be the people who acknowledge in word and deed Christ's lordship. The New Testament indicates that the Lord entrusted a great mandate to his church. As God's people are faithful in carrying out their corporate task, the church brings glory to God.

What specifically is the ministry of the church? Theologians commonly summarize our vocation by appeal to three Greek terms, *martyria* or *kerygma* (witness), *koinonia* (fellowship), and *diakonia* (service).[2] However, this summary omits the foundational ministry—worship—and fails to see the important connection between proclamation and service as constituting one ministry directed toward the world. Consequently, as a more complete description of the church's mandate we offer an alternative. In our common life we are to seek to be a true community of faith, manifesting the community bond in corporate worship, mutual edification, and outreach to the world.

Worship

The mandate Christ has given to the church includes worship. Although we may worship God privately in many ways, worship is also to be a dimension of the church's corporate life. Hence, the author of Hebrews admonished the community not to give up meeting together (Heb. 10:25). And Paul issued instructions to guide Christians when they "come together" (1 Cor. 14:26). We are to be a worshiping community, offering to God the glory due his name. For this reason we may appropriately speak of the church as being "gathered to worship."

The focus of worship. Basically, worship means attributing worth to the one who is worthy.[3] The worship dimension lifts the attention

---

2. E.g., Dale Moody, *The Word of Truth* (Grand Rapids: Eerdmans, 1981), 428-33. See also, Harvey Cox, *The Secular City* (New York: Macmillan, 1965), 125-48.

3. "To pay divine honors to; to reverence with supreme respect and veneration; to perform religious service to; to adore; to idolize." *New Websters Dictionary of the English Language* (No city: Delair, 1971), 1148.

of the believing community to the God who constitutes us as his people. Hence, Ralph Martin defines worship as "the dramatic celebration of God in his supreme worth in such a manner that his 'worthiness' becomes the norm and inspiration of human living."[4]

The biblical writers instructed their readers about the focus of such worship. They encouraged the worshiping community to ascribe worth to God for who he is and for what he does.

We are to worship God for who he is. Repeatedly the biblical authors enjoined their readers to acknowledge God because he is the Holy One. The psalmist admonished: "Ascribe to the LORD the glory due his name; worship the LORD in the splendor of his holiness" (Ps. 29:2; see also 96:8; 1 Chron. 16:29). In so doing we consciously join with the angelic hosts who continually proclaim, "Holy, holy, holy is the Lord God Almighty, who was, and is, and is to come" (Rev. 4:6-8; see also Isa. 6:3).

The Scriptures also caution us to worship God because he is the Creator. In his vision of the heavenly court, John observed the twenty-four elders (who symbolize the whole people of God) declare, "You are worthy, our Lord and God, to receive glory and honor and power, for you created all things, and by your will they were created and have their being" (Rev. 4:11). As the Creator, God is powerful and therefore worthy of awe and praise (Ps. 29:3-10).

Above all, however, the biblical people of God were to worship him because of his saving acts. The Old Testament continually admonished Israel to worship God because he had graciously entered into covenant with them (1 Chron. 16:15), and as a result, he had done great wonders (v. 12), especially in rescuing them from their enemies. According to the New Testament, the focal point of God's saving work is Jesus. Because of his role in salvation, the risen Lord is now the recipient of worship. John the seer observed the living creatures and the elders praising the Lamb: "You are worthy to take the scroll and to open its seals, because you were slain, and with your blood you purchased men for God from every tribe and language and people and nation." (Rev. 5:9).

---

4. Ralph Martin, *The Worship of God* (Grand Rapids: Eerdmans, 1982), 4.

Through its corporate worship life, the community gathers to commemorate the foundational events of our spiritual existence, at the center of which is the action of God in Christ delivering humankind from the bondage of sin. In so doing we extol God's great love. We glorify the God who is eternally the community of love and especially the Father who "so loved the world that he gave his one and only Son" (John 3:16).

The means of worship. The biblical writings offer insight as to what activities can serve as vehicles for our worship. The Bible provides precedence for the use of a variety of means to facilitate the worship experience. Especially useful are music, declaration, prayer, and symbolic acts.

(1) Perhaps no activity is more central to biblical worship than *music*. Indeed, singing and worship have been integrally connected since God first constituted Israel as his people. Thus, when God rescued them from the Egyptians, Moses and the people sang their praises to him. They acknowledged God as their strength, song, and salvation (Ex. 15:1-18). The practice of singing begun among the ancient Hebrews continued into the New Testament church (Matt. 26:30; 1 Cor. 14:26; Eph. 5:19).

Israel's singing on the day of the exodus was surely correct, for music is a natural human response to the saving experience. Hence, the psalmist declared, "Come, let us sing for joy to the LORD, let us shout aloud to the Rock of our salvation. Let us come before him with thanksgiving and extol him with music and song" (Ps. 95:1). We engage in this act of worship because of our joy in the Lord. Again the psalmist wrote, "It is good...to make music to your name, O Most High...For you make me glad by your deeds, O LORD; I sing for joy at the works of your hands" (Ps. 92:1,4). But above all, we make music in worship, because God delights in us as we respond in this manner to his great salvation. The ancient psalmist knew this as well: "Praise the LORD. Sing to the LORD a new song, his praise in the assembly of the saints. Let Israel rejoice in their Maker; let the people of Zion be glad in their King. Let them praise his name with dancing and make music to him with tambourine and harp. For the LORD takes delight in his people; he crowns the humble with salvation" (149:1-4). In this joyous expression of worship, all kinds of musical instruments may be used—trumpet, harp, lyre, tambourine, strings, flute, even cymbals! (150:3-5).

It is not surprising that music is an important vehicle of worship expression. Although its forms may vary among cultures, music seems to be a universal part of human life. Music offers people a medium through which to give expression to the broad dimension of their being. Song can incorporate the cognitive aspects of life, expressing in lyrics and in the structure of the music the composer's conception of the world. But music also reflects the noncognitive. It captures feelings, emotion, and mood, thereby giving expression to what cannot be said through words alone. The music people create reflects their deepest thoughts and feelings, their greatest concerns and fears, their highest hopes and expectations. And music serves to confirm in ourselves and others the emotions and aspirations it captures.

Consequently, it is fitting that the people of God express their Christian consciousness through music. In so doing we offer to God our emotions in addition to our creeds, our feelings as well as our beliefs. We offer to him the joy we sense because of his goodness; we share in the sorrow and pain Christ bore on our behalf; and we anticipate the glory of the great eschatological day when our Lord will return. Giving expression to these feelings can all be worship, in so far as it is intended to honor the triune God and is offered to him by his covenant people.

(2) Although in its experience of worship the Old Testament community focused on music, center stage in Christian worship is reserved for *declaration*. The gathered community comes together to speak and to listen.

Like that of music, the foundation for declaration as a dimension of worship lies in the Old Testament. In ancient Israel singing and declaring were readily linked together. This is evident, for example, in David's song of thanks: "Sing to him, sing praise to him; tell of all his wonderful acts....Sing to the Lord all the earth; proclaim his salvation day after day" (1 Chron. 16:9,23; see also Ps. 96:2-3). Such declarations connected to singing could even be loud and boisterous:

"Come, let us sing for joy to the Lᴏʀᴅ; let us shout aloud to the Rock of our salvation" (Ps. 95:1).

Declaration was central not only in the ancient Hebrew community, but also in the church. Just as God had chosen Israel to proclaim his gracious salvation, so also he has called us to this glorious ministry. The author of Hebrews indicated that such declaration constitutes one dimension of the appropriate Christian sacrifice: "Through Jesus, therefore, let us continually offer to God a sacrifice of praise—the fruit of lips that confess his name" (Heb. 13:15).

Our declarations of praise, like the music we offer to God, are to focus on his great salvation. Peter, invoking language reminiscent of the Old Testament, wrote, "But you are a chosen people, a royal priesthood, a holy nation, a people belonging to God, that you may declare the praises of him who called you out of darkness into his wonderful light" (1 Pet. 2:9).

Declaration includes telling each other about the greatness and goodness of God. It also means corporately extolling God for who he is and what he has done. In corporate worship, however, declaration entails as well the proclamation of God's word. In the ancient communities, such declarations often took the form of prophetic utterances (1 Cor. 14:1-5,26-32). But a central place was also given to the reading and explication of the Torah (Neh. 8:1-9) or of the Scriptures (1 Tim. 4:13). This biblical tradition forms the foundation for the contemporary sermon.

The Protestant churches have tended to place the sermon at the heart of worship. This practice is correct insofar as it highlights the central role of the Scriptures in community life and the importance of understanding Scripture for community vitality. But implicit in the sermon is also its role as a specific way in which the people of God declare his goodness. As the church gathers to hear the sermon, they are celebrating the divine provision of instruction in the present as an outgrowth of the Spirit's formulation of the Bible in the past.

(3) Corporate worship includes *prayer*. Fundamentally, prayer is an aspect of declaration—specifically, declaration directed to God. In prayer the community turns the focus of its address away from humans to the God who is the foundation of its existence.

The declaration to God that occurs within the context of corporate worship life ideally consists of four elements. Although every prayer need not include each, the ongoing prayer life of the church ought to encompass all four aspects. The elements listed in their logical order construct an acrostic with the word ACTS: adoration, confession, thanksgiving, and supplication.

Simply stated, adoration means praising God for who God is. This follows the model of the Lord's prayer, which begins, "Our Father in heaven, hallowed be your name" (Matt. 6:9). In keeping with Jesus' directive, the faith community verbalizes to God the glory due him. This aspect of prayer centers on the nature of God, as the church praises God because of his perfect character. The offering of praise to God is beneficial to the church, in that adoration is a safeguard against idolatry and false pride. More importantly, God delights in the praise of his people, for such adoration is a symbol of our response of love to our gracious Creator and Redeemer.[5]

Jesus' model prayer enjoins his followers to engage not only in adoration but also in confession: "Forgive us our sins" (Luke 11:4). In corporate confession we acknowledge our human failure and express agreement with God concerning it, namely, that it is displeasing in his sight. The Bible indicates that confession is important as a prerequisite to the reception of God's forgiveness and spiritual provision (Jer. 5:25; Ps. 66:18; Matt. 6:14-15). Confession may also open the way to receive God's word. The experience of Daniel serves as an example. The divine messenger came to him, while Daniel was "speaking and praying, confessing my sin and the sin of my people Israel" (Dan. 9:20).[6]

Adoration and confession form a natural progression. As we catch a vision of God in all his glory, we are drawn to see our own sinfulness. Isaiah experienced this progression. As he saw the Lord "high and lifted up" and the angels singing, "Holy, Holy, Holy is the

---

5. For an interesting, although overstated discussion of the significance of praise for spiritual living, see Paul E. Billheimer, *Destined for the Throne*, (Fort Washington: Christian Literature Crusade, 1975), 115-126.

6. For a statement of the principle underlying the relationship between confession and the reception of divine gifts, see Don E. Saliers, *The Soul in Paraphrase* (New York: Seabury, 1980), 64-65.

Lord," he came to an awareness not only of his sin but also that of his people (Isa. 6:1-6).

As the community acknowledges human sinfulness, the ensuing reception of forgiveness (1 John 1:9) produces a grateful heart, leading to prayers of thanksgiving. Such prayers move beyond the experience of being forgiven to express gratitude to God for all that God has done and is doing (1 Thess. 5:18). This dimension of prayer ought not to be confused with adoration, however. Adoration praises God because of his character, whereas thanksgiving is the expression of gratitude for what God does on behalf of the church and the world. Thanksgiving arises from the reception of God's gifts; adoration centers on the Giver.[7]

Adoration, confession, and thanksgiving embolden the people of God to engage in supplication. This dimension of corporate prayer entails petitioning God concerning human need (Phil 4:6). Here the church sets before the loving heavenly Father the needs of the people of God locally and universally (1 Thess. 5:25) and the needs of the world itself (1 Tim. 2:1-4).

(4) A final vehicle for corporate worship is *symbolic act*. Unfortunately, this dimension is often overlooked in Protestant worship. The traditional Protestant discomfort with symbolism is understandable given the context of medieval church practice out of which the Reformation emerged. Nevertheless, symbolism is an important part of human life. And symbolic acts are implicitly present even in the simplest worship services.

The central symbols in the life of the church are the ordinances, which symbolize the gospel. These warrant a more complete discussion, and therefore become the explicit point of discussion in chapter 19.

In its worship life the church employs many less obvious symbolic acts. These can include the simple handshake, which is so integral a part of Western culture. When warm and heartfelt, this act can extend to others the welcome, friendliness, and acceptance we have re-

---

7. For a similar distinction, see James Hastings, ed., *The Great Christian Doctrines* (Edinburgh: T. & T. Clark, 1915), 133. See also John H. Wright, *A Theology of Christian Prayer* (New York: Pueblo, 1979), 58-61.

ceived from God. Hence, it becomes a way of indirect praise to God for his goodness. Similarly, the practice of forming a circle and joining hands, especially following the Lord's Supper celebration, can be a symbolic act of worship. Through this practice, we express our unity within Christ's body and bear silent praise to the Spirit who fosters this unity.

Perhaps more obvious as a symbolic act of worship is the manner in which many congregations collect the financial gifts of the worshipers. Often the ushers pass baskets through the congregation and then bring the collected money to the front. In this manner we offer our corporate gifts to God in one community act. In addition to the corporate act, even the giving of money can be symbolic, as we allow the gift to be an expression of our gratitude to God for his goodness to us as a people. The financial gift can also serve as a representation of our entire selves, a sign that in this act we are offering not only the monetary gift but all that we have and are.

We do well to foster a heightened use and awareness of symbols in our corporate worship.

Edification

Jesus entrusted a joyous responsibility to his followers. We are to "worship the Father in spirit and in truth" (John 4:23), that is, to attribute worth to our God and Savior. Our Lord also mandated that we follow his example in washing one another's feet (13:12-17). Hence, the work of the church also includes edification—that we care for one another within the body of Christ and build each other up, so that all believers might become spiritually mature (Eph. 4:11-13).

Aspects of edification. The dimension of edification means that as the corporate people of God we take seriously our calling to be a fellowship of mutuality. Mutuality means that we sense a fundamental oneness with each other. This oneness includes being bound together by shared values and by our participation in a common mission.

Mutuality also encompasses more relational dimensions as well. It entails that we develop within the group meaningful relationships with one another. The relationship we share means that we sense sympathy, compassion, and empathy for each other, that we "rejoice with those who rejoice" and "mourn with those who mourn" (Rom. 12:15). Mutuality means likewise that we seek to live in harmony with each other (12:16), intercede for each other, care for each other, and minister to the needs of one another (12:13).

The demands of the life of discipleship in a fundamentally inhospitable environment heighten the importance of mutuality. We desperately need the support of others who share the same vision of God acting in the world and who are therefore dedicated to one another as we participate together in that divine activity.

Basically, the church fulfills its edification responsibility as its members minister to the needs—both material and spiritual—of others in the fellowship. Such ministry includes sharing the burdens of those who are facing difficulties (Gal. 6:1-2), encouraging and admonishing each other (Heb. 10:24-25), and nurturing those who are new or weak in the faith (Rom. 14:1,19). Such edification is crucial to all believers. The Christian life is not merely an individual struggle for perfection. Rather, it is in an important sense a community project.

Our edification ministry means not only that we give support to one another, but also that we become accountable to each other. Accountability does not mean that we sacrifice personal responsibility or give up the freedom of the individual Christian in blind obedience to the group or to dictatorial leaders. It does suggest, however, that we take seriously our interrelatedness as a believing community. What each of us does and how each of us lives affects the entire fellowship. Especially the wilful, blatant sins of church members cast a shadow over our common testimony to the gospel. For this reason, Peter admonished his readers to be holy in all their actions: "Live such good lives among the pagans that, though they accuse you of doing wrong, they may see your good deeds and glorify God on the day he visits us" (1 Pet. 2:12). Conversely, we share a common interest in spiritual growth—desiring that the eyes of all believers be enlightened to know the hope to which God has called us (Eph. 1:18). And we gladly become accountable to one another, because we know that each of us can be an instrument of the Spirit's work in fostering maturity in us.

The people of God use many vehicles for edifying one another. Obvious examples include the preaching and teaching that occurs within church life. Not only do they become the channels for instruction as to how we should live, preaching and teaching form the primary means for instilling and maintaining the common commitment to the shared values and mission of the community.

Not to be overlooked, however, are structures designed to foster mutual nurture—inquirer classes, small care circles, and larger fellowship groups. By bringing members of the church together, these occasions promote mutuality. They offer opportunities for fostering meaningful relationships and strengthening bonds of support and accountability.

Finally, even involvement in the other two aspects of the church's mandate—worship and outreach—serve its edification ministry. As we join together in carrying forth our common task, whether in celebrating the greatness of God or in ministering to the world, mutuality is enhanced. Common activity can be a means to solidifying the bonds that tie us to each other and to fostering growth within our lives.

The church as a praying people. Foundational to the edifying mandate, however, is yet another vehicle—prayer. The church carries out its edification mandate as it functions as a praying people, practising the art and privilege of intercession (James 5:16).[8]

The activity of intercession is based in part on the biblical concept of the priesthood of the believers.[9] In a special and important way each Christian is to function in the church as a priest. The Old Testament provides the context for understanding this function. Among the ancient Hebrews, priests were charged with the role of offering sacrifices to God on behalf of the people and interceding before God on behalf of others. As a kingdom of priests purchased by Christ (Rev. 5:10), the New Testament people of God have been entrusted

---

8. See, for example, Stanley J. Grenz, *Prayer: The Cry for the Kingdom* (Peabody, Mass.: Hendrickson, 1987).

9. For a discussion of this concept and its basis in the Old Testament role of intercessors, see Lukas Vischer, *Intercession* (Geneva: World Council of Churches, 1980), 25-27, 48-49.

with a similar role, namely, the glorious privilege of praying for each other.

Jesus' own example is especially instructive for our understanding of intercession. In the upper room he articulated his concern for all disciples: "My prayer is not that you take them out of the world but that you protect them from the evil one. They are not of the world, even as I am not of it. Sanctify them by the truth; your word is truth" (John 17:15-17). Following Jesus' example, we will not petition God that our friends experience a life of ease—that they be spared all the trials of life. Rather, the focus of our intercession is that God protect them from the evil one as they live in the midst of the world and that they be sanctified, built up by the truth which is God's word.

The New Testament epistles are filled with examples of intercession (Rom. 15:5-6,13; 2 Cor. 13:7; Eph. 3:16-19; Eph. 6:18; 1 Thess. 3:10-13; 5:23; 2 Thess. 2:17; 3:5,16; Heb. 13:21). In fact, nearly every Pauline letter begins with prayer for the Christians whom Paul was addressing (Eph. 1:15-19; Phil. 1:9-11; Col. 1:9-12; 2 Thess. 1:12; Philemon 6).

Central to all intercession is the desire that believers come to know and reflect the divine will. God's primary will for each Christian is that we all attain spiritual maturity—growth in faith, knowledge, doctrine, character, and speech (Eph. 4:13-15)—so that we may radiate the reality of Christ. Following the New Testament pattern, we pray for one another, petitioning God that the Spirit might be at work in our lives, causing us to grow as we are built up in the faith and in our knowledge of Christ. We pray that we might all hold fast to correct doctrine, that our character may increasingly conform to that of Jesus, and that our speech may always be the truth seasoned with love.

In addition to his intention that all believers become mature, God desires that each Christian be active in a specific place of service. Knowing this, our intercession also includes the request that the Spirit both illumine our brothers and sisters to find their calling and strengthen them to be faithful in their God-given responsibility.

The church as community to its believers. Prayer lies at the foundation of the church's edification mandate. But at the heart of this task is the role of the church as community to one another.

The Enlightenment fascination with individualism led thinkers in the modern era to place the community dimension of the church's mandate on the periphery. However, the waning of the focus on individualism in recent years has sparked a renewal of interest in the concept. Thinkers in various disciplines now assert that our understanding of the human phenomenon must reflect a more adequate account of the social dimensions of life.[10] One such thinker, Robert Bellah, offered an appropriate description: A community "attempts to be an inclusive whole, celebrating the interdependence of public and private life and of the different callings of all." Hence, it "is a group of people who are socially interdependent, who participate together in discussion and decision making, and who share certain *practices*...that both define the community and are nurtured by it."[11]

The contemporary concept of community offers a means for understanding the edification mandate of the church. It suggests that the church is essentially a people who act as community to one another. Of course, the church engages in its community function as it fosters sharing, caring groups, as well as opportunities for believers to enjoy fellowship with one another. But theologically more important is the deeper manner in which the church is a community. As a community of memory and hope, it fosters identity formation within believers.

(1) The church brings into its purview past, present, and future. In so doing, it functions as a community of memory and hope.[12]

---

10. Daniel A. Helminiak, "Human Solidarity and Collective Union in Christ," *Anglican Theological Review* 70/1 (January 1988): 37.

11. Robert N. Bellah, et al. *Habits of the Heart: Individualism and Commitment in American Life* (Berkeley: University of California Press, 1985), 333.

12. Drawing from the work of earlier thinkers, including Royce, contemporary secular communalists acknowledge the presence in the wider society of such communities. For a short overview, see "Josiah Royce," in the *Dictionary of Philosophy and Religion*, ed. William L. Reese (Atlantic Highlands, N.J.: Humanities Press, 1980), 498-99.

The church is a community of memory.[13] It has a history, which in an important sense constitutes it. The church community keeps its past alive by retelling its story. This constitutive narrative articulates primarily the biblical drama of salvation centering on Jesus of Nazareth. But the church's narrative includes as well the stories of the great people who have left a lasting legacy of faith to subsequent believers (Heb. 11). In retelling its ongoing narrative, the church offers examples of persons who have embodied and exemplified the meaning of the gospel, which stands at the heart of the faith community.

The gaze of the church community encompasses the future as well. The telling of the biblical drama which climaxes in the consummation of history leads believers to anticipate the continuation and further development of God's activity among his people. This vision of God's future brings the community to sense that it is moving ever onward toward a goal—the enjoyment of full community—which lies yet before it in the future. Through this focus on the future, the church functions as a community of hope.

By keeping before its members the grand sweep of God's actions from the past to the future—whether through preaching and teaching or in less direct ways such as liturgy and music—the church edifies its members. It provides a transcendent vantage point for life in the present, thereby supplying a context of meaning that can allow us to connect our personal lives with the life of a larger whole. And it facilitates us in seeing our efforts as being contributions to that whole. This edifying ministry strengthens faith and equips the faithful to be the people of God in the present context.

Paul provided a pattern for such edification. He admonished his readers to remain steadfast, because the vision of their future resurrection as an extension of Christ's resurrection in the past means that their efforts carry eternal significance (1 Cor. 15:58).

---

13. In *The Problem of Christianity*, Josiah Royce (1855-1916) explored the idea of one vast "community of interpretation," not so much as a present reality but as a task to which we ought to be loyal. Anticipating contemporary writers such as Robert Bellah, he spoke of community in religious terms, as a community of memory and hope, faith, and redeeming grace.

Also important to community life is the provision of qualitative meaning to time and space, and to persons and groups.[14] By means of the cycle of the church calendar year, the faith community raises our sights above the apparently meaningless flow of time. By linking the day, the week, the season, and the year with the sacred story of divine redemption, the church presents time as a meaningful whole. This connection is facilitated as well by practices of commitment.[15] Through these rites the church initiates new believers into its circle, and all members repeatedly reaffirm their presence in the church community. As we will see in chapter 19, baptism and the Lord's supper function as our primary community commitment rites.

(2) The church edifies its members by serving as a community of memory and hope. In so doing it also provides a foundation for identity development in its members.

Contemporary communalists point out that personal identity formation requires collective representations, the group-based symbols with which individuals identify. These provide a collection of shared meanings and values which is crucial to the inculcation of ideals in its members.[16] Because meaning is not an individual matter but rather is interpersonal or relational, the group is crucial for the process of personal identity development.[17] This occurs through the telling of a personal narrative, the story which makes sense of our lives.[18] But any such story of a person's life is always embedded in the story of the communities in which the person participates,[19] for traditions mediated by communities, and not individuals, are the carriers of rationality. The community transmits to the individual the transcending story, as the community carries from generation to generation

---

14. Contemporary communalists emphasize the importance of this dimension. See, for example, Bellah, *Habits of the Heart*, 282.

15. Ibid., 152-54.

16. Emile Durkheim, *The Division of Labor in Society*, trans. George Simpson (New York: Macmillan, 1964), 277.

17. He states his case in George Herbert Mead, *Mind, Self and Society from the Standpoint of a Social Behaviorist*, ed. Charles W. Morris (1934; Chicago: University of Chicago Press, 1962).

18. Bellah, *Habits of the Heart*, 81.

19. See, for example, Alisdair MacIntyre, *After Virtue*, second edition (Notre Dame: University of Notre Dame Press, 1984), 221.

and from group to individual traditions of virtue, common good, and ultimate meaning—that is, of character and values.[20]

As a community of memory and hope, the church facilitates the development of the self of its members. Central to the theology of Paul and the New Testament in general is the declaration that to be a Christian means fundamentally to be united with Christ. This union entails not only mental assent to a set of doctrines, but also embodying in our beliefs, attitudes, and actions the meanings and values that characterized Jesus' own life. In this process of embodiment the Christian faith community is crucial. The believing fellowship transmits the redemptive story, which it recounts in word and deed. Thereby it mediates to believers the framework for the formation of personal identity, values, and world view. In addition, however, through its life under the direction of the Spirit speaking through the Scriptures, the community of believers offers its members not only the cognitive framework for initial identity formation, but also practical instruction concerning the life of discipleship from which we derive our ongoing identity.

As Christians we enjoy not only a personal, but also a shared identity. This identity becomes ours as we exemplify the goal for which we were created. God desires that we reflect his own image—that we exemplify the pattern of life which characterizes the triune God. As we have argued repeatedly in these pages, because God is a social reality, it is only in relationship—in community—that we are able to reflect the divine nature.[21] Hence, we can only exemplify the divine image within the context of community, specifically, the community of the people who together acknowledge the lordship of Jesus the Christ. For this reason, we are dependent on the community of Christ in the task of reflecting the image of God. The church extends fellowship to its members and binds all believers to each other and to the common whole. Thereby the church facilitates our understanding

---

20. E.g., George Lindbeck, "Confession and Community: An Israel-like View of the Church," *Christian Century* 107 (May 9, 1990): 495.

21. For a discussion of the implications of the social Trinity for the concept of the image of God, see Cornelius Plantinga, Jr., "Images of God," in *Christian Faith and Practice in the Modern World*, ed. Mark A. Noll and David F. Wells (Grand Rapids: Eerdmans, 1988), 59-67.

ourselves as the people of God, which people we are by virtue of God's grace given to us in Christ.

Insofar as we take part in the life of the community of Christ's followers we are the image of God. The community, therefore, is vital for our understanding of our personal and corporate identity. Through our loyalty to Christ and within the context of the faith community, we enjoy a common life marked by unity with Jesus. In this common life we seek to be a true community of faith.

Outreach

As the people of God we do not exist only to worship God and build up one another. We also exist to minister to the world around us. Indeed, no true community of faith can fail to set its sights outward—toward the world in which it is called to live. Foundational to our corporate existence is a vision of the whole human family reconciled to God, one another, and creation. Consequently, we direct our energies toward those who lie beyond our fellowship. In so doing, we are obedient to the outreach mandate Christ entrusted to the church. Thereby we bring glory to the triune God.

Christ calls us to reach out to the world. But what constitutes this ministry? What exactly is outreach?

Outreach as evangelism. One central hallmark of the evangelical movement has been the emphasis on evangelism as the focus of the church's outreach mission. While this emphasis is surely correct, we must look more closely at what constitutes the evangelism endeavor of the people of God.

(1) It is obvious to most Christians that evangelism entails proclamation. Evangelicals have often simply equated evangelism with the verbalization of the good news, asserting that the outreach mandate of the church lies squarely on the task of declaring the gospel message (the *evangelion*) throughout the world. As the foundation for such an equating of evangelism with proclamation, we need look no further than the great commission itself. The longer ending of Mark's Gospel, for example, cites Jesus as commanding proclamation: "Go into all the world and preach the good news to all creation" (Mark 16:15). Likewise, we may look to Jesus' prophecy that this

mission will be accomplished in the present era: "And this gospel of the kingdom will be preached in the whole world as a testimony to all nations, and then the end will come" (Matt. 24:14). As Paul correctly concluded, "How, then, can they call on the one they have not believed in? And how can they believe in the one of whom they have not heard? And how can they hear without someone preaching to them?" (Rom. 10:14).

Viewed in this context, evangelism is announcement. But what do we announce? Evangelicals often suggest that our proclamation focuses on the plan of salvation. However, in recent years New Testament scholars have reminded us that Jesus' preaching centered on the kingdom of God, and he issued a call for response. Mark capsulized: "After John was put into prison, Jesus went into Galilee, proclaiming the good news of God. 'The time has come,' he said. 'The kingdom of God is near. Repent and believe the good news!'" (Mark 1:14-15). As Mortimer Arias concluded, "Jesus' evangelization, then, was *kingdom evangelization.*"[22] In the context of the announcement of the divine reign, he called his hearers to participate in the community of God.

Following Jesus' example, we announce that God has intervened in history to effect our salvation. In the words of Harvie Conn, "Evangelism announces the liberating work of God as in Christ He fashions a new humanity."[23] God's intervention means that his reign has dawned, is present, and will arrive in its fullness. God is acting toward the fulfillment of his purpose for creation, namely, the establishment of the new community of reconciliation. In our proclamation, therefore, we lift up a new world view, a view of the world under God. And we assert that acknowledging the God who is at work in the world is the only sure alternative to the myriad of competing loyalties, which despite their lure fall short of ultimacy.

While evangelism includes telling "the old, old story of Jesus and his love," it encompasses more than verbal proclamation. Rather

---

22. Mortimer Arias, *Announcing the Reign of God* (Philadelphia: Fortress, 1983), 3.
23. Harvie Conn, *Evangelism: Doing Justice and Preaching Grace* (Grand Rapids.: Zondervan, 1982), 32.

than constituting its totality, verbal proclamation is but one central aspect of evangelism.

(2) In addition to proclamation—the announcement of the reign of God—evangelism is presence. Evangelism occurs as the Holy Spirit fashions us into the eschatological community in the world. The very presence of the covenant people stands as a sign that God has acted, is acting, and will act.

The church constitutes a sign to the world in various ways. For example, it points to the divine reign when it gathers for worship. As we lift our voices to God, we offer in the midst of the fallenness of the present the praise that will reverberate through all creation on that great eschatological day. Our praise is a reminder to all that God has not forsaken his creation to the forces of evil. Rather, the existence of the church declares that Christ has come and has instituted the new community; that the Spirit is here and is constituting us as God's people; and consequently God will act decisively to bring his purpose to completion.

The church is a sign likewise when it lives as a community in the world. As those who have responded to the gospel call and acknowledge the lordship of Christ, we seek to model what it means to live under the guidelines of the divine reign. Kingdom principles include peace, justice, and righteousness. But above all, the divine reign is characterized by love. Consequently, by being a true community of believers, we indicate what the reign of God is like; it is the community of love.

Living as a community carries with it a prophetic dimension. Insofar as we model community, our presence bears prophetic witness to the world. It issues an implicit call to society to measure itself against the divine reign under which it too must stand and against which it will be judged. This presence is itself a prophetic evangelization of the world, for it carries the implicit call to the world to acknowledge the lordship of the God who has established us as his people.

Our presence in the world as a community also carries with it an implicit personal evangelistic component. Personal reception of the gospel includes becoming aware of one's need and discovering that Christ is the answer to that need. The greatest need of all people is

reconciliation and participation in God's community. Such awareness of the truth, however, does not come solely through verbal proclamation. Rather, the gospel must also be embodied—credibly
demonstrated—if others are to see and acknowledge the truth of the
gospel. When the people of God live as the foretaste of the eschatological redeemed community, they draw others to the crucial awareness of personal need as well as of God's provision. For this reason,
truly being the presence of the community of Christ in the world is
central to our evangelistic mission. As Harvie Conn noted, "At the
center of evangelism should be an answer—the kingdom of God
embodied in a community of salvation and sharing."[24]

(3) The goal of evangelism is disciple-making. Jesus did not call
us to the task of evangelism with a view toward making converts,
but disciples. Indeed, in Matthew's version of the great commission
he defined our mandate as disciple making: "Therefore go and make
disciples of all nations, baptizing them in the name of the Father and
of the Son and of the Holy Spirit, and teaching them to obey everything I have commanded you" (Matt. 28:19-20). This commission is
in keeping with our Lord's own practice. During his earthly ministry,
he was never satisfied with mere confession (Matt. 7:21; Luke 6:46)
but always called people to costly discipleship (Luke 14:25-33).

Jesus' call to discipleship lay within the context of his proclamation of the divine reign. He desired that in response to his kingdom
message his hearers acknowledge the lordship of the King and as a
consequence become his disciples. The community of Christ, therefore, is the fellowship of Jesus' disciples. For this reason the church
welcomes within its boundaries all who declare their allegiance to
the Lord Jesus, and as those who desire to follow him, hold fast to
their acknowledgment of Jesus.

The fellowship of Jesus' followers is not merely a loose coalition
of individuals who acknowledge Jesus, however. Rather, it is a community of disciples who seek to walk together in accordance with the
principles of the kingdom. As Christ's church, we desire to live out
in the present the final reality that will come at the end of history,
namely, the reconciled community. This forms the ultimate reason

---

24. Ibid., 30.

why the goal of evangelism is disciple making. The Spirit directs his great creative work toward establishing the eschatological community, a people who are bonded together by their mutual obedience to the God revealed in Jesus. It is their commitment to living as Jesus' disciples which facilitates the mutuality that characterizes the community they form.

(4) In the evangelism task, prayer is crucial. Our prayer begins with intercession for individuals who have not as yet acknowledged Jesus as Savior and Lord. Such prayer is motivated by biblical teaching. According to the Scriptures, God desires that all persons repent and come to know the truth (2 Pet. 3:9; 1 Tim. 2:4). To this end, God has acted in Christ on behalf of the reconciliation of all (2 Cor. 5:18-21). Many remain unreconciled, however, because they are blinded by Satan and therefore cannot see the truth of the gospel (2 Cor. 4:4). In his ministry Christ defeated and bound Satan, so that Satan's captives can be freed (Luke 11:17-22; Heb. 2:14-15). To this end they must experience the Spirit's convicting work (John 16:8-11), which produces an awareness of their sinfulness and need for redemption. And they must hear a convincing proclamation and demonstration of the gospel (Rom. 10:11-15; 1 Cor. 1:21-25; 2 Cor. 5:18-20).

We direct our prayer toward the implementation of this important process. In prayer we focus the power of God on whatever is blocking others from coming to faith. We request God to send proclaimers and "embodiers" of the gospel. We claim God's promise to bless the proclaimed word (Isa. 55:11).[25] And we invoke the power of God to overcome Satan's blinding, thereby freeing the will of "the warping influences that now twist it awry," to use the words of S. D. Gordon.[26]

In the evangelism enterprise our prayer also encompasses the world. We intercede for political leaders, invoking on their deliberations the Spirit of wisdom in the cause of that peace which is conducive to the spread of the gospel (1 Tim. 2:1-3).[27] In addition, we

---

25. See Watchman Nee, *The Prayer Ministry of the Church* (New York: Christian Fellowship Publishers, 1973), 104-107.

26. S. D. Gordon, *Quiet Talks on Prayer* (London: Revell, n.d.), 192-93.

27. The World Literature Crusade, which has as its goal the blanketing of the earth with the gospel of Christ, suggests seven petitions appropriate for Christians to offer with respect to world leaders. See Dick Eastman, "The Sevenfold World Leaders Prayer Focus," in the World Literature Crusade pamphlet, "Kings and Presidents."

petition God that the church may accomplish the task of proclaiming the good news to the entire world, in accordance with Jesus' declaration (Matt. 24:14). While including this grand request, our intercession rightly focuses on specific proclaimers. In keeping with our Lord's command to his disciples, we petition "the Lord of the Harvest to send laborers into his harvest field" (9:38). And we intercede for those who have answered his call. We ask that their words be energized, so that the message will spread, and that they be protected from their enemies (2 Thess. 3:1-2).[28]

Outreach as service. The mission of the church includes inviting others to make the "good confession" and thereby enter into the fellowship. Our task, however, is not limited to the expansion of the church's boundaries. Rather, it includes sacrificial ministry to people in need. Outreach, therefore, entails service.

(1) Most Christians are convinced that Christ calls the church to serve the world in his name. Nevertheless, a heated debate has transpired over the last hundred years concerning the extent to which service is a legitimate part of the church's outreach mandate. More specifically, the focus of the discussion has been on the relationship between evangelism and social action.

Some Christians see no connection whatsoever between evangelism and social action. Consequently, they reject the latter categorically. Claiming that it is a distraction, they argue that social concern can only divert attention, energy, and finances away from the true task of the church, which they see as "saving souls." Often this position is coupled with a pessimistic appraisal of the future of the world and the anticipation that the Lord's return will occur soon. Hence, proponents often agree with the position espoused by the great evangelist Dwight L. Moody. Comparing the world to a wrecked vessel, he declared, "God had commissioned Christians to use their life boats to rescue every man they could."[29] Moody maintained further

---

28. Eastman offers an alternate list of proper requests: workers for the harvest, open doors, abiding fruit and strong support base. See Dick Eastman, *The Hour That Changes the World,* (Grand Rapids: Baker, 1978), 153-57.

29. Richard K. Curtis, *They Called Him Mister Moody* (Garden City, N.Y.: Doubleday, 1962), 266-67.

that humans would overcome poverty when they replaced indolence with diligence.[30]

Others who find no place for social concern in the evangelistic endeavor do not reject it completely. Rather, they argue that legitimate concern for the needy is the result of evangelism. It is an indication that the gospel has taken firm root, just as in the case of Zacchaeus after his encounter with Jesus (Luke 19:8-9). "Changed people will result in a changed world," they argue; consequently, the church should focus its resources on evangelism, not social action.

While some Christians find little or no place for social action in the church's mandate, others are not so quick to reject service as a legitimate part of community outreach. Acknowledging that "hungry people cannot listen to sermons," they view social action as a bona fide preparation for evangelism or even a manifestation of evangelism.[31] Their emphasis, however, remains on proclamation as the focus of the church's outreach ministry.

Others elevate social action to the same plane as proclamation, arguing that the two activities should be carried on simultaneously. John Stott, for example, argues that social involvement as a "partner" of evangelism, for "the two belong to each other and yet are independent of the other."[32] Much of Christian missionary work has reflected the idea that concern for the needy is a partner with verbal evangelism. In keeping with this belief, missions often encompass medicine, education, and proclamation.

In recent years, however, many thinkers have come to acknowledge an even stronger connection between proclamation and service. They declare that social action is an essential element in evangelism, so that where Christians do not express concern for the needy the gospel has not yet been proclaimed. On this basis some

---

30. David O. Moberg, *The Great Reversal: Evangelism and Social Concern*, revised edition (Philadelphia: J.B. Lippincott, 1977), 32.

31. See, for example, J. Herman Bavinck, *An Introduction to the Science of Missions*, trans. David Hugh Freeman (Grand Rapids: Baker, 1960) as described by John Stott, *Christian Mission in the Modern World* (Downers Grove, Ill.: InterVarsity, 1975), 26-27.

32. Stott, *Christian Mission*, 27.

refuse to dichotomize the mission of the church into these two categories.[33]

Finally, some Christians have concluded that social action and evangelism are indivisible. This may simply mean that evangelism is itself social action. The proclamation of the gospel brings about a church consisting of "the despised, the weak, the foolish, the slave, the man of another race, along with the noble, the strong, the wise, the free, and the native born." Thereby the gospel confronts society with "a new norm of what it means to be human."[34] This may also mean, however, that social action is evangelism. Hence, some voices today assert that the church need only seek to minister to the needy, for this alone is its outreach mandate.

(2) We propose that the involvement of the church in social action is crucial regardless of its relationship to evangelism. It is a natural extension of Jesus' own ministry as entrusted to us. Hence, in embarking on a ministry of service, the church is simply continuing the mission of Jesus himself.

Our Lord did not describe his task as proclamation in isolation but as proclamation in the context of service. He applied to himself the great prophecy of Isaiah: "The Spirit of the Lord is on me, because he has anointed me to preach good news to the poor. He has sent me to proclaim freedom for the prisoners and recovery of sight to the blind, to release the oppressed, to proclaim the year of the Lord's favor" (Luke 4:18-19). True to his word, Jesus engaged in service to people in need. The sick, the outcasts, the demon-possessed, the sinful, and the sinned against found in him a friend and healer. Through his acts of compassion, Jesus demonstrated the presence of the kingdom (Luke 11:20). Then prior to his death he promised the disciples that they would carry on his work, doing even greater things than they had observed (John 14:12).

---

33. See, for example, Arias, *Announcing the Reign of God*, 3, 107; Orlando E. Costas, *The Church and Its Mission: A Shattering Critique from the Third World* (Wheaton, Ill.: Tyndale House, 1974), 308-309; Orlando E. Costas, *The Integrity of Mission: The Inner Life and Outreach of the Church* (San Francisco: Harper and Row, 1979), 73-75.

34. William J. Richardson, *Social Action vs. Evangelism: An Essay on the Contemporary Crisis* (South Pasadena, Ca.: William Carey Library, 1977), 36.

Involvement in service likewise arises out of a wholistic conception of the gospel. Those who deny a connection between evangelism and service articulate a gospel directed only to one dimension of the human predicament. For them the good news is for the individual, and it facilitates spiritual reconciliation—reconciliation with God. If they are at all interested in social action, proponents of this position advocate what Vernon Grounds calls a "policy of indirect influence."[35] Seeing the gospel as individual in its address, they find it only incidentally social in its application, specifically as an outworking of its impact on saved individuals.

The biblical gospel, however, is explicitly social. It focuses on reconciliation with God, of course. But reconciliation is a social reality, for we are in right standing with God only as we are likewise being brought into right relationship with others. Consequently, the gospel is also essentially social in application. It demands that reconciliation with God be embodied in social relationships, even in earthly social institutions such as family, business, and government.[36] The gospel is the announcement of the presence of God's reign which establishes community. The community God is creating is a reconciled people who are concerned about compassion, justice, righteousness, and, above all, love. Hence, it is a community interested in social fellowship.

Like evangelism, therefore, service is kingdom work. Through our activities in the world, we seek to be instruments of the Holy Spirit in advancing the lordship of Christ in all facets of human life.

(3) Christ has called us to a ministry of service. But what is this task? Following Jesus' example leads us to a ministry of service that focuses on meeting the needs of the less-fortunate of the world. Like the good Samaritan, we bind up the wounds of the injured and outcast of the world. Yet Christians have increasingly come to the conclusion that service to the world demands that we move beyond binding wounds to become the advocates of the wounded by attempting to foster structural changes in society.

---

35. Vernon Grounds, *Evangelicalism and Social Responsibility* (Scottdale, Pa..: Herald, 1969), 7.
36. Ibid., 8.

Involvement in structural change arises from concern for the victims of social ills. By changing structures, we seek to lessen the likelihood of injury in the future. Beyond this people-centered motivation, the fostering of structural change is mandated by fidelity to the kingdom. As the eschatological community loyal to Christ, we desire that society reflect to an increasing extent the principles that characterize the reign of God.

Because it is a continuation of the ministry of Jesus and a sign of the presence of the reign of God, service is an end in itself. While it may serve as a catalyst for the conversion of those who receive our service, such work is not merely a means to the expansion of the church. Therefore, we must continually check our motives as we serve the world. Harvie Conn cautioned his readers against making verbal proclamation the hidden agenda of service. He called for the construction of ministry models "that do not manipulate situations into opportunistic occasions for springboard evangelism, models that do not make service and justice into some sort of pre- evangelism"[37]

(4) Just as it is crucial to the evangelism enterprise, prayer is also indispensable to our service as the people of God in the world. The gospel is not only directed to the reconciliation of individual human beings with God, but also to reconciliation among the human family and between humankind and the created order. For this reason, the task of the people of God in partnership with the Holy Spirit includes the advancement of God's rule as we serve the world and seek social justice. The quest for social justice, however, is a spiritual activity for which prayer is a powerful spiritual resource.

In the midst of the evil present in contemporary society, we petition God in accordance with the prayer of our Lord, "your kingdom come, your will be done on earth as it is in heaven" (Matt. 6:10). Donald Bloesch aptly described the intimate relationship between prayer and service:

> Although it is the highest form of action, prayer is not the only
> form of Christian action. Deeds of loving kindness and works of

---

37. Conn, *Evangelism*, 50.

social reform also comprise a necessary part of Christian life, but they must always be informed by prayer. It can be said that the glory of God is the goal of prayer; social service is the fruit or consequence of prayer.[38]

Service arises out of an awareness of the "not yet" status of the world in every current form. The arrival of the fullness of God's kingdom awaits the future eschaton. In the meantime the vision of that great future day provides both the motivation and the blueprint for Christian service. Prayer is a crucial means God uses to bring us to understand the church's task. Through prayer bathed in the Scriptures, we discern God's will in the situations we face. In prayer, we view specific aspects of the current world order in the light of the biblical vision of the future new order. As we petition the coming of God's rule, the Spirit illumines our minds to see what the will of God might mean for the social structures of our world. Through prayer we perceive the shortcomings of our world in the backdrop of God's purposes. In fact, as Kenneth Leech observed, "Prayer which lacks this future orientation is bound to become settled and at ease, a victim of that false peace against which the prophets constantly warn us."[39]

In prayer we catch the vision of God's future for the sake of action in the present. Through prayer the new order becomes a part of our own action-motivating vision. Prayer, however, is more than an envisioning of the future; it also provides resources for battle.

In the attempt to minister to human social needs, we soon discover that we are facing immovable structures which lie beyond our ability to affect. If we are to overcome these structures, we require the resources of God. In this context, prayer is crucial. As Paul admonished his readers:

> For our struggle is not against flesh and blood, but against the rulers, against the authorities, against the powers of this dark world and against the spiritual forces of evil in the heavenly realms.... and pray in the Spirit on all occasions with all kinds of prayers and requests. (Eph. 6:12,18)

---

38. Donald G. Bloesch, *The Struggle of Prayer* (San Francisco: Harper and Row, 1980), 131-32.
39. Kenneth Leech, *True Prayer* (New York: Harper and Row, 1980), 68.

Petition plays a vital role in the struggle against the powers. Through this activity we tap the power of God—the power of the kingdom—which alone is able "to demolish strongholds" (2 Cor. 10:4). By means of prayer, we are strengthened for service. And we are renewed in faith, despite the trials of kingdom work in this fallen world. Above all, however, our petition becomes the cry for God to act in the situation—the cry for the coming of his reign into the present. Ultimately, only God's power is sufficient to overcome the "spiritual forces of evil." Prayer lays hold of and releases God's willingness and power to act in accordance with his will—the kingdom of God—on behalf of the creation, which God loves.

Worship, edification, and outreach through evangelism and service—these constitute the mandate of the church. As we are obedient to this mandate we are the eschatological covenant community in the world. Thereby we bring glory to the triune God. Through participation in this great responsibility, we give tangible expression to our commitment to the Lord Jesus, which commitment lies at the foundation of our corporate covenant. Community life is intended to intensify our loyalty to Christ. Our Lord ordained certain practices of commitment, which symbolize and strengthen us for the task of being his people in the world. To these we now turn our attention.

19 Community Acts of Commitment

Then Jesus came to them and said, "All authority in heaven and on earth has been given to me. Therefore go and make disciples of all nations, baptizing them in the name of the Father and of the Son and of the Holy Spirit, and teaching them to obey everything I have commanded you." (Matt. 28:19-20)

Outline

The Working of Baptism
  Baptism as a divine act
  Baptism as a human act
  Baptism as a divine-human act
The Subjects of Baptism
  Baptism and faith
  Infant versus believer's baptism
The Mode of Baptism
The Lord's Supper: Reaffirming Our Identity
  The Presence of the Lord in the Celebration
    The development of transubstantiation
    The Protestant reaction
  The Meaning of the Lord's Supper
    The question of terminology
    The orientation to the past
    The orientation to the future
    The orientation to community
  Our Presence at the Lord's Supper
    The importance of our presence
    The presence of others at the table

The church is the eschatological covenant community. It is a special people—those who through their life and witness are a sign of the divine reign. Above all, this covenant people is a community, called to reflect the nature of the triune God himself, which is love. In the context of its worship, the community employs a variety of symbolic acts that carry great significance. Because certain of these practices symbolize the gospel itself, they serve as vehicles by means of which we confirm our participation in the grace God offers us through Christ and consequently in the fellowship of the covenant people. These practices are community acts of commitment.

In this chapter we turn our attention to the symbolic acts through which we celebrate God's salvation, declare our allegiance to Christ, and affirm our presence in his church. Although each of these is unique and fulfills a special role, they share certain common features. Consequently, we begin our discussion by setting forth a general understanding of the acts of commitment. This discussion then forms the context for viewing the specific acts the church practices in obedience to the command of Christ: baptism and the Lord's supper.

Acts of Commitment and the Church

At the heart of the life of most church traditions is a group of sacred acts. In our attempt to assist the church in reflecting on its faith, we must bring these acts under our purview so as to construct a theological understanding of their place in community life. Our task is to construct a systematic-theological foundation for their use in the church.

The Function of Acts of Commitment

In our intent to construct a systematic-theological context for the use of practices of commitment, we are confronted immediately with the question of their function. This discussion takes us to the heart of the disagreements among Christians concerning the rites Christ left to us.

Differences concerning the function of the sacred practices emerge when Christian thinkers discuss terminology: What term best serves as the general category for the various sacred practices of the church? Because words are significant as carriers of meaning, we must raise this question. What word capsulizes the fundamental nature and purpose of these practices? How should we describe the basic function of the acts of commitment?

Sacrament or ordinance. Initially, the terms theologians chose to denote the sacred practices were a function of the larger linguistic context in which the church tradition they represented developed. During the early centuries the dominance of the Greek language led to the widespread use of *mysterion* (from which we derive the English "mystery").[1] For this designation, the Greek Fathers appealed

---

1. John Chrysostrom, for example, referred to the Eucharist (Lord's supper) as a "mystery." *Homilies on 1 Corinthians*, 7.1, as cited in Timothy Ware, *The Orthodox Church* (New York: Penguin Books, 1983), 281. "Mystery" remains the normal designation for the sacraments in the Orthodox Church. See Anthony M. Coniaris, *Introducing the Orthodox Church* (Minneapolis: Light and Life Publishing Co., 1982), 126-27. Hence, baptism may be called the "mystery of water." Alexander Schmemann, *Of Water and the Spirit* (n.c.: St. Vladimir's Seminary Press, 1974), 40.

to certain New Testament texts that contain the word, such as Paul's description of his work as the administration of the divine *mysterion*, the grace of God (Eph. 3:2-3).[2]

In contrast to their Eastern colleagues, theologians in the West, for whom Latin and not Greek was the vernacular language, used the term *sacramentum* (from which is derived the familiar English word "sacrament"). In so doing they baptized a secular concept. A *sacramentum* was the oath of fidelity and obedience to one's commander sworn by a Roman soldier upon enlistment in the army. Or the term could designate a bond money deposited in a temple pending the settlement of a legal dispute.[3] Latin Christians saw in this term the central significance of their sacred observances. From the secular foundation of the term they drew the ideas both of solemn religious observances and of sacred objects.

Soon, however, the idea of a sacrament as an oath of fidelity was overshadowed. The trend began as early as Augustine. This great church father differentiated between the sacrament itself and the grace the Spirit imparts. As a consequence, theologians derived from his thinking the widely held understanding of a sacrament as an outward, visible sign of an inward, invisible grace.[4] The Augustinian conception opened the way for theologians to seek to determine the relationship between the outward sign and the inward reality. Their quest eventually led to the conclusion that a close, integral connection exists between the two dimensions of the great sacramental mystery.

By the late Middle Ages, an elaborate ecclesiastical system had developed around the sacred rites. The system was held aloft by two important pillars, sacramentalism and sacerdotalism.[5]

Church life centered on the sacred practices (sacramentalism). The church faithful looked to the rites of the church which they be-

---

2. Heron notes, however, that in such texts *mysterion* does not refer to sacred rites, but to the hidden things of God disclosed in Christ. Alasdair I.C. Heron, *Table and Tradition: Toward an Ecumenical Understanding of the Eucharist* (Philadelphia: Westminster, 1983) 55.

3. Ibid., 69.

4. J.N.D. Kelly, *Early Christian Doctrines*, revised edition (San Francisco: Harper and Row, 1978), 422-23.

5. For a discussion of this system, see Heron, *Table and Tradition*, 89-91.

lieved were able to infuse divine grace into the participants. A sacrament was a cause of grace, in that it was God's chosen means of dispensing grace to humans. Theologians did not understand grace as God's gracious presence but as a reality distinct from God, a supernatural power God infuses into the soul. Further, this grace came without regard to the spiritual condition of either participant or administrator (the priest). So long as the recipient did not resist the working of God in the sacraments, when duly administered these acts infused grace by their very operation (*ex opere operato*).

Because the working of the sacraments rested on their being dispensed by a duly consecrated officiator, the ordained clergy administered sacramental church life (sacerdotalism). Medieval theologians theorized that through ordination God endowed each priest with a special power, the ability to transform the physical elements used in the sacraments (water; bread and wine) from something mundane into a means of grace. The priest's action therefore constitutes a true sacrament, an act through which God infuses grace into the communicants. Sacerdotalism ultimately meant, however, that the clergy are the chosen instruments of God, the channels of divine grace.

The medieval sacramentalism came under attack in the Reformation. Although agreeing that the sacred rites infuse spiritual vitality into the participant, Martin Luther rejected the claim that they did so *ex opere operato*. He declared that a valid sacrament required more than the power of the priest. It demanded faith of the participant.

In the eyes of some, however, Luther had not gone far enough. Despite his insistence of the necessity of faith for the working of a sacrament, they believed that Luther still allowed a magical outlook toward the church's rites. Consequently, critics concluded that sacrament retained too many overtones of the older associations to be salvaged. A radical break must be made with sacramentalism, they argued, and this break could not be accomplished without a rejection of the word itself.

Among certain of the radicals, including the English Baptists, the term " ordinance" gained wide usage as a replacement for the rejected designation. Derived from the verb "to ordain," an ordinance is simply a practice which Christ ordained. Thus, the word designates those special acts which the Lord himself instituted.

Bound up with the designation " ordinance" are certain aspects of the distinctive theology of the acts of commitment which developed among the radical Protestants. At the heart of this theology was a focus on obedience. Believers participate in the ordinances out of a desire to be obedient to the one who ordained these acts for the church. The ordinances, therefore, are signs of obedience.

The dimension of obedience, in turn, naturally led to another focus of the radicals' understanding of these acts. Because they are signs of obedience, the rites are basically human, and not divine acts. Rather than God's imparting grace to the communicant through the act, an ordinance provides occasion for the participant to bear testimony to the spiritual truths symbolized in it. This outlook, of course, provides an even more thorough-going expression of Luther's insistence on the necessity of faith to the working of a sacrament. Unless the symbolized spiritual realities are present in the life of the participant, the acts are meaningless.

Radical Protestants such as the Baptists were justified in reacting against the overemphasis on the sacraments and the magical understanding of their workings that characterized medieval ecclesiology. Unfortunately, during the rationalistic age in which the movement initially flourished, many free church thinkers came to the conclusion that the acts of commitment are merely ordinances. The sole purpose of these acts is to serve as a means for us to demonstrate obedience to Christ.

Viewing the acts of commitment as merely ordinances can be as inappropriate as the magical understandings that the change in terminology was intended to avoid. Under the rationalistic impulse, use of the term " ordinance" has led some thinkers to reject any connection between the sacred practices and divine grace. In so doing, they attach less significance to the ordinances than is present in the New Testament itself. And by reducing these rites to mere symbols, they risk devaluing them. It is interesting to note, for example, that many Baptists, whose denominational name derives from the ordinance, often view this act as having no real importance beyond forming the entrance into the local church.

Recent decades, however, have shown signs that entrenched loyalties to older positions may be giving way to a willingness to learn from a variety of traditions.[6] Among those who favor the term " ordinance," certain British thinkers have launched a movement toward a deeper theology of the sacred practices. These theologians are attempting to develop an alternative to both medieval sacramentalism and the modern rejection of any sacramental understanding.[7] Their endeavor offers a basis for us to reaffirm a sacramental significance for the acts of commitment, while retaining the primacy of the designation " ordinance."

The meaning of ordinances. Our understanding of the function of the ordinances arises from the meaning of both terms that developed in the Western Christian tradition to refer to these sacred practices. While designating the acts " ordinances" we can also draw a dimension of their significance from the original meaning of the term "sacrament."[8]

Our primary understanding of the sacred practices arises from the designation " ordinance." As his obedient disciples, we naturally desire to continue those practices which Christ ordained for us to follow. We practice the ordinances, therefore, as the primary divinely ordained means for us to declare our loyalty to Jesus as Lord.

Calling these acts " ordinances" keeps our focus on the connection between the sacred practices and both Christ's command and our obedient response. Yet the question arises, Why did Jesus ordain these acts? We respond by noting that Christ commanded us to observe these acts because participation in them is of benefit to us. As

---

6. Perhaps the most important indication of this trend among mainline denominations is the 1982 consensus statement *Baptism, Eucharist and Ministry*, Faith and Order Paper no. 111, World Council of Churches (Geneva, 1982).

7. See for example, George R. Beasley-Murray, *Baptism in the New Testament* (Grand Rapids: Eerdmans, 1962).

8. Although we may not totally agree with his characterization, Thomas Howard provides an example of how we can draw together aspects of each emphasis: "In the sacraments of the church we find focused, articulated, set forth, and mediated to us, in obedience to the Lord's example and command, the great mysteries of Creation, Fall, and Redemption." Thomas Howard, "A Call to Sacramental Integrity," in *The Orthodox Evangelicals*, ed. Robert E. Webber and Donald Bloesch (Nashville: Thomas Nelson, 1978), 140.

Calvin rightly declared, "they have been instituted by the Lord to the end that they may serve to establish and increase faith."[9]

The importance of the acts of commitment for establishing our faith is accepted by nearly all Christian traditions.[10] Crucial differences emerge, however, when we ask about the means: How does the Lord strengthen us through these acts?

We maintain that the primary significance of the acts of commitment lies in the root meaning of *sacramentum*. As its original use as an oath of allegiance indicates, through the sacred practices we affirm our fidelity to our Lord Jesus Christ. These acts provide a significant means for us to confess our faith.

We must take this idea a step farther. Through these acts, we confess our faith in a special manner. They are enacted pictures or symbols of God's grace given in Christ. Therefore as thinkers including Augustine and the Reformers declared, acts of commitment become visual sermons, the Word of God symbolically proclaimed.[11] Through our participation we not only declare the truth of the gospel, however, we also bear testimony to our reception of the grace symbolized. Hence, through these rites, we "act out" our faith. The acts of commitment become enactments of our appropriation of God's action in Christ. As we affirm our faith in this vivid symbolic manner, the Holy Spirit uses these rites to facilitate our participation in the reality the acts symbolize.

Although this functioning of acts of commitment may sound foreign to modern ears, it is wholly in keeping with the understanding of symbols that characterized the biblical world. The Baptist scholar Wayne Ward capsulized that outlook: "In biblical thought, Old Testament and New, a symbol actually participated in the reality which it signified. A name, a word, or sign actually *was*, in some measure, the thing which it signified. The name *was* the person."[12] In keeping

---

9. John Calvin, *Institutes of the Christian Religion* 1559 edition, 4.14.9., in *The Library of Christian Classics* volume 21, ed. John T. McNeill, trans. Ford Lewis Battles (Philadelphia: Westminster, 1960), 1284.

10. Exceptions include the Salvation Army and the Quakers, who do not practice the traditional acts of commitment.

11. Calvin, *Institutes of the Christian Faith*, 4.14.4. in *Library of Christian Classics*, volume 21, 1279.

12. Wayne Ward, "Baptism in a Theological Perspective," *Review and Expositor*, 65/1 (winter 1968): 44.

with this, the biblical authors assumed that the symbolic acts they practiced in some sense facilitated participation in the reality signified by the rites. Hence, Ward added: "...to be baptized 'into the name of Jesus' meant to be baptized into Jesus himself, to belong to him, and to be incorporated into the very sphere of his personal being. To be baptized into his death actually meant to participate in the death of Christ."[13]

The acts of commitment we practice in the church are ordinances. We continue to observe these acts because Christ ordained their use. Our Lord gave us the ordinances for a purpose, namely, to be the means to express our loyalty to him in a vivid, symbolic manner. Because they are oaths of loyalty—beautifully symbolic vehicles for confessing our faith in Christ—they are closely bound up with the reality they symbolize and are channels of the Holy Spirit at work in our lives. And they are sermonic pictures that graphically depict the truth we verbally declare in the gospel message.

Commitment acts and community. The ordinances are oaths of fidelity. Because of this, the meaning of the sacred practices lies in their use as acts of commitment within the context of the community of Jesus' disciples. This observation takes us back to the basic understanding of the church as the eschatological covenant community outlined in the previous two chapters.

We suggested in chapter 17 that fundamental to our understanding of the church is its nature as a community. Specifically, the church is a community of memory and hope, for it links the present to the past and the future. In so doing it strengthens our sense of identity as members of Christ's fellowship. The sacred practices function as vehicles of the Spirit in this identity-forming process. These acts constitute practices of commitment,[14] by means of which we initially affirm and repeatedly reaffirm our inclusion in the community.

As a *community of memory*,[15] the church keeps its past alive by retelling its story, which focuses primarily on the biblical drama of

---

13. Ibid.

14. Robert N. Bellah, et al., *Habits of the Heart: Individualism and Commitment in American Life* (Berkeley: University of California Press, 1985), 152-54.

15. "Josiah Royce," in *Dictionary of Philosophy and Religion*, ed. William L. Reese (Atlantic Highlands, N.J.: Humanities Press, 1980), 498-99.

salvation. The acts of commitment link Jesus' contemporary follow-ers with the biblical narrative, at the heart of which is his life, pas-sion, and resurrection. These practices recount in a dramatic, symbolic manner the Christian declaration that God was in Christ reconciling the world to himself. Hence, they are vivid memorials, recalling to our minds the work Christ accomplished.

Their meaning goes beyond this general declaration, however. In addition, participation in the acts facilitates symbolic participation in the saving events which form the foundation for our identity as per-sons united with Christ. The acts of commitment, therefore, transport us into the past. Through these symbols we reenact our death and resurrection with Christ. Thereby the Spirit vividly reminds us of our union with Christ and confirms in us our identity as new persons in Christ.

The church is likewise a *community of hope*. It lifts our gaze from the past to the future. In our celebrations, we view not only God's past salvation, but his eschatological future as well. One day the ris-en and exalted Lord will return in glory. This event will mark the consummation of his story and the transformation of his followers (together with all creation) into his likeness through the resurrection. The acts of commitment are a powerful means of sustaining this vi-sion in us. They provide a symbolic declaration that God will one day bring his work to completion in the world and that our true iden-tity lies in that event: We are what we will be.

Through the sacred practices we not only announce this truth, we also symbolically participate in that grand event. As we celebrate in the midst of the brokenness of the present the glorious fullness of that future day, we proleptically participate in it.

In short, participation in the ordinances facilitates the symbolic retelling of the old, old story of God's action in Jesus and the decla-ration of his glorious future. As we tell the story, we are transported into the past, and we anticipate the future. We symbolically experi-ence Christ's death and resurrection, which constitutes the founda-tion for our own future triumph over sin and death. As we are reminded of the past and are caught up in the vision of God's future, we gain a sense of the connectedness of all history. Through this, the

Spirit confirms in us that we are moving ever onward toward full participation in God's intention for us. This reminder provides a transcendent vantage point and a sense of our ultimate identity through which the Spirit empowers us for living in the here and now.

The Number of Commitment Acts

The ordinances are an important vehicle through which the Spirit provides a transcendent vantage point for life in the present. But what specific practices function in this manner? What rites ought we to include among the acts of commitment?

The historical question. Theologians representing different Christian traditions have offered differing answers to the question of the number of sacred practices. Until the Middle Ages, there was some fluidity concerning which rites were counted among the sacraments. Nevertheless, both the Eastern[16] and Western[17] churches emphasized seven acts: baptism, confirmation, confession or penance, Eucharist, ordination (orders), marriage, and the anointing of the sick (last rites). In 1274 the Council of Lyons affirmed the seven sacraments as the official teaching of the Roman Catholic Church.

In rejecting the sacramental system of the medieval church, the Reformers also took issue with the medieval list of sacraments. They reduced the number to two: baptism and the Lord's supper.[18]

Certain participants in the radical reformation (commonly known as Anabaptists) included a third, foot washing, as well. They viewed this practice as a sign of true humiliation and a symbol of the washing of the soul in the blood of Jesus Christ.[19] Yet even its proponents never elevated foot washing to the significance accorded to the other two acts.[20] And they generally practiced this rite only in the context of an extended Lord's supper celebration.

---

16. See, for example, Anthony M. Coniaris, *Introducing the Orthodox Church: Its Faith and Life* (Minneapolis: Light and Life Publishing Co., 1982), 124.

17. John A. Hardon, S.J., *The Catholic Catechism* (Garden City, N.Y.: Doubleday, 1966), 446-47.

18. Luther may have viewed confession as also sacramental (perhaps through its connection with the Eucharist).

19. See, for example, The Dordrecht Confession of the Mennonites (1632), article 11, in *Creeds of the Churches*, ed. John H. Leith, third edition (Atlanta: John Knox, 1982), 302.

20. Ibid.

Two acts of commitment. In the light of this historical disagreement about the actual number of sacraments, we ask, On what basis ought we to decide which practices are genuine acts of commitment? Which specific rites ought we to place at the center of community life? Our previous discussion concerning the function of the acts of commitment provides insight for determining which rites ought to be included among the sacred practices of the community.

As we concluded above, acts of commitment are fundamentally ordinances. Consequently, each rite must carry the command of Jesus himself. There must be biblical evidence that the early community practised the act in conscious obedience to the Lord.

Acts of commitment are likewise symbols of the gospel. They constitute fitting vehicles for expressing our commitment to the Lord Jesus Christ. In addition to carrying the precedence of the early church, therefore, each act must depict in a symbolic manner the central story of Jesus and our union with him. Any such practice must be so closely linked to the gospel message, so that it becomes a symbol for the truth of the good news it embodies.

When measured by these criteria, many of the rites observed by certain Christian traditions do not qualify as acts of commitment in the sense of gospel ordinances. We might possibly find in practices such as confirmation, confession, marriage, ordination, and the anointing of the sick a representation of certain aspects of the gospel. Nevertheless, we fail to discover explicit foundation in the corporate life of the New Testament community for treating them as acts of commitment. In the case of foot washing, in contrast, we could point to an explicit ordination by our Lord. After Jesus washed the disciples' feet in the upper room, he commanded: "Now that I, your Lord and Teacher, have washed your feet, you also should wash one another's feet. I have set you an example that you should do as I have done for you" (John 13:14-15). Yet the early church did not understand this statement as enjoining on the community the physical act of foot washing. Nor does the rite reenact the heart of the gospel, namely, our death and resurrection with Christ, even though it represents the kind of humility that we should emulate.

Baptism and the Lord's Supper, in contrast, stand above the others as bonafide ordinances. The foundation for both lies in the Lord's command as followed by the apostolic churches. The early community clearly practiced baptism (Acts 2:41; 8:36; 10:47-48) in continuity with what Jesus himself had ordained (Matt. 28:19-20). The Lord's supper likewise became an integral part of worship (1 Cor. 11:17-34). Christians observed it in conscious attempt to obey the Lord's own intent (Luke 22:19).

Not only were baptism and the Lord's Supper ordained by Christ himself, both constitute appropriate symbols of the central aspects of the gospel story. They vividly portray Jesus' death and resurrection as God's provision for human sin. In addition, they provide a fitting means for us to symbolize our commitment to Christ, our participation in his death and resurrection, and our anticipation of the full reception of salvation at the eschatological consummation of God's program.

To summarize: As symbols of his story which is now our story, baptism and the Lord's supper form the practices of commitment within the community of faith. Through these two acts we enact our faith as we symbolically reenact the story of redemption. We memorialize the events of Jesus' passion and resurrection, we bear testimony to the experience of union with Christ which we all share in the community, and we lift our sights to the grand future awaiting us as participants in the covenant community of God.

Within the context of this general understanding we now look more closely at each of the two acts of commitment.

Baptism: the Seal of Our Identity

Most Christian churches practice an initiatory rite, in which water is applied to the participant as a symbol of certain spiritual truths bound up with our new status as participants in the community of Christ. Despite the nearly universal practice of the act, baptism has been a source of disagreement among Christian traditions. Consequently, we must attempt to set forth our theology of baptism in the context of the perplexing questions over which theologians disagree.

677

Background and History

The terms "baptize" and "baptism" are transliterations from the Greek words, *baptizo* (verb) and *baptisma* (noun), referring to the action of washing with, or plunging into (literally, surrounding with) water. Some scholars have attempted to trace the practice to various sources, including certain Jewish and pagan rituals. Rather than looking to these, the New Testament authors claim the precedence (Matt. 3:13) and command (28:19) of Jesus, arising out of the ministry of John the Baptist, as the genesis of the Christian rite and the authority for its practice.

The practice of both John the Baptist and the early church probably included the dipping of the participant in the baptismal water (Acts 8:38-39), although some scholars suggest that pouring water over the candidate may also have been used.[21] At baptism the early church invoked the name of "the Lord Jesus" (Acts 19:5) or the trinitarian formula (Matt. 28:19), for it was "into the Lord" that the participant was symbolically placed through this rite.

In the patristic era the church developed specific instructions for baptism. The *Didache*, for example, stipulated the type of water to be used (preferably a running stream of cold water). Later writings reveal the growth of an involved initiation process, necessitated as the church sought to incorporate a large number of converts from pagan backgrounds.[22]

Sometime after the second century the baptism of infants and the mode of sprinkling were introduced. However, believer's baptism (the rite as a profession of the personal faith of the participant) and immersion (placing the participant fully under water), continued in general use up to the Middle Ages. By the time of the Reformation infant baptism by sprinkling had gained ascendancy throughout the Western church, with the notable exception of the sixteenth-century radical reformers (the Anabaptists). Despite the widespread preference for the sprinkling of infants, nearly all Christian traditions ac-

---

21. J.G. Davies, *The Architectural Setting of Baptism* (London: Barrie and Rockliff, 1963).

22. For a sketch of this initiation process, see Laurence Hull Stookey, *Baptism: Christ's Act in the Church* (Nashville: Abingdon, 1982), 101-15.

knowledge the propriety of believer's baptism by immersion, and this is the sole practice of several groups.

The Meaning of Baptism

The New Testament writers used several types from the Old Testament to describe what baptism means. These include the Exodus (1 Cor. 10:1-2), circumcision (Col. 2:11-12) and the flood (1 Pet. 3:19-21). Of greater importance for Christian baptism than these Old Testament events are the death and resurrection of Jesus (Rom. 6:3-5). The relationship of the rite to the story of Jesus lies at the basis of its meaning as an act of commitment for our perpetual use.

The symbolic significance of baptism. The initiatory act of commitment is a symbolic enactment of the gospel. Through it, we both announce the importance of Jesus' story for all believers and offer our own initial public confession of faith in Christ. In baptism we give symbolic expression to the meshing of our individual story with the narrative of Jesus and hence with the story of the faith community. In so doing, we express through baptism several related truths.

(1) Above all, baptism symbolizes our spiritual union with Christ. This union entails our participation in Good Friday and Resurrection Sunday—our death to the old, sinful life and our being raised to new life (Rom. 6:3-8). Through baptism we declare that Jesus' story now constitutes our own identity and life. And we anticipate our full participation in his resurrection at the eschatological renewal.

The concept of participation in the death of Christ links baptism to the forgiveness of sins (Acts 2:38; 1 Pet. 3:21), which Christ died to effect. The imagery of washing is of significance here. Just as physical washing puts off filth from the body, so also our participation in the death of Christ, symbolized by baptism, puts off sin. Similarly, baptism is linked to the new birth and the reception of the Spirit (1 Cor. 12:13), for participation in Christ's resurrection means that the Holy Spirit is now present in our lives. He acts as the pledge and power of our future resurrection (Rom. 8:11; 2 Cor. 1:22; 5:5; Eph. 1:13,14).

(2) Bound up with our confession of faith is a transfer of loyalties—the replacement of former allegiances by a new allegiance to

Christ as Lord. This transformation of loyalty places us in a new fellowship, the community of those who confess the Lord Jesus. Hence, our union with Christ includes presence within his body, the church (1 Cor. 12:13). At baptism we enter the community of believers concretized in the local congregation. As baptized persons we are members of the community of faith, which means we share the one story of the people of God.

(3) Finally, as a sign of our union with Christ in his resurrection, baptism symbolizes the confirming of a covenant with God.[23] Participation in the rite is a public act in which we enact the pledging of ourselves to God (1 Pet. 3:21). Through it, we declare our intention to follow the pathway of discipleship.

The eschatological orientation of baptism. In linking the participant with Christ's death and resurrection, baptism carries an eschatological orientation. The act points beyond our initiation into the Christian life to the goal of God's saving activity. This goal includes glorification—the transformation of all believers at the Lord's return (Rom. 8:11; 1 Cor. 15:51-57) and our participation in the eschatological community of God. En route to that goal lies the process of sanctification, as the Spirit continually renews us in our Christian walk (2 Cor. 3:18; Rom. 8:9).

Baptism is eschatological in orientation likewise in that it is practised with a view toward participation in the kingdom of God, the glorious eschatological fellowship of God with his people. Just as Jesus' story did not end on Resurrection Sunday—Christ will return to earth in glory to reign—so the believer's story is not consummated in baptism. Rather, this act points to the coming of God's reign and symbolizes our hope of participating in that eternal community. For this reason, Paul described the presence of the Spirit, whose coming on the believer is symbolized by baptism, as a pledge of the reception of God's full salvation at Christ's coming (2 Cor. 1:22; 5:5; Eph. 1:14).

Baptism and the community. Above all, however, baptism is oriented toward our participation in community. As an act of commit-

---

23. See Bo Reicke, *The Epistles of James, Peter and Jude*, volume 37 of *The Anchor Bible* (Garden City, N.Y.: Doubleday, 1964), 106-107, 139.

ment, it marks our initiation into the narrative of the Christian fellowship. This rite inducts the new believer into the shared practices of the believing community which is defined and ruled by the story of Christ's life, death, and resurrection.[24]

The church, therefore, rightly sees in baptism the symbol of the new birth. Our spiritual birth mediates to us the new identity that all initiants into the church enjoy. baptism represents the change of context that has resulted in the believer now belonging to the family of God. No longer do we define our lives in accordance with the categories of the old community. Rather, we see ourselves as those who have passed from the rulership of sin and its condemnation into the fellowship of the people of God, who enjoy reconciliation with our God and therefore with each other.

The new identity symbolized by our baptism carries ethical demands. We must now live out the new identity God freely bestows on us. Corporately we must now allow the Spirit to transform us into the community of those who belong to God. Individually we must truly reflect our identity in Christ. In short, we must seek to live in accordance with who we will be.

The impact of baptism. Because it signifies our union with Christ, participation in his church, and our public covenant with God, baptism is a visual word of proclamation. This act declares the death and resurrection of Christ on behalf of sinners, and it anticipates his return in glory. As a gospel proclamation baptism is to be a channel for the working of the Holy Spirit in the lives of those present. Through this rite, the Spirit issues a call to response. For this reason, baptism carries great impact.

(1) Obviously, baptism ought to have a powerful impact on the one being baptized. For this person the celebration of the ordinance should be a day to remember. It should be a powerful motivation for godly living throughout life, as we subsequently recall the day of our baptism and thereby are reminded both of the commitment we made to Christ and the presence of the Holy Spirit sealed to us on that day.

---

24. For the development of this idea, see, for example, L. Gregory Jones, *Transformed Judgment: Toward a Trinitarian Account of the Moral Life* (Notre Dame: University of Notre Dame Press, 1990), 137-39.

Through his repeated reminders of our baptismal experience, the Spirit also admonishes us concerning the importance of living a holy life, a life conforming to the confession we made that day. And he strengthen us in our Christian walk.

(2) In addition to being a day to be remembered for the one taking this step of obedience, baptism ought have a powerful impact on the baptizing community. The presence of the baptismal candidate in the water is a reminder that the new birth is but the beginning of a life of growth in character and service. In sponsoring this ordinance, the community is assuming the responsibility of edification and support for the person being baptized, as well as for all others God has entrusted to its care. Likewise, as the baptismal candidate reminds us of the many in the world who have not yet responded to the gospel, the Spirit calls the community to realize anew that the task of outreach given by the Lord is not yet complete. Consequently, he admonishes us to be vigilant in seeking to proclaim the good news to all people.

Not only does the Spirit issue a call to the baptizing community as a whole, he speaks as well to each Christian present. As we watch the baptism of another, we are reminded of our own baptismal vow. Through this reminder the Spirit calls us to renew the covenant with God we made on the day of our baptism (Rom. 6:1-2, 11-13) and to dedicate ourselves anew to live a holy life.

(3) Finally, through baptism the Spirit issues a call to any persons present who have not yet come to faith. Baptism depicts the good news of the death and resurrection of Jesus for the sins of the world and the necessity of personal conversion. Consequently, when coupled with appropriate explanatory remarks, this rite is the Spirit's call to make the same confession being affirmed by the participant and the community.

The Working of Baptism

Despite broad agreement concerning the meaning of baptism, the various Christian traditions find themselves at odds as to exactly how God's goal is accomplished in the act. Pedobaptists (those who practice infant baptism) emphasize God's working in baptism. Traditions favoring believer's baptism tend to view the rite as almost exclusively a personal human response. Over the last three centuries, proponents of each position have disagreed concerning which alternative embodies the correct theology of baptism. We must look closer at this debate.

Baptism as a divine act. The majority of Christian churches emphasize the divine side of baptism. They view the rite as above all the work of God. Despite this agreement, however, different traditions understand God's agency in baptism in a variety of ways.

Some suggest that through the rite the Spirit accomplishes regeneration. This view is known as baptismal regeneration. In the Middle Ages, theologians asserted that baptismal regeneration occurred *ex opere operato*: Through the rite itself God produces what baptism signifies. Baptismal regeneration survives in some form in the contemporary expressions of the more sacramental traditions, including the Roman Catholic and Eastern Orthodox Churches and among certain Lutherans,[25] all of whom apply this understanding to infant baptism. It is also the position of certain followers of the nineteenth-century American leader, Alexander Campbell. The Campbellite churches, however, generally practice believer's baptism only.

Churches which agree concerning the basic idea of baptismal regeneration nevertheless differ concerning the results of the Spirit's work in that act. Roman Catholic theology speaks of the efficacy of baptism to remit both original sin and the actual guilt brought by sin. At the same time, the virtues of faith, hope, and love are poured into the participant.[26] The Orthodox Church, in contrast, speaks of the regeneration worked in baptism as divinization. The participant partakes of the divine nature and from then on is a carrier of the very life of God.[27]

Many Protestants deny any direct correlation between baptism and the regeneration of the participant. Consequently, they offer alternatives to baptismal regeneration. Many Lutheran theologians

---

25. E.g., Mark Ellingson, *Doctrine and Word: Theology in the Pulpit* (Atlanta: John Knox, 1949), 141-45; Carl Braaten, "Baptism," in *Christian Dogmatics*, ed. Carl Braaten and Robert W. Jenson, two volumes (Philadelphia: Fortress, 1984), 2: 315-33.

26. Hardon, *Catholic Catechism*, 506-511.

27. Coniaris, *Introducing the Orthodox Church*, 131.

view the rite as the sign of God's claim on an individual prior to personal response.[28] While accepting this emphasis,[29] theologians in the Reformed tradition tend to see the significance of baptism in the context of covenant theology. Baptism is the sign and seal of the covenant God makes with his people, or which God's people make with their Lord.[30] Salvation, they assert, is not accomplished through baptism (as proponents of baptismal regeneration claim) but through election.[31] Hence, as Daniel Migliore noted, "infant baptism is a sign of *covenantal responsibility* as a community of faith and most especially as parents of this child."[32]

Baptism as a human act. The concept of baptism as covenant is likewise present among some who practice believer's baptism.[33] However, they tend to emphasize the human aspect of the covenant sealed in the rite. Out of this understanding have developed two alternative, but related outlooks toward baptism. Some believer's baptists describe the act as a significant, divinely given means of responding personally to the gospel.[34] Others view it as a public testimony to an inner spiritual transformation.[35] In either case, baptism is linked to discipleship. It is a public affirmation of a person's conscious decision to place himself or herself under the lordship of Jesus. In this, Jesus' baptism serves as a model, and the disciple is often said to be "following the Lord in baptism."

Some groups have taken this change in understanding (baptism as a human response, not a divine act) a step farther, viewing the prac-

---

28. This concept is present in other traditions as well, including the Orthodox, e.g., Coniaris, *Introducing the Orthodox Church*, 129. Brunner suggests that baptism points to the grace of God which precedes all preaching and all faith. Emil Brunner, *The Christian Doctrine of the Church, Faith, and the Consummation*, trans. David Cairns (Philadelphia: Westminster, 1962), 57.

29. E.g., Daniel Migliore writes, "Infant baptism, responsibly practised, is a sign of *God's gracious initiative* in creation and redemption." *Faith Seeking Understanding* (Grand Rapids: Eerdmans, 1991), 219.

30. Geoffrey W. Bromiley, *Children of Promise* (Grand Rapids: Eerdmans, 1979), 38-51.

31. Many Reformed thinkers find in this covenantal view a basis for the practice of infant baptism. The extent of election is wider than the circle of those who consciously believe, they argue. This gives warrant for the baptism of infants. See, for example, Hendrikus Berkhof, *Christian Faith*, trans. Sierd Woudstra (Grand Rapids: Eerdmans, 1979), 355.

32. Migliore, *Faith Seeking Understanding*, 219.

33. Paul K. Jewett, *Infant Baptism and the Covenant of Grace* (Grand Rapids: Eerdmans, 1978).

34. Beasley-Murray, *Baptism in the New Testament*, 263-305.

35. Millard J. Erickson, *Christian Theology* (Grand Rapids: Baker, 1985), 3:1096.

tice as not essential to the Christian faith. Certain denominations view baptism as optional rather than required for local church membership. A few have gone so far as to discontinue totally the practice (e.g., the Salvation Army and the Quakers).

Baptism as a divine-human act. Our discussion of the function of the acts of commitment suggests that both of these traditions are expressing an important aspect of baptismal theology. To see how this is the case, we must appeal to the significance of the designation " ordinance" and to the intention Christ had in commanding this practice as an oath of fidelity.

As an act of commitment, baptism is an ordinance, a rite we follow as a sign of obedience to Christ. Baptism is the divinely given means by which we make our initial public confession of faith in Christ. In baptism, we also declare our intention to set out on the road of discipleship. The dimension of the act as an ordinance focuses on the human element. The sacred practice is the believer's response to the gospel call to follow Jesus.

Baptism, however, is more than a mere demonstration of our obedience, it is a meaningful oath of fidelity. Our Lord ordained this act because he knew that it is of great benefit for us as we embark on the road of discipleship. Baptism is to be a day to remember. Through this act the Spirit admonishes us to live in fidelity to Christ, and he strengthens us for the task of following our Lord.

In a sense, baptism is analogous to a public wedding. For a couple being married, reciting vows in the presence of witnesses becomes a day to remember. It is a focal point for their initial commitment to each other. Their public declaration of covenantal love both strengthens them to live in faithfulness to each other and throughout life draws their attention to the covenant they made on that day. In a similar manner, the Holy Spirit can use our baptism to strengthen our commitment to Christ.

The Subjects of Baptism

Historically the most volatile aspect of the baptismal controversy focused on the question concerning the subjects of baptism: Who may we properly baptize? More specifically, should we reserve baptism for those who can make a personal confession of faith through this act (believer's baptism)? Or is this rite also for infants who will only later be able to join the Christian community in its confession?

Baptism and faith. We can develop our response to the question of the proper subjects of baptism only after we place it in the context of a deeper issue, the theological question of the relationship between baptism and faith.

It is obvious that some members of the household of faith never undergo Christian baptism. We need only mention the many Old Testament saints and certain pre-Easter converts. (Some theologians would add special cases, such as persons dying in infancy.) Further, baptism itself is no guarantee of participation in God's eschatological rule, for it is possible for a baptized person to abandon Christ's community (Matt. 13:20-21; John 15:1-6; Heb. 6:4-5; 1 John 2:19).

When taken as a whole, however, the thrust of the New Testament clearly places a connection between baptism and faith. During the church age, faith expressed in baptism is so closely linked with the new birth that the two are virtually inseparable. In keeping with this, most Christian traditions set baptism as a requirement for church membership.

The apostolic church never separated conversion from baptism, and the early believers always considered inward faith and baptism as its public confession in connection with each other. They saw faith and baptism as two sides of an undivided whole. This understanding lies behind the texts that seem to attribute saving significance to baptism or indicate that faith expressed in baptism constitutes a necessary prerequisite for entrance into the kingdom (Acts 2:38; 8:35-36; Mark 16:16, 1 Pet. 3:21; Gal. 3:25-27).

How are we to understand this close connection between baptism and faith in the early church? According to the New Testament, faith is not merely a private event; it must come to public expression (James 2:14-26). Baptism is the God-given means for our initial outward confession of inward faith. This act is a public declaration of personal faith in Jesus Christ as Lord.

Infant versus believer's baptism. Despite a lively discussion and the publication of countless writings on the subject, the last three centuries have produced no consensus in the debate between pedop-baptists and believer's baptists.

Until recently, pedobaptists sought to find references to the prac-tice in the New Testament, especially in the so-called household texts (Acts 10:24; 16:15; 16:31-34; 18:8; 1 Cor.1:16). Careful exe-gesis, however, has netted the conclusion that the inclusion of infants in such baptisms, while possible, is remote.[36] Many scholars now agree that there is no direct evidence of infant baptism in the first century.[37] Beyond textual arguments pedobaptists appeal to theolog-ical support, as noted in the previous section, and to the weight of ec-clesiastical tradition.[38]

Believer's baptists have often sought to give evidence that the New Testament bans infant baptism. However, because of the ab-sence of the practice in the first century, we can find no specific text that directly discusses the practice.

More importantly, Baptists appeal to the New Testament to de-fend believer's baptism as the primary, if not the only proper prac-tice. It does appear likely that the early church practiced believer's baptism exclusively. Pedobaptists, however, point to the first-centu-ry missionary situation to explain why the first generation Christians baptized only adults. What practices the church should develop in the case of the second generation is an issue the New Testament did not address, they conclude.

In addition to the biblical argument in favor of believer's baptism, its advocates reject infant baptism as an inferior, even dangerous practice. Infant baptism is performed by necessity in the absence of the participant's conscious personal faith. Consequently, the act is either reduced to a mere "baby dedication" or it is inflated to a regen-erative act which encourages confidence in baptism rather than in Christ.[39] Further, critics argue that infant baptism subverts the con-

---

36. See Beasley-Murray, *Baptism in the New Testament*, 306-86; Stanley Grenz, *Isaac Backus-Puritan and Baptist* (Macon, Ga.: Mercer University Press, 1983), 293 n. 94.

37. E.g., Ellingsen, *Doctrine and Word*, 144; Stookey concludes: "The desire to find New Testa-ment warrant for the baptism of infants has resulted in exegetical violence." *Baptism: Christ's Act in the Church*, 47.

38. The Lutheran theologian, Ellingsen, for example, declares, "Ultimately those who advocate infant baptism can make their best appeal to the predominance of the practice throughout the church's history." *Doctrine and Word*, 144.

39. Henry Cook, *What Baptists Stand For*, third edition (London, 1958), 225, 243.

cept of the church as the fellowship of believers entered by conversion, for the practice declares that entrance into the church comes by some other basis than personal faith alone.[40] Baptists point out as well the fallacy of seeing infants as in some sense church members, while denying them the privileges of this status, such as presence at the Lord's table, until after confirmation.[41] Infant baptism is also harmful because it denies the child the divinely ordained means of declaring conscious and responsible belief in Jesus Christ later in life.[42] And it fosters the separation of conscious faith from baptism, in that baptism occurs before the experience of personal faith in Jesus Christ. Finally Baptists argue that infant baptism is dangerous, because historically the practice has opened the way to a national church which extends the boundaries of the faith community to the political boundaries of the land.[43]

These considerations are weighty. More crucial, however, is the theological problem infant baptism poses. The rite is simply inappropriate to convey the New Testament meanings essentially connected with baptism. Baptists claim that the faith Luther declared as necessary for validating any sacrament is the personal faith of the candidate, which is simply not present in infant baptism.

Pedobaptists have not been without response to this criticism. Today theologians generally accept that Infant presupposes some type of profession of faith.[44] But pedobaptists have refused to limit their understanding to the personal faith demanded by Baptists. Luther dealt with this problem by speaking of infant faith, postulating that in some sense faith is present in the infant at Infant. Other traditions, including the Reformed and Methodist churches, rely on the presence of collective faith (the faith of the baptizing community) or even proxy faith (the faith of the parents or godparents) to legiti-

---

40. Ibid., 246, 243.

41. Augustus Hopkins Strong, *Systematic Theology* (Philadelphia: Griffith and Rowland, 1907), 952; Henry C. Vedder, *A Short History of the Baptists*, second edition, (Philadelphia: American Baptist Publication Society, 1907), 27-28. This practice, however, has never been employed by the Orthodox Church and is currently under debate in several Protestant churches.

42. Strong, *Systematic Theology*, 957; Wayne E. Ward "Baptism in Theological Perspective." *Review and Expositor*, 65 (winter 1968): 47.

43. Strong, *Systematic Theology*, 957; Ward, "Baptism in Theological Perspective," 48.

44. For a statement by a Roman Catholic, see Hardon, *The Catholic Catechism*, 180; see also *Baptism, Eucharist and Ministry*, 3.

mize infant baptism. The rite, therefore, points to the time (such as confirmation) when the child will come to confess the faith now being declared by the baptizing community or their representatives.

These suggestions from pedobaptist traditions, however, miss the central point. As we concluded above, baptism is the God-given means whereby we initially declare publicly our inward faith. If this is the case, believer's baptism is obviously superior. Infant baptism simply cannot fulfill this function. Because it cannot be an outward expression of inward faith, infant baptism also loses its value as a day to be remembered. Believer's baptism, in contrast, does offer the means to confess personal faith. For this reason, it deserves to be the standard practice in the church.

The Mode of Baptism

Historically less explosive but nevertheless controversial is the question of the proper mode of baptism. Christian churches have practised three major modes: sprinkling, pouring, and immersion.

Sprinkling dominates among most Protestants and in the Roman Catholic Church, although immersion is often allowed. Certain Anabaptist groups use pouring. Although the Eastern Orthodox Church immerses babies,[45] the Baptist tradition has been the strongest advocate of immersion.

Although immersion has been and remains the dominant practice in the believer's Baptist tradition, these churches have not emphasized the specific mode to the same degree as the proper subjects of baptism. As an example we may cite the group which many historians place at the beginning of the modern Baptist movement. Following the lead of John Smythe, these General Baptists practiced pouring during the first three decades of their existence (1609-1641), before accepting immersion from the Particular Baptists. In addition, certain members of the wider believer's Baptist circle, the heirs of the Continental Anabaptist movement, have never practiced immersion. (A movement toward immersion did develop among the Men-

---

45. According to Timothy Ware, "Orthodoxy regards immersion as essential." Ware, *The Orthodox Church*, 284.

nonites in Russia through contact with German Baptist missionaries.)

Traditionally immersionists have based their position on the claim that immersion was the mode of the New Testament church. The word *baptism* is not an indigenous English word. It is the transliteration of a Greek term *baptizo* which means "to immerse," in contrast to the word *hrantizo*, "to sprinkle." The descriptions of baptisms in the New Testament also point to immersion as the favored mode (Acts 8:39; Matt. 3:16). This thesis finds support in the statement in the Fourth Gospel that John the Baptist performed the rite where large amounts of water were available (John 3:23).

Nonimmersionists do not deem this exegetical evidence conclusive. They point out that *baptizo* is broader than its literal meaning, for it is also used occasionally in a figurative sense (Mark 7:4; Mark 10:38-39; Luke 11:38; 1 Cor. 10:2). Further, although the descriptions of New Testament baptisms indicate that baptism occurred with both the officiator and the candidate standing in water, they do not state explicitly what happened in the act. In fact, critics argue, early Christian art may indicate that water was poured on the head of the baptismal candidate standing in a river or body of water.[46]

In part the question rests on whether or not a specific mode is central to the rite. Many immersionists claim that without the proper "New Testament mode," no baptism has occurred. Those who practice other modes counter this claim by suggesting that baptism is constituted by the presence of water coupled with the pronouncement of the divine name, and not the amount of water.

Taking such criticisms seriously, some immersionists only propose that immersion is the superior mode. We may derive its superiority not only from New Testament evidence but also from the value of the rite as a sign of gospel truth. Immersion most clearly depicts what the ordinance of baptism is meant to signify, namely, the death and resurrection of Jesus and the believer's union with Christ. If baptism is an enactment of the story of Jesus and our participation in

---

46. Davies, *The Architectural Setting of Baptism.* Some suggest, however, that these art works are symbolic and not actual depictions of ancient baptismal practices; the pouring of water symbolized the coming of the Spirit related to baptism.

that story, then immersion is its clearest symbol. Submersion in water appropriately indicates death. And the bursting forth out of the watery grave illustrates resurrection life.

Nonimmersionists respond by pointing out the symbolic value of other modes: the cleansing from sin symbolized by sprinkling (Titus 3:5; Heb. 10:22; 1 Pet. 1:2; Ezek. 36:25; Isa. 52:15) or the coming of the Spirit associated with pouring (Joel 2:28; Acts 2:1-2,38). We ought not to discount these suggestions. Nevertheless, we conclude that of the three modes immersion carries the strongest case—exegetically, historically, and theologically.[47] Therefore under normal circumstances it ought to be the preferred, even the sole practice of the church.

The Lord's Supper: Reaffirming Our Identity

In addition to baptism, most Christian churches practice a second act of commitment which focuses on bread and the fruit of the vine (wine or grape juice). In contrast to the rite of initiation, which can only occur once, Christians observe this second practice repeatedly—yearly, quarterly, monthly, even weekly or more often. Our participation in the second act of commitment constitutes a repeated reaffirmation of what we initially declared in baptism—namely, our new identity in Christ.

Despite nearly universal agreement from the first century to the present that Christians are to participate in this act, there is wide disagreement about the theology lying behind the practice. In fact, although baptism has been the subject of much discussion throughout the history of the church, of the two acts the repeated rite has generated greater controversy.

Disagreement arises already at the level of the proper designation for this act of commitment. The traditional Roman Catholic term is "Mass," which may originally have been derived from the closing words of the Latin liturgy.[48] To replace the Catholic connotations of the act as an offering to God with the idea of a shared meal, the Re-

---

47. This is the conclusion even of nonimmersionists such as Stookey, *Baptism: Christ's Act in the Church*, 166.
48. Heron, *Table and Tradition*, xii.

formers deliberately substituted the name "the Lord's Supper" (1 Cor. 11:20). Alternately, Protestants refer to the rite as "Holy Communion," or simply "Communion," thereby emphasizing the dimension of sharing in fellowship with Christ (or one another) through this act. In recent ecumenical discussions the designation "Eucharist" derived from the Greek *eucharisto* ("to give thanks") and dating to the patristic era[49] has gained widespread use.

The Presence of the Lord in the Celebration

Of the various issues theologians have discussed none has been more contested than the question about the presence of the Lord at the celebration: In what sense is Christ now present at the meal he ordained? While discussed by Christians from the early centuries, this question came to heated debate in the Reformation.

The development of transubstantiation. In a sense, we might see the Reformation as a dispute over the Eucharistic presence of Christ. In no uncertain terms the Reformers rejected the Roman Catholic conception of the Eucharist as a Mass. At the heart of this conception was the doctrine of transubstantiation. Although this teaching first gained definitive form in the late 1200s, in devising this theory, medieval theologians were merely bringing to a culmination a long trajectory of thought that focused on Christ's real presence at the Eucharist in the bread and wine.

As early as the second century, Christian teachers such as Justin Martyr insisted on a literal interpretation of Jesus' words of institution as reported in the New Testament accounts ("This is my body." "This is my blood.").[50] Later thinkers, including Cyril, John Chrysostom, and Ambrose, suggested that some miraculous change lay behind this phenomenon. The medieval schoolmen sought to clarify how this change transpired. In the eleventh century, theologians commonly spoke of a change in substance occurring in the bread and wine. By about 1150 the term "transubstantiation" came into use to

---

49. E.g., *Didache* 6.5, trans. James A Kleist, *Ancient Christian Fathers* (New York: Paulist, 1948), 6:20; Justin Martyr, *First Apology*, trans. Thomas B. Falls, *The Fathers of the Church* (Washington, D.C.: Catholic University of America Press, 1948), 6:105-106.

50. Justin Martyr, *First Apology*, 66.2, 66.3.

describe the nature of this change. But it was left to Thomas Aquinas (1224-1274) to hone the tradition into its final form.

Behind Aquinas's explanation of the miraculous change in the elements lay the differentiation among the terms "material," "substance," and "accidents" he apparently derived from the ancient Greek philosopher Aristotle. "Material" is merely the unformed physical matter inherent in all things. "Substance" refers to the unchanging essence of any existing reality, the "form" (to use Aristotle's term) which constitutes an object's identity. Finally, "accidents" are the nonessential outward characteristics (the *species*), which give anything its appearance and which can and often do change but do not thereby alter the underlying essence.

Aquinas applied this distinction to the Eucharist in a surprising fashion. During the Mass the bread and wine undergo a miraculous change. Rather than altering their accidents while retaining their essence, as in normal physical processes, the elements experience a change in essence while remaining unchanged in their accidents. This miracle indicates why the color, taste, and texture remain those of bread and wine. Despite the lack of change in accidents, the substances have indeed undergone a transformation. They became the actual body and blood of Christ. Hence, "under" the outward appearance (*subspecies*) lies a transformed essence, the real presence of Jesus himself.

The change in the communion elements means that Christ is physically present at the Eucharist. The bread and wine become his body and blood. Consequently, in the Mass the communicant ingests the body of Christ.

The doctrine of transubstantiation formed the theoretical foundation for understanding the Mass as a sacrifice. According to medieval theology, the Eucharist is not only an act of God who infuses grace into the communicant. It is also a human response, a sacrifice offered to God. In setting forth this understanding, the late medieval schoolmen took a step beyond the earlier teaching about the sacrificial nature of the rite. From John Chrysostom to Peter Lombard thinkers had spoken of the Eucharist as a sacramental sharing in Christ's completed sacrifice on the cross. Later theologians, including Thomas Aquinas, came to see the Eucharist as a sacrificial offering in its own right.[51] Thereby they provided the theological foundation for the deeply rooted medieval conviction that the celebration of the Mass was itself a meritorious act.[52]

The Protestant reaction. The Reformers vehemently rejected the Eucharistic understanding of the Roman Catholic Church. For them, the sacrament was not a cause of an actual infusion of grace. Nor could the rite be offered to God as a human work, a sacrifice. Luther insisted that the Eucharist was a sign of God's promise given to faith and directed toward faith, which we can only receive from God as a testament or promise.

Their radical reorientation of the rite necessitated that the Reformers return to an earlier point in the development of church Eucharistic theology. They needed to begin again to carve out an understanding of the presence of Christ at the celebration. Although they agreed that transubstantiation was an inadequate and ill-conceived explanation, they were not of one mind as to what to offer in its stead. Three viewpoints emerged.

(1) Martin Luther stood closest to the Roman Catholic position. He agreed with the realist intention of the medieval theologians: Because our Lord is physically present in the communion elements, the communicants ingest Christ's body. But Luther resented that the schoolmen had made transubstantiation into a dogma. He doubted that a change occurs in the substance of the communion elements. The communicants ingest bread and wine, he taught. Nevertheless, Christ's body and blood are present in the elements. Christ is not present instead of bread and wine, but with them. The communicants ingest the Lord's body and blood *under* and *with* the communion elements, with the substance of the physical realities. Hence, Luther proposed the term *consubstantiation* (Latin: *cum* = "with") to denote the mystery of the Eucharist.

Although Lutheran and Roman Catholic theologians disagreed concerning the means, they found basic agreement concerning the

---

51. See Thomas Aquinas, *Summa Theologica* 3.79.5-7, trans. Fathers of the English Dominican Province, three volumes (New York: Benziger, 1947), 2:2483-85.
52. For this conclusion, see Heron, *Table and Tradition*, 106.

result: Christ is physically present at the Lord's Supper, present in the communion elements. Luther's conception of this real presence was facilitated by a Christological consideration. He argued that through the "communication of attributes" (*communicatio idiomatum*) Christ's human nature shares in the qualities of his divinity, including omnipresence. Therefore the human Christ, who is both in heaven and everywhere in the universe, is localized in the bread and wine of the Eucharist. These elements reveal Christ's presence here for us.

(2) Contemporaneously with Luther another great reformer, Huldreich Zwingli, was at work in Switzerland. Because he was not so firmly rooted in medieval piety and theology as was Luther,[53] the great Swiss reformer proposed an even more radical break with the doctrine of transubstantiation.[54] His German colleague never challenged the idea of Christ's real presence in the elements and hence maintained the focus on the more objective aspect—Christ's promise to us in the Eucharist. Zwingli, in contrast, emphasized the other side of the Eucharistic celebration—the subjective dimension. Rather than being in any way a Mass, an offering to God, Zwingli claimed that the Lord's Supper is a memorial meal, a vivid act of remembrance through which we memorialize Christ's sacrifice.

Moreover according to Zwingli our participation in the communion elements does not mediate communion with the real flesh and blood of Christ. Christ's presence is not "in" the bread and wine at all. The glorified body of the risen Lord is localized in heaven at the right hand of the Father. Therefore he cannot be present on earth in the elements.

Rather than our Lord being physically present in the bread and wine, Zwingli argued that Christ is spiritually present. His presence resides in the believing community who remember the Lord's sacrifice. Christ chooses to be present because believers have gathered in his name. In this manner, the Zurich reformer moved the focus of the celebration from the elements and the words of institution ("This is my body." "This is my blood.") which formed the high point of the

---

53. Heron offers this reason. Ibid., 115.
54. Zwingli outlined his position in his *Commentary Concerning True and False Religion* (1525).

Mass. Rather than the bread and wine being the central sign of Christ's presence, Zwingli elevated the whole action of the community in accordance with Jesus' words, "Do this in remembrance of me."

Their different understandings of the Eucharist perpetrated an irresolvable rift between the two reformers. They bequeathed to the next generation the task of reconciling the two positions. In this context, the mantle of theological leadership fell to John Calvin.

(3) The Geneva reformer tackled the Eucharist dispute in his *Short Treatise on the Holy Supper* (1540). In the closing chapter, "The Present Dispute,"[55] he set forth what would become the foundation for his mature thinking on the subject.

With Luther, Calvin concluded that when we receive the sacrament in faith, "we are truly made partakers of the real substance of the body and blood of Jesus Christ."[56] When visualizing how this occurs, the reformer broke with the Middle Ages and invoked the mediatorial work of the Spirit. "Not to diminish this sacred mystery," he surmised, "we must hold that it is accomplished by the secret and miraculous virtue of God, and that the Spirit of God is the bond of preparation, for which reason it is called spiritual."[57]

His appeal to the Spirit facilitated Calvin in charting a middle position. He agreed with the Roman Catholic theologians and Luther that Christ's presence at the Eucharist is focused on the communion elements. However, he denied that this entails the real presence of the Lord's physical body. Here he agreed with Zwingli that Christ in his human nature is localized in heaven.[58] Rather, that postulating a real presence, the Geneva reformer spoke of Christ's *spiritual* presence in the elements. The heavenly Christ meets the believer in the bread and the wine. But this great communion with Christ is facilitated by the Spirit. The Holy Spirit unites us with the Lord across the

---

55. John Calvin, *Short Treatise on the Holy Supper*, in *Calvin: Theological Treatises*, in *Library of Christian Classics* volume 22, ed. John Baillie, John T. McNeill, Henry P. van Dusen, trans. J.K.S. Reid (London: SCM, 1954), 163-66.

56. Calvin, *Short Treatise*, 166.

57. Ibid.

58. On this basis, Calvin denied the doctrine of the real presence in articles 21-26 of the *Consensus Tigurinus* or the "Zurich Consensus" he hammered out with Bullinger in 1549. For a short history, see Heron, *Table & Tradition*, 133-34.

great distance between our location on earth and his presence at God's right hand.

The Meaning of the Lord's Supper

The discussions of the 1500s form the context for the development of distinct Christian ecclesiological traditions, which are only now beginning to find resolution. Within this context of confessional division among Christians concerning the Eucharistic celebration, we must seek to set forth our theology of this act of commitment.

The question of terminology. We begin our quest for the meaning of the rite by returning to the question of the proper designation for the act.

The several terms preferred by the various Christian traditions focus our attention on the dimensions of the meaning of the act. As we will develop further, the rite is a "communion," for through it we symbolically enact our fellowship with Christ and with one another in the faith community. Likewise, it is a Eucharist, for it is a joyous celebration of thanksgiving for what God has done and will do.

Of the alternatives, however, we prefer the designation "the Lord's Supper." This term anchors our practice in the table fellowship that Jesus shared with his followers. Of these occasions, the most important was our Lord's institution of its perpetual celebration at the last meal he shared with the Twelve.[59] Consequently, in so far as it is an enactment of the Last Supper, the designation "the Lord's Supper" emphasizes the function of this rite as an ordinance, an act of commitment Christ has given for us to follow.

The orientation to the past. Despite their differences, the several positions that formed the focus of debate in the sixteenth century had one important feature in common. They all moved from the past to the present, seeking to explain how a past event can become a present reality.[60] Hence, the discussion participants debated the

---

59. For a discussion grounding the Lord's supper in the Jewish Passover celebration, see Markus Barth, *Rediscovering the Lord's Supper* (Atlanta: John Knox, 1988), 7-27.

60. This is the judgment of Heron, *Table and Tradition*, 152-54. Wainwright affirms the same basic viewpoint, albeit suggesting that the older treatises focused the discussion on the three aspects which follow in our paragraph. Geoffrey Wainwright, *Eucharist and Eschatology*, American edition (New York: Oxford, 1981), 1.

question concerning the relationship between Jesus' death and the sacrificial aspect of the Eucharist. They attempted to describe the ontological presence of Christ at the sacrament. And their deliberations focused on the outworking of the sacrament in fostering a present union of the individual communicant with the Lord.

At one level, the focus from past to present is correct. As the designation "the Lord's Supper" suggests, the celebration does draw our attention to what God has done. In fact, this past orientation is foundational to the significance of the meal. However, we must look further at the manner in which the Lord's Supper is a celebration of the past, before enveloping this past orientation within a broader perspective which augments our understanding.

(1) Forming the basis of the meaning of the act is the function of the Lord's supper as a memorial meal. Through our gathering at his table we reenact the Last Supper, when our Lord instituted our practice and explained its significance. By means of this reenactment, we fulfill our Lord's command, "Do this in remembrance of me."

In this way, we symbolically enter into the story of our Lord. We vividly remember Jesus' significant life. We sit with the disciples in the upper room and recall Jesus' teaching about the pathway to life and about his death as the provision for spiritual vitality. We call to mind the table fellowship he shared with publicans and sinners, which stood as a sign of the kingdom and of the new community he was inaugurating. We remember as well his sacrificial death, recalling this climax to our Lord's great example of humble service to others and complete obedience to the Father. In bringing us to remember our Master in this way, the Spirit rekindles our devotion for the Lord, renews us in our commitment to discipleship, and strengthens us for living as Christ's followers in the present.

(2) As a remembrance of Christ, the Lord's Supper is likewise a gospel proclamation. Through our eating and drinking, we proclaim in a symbolic manner "the Lord's death" (1 Cor. 11:26). This proclamation includes the declaration of the simple fact that Jesus died—that Jesus sacrificed his life. This is reenacted in the broken bread

which speaks of the giving of his body and in the poured wine which refers to the shedding of his blood.

When observed within the context of the Old Testament conception of sacrifice, this act declares not only the fact of Jesus' death but also its meaning—why Jesus died. The poured wine refers to the giving of Jesus' life for sin in order to seal a new covenant between God and his people, for "without the shedding of blood there is no remission of sins" (Heb. 9:22; Mark 14:24 or Matt. 26:28). In addition, through our eating and drinking—which is simultaneously an individual and a corporate act—we personalize Jesus' death: He suffered for us, and specifically *for me* (John 6:54).

(3) As we eat and drink at the table, the Lord's Supper becomes an enactment of our participation in Christ himself (1 Cor. 10:16). Eating and drinking form appropriate symbols of this participation. The acts of ingestion represent the central dimension of personal faith, namely, that faith is the reception of God's gracious provision in Christ. Just as the act of ingesting bread and wine is merely the means of taking food to ourselves for physical vitality, so also faith is essentially the appropriation of Christ's completed work on our behalf for our spiritual vitality.

The orientation to the future. The debate partners of the sixteenth century correctly saw that the past event of Jesus' death forms the foundation for the meaning of the Lord's Supper celebration. They did not sufficiently emphasize, however, an equally significant dimension of the act, its future orientation. This dimension was rediscovered in the twentieth century, which marked a turn to the future in theology in general and eventually in ecclesiology in particular.[61]

The future dimension is evident in Jesus' promise at the institution of the Lord's Supper: "I tell you, I will not drink of this fruit of the vine from now on until that day when I drink it anew with you in my Father's kingdom" (Matt. 26:29). Through this promise, our Lord invites us to see his sacrificial death within the grand sweep of the bib-

---

61. Hence, the recent consensus statement declares, "The Eucharist opens up the vision of the divine rule which has been promised as the final renewal of creation, and is a foretaste of it." *Baptism, Eucharist and Ministry*, 14.

lical drama. This narrative moves from the past to the future, climaxing in the end of history. The Lord's Supper, therefore, is a celebration of the story of Jesus in its finality and totality, from cross to crown.

When in the Lord's Supper we commemorate the great saving event of Jesus' death, therefore, we do not merely look to the past. On the contrary, this event occurs in the context of Jesus' promise of a future "drinking anew" in the kingdom. Therefore, it directs our attention to the future. In the Lord's Supper we remember Jesus' sacrificial death and through the enactment symbolically participate in that event. But we remember the event in accordance with its promissory significance.

According to the New Testament, therefore, the significance of the Lord's Supper lies in its relationship to the future as grounded in the past.[62] Through its link to the future fulfillment of Jesus' promise, the past event of Christ's death constitutes our identity. As the reappropriation of that identity, the Lord's Supper draws us into the future. There we meet the risen Jesus who has gone before us into God's eschatological kingdom through his resurrection, which we will one day share.

The orientation to community. The turn to the future characteristic of twentieth-century theology provides a helpful orientation point for a contemporary understanding of the presence of the Lord in the Lord's Supper. Yet, alone it is insufficient. Our understanding of the presence of the Lord at the communion observance must join the future focus with another concept, the idea of community that lies at the center of our systematic theology. We assert that ultimately it is from the perspective of the eschatological community that the Lord is present with his people.

The future that Jesus promises us is a special future. It is characterized by fellowship. In the upper room he promised his disciples that he would one day drink the cup with them "anew." In this way, he directed them toward the time when he would enjoy a greater

---

62. This thesis is developed in Wainwright, *Eucharist and Eschatology.* See also Heron, *Table & Tradition,* 23, 54.

communion with his disciples in the kingdom. Jesus' promise is likewise for us. He promises that we too will participate in a grand communion with our Lord in the eschatological community of God.

In the supper we not only anticipate communion with the Lord as a hope for the distant future. We also experience the future community proleptically in the present. Through the Holy Spirit, Jesus' promise of an eschatological fellowship becomes a present reality. Our Lord comes among us and communes with us. In this sense, therefore, the celebration is an experience of present community.

As a symbol of community with our Lord, participation in the supper signifies our reaffirmation of Christ's lordship. Through our presence at the Lord's table we publicly confess our loyalty to Christ. Through this act, we are owning once again the pledge or covenant we made at our baptism. As this occurs, the Spirit declares and strengthens our unity with Christ. For this reason, our celebration carries grave ethical implications. It is a reminder that we can serve no other gods (1 Cor. 10:18-22), that no loyalty dare usurp the place of Christ.

The Lord's Supper is not only a symbol of present community with Christ but also with one another within Christ's fellowship. For this reason, the act is intended to express the unity of all believers in the one body. Paul indicated that the one loaf of bread symbolizes this oneness of the fellowship (1 Cor. 10:17). Our corporate eating from the single loaf symbolizes our common participation in communion with Christ. This aspect of the celebration also entails an ethical demand, as the Spirit reminds us that we belong to each other and consequently are to be concerned for the welfare of one another.

Through the Spirit's ongoing act of constituting the church as the eschatological community, Christ is present. The presence of Christ through the Holy Spirit transforms our observance of the Lord's Supper from merely a solemn memorial of our crucified Savior into a joyous celebration of the risen and returning Lord who is present among us. The Lord's Supper is, therefore, a communion with Christ and each other. We reaffirm our faith, reenvision our hope, and declare anew our love to the Lord of the future who communes with us in the present by his Spirit, As we do so, we must thank God for the great salvation which is ours because of his grace. Hence, the Lord's Supper is a Eucharistic celebration, that is, a joyous declaration of thanksgiving to the Father through the Son by the power of the Spirit.

Our Presence at the Lord's Supper

The presence of the Lord with his celebrating people at the Lord's Supper mandates that we take the rite seriously. This means that the Eucharist must become a significant aspect of the worship life of the church. It means as well that we give due consideration to the question of our presence at the table.

The importance of our presence. We participate in the Lord's Supper at Jesus' own invitation. The Master's summons endows the ordinance with a significance which mandates our regular presence at the community celebration.

Above all, the communion meal is an ordinance. The early community observed the Lord's Supper because they knew that Christ himself had instituted its practice. In continuity with the first Christians, our participation in the Lord's Supper stands as an act of obedience. Presence at the table offers us a means whereby we declare in a symbolic manner our ongoing obedience to Christ.

When we observe the Lord's Supper as an act of obedience, it also serves as a repeated affirmation of loyalty to our commanding officer. By our participation in this act of commitment, the Holy Spirit powerfully reminds us of who we are as persons in Christ, of our covenant with God and one another, and of our participation in the community of God.

Because presence at the Eucharist entails our renewal of the covenant with God, baptism properly precedes participation in the Lord's Supper. As we noted earlier, baptism is the God-given means by which we initially confess publicly our faith in Jesus and thereby enter into covenant with God and with the people of God. The reaffirmation of our personal loyalty to Christ inherent in the Lord's Supper presupposes our initial declaration of loyalty made in baptism.

Through the Lord's Supper the Spirit also strengthens us for Christian living. He reminds us of Jesus' example and admonishes us to follow our Lord's model. Through the repeated symbolic reminder of the good news of forgiveness in Christ, the Holy Spirit refreshes us in the midst of our failure and sin. At the same time, through our eating and drinking, the Spirit reminds us of Christ's power available each day and thereby encourages us to appropriate this divine resource. As the Spirit reminds us of Jesus' soon return, he provides motivation to hopeful, watchful service until that great day.

The presence of others at the table. A final point of difference among Christians lies in the matter of who should participate at the Lord's table.

As we have concluded earlier, the Lord's Supper is not a means of grace that works apart from faith (*ex opere operato*). Instead, it is a symbol of spiritual truth and a reaffirmation of loyalty to Christ. Only believers can testify to the gospel reality depicted by this act. Likewise, only those who are in fellowship with God are able to reaffirm personal loyalty to Christ by this act. For these reasons only Christians ought to partake of the elements (1 Cor. 11:27).

At the same time, however, others may nevertheless be present during the celebration as nonparticipating observers. Because the Lord's Supper vividly proclaims the essential truth of the gospel, the Spirit can issue a call to any present who are not yet believers. As they see the enactment of the Lord's sacrifice and renewal of the covenant with the Lord believers thereby make, the Spirit calls them to come to Christ in faith and receive the salvation available through him.

Our Lord instituted two acts of commitment— baptism and the Lord's Supper—for the sake of his church in the world. These practices provide public occasions initially to confess and subsequently to reaffirm our loyalty to Christ. Through them we also publicly affirm our presence within his community and our desire to be involved in the work of the people of God. In order to facilitate its ministry in the world, Christ's community organizes itself. The acts of commitment form one aspect of that organization. A larger aspect is development of organizational structures within the body of Christ. We now explore this dimension of our corporate life.

20

The Organization for Community Life

It was he who gave some to be apostles, some to be prophets, some to be evangelists, and some to be pastors and teachers, to prepare God's people for works of service, so that the body of Christ may be built up until we all reach unity in the faith and in the knowledge of the Son of God and become mature, attaining to the whole measure of the fullness of Christ. (Eph. 4:11-13)

Outline

To be effective in carrying out its purposes, every human community must organize itself. Community organization includes practices of commitment which integrate new members into the body and provide opportunities for members to reaffirm their loyalty to the corporate vision. Organization includes likewise the development of structures within the community. Ultimately, the goal of such structures is to facilitate community life.

The church is a special community; it is the people of God. As this corporate people, our purpose is to bring glory to the triune God by fulfilling the mandate our Lord entrusted to us—worship, edification, and outreach. According to the foundational documents of our community life, the Scriptures and especially the New Testament, Christ ordained two practices of commitment. Did the risen Lord through his apostolic mouthpieces also enjoin additional dimensions of community organization? Is there a New Testament church structure that we are to follow today?

In this chapter, we delineate our theology of church organization. We attempt to set forth a structure that can channel the energy of the community toward fulfilling the vocation Christ has given us. With this goal in view, we seek principles from the Bible and insight from the Christian heritage to direct us in our attempt to organize ourselves for the task of being the people of God in the contemporary world.

We raise the question of community organization in four aspects of church life: membership in the community, governmental structure of the community, leadership for the community, and ordination by the community.

Membership in the Community

Every community has boundaries, regardless of how ill-defined, fluid, and fuzzy they may be. Consequently, every community must develop some understanding of what constitutes inclusion within its life. The need to define boundaries may take various forms, ranging from loosely constructed inclusion guidelines to elaborate criteria for membership codified in a constitution document.

Like other communities, the community of Christ is a "bounded set," a social group with certain boundaries. In this sense Christ's community takes on an institutional form. But what determines inclusion in the church? To what degree is the fellowship of Christ's disciples an institution with a specific membership and defined criteria for inclusion?

Community Membership in the First Century

The picture of the early fellowship that emerges from the New Testament suggests that a somewhat informal understanding of church membership prevailed among the first believers. In contrast to the elaborate codified statements of inclusion requirements often used by churches today, the book of Acts simply states that persons were "added to their number" (Acts 2:41). Indeed, "the Lord added to their number daily those who were being saved" (v.47). Later Luke reported that "the number of disciples in Jerusalem increased rapidly" (Acts 6:7), but he did not elaborate as to how the early congregation kept records of its membership. Letters of commendation, similar to contemporary letters of transfer between congregations, were, however, carried from one locale to another (1 Cor. 16:3; 2 Cor. 3:1; 3 John 5-9).

The formalized membership processes which most church traditions now take for granted find their genesis in historical developments, especially the elaborate baptismal practices the persecuted church developed in the late second century.[1] Although membership procedures may have been less formalized in the New Testament, early believers held inclusion in the church in high esteem. In contrast to the modern emphasis on the individual, belonging to a larger corporate whole was an important dimension of life in the ancient world. Consequently, early believers understood themselves as those who had been personally incorporated into the larger community (Acts 8:14-17; 18:24-27; Rom. 15:26-27). This understanding lay behind Paul's organic conception of the church as the body of interdependent believers, all of whom contribute to the functioning of the whole (1 Cor. 12:12-27). The idea of a self-sufficient, isolated Christian was inconceivable to first-century believers. In their understanding the individual believer and the community were intertwined.

First-century Christians viewed the faith community as the sphere of a unique divine presence at work in the world. Consequently, exclusion from the Lord's congregation was a serious matter. Rather than merely the formal striking of a name from the church roll, excommunication marked the cessation of fellowship. The act meant that the congregation had severed the bond with the wayward member (Matt. 18:17; 1 Cor. 5:13). Expulsion was not merely the breaking of ties with a company of humans; it also marked excommunication from Christ. To be expelled from Christ's church

---

1. For an overview, see J. G. Davies, *The Early Christian Church* (Grand Rapids: Baker, 1980), 103-104. For a description of early church practices, see *Didache*, 7, trans. James A. Kleist, *Ancient Christian Fathers* (New York: Paulist, 1948), 6:19; Justin Martyr, *Apology* 1.61 trans. Thomas B. Falls, *The Future of the Church (Washington,* D.C.: Catholic University of America Press, 1948), 6:99-100.

entailed removal from the sphere of the Lord's presence and protection. The world was the location of Satan's dominion. For this reason, to be placed outside the church potentially meant to come once again under Satanic attack (1 Cor. 5:5).

Baptism and Community Membership

First-century believers viewed membership in the faith community as a serious matter. Repeatedly in church history attempts have been made to recapture the pristine understanding. In a sense, the Reformation as a whole was a reaction in the name of the New Testament against the medieval ecclesiology which Protestants claimed had imposed an alien structure on the original approach to community life. The new turn that developed in the Protestant movement forms a signpost for our attempts today to provide a theological understanding of church membership.

The legacy of the Reformation. The reforming impulse within mainstream Protestantism reached its apex in the English Puritan movement, especially with the proponents of congregationalism. These thinkers came to see the local congregation as a company formed and maintained by a corporate covenant with God. They viewed membership in a local church as important, therefore, because it meant inclusion within a covenanting people, and exclusion constituted being cut off from the covenant.

We would do well to regain the sense of the importance of our inclusion in Christ's company that characterized the New Testament church and which the Puritan congregationalists sought to recover. A contemporay theology of church membership, however, must take seriously our changed situation. Unlike the early church, we are not the first generation. Interposed between the situation of the first Christians and ours is a theological debate as to who actually qualifies for inclusion within the corporate community. This question, in turn, takes us back to the nature of the church itself.

The pure church ideal. Nearly all Christian traditions set baptism as the main prerequisite for church membership. As a sign of entrance into the community of Christ, this rite initiates a person into the church. At this point, however, the differences between pedobaptists and believer's baptists about the proper candidates for baptism reemerge (see chapter 19).

Their distinctive understanding of the initiatory rite as the confession of personal faith leads believer's baptists to argue that church membership is only for those who are able to make a conscious declaration of faith. Infants cannot be included, because they have not yet reached the stage in life in which they are able to bear witness to personal conversion or to express consciously chosen loyalty to Christ. Because infants are not proper candidates for baptism, they cannot be members of the baptized community.

Believer's baptists claim that their position is the logical outworking of the Puritan principle of "regenerate church membership." This principle rests on the supposition that the church is a covenant community, the company of the redeemed. If this is the nature of the church, it follows that the church properly consists only of those who give evidence of regeneration (or election). Building from their congregationalist forebears, believer's baptists understand this to mean that we must reserve inclusion in the church for conscious disciples of Christ. As a consequence, they seek to live out in practice as far as is possible the "pure church ideal," that is, to maintain churches consisting of the truly regenerate (or elect) alone. What may appear to be rigid membership requirements among believer's baptists, therefore, is not motivated by a spirit of legalism, but by the desire to ensure as far as possible that only those who are truly Christ's disciples be church members.

By extending to infants the privilege of baptism, which is the sign of entrance into the church, pedobaptists readily suggest that persons can in some sense be church members from infancy. As a consequence, pedobaptist theology often pictures the church as a mixed company, not merely in practice but also in its essence. Pedobaptists in Reformed churches, for example, argue that church membership is for "the elect and their children."[2] Although they hope that these

---

2. Hence, the architects of the early Reformed tradition appealed this understanding of the church in setting themselves apart from the Anabaptists: "We condemn the Anabaptists, who deny that young infants, born of faithful parents, are to be baptized. For, according to the doctrine of the Gospel, 'to such belongs the kingdom of God' (Luke xviii. 16), and they are written in the covenant of God (Acts iii. 25). Why, then, should not the sign of the covenant of God be given to them? Why should they not be consecrated by holy baptism, who are God's peculiar people and are in the Church of God?" Second Helvetic Confession (1566), 20, in John H. Leith, *Creeds of the Churches*, third edition (Atlanta: John Knox, 1982), 169.

children are themselves also elect and therefore will eventually demonstrate the signs of election, Reformed thinkers can offer no guarantee that this will indeed be the case. Unless the community imposes strict guidelines for excommunicating the nonelect from their roles (which most churches find runs counter to Christian charity), the church always remains a mixed company.

The mixed nature of the church is no less evident in traditions holding to baptismal regeneration. Baptized infants are in some sense regenerated, proponents theorize, either because God works through the sacrament (Roman Catholics) or because he works in correspondence with it (some Lutherans). In this manner, advocates of this position maintain a certain fidelity to the principle of regenerate church membership (albeit not intentionally). They differ with believer's baptists, however, concerning what is entailed in that regeneration. And they generally acknowledge that those once baptized can lose their regenerate status.

In the end, the elaborate theological arguments of pedobaptists for including infants within the church remain unconvincing. The conscious, heartfelt dedication of a person to a life of discipleship marks a qualitative jump in the level of participation in community life. Even pedobaptist traditions acknowledge this principle, for they generally add to infant baptism subsequent rites of passage such as confirmation.

Believer's baptists remind the church that we ought to give due seriousness to the personal declaration of faith and the decision to embark on the path of discipleship. Children of church members have a special claim on the watchcare and nurture of the community.[3] Nevertheless, we cannot view children as participants in the church until they give personal and conscious expression to the faith of the community.

Initiation into the community. Uniting with a local congregation (which is the visible expression of Christ's church) forms the final step in the process of initiation into the company of the people of God. This process begins with personal faith in Christ as Savior and

---

3. For a discussion of this from a believer's baptist position, see Marlin Jeschke, *Believer's Baptism for Children of the Church* (Scottdale, Penn.: Herald, 1983).

Lord, is publicly expressed in water baptism, and culminates in formal church membership. Yet we must be careful never to reduce this act to the level of joining of a club or organization. It is rather the sealing of a covenant with like-minded persons to walk in common commitment as Jesus' disciples.

Above all, initiation into the church is incorporation into a community. It means participation in a body of people who share a story, a vision, and a mandate. The process of initiation into the church of Christ, therefore, comes about through the triad of inward personal faith, its outward expression in baptism, and formal membership in a local congregation. Faith marks our acceptance of the story of Jesus for us. Baptism symbolizes our transfer of loyalties. And church membership marks the public meshing of our personal story with the story of God's people.

Baptism after the First Century

As we noted already, we no longer live in the era of the first generation of Christians. Sometime after the end of the first century, the main trajectory of Christian tradition incorporated the practice of infant baptism as a means to respond to the problem of the second generation. It became a way of linking children of believers to the community of faith. Since then, the vast number of the people of God simply have not experienced believer's baptism, which appears to have been the practice of the New Testament era. Even many proponents of believer's baptism distinguish between personal faith, baptism as its public expression, and membership in a local church, both temporally and theologically. Our changed environment produces a crucial problem: How ought believer's baptists and pedobaptists to view each other?

Sectarianism versus denominationalism. In recent centuries theologians have practiced two contrary alternatives. The first, sectarianism, emphasizes the *visible* church. Believer's baptist sectarians see this rite as the definitive mark of a true church, implying thereby that only believer's baptist congregations are true churches.[4] If other churches are false, it follows that pedobaptists are in some sense not church members.

The second alternative, denominationalism, appeals to the concept of the *invisible* body of Christ. According to proponents of this view, the true church consists of all the redeemed, regardless of ecclesiastical affiliation or lack of the same. Baptism, in turn, becomes a matter of polity, which the various churches may determine for themselves.

Denominationalism has one great advantage. It allows us to affirm fellowship with Christians in churches with which our congregation has no formal fellowship. This advantage, however, often leads to the deprecation of baptism. As the initiation ordinance is separated from conversion and linked solely to membership in a local church, it loses its meaning as a sign of an important theological truth about the nature of salvation.

This second approach has become widespread among believer's baptists in recent years. Many link baptism with reception into the church and disjoin the ordinance completely from conversion. Several years may separate baptism/church membership from the initial conversion experience. In this way the ordinance becomes an unnecessary appendage to one's personal encounter with Jesus Christ, interpreted as the point of repentance and faith.

Beyond denominationalism. The current situation demands an outlook that follows neither alternative described above. Against the denominationalist impulse, we must restore the significance and importance of baptism, both in theory and practice. We must reunite the symbol with the conversion experience which it symbolizes. Against the sectarian impulse, we must restore baptism without "unchurching" the rest of Christendom.

Two considerations offer a way forward in this apparent impasse. First, God's grace is not bound by structures which can so easily become legalistic means of "works righteousness." This means that the God who is able to work in spite of all human ignorance and error can

---

4. Perhaps the most influential expression of this position is Landmarkism, which has its roots in the nineteenth century. Landmarkists claim that Baptist churches are the only true churches in the world and the only church is the local organization. For a description of the tenets of Landmarkism, see H. Leon McBeth, *The Baptist Heritage* (Nashville: Broadman, 1987), 450-51.

utilize practices that seem to be an inferior reflection of the original initiation rite in order to carry out his own purposes.

Second, always present in baptism is a future orientation. The initiation rite is practiced with a view toward participation in the future kingdom of God. This future orientation is most readily evident in believer's baptism. In this act the individual pledges allegiance to Christ, whose rulership is the meaning of the kingdom. Yet infant baptism is not totally devoid of a future orientation. Pedobaptists baptize infants with a view toward their future participation in the kingdom, which will be marked by a coming to faith at some point in the future. This, which inheres in the hope of kingdom participation, unites Christians despite our differences over the proper subjects of the initiatory rite.

Believer's baptists and pedobaptists represent two distinct Christian traditions with two differing ecclesiologies. Yet these differences, as important as they are, do not require that each group excommunicate the other. Specifically, our commitment as believer's baptists to what we see as the biblical sequence (personal faith expressed in believer's baptism leading to inclusion in the church) does not require that we either reduce the importance of the rite of initiation or conclude that all persons baptized in infancy are outside of Christ's church.

Community Structures

Paul challenged the Christians in Rome to see a positive role for government. God ordained government to benefit human community (Rom. 13:1-7). What is true of government in general is especially valid in the church. Beginning in the apostolic era, the people of God have continually known the importance of organization for the purpose of facilitating the ministry given by Christ. The impulse toward organization leads to establishing church government structures. In pursuing the proper mode of government, however, we must look at how churches fit together into a unified whole and at how each local congregation may best be organized. To this end, we view the local church first in its associational context and then in itself.

The Government of the Community

As we noted in chapter 17, no visible fellowship of Christians is an entity solely to itself. Rather, each is the church of Jesus Christ in miniature. Throughout Christian history, believers have acknowledged this principle by constructing lines of connection among the various communities of faith. In so doing local fellowships have seen themselves as participants in the wider community of faith. Such participation, however, demands some type of organizational structure for the churches in their associational context.

Models of government. The practical question, "What mode of government should characterize the church in its universal expression?" has been perennially divisive. Three basic models have appeared and reappeared through the course of history—the hierarchical, the representative, and the independent. Each of these continues to claim adherents today.

The hierarchical (or episcopal) model may constitute the longest continuously practiced system of church government within the mainline Christian traditions. It is exemplified today by the Roman Catholic Church and the Anglican fellowship.

In the episcopal system, a group of clergy, generally called "bishops" (Greek: *episcopos*) mediate Christ's authority to the people of God. These leaders exercise oversight in the Church[5] as an extension of, or in continuity with the authority of the apostles. As a consequence, each local gathering of the faithful (or parish church) participates in the one Church because the local body is in fellowship with (comes under the supervision of) a bishop of the Church.[6]

---

5. Hence, according to Roman Catholic polity, inherent in the episcopacy is "the right to govern and direct the people of God according to the norms of worship and conduct that are binding on the consciences of the faithful. John A. Hardon, S.J., *The Catholic Catechism: A Contemporary Catechism of the Teachings of the Catholic Church* (Garden City, N.Y.: Doubleday, 1975), 222.

6. This is the case even in those communions, such as the Episcopal Church in the USA, in which the laity exercise a role in church governance. Dawley writes, "As its name indicates, the polity of the Episcopal Church is one where the ministers of ordination and chief governance are bishops....The ministry in all Churches of the Anglican Communion...is one in which bishops in the succession of the historic episcopate occupy an essential place. It is natural, therefore, that the chief unit of church life should still be the ancient *diocese*, an area consisting of the parishes and people under the care of the bishop." Powel Mills Dawley, *The Episcopal Church and Its Work*, revised edition (New York: Seabury, 1961), 114.

In the Roman Catholic Church, one office is supreme, that of the Bishop of Rome who is more commonly known as the pope. Although historically British Anglicans look to the English monarch as the head of the church, the focus of authority lies with the collegial leadership of the college of bishops under the direction of the Archbishop of Canterbury. The Episcopal Church in the USA, retains the focus on the bishops while adding a representative aspect. The national legislative body is the General Convention. All acts of the convention must be passed by the House of Bishops (composed of all bishops of the Church) and the House of Deputies (consisting of priests and lay people from each diocese) body.[7]

Whereas the hierarchical model represents the Roman Catholic legacy, the representative (or presbyterian) model is indicative of the Reformed tradition. In its expression among the English Presbyterians in the Puritan era this system was modeled along the pattern of the fledgling English Parliament.

According to presbyterian polity, a group of persons, often called "presbyters" (Greek: *presbuterios*), mediate Christ's authority to the congregations. The presbyters are the representatives of the local fellowships, who delegate to their leaders this representative authority. In practice, a series of assemblies may exercise this governing authority. Leaders represent local congregations in the regional presbytery or classis. The presbyteries, in turn, select representatives to the synod, as well as to the General Assembly, which is the highest body of authority.[8]

The hierarchical system is based on the premise that Christ's authority flows to the congregations through ordained persons who are ultimately responsible for the church as a whole. Representative structures embody the premise that the people delegate Christ's authority to a body of persons—both clergy and laity—who then act on their behalf. According to the independent model, in contrast, Christ's authority functions immediately in each local fellowship (hence, the designation "congregational"). Each church is directly

---

7. Ibid., 100.

8. See, for example, *The Divine Right of Church Government* (1799; New York: R. Martin, 1844), 171-72.

accountable to its Lord and in this sense is autonomous (that is, responsible under Christ for its own affairs). The congregations band together in associations, to which they are accountable, but associational authority is advisory, rather than legislative. The decisions of an association require the concurrence of the local congregation.

While various groups throughout church history have followed the independent model, it remained on the fringe of Christian tradition until the Reformation. Luther advocated a type of congregationalism, but he was also open to maintaining the episcopacy[9] (as was Melanchthon).[10] More so than Luther, the English Puritan movement formed the context for the development of congregationalism. English congregationalism received an important impetus from the rising democratic spirit, which paralleled its own development.

The congregational impulse formed the motivation for an important change of nomenclature. Most ecclesiastical traditions readily speak of the whole of which each congregation is a part as the "Church." Congregationalists, in contrast, are reticent to use this term for any body beyond the local fellowships. Hence, whereas we can speak of the Roman Catholic Church, or even the Presbyterian Church, many suggest that there is no Baptist Church, only Baptist churches. Rather than a "Church," Baptists and participants in certain other traditions denote the wider fellowship as a "conference," "convention," or "association" of churches.

New Testament considerations. In the era following the Reformation each of the three models could boast strong advocates who argued from the New Testament that their position was either the only model that could claim biblical precedence or at least the best reflection of the pattern that developed in the early church. Today, however, it is fashionable to admit that the evidence from the New Testament is inconclusive[11] and therefore that all three models of church structure find their genesis in tendencies noticeable already in the first century.

---

9. See Paul D.L. Avis, The *Church in the Theology of the Reformers* (Atlanta: John Knox, 1981), 109-14.

10. Wolfhart Pannenberg, *The Church*, trans. Keith Crim (Philadelphia: Westminster, 1983), 86.

11. This position is even argued by Erickson. Millard J. Erickson, *Christian Theology*, three volumes (Grand Rapids: Eerdmans, 1983-1985), 3:1084.

We ought not interpret the inconclusiveness of recent discussions of New Testament polity as suggesting that the Bible offers no guidance in this matter. On the contrary, the biblical documents provide insight into the church life of the earliest communities. From this pattern we may draw principles to guide our construction of governmental structures.

(1) One recurring theme throughout Acts and the epistles is the principle of congregational autonomy. In the New Testament era we discover individual congregations making decisions apart from external control.

The church in Antioch, for example, exercised the prerogative of commissioning Paul and Barnabas into missionary service (Acts 13:1-4). Upon the completion of their travels the two missionaries returned to make a report to the local fellowship (14:27). The Jerusalem council took upon itself the task of sending a letter of instruction to the gentile churches (15:22-29). Yet this body was instigated by the incentive of the Antioch church (which would be one of the recipients of that letter), which dispatched messengers to the mother congregation (15:2-3).

In keeping with the idea of independency, Paul admonished the Corinthian congregation to take charge of its own internal problems. They were to address the schism within its ranks (1 Cor. 1:10). They were to assume jurisdiction for the observance of the Lord's Supper (11:33-34). And reminiscent of Jesus' own instructions (Matt. 18:15-17), they were to maintain membership purity (1 Cor. 5:4-5; 12-13).

(2) While central to the biblical understanding, autonomy of the local church never degenerated into congregational individualism. Rather, in the New Testament interdependency functioned as a counterbalancing norm.

The participants at the Jerusalem council assumed that their decision would be honored by churches on both sides of the controversy. The same principle is displayed in Paul's repeated call to local fellowships to acknowledge the authority Christ had invested in his apostles or to receive apostolic representatives such as Timothy and Titus. In fact, Paul instructed the churches to acknowledge their common unity in all matters. In keeping with this principle, the apostle appealed to what was practiced in all churches as carrying a certain authority (1 Cor. 11:16; 14:33). His desire that the Gentile congregations be bound together with the mother church through a practical demonstration of unity was perhaps one motivation lying behind Paul's determination that they take up a collection for the Jerusalem saints.

Balancing autonomy with the associational impulse. As in the first century, these two New Testament principles—congregational autonomy and the associational impulse—lay the foundation for the organization of the contemporary people of God.

(1) The principle of autonomy means that within the larger whole, each congregation is self-governing. Each body of believers looks after its internal matters.

Each fellowship possesses what we may call "church powers." These include the "power of membership." Each congregation has the prerogative to welcome new participants into the covenantal relationship, to write letters of commendation or transfer to sister congregations on behalf of members who relocate, and to exercise discipline within the context of the church covenant. Local church discipline may even entail breaking fellowship with those who remain in violation of the covenant.

Included as well is the "power of mandate." The Lord has charged each group of believers to fulfill within its own context the threefold mandate of worship, edification, and outreach entrusted to the church as a whole. To this end, each congregation retains the "power of organization." This includes the prerogative to select officers for the local assembly (Acts 6:1-5) and to ordain leaders for the entire church, within the context of the advice of sister congregations (Acts 13:1-4; 1 Tim. 4:14).

(2) Balanced with congregational autonomy is the principle of association. Although possessing church powers, no congregation is an end to itself. Each is a participating partner with all other fellowships in a larger whole. Hence, all congregations are important for the life and ministry of each, and each local body is crucial for the life and ministry for the whole people of God in the world.

With a view toward this reality, each congregation should give expression to its participation in, and responsibility to the larger whole by means of voluntarily joining with sister churches in an associational framework. Associations of various types facilitate us as we seek together to determine the Lord's will for his church. They likewise promote a wider experience of fellowship. And through associations congregations are able to combine resources in order to engage in the task common to the entire people of God.

In addition to its practical advantages, the inclusion of local congregations within the wider association is theologically significant. Each local fellowship is to be the church of Jesus Christ in miniature. Yet this does not mean that any congregation can be a church of Jesus Christ in isolation. Associations of churches on various levels—regional, national, international—give expression to the importance of wider Christian fellowship, unity, and reciprocal dependence. Understood in this context, cooperation through association ties becomes an inevitable outworking of the impulse of each congregation to participate in that whole of which it is the local expression.

Government Within the Communities

Each fellowship of believers is to be the church of Jesus Christ in miniature. For this reason, each is to engage in the ministry of the whole people of God. Just as organizational structure is necessary for facilitating the working together of the churches, so also each congregation must develop an internal structure for the sake of facilitating its members in carrying out their common task. The question of church government, therefore, demands not only consideration of how the local congregations are connected with each other, but also how the local fellowship organizes itself for the purpose of its mission.

The congregationalist dilemma. In many cases, local structure follows naturally from the system adopted by the wider ecclesiastical tradition. In hierarchical bodies the ultimate decision-making prerogative for each local church may reside with the bishop under whose watchcare it rests (and by extension with the clergy who minister in the parish).[12]

Similarly, the representative model often extends to local church structure. A governing board (the session or the consistory) made up of both the ruling elders (lay persons) and the teaching elders (clergy) assume responsibility for the congregation.

In contrast to Episcopal and Presbyterian churches, those following the independent form are not always consistently congregational. The roots of this inconsistency lie in the discussions of their English forebears in the late sixteenth century. In a day when kings and councils decided the will of God, they asserted the radical idea that the church is constituted by the voluntary covenant of converted believers, who as an entire company under the guidance of their leaders discern Christ's will. The early congregationalists, however, were divided as to the outworking of this principle in the relationship between the members of a local congregation and their leaders.

Some congregationalists favored what we may call semi-Presbyterianism. This theory invests the local elders with the final authority in the congregation. Others perceived that the democratic impulse that yielded the principle of congregational autonomy must be applied within the fellowship itself. Somewhat parallel to the wider political concept capsulized in the slogan, "The voice of the people is the voice of God," they theorized that final authority in the church resided with the people as a whole. We know this position as democratic congregationalism.

The foundation of democratic congregationalism. In recent years, ideas that logically lead to democratic congregationalism have gained widespread acceptance throughout the church. The consensus statement, *Baptism, Eucharist and Ministry*, for example, declares, "Strong emphasis should be placed in the active participation of all members in the life and the decision-making of the community."[13]

---

12. This is especially true in the Roman Catholic Church. However, even in the Episcopal Church, in which local congregations exercise much autonomy, the bishop in the diocese retains "the pastoral responsibilities of a Father-in-God to the people in Christ." Dawley, *The Episcopal Church*, 114-15. Likewise the fixed norm and standard for worship in each congregation is the *Book of Common Prayer*. Ibid., 84.

13. *Baptism, Eucharist and Ministry*, Faith and Order Paper number 111 (Geneva, 1982), 26.

More importantly, proponents of democratic congregationalism see this model as the outworking of certain biblical principles rediscovered in the Reformation.

(1) The foundation for democratic governmental structures resides in Jesus' own teaching concerning how his disciples should relate to each other. He repeatedly drew a contrast between the attitudes of authoritarianism and overlordship characteristic of the Gentiles and the Pharisees, and the spirit of mutuality that he desired for his followers (Mark 10:42-43). Rather than looking for special status, his disciples were to remember that Christ is their sole master and they are all sisters and brothers (Matt. 23:8). This egalitarian strand in Jesus' teaching is best lived out in church life through democratic congregationalism.

(2) Proponents of this model of polity appeal likewise to New Testament practice. According to the Book of Acts many decisions pertaining to ministry and structure were made by an entire congregation. The whole people were involved in the choosing of Judas's replacement (1:23-26), the selection of the first deacons (6:3-6), and the commissioning of Paul and Barnabas (13:3). Similarly, the Jerusalem council did not involve merely a select few, but the entire congregation (15:22).

Critics can cite Paul's appointment of elders for the churches in Asia Minor (Acts 14:23) as a counterexample to democratic congregationalism. However, we must placed this incident in the context of the procedure followed by the Jerusalem congregation in selecting the seven (6:3-6). Paul's act may have included the ratification of the choice by the churches. If not, it may have been a temporary expediency at the founding stage of the new congregations.

The practice of addressing epistles to entire churches rather than to their leaders reinforces the impression of the ultimate importance of the people as a whole in the life and decision-making of the local congregations.[14]

---

14. Erickson rightly notes that the epistles addressed to individuals—Philemon, 1 & 2 Timothy, Titus—were intended primarily for these persons and not for congregations under their care. Erickson, *Christian Theology*, 3:1082, citing Edward T. Hiscox, *The New Directory for Baptist Churches* (Philadelphia: Judson, 1894), 155ff.

(2) In addition to its foundation in Christ's teaching and the witness of New Testament practice, proponents claim that democratic congregationalism is the consistent outworking of a grand Protestant hallmark. At the heart of Luther's reform[15] lay a great principle, the priesthood of all believers.

The Reformers did not invent the idea of believer priesthood, however. Instead it arises from the teaching of the New Testament itself. The Scripture writers spoke of all believers as priests (1 Pet. 2:5; Rev. 1:6; 5:10; 20:6). All may approach the throne of grace through Christ (Heb. 4:15-16; 10:19-20). For this reason, the disciples of Christ were to acknowledge no mediatory hierarchy among them (Matt. 23:8-12; Mark 10:42-44; 1 Tim. 2:5). On the contrary, each believer has the privilege and responsibility to engage in priestly functions, such as offering spiritual sacrifices to God (Heb. 13:15; Rom. 12:1; 1 Pet. 2:9) and interceding for others (1 Tim. 2:1,2; 2 Thess. 3:1; James 5:16).

In the Reformation, this biblical emphasis resurfaced in the context of the crucial question of access to God and God's available grace. Medieval church life centered on the clergy, who supposedly were the instruments of the church in mediating both divine grace to the people and their offerings and prayers to God. The Reformers, however, reintroduced the radical idea of unmediated access. Because of the work of the one Mediator, we experience God's grace directly. Consequently, all believers are priests, enjoying access to God through Christ without any human go-betweens. For Luther and others, the concept of believer priesthood also meant that our Lord has entrusted all Christians with the gospel and with the task of ministering the gospel to others.[16]

Proponents of democratic congregationalism claim that the local church is the context in which we are to give concrete expression to the doctrine of believer priesthood. Such expression includes the participation of all members in the fulfillment of the church's mandate—worship, edification, and outreach. We are all to use our spiritual gifts for the benefit of the whole (1 Cor. 12:7; 1 Pet. 4:10-11).

---

15. Avis, *The Church in the Theology of the Reformers*, 95.
16. See ibid., 95-102.

Believer priesthood must come to expression in the decision-making process as well. The church's mandate is a common responsibility and not merely the task of a special clergy class. In the same way diligent discernment of Christ's will for the church is a matter for the concern of all, not merely a few. Church business meetings, when properly conducted and understood, therefore, are a spiritual experience. The people of God gather to do the business of God—to determine the Lord's will for the congregation.

The democratic congregational ideal in practice. The representative model took as its pattern the parliamentary system of political government that arose in sixteenth century England. Democratic congregationalism, in contrast, found its ideal in the town meeting. Just as every citizen participates in the decision-making process, within the local community the entire membership comes together to seek their Lord's will.

This comprises the central principle of democratic congregationalism. The entire company of believers discerns Christ's will for his people. The corporate decision-making process envisions a working together of leaders and people. By teaching and personal example, leaders equip the whole people for their task (Eph. 4:11-13), and they offer information and advice so that the people can reach spiritual decisions. Each church member, in turn, is responsible to become an active, informed, conscientious church member, to shoulder the responsibilities of membership in the covenant community, and above all to be sensitive to the Spirit's leading.

As lofty as it appears in theory, democratic congregational ideal is difficult to maintain in practice. One potential problem lies with congregational meetings themselves. In the decision-making process the earnest search by the people to determine corporately the Lord's will readily degenerates into majoritarian voting procedures with factions vying for control. The apathy of the membership, evidenced by declining participation in congregational meetings, can likewise render congregational rule ineffective. As churches become larger the practicality of the congregational meeting grows more difficult, for it is impossible for a great number of people to participate actively in this system of government. Democratic congregationalism is the active role of all in the corporate determination of Christ's will, not the rule by the voting majority at meagerly attended church meetings. In our day this model is becoming an increasingly illusive ideal.

Democratic congregationalism plagued with another potential problem as well—the actual role and authority of leaders. How forceful should the pastor be, for example, in seeking to direct the congregation toward the fulfillment of its mandate? Or given the decline of the congregational meeting, how many decision-making prerogatives should the central church council exercise?

Difficulties such as these have lead to a resurgence of semi-Presbyterianism within traditionally congregational churches. Sometimes it takes the form of a clericalism in which a strong pastor exercises almost full control over the church program. Other times a board of elders, which often becomes self-perpetuating and hence beyond the control of the congregation, exercises absolute authority over congregational matters.

Trends such as these pose a difficult question: At what point does democratic congregationalism become semi-Presbyterianism? We conclude from what we have said thus far that a congregation may delegate to its leaders whatever decision-making prerogatives it finds expedient for facilitating their corporate ministry. The people as a whole, however, must retain final authority for the exercise of church powers—membership, mandate, and organization (including selection of local officers and ordination).

Leadership for the Community

Christ has entrusted the ministry of the church to the people as a whole. For this reason, every believer should be a ministering priest, actively serving with the gifts bestowed by the sovereign Spirit and in accordance with his or her calling. To facilitate an effective corporate ministry, church organization provides the community with the leadership of capable persons. Such leadership serves the local communities and by extension the community as a whole.

Offices in the Communities

The congregational model of church life begins with the local fellowship viewed as the church of Jesus Christ in miniature. The purpose of church government is to facilitate the whole people under the guidance of their leaders in discerning and discharging the will of Christ. Crucial to this model, therefore, is the selection of leaders who expedite the working together of the people within the fellowship. But exactly what congregational offices are central to the accomplishment of this task?

Church offices in the New Testament. In his greeting to the Christians at Philippi, Paul indicated the presence in the early churches of two basic types of offices—bishops and deacons (Phil. 1:1).

The first office Paul mentioned may have had its genesis in a blending of the Greek and the Hebrew traditions. Its nature arises from the two terms the New Testament writers used to speak of it. The designation "bishop" (Greek: *episcopos*) means "one who supervises" (see Acts 20:28; 1 Tim. 3:1-2; Titus 1:7). Hence, this office "almost always related to oversight or administration."[17] Scholars differ as to the exact genesis of the biblical use of this term, whether it arose from secular Greek office structures, from temple or synagogue overseers in Judaism, or from the Qumran sect.[18] The alternate term, presbyter (Greek: *presbuteros*) or elder (Acts 20:17; 1 Tim. 5:17-19; Titus 1:5; James 5:14; 1 Pet. 5:1ff) could refer either to chronological age or special status within the community.[19] Its use as an office designation in the New Testament may reflect Greek influence. In Sparta, for example, a member of the word group was a political title denoting the president of a college.[20] More important, however, was the Hebrew background. Bornkamm noted that elders are presupposed in "all strata of the OT tradition," their origin lying

---

17. Joachim Rohde, "episcopos," in the *Exegetical Dictionary of the New Testament*, ed. Horst Balz and Gerhard Schneider, English translation, three volumes (Grand Rapids: Eerdmans, 1991), 2:36.

18. Ibid.

19. Joachim Rohde, "presbuteros," in *EDNT*, 3:148.

20. Guenther Bornkamm, "presbus...," in the *Theological Dictionary of the New Testament*, ed. Gerhard Kittel and Gerhard Friedrich, trans. Geoffrey Bromiley (Grand Rapids: Eerdmans, 1968), 6:653.

"in the most ancient patriarchal period when Israel was made up of tribes."[21]

In certain New Testament texts, we find bishop and elder used interchangeably (Acts 20:17-28; Titus 1:5,7). This suggests that in the early church they were likely not two offices, but merely alternate designations for the same position.[22]

The New Testament writers gave some indication as to the functions that first century elders fulfilled. Bishop suggests a supervisory task. These leaders carried the responsibility of directing the ongoing functioning of the congregation in the various aspects of its corporate ministry. They were to "shepherd" or guide the people of God (Acts 20:28; 1 Pet. 5:2). And they were to coordinate congregational ministry (1 Tim. 3:5; 5:17), providing administrative leadership which included involvement in ministry.

Elder suggests a spiritual task. Their position in the congregation meant that they would fulfill certain ministries, such as anointing the sick (James 5:14). Spiritual oversight also meant preaching, teaching, admonishing, and guarding against heresy (Titus 1:9). Because of the grave responsibilities involved, the office was to be filled only with persons who met strict qualifications (1 Tim. 3:1-7).

Working alongside of the bishops were a second group of officers, called deacons or helpers (Greek: *diakonos*). The verb from which this noun arises means basically "to wait on someone at table"[23] (Luke 12:37). From this basic meaning grew the wider sense of service,[24] including "to minister to the needs of another" (Matt. 4:11; 1 Tim. 1:18) or "to render assistance or support" (Matt. 25:44). Consequently, a deacon could be a table waiter, a servant, or an assistant.

Within the specific context of the early church, the New Testament writers used the term *diakonos* in several ways. It could refer to the apostolic service of proclamation, charitable service in the

---

21. Ibid., 655.

22. Rohde, "episcopos," in *EDNT*, 2:36. Milne writes, "It is now generally accepted among scholars of all traditions that the Greek words *episcopos* (bishop) and *presbuteros* (elder) are equivalents in the NT." Bruce Milne, *Know the Truth* (Downers Grove, Ill.: InterVarsity, 1982), 241.

23. Alfons Weiser, "diakonos," in *EDNT*, 1:302; Herman W. Beyer, "diakoneo..." in *TDNT*, 2:82.

24. Beyer, "diakoneo..., in *TDNT*, 2:82.

congregation, or the ministry of the church as a whole.[25] Most significant for our discussion of church organization is its use as a designation for a specific office, the deaconate.

There is not an abundance of evidence as to how deacons functioned in the early communities. Nevertheless, it appears that the initial impetus that led to the eventual establishment of this office occurred in the Jerusalem church.[26] The congregation selected seven people to assist with some of the organizational and service responsibilities, in order that the apostles could devote themselves fully to their primary function of providing spiritual leadership (Acts 6:1-4).

What arose in Jerusalem as a pragmatic response to a specific need the Pauline churches subsequently institutionalized. By the time of the writing of the Pastoral Epistles (1 and 2 Tim., Titus), "helper" had become an official designation for those functioning as assistants to the overseers. Some helpers may also have acted as apprentices who would eventually serve as overseers themselves. As in the case of bishops, all who were appointed as deacons needed to be people of high character (1 Tim. 3:8-12).

Statements about bishops and deacons in the New Testament suggest that the churches may have developed a twofold office structure. Local leadership responsibilities were shared by a group of elders or bishops. (The New Testament generally uses the plural form when referring to holders of this office.) The overseers provided supervision and spiritual guidance to the congregation. Assisting these leaders were the helpers, who took care of some of the administrative and pastoral tasks.

Church offices in the ecclesiastical tradition. Soon the two-tiered organizational structure of the New Testament churches gave rise to the three-tiered system which has predominated in Christian history.[27] This development began within local congregational life. The bishop became the leader of the community, ordained to proclaim

---

25. Weiser, "diakonos," in *EDNT*, 1:302-303.

26. Norman H. Maring and Winthrop S. Hudson, *A Baptist Manual of Polity and Practice* (Valley Forge, Pa.: Judson, 1963), 111-12.

27. For a sketch of this development, see *Baptism, Eucharist and Ministry*, 24.

the Word and preside at the local eucharistic celebration. At the Lord's table, the bishop was surrounded by the college of presbyters and by the deacons. In this manner the office of bishop came to be separated from that of the presbyters.

The three-tiered structure moved away from the life of the local community. The bishop became the leader of the church in a metropolitan area which comprised several eucharistic communities. As this occurred, the local fellowships were left under the care of presbyters (eventually, priests). As assistants to the bishops, the deacons likewise took on functions beyond the local churches.

The Reformers once again anchored the office structure in the local church. This change formed the foundation for the reemergence of a two-tiered model, which was later adopted by many Protestant churches. For example, the Baptists in seventeenth and eighteenth century North America practiced a relatively uncomplicated polity. Whenever possible, a local congregation sought out a gifted person to fulfill various pastoral duties, including preaching and evangelism. This person, generally ordained by the congregation as an elder (or pastor) often remained in office for life. To assist the elder in the more mundane church affairs, the fellowship set apart a group of deacons.

The nineteenth century was an era of change. Congregations grew in size, acquired property, and added new programs. Pastors became better educated and increasingly mobile. The changes resulted in more complex church structures. Congregations added additional boards, charging them with the administration of the expanded programs and facilities. The deacons, in turn, gained more influence and importance in the local congregations, becoming the leaders who remained behind as pastors came and went. Today deacons are charged with "the spiritual well-being" of the congregation. Consequently, they fulfill many of the spiritual functions of the biblical overseers.

New Testament offices and today's church. The context of church life has changed greatly since the first century. Yet the two-tiered system prevalent in the New Testament churches offers an important foundation for contemporary organization, regardless of the exact terms used to designate offices and the exact responsibilities officers fulfill.[28]

To facilitate the ministry of the whole people, each congregation should delegate to a group of spiritual persons the responsibility of providing supervisory leadership over the activities of the church. The primary task of these leaders is to guide the people in the focal areas of congregational mission. As needs arise the church may select helpers to assist the supervisory leaders in carrying out their responsibilities.

Central to the organizational structure of a church, therefore, is a group of leaders that form the major advisory body (church board), which is directly accountable to the congregation. The central role of the church board is to provide spiritual leadership and direction to the church in its program of ministry. Included on this board are the pastor(s) and the moderator or church chairperson, who leads both the church business meetings and the church board meetings. Also included are those persons who serve because of their supervisory responsibilities for the various aspects of the congregational mandate (worship, edification, and outreach). Finally, the board may include at least one member who oversees the church physical resources. In this manner each member of the church board is providing responsible leadership in the life of the congregation.

Final authority remains with the people as a whole, for they are the selecting body. The entire church calls pastors for an indefinite length of service. All other officers serve for terms of definite length. The congregation selects officers on basis of stringent criteria: spiritual qualification (1 Tim. 3:1-7), giftedness and interest, and proven effectiveness in other tasks. Structured under the church board and serving with its members are the various "helper" offices. These are added by the congregation according to perceived needs with the purpose of assisting the church leaders in carrying out their tasks. Helpers may be organized into standing committees, each of which coordinates a specific aspect of the life of the church (worship committee, outreach committee, edification committee, plus a physical

---

28. For a fuller delineation of this proposal, see Stanley J. Grenz, *The Baptist Congregation* (Valley Forge, Pa.: Judson, 1985).

resource committee). The overseer responsible for a specific area may chair the corresponding standing committee and serve as the liaison between it and the church board. Persons selected as helpers must meet similar spiritual criteria (1 Tim. 3:9-11).

Offices of the Community

The need to facilitate the involvement of the people in the church's mission lies behind the establishment of offices in the local community of believers. Does this need also give rise to office structures beyond the congregational level? Are there also "intercongregational offices," roles which transcend the local assembly?

The New Testament background. The New Testament documents yield evidence to the presence in the early church of persons whose influence was not focused in a single congregation. Their service transcended local boundaries. One such office was "apostle." Paul, for example, exercised a certain amount of influence in the churches he founded, which he repeatedly defended in his epistles in the face of rebellious elements. Likewise, in his first epistle John declared that one mark of all true churches is doctrinal purity understood as loyalty to apostolic authority and teaching.

Assistants who acted as emissaries of the apostles and therefore shared in their ministry form a second example of persons whose service went beyond any one congregation. For example, under Paul's directive Titus appointed elders—whether by supervising an election or by direct personal selection—for the missionary churches of Crete (Titus 1:5), a task which Paul had earlier fulfilled in a similar context (Acts 14:23).

In the Ephesian epistle, Paul lists four categories as Christ's gifts to his church: apostles, prophets, evangelists, and pastors and teachers. Here, the apostle has the church in general and not any specific congregation in view, indicating that such persons minister in the context of the whole. Apostles played a significant foundational role in the early church as the guardians and pioneer propagators of the gospel. Prophets served as mouthpieces for special divine communication. Evangelists carried on itinerant missionary work, using churches established by the apostles as a basis (for example: Apollos in Acts 18:27-28). The example of Timothy's sojourn in Ephesus suggests that pastors and teachers worked more directly within a specific locale for an extended period of time in order to edify the congregation through this focused ministry.

The pastoral office. There is much debate as to whether Christ intended that the offices of apostle, prophet, and evangelist continue throughout church history.[29] Nearly universally recognized, however, is the ongoing importance of the pastoral office, regardless of how different traditions choose to designate it.

We maintain that the pastor/teacher Paul mentioned in the Book of Ephesians and Timothy exemplified during his stay at Ephesus provides the foundation for the central dimension of this office. The pastor exercises leadership within a local congregation, but with ramifications beyond the local setting.

Like Timothy's sojourn in Ephesus, most generally a pastor serves a local church. Within the local setting the pastor functions within the framework of the local leaders (the pastoral staff and the church board). At the same time the pastor's ministry is one of greater depth because of the "full-time" status involved. Paul's injunctions to Timothy indicate the scope of pastoral responsibilities. Included are the general responsibilities of the eldership, including administrative oversight, congregational leadership, and "shepherding." These are augmented by such activities as leading worship, teaching, preaching, and evangelism. All pastoral activity occurs in the context of an ultimate objective, namely, preparing "God's people for works of service" (Eph. 4:12).

In these various ways, the pastor serves as visionary to the people. Fundamentally, the pastoral office is to facilitate the well-functioning of the community. To this end, the pastor keeps before the mem-

---

29. In the context of their rejection of the concept of apostolic succession, many Protestants claim that the apostolic office was for the first century only. Hence, Milne writes, "To claim apostolic *office* today is a misunderstanding of biblical teaching and in practice offers a serious challenge to the authority and finality of the divine revelation of the NT." *Know the Truth,* 218. Dispensationalists sometimes argue that the offices of apostle, prophet, and evangelist were given for the stage of church history prior to the fixing of the canon. Recent charismatic scholarship, however, has revived the idea of the presence of all these offices in the contemporary church. See, J. Rodman Williams, *Renewal Theology: Systematic Theology from a Charismatic Perspective,* three volumes (Grand Rapids: Zondervan, 1992), 3:164-77.

bers the vision of the community ideal, the design of God toward which the local fellowship directs its energies. This visionary role includes keeping alive the past by retelling the foundational community narrative—the story of Jesus. It includes as well, keeping the future always in view by embodying in word and symbol the glorious divine purpose that one day God will realize in his renewed creation.

The pastor is sent by the Lord into a specific congregation for service to that body for an indefinite period of time. Yet in addition to this primary role within the local congregation, the pastoral office generally carries implications for ministry beyond the local fellowship.

The wider ministry may be merely the informal authority of spiritual office within both the civil locale of residence and the ecclesiastical arena of sister churches and associational connections. In associational life all pastors exercise an informal authority merely because of their spiritual leadership role in a cooperating church.

The wider pastoral responsibility, however, may take the form of a more formal ministry. We entrust explicit leadership to persons serving as association officials, area ministers, chaplains, and teaching faculty at theological colleges. These associational roles are extensions of the pastoral office, for such persons continue to provide pastoral ministry for the sake of the churches of the associations they serve.

Ordination by the Community

Nearly all Christian traditions acknowledge the importance of setting aside leaders on behalf of the entire people of God. Most traditions likewise incorporate into church life some specific pattern as the means of designating community leaders. We generally speak of this process as ordination.

Despite widespread acceptance of the practice of ordination, there is a variety of understandings among Christian traditions about its meaning. One basic difference focuses on the question concerning the exact offices to which persons ought to be set apart by this special act. Is ordination best understood as the installation of certain persons to the offices of the universal church—bishop, presbyter, and deacon? Or does ordination refer to the setting apart of persons as pastors (and perhaps deacons) for local congregations?

As this question suggests, the disagreement concerning the proper subjects of ordination is an outworking of the more fundamental discussion of the nature of the church offices themselves. Despite disagreements concerning these matters, most Christian traditions agree that persons who enter pastoral ministry must be set apart for this task by Christ's church. Therefore, we focus our attention on pastoral ordination.

The Basis for the Practice of Pastoral Ordination

The ordination of persons for pastoral oversight has been a central practice of church life throughout the Christian era. Although centuries of church tradition support the act, we need to look behind ecclesiastical practice to inquire concerning the deeper foundation for ordination as an ongoing practice in the community.

The biblical foundation for ordination. The practice of publicly setting apart leaders for the people of God has its roots in the Bible. Both ancient Israel and the New Testament church selected leaders.

Already in the Old Testament the act of laying on hands, which is widely practiced today in conjunction with ordination, signified in certain cases the investment of a person with leadership responsibility and authority. Under the command of God, Moses laid hands on Joshua in the presence of the priest and the community (Num. 27:18-23). A parallel act among the ancient people was that of anointing with oil. This practice symbolized the entrance of a person into a leadership role. Three offices were especially associated with the rite of anointing—prophet, priest, and king.

As important as the practices of ancient Israel may be, Christians find the primary biblical foundation for the ongoing practice of ordination in the New Testament community. The use of this act in the early church was anticipated by Jesus' appointing twelve persons from among his disciples to play a special role in his mission (Mark 3:13-14). Later, the loss of Judas from the group precipitated the action of the disciples in the upper room which added Matthias to the ranks of the twelve (Acts 1:21-23).

In keeping with the precedence established in the calling of the twelve apostles, the early churches set apart persons to specific offices. The Jerusalem church commissioned the seven through the act of laying on of hands (Acts 6:6). Later, the Antioch congregation used the same act to set apart Barnabas and Paul for missionary service (13:1-3).

Perhaps the paradigmatic biblical example to which we can appeal for the practice of pastoral ordination is the experience of Timothy. This incident suggests that two elements—a divine personal call and the confirmation by a local fellowship—worked together in bringing Timothy into pastoral ministry. New Testament references suggest that the ordination of this young associate of Paul was precipitated by Timothy's own reception of a special divine call, mediated through a prophetic pronouncement about his future service (1 Tim. 1:18; see also the similar case of Paul and Barnabas recounted in Acts 13:2-3). The subsequent public act of ordination confirming the call consisted in the laying on of hands by the elders of a local congregation (1 Tim. 4:14).

Fitting the various statements together, we conclude that in the New Testament era ordination was related to the gift of the empowering Holy Spirit (1 Tim. 4:14; 2 Tim. 1:6,7). It marked a public commissioning of a servant of God (Acts 13:3; see also, Num. 27:18-23). Hence, as a public acknowledgment of the Spirit's action, the early church set apart persons whom the sovereign Spirit had selected and endowed for the fulfillment of special leadership tasks in service to the people of God.

The theological foundation for ordination. The biblical documents provide a historical precedence for ordination. For the specific *raison d'etre* for its use in the church, however, we must turn to the broader sweep of God's action in history. What we have outlined concerning the nature of the church in the divine program and the role of leaders in the church provides the sytematic theological context for our continuance of the practice.

(1) Ultimately, we continue to ordain because this act serves an important function within God's program in history. Our Creator-Redeemer God is at work bringing all creation to his intended goal, namely, the establishment of the glorious community of the triune God. As the Completer of the divine activity in the world, the Holy Spirit sovereignly calls persons to places of service in behalf of Christ and endows them for ministry within his program for human history.

One crucial area of service is leading God's people in their involvement in the divine program. Ordination is the act by which the community recognizes and confirms the presence of this call, as well as the Spirit's endowment, in a particular individual. Hence, ordination serves the Spirit's intent to provide gifted leadership for the ongoing work of God's people in service to his purposes in the world.

(2) Closely linked with the foundation in the divine program for history is the ecclesiological basis for ordination. This act is embedded in the life of the church.

As we have argued in chapter 17, the focal point of God's action in the present age lies with the church. We are to be the eschatological covenant community, the sign to the world of the coming consummation of God's program for creation, and the image of the triune God himself. Obedience to this mandate is the responsibility of the entire people. However, because we are a community, for the fulfillment of our task we are dependent on capable leadership. We need persons who can facilitate, expedite, and coordinate our individual contributions for the sake of our common task. Ordination finds its significance in this context. It is the act by means of which the community sets gifted persons in leadership for the effective working of the whole membership toward the completion of their common purpose.

From its beginning, the community has set apart by a public act persons whom the Lord of the church through his Spirit calls to provide pastoral leadership. Just as the Spirit calls persons into leadership service throughout the church age, so also he intends that the church continue to practice this public act.

The foundation of the act within its ecclesiological context means that the function of pastoral leadership is itself tied to the community. As the recent consensus statement *Baptism, Eucharist and Ministry* declared, "ordained ministry has no existence apart from the community."[30] Hence, the central task of the ordained person lies in the leadership role of the pastoral office. Again to cite the words of *Baptism, Eucharist and Ministry*, "The chief responsibility of the ordained ministry is to assemble and build up the body of Christ by proclaiming and teaching the Word of God, by celebrating the sacraments, and by guiding the life of the community in its worship, its mission and its caring ministry."[31]

Because it is grounded in the life of the community, ordination to pastoral ministry arises out of the priesthood of all believers. All members share the ministry of the community. To this end, all are called and ordained by the Holy Spirit to ministry. Baptism is the sign of our universal ordination, for this act signifies our new birth by the Spirit, our new identity as disciples of Jesus, and our new relationship to one another as participants in the one fellowship of Christ. Ordination to pastoral ministry, therefore, is embedded in the Spirit's universal calling of all to the ministry of the church and his universal endowment of all for this task.

Within this larger context of universal ministry, the Spirit calls certain persons to the pastoral office. Thereby he provides leaders for the work of the "holy priesthood" (1 Pet. 2:9) which is the whole community. In short, therefore, we ordain persons to pastoral leadership in order that they may serve on behalf of the people. As Daniel Migliore noted, "ordination is properly understood *missiologically rather than ontologically.*"[32] Ordination does not facilitate an ontological change in the clergy, elevating them above other Christians. Instead, the act commissions a person into leadership for the sake of the mission of the entire people of God.

---

30. *Baptism, Eucharist and Ministry*, 22.
31. Ibid.
32. Daniel L. Migliore, *Faith Seeking Understanding: An Introduction to Christian Theology* (Grand Rapids: Eerdmans, 1991), 228.

The Significance of Ordination

The practice of ordination in the church carries the precedence of the ancient communities of faith. It is also embedded in the drama of God's saving activity and in the church as the focus of that activity in the present age. Understood in this context, the practice carries great significance.

The meaning of the act. To enter into pastoral ministry a person must meet two conditions: a personal call from the Lord of the church through his Spirit and the confirmation of that call by the faith community.[33] Ordination is connected with the second condition. It is, as Luther suggested, an ecclesiastical ceremony through which the community ratifies the call and election of the minister.[34] As a confirmatory act, ordination is significant for the person ordained, for the ordaining community, and for the wider society.

(1) Ordination is a significant event for the new church leader. It is a public confirmation by the faith community that the call to pastoral ministry which the ordinand has personally sensed is indeed a call from the Lord of the church.

The importance of such a confirmation arises out of the interdependency of the individual believer and the community. The Lord does give direction to his disciples individually. Nevertheless, the confirmation and consensus of the body of believers assists individuals in determining the extent to which they have correctly perceived the moving of the Spirit.

Further, ordination is the act whereby the community publicly recognizes that the Holy Spirit has invested the ordinand with certain gifts for ministry leadership.[35]

(2) Ordination is likewise significant for the church itself. In this sense, the practice is a commissioning. By means of this act the community places a person into a significant area of service within its life and ministry. Inherent in the commissioning is the commitment by

---

33. This Reformed and free church emphasis has gained wide recognition among the various church traditions. See, for example, *Baptism, Eucharist and Ministry*, 31. See also Migliore, *Faith Seeking Understanding*, 227.
34. For this interpretation of Luther, see Avis, *The Church in the Theology of the Reformers*, 105.
35. *Baptism, Eucharist and Ministry*, 30.

both the church and the ordinand to a new relationship, namely, that of leader and coworkers.

(3) Ordination is finally a public act in the widest sense of the term, for it is directed toward the world. Through ordination, the community declares that the ordinand is now installed into a pastoral position. As a leader of the church, this person will engage in ministry beyond its confines. The ordained leader will minister in and to the world.

Although not the case in the first century, our society recognizes clergy status. The pastoral office carries acknowledgment not only in the ecclesiastical, but also in the civil sphere. In ordination, therefore, the church bears public witness that it has entrusted the ordinand with the pastoral office. Therefore this person should be acknowledged as such in whatever ways society relates to clergy.

The ordaining body. Ordination is the act whereby the community publicly declares that the ordinand is gifted, commissioned, and installed in pastoral ministry. Who actually sets a person in this leadership role?

At the heart of any truly Christian theology of ordination is the recognition that ultimately the Lord of the church ordains leaders for his people. This recognition arises out of the nature of the general work of the Master in the lives of his disciples. Through his Spirit, Christ continues to call his servants to fulfill a vocation in his service, to set them in the positions he desires, and to endow them—as the one who baptizes with the Spirit—for the fulfillment of their vocation. Within this action of the Lord in the lives of all lies his work in the case of those he designates for pastoral leadership.

Ordination is the Lord's prerogative. Yet the question still remains as to identity of the earthly vehicle for the accomplishment of his will. We have already argued that Christ's authority functions immediately in the local congregation. It follows that ordination is in the final analysis a prerogative of the visible fellowship. As the local community ordains persons for pastoral ministry, they serve as the channel for Christ's ordaining through his Spirit. This focus is symbolized by the participation of the congregational leaders in the central rite of the event, the laying on of hands.

Ordination, however, is not directed solely toward leadership in the local congregation. Rather, by this act a person is set aside for a ministry for the entire church. Consequently, in ordaining pastoral leaders a local congregation does not act merely on its own authority and for itself, but on behalf of the whole community of Christ. The participation in the laying on of hands by all ordained persons present symbolizes that the act of ordination extends to the entire church and that the ordained function overflows the local church boundary. Because of the participation of the whole church in the act of the local fellowship, sister congregations acknowledge the properly conducted ordination administered by another church.

The ordaining event. An ordination service may consist of many different elements, including music, a sermon, even perhaps the Lord's Supper. The focal point of the event, however, lies elsewhere. The ordaining act consists primarily in a prayer coupled with a symbolic act, the laying on of hands.

At the heart of the ordaining event is the prayer of the community. Foundational to the prayer is the corporate acknowledgment of the Spirit's sovereignty in calling persons to ministry. This recognition, in turn, leads the community to thank God for his ongoing provision of leadership for his people represented by the calling of the ordinand. The focus of the prayer is an invoking of the Spirit's presence in the ministry of the new leader and through that ministry in the life of the faith community itself. The community therefore intercedes for the ordinand, petitioning God that the new leader be empowered by the Spirit for the new relationship now being established between the leader and the people of God. By interceding for its leaders, of course, the community likewise petitions for its own well-being as a people with a mandate.

Coupled with the prayer is a symbolic act, which symbolizes the granting of the request by the Lord who endows with the Spirit. In keeping with its biblical use, the laying on of hands symbolizes the coming of the Spirit on the ordinand as the empowerment for the task of pastoral leadership.

Through the act of ordination, the community commissions a person for pastoral ministry. Contrary to the emphasis on the mediation of divine grace which characterized the understanding in the Middle Ages, many Christian traditions today acknowledge that the primary function of the ordained person is that of servant leadership.[36] Through ordination, therefore, a person is set apart for service.

In fulfilling a leadership role in the church, the ordained person seeks to be a servant to the people. Indeed, the fundamental task of pastoral leaders is that of leading the whole people of God in service (Eph. 4:11-13). Consequently, rather than being set in a position of dominance over the people, the ordained person stands with them as together they seek to be obedient to the Lord of the church. The consensus document put the point well: "ordained ministers must not be autocrats or impersonal functionaries." Rather they are to "manifest and exercise the authority of Christ in the way Christ himself revealed God's authority to the world, by committing their life to the community."[37]

All church leaders must keep in mind that service is the goal and intent of each office in the community. But in this, pastors are to lead the way. They are to be "examples to the flock" (1 Pet. 5:3) "in speech, in life, in love, in faith and in purity" (1 Tim. 4:12). In short, they are to be models to the congregation of Christlike character and servanthood. As those chosen by the Spirit and endowed with special responsibilities, these persons have been entrusted with leadership authority. Their positions, however, do not entail license to promote selfish or even personal goals. Rather they are to enter into office with all humility and with the intent of seeking the good of the whole.

Ordained persons can find encouragement in the New Testament for their task of acting as servant leaders. Peter, for example, appealed to elders to be willing and eager servants, who are not greedy and do not "lord it over" those entrusted to them (1 Pet. 5:1-3). Above all, the New Testament sets before us the example of Christ. He declared that those who would lead his people must be humble

---

36. For a recent example, see Migliore, *Faith Seeking Understanding*, 229.
37. *Baptism, Eucharist and Ministry*, 23.

servants (Mark 10:42-43). And he illustrated his teaching with his own example of humble service on our behalf (2 Cor. 8:9; Phil. 2:6-8).

The Christlike spirit of humble service is to predominate at all levels of governmental deliberation as the people of God seek consensus concerning the Lord's will for his church.

Church governmental structure is not an end in itself. Rather, it is a means whereby the community organizes itself for the fulfillment of the corporate mandate. Through office structures the Holy Spirit seeks to provide capable leadership for the sake of the ministry of the whole people. Each congregation, as well as associations of churches, ought to develop structures which best meet their own needs. Yet the principles practiced by the early communities have enduring value and therefore are worthy of emulation.

Regardless what organizational model we utilize, we must keep uppermost in our minds that the goal of church government is to facilitate the whole people of God in discerning and discharging the Lord's will. Only as we obey Christ can we indeed be the eschatological covenant community God intends us to be. Our goal is to embody and advance the program of God until our Lord returns. Hence, the church exists for the sake of eternity.

Because the goal of the church transcends the present, our systematic theology remains incomplete. Lying yet before us is the task of articulating the wider context in which our ecclesiology is set. To accomplish this, we now turn our attention to the final theological focus, eschatology.

Part 6
Eschatology
The Doctrine of Last Things

In its classical form, the systematic treatment of Christian theology concludes with eschatology or the doctrine of last things. In a sense the nomenclature "last things" is inappropriate. We tend to interpret it in either a temporal or a logical sense. Thus, "last" means what comes last in the historical sequence—what will be our experience only at the end of history. Or "last" means what comes at the end of the sequence of topics and therefore may be of least importance. In this manner, thinkers often relegate eschatology to the fringes of theological reflection.

Contrary to either of these interpretations, however, we must understand "last" in the older sense depicted by the Greek term *telos* ("goal"). In the doctrine of last things we speak about God's goal or purpose for his activity in the lives of individuals, in human history, and in creation. We devote this final section of our systematic theology to reflection on the last things understood in this manner. We articulate the divine intention that lies behind God's actions.

Our treatment of eschatology comes in four chapters. We look first at God's intention for us as individuals (chapter 21). This dimension is often labeled "personal eschatology." Here our quest is to know what lies beyond death. Does death draw our existence to a meaningless, or even sinister close? To this question, the Christian faith responds by declaring that God's plan is that we overcome death through the resurrection.

Next we turn to "corporate eschatology" (chapter 22), the articulation of God's intention for humankind as a whole and for human history. Does history end in a meaningless catastrophe? Or is our corporate story going somewhere? In response, we appeal to the biblical understanding of the directedness of history. God is directing our human story toward the fulfillment of his design. This truth is evident above all in the hope of the eschatological return of Christ as the climax of history.

The third dimension of "last things" is God's intention for the entire cosmos (chapter 23). In the cosmic aspect of eschatology we look to the eternity that lies beyond history. God is directing all creation toward his final goal, namely, the eternal community in the new heaven and the new earth.

Finally, we bring the discussion to a close by discussing the intent of eschatology (chapter 24). By so doing, we likewise draw together the entire volume, setting forth the goal of the systematic theology we have outlined throughout the treatise.

21

The Consummation of Personal Existence

For I am convinced that neither death nor life ... neither the present nor the future ... will be able to separate us from the love of God that is in Christ Jesus our Lord. (Rom. 8:38-39)

Outline

Eschatology is the exposition of the goal toward which the triune God is bringing his creation. Within the more general topic lies the specific focus which we call "personal eschatology." This aspect treats the consummation of God's plan as it concerns us as individuals. The focus of personal eschatology, therefore, is the crucial question concerning the meaning of life: Is personal existence ultimately meaningless? Or does God have a purpose for our individual human lives? Is there a goal which he will realize in us and thereby bring our existence to its culmination?

Our discussion naturally begins with the phenomenon of death. From the human perspective, this event marks the end of personal life. However, the good news of the gospel is that our existence does not necessarily end in death. For this reason, after raising the question of death's significance, we explore the theological assertion that our lives have an actual culmination beyond death, specifically in what the Bible calls "resurrection." With this hope in view, we then conclude our exploration by inquiring about the hope we have in the face of death (the intermediate state).

The Significance of Death

Death is a universal human phenomenon: All people die. Personal eschatology is the reflection on faith's response to the seeming finality of death. En route to articulating our hope beyond death, we must look more closely at this phenomenon, placing it in a theological context.

The Problem of Death

In spite of—or even because of—the universality of this experience, death is a great mystery, perhaps the greatest mystery of human existence. As a mystery, death is problematic to humans.

The problem of definition. One problem we encounter when we reflect on death is the biological phenomenon itself. Despite great advances in medical science, we have not been able to determine exactly what death is. This difficulty emerges in attempts to devise a comprehensive means of ascertaining when death occurs.

The traditional understanding of death equated the extinction of life with the cessation of the two main "vital signs," breathing and heartbeat. Although these criteria remain useful in the majority of situations, the traditional view is not sufficiently sophisticated to function as an all-encompassing definition. A significant minority of comatose patients would be deemed dead by the older standard, for their breathing is not spontaneous. Yet many of them will regain consciousness.[1]

The shortcomings of the older view have led in recent years to a focus on brain activity as the central indication of life and death. In 1968 a Harvard Medical School committee was among the first to articulate such a definition, which it offered as an alternative in cases of comatose patients. It suggested that a person be declared dead if the following criteria are met: unreceptive and unresponsive (that is, in a state of irreversible coma); lack of movement or breathing when the mechanical respirator is turned off; no demonstration of reflexes; a flat electroencephalogram for at least twenty-four hours, indicating no electrical brain activity (assuming that the person has not been subjected to hypothermia or central nervous system depressants).[2]

In the wake of widespread acceptance of the Harvard Committee definition, a United States government commission proposed in 1981 the Uniform Determination of Death Act. It brings the traditional view together with the newer focus on the brain. According to

---

1. William E. Phipps, *Death: Confronting the Reality* (Atlanta: John Knox, 1987), 14.

2. As reported in Willard Gaylan, "Harvesting the Dead," reprinted in *Moral Issues and Christian Response*, ed. Paul T. Jersild and Dale A. Johnson, second edition (New York: Holt, Rinehart and Winston, 1976), 352.

this model law, a person is dead who has sustained either "irreversible cessation of circulatory and respiratory functions" or "irreversible cessation of all functions of the entire brain, including the brain stem."[3]

Although helpful, the newer definitions have not solved all the problems in defining death. The brain stem, which regulates breathing and blood circulation, may give off sporadic EEG signals long after the cerebrum, the seat of memory and consciousness, ceases to function. Consequently, many persons who will never recover cognitive functions, that is, who are in a permanent vegetative state, cannot be declared dead and are maintained on artificial support systems. This situation has led some thinkers to call for a narrowing of the definition of death to the irreversible cessation of spontaneous cerebral functions.[4]

Medical science has made progress in the attempt to determine what constitutes physical death. Yet no one has been able to penetrate completely the mystery. Death—even in its biological dimension—remains an enigma.

Death and the meaning of life. The death of a human being is more than the cessation of the functioning of a biological organism. It is the end of a personal life. As Helmut Thielicke noted, "Human death transcends biological death…to the same degree that man as a creature of personhood transcends his own quality as a biological being, as a mammal."[5] As a consequence, more problematic than the determination of an all-encompassing definition of the physical phenomenon is the personal aspect of death.

The discussion of death brings us to a dimension of the difference between humans and other earthly life forms. We die not only as creatures, but also as persons. Therefore, all attempts to define bio-

---

3. President's Commission for the Study of Ethical Problems in Medicine and Biomedical and Behavioral Research, *Defining Death: A Report on the Medical, Legal, and Ethical Issues in the Determination of Death* (Washington, D. C.: Government Printing Office, 1980), 73, as cited in Phipps, *Death*, 15.

4. E.g., Robert Veatch, *Death, Dying, and the Biological Revolution* (New Haven: Yale University Press, 1976), 76.

5. Helmut Thielicke, *Death and Life*, trans. Edward H. Schroeder (Philadelphia: Fortress, 1970), 186.

logical death will ultimately fail to put us in touch with the full significance of this event.

Although we share mortality with all living things, in one aspect our experience of death differs from that of other creatures. In contrast to plants and animals, humans are conscious of their mortality and can reflect on it. Not only are we aware of death as a general fact of existence, throughout our lives we carry the knowledge that we will die, that we are en route to the day when we too will share this fate. Humans encounter what Max Scheler called "the experience of life's directedness toward death."[6] Because we can contemplate our own death, its shadow darkens our path even as we live.

Our ability to reflect on our own death brings to light the deeper dimension of this phenomenon. Not only is death the cessation of biological functioning, it marks the end of a personal life. In this way, death calls personal existence into question. As the termination of a person's life, death speaks as it were the final word. Death, so it seems, undermines all our attempts to find meaning for our own lives. In the end, we all die. Whatever significance we may have constructed for life is abruptly breached. As the psalmist declared, "What man can live and not see death, or save himself from the power of the grave?" (Ps. 89:48).

The dark shadow that death casts across personal life suggests that life is a meaningless absurdity. This was the conclusion of the Preacher: "All share a common destiny—the righteous and the wicked, the good and the bad, the clean and the unclean, those who offer sacrifices and those who do not" (Eccl. 9:2). They all "join the dead" (v.3).

In death, therefore, we face an enigma more problematic than the cessation of the functioning of a biological organism. We are confronted with a crisis of meaning produced by our inevitable death. As Ernest Becker poignantly observed, "The irony of man's condition is that the deepest need is to be free of the anxiety of death and an-

---

6. Max Scheler, "Tod und Fortleben," *Schriften aus dem Nachlass* (Berne, Switzerland, 1957), 1:30, as cited in Eberhart Juengel, *Death: The Riddle and the Mystery*, trans. Iain and Ute Nicol (Philadelphia: Westminster, 1974), 14.

nihilation; but it is life itself which awakens it, and so we must shrink from being fully alive."[7]

Does our Christian faith commitment shed light on the phenomenon of death? Does death carry any genuine significance, or is it indeed the ultimate absurdity?

The Biblical Trajectory

We begin our search for the significance of death with the biblical documents. In the Scriptures we discover a trajectory of thought concerning death which climaxes in the discovery that death is ultimately understandable only in the light of God's purposes as revealed in Jesus Christ.

The Old Testament: death as ambiguous. As the ancient Hebrews reflected on death, they found it to be a two-sided or ambiguous phenomenon. It is the natural end to life, as well as an enemy. Death's ambiguity emerges in stark contrast to the strong Old Testament affirmation of life.

The Hebrews placed great value on human life. They viewed a long, full life with an assured posterity as among God's best gifts to his people (Ps. 128). Life is of such value because it is connected with God. According to the Old Testament, God is the living one, the fountain of life. He is also the ruler over life, the one who gives life and takes it away (1 Sam. 2:6; Job 1:21). The ancient people did not perceive God's rulership over life only in each human being (Job 34:14-15), but also in nature as a whole (Ps. 104:27-30). The connection between life and God carried a practical implication: Obedience to God's word is the key to enjoying life, for obedience enhances personal living (Deut. 5:16; Prov. 3:1-2; 9:11; Isa. 55:3).

In contrast to this strong affirmation of life, the Hebrews shared with other cultures an ambiguous attitude toward death. On the one hand, they understood death as the inevitable result of the aging process. As such, like life itself, it is from God (1 Sam. 3:6). Therefore, to die "old and full of years" is one of the highest blessings God could bestow upon the righteous person. On the other hand, the an-

---

7. Ernest Becker, *The Denial of Death* (New York: Free Press, 1973), 66.

cients also viewed death negatively. The Old Testament spoke of it as an evil, an alien power over which humans have no control (2 Sam. 22:6; Ps. 89:48).

The Hebrews also viewed the situation of the dead as ambiguous. Some Old Testament texts declared their fate in nonspeculative, somewhat positive terms. The one who dies is simply "gathered to his fathers" (Gen. 49:33). The biblical authors commonly used the word *Sheol* to refer to the place of the dead. References to Sheol, however, heighten the ambiguity that surrounds the dead. Sometimes *Sheol* is quite neutral in tone, for it connotes "the grave" as the place which awaits all persons (Gen. 37:35). Elsewhere it takes on more sinister dimensions (Hos. 13:14). This more negative aspect of the grave led the Old Testament saints to raise the crucial question of personal existence beyond death: "If a man dies, will he live again?" (Job 14:14).

Rather than an ascent to God, as in strands of ancient Greek thought, the Hebrews viewed *Sheol* as a place of descent. The Old Testament authors sometimes used spatial imagery to depict it. The dead are in the depths, in contrast to the heights of heaven (Job 11:8). Persons "go down" into *Sheol* (Job 21:13; Ps. 55:15; Prov. 15:24; Ezek. 31:15-17). Consequently, it is a pit (Isa. 14:15; Ezek. 31:14), perhaps located beneath the earth (Ps. 63:9; Ezek. 32:18). Despite the use of spatial imagery, the Hebrews may actually have conceived of *Sheol* as more of a state than an actual place.[8]

Although at times *Sheol* was depicted in neutral terms, the Old Testament writers more generally suggested that the experience is negative. It means separation from the presence of God. The dead cannot praise Yahweh (Ps. 6:5). Rather, they "go down to silence" (115:17). When musing on his impending death, Hezekiah declared that to die means never again to see God in the land of the living (Isa. 38:10-11). Generally, the Old Testament writers spoke of *Sheol* as a permanent, unalterable fate (Job 7:9). The dead cannot hope in God's faithfulness (Isa. 38:18).

Despite the negative nature of the situation of the dead, a hope in the face of *Sheol* came to expression in the Old Testament. Perhaps

---

8. George Eldon Ladd, *The Last Things* (Grand Rapids: Eerdmans, 1978), 32.

it is ultimately only the place for the unrighteous, not the righteous. The Psalmist was confident that the wicked "return to the grave," whereas the hope of the afflicted will never perish (Ps. 9:17-18). Elsewhere he petitioned God that he not be put to shame, because he cried out to God. The wicked, in contrast, deserve to be shamed and to lie silent in *Sheol* (31:17), and those who trust in themselves are destined for *Sheol* (49:13-14).

The Old Testament community came to the conclusion that the forces of death and *Sheol* may not speak the last word. On the contrary, God had shown to his people the path to life by means of which they might avoid this fate (Ps. 16:8-11; Prov. 15:24). Consequently, the righteous psalmist could anticipate future bliss: "You guide me with your counsel and afterward you will take me into glory" (Ps. 73:24).

The saints knew yet a greater source of hope, however—God himself. *Sheol* is not beyond God's cognition (139:8). Therefore, God can save the righteous from its power and bring them into his own presence. The psalmist expressed this hope: "God will redeem my soul from the grave, he will surely take me to himself" (49:15; see also 86:13). But perhaps the grandest expression of hope came in Hosea. God interrupted his recounting of Israel's history of unfaithfulness to declare, "I will ransom them from the power of the grave [*Sheol*]; I will redeem them from death. Where, O death, are your plagues? Where, O grave, is your destruction?" (Hos. 13:14).

The Old Testament writers never separated the hope for eventual salvation beyond the grave from bodily existence. Hebrew anthropology could not envision human life in any other form, including existence in some sort of disembodied state. This was pronounced in Elijah's bodily ascension into heaven, who as God's chosen, righteous prophet escaped *Sheol* entirely (2 Kings 2:11). Hence, Job spoke for the entire tradition when he affirmed: "I know that my Redeemer lives, and that in the end he will stand upon the earth. And after my skin has been destroyed, yet in my flesh I will see God; I myself will see him with my own eyes—I, and not another. How my heart yearns within me!" (Job 19:25-27).

During the exile, the hope for divine salvation for the righteous led to the expectation of an eschatological resurrection. The angelic messenger informed Daniel about this great future event: "Multitudes...will awake: some to everlasting life, others to shame and everlasting contempt" (Dan. 12:2). But concerning the situation of dead who await that great day, Daniel gained no information, only that they now "sleep in the dust of the earth."

The New Testament: hope in the face of death. The New Testament witnesses to an event that brought a new perspective from which to consider the significance of death: God's power has raised Jesus of Nazareth from the dead.

For the New Testament authors, viewing death in the light of Jesus' resurrection eliminated all ambiguity. The negative appraisal that we discovered in the Old Testament was consistently applied in the New. The author of Hebrews, for example, depicted death as a sinister force lying under the power of Satan and striking fear in human hearts (Heb. 2:14). Jesus himself knew death was an enemy. In the Garden of Gethsemene he expressed his desire for companionship, and on the cross cried out in godforsakenness (Mark 14:32-36; Heb. 5:7; Mark 15:37).

The negative appraisal of death was especially pronounced in Paul. The apostle made a direct connection between death and sin. Death entered the world through human sin (Rom 5:12), and it continues to be sin's outworking (6:23). In fact, sin and death form a law at work in us, an alien power to which we are slaves (7:21-25; 8:2; see also 7:5; James 1:15). Paul also specified the link between the two. Death is the vehicle through which sin reigns (Rom. 5:21), while sin gives death its sting (1 Cor. 15:56).

New Testament writers developed the Old Testament theme of the alien nature of death but clarified and enlarged the ancient hope. *Sheol* (or Hades, its Greek counterpart) does not speak the last word, for God is greater than the power of death. The documents speak with one voice in declaring that despite death's power, Christ our Savior "has destroyed death and has brought life and Immortality to light through the gospel" (2 Tim. 1:10). The pathway to life known to the Old Testament saints has been revealed in Jesus. As a consequence, if we believe in the one who sent him (John 5:24) and keep his word (John 8:51), we have already passed from death to life (1 John 3:14) and will not see death. For believers who are alive at the end of history, this spiritual truth will also be physically experienced. They will escape biological death, for they will be raptured to meet their returning Lord in the air (1 Thess. 4:13-17; see also John 21:22-23).

Eternal life is our present possession. Nevertheless, the final victory over death lies in the future. Death remains our last enemy (1 Cor. 15:26). It will only be overcome when our mortal bodies are clothed with immortality (vv.54-55). Then God himself will banish death from our experience (Rev. 20:14; 21:4,8).

Jesus' resurrection introduced one additional factor into the New Testament understanding of death. It relativized that experience. The biblical authors not only expressed hope beyond death, but also in the face of death. Although it remains an enemy, death is now a conquered foe. For this reason the prospect of dying and the thought of our own death no longer hold terror for us. The New Testament declares that death does not leave believers in a state of separation from God's love (Rom. 8:34-39). We are not abandoned in death, but are surrounded by the nearness and love of God. Hence, "to depart" means to be "with Christ" (Phil. 1:23).

Relativized in this manner, death is no longer the greatest possible tragedy. On the contrary, it can even become a special way of sacrifice. For those who are killed because of their testimony to Christ, death is the means of sharing and recapitulating the great sacrifice of Christ (2 Tim. 4:6; Phil. 2:17; Rev. 6:9).

In short, the good news of the New Testament is the assertion that one man has already triumphed over death. One day this triumph will be complete, and death itself will be eliminated from human affairs. Consequently, death no longer is ambiguous. It is a sinister foe connected to sin and therefore the greatest enemy of humankind. Yet this enemy is in principle a defeated foe. As a result, rather than separating us from God's love, death can become a way of glorifying Christ as we give testimony even in death to the grace God has shown us in Jesus.

The Theological Significance of Death

These biblical themes provide the context in which we can understand the significance of death. To see this phenomenon correctly, we must view it in the light of God's ultimate intention for his creation as revealed in Jesus Christ.

Death and the biological realm. Reflection on the significance of death confronts us immediately with the apparent naturalness of the phenomenon. Death is universally present throughout the earthly biosphere. Does it therefore follow that death is a natural aspect of the biological realm? Is death simply the natural end to earthly existence?

The question of the naturalness of death can never be adequately answered by the sciences. Through biological inquiry we can substantiate *that* all creatures are mortal. However, we can never reach a conclusion as to whether all creatures are *naturally* mortal, if the term "natural" refers not only to what is, but also to what ought to be. The introduction of considerations of "ought" moves us into the realm of intention—ultimately, the intention of the Creator. Hence, raising the question of ought demands that we see the matter from the theological—specifically eschatological—perspective.

Viewed theologically—from the vantage point of God's eschatological goal—we conclude that death is unnatural. It is contrary to God's purpose for his creation. John's vision of the eschatological renewal revealed God's intention. He saw that " death and Hades were thrown into the lake of fire" (Rev. 20:14). By means of this imagery the inspired seer anticipated the eventual banishing of death from the new creation (21:4). Death can have no place in the new order because God himself will dwell with his people (21:3), and his presence means the reign of life. Ultimately death is unnatural because it is contrary to our divinely-given destiny, God's purpose that we enjoy community with him.

Death as loss of community. Our foundation for concluding that death is unnatural suggests an appositional relationship between death and community. Rather than being a natural dimension of creation, Paul declares that death is the product, consequence, and instrument of sin. In chapter 8, we spoke of sin as failure, specifically, failure of community. We must now explore this connection between death, sin, and community.

In the Bible, death is not merely the end of a biological organism, but the awful outworking of our human destruction of God's intention. According to the Bible, the opposite of death is not merely physical life or biological functioning, but eternal life. It is existence in the presence of, and in accordance with the will of God.[9] Sin is the failure to live according to this divine intention. As a result, Sin leads to death, understood not merely as loss of physical life, but more importantly as separation from God.

God's ultimate goal for his creation is community, that we enjoy eternal fellowship with him, one another, and our environment. Sin, in turn, is the destruction of this purpose. Death's connection to sin means that death is also antithetical to community. The condition that sin produces is eternal loss of fellowship. Death is the breach in community with God, which entails as well a breach in fellowship with others and with the physical environment, leading to biological death.

The ancient Hebrews perceived death's opposition to community. The Old Testament writers declared that *Sheol* cuts a person off from fellowship with God. Those in *Sheol* cannot praise God or hope in him.

We must take this observation a step farther. Insofar as it means the loss of community, death entails isolation. Death means the loss of relationship; hence, it is the epitome and final expression of the tendency toward radical individualism. Biological death functions as a vivid sign of this dimension of death. Even though a person may die surrounded by a crowd of people, in the end death is an individual matter. Each human goes through death totally alone. No one can experience death for someone else, and no one can travel through death accompanied by another.

---

9. See, for example, Rudolf Bultmann, "zoe," in the *Theological Dictionary of the New Testament*, ed. Gerhard Kittel, trans. Geoffrey W. Bromiley (Grand Rapids: Eerdmans, 1964): 2:863-64. See also, Hans-Joachim Ritz, "bios," in the *Exegetical Dictionary of the New Testament*, ed. Horst Balz and Gerhard Schneider, English translation (Grand Rapids: Eerdmans, 1990), 1:219, and Luise Schottroff, "zoe, in EDNT, 2:105-106.

The experience of dying alone points to a deeper aspect of the individualizing nature of death. To be a person means to have a history or an identity narrative. As we noted earlier, a personal narrative is never merely the story of an isolated individual. On the contrary, because our narratives are always embedded in the story of a people or world in which we participate, an isolated individual (were such a situation possible) would have no story.

Marking as it does an abrupt end to one's personal story, death inaugurates just such a situation. It means that we now lack an ongoing narrative. This breach in our story does not arises only because the dead are cut off from their own lives, but also because they are separated from the living community in which our personal narratives are embedded. This separation is radical, for death calls into question whatever meaning we sought to devise in life, thereby casting the shadow of meaninglessness over our entire previous existence. Therefore, death constitutes a breach of community, a fall into isolation, a loss of identity.

Death's loss of ultimacy. Death remains with us until the eschatological renewal. Even believers must pass through death with its potential for destroying meaning and personal identity. Yet Jesus' revelation of the divine purpose for us has facilitated a fundamental change in our understanding of death. While not shedding its awfulness as "the last enemy," death is no longer the ultimate foe it once was. It has lost its ultimacy; it does not speak the last word and thereby negate our existence.

Death's loss of ultimacy is observable in the new manner in which we appraise its potential. While admitting that this foe retains great power, we view death as ultimately impotent. Because God has given us eternal life, death has lost its terror. It cannot fulfil its threat to destroy community with God for all eternity. Instead, we look beyond death to an eternal future in God's presence. We are no longer disquieted by the isolation that death effects. Because we are destined for fellowship with God, we know that death no longer marks the end of our existence. Rather than listening to death's siren call, therefore, we entrust ourselves to God's promise which is already present within us through the indwelling Spirit.

Because we can look beyond death to the eternal community God promises us, we are confident even in the face of death. Death is no longer the isolating, solitary experience it once was. On the contrary, Jesus has tasted death for us, and as a consequence we do not die alone. Even in death we enjoy community, for we are surrounded by God's love in Christ.

Having lost its ultimacy, death now can carry positive significance. Divested of its sting, the last enemy of humankind now functions as a metaphor of the transformation that occurs through conversion, symbolizing our forsaking of the old estranged manner of living. Our old foe, which as the end of personal existence once cast the shadow of meaninglessness over life, now marks the completion of our earthly vocation in service to God (2 Tim 4:7). The sinister power which formerly led to the shadowy realm of *Sheol* can even become a source of blessing. Death is the entrance into rest, even release from the cares and sufferings of life. As the angel declared in John's vision, "Blessed are the dead who die in the Lord from now on." To which the Spirit replied, "Yes,...they will rest from their labor, for their deeds will follow them" (Rev. 14:13).

For the martyrs, the experience that meant descent into the abode from where no one could ever hope to praise God, has become a vehicle through which to offer the sacrifice of their very life in praise to the one who suffered for us all. No wonder Paul could conclude that for him to die would be "gain" (Phil. 1:21). Through his death as a martyr he would pour out his life as a drink offering to God (2 Tim. 4:6).

Overcoming Death in the Resurrection

We declare that God's purpose for creation is life—participation in God's eternal community. As the bearer of that life, Jesus rendered death a defeated foe. We will one day fully overcome death's threat to our personal existence as God brings us into complete fellowship with himself, one another, and all creation.

This fundamental Christian assertion raises the question of means: In what manner do we finally overcome death? What event will inaugurate our eternal participation in community? The answer of the

Christian message is capsulized by the metaphorical word *resurrection*. We will overcome death on the great eschatological day when we join Christ in the experience of resurrection.

Our hope is that we will participate in the eschatological renewal God has planned for his creation. Because our participation is facilitated by nothing short of the resurrection, this occurrence marks the culmination of personal existence. Our affirmation, however, requires further elaboration. We begin by exploring the nature of the life that marks the culmination of our existence. Then we view the actual event which mediates that culmination.

The Nature of Culminated Personal Life

The Christian message declares that ultimately personal life culminates in the resurrection. This expectation, however, is not universally held today. We must delineate the Christian hope of resurrection in the context of other eschatological visions.

Contemporary visions of the culmination of life. The ascendancy of the natural sciences and the scientific method has led many people in the modern era to conclude that there is no culmination to personal life; our existence ends in death. We have already argued against this position on the basis of God's intention that we enjoy eternal community. However, we have not yet fully described the community that lies beyond death. The nature of our divinely given destiny remains a point of controversy today.

(1) One prominent view understands the community beyond the grave as union with the divine reality. Advocates of this position, which is often called *monism*, generally understand God in somewhat impersonal terms. Union with the Absolute, therefore, entails the dissolution of human personal distinctions as well as the distinction between God and creatures.

Although typical of Eastern religions, monism, the expectation of the melding of personal life into the divine, is also present in certain strands of contemporary Christian teaching. Process theology, for example, has no place for an actual personal existence beyond this life. Rather, our lives continue only in that they have become aspects of the experience of God. By means of the idea of prehension ("a feeling of that which is other than the self"[10]), process thinkers imagine an eternity in which the multiplicity of human subjectivities achieve a unity (which is God).[11]

Feminist theologian Rosemary Radford Ruether articulated an even more obviously monistic vision. She saw death as "the final relinquishment of individuated ego into the great matrix of being." For her, the Absolute is a "great collective personhood...in which our achievements and failures are gathered up, assimilated into the fabric of being, and carried forward into new possibilities."[12]

The anticipation of a postmortem union with the divine does not give sufficient place to personal life. Monistic visions blur all personal distinctions, for in the end they allow for no eternal differentiations not only among humans but also between God and creatures. Thereby they undermine the ultimate personal character of God and the personal nature of human life.

In losing personhood, monism also destroys community. By its very nature, community entails fellowship among persons. This is evident already in the divine life, which is the community of the trinitarian persons. Failing to give sufficient place to personal life, monism is unable to provide a valid understanding of the community that forms the consummation of that life.

(2) As a step beyond monism, reincarnation seeks to give more serious attention to personal life. At death we do not immediately blend into the divine, for the person reemerges in a new earthly form. The chain of rebirths can continue indefinitely as the soul either progresses or regresses from one earthly life to the next.

Strictly speaking *reincarnation* fails to function as an eschatological vision. If a series of rebirths is never-ending, there is no culmination of the personal life (only the eternal cycle of rebirth—death—rebirth), and consequently life is ultimately meaningless. If however the cycle of death and rebirth does eventually end (such as with a loss of personal identity in the divine Absolute) reincarnation is merely the means to a basically monistic culmination.

---

10. Marjorie Hewitt Suchocki, *God—Christ—Church* (New York: Crossroad, 1984), 179.
11. Ibid., 190.
12. Rosemary Radford Ruether, *Sexism and God-talk* (Boston: Beacon, 1983), 258.

Whether or not it is understood in monist terms, reincarnation is beset with difficulties. The teaching does not take seriously earthly, bodily existence. It assumes that the real person is the nonmaterial soul which migrates from body to body. Therefore, the body does not participate in our essence, but is merely the vehicle through which the soul functions temporarily. Likewise, this teaching does not take seriously individual embodied existence as constituting personal identity. Reincarnation denies that it is the individual embodied life that comes to culmination in the eschatological community. Rather, any specific life—any one identity narrative—is but a stage in the development of the soul which transcends it. By denying the eternal significance of individual life, reincarnation loses the culmination of personal life in community.

(3) In contrast to reincarnation, a third vision, the *immortality of the soul*, seeks to give serious attention to individual human existence. According to this view, personal life culminates when at death the soul discards the body that housed it and thereby attains its eternal blessedness. The ancient Greek philosophers were imbued with this vision. Perhaps the classic statement is Plato's description of Socrates' death in the *Phaedo*. His thesis is that death merely completes the liberation begun through philosophical reflection. It frees the soul from the contaminating imperfections of the body so that it might penetrate the world of the eternal ideas to which it belongs.[13]

The idea of the soul's immortality has been highly influential throughout Christian history. Certain Christian thinkers assert that at death the individual soul enters into the fullness of eternity, however that fullness is to be understood.

Despite its influence, the doctrine is problematic. It suggests that immortality is somehow intrinsic to the soul, rather than being God's gift. Further, this teaching suggests that it is the body, not death, that must be overcome.[14] In so doing it postulates that the seat

---

13. Plato, *Phaedo*, 64a-67b, in *The Collected Dialogues of Plato*, ed. Edith Hamilton and Huntington Cairns (Princeton: Princeton University Press, 1961), 46-49.

14. Oscar Cullmann, *Immortality of the Soul or Resurrection of the Dead* (London: Epworth, 1958), 6.

of human sin resides in the body, so that our physical aspect is beyond redemption.

Similarly, the doctrine of the immortality of the soul presupposes a dualistic anthropology which suggests that our essence resides in the soul apart from the body. This teaching contradicts both biblical and contemporary understandings of the nature of the human person. In addition, the idea suffers from a debilitating difficulty. If we experience the fullness of eternity without the body at death, then different persons enter into the human destiny at different points in the flow of time, rather than together at the end of time. This means that the eternal life that culminates personal existence is an individual experience and not truly a social reality.[15] So understood, however, eternal life is not the eschatological community of the redeemed.

The Christian hope. In the midst of alternative expectations, the Christian message offers a unique vision of the culmination of personal existence. Beyond death, we declare, lies the resurrection of the righteous who through this corporate event share together in the eternal community.

The hope of resurrection lies at the apex of the biblical reflection on personal eschatology. The ancient Hebrews raised the question, "If a man dies, will he live again?" In response, several biblical authors expressed confidence that somehow God would overcome *Sheol* and bring his saints to himself. Yet it was to the apocalypticists that God gave the insight that the means whereby he would accomplish this great act was through the resurrection. The New Testament bears witness that this apocalyptic expectation formed the foundational hope of the early Christian community.

Our hope in the face of death is that one day God will raise us to the higher plane of existence we call eternal life. We will attain to the goal of our being, which is the enjoyment of eschatological community with God, one another, and creation. *Resurrection* is an appropriate word to describe this higher plane of existence. It reminds

---

15. A variation of this argument has been advanced by Wolfhart Pannenberg. See Stanley J. Grenz, *Reason for Hope: The Systematic Theology of Wolfhart Pannenberg* (New York: Oxford, 1990), 194-95.

us that the goal of creation which we will one day enjoy involves both continuity and discontinuity with our present existence.

The theme of sameness and difference—continuity and discontinuity—is evident in Jesus' resurrection, which is the model for ours. His followers were convinced that the risen Lord who appeared to them was the same Jesus they had known. His body bore recognizable resemblances, including the scars from the crucifixion (John 20:27). And his mannerisms indicated that he was indeed Jesus. At the same time, the risen Lord was not immediately recognizable to them. He had not merely been restored to his former earthly existence but was transformed into the life of the age to come.

The same interplay of sameness and difference that characterized Jesus' resurrection will be evident in ours. This event will mark a degree of continuity with the present. As the term itself indicates, the resurrection focuses on the body, and by extension, on personal existence. This suggests that the eschatological community which is the goal of the resurrection will be a fellowship of persons. It indicates as well that God's intention is not to rescue us from the body or the earth. Rather, we will participate in the eternal community as the embodied, earthly creatures that we are.

The idea of resurrection also evidences a fundamental discontinuity with our current existence. We enter into the fullness of God's design only through a radical change. This change is, of course, ethical: our susceptibility to sin ("flesh") must be rooted out, replaced by complete conformity to Christ ("spirit"). This change is likewise physical: our mortality—our susceptibility to disease and death—must be transformed into immortality.

Paul, who provided the most extensive discussion of the resurrection, spoke of this event in these exact terms. That glorious event will transform our mortality into immortality and our perishability into the imperishable; what is sown in dishonor and weakness will be raised in glory and power (1 Cor. 15:42-43). As wheat emerges from seed, so also our resurrection body will be fit for life in the eschatological community (15:37-38; see also, Mark 12:24-27). Consequently, to refer to what lies beyond the resurrection, the apostle used the apparently self-contradictory term "spiritual body" (1 Cor.

15:44). Paul did not mean "a body made of spirit," as if this were some new substance, but rather as Ladd pointed out "a body transformed by and adopted to the new world of God's Spirit."[16]

The resurrection is a trinitarian act. Like the other works of God, the Father raises the dead according to the pattern of the Son and by the power of the Holy Spirit (Rom. 8:11). Hence, the Spirit, as the Completer of God's work in the world, is the immediate facilitator of this event. Through the Spirit's life-giving presence God will raise us to full participation as embodied creatures in the divine relationship shared between the Father and the Son. Because God will give life to our mortal bodies, his final gift of full redemption will encompass our personal lives in their entirety—as embodied persons. We will enjoy personal, embodied existence throughout eternity.

The biblical vision of the culmination of personal life focuses on the resurrection. We must now ask, Is such a vision possible?

The Possibility of the Resurrection

The message of the resurrection was a stumbling block to the Greek thinkers whom Paul encountered in Athens: "When they heard about the resurrection of the dead, some of them sneered" (Acts 17:32). Imbued with the belief that the body was the prison of the soul, the philosophers found ludicrous the idea that the soul would be reunited with the body for eternity.

In the modern era, the resurrection hope has become a theological embarrassment. The difficulty no longer arises from the apparent contradiction of the doctrine to the philosophical idea of the soul as the essence of the human person. Modern thinkers have largely discarded the notion of a substantial soul. Rather, the hope of resurrection appears incompatible with contemporary understandings of what constitutes the identity of a person. Thinkers now suggest that continuity of personhood through time is based on such factors as bodily identity, memory, and similarity of character or mental characteristics.[17] The expectation of an eschatological resurrection rais-

---

16. Ladd, *The Last Things*, 83.
17. Stephen H. Travis, *I Believe in the Second Coming of Jesus* (Grand Rapids: Eerdmans, 1982), 164.

es the difficult question concerning the possibility of the continuity of a person through death leading to the resurrection at the end of time.

We may illustrate this difficulty by viewing the specific problem of identity of the material substance of a person's body. Death sets in motion the decomposition process, through which the elements of the body return to the earth to become the foundation for the life of other organisms. The doctrine of resurrection, however, appears to teach that the body will be reconstituted. How is this possible, given the fact that between death and resurrection the elements of that body will become part of subsequent living organisms? If the body disintegrates at death, how can we assert that the dead person will be raised to life as demonstrably the same person?

This question poses a problem for the conception which Wolfhart Pannenberg labeled the restorationist theory.[18] The Christian hope of resurrection, however, does not assert that the earth gives back the dead as they were. The eschatological event is not the resuscitation of corpses, resulting in a return to earthly existence. Rather, resurrection signifies the elevation of a person to that higher plane of existence which we can only describe as community—complete fellowship with God and others on the new earth that God himself is creating out of the old.

Rather than lacking intellectual credibility, the biblical anticipation fits better with contemporary anthropological understandings than do the alternative visions. The human sciences have reached a virtual consensus that the body is constitutive of humanness. We are embodied creatures, not just immortal souls housed for a time within bodies. Only the hope of resurrection takes seriously this holistic understanding of the human person. The doctrine of the resurrection affirms that we do not enter into the fullness of eternity apart from the body, but only in the body. Social scientists are likewise becoming increasingly aware of the corporate dimension of human life. We are not isolated individuals, but social beings. This understanding also fits best with the resurrection hope, which declares that we do

---

18. For his discussion of this viewpoint, see Wolfhart Pannenberg, "Constructive and Critical Functions of Christian Eschatology," *Harvard Theological Review* 77 (1984): 130.

not experience the culmination of personal existence alone, but corporately.

After we have pursued all considerations, however, the fundamental basis for the Christian's hope is the nature of the God revealed in Christ. Jesus reminded the Sadducees who denied the resurrection, "God is not the God of the dead, but of the living" (Mark 12:24-27). Stephen H. Travis rightly concluded from this text, "I believe that death will be overcome by life because I believe in God—the kind of God whom Jesus shows us, the God to whom we human beings matter. It is impossible to imagine this God scrapping what is precious to him."[19]

The New Testament writers testified that the means whereby God will draw us to himself is best described by the term "resurrection." Exactly how God will perform the miracle lies beyond human knowledge. Yet the one who called the world into existence out of nothingness is capable of bringing us to the new creation.

While God's method of bringing us into fullness of life remains unknowable, that he will do so is clearly evident. Believers already experience the foretaste of the resurrection. The New Testament writers remind us that the Holy Spirit dwelling within is the down payment or guarantee of the future fullness of life (Eph. 1:14; Rom. 8:23).

Hope in the Face of Death

The Christian message puts forth the resurrection as the means whereby God will bring us to the full enjoyment of community. One glorious day we will join Christ in the Easter experience. But what solace does this hope offer to us as we contemplate our own death? What happens immediately at death?

Competing Visions of Life After Death

While sharing the common resurrection hope, Christian thinkers have not been in agreement concerning how that hope impacts our

19. Travis, *I Believe in the Second Coming*, 168.

understanding of what lies immediately beyond death's door. There are several visions of life after death.

Death as the entrance into eternity. One proposed vision collapses death and resurrection into one event. At death, its proponents claim, a person immediately experiences the elevation into eternal life to which the hope of resurrection points.

The roots of this position lie in a late medieval discussion of what happens to the soul at death.[20] Pope John XXII had theorized that the human soul does not enjoy the beatific vision until the eschatological judgment but simply sleeps after death. In an edict of 1336, however, John's successor, Benedict XII, declared that the souls of the righteous enjoy face-to-face contemplation of the divine essence beginning with death. The souls of the wicked, in contrast, descend to hell, even though they will give an account of their deeds on judgment day.[21]

A more recent reworking of this medieval position avoids the differentiation between eternity and the intermediate state implicit in Benedict's edict. According to the newer position, death does not merely place us in a realm in which we already experience what will become our eternal destiny. Rather, death forms the boundary line between time and eternity. At death a person immediately receives the heavenly, resurrection body[22] and gains the final state.[23] Or death places us immediately at the end of history, at the judgment, and in the realm of the eternal kingdom.[24]

Although helpful, this position entails a potentially fatal risk. Wolfhart Pannenberg, for example, rejects the " resurrection in death" position on the basis of what he finds to be the inner logic of the biblical conception of resurrection.[25] Insofar as each person pur-

20. See Hans Schwarz, *On the Way to the Future*, revised edition (Minneapolis: Augsburg, 1979), 232

21. *Constitution Benedictina*, in *The Church Teaches: Documents of the Church in English Tradition*, trans. John F. Clarkson, et al (St. Louis: Herder, 1955), 349-51.

22. This is the position of Travis, *I Believe in the Second Coming*, 175.

23. See for example, W. D. Davies, *Paul and Rabbinic Judaism* (London: S.P.C.K., 1955), 317-18.

24. A recent proponent of this view is Paul Althaus. For a discussion of his position, see G. C. Berkouwer, *The Return of Christ*, trans. James Van Oosterom (Grand Rapids: Eerdmans, 1972), 38-40.

25. See Grenz, *Reason for Hope*, 194-95.

portedly experiences eternal life at death, this experience is by necessity a purely individual reality. In this manner, proponents separate the consummation of individual life from its social or corporate context. The biblical conception, in contrast, places our individual entrance into eternity in the context of the one general resurrection.

Soul sleep. The roots of a second vision of what lies immediately beyond death may also be found in the discussions of the early 1300s. Several thinkers have developed further the suggestion of John XXII that the human soul simply sleeps after death, awaiting the eschatological judgment and the eternal state beyond.

Adherents of soul sleep do not only claim the statement of the medieval pope but more importantly the legacy of Martin Luther. In his musings, the great Reformer appealed to the experience of sleep in order to illume what lies between death and resurrection: "For just as a man who falls asleep and sleeps soundly until morning does not know what has happened to him when he wakes up, so we shall suddenly rise on the Last Day; and we shall know neither what death has been like or how we have come through it."[26] Elsewhere, he offered a similar picture of his own status while waiting for the resurrection: "We are to sleep until he comes and knocks on the grave and says, 'Dr. Martin, get up.' Then I will arise in a moment and I will be eternally happy with him."[27]

Proponents of soul sleep claim a biblical foundation for their view. The writers of Scripture did use the term "sleep" to refer to the dead (1 Kings 2:10; John 11:11; Acts 7:60; 13:36; 1 Cor. 15:6,18,20,51; 1 Thess. 4:13-15). However, critics are quick to point out that such texts do not supply definitive knowledge concerning the state of the dead; the word is simply a first-century euphemism. Further, soul sleep presupposes that the human person is a substantial dichotomy of soul and body, necessitating a spiritual repose in

---

26. Martin Luther, *D. Martin Luthers Werke*, Kritische Gesamtausgabe (Weimar, 1883-), 17/2: 235, as cited in Paul Althaus, *The Theology of Martin Luther*, trans. Robert C. Schultz (Philadelphia: Fortress, 1966), 414.

27. Luther, *D. Martin Luthers Werke*, 37:151, in Althaus, *The Theology of Martin Luther*, 415.

which the immaterial part sleeps while the material body disintegrates in the grave.

Despite difficulties such as these, when we keep in mind its metaphorical intent, soul sleep highlights the biblical theme of the blissful rest of the righteous dead who are kept with God awaiting the resurrection.

Conscious existence of the soul. Before the twentieth century many theologians sought to reconcile the twin themes of the immortality of the soul and the resurrection of the body.[28] To this end, they envisioned the intermediate state as a disembodied, personal, conscious existence of the soul between death and the eschatological event that marked entrance into the eternal state. The continuation of personal existence in the form of the disembodied soul also solved the problem of the continuity of the person between death and the resurrection. After its separation from the body, the soul carries with it the "construction plan" for the resurrection body.

The acceptance of a conscious existence in the intermediate state has led some theologians to consider what such an existence must be like. The most obvious alternatives are a place of bliss and a place of torment. Roman Catholic doctrine adds several other locations to which a soul may journey at death, the most important of which is *purgatory*. At death, most Christians enter a place of purifying suffering, where they are fitted for heaven by the expiation of all remaining guilt.[29]

Protestant thinkers have been quick to point out the problems with the idea of purgatory. Although some find in the concept a certain theological appeal,[30] purgatory is nowhere explicitly taught in Scripture.[31] On the contrary, the book of Hebrews capsulizes what seems to be assumed in the New Testament, namely, that death brings a certain finality to human life: "It is appointed unto man once to die

---

28. James Addison, *Life Beyond Death in the Beliefs of Mankind* (Boston: Houghton Mifflin, 1931), 202.

29. For a recent delineation of this view, see Zachary J. Hayes, "The Purgatorial View," in *Four Views on Hell*, ed. William Crockett (Grand Rapids: Zondervan, 1992), 93.

30. Clark Pinnock, for example, finds a certain appeal to the idea. See his response to Zachary Hayes in *Four Views on Hell*, ed. Crockett, 127-31.

31. This point is raised by both John Walvoord and William Crockett in their responses to Hayes, in *Four Views on Hell*, ed. Crockett, 119-26.

and after that comes judgment" (Heb. 9:27). The doctrine of purgatory, in contrast, fails to take seriously the definitive nature of earthly existence for our eternal destiny.

All views positing a conscious existence of the soul beyond death potentially share the theological problem Protestants find reprehensible in the Roman Catholic doctrine of purgatory. In various ways all these views play down the finality of earthly life. Lying behind the postulate of a postmortem abode for the soul is dichotomist anthropology dividing the human person into two substantial entities, soul and body, and elevating the soul as the true bearer of personhood. This anthropology risks placing our confidence for surviving death in the innate immortality of the soul.

More critically, placing the soul in any state of conscious existence beyond death means that the disembodied soul participates in new experiences apart from the body (such as disembodied cognition of events happening on earth, disembodied relationships with other souls, or disembodied experiences of bliss or torment). But because the soul brings with it these additional postmortem experiences, the resurrected person who meets God at the judgment is not identical with the earthly person.[32]

Biblical Insight into the Intermediate State

With these alternative visions in mind, we return to the biblical documents. Specifically, we ask: Is the intent of the Bible to call us to formulate our hope in the face of death by anticipating conscious existence beyond the grave? Do we consist of immortal souls that survive death and exist in an intermediate state?

The Old Testament concept of Sheol. The authors of the Old Testament historical books repeatedly used the term *sleep* to refer to death (1 Kings 2:10; 11:43). This use, however, is probably merely a euphemism rather than an explanation of what happens at death. Consequently, the focal point for our search for insight into the status of the dead from the Old Testament lies with the concept of *Sheol*. We noted earlier the ambiguous nature of the reality to which this

---

32. For this observation I am indebted to Wolfhart Pannenberg's lectures on eschatology. See, Grenz, *Reason for Hope*, 194.

term points. What remains is to determine the status of those in *Sheol*: Is this a place inhabited by the souls of humans who died?

Whatever and wherever it may be, Old Testament writers said little about inhabitants of *Sheol*. Sometimes they were called the *rephaim* (Ps. 88:10), a word which can be loosely translated "shades." George Eldon Ladd explained that *raphaim* does not refer to disembodied spirits of human beings but to "some kind of a pale replica of man himself."[33] The ancient Hebrews, therefore, understood death as introducing at best only a shadowy existence (Eccl. 9:10). Consequently, *Sheol* is not the repose of the essential person after death. Nor did the Old Testament writers see it as a place of bliss.

The New Testament basis for an intermediate state. The New Testament promises to be a more fruitful biblical source for understanding what lies immediately beyond death. We noted already that in certain texts the biblical writers used the euphemism "sleep" to refer to death. More important for our conception of the situation between death and resurrection are the texts that seemingly comment on the actual state of the dead.

Certain texts merely allude to some type of continuation of personal life after death (Phil. 1:20-24). However, a few others seem to offer clear indication that the intermediate state entails an abode of conscious, temporal existence. We must look more closely at these.

(1) Some thinkers find just such detail in the narrative of the rich man and Lazarus (Luke 16:19-31), which seems to indicate that the intermediate state includes a place of torment for the wicked (Hades, the Greek substitute for *Sheol*) and a blessed abode for the righteous ("Abraham's bosom"). Although many proponents of this view argue that the story is historical, other scholars understand it as a parable.[34]

The story's parabolic nature is indicated by the stylized name of the major character, Lazarus ("God has helped"). This name forms a notable contrast to the nameless status of the rich man. This name and his presence in Abraham's bosom link Lazarus with the late Old Testa-

---

33. Ladd, *The Last Things*, 32.
34. See ibid., 33-34.

ment hope that the righteous will not be consigned to *Sheol*, but somehow will enjoy God's presence beyond death. In addition, the narrative cannot be historical because it contradicts the biblical teaching concerning the judgment. By placing the rich man in hell and Lazarus in a state of bliss, the story assumes that for these two persons, the final judgment has happened already—at death, rather than at the last day. More significantly, by focusing on the stinginess of the rich man and the poverty of Lazarus as the sole reason for their postmortem condition, the story presents economic standing, not righteousness, as the criterion for status in the hereafter. It suggests that those who experience poverty in this life deserve comfort in the next.

If the narrative is indeed a parable, we must look to its central theme, rather than deriving theological meaning from other aspects that may simply be "local color." Two themes immediately present themselves. The story may be an illustration of Jesus' repeated teaching that in the kingdom the last shall be first and the first last. God's justice may mean that the disadvantaged here will be advantaged in the next life. Where and how the great "kingdom reversal" occurs is not the point of the story.

More likely, Jesus intended that we look to the end of the story for its meaning. The torment the rich man experiences leads him to think about his brothers who are yet alive. As the narrative ends, Abraham declares that they will not believe, even if one rises from the dead. The brothers represent the unbelieving Jewish leaders to whom Jesus directed the story: Even Jesus' resurrection will not convince his enemies. As Ladd concluded, rather than the actual fate of the rich man and Lazarus and by extension the state of the dead, "the parable is about the hardness and obduracy of the Jews who refuse to accept the witness of Scripture to the person of Jesus."[35] As to the picture Jesus painted of contrasting bliss and torment, we do well to conclude with Stephen Smith: "Perhaps the most such imagery is intended to teach is the real and eternal consequences resulting from our beliefs and consequent life styles."[36]

---

35. Ibid., 34.
36. Stephen M. Smith, "Intermediate State," in the *Evangelical Dictionary of Theology*, ed. Walter A. Elwell (Grand Rapids,: Baker, 1984), 562.

(2) Paul's anticipation of a "tent not made with hands" beyond death (2 Cor. 5:1-9) also seems to provide insight into the intermediate state. Some exegetes interpret the apostle's reference to a "heavenly dwelling" as indicating that at death believers enter conscious existence with God in heaven. This suggests that the intermediate abode of the righteous is of a higher order than our present earthly experience.[37]

In contrast to this view, the traditional interpretation understands Paul as referring to the resurrected body and not a location in the intermediate state. The "further clothing" the apostle anticipated will come when what is mortal is "swallowed up by life." Read in the light of Paul's clear statements about the resurrection (1 Cor. 15:50-53), he could not have envisioned this event as occurring prior to the last day. The "further clothing" can only be the immortal body we will receive at Jesus' return. Hence, in this text Paul was voicing his preference for the experience of resurrection (the clothed state) over that of death (the potentially unclothed condition).

(3) Jesus' promise to the thief on the cross, "Today you will be with me in paradise" (Luke 23:42-43), must likewise be exegeted with care. We must be careful not to isolate this statement from the thief's request that he receive a place in the messianic kingdom ("Remember me when you come into your kingdom"). The thief had become convinced the Nazarene was the Messiah who despite imminent death would somehow come into his rightful rule. As a result, the criminal expressed confidence that Jesus could grant him participation in the kingdom. (The thief's request, therefore, is an instance of the New Testament answer to the Old Testament question as to whether the righteous dead will participate in the future reign of Messiah.)

Jesus did not respond by speaking of the messianic kingdom, but by promising the thief that he would enjoy the Lord's presence even in death ("today"). The focal point of Jesus' reply was not the location of the two beyond death ("paradise"), but the promise of his personal presence ("Today you will be with me"). The intention of the

---

37. See, for example, William Lane Craig, "Paul's Dilemma in 2 Corinthians 5: 1-10," *New Testament Studies* 34 (January 1988): 145-47.

text, therefore, is not to spark speculation concerning what and where paradise is. Rather, it ought to lead to the confidence Paul later expressed, namely, that death cannot separate the believer from God's love (Rom. 8:38-39), because even in death the believer is "with Christ" (Phil. 1:23).

The biblical conception of life beyond death. We must be cautious in approaching all texts that some theologians interpret as providing information about the status of the dead. As Helmut Thielicke concluded, "such statements of Scripture by no means entail a doctrine of immortality or the presupposition of some division of the I."[38]

The biblical authors offered only sketchy information about the situation of the dead. We know that all humans will be present at the eschatological judgment (Rom. 14:10; 2 Cor. 5:10; 2 Pet. 2:9). Consequently, death does not simply mark the end of personal life. Beyond this general statement, from Scripture we glean a special hope for believers.

Above all, because we know that at his return we will be united with our Lord, we may rest assured that even in death we are secure. Our greatest enemy is powerless to separate us from the love of God which is ours in Christ. Consequently, in the extremity of death, we remain surrounded by God's loving presence.

G. C. Berkouwer concluded that the primary concern of the doctrine of the intermediate state lay precisely "with the reality of the promise that not even death could separate the believers from communion with Christ."[39] This communion, however, does not rest on anything intrinsic to us as humans. Rather, in death as in life we are dependent on our Lord. As a consequence, we must avoid speculating about the nature of that postmortem communion. Again Thielicke was correct in warning us: "The form in which 'I' am to be with him (somatic or psychic, intermistic or in eternal continuity) is no more a valid object for my questioning than is my authorization to analyze psychologically the state of the I which is the subject of faith."[40]

---

38. Thielicke, *Death and Life*, 217.
39. Berkouwer, *The Return of Christ*, 59.
40. Thielicke, *Death and Life*, 216.

The New Testament writers presented one additional theme, however. Because in death we are surrounded by God's loving presence, the righteous dead are "resting from their work" (Rev.14:13). To this description we might add "blissfully," for we know that at the resurrection the fruit of our labors, which cease in death, will be revealed. However, the New Testament never emphasized this "bliss" in any way that detracts from the priority of the resurrection. Rather, in the New Testament understanding the believer does not enter into the completion of salvation in some intermediate state at death, but only at the coming of the Lord at the consummation of history (Matt. 25:34; 1 Pet. 1:4-5). As Ladd rightly concluded, while the condition of the righteous dead may be described as blessed, "the entire Bible witnesses to the fact that the final redemption must include the resurrection and the transformation of the body."[41]

The Situation of the Righteous Beyond Death

Christ's disarming of death has led many Christians to develop an understanding of life after death which reflects more the Greek than the biblical spirit. Just as Socrates welcomed death as the great liberator and the goal of his entire life, so also some Christians look to death as the gateway to a higher existence. Rather than a positive friend and the doorway to a better afterlife, however, the biblical view begins with the assertion that death remains a foe which will only be overcome on the great eschatological day. If death remains an enemy even while en route to its final defeat, what about the saints who have experienced death?

The foundation: Hope for resurrection. In seeking to discern what happens immediately at death, we must always maintain the biblical emphasis on the resurrection. The goal of our hope is the resurrection, not an intermediate state. The resurrection, not death, is the doorway to participation in the fullness of life. Only the assurance of joining Christ in resurrection unmasks the mystery of death and dissipates the terror of the unknown realm beyond death. This assurance alone provides the foundation for confidence in the face of

---

41. Ladd, *The Last Things*, 39.

death. When walking through the valley of the shadow of death, we need fear no evil because the one who has already gone through death accompanies us (Ps. 23:4).

The conclusions we draw concerning the status of the dead can only be the outworking of our hope for participation in the resurrection. The primacy of the resurrection reminds us that the dead are not annihilated, for all appear at the eschatological judgment. The focus on the resurrection reminds us as well that theirs is not a "normal" existence, for it is not in accordance with God's intention for humankind which includes the physical or bodily aspect of human life.

Our elevation of the resurrection as the culmination of personal life suggests that the dead are "held by God." Death does mark the end of earthly life, but not the end of personal existence. Through death God retains the personhood of the dead until the eschatological judgment. At that point they reappear with the marks of personal continuity—bodily identity, memory, and similarity of character or mental characteristics—intact.

In the end, the intermediate state is God's act of holding fast to his creatures. The unrighteous are kept *by* God unto judgment and eternal death. The righteous are kept *with* God unto resurrection and eternal life, surrounded by God's love and blissfully resting. Our hope of survival through death, therefore, is not our doing; nor is it the outworking of any supposed immortality we possess intrinsically. Rather, just as in our life here on earth, we can only trust in God's willingness to hold fast to us. As Helmut Thielicke noted, "The emphasis here is not on some quality of mine that outlasts death, but on the quality of my Lord not to desert me."[42]

The realm beyond death. The intermediate state, then, is God holding us fast until the resurrection. But what is the actual situation of the dead?

Crucial to any helpful conception of the intermediate state is our understanding of time and eternity. We cannot grasp fully how time is present to eternity. Nevertheless, two erroneous conceptions mark the boundaries which we must not transgress. We dare not divorce

---

42. Thielicke, *Death and Life*, 215.

eternity from time,[43] making eternity into a never-ending state of rest or quiescence disconnected from time. Likewise, we ought not collapse eternity into time so that eternity becomes merely an endless succession of temporal units. Rather, as Hans Schwarz suggested, "Eternity is…the fulfillment of time in perfection."[44] Death, in turn, marks the boundary not only of earthly life, but consequently between the earthly and the eternal experiences of time.

We can readily apply this understanding to the question of the intermediate state. From the perspective of those who remain on earth, the dead person appears to be "sleeping" in the grave. This apparent situation arises from the nature of death as the point which halts personal participation as an agent in the ongoing flow of earthly time. The dead person is no longer involved in earthly events. Beyond the flow of disconnected events characteristic of earthly time, the dead person has been transferred into the realm of eternity. Therefore, he or she senses no gap between death and the eschatological resurrection.

This does not mean that the dead immediately experience the resurrection, however. Being uninvolved in earthly events does not mean that they are completely disconnected from these occurrences. On the contrary, while not active agents in earthly events, in a special sense the dead are aware of what is happening on earth. Yet we must understand this cognition by appeal to their changed perspective toward time.

We experience events as travellers through time from the present into the future and therefore as disconnected units en route to the end. In eternity, however, we will know earthly time as the unified whole which from God's perspective it actually is. Seen from the perspective beyond earthly time, the dead share God's composite perspective. They are not conscious of earthly events as isolated occurrences but as integrated into a whole. They perceive events from the vantage point of the eschatological completion of God's program in the resurrection, that is, in their interconnectedness.

---

43. For a critique of this understanding, especially as an argument against the idea of an intermediate state, see Berkouwer, *The Return of Christ*, 40-46.

44. Schwarz, *On the Way to the Future*, 229.

A specific situation may serve to illustrate this concept. We often inquire as to whether a deceased loved one might be aware of our grieving in the face of his or her death. This person is aware, we assert. But he or she is not cognizant of our grief in the manner that characterizes earthly awareness, namely, as an isolated event in the process of time. Rather our loved one knows our grief in the context of the whole of time, specifically as it is eschatologically overcome in the joy of our reunion in the resurrection.

In the face of the meaninglessness of our existence which apparently ends in death, we declare the good news that we will one day share in Christ's resurrection. This event which marks the culmination of personal life in the great eschatological community is not an isolated, individual experience. Rather, the resurrection is also a corporate or social event that will occur when our risen Lord returns in glory to bring human history to its climax. To this culmination of corporate life in the second coming we now turn our attention.

22 The Consummation of History

The seventh angel sounded his trumpet, and there were loud voices in heaven, which said: "The kingdom of the world has become the kingdom of our Lord and of his Christ, and he will reign for ever and ever." (Rev. 11:15)

Outline

The doctrine of last things is the systematic-theological exposition of the goal toward which the triune God is bringing his creation. Eschatology includes reflection on the consummation of God's plan for individual humans. The study looks as well, however, to humans in general or humankind as a corporate reality. For this reason, we must turn our attention beyond personal eschatology to what we may call "corporate eschatology."

The corporate aspect of eschatology readily emerges from its connection with history. The human story is a proper topic for the doctrine of last things, because the divine saving activity transpires within the flow of events in time. In fact, seen in its entirety, history is the narrative of God at work in the world. In this context, the doctrine of last things is the systematic-theological reflection on history as the narrative of God's activity in bringing humankind to God's intended goal. Corporate eschatology is reflection on history from the perspective of the consummation of the human story in accordance with God's plan.

The corporate aspect of the doctrine of last things emerges as well from the social nature of humankind whose history we bring under the purview of faith. Humans are not isolated individuals writing purely individual stories. Rather, we are social beings whose individual narratives intersect and who share a common narrative, the story of humanity. Consequently, in the doctrine of last things we consider the corporate dimension of human existence in the light of the consummation of the divine plan.

Our examination of God's ultimate purpose for humankind leads us to three questions. First, we inquire about human history itself: Is our corporate story truly going somewhere, so that history is meaningful? In the first section of the chapter, we set forth the affirmative answer to this inquiry inherent in the Christian message. We conclude that human history has a divinely intended fulfillment. God is directing our corporate story toward its consummation in the kingdom of God, the eschatological community.

On the basis of our response to the first question, we raise the second: When does God establish his kingdom, the eschatological community, among us? Our answer invokes the contemporary idea of the already/not yet. The community which is God's kingdom is already among us, but its consummation awaits us in the future.

With this in view we move to the third question, How will the end arrive? Here, we tackle the controversial issue concerning the process that will bring history to its culmination. We assert that human history reaches its climax in the return of Christ.

The Meaning of History

According to culture commentator Christopher Lasch, one of the chief hallmarks of our world is the growing conviction that many things are now coming to an end: "Storm warnings, portents, hints of catastrophe haunt our times. The 'sense of ending,' which has given shape to so much of twentieth century literature, now pervades the popular imagination as well."[1] The contemporary sense of ending marks a profound, even monumental change that has accompanied the breakdown of the modern era. We are witnessing the shattering of the tenacious illusion of unbridled optimism that lay at the heart of the modern world view.

What does Christian theology say in the midst of this contemporary situation? Are all things indeed coming to an end? In the light of the

---

1. Christopher Lasch, *The Culture of Narcissism: American Life in an Age of Diminishing Expectations* (New York: Norton, 1978), 3.

portents of gloom rampant in our world, can we truly speak of a corporate human story, a unified narrative that encompasses all humankind? If so, what is the *telos* toward which human history is moving?

Christian Hope in a Changed Context

Building from the hopeful nature of the Christian ethos that formed the foundation for Western culture, the era from the Enlightenment to the 1900s was largely an optimistic period of history. Philosophers, theologians, and historians constructed sketches of the human story, at the heart of which they found the idea of progress. Although differing in content, secular and Christian thinkers agreed that humankind could anticipate a glorious future.

Today, however, this situation has changed. The Christian message of hope no longer parallels the general expectations of our society. Being a hopeful people now runs counter to the mood of the culture in which we live. To set the context for our discussion of the Christian conception of history, we must review how the shift from hope to despair occurred.

From optimism to pessimism. Beginning in the Enlightenment, the unfaltering belief in the inevitability of progress became a cardinal doctrine of the faith of modern culture. Self-evident to all was the assumption that careful application of the scientific method could only result in a continuous advancement in knowledge. As knowledge increased, humans would both gain increasing control over the realm of nature and progressively surmount each social ill we face. In keeping with this attitude, "progressive" became the codeword of the modern era. It was the criterion for all activity and the chief acclamation designating what our culture elevated as good and righteous.[2]

The heyday of the modern era came in the 1800s, the century of optimism and progress. People anticipated unending expansion and development. No obstacle seemed so insurmountable that it could not be overcome by the onslaught of the forces of human advancement. In this optimistic context various types of utopianism flourished. Christian progressivism suggested that the advancing spread

---

2. See, for example, Ernest Lee Tuveson, *Millennium and Utopia*, Harper Torchbooks edition (New York: Harper and Row, 1964), 1.

of the gospel throughout the world would result in the triumph of the faith and the advent of a better day. Its heretical cousin, Marxist utopianism, offered a secularized alternative, anticipating that the class struggle would result in the victory of the proletariat.

As the 1900s unfolded, a significant reversal occurred in the general expectations for the future. The optimism of the 1800s gave way to a new, somber mood—pessimism. This phenomenal shift in attitude began in Europe at about the time of World War I and slowly spread to North America. Its onward march was abetted by the Second World War,[3] major conflicts in Korea and Vietnam, and skirmishes in many parts of the world.

The tenacity of militarism was but one sign that a host of grave problems threatened not only us personally, but even the existence of life itself on earth. An entire generation grew up under the specter of nuclear war, the menace of worldwide famine, and dire predictions that overpopulation and commercial exploitation would strain our environment beyond its capacities. The world was thrust into the throes of unrelenting crises—energy shortages, forebodings of financial and economic ruin, epidemics such as AIDS, and most ominous of all, portents of ecological disaster. Not only could these perilous realities undermine the fabric of stable society in the present, they also cast a sinister shadow across the very future of humankind and the earth as a whole.

Broad access to information characteristic of our technologically advanced age facilitated widespread awareness of our crucial problems. As a consequence, people now find themselves faced with the brute possibility of a cosmic catastrophe: The world could indeed come to an end.[4] This realization has produced a profound crisis in

---

3. The German Old Testament scholar Klaus Koch notes the importance of World War II to the rise of pessimism in Europe. After the outbreak of this war, "nearly all discerning Christians had finally lost faith in a divinely willed progress in history," so much so that "longing for the speedy approach of the kingdom of God in time became suspect." *The Rediscovery of Apocalyptic* (London: SCM, 1972), 67-68.

4. This characteristic of the contemporary *Zeitgeist* has been noted by many thinkers. See, for example, Paul D. Hanson, "Introduction," in *Visionaries and Their Apocalypses*, ed. Paul D. Hanson, *Issues in Religion and Theology* number 4 (Philadelphia: Fortress, 1983), 3. See also, Hanson's article, "Old Testament Apocalyptic Reexamined," in *Visionaries and Their Apocalypses*, 37.

the contemporary *Zeitgeist*. For the first time since the dawn of modernity, there is widespread questioning of the central dictum on which the modern world was founded—progress through ever increasing technological and social advancement. The well-ordered world view that sustained Western society for three centuries is collapsing.

Like generations before us, people today continue to anticipate the future. In contrast to their modern forebears, however, they no longer view the future as the glorious new order to be greeted with hope. Rather, in their eyes it is the catastrophic end of the world, a prospect which they dread.

Accompanying the sense of despair in the face of the future is a parallel loss of the past. In contrast to earlier ages, people today no longer find direction through a sense of historical continuity. They are not conscious that they belong to a succession of generations uniting past, present, and future.

In discarding both the future and the past, our society has lost its sense of history. Until recently, the assumption that we participate in a whole that unifies all generations since the beginning of time was an unassailable postulate. This basic idea once facilitated people in understanding themselves, for they knew that their lives were embedded in history. Today the situation is gravely different. The assumption that humankind is a unity has been discarded. As a consequence, people today no longer build their lives on a felt sense of historical rootedness.

Alienated from the past and hopeless in the face of the future, people cling the present—more specifically, to the isolated self in the present. In response to the loss of historical consciousness, they resign the external world to its fate and turn their gaze to their own private, inner worlds. Lasch has poignantly termed the flight into the present existence of the isolated self "the culture of narcissism."[5]

The challenge of a pessimistic world. How are we as Christians to respond to the pessimism and narcissism of our culture? What message do we offer? The task of the contemporary theologian is to ar-

---

5. Lasch, *The Culture of Narcissism*, 7.

ticulate the significance of the Christian confession of Jesus' lordship in the midst of this situation.

The current reawakening in our society to the possibility of the end of the world and the despair that this awareness has provoked offer a grave challenge to the people of God. We agree that "the end of all things is near" (1 Pet. 4:7). But in contrast to the sense of doom that characterizes people around us, we anticipate a glorious future beyond the climax of history. We declare that the curtain of our age will be brought down by nothing less than the glorious return of the risen and exalted Lord Jesus Christ, whose life, death, and resurrection form the foundation of our identity. We assert that this event, which a mere generation ago moderns held up to ridicule on the basis of the prevailing belief in optimism and progress, is the only genuine hope possible in a world despairing of the future and disconnected from the past. On the basis of our confession of faith in Christ as the returning Lord, our task is to set forth an understanding of history as meaningful in an era devoid of meaning. History has significance, we declare, because it is rushing ever onward toward the culmination of God's work in the world. Yet we ask, What exactly is the divine purpose toward which history is moving? What is the content of our message of hope for history?

To develop our answer to this question, we must return to the Bible. Specifically, we look to the biblical trajectory through which God led his people to affirm the idea of a unified human history. In short, we inquire concerning the corporate eschatology of the biblical people of God.

Corporate Eschatology and the Biblical Message

The anticipation of a climax to human history—a corporate eschatology—lies at the heart of Scripture. Running throughout the Bible is a narrative, the recounting of the acts of the sovereign Lord of history accomplishing his goal. The central carrier of this narrative is an outlook toward history developed by a specific trajectory of biblical revelation. This trajectory began with the great prophets of the Old Testament and reached its apex in the apocalyptic movement which cradled the ministry of Jesus and the New Testament. This prophetic-apocalyptic vision of history forms the heart of our corporate eschatology.

The prophetic vision. Broadly understood, the prophetic outlook dates to the early stages of Israelite history. With the establishment of the monarchy, however, prophets took on a new role which was political as well as religious.[6] God called them to hold the king accountable to the divine ideal for the office of earthly rulership. Central to the prophetic message was the proclamation of Yahweh's desire for justice, the theme that eventually led to the expectations of a catastrophic in-breaking of God to establish salvation and mete out judgment.

The quest for justice was embedded in the Hebrew psyche from the beginning of nationhood. Through much of its history, Israel was an oppressed people. The deliverance from Egyptian bondage and the emigration to the Promised Land did not bring about complete justice. Internal and external factors complicated the attainment of the ideal. The Israelites did not live in accordance with their covenant with God, and the nation was continually buffeted by neighboring and indigenous peoples. These factors led many in Israel to look to the inauguration of the kingship as the vehicle through which justice would finally be established. However, in the face of repeated military pressure from powerful neighbors and because they fell prey to the temptation to use political position for selfish gain, Israel's kings were either unable or unwilling to maintain justice in the land.

In the midst of this growing discontent and later as the divided kingdom came under the dominance of Assyria and Babylonia, the prophets increasingly directed the hopes of the faithful away from the present rulers and toward the future. A king would come in the name and power of Yahweh to bring justice to the nation. In this way God would vindicate his name and establish his glory.

Although it would be the work of God, there was also a role for the people to play in the coming of the great event. God would establish justice only after the people had prepared themselves. The prophets, therefore, broadened their task. They called Israel to repent

---

6. H. H. Rowley, *The Relevance of Apocalyptic*, second edition (London: Lutterworth, 1947), 14.

from all unfaithfulness and to live righteously in view of the great deed that God would accomplish in the future.

The later prophets knew as well that God's act of self-vindication could not be an isolated, national event. In fact, as early as the call of Abraham, God had promised that this nation would be the means of blessing to the entire world (Gen. 12:1-3). Consequently, the demonstration of the divine glory must occur in the presence of all nations. This was only right, for the oppression of Israel by the surrounding nations had called Yahweh's honor as the God of Israel into question.

As their expectations for the establishment of justice within history were repeatedly dashed, prophetic voices grew increasingly pessimistic in their view of the present world. Articulators of the hope of restoration lifted their gaze beyond history to the eternal, cosmic realm. Divine salvation would not come in the ongoing history of the nation. Instead, the seers began to look to a divine act breaking into history and establishing a new creation. This shift in outlook gave birth to a new and deeper understanding of the drama of human history—apocalypticism.[7]

The apocalyptic vision. The concepts of a corporate eschatology and a climax to human history which arose among the prophets were advanced by the apocalypticists. The apocalyptic style flourished between 200 B.C. and 100 A.D. first within Jewish and later within Jewish-Christian circles. Although most of the apocalyptic writings were not included in the canon, the *genre* is represented in the biblical books of Daniel and Revelation, and in sections of Isaiah, Zachariah, and the synoptic Gospels. In addition, the prophetic-apocalyptic view of history formed an important aspect of the thinking of the New Testament writers.

The apocalyptic vision focused on world history as the stage on which a cosmic drama is being played out.[8] This drama pits God and the hosts of heaven in a fight against Satan and the forces of evil. The

---

7. Paul D. Hanson, "Old Testament Apocalyptic Reexamined," in *Visionaries and Their Apocalpses,* 58.

8. For a recent discussion of these and other common apocalyptic themes, see Koch, *The Rediscovery of Apocalyptic,* 28-33.

climax of world history brings the replacement of all earthly empires, which are in the service of Satan, with the eternal kingdom of God.[9] Presently the outcome of this conflict may appear to be in doubt, but it is not. The transformation from the world kingdoms to the kingdom of God will transpire when God asserts his sovereignty. Hence, lying behind the apocalyptic vision was the belief that ultimately God is in control of history.[10]

The apocalypticists declared that the kingdom of God is a future reality. It is nevertheless present, albeit in concealed form, as a hidden power currently at work in bringing the end to pass. The apocalyptic world view anticipated the soon overthrow of current earthly conditions, that is, the imminent, catastrophic end of the world. The grand cosmic event that signals the end will be preceded by the dominion of evil, a time of unprecedented persecution for the righteous, as well as widespread disaster and human suffering.[11] Hence, the anticipated future forms a contradiction to, rather than merely a continuation of the present.[12] The climactic event reveals the divine glory as well as the divine power over the spiritual hosts and world history. Then, in the new eon the faithful saints of God will participate with the good angels in the eternal kingdom, sharing thereby in the glory of the age to come.

The apocalypticists' message went beyond that of transmitting knowledge of future events and of assessing the current situation in the light of the future. It had ethical importance for the present. The coming of God's power in judgment and salvation means that a line will be drawn between humans. This line even cuts through the people of God, for the righteous will be divided from the apostate. Consequently, the apocalyptic world view fostered a sense of urgency.[13] Its message is an admonition to the faithful to remain firm to the end and to endure persecution during the short season of satanic sway in view of the glory to follow. At the same time, the message was a warning of impending doom to the ungodly nations and to the apos-

---

9. Rowley, *The Relevance of Apocalyptic*, 165.
10. Ibid., 151.
11. Ibid., 155.
12. Ibid., 35.
13. Ibid., 170.

tate. Such doom is sure to transpire when the kingdom of God replaces the kingdoms of the world.

While not encompassing all that the Bible says about human history, the prophetic-apocalyptic vision constituted a central theme. This view was shared by Jesus and the disciples, and it provided both the context and the categories for the earliest formulation of the gospel message. Imbued with the apocalyptic hope, the New Testament writers bequeathed to the church and to Christian theology the vision of God's grand action in bringing history to its purposeful end. The New Testament inaugurated one crucial innovation, however. The event which will mark the climax of human history is the return of the crucified and risen Jesus.

The Significance of History

The trajectory of biblical revelation we have outlined above set forth a specific understanding of history. It declared that the human story is one, corporate narrative. History moves from the primordial past which marks its beginning to the immanent return of Christ with which it will end. Because it is directed toward a goal or end, history is meaningful. It is the story of God's activity in bringing his purposes to pass.

Can we say more about the significance of history? Is there a theme running through the entire human narrative which gives it its ultimate meaning?

The basic characteristics of history. Before we can offer our answer to this question we must make explicit the assumptions about the nature of history which lie behind the prophetic-apocalyptic conception outlined above.

The biblical conception of history stands out more clearly when it is placed in the context of two influential alternatives. In contrast to the cyclical understanding that dominated the other ancient religious traditions, Israel bequeathed to the church and consequently to Western culture a linear view of time and with it a historical consciousness. Likewise, contrary to the human-centered view of modern secular progressivism, Christian faith sets forth a theocentric understanding of history; the acting subject who unites the narrative into one story is God himself.

(1) Israel came to understand time as linear. This discovery formed a radical innovation in comparison to the conception of other ancient religious traditions which reflect a cyclical view of time.[14] According to the cyclical outlook, life follows a rhythmic pattern, a circle of a finite number of events that occur repeatedly and with observable regularity.

The religions of Israel's neighbors were characterized by a cyclical understanding of time. The worship life of the Canaanites, for example, focused on two gods who were associated with the major seasons of the year. In early summer as the coming drought began to dry out the vegetation, religious rituals lamented the death of the fertility god Baal and the triumph of Mot the god of death. Then as the winter rains began to replenish the dry ground bringing the promise of good crops, the Canaanites celebrated Baal's rebirth.[15]

God directed Israel to view life in a different manner. Events did not merely follow a repeatable pattern. Rather, each was a unique occurrence, and together these events were a trajectory which had a beginning and would have an end. Hence, occurrences formed a history—a narrative.

The foundation for Israel's unique historical consciousness lay in a unique theological outlook. The Old Testament writers were strictly monotheistic. They proclaimed that there is ultimately only one God (Yahweh)—not the several gods of Israel's neighbors. Further, Yahweh is not merely a tribal deity but the God of all humankind. The implications of this universally directed monotheism were profound. It facilitated Israel in seeing history as the linear activity of the one God who is asserting his rulership over all the nations. The historical trajectory of God's actions ran from creation to final redemption, from the primeval garden to that day when the earth will be "filled with the knowledge of the glory of the LORD as the waters cover the sea" (Hab. 2:14; see also, Ps. 102:15; Isa. 66:18-19).

---

14. Karl Loewith, *Meaning in History* (Chicago: University of Chicago Press, 1950), 19.

15. Hans-Joachim Kraus, *Worship in Israel: A Cultic History of the Old Testament*, trans. G. Bushwell (Richmond, Va.: John Knox, 1966), 38-43.

The ancient people of God bequeathed this linear view to the early church and the Christian tradition.

(2) Western culture inherited the Hebrew legacy of linear history. Under the impulse of humanism, thinkers, especially in the modern era, separated the biblical idea of linear history from its theological moorage. Modern historians exchanged the God-centeredness of the biblical vision for a human-centered understanding,[16] the idea of inevitable human progress. The results were disastrous. In making humankind the subject of history, they brought the goal of history into the historical process itself, thereby eradicating its transcendent reference point. When clouds began to darken the horizon of the future, the idea of progress faltered. With the historical consciousness robbed of its foundation in the vision of a glorious goal beyond time, pessimism loomed as the only possible response.

In contrast to secular progressivism, the linear view of time that Israel passed on to the church places history on a theocentric foundation. History is more than the story of human acts. It is the narrative of God's action in bringing creation to his intended goal. Because the unity of history lies in the activity of the one God, biblical faith admits that we can never attain the goal of history on our own. History is not our story—the story of the progress of humankind. Rather, through his saving action God himself brings history to its fulfillment.

This understanding of linear time as the story of the unfolding of God's purposes for humankind provides Christian eschatology with its message of hope in the midst of a pessimistic world. The Bible presents history as meaningful, for it is directed toward a goal; it is going somewhere. This "somewhere" is not an illusive human utopia in history, which we are ultimately powerless to create. Rather, history's goal is nothing less than the realization of God's purposes for his creation. The grand culmination of history arrives only because God stands at the end of the human story. By his grace, he is ordering our story to its intended goal, which will be realized when Jesus returns in glory.

---

16. For a discussion of the development of this historical shift, see Hans Schwarz, *On the Way to the Future*, revised edition (Minneapolis: Augsburg, 1979), 19-23.

History *as God at work establishing community.* The goal or *telos* of history is the accomplishment of the divine plan for humankind. The Bible leaves no doubt as to the content of God's goal for human history.

According to the Scriptures, God is directing history toward his glorious reign, the presence of God's will throughout the earth. This goal forms the central petition of the Lord's Prayer: "your kingdom come, your will be done on earth as it is in heaven" (Matt. 6:10). As we have noted repeatedly in these pages, the content of the divine reign is community. Hence, the goal of God's activity in the world is to establish community. The actualizing of his purposes leads to reconciliation and fellowship.

The establishment of community forms a unifying, central theme of the entire Bible. The biblical story reaches its climax in John's picture of the new heaven and new earth—the eternal community which is the *telos* of history. The vision of the inspired seer who wrote the Book of Revelation, however, marks the culmination of a long history of promise that stretches back to the Garden of Eden and encompassed the prophetic and apocalyptic anticipation.

The seer looked to an eon beyond the present which will mark the completion of the divine program in human history. The future new order will be characterized by reconciliation and harmony. Its inhabitants will live in fellowship with each other, with creation, and most importantly with God. John envisioned the new order as a human society, a city, the new Jerusalem (Rev. 21:9-21). In that city, nature will again fulfil its purpose of providing nourishment for humans (22:1-4). Most glorious of all, however, God will dwell with us on the new earth (21:3; 22:3-5).

Taken as a whole, the Scriptures assert that God's program is directed to the bringing about of a redeemed people living within a redeemed creation enjoying fellowship with their redeemer God. Consequently, the goal of our corporate human story is the union of the one new humanity in Christ (Eph. 2:15), the fellowship of those whom Christ purchased for God "from every of tribe and language and people and nation" (Rev. 5:9). The New Testament authors boldly declared that this goal will only come to pass when Jesus returns.

The Presence of Community
In and Beyond History

Christian eschatology declares that history is meaningful. It is the story of God's activity in bringing creation to his intended goal. The goal toward which all history is rushing is the return of Christ, which will mark the establishment of community and hence the ultimate realization of God's will, which is his reign. With this end in view, we now inquire concerning the presence of the future in history.

In chapter 17 we noted the debate among New Testament scholars as to what Jesus taught about the kingdom. Thinkers concluded that in our Lord's mind the kingdom of God embodied the idea of God's self-disclosure, God's sovereign activity, his ultimate intervention in human affairs. The discussion in the twentieth century led to an uneasy consensus that Jesus saw this divine reign as inaugurated but not consummated. The kingdom, in other words, is "already" but "not yet."

The consensus among New Testament scholars leads to the theological conclusion that the goal of history is both already present but also not yet here. God has acted on our behalf, but the consummation of this divine intervention lies yet in the future. As we have seen, the divine goal for history is God's establishing of community. God has acted within history with this specific purpose in view, namely, that we enjoy fellowship with him, with each other, and with creation. The focus of God's historical action was the coming of Jesus Christ. The consummation of God's historical action, which occurs at Christ's return, will mark the final arrival of community in the new creation. Nevertheless, community is in some sense a present reality. We now explore this conclusion.

History's Goal as "Already"

Since the coming of Jesus the kingdom of God has been present in human history in a partial manner. The presence of the kingdom means that community can be a present reality, even though in its fullness true fellowship comes only at the culmination of history.

793

This assertion constructs a bridge between our present and God's reign. All true experiences of community are an expression of the divine will. In our enjoyment of fellowship with God, among humans, and toward creation, God's will is done and God comes to rulership. The kingdom, however, is always God's work—God's gift to us. Therefore, wherever genuine community emerges in the midst of our fallen world God is present and working.

The link between our present and God's reign means that the experiences of fellowship and reconciliation we now enjoy are signs of the grace of God operative in the face of the brokenness of the present. As signs of God's activity in the world in establishing community, they mediate a transcendent meaning to history from within history. They remind us that present events are meaningful as they are linked to the story of God, who is at work establishing community in the world. Experiences of community in the present offer us a foretaste of the eschatological fellowship we will one day enjoy with God, one another, and the redeemed creation.

The connection between present expressions of community and the divine reign carries practical implications. It links the building of community to the work of the kingdom. Aware that ultimately community in every form is God's gift, we can celebrate the goodness of our God as it is embodied in each experience of community in the present world.

The implications of the connection between community and the kingdom move beyond celebration, however, to active participation. As Christians we may join with others in seeking to facilitate true community on a variety of levels—including the political, societal, and familial, in addition to the ecclesiastical. Wherever people are promoting wholesome relationships in the midst of a fallen world, Christians should be providing active assistance, knowing that we are thereby engaging in kingdom work. In fact, we alone are cognizant of the true significance of such community building efforts. Through our awareness of the biblical vision we can relate them to the God who is ultimately the only foundation for, and facilitator of true community. With this in view, we engage in efforts to strengthen such institutional expressions of community as the family or the neighborhood, participate in civic organizations which foster human relations, and support legislation designed to enhance community among humans or human care of the earth.

Although community building occurs in many aspects of human life, in this age the focal point of the divine establishing of community is the church, the fellowship of Jesus' disciples. In Part 5 (ecclesiology) we explored this central aspect of the "already" of the kingdom. As the community of the people of God, the church is a sign of God's reign. Insofar as the church engages in its mandate, it advances the principles of the kingdom which lead to the fostering of community. In so doing the church serves as the focus of the proleptic experience of fellowship, existing in the world as the reconciled and reconciling community of Christ. It provides the primary context for our present experience of community, and its doors remain open for anyone who would enter into fellowship with God through Christ and hence join our community.

History's Goal as "Not Yet"

God is intervening in human affairs. However, the consummation of his activity awaits us in the future. Consequently, the ultimate establishment of community is not yet here, not yet a reality. It will come only as history reaches its culmination in the return of Christ. This assertion leads us to inquire, What will characterize that great future reality?

The eschatological fullness of what is now partially present will complete what God has already begun in history. It will come, therefore, as God's gracious gift. At the same time, the eschatological event will stand over against that history of which it is the climax. In short, the consummation—Christ's return—will entail both grace and judgment.

The end as grace. Christ's return at the end of history will come as the culmination of God's work on behalf of humankind. As the completion of what God has already begun, it will be a gracious act. By his grace, God will establish community in its fullness.

Although within history we enjoy experiences of fellowship with God, one another, and creation, our present experience is only partial. We anticipate the coming of the fuller reality on that day when Christ returns. Only then will human history attain its goal, as God graciously establishes fully the community he has been fostering throughout history. Only then will the meaning of history be complete and totally visible. Only then will we see clearly the scarlet thread of the divine hand running through the entire human story. Then we will marvel at the intricate manner in which our history was indeed "his story."

The end as judgment. The eschatological culmination is God's gracious act bringing to completion what he is already inaugurating among us. At the same time, however, the second coming of Jesus constitutes God's judgment on the human story.

God's judgment on human history is inherent within the establishment of community itself. The glorious fellowship that we will enjoy with God, one another, and creation at the end of history will accentuate the failure of sinful humankind within history. It will form a stark contrast to the fallen human condition. In the blazing light of God's community we will see clearly the alienation caused by human sin. The glory of community will show in stark relief our enmity against God, each other, and creation. We will perceive how we lived in hurtful distrust of God, how we built walls among ourselves, and how we ill-treated creation. Even seemingly worthy human attempts to create community will show themselves as only the pale replications of the genuine divine community.

When Christ returns, the eschatological consummation of history will stand as a judgment on history. Yet its role in judgment begins already. Throughout this age the fullness of community—the kingdom—stands over us as an ever-present, transcendent ideal. It remains always the "impossible possibility," to borrow the appropriate description coined by Reinhold Niebuhr.[17] The vision of God's perfect fellowship provides the ideal for all human social interaction. At the same time, the fullness of community also reminds us of how short of the mark our efforts always are.

---

17. Reinhold Niebuhr, *An Interpretation of Christian Ethics*, Living Age edition (New York: Meridian, 1956), 97-123.

Even in judgment, however, grace remains present. Precisely as it forms God's judgment on history, the eschatological consummation remains an expression of his grace. The depth of community we are incapable of establishing God bestows on us as his gift. The divine gift of fellowship begins in the present, as it enters our experience within the fallen world. Then on that great day when Jesus returns, God will graciously bring us to enjoy community in its glorious fullness for all eternity.

The Climax of History

History is the story of God's activity in establishing community. Consequently, our corporate human narrative is incomplete. It is moving toward the consummation of God's work at the great eschatological day when our Lord returns. Yet we ask, What specific events must transpire as we move toward the consummation of history? For many Christians, this is the central question of eschatology, which they understand as the quest for the biblical chronology of the end.

Often theologians, especially those in the Reformed tradition, set forth their answer to the question of chronology by providing a specific understanding of the thousand year reign of Christ mentioned in Revelation (Rev. 20:1-8). For this reason, we turn our attention to the chronology of the end in the context of the debate about the millennium.[18] We must look first at the roots of the millennial concern, then summarize the contemporary alternatives, before delineating our own expectations.

Apocalyptic and Millenarianism

The apocalyptic thinkers continued the exploration begun by the prophets into the relationship between the eternal destinies of individual humans and the destiny of the corporate nation. Daniel drew the two eschatological themes together through the idea of resurrection. At the end of the age, the righteous and the unrighteous will rise

---

18. For a fuller delineation of this issue, see Stanley J. Grenz, *The Millennial Maze* (Downers Grove, Ill.: InterVarsity, 1992).

from their graves in order to face judgment. The righteous will join the nation of Israel to share the blessings of the eternal messianic kingdom which would be located on this earth.[19]

Beginning in the second century B.C., however, Daniel's viewpoint began to be altered.[20] The apocalypticists became conscious that the earth, although purified, could not be the fitting location of an eternal messianic kingdom. Two possible solutions to this problem came to the fore. The one moved the focal point of the kingdom from earth to heaven, substituting the image of a heavenly Jerusalem for the earthly as the seat of the messianic rule.[21] The other reduced the messianic kingdom to a temporal reality and transposed the goal of the resurrection to an eternal, heavenly realm.[22]

The disagreement as to whether the messianic kingdom was eternal and heavenly or temporal and earthly brought a corresponding division within the ranks of the apocalypticists concerning the placement of the eschatological judgment. One alternative—that of an eternal messianic kingdom in the eternal new heavens and new earth—demanded that the judgment precede and initiate the messianic rule. The other—that of a temporal, earthly kingdom—shifted the judgment to the end of that era.[23]

The vision of the millennium within the last canonical book (Rev. 20:1-8) brought the question debated by the ancient apocalypticists into Christian theology. Do the second coming of Christ and the resurrection of all humankind, together with the eschatological judgment and the inauguration of the eternal kingdom, occur as one grand event? Or are they separated by a temporal messianic rule lasting a thousand years? In other words, does the eternal kingdom of God come as the catastrophic end to human history in an unmeditated fashion, or are we to expect an interregnum of a thousand years, a golden age on earth? And how does the millennial vision of Revelation 20 fit with the transformation of the Jewish expectations for a

---

19. See, for example, R. H. Charles, *Eschatology: The Doctrine of a Future Life in Israel, Judaism and Christianity*, revised edition (1913, New York: Schockenn, 1963), 247-48.

20. Ibid., 209-10, 245-51.

21. Ibid., 210, 245.

22. Ibid., 248, 250-51.

23. Ibid., 289-90.

temporal messianic kingdom into the New Testament emphasis on the present kingship of Jesus?[24]

The Millennium in Christian Theology

Throughout church history, theologians have differed concerning the proper interpretation of John's vision of the thousand years. Several early church fathers were millenarian, anticipating an earthly reign of Jesus prior to the consummation of God's program. Under the influence of Augustine the other tradition, which anticipates no such interregnum, came to dominate. However, in Puritan Reformed theology the question of the millennium emerged as the crucially divisive issue, an issue which was subsequently bequeathed to evangelicals.

Although there are differences of detail within each, three basic positions—postmillennialism, amillennialism, and premillennialism (subdivided into two types)—encapsule the current discussion within evangelicalism. The nomenclature popularly used to delineate these basic positions arises from the answer given by each to the question concerning the time of Christ's return relative to the millennium.

Postmillennialism. As the name suggests, adherents of postmillennialism anticipate that the eschatological return of Christ will occur *after* an earthly golden age, which John pictured as a thousand year reign of Christ. Hence, the second coming is "postmillennial."

This viewpoint emphasizes the continuity between the current era and the golden age. The thousand years will be a period of time much like our own, but with a heightened experience of goodness, due to the pervasive influence of Christian principles throughout the world. Postmillennialists also emphasize human involvement in the advent of the thousand years. Although the golden age comes as the work of the Holy Spirit, God uses human efforts in advancing its coming.

The eschatological chronology of postmillennialism includes the following elements: As the gospel spreads throughout the earth and

---

24. For a window into the current discussion of this issue, see, T. Francis Glasson, "The Temporary Messianic Kingdom and the Kingdom of God," *Journal of Theological Studies* 41/2 (1990): 517-25.

brings its divinely-intended and Spirit-energized results, evil (and perhaps its personal representation in the form of Antichrist[25]) is eventually routed and the millennium arrives. During this era the nations live in peace, for Satan is "bound" and thereby evil is temporarily restrained. After the thousand years have ended Satan is loosed to lead a short-lived rebellion, the final conflict of evil with righteousness,[26] whether this be understood as a spiritual battle of truth against error[27] or in terms of political persecution.[28] Satan's rebellion is ended by the triumphal return of Jesus. The second coming is followed by the general resurrection, the judgment, and the eternal state—heaven and hell.

Amillennialism. The word *amillennialism* means "no millennium." Its proponents do not anticipate an earthly golden age in the future but find some other significance to the symbol in John's vision. The figure may refer to a specific period of time in the past during which Christ held sway in his church.[29] Or it could symbolize the church age in its entirety, so that the reign mentioned is either one dimension of the experience of the church as a whole[30] or of the individual believer.[31] Others interpret the thousand years as the reign of departed saints in the heavenly realm during this age.[32] Or it may be a vision of the eternal kingdom of God. In any case, all amillennialists anticipate that the second coming of Christ will mark the beginning of eternity without an intervening interregnum.

---

25. Hence, for example, Augustus Hopkins Strong, *Systematic Theology*, three volumes (Philadelphia: Griffith and Rowland, 1907), 3:1008.

26. Ibid., 1009; For a lengthier discussion of this question, see Loraine Boettner, *The Millennium* (Philadelphia: Reformed, 1957), 67-76. The expectation of a final apostasy is not universally held among postmillennialists.

27. J. Marcellus Kik, *An Eschatology of Victory* (Philadelphia: Presbyterian and Reformed, 1974), 238.

28. E.g., Jay Adams, *The Time Is at Hand* (Philadelphia: Presbyterian and Reformed, 1974), 86-88.

29. See, for example, Adams, ibid.

30. See G. C. Berkouwer, *The Return of Christ*, trans. James Van Oosterom (Grand Rapids: Eerdmans, 1972), 314-15.

31. See, for example, William Cox, *In These Last Days* (Philadelphia: Presbyterian and Reformed, 1964), 68-71.

32. For a discussion of this position, see Oswald T. Allis, *Prophecy and the Church* (Grand Rapids: Baker, 1972), 5. See also Benjamin B. Warfield, *Biblical Doctrines*, reprint edition (Edinburgh: Bannner of Truth, 1988), 649.

Of the major eschatological chronologies, the amillennial is the simplest.[33] The time between the two advents will be characterized by a mixture of good and evil. At the close of the age, this conflict will intensify as the church completes its mandate of evangelism and the forces of evil coalesce (perhaps in the appearance of the antichrist). In the midst of a final, intense time of persecution of the church, Christ will appear in the fullness of his glory. At the Lord's return a conglomeration of events will occur,[34] which complete his redemptive work.[35] These include Christ's victory over the forces of evil (Antichrist), the general resurrection, the judgment, and the transformation of creation into the eternal state. For the saints of all ages resurrection will mean that they, together with believers on the earth, meet the descending Lord and enter into the eternal kingdom of the new heaven and the new earth. For the wicked, resurrection facilitates their appearance before their judge (together with the wicked on the earth), followed by banishment into eternal condemnation.

Premillennialism. Premillennialists expect the return of the Lord prior to the thousand year period. Thus, Christ's coming is "premillennial." Jesus will be physically present on the earth to exercise world dominion during his thousand year reign.

In contrast to postmillennialist, proponents of this view emphasize the discontinuity between the current age and the thousand years. This discontinuity means that human agency plays little role in the coming of the golden age. Rather, the millennium arrives as the gift of divine grace and only after a catastrophic act of God that brings the present eon to a close.

The general premillennial chronology anticipates that the present age will climax with a period of tribulation followed by the return of Jesus Christ. The second coming will mark the judgment on the Antichrist and the resurrection of the righteous. At the Parousia Satan will be bound, and the era of peace and righteousness will commence on the earth. After the millennium, Satan is freed from his prison. He

---

33. For the typical amillennial scenario, see Floyd Hamilton, *The Basis of Millennial Faith* (Grand Rapids: Eerdmans, 1952), 35-37.
34. See, for example, Cox, *In These Last Days*, 59-67.
35. Louis Berkhof, *The Second Coming of Christ* (Grand Rapids: Eerdmans, 1953), 83.

gathers the unbelieving nations in a rebellion against Christ's government. His treason is short-lived, however, for it is squelched by fire from heaven. Then come the general resurrection (including the resurrection of the unrighteous), the judgment, and the eternal state.[36]

Two distinct groups claim the legacy of premillennialism. Historic premillennialists[37] assert that theirs is the variety that has been present in the church since the patristic era. Its proponents anticipate a time of tribulation directed against the church, climaxed by Christ's coming to rescue his disciples from the forces of evil. The millennium, in turn, is a time for God to bless Christ's faithful followers.

As their name suggests, dispensational premillennialists tend to divide human history into distinct periods of time or "dispensations." More importantly, they differ from their historic premillennial cousins on the basis of their understanding of which people will be the focus of God's attention in the future tribulation and millennium. Rather than viewing these epochs as aspects of God's program for the New Testament church, dispensationalists generally find their significance in God's intention for national Israel.

According to the dispensational understanding, during the tribulation God will prepare Israel to accept their Messiah. Consequently, the majority of dispensationalists hold to the pretribulational rapture.[38] The current age will one day be brought to a close by the secret "meeting in the air," by means of which Jesus takes his (true) church to heaven to stand before "the judgment seat of Christ" and to celebrate "the marriage supper of the Lamb" (Rev. 19).[39] Meanwhile on earth the appearance of the Antichrist marks the beginning

---

36. J. Dwight Pentecost, *Things to Come*, (Findlay, Ohio: Dunham, 1958), 547-83.

37. Historic premillennialists writings include Clarence Bass, *Backgrounds to Dispensationalism* (1960; Grand Rapids: Baker, 1977); Millard Erickson, *Contemporary Options in Eschatology: A Study of the Millennium* (Grand Rapids: Baker, 1977); and D. H. Kromminga, *The Millennium* (Grand Rapids: Eerdmans, 1948).

38. Some dispensationalists, however, argue that the rapture is mid-tribulational, that is, that the first three and one-half years of the tribulation precede the rapture. For a presentation of this position, see Gleason L. Archer, "The Case for the Mid-seventieth-week Rapture Position," in *The Rapture: Pre-, Mid-, or Post-tribulational* (Grand Rapids: Zondervan, 1984), 113-45.

39. See Pentecost, *Things to Come*, 219-28.

of the tribulation. During this time the archenemy of Christ rules over the world, and God pours out his wrath on the earth.

The tribulation period climaxes with a military conflagration in Palestine,[40] in the midst of which Christ returns with the armies of heaven and routs his enemies.[41] Israel acknowledges Jesus as Messiah, and the thousand-year kingdom is established on the earth, during which time Israel will enjoy presence in the land of Palestine and prominence among the nations.[42] Hence, just as the tribulation is the time of "Jacob's trouble," so also the millennium will be the time during which God will pour out unparalleled blessings on Israel. National Israel, therefore, not the New Testament church, is prominent in the dispensationalist understanding of the vision of the thousand years.

The Deeper Issue of Millennialism

We ought not minimize the exegetical question concerning the proper interpretation of the vision of the thousand years. Yet theologically more significant is the deeper conviction concerning human history each of the three major millennial positions illustrates. Each embodies a response to the practical question as to the attitude that ought to characterize the church of Jesus Christ as it seeks to fulfil its mandate in the world. Each of these basic theological attitudes offers insight into the heartbeat of the Spirit which transcends them all. We may stylize these differing outlooks toward history as optimism, pessimism, and realism.

Postmillennial optimism. Postmillennialism sets forth a basically optimistic outlook toward history and our role in the attainment of God's program. The evil one attempts through seduction, treachery, or persecution to thwart the onward movement of the divine purposes. Nevertheless, the people of God will be successful in the comple-

---

40. The classical dispensationalist scenario is summarized by Dallas Seminary theologian Robert P. Lightner in the column, "Dallas Seminary Faculty Answer Your Questions," *Kindred Spirit* 15/1 (Spring, 1991): 3.

41. Pentecost, *Things to Come*, 358. For detailed dispensationalist descriptions of the military intrigue at the end of the tribulation, see Pentecost, *Things to Come*, 318-58; See also Hal Lindsey, *The Late Great Planet Earth*, Bantam edition (New York, Bantam Books, 1973).

42. See, for example, Pentecost, *Things to Come*, 508-11.

tion of the divinely given mandate. Christ will reign over the world through his obedient church, and the principles of peace and righteousness permeate the whole earth.

In keeping with this optimistic outlook toward world history, postmillennial theologies emphasize the continuity between the present order and God's reign. The future kingdom is a heightening of forces already at work in the present. The "golden age" is the product of concursive action, as human agents cooperate with the divine Spirit in bringing God's goals to pass.

At its best, then, the postmillennial world view leads to engagement in the world.[43] Postmillennialism forms a reminder that before the people of God can become the church triumphant we must be the church militant. En route to the dawning of the golden age there are battles to be won. And because the divine power is now at work through the church, that golden age may be "just around the corner."

In this manner, postmillennialism is the voice of the Spirit calling us to confident engagement. We can be optimistic, because God is sovereign over history and is actively bringing his sovereign goal to pass. In the cosmic battle, we have joined the cause that will in the end be victorious. Through Christ this sovereign God has commissioned us to participate in the advance of the divine reign and the establishment of community. Knowing this, we ought to be motivated to redouble our commitment to work and pray, in order that his will might be done on earth as it is in heaven.

Premillennial pessimism. As nineteenth century American theological history so aptly demonstrates, left unbridled, postmillennial optimism runs the risk of separating itself from its proper source and thereby degenerating into blind utopianism. The awareness of our role in cooperating with the God of history can easily lead to a sense that we are the determiners of our history. And the proclamation of the kingdom of God as the goal of historical activity can unfortu-

---

43. It is no historical accident that by and large the great thrusts toward worldwide evangelistic outreach and social concern in the modern era were launched by a church imbued with the optimism that characterizes postmillennial thinking. See for example, the discussion of Puritan missions in Iain H. Murray, *The Puritan Hope* (London: Banner of Truth Trust, 1971), 131-83, esp., 149-51, 178. See also, John Jefferson Davis, *Christ's Victorious Kingdom* (Grand Rapids: Baker, 1986), 118-19.

nately be transformed into efforts to produce the kingdom of God within history. Consequently, in the midst of our confident acceptance of our mandate, we need to hear what the Spirit is saying to the churches through premillennialism. In contrast to the optimism of postmillennialism, premillennialists display a basic pessimism concerning history and the role we play in its culmination. Despite all our attempts to convert or reform the world, prior to the end Antichrist will gain control of human affairs, premillennialists reluctantly predict. Only the catastrophic action of the returning Lord will bring about the reign of God and the glorious age of blessedness and peace.

In keeping with this basic pessimism concerning world history, premillennial theologies emphasize the discontinuity, or even the contradiction, between the present order and the kingdom of God. They likewise elevate the divine future over the evil present. The kingdom is the radically new thing God will do. However it may be conceived, the "golden age" comes as God's gracious gift and solely through God's action. Simply stated, premillennial pessimism reminds us that ultimately the hope of the world rests in God, and not in our feeble actions.

Amillennial realism. Convinced of the truths found in pre- and postmillennialism but lacking their historical focal point, amillennialists are drawn to the ethos of each of the millenarian positions, while in the end rejecting both. They seek to balance and blend the two into a nonmillenarian outlook. The result is a world view characterized by realism.

Victory and defeat, success and failure, good and evil will coexist until the end. The future is neither a heightened continuation of the present, nor an abrupt contradiction to it. The kingdom of God does not come by human cooperation with the divine power currently at work in the world, but neither is it simply the divine gift for which we can only wait expectantly.

Consequently, both unchastened optimism and despairing pessimism are illegitimate. Rather, the amillennialist world view calls the church to realistic activity in the world. Under the guidance and empowerment of the Holy Spirit the church will be successful in its mandate; yet ultimate success will come only through God's grace. The kingdom of God arrives as the divine action breaking into the world; yet human cooperation brings important, penultimate results. Therefore, God's people must expect great things in the present; but knowing that the kingdom will never arrive in its fullness in history, they must always remain realistic in their expectations.

Our ultimate hope. Amillennial realism lifts our sights above the merely historical future to the realm of the eternal God. It reminds us that the kingdom of God is a transcendent reality which can be confused with no earthly kingdom prior to the final transformation of creation. No earthly city can ever hope to become the New Jerusalem, except through a radical transformation of human nature and of the universe, which through the fall unwillingly participates in the human predicament.

Because of the cosmic dimensions of the vision of corporate eschatology, our ultimate goal is not a golden age on earth, whether preceding or following the return of Christ. Rather, we await with eager anticipation a glorious eternal reality, the new heaven and new earth. This alone forms the complete fulfillment of the promises of land and physical blessings God announced to ancient Israel and the promise of the fullness of our participation in eternal life proclaimed in the New Testament. Only with the coming of the gloriously recreated cosmos will God make his dwelling with us. And only on the redeemed, transformed creation will we experience full community with nature, with each other, and most importantly with God our Creator and Redeemer.

This radically transcendent kingdom is at the same time radically immanent.[44] God has broken into our world. He has brought us into participation in his already inaugurated explosion into the earthly realm. Therefore, in the midst of the brokenness of life we can celebrate the new life of the Spirit.

---

44. This is the consensus reached by the newer research into the kingdom of God in the teaching of Jesus. See, Bruce Chilton, "Introduction," in *The Kingdom of God in the Teaching of Jesus*, ed. Bruce Chilton, *Issues in Religion and Theology* 5 (Philadelphia: Fortress, 1984): 25-26.

The Era of the Immanent End of History

History is the story of God's activity in bringing humankind to his desired goal. The proleptic presence of community within history raises the question of corporate eschatology: When will the community we now partially enjoy be fully present? When will history reach its consummation? To respond to this question, we must turn our attention to the Scriptures, especially the New Testament. We inquire about the New Testament conception of the end of the age. The biblical writers declared that ours is the age of the immanent consummation of history. What does this mean?

The biblical understanding of our age. The biblical writers repeatedly spoke about the end of history. They declared that one day, God will bring his program for humankind to completion in the glorious return of Christ which will inaugurate the full establishment of community. New Testament assertions about the events that must transpire in the future arose from a specific conception of the nature of the present era. The early believers understood our age as the eschatological day, the day of immanent fulfillment and of Christ's reign.

(1) Lying behind the writings of the New Testament is the presupposition that the world has entered a special, eschatological era. This age is bounded on the one side by the Christ-event (the advent, life, death, resurrection, and ascension of Jesus of Nazareth and the outpouring of the Holy Spirit) and on the other side by the consummation (the return of Christ in victory and judgment). When viewed from the Old Testament perspective of promise, this is the time of fulfillment (1 Pet. 1:10-12). These are "the last days," the final era before the consummation of God's activity in the world.

The biblical writers presented the age between the ascension and the consummation as a two-sided era. On the one hand, we will witness a regrouping of the forces of evil. Persecution, heresy, deception, and seduction will increase as the Evil One mounts an onslaught against the message of God's universal rule. The enemy will seek to resist the advancement of the church into the domain of darkness. He will also attempt to neutralize the ranks of the church. The marshaling of the forces of evil will be partially effective, for many will fall away, be deceived, or lose heart. On the other hand, our era will also be marked by the progress of the gospel. The Spirit-empowered church will complete its mandate before the end comes.

The early Christians were convinced that they were already witnessing the presence of both dimensions. The forces of evil were regrouping, even as the gospel was spreading throughout the world. According to the New Testament authors, these events constituted signs that the special eschatological age had indeed dawned. Consequently, they believed that the last days were already upon the world (1 John 2:18-19).

(2) The expectation concerning future events that characterized the outlook of the early church arose likewise from their belief in the universal lordship of Christ. The New Testament believers knew that if Jesus is Lord, he must be Lord over every power in the universe. If he is indeed Lord, however, the eschaton must be a real historical event. The day must come when Jesus acts to vindicate those who now acknowledge his lordship and to exercise dominion over every cosmic power. One day he must bring victory not only over those who persecute the church but also over every power hostile to humankind, including our great cosmic enemy, death. Because of their hope for this victory, the apostles saw Christ's return to raise the dead as *the* crucial future event.

The eschatological timetable. The New Testament insight into the nature of our era as the age of fulfillment and of the reign of Christ leads us to speak of the eventful climax to human history. Nevertheless, the question still remains: How will history come to its end?

Taken as a whole, the witness of the Scriptures allows us to offer a simple summary of the glorious climax of human history. The Bible is clear that the central event with which the corporate human story closes is the final triumph of good over evil. This means that the forces of evil will regroup for a final onslaught, only to be routed by the victorious return of Jesus Christ himself. At that glorious event the corporate people of God will be united with their Lord, a union facilitated by the resurrection. This eschatological event will be the doorway to our enjoyment of an eternal presence with our God.

Beyond providing us with this insight into the future, the biblical documents do not provide dates and detailed sequences. We cannot glean from the Scriptures a group of isolated incidents that together form a series of mileposts from which we can construct an "end times check list." Nor can we determine what length of the distance from the first coming to the second the world has traversed. On the contrary, we can only say with the New Testament writers, "The time is near" (Rev. 22:10).

Rather than a detailing of history written before the time, eschatological statements in the Bible are ultimately expressions of hope, understood in the Greek sense of sure expectation and certainty. They are declarations as to what must certainly transpire. As expressions of hope, eschatological assertions are fundamentally statements of grounded expectation, based on an understanding of the nature of reality, history, and our present situation.

The eschatological consummation will occur: The Lord will certainly return. While the end is sure, the path to the realization of God's ultimate purpose for creation is in some sense open. History is in part contingent; it includes risks. War may lead to a doomsday holocaust, or our misuse of the environment may usher in an ecological disaster. God himself is the author of the openness of the historical process, for he calls us to participate in history. God's purposes for humankind will surely be realized; yet he invites us to be agents in his historical work. This theme is evident in Peter's admonition to his readers to hasten the day of the Lord (2 Pet. 3:12).

The eschatological assertions of the Bible intend to inspire hope within us. As a people of hope we can engage with confidence in the work of consummation. Through the Scriptures, God sets before us a vision of the coming community, which he bestows and will bestow on his creation as a gracious gift. This God stands before us— in the future—beckoning us onward. In hope, therefore, we can direct our efforts, including our prayers[45] and our actions, toward the advance of God's program in the world. We can be steadfast at each step en route to the return of our Lord, knowing that our involvement in the corporate human story carries eternal significance (1 Cor. 15:58).

---

45. See Stanley J. Grenz, *Prayer: The Cry for the Kingdom* (Peabody, Mass.: Hendrickson, 1988).

Christians assert that history is meaningful. Our human story will reach its climax in the return of the Lord Jesus Christ. God's purposes do not end with humankind, however. Rather, they encompass all creation. To this wider dimension of eschatology we now turn.

23

The Consummation of God's Cosmic Program

Then I saw a new heaven and a new earth, for the first heaven and the first earth had passed away, and there was no longer any sea. I saw the Holy City, the new Jerusalem, coming down out of heaven from God, prepared as a bride beautifully dressed for her husband. And I heard a loud voice from the throne saying, "Now the dwelling of God is with men, and he will live with them. They will be his people, and God himself will be with them and be their God." (Rev. 21:1-3)

Outline

The Christian message proclaims that God is active in bringing his purposes to pass. He desires that we overcome death through participation in Christ's resurrection and thereby enjoy eternal life. He intends that our common human narrative culminate in the glorious return of the Lord Jesus Christ. At the same time, God's purposes are greater than either our individual existence or the human story. He is directing his activities to a goal which is ultimately cosmic in scope, one which envelops all creation. God's program for the cosmos culminates in the eternal community of the new creation.

Our exposition of "cosmic eschatology" begins with the question, What marks the transition from the present order to the eternal reality? According to the Bible, the new creation does not arise through cosmic evolution or by means of human progress. Rather, it comes with a climactic event, the eschatological judgment of all creation.

When we consider the judgment, a second question arises: Is there a dark side of the consummation? Will all creation participate in the new order, or will some humans be left out? And if some do not participate, what will be their situation?

As important as this theme is, however, the consummation of creation will not be primarily destruction. Rather, God will incorporate the cosmos into the transformation that was displayed in the resurrection of Jesus and inaugurated by that event. Our chapter closes, therefore, with a discussion of the joyous eternal reality we will share.

The Transition from Creation to New Creation

God is directing his actions toward an all-encompassing goal, the transformation of the entire cosmos into the glorious eternal community of the new creation. What precipitates that transformation? What marks the transition from the present order to the new order God intends for his creation? The Christian eschatological vision answers with the word "judgment." Creation becomes new creation only as it is transformed at a day of reckoning.

The Judgment of the Cosmos

In chapter 22 we noted that the eschatological consummation of history comes as judgment on the human story. This principle holds for the entire cosmos. En route to the new creation, all creation must pass through judgment.

The certainty of cosmic judgment. Judgment is one of the most recurring themes in the Bible. God does not simply abandon his creation, but directs the entire cosmos in accordance with his own purposes. In addition, he calls creatures to account. Judgment encompasses both of these dimensions of God's ordering of creation. God's exercise of judgment over creation is pervasive. Especially important to the biblical writers is the reckoning God requires of the cosmic powers. In their struggle against polytheism, the Old Testament writers asserted that God acts in judgment on the gods of the nations (Ex. 12:12; Num. 33:4; Jer. 10:14-15).

The New Testament writers spoke of God's judging the heavenly beings. For those who fell into wickedness this is already a past event (2 Pet. 2:4; Jude 6). Nevertheless, there remains yet a future aspect of the judgment for both demons and angels (Matt. 25:41). And believers will participate in this event (1 Cor. 6:3). The divine judgment of the cosmic forces is also related to Christ's work, for in his death Jesus "made a public spectacle" of the powers and authorities (Col. 2:15). Above all, however, God will bring the devil to the day of reckoning, leading to his banishment from the new creation (Rev. 20:10).

The judgment focuses on moral creatures and cosmic forces. Yet the biblical authors also spoke of an eschatological judgment of creation itself. In a poignant description, Peter appealed to the Genesis flood as a foreshadowing of this future catastrophe: "By water also the world of that time was deluged and destroyed. By the same word the present heavens and earth are reserved for fire, being kept for the day of judgment and destruction of ungodly men" (2 Pet. 3:6-7). On the day of the Lord, he explained, "The heavens will disappear with a roar; the elements will be destroyed by fire, and the earth and everything in it will be laid bare" (v. 10).

The purpose of cosmic judgment. We can readily understand the severity of the judgment God reserves for the evil cosmic powers. Because they have worked in opposition to the divine purposes for creation, they cannot participate in the new order God will fashion. Less comprehensible, however, is the necessity for eschatological judgment on the physical creation, which Peter described. Why must the transition of the physical universe from creation to new creation come by way of judgment? Two considerations shed light on this necessity.

(1) The eschatological event is linked to the liberation of creation from its present situation. In an insightful text, Paul reminded his readers that not only humans, but also the physical world now exists in a state of bondage:

> "For the creation was subjected to frustration, not by its own choice, but by the will of the one who subjected it, in hope that the creation itself will be liberated from its bondage to decay and brought

> into the glorious freedom of the children of God. We know that the
> whole creation has been groaning as in the pains of childbirth right up
> to the present time." (Rom. 8:20-22)

Although the apostle provided few details, he indicated that even in its physical dimension, the cosmos does not yet fully reflect God's intention.

The aspect that Paul singled out is the power of decay which we see at work in creation. Decay and death are a natural part of the present order, of course. When we view them in accordance with God's eschatological purpose and desire, however, the presence of decay is not "natural." Decay and death do not belong to the fulfillment to which God intends to bring creation. The new creation emerges only after the physical cosmos undergoes a transformation through which it is liberated from decay. We know this transformation as God's eschatological judgment. On that day, the Creator will purge from the physical realm all decay-producing elements, thereby freeing the cosmos from bondage.

(2) The second consideration builds on the first. Judgment is God's means of preparing the physical realm for the fellowship he intends to share with all creation. God's ultimate intention is to establish eternal community with his creatures. According to the vision of the seer of the Apocalypse, God desires to make his dwelling within creation (Rev. 21:1-3). He purposes to create a new realm in which he enjoys fellowship with his redeemed people on the earth.

In order for it to become the home to this new community, the cosmos must be changed. God's presence necessitates a radical transformation. The presence of the eternally unchanging one requires that the physical realm be cleansed from the power of decay. The presence of the one who is life requires that the cosmos be purified from the power of death. Only when it has been transformed can all creation offer complete and worthy praise to the Creator.

The presence of redeemed humankind in the new creation likewise necessitates a radical transformation. Our entrance into eternal fellowship with God occurs only as we undergo resurrection. Through this event God will gloriously change our perishable, mortal bodies. Glorified immortal persons cannot inhabit an earth characterized by decay and death. For this reason, God must reorder the earth so that it becomes a fitting environment for us. The eschatological judgment, therefore, is God's act of transforming the old cosmos into the new, for the sake of his purpose of establishing the eternal community of a redeemed humankind enjoying the presence of their Redeemer God as they dwell in harmony with the renewed creation.

The Judgment of Humankind

God's purposes encompass all creation. Consequently, the judgment that marks the transition from the old to the new extends to the entire cosmos. Nevertheless, God's activity in the world focuses on humans, for as the perpetrators of the failure we call sin, we are the aspect of creation needing reconciliation. It comes as no surprise, therefore, that humans are the focus of the theological theme of judgment. As Christians we confess that all people, both the living and the dead, will face divine judgment (Acts 10:42; 2 Tim. 4:1; 1 Pet. 4:5). For humankind, like the cosmos in general, this eschatological event forms the transition from the old to the new creation.

The certainty of our judgment. The expectation that all humans will face judgment is present throughout the biblical literature. Nevertheless, the people of God grew in their understanding of the inevitability of the divine reckoning.

In the early stages of their history, the ancient Hebrews were primarily aware of judgment as a present reality. They knew that sin brought evil consequences. They knew as well that God could and did mete out punishment on wicked nations. They had seen, for example, the plagues he had sent upon the Egyptians. They themselves had been the instruments of his judgment on the Canaanites when they conquered the land. For Israel, God's punishment of the wicked meant that judgment had a positive aspect. Through such events Yahweh liberated the Israelites from their enemies, justified his own claim to deity, and exonerated his faithful people.

The prophets heightened the awareness of the present dimension of judgment. In addition, however, they turned attention to the future. The prophets proclaimed a coming day of the Lord—a judgment in history. In that grand event Yahweh will judge the nations

(Amos 1:2; Joel 3:2), thereby vindicating his name and his people. Yet contrary to the expectations of many in Israel, the future judgment will also be a dark day, as God calls his own people to account (Amos 9:1-4; Mal. 3:2-5).

As the prophets increasingly directed their anticipation to an eschatological reign of the Messiah, the expectation of a future judgment in history came to be eclipsed by that of a final judgment at the end of history. This focus on an eschatological day of reckoning added an individual dimension to the corporate understanding of judgment. Although it appeared that the wicked flourished and the righteous suffered, the prophets assured Israel that divine justice will prevail in the future judgment.

This anticipation led godly thinkers to ask whether and on what basis the saints of previous generations will participate in the eschatological reign of the Messiah. God's messenger revealed to Daniel that both the righteous and the wicked will face final judgment to receive eternal blessedness or damnation (Dan. 12:2).

The prophetic-apocalyptic expectation formed the context for the teaching of Jesus and the early church. Both our Lord and the apostles declared the certainty of a day of reckoning for all persons (Matt. 11:24; 12:36; Rom. 14:10; 2 Cor. 5:10; Heb. 9:27; 2 Pet. 2:9; 1 John 4:17). While the New Testament writers echoed the anticipation of Israel's prophets, they also set forth a decisively new dimension, namely, the identity of the eschatological judge. In his vision, Daniel had seen "one like a son of man"—a human figure—to whom God gave the prerogative of judgment (Dan. 7:13-14). The New Testament community declared that this eschatological judge is none other than the crucified Jesus. Their belief had its genesis in our Lord's own self-consciousness. As we noted in chapter 12, he announced himself as the Son of man who will one day come in judgment (Mark 14:62).

The New Testament witness to the identity of the judge adds a new dimension to the certainty of the final judgment. The exaltation of the crucified one to the right hand of the Father constitutes God's affirmation of Jesus' righteousness in the face of his opponents (Acts 2:36). Although God has pronounced his confirmation of Jesus, our

Lord must be vindicated throughout the whole cosmos. This can only occur when God publicly displays that in Jesus all things do have their connection (Col. 1:17). As the event that marks the transition from the old to the new creation, the eschatological judgment is God's final vindication of Jesus.

The certainty of the judgment arises not only from the movement of salvation history toward the vindication of Jesus, but from the character of God himself. Rather than facilitating the retribution of a wrathful God, as some suggest, our presence at the judgment is a sign and outworking of God's love. God created us with the intent that we should willingly respond to his gracious invitation of reconciliation and fellowship. The judgment indicates the seriousness with which God views our response to his call.

The time of our judgment. As we have already noted, the biblical authors spoke of both a temporal and an eschatological dimension of judgment. God calls us to account in the present, and we will give a final account at the return of our Lord.

(1) We have already reminded ourselves that the idea of temporal judgment was an important Old Testament theme. However, the presence of judgment within history—understood as God calling humans to account—was also an important New Testament teaching. Paul, for example, declared that God is continually exercising judgment over the ungodly. As humans practice iniquity, God consigns them to the debilitating results of their sin (Rom. 1:24-28). In many cases we simply reap what we sow (Gal. 6:7-8).

In addition to this somewhat passive aspect of judgment, God's present reckoning takes on a more active role. As God's people proclaim and live out the gospel, the light of God shines on human wickedness (John 3:18-20). Thereby the evil deeds of the godless which once passed unnoticed can no longer be hidden. They are made visible through comparison with the proclamation of the divine standard for human life and conduct.

The New Testament writers also spoke of a present experience of accountability and judgment for the community of Christ. On certain specific occasions in the early church, God brought punishment to the perpetrators of grievous sins (Acts 5:1-11; 1 Cor. 11:30). The present judgment is not merely negative in its intent, however. God's judging activity is also remedial or preventative, having as its goal that we be spared future condemnation (1 Cor. 11:32). Further, it is a sign of God's fatherly discipline, so that we might grow spiritually (Heb. 12:5-11) and be more productive in his service (John 15:2).

(2) Ultimately, the present experience of judgment takes its significance from the reality of an eschatological day of reckoning. Exactly when will this event transpire? Evangelical theologians differ over this matter. Their opinions are influenced in part by their understanding of the millennium.

Many premillennialists anticipate a series of eschatological events of reckoning. Immediately at his return, Christ will judge the peoples of the earth (Matt. 24:31-46). This is not the final day of reckoning, however, the judgment of the living and the dead. The "great white throne judgment" does not occur until after the millennium (Rev. 20:11-15). Classical dispensationalists add at least one additional judgment to these two. During the tribulation period, our Lord judges the believers, who were raptured to meet Christ in the air (1 Thess. 4:16-17).

In contrast to the multiple judgments premillennialists anticipate, amillennialists and postmillennialists generally look for only one judgment. They understand the various New Testament texts as providing unique perspectives on the single judgment of all humankind that will occur at Christ's return. This simpler expectation not only seems more in keeping with the biblical witness, but is also more reflective of the nature of the eschatological judgment.

The basis for judgment. The witness of the Bible is that all will stand at the judgment. But what will be the basis for the reckoning that we will all give to God? And is there one standard by means of which God will measure all humankind?

From the issuing of the first instructions to Adam in the Garden of Eden (Gen. 2:15-17) to the vision of the final judgment in the Apocalypse (Rev. 20:11-15) the biblical authors declare that we will be judged according to our works (Jer. 17:10; 32:19; Matt. 16:27; Rom. 2:6; 2 Cor. 5:10; Gal. 6:7-8; Rev. 22:12). Among the works which Jesus cited as leading to condemnation include the accumulation of earthly possessions to the exclusion of true wealth (Mark 10:17-31; Luke 12:13-21), lack of care for the disadvantaged (Matt. 25:31-46), and unwillingness to forgive (18:21-35).

This broader theme of judgment according to deeds forms the context for raising the question concerning the standard for judgment.

Several New Testament texts suggest that God will use different standards in judging the people of the world. According to Paul, the Jews will be condemned by the law which they possess, whereas the Gentiles who do not have the law will be accused by their own consciences (Rom. 2:12-16). At the end of his parables enjoining watchfulness, Jesus declared that the servant who knowingly disobeys his master will suffer greater punishment that the one who disobeys in ignorance. He then concluded with this principle: "From everyone who has been given much, much will be demanded; and from the one who have been entrusted with much, much more will be asked" (Luke 12:48). Jesus raised a similar point with the Jews, declaring that on the day of judgment his own message will condemn those who reject his words (John 12:48). The author of Hebrews applied this principle to those recipients of the gospel who reject Christ: "Anyone who rejected the law of Moses died without mercy on the testimony of two or three witnesses. How much more severely do you think a man deserves to be punished who has trampled the Son of God under foot" (Heb. 10:28-29).

As the foregoing examples indicate, texts that present differing standards generally do so in the context of the negative outcome of judgment (condemnation). When the biblical writers include as well the positive aspect (the possibility of commendation, blessing, and vindication), they indicate that all humankind will be measured by one standard, conformity to the divine will. Paul's words to the Romans are an example: "To those who by persistence in doing good seek glory, honor, and immortality, he will give eternal life. But for those who are self-seeking and who reject the truth and follow evil, there will be wrath... There will be...glory, honor, and peace for everyone who does good" (Rom. 2:7-10).

The biblical focus on the divine will suggests that judgment is related to community. The standard against which God judges us can be nothing other than his own purpose or goal for humankind. His intention is that we live in fellowship with him, with each other, and with all creation. To the extent that we pursue community, our lives glorify God and therefore are consistent with his divine standard. The Lord greets such consistency with "glory, honor, and peace," even "eternal life," as Paul indicated.

In this connection, Christ is the standard for judgment. As we noted in chapter 10, Jesus revealed the divine design for humankind, namely, that we live in fellowship with, and obedience to God. Because he shows us what it means to be human, our Lord is the standard in comparison to whom our lives are measured.

The emphasis on the divine will as the standard of judgment assists us as well in understanding the manner in which believers will be involved in the act of judging (Matt. 19:28; Luke 22:30; 1 Cor. 6:2; Rev. 20:4). We are those in whom and among whom the Holy Spirit is creating obedience to God's intent to establish community. As a result, our lives bring to light the failure of moral creatures who do not live in accordance with God's desire.

Our presence at the judgment. At the final day of reckoning God will judge all humans according to their works. Obviously that judgment will result in God's just condemnation of the wicked. Less clear is how this biblical theme offers hope that anyone might attain entrance into God's eternal community.

Some Christians solve this apparent problem by surmising that believers will be exempted from the day of reckoning. Were we present at the judgment, our works could only elicit a sentence of condemnation. Therefore, we can only attain entrance to the kingdom by avoiding the final judgment. Proponents can marshall certain biblical texts in support of this view. Paul, for example, urged the Corinthians to judge themselves so that they will not come under judgment (1 Cor. 11:31). As we have seen, however, the assertion that we will not stand before God contradicts a theme that runs throughout Scripture: We will all face God's judgment. Rather than exempting us from the day of reckoning, Peter warned that judgment actually must begin with the community of Christ (1 Pet. 4:17).

Other theologians appeal to the connection between actions and character. Judgment by works is appropriate, because outward deeds reveal our inward spiritual state. Hence, believers' works give evidence to the presence in their lives of true faith (Gal. 5:6). This conclusion is a natural outworking of the principle Jesus offered in warning his hearers concerning false prophets: "By their fruit you will recognize them" (Matt. 7:16).

While this understanding is surely correct, it must be augmented by a further biblical theme. As we noted earlier, the New Testament writers introduced a great innovation into the Old Testament expectation. They knew the judge. The one who calls us to account is the God whom we have come to know in Christ. The one before whom we will stand on the last day is none other than the one who has extended his saving love toward us. In fact, God has already judged our sins in Jesus' death (Rom. 3:21-26; 8:1, 31-34). Consequently, all who are in Christ can face the day of reckoning without fear, because we will not come under divine condemnation (8:31-34).

Although our eternal destiny will not be at stake, we will nevertheless be present at the judgment. If this is so, then what purpose could judgment entail in our case? For us the day of reckoning will complete the process of sanctification leading to glorification. Judgment, therefore, will be an act of purging. God will test our works in order that he might remove all the dross (1 Cor. 3:13-15).

In addition to this somewhat negative function, the judgment will also serve a positive purpose. It will mark our vindication as Jesus' followers. Through the ascension, God installed Jesus as the Lord of the cosmos and the Son of Man. Our Lord's return as judge of the world will mark his universal, public vindication. We will share in that glorious event, for the cosmic judgment that constitutes Jesus' vindication will likewise be the vindication in the presence of all the cosmic powers of those who have confessed his name. For us, therefore, the return of Christ in judgment is a source of hope (1 John 4:17).

While a foundation for hope, the eschatological judgment will also entail surprise. The divine act of reckoning does not bypass the company of God's people. God's judgments in Old Testament history did not merely call Israel's neighbors to account. It moved through the chosen nation as well. So also the eschatological judgment will not merely affect humankind in general. It will also cut through the center of the church (1 Pet. 4:17). As Jesus warned, not all who call him "Lord" will enter the kingdom. To some he will respond, "I never knew you" (Matt. 7:21-23).

The nature of the judgment. In attempting to understand the eschatological judgment, we must be careful not to confuse our sometimes fanciful picture of the event with the event itself. We often conceive of the great day of reckoning as a vast host of individuals lining up to pass single file by the judge's bench in order to hear the pronouncement of condemnation or acquittal. The images in the New Testament form a marked contrast to this picture. The biblical writers described judgment as occurring swiftly, even instantaneously. More significantly, they presented this event not so much as a pronouncement of some previously unknown verdict but as bringing to light hidden realities. What we do not now see or acknowledge will be disclosed publicly (Luke 8:17).

The public disclosure of now hidden realities will constitute a vindication of God himself. In this age, it appears that God is slow to act in the cause of justice. His apparent slowness calls into question God's power, his willingness to act, and even his existence. Evil, not God, appears to be sovereign. God's apparent impotence is manifested whenever the wicked prosper and the righteous suffer (see Ps. 73:1-16). Most tragic of all, the Righteous One suffered at the hands of the wicked. As an extension of Jesus' suffering, his followers suffer at the hand of God's enemies.

One day, however, we will witness a great reversal, as God acts to overturn this situation. Just as in raising Jesus from the dead God passed judgment in favor of his righteous Son, so also he will one day pass judgment on behalf of the righteous (Luke 18:1-8). This action will vindicate God as the one who in his good time does indeed bring to justice his enemies and those who persecute his people (2

Pet. 3:3-10). Thereby, he demonstrates his wisdom and righteousness even to the cosmic powers (Eph. 3:10).

The eschatological reversal not only involves the righteous children of God, it also affects human social conditions. When God acts in judgment, he will overturn the power structures of society. At the present time the powerful appear to be in control of the affairs of life. On that day all will see that the sovereign God has sided with the powerless, for the Lord will champion the cause of the down-trodden. Jesus' promise that "the first will be last and the last will be first" will be fulfilled, as in the final judgment worldly standards give way to the divine criterion. Then all will see that God does not measure success as power and earthly prestige, but in accordance with humble servanthood and service to one another as well as the needy (Matt. 25:31-46; Mark 10:35-45).

Coming as the culmination of history, the judgment brings to light the unity of the cosmic story and our participation in it. What appears to be a fragmented flow of disconnected events hides a unifying thread. God has placed this unity—the *Logos*, the foundational principle of life—within all reality. On that day, all humankind will see plainly that Jesus of Nazareth is the link that brings unity to all of life. This historical person revealed God's loving heart as well as our human vocation.

At the judgment, our lives will be scrutinized in accordance with the unifying principle of all history as revealed in Jesus. The comparison of how we have lived with the revelation of the unity of life will result in a "shrill dissonance." We will see plainly the great gap between God's pattern for our lives and the actual way we lived.

In short, the judgment is not a capricious or arbitrary assigning of eternal fates to individuals. Rather, it is God's public revelation of the significance of all history. This cosmic disclosure will indicate the extent to which our individual histories reflect and incorporate the meaning of God's history. The judgment will indeed be a day of surprises!

Eternal rewards. Viewing the judgment as the measuring of individual histories in the light of God's cosmic activity leads to the question of rewards. Will God reward us at the judgment? If so, in what sense are we to hold this expectation?

The New Testament writers gave some indication that believers will receive rewards on the day of judgment. Paul, for example, appealed to future reward and loss as a basis for challenging his readers to sober Christian living (1 Cor. 3:10-15). Occasionally the writers referred to various "crowns" that God will bestow on believers. And Jesus himself incorporated the concept of rewards in his teaching (Matt. 25:14-30).

Providing a counterbalance to the anticipation of rewards, however, is another biblical theme. Absent in the eternal kingdom are the distinctions among people so prevalent in this age. In the parable of the workers, for example, the vineyard owner rewards the late-comers with the same generous wage he gives to those who worked the entire day (Matt. 20:1-16).

Not only must we temper the idea of rewards by the egalitarianism of the New Testament, we must recognize in it certain theological problems. The expectation of rewards risks introducing an impure motivation into Christian service. True biblical spirituality necessitates that we serve God out of love for the one who saved us, not because we desire to be exalted above others. Further, the concept of rewards runs the danger of perpetuating the class systems so prevalent in this world, as we give the impression that the kingdom will be ruled by the privileged few—the "rewarded"—just as human societies are.

Despite its dangers, we ought not to abandon entirely the expectation of eternal rewards. It reminds us that our labors in service to the Lord have eternal significance, for he promises to reward his faithful followers (1 Cor. 15:58).

We can avoid these potential theological difficulties as we keep in mind the dimension of surprise in the judgment. Our Judge uses a criterion that differs from the world's standards. As a result, those who in this life appear to be the lowly and the unimportant are the very persons the Lord may elevate above others whom we esteem as the most prominent. This principle applies to motives as well. Those whose labors have been motivated by purely selfish ends will be surprised when the Lord rewards others. As Jesus repeatedly declared, the path to greatness in the kingdom follows the route he himself pioneered, self-sacrifice in service to others.

Finally, the principle of divine justice assuages the sensitivities of the powerless. Because the mark of greatness in the kingdom is humble servanthood, the eternal society will be free from the domination by the powerful that is evident in human society. The prominent persons in God's new order will be those who are servants of all.

To summarize: the judgment is the public, cosmic revealing of the truth of reality. This revelation will bring surprise and joy to some, as they are welcomed into eternal bliss and receive the rewards of their labors. For others, this day will come as a shock, for they will see clearly the ultimate failure of their lives. The shock of judgment will begin within the believing community, as some discover that although they are saved they rendered only meager service to the Lord (1 Cor. 3:15).

The Dark Side of the Judgment

The judgment will mark the revealing of now hidden realities. Above all, it will bring to light that God created us for community. The anticipation of a day of reckoning raises the question of possible failure. The New Testament believers understood that for the enemies of God the eschatological event will result in exclusion from community with their Creator (Luke 13:25-29; Matt. 22:13; Rom. 6:21; Phil. 1:28; 3:19; 1 Thess. 5:3; 2 Thess. 1:8f).

Is this failure beyond repair? Will some never realize their destiny throughout all eternity? Or is exclusion from community merely temporal, so that all will eventually participate in God's new creation? And if the potential for an eternal exclusion form our destiny is true, what form will it take?

Universalism

Nearly all Christian thinkers agree that our loving God wants all to be saved, but there is also a dark side to the good news because God's justice requires that he not overlook human failure. Theologians disagree, however, as to the intent and extent to which God's justice must operate.

Some argue that God's sentence of condemnation is remedial and consequently not irrevocable. Like a great pedagogue, God condemns in order that he might bring all to salvation. In the end God will gather every person into his eternal fellowship (hence, the name "universalism"); all persons will be restored to God (hence, the designation "the doctrine of *apokatastasis*").

The place of universalism in the church. Universalist ideas were present in the church by the early 200s. The most celebrated early advocate was the Alexandrian church father, Origen (185-254). He suggested that even Satan himself would eventually be welcomed into everlasting bliss.[1] Patristic proponents held that the universal restoration occurs through Jesus Christ.[2] All will be saved, Origen argued, because through the reconciling power of the resurrected Christ God's love eventually wins over all creaturely resistance.[3]

The church condemned Origen's universalism, and the teaching fell into disfavor in the Middle Ages. Yet this viewpoint has refused to disappear. Since the Enlightenment, the doctrine of *apokatastasis* has gained considerable following. Many liberal theologians in the 1800s followed the lead of Friedrich Schleiermacher[4] and were influenced by this alternative to the traditional doctrine of hell.[5]

Although several leading twentieth-century theologians were universalists, others preferred to be more cautious. Karl Barth, for example, remained somewhat ambivalent so as not to place limits on God's grace.[6] Whereas universalism demands that God's grace

---

1. For a description of Origen's position, see R. P. C. Hanson, *Allegory and Event: A Study of the Sources and Significance of Origen's Interpretation of Scripture* (London: SCM, 1959), 335.

2. John Sanders, *No Other Name: An Investigation into the Destiny of the Unevangelized* (Grand Rapids: Eerdmans, 1992), 81.

3. For this characterization, see G. C. Berkouwer, *The Return of Christ*, trans. James Van Oosterom (Grand Rapids: Eerdmans, 1972), 390.

4. Friedrich Schleiermacher, *The Christian Faith*, second edition, ed. H. R. Mackintosh and J. S. Stewart (Edinburgh: T. & T. Clark, 1928), 539-60, 720-22.

5. See, for example, Albrecht Ritschl, *The Christian Doctrine of Justification and Reconciliation*, ed. H. R. Mackintosh and A. B. Macaulay, reprint edition (Clinton, N.J.: Reference Book Publishers, 1966), 125-39.

6. Karl Barth, *Church Dogmatics*, trans. G. W. Bromiley (Edinburgh: T. & T. Clark, 1961) 4/3.1: 477-78.

reach all, he argued, its denial limits the ability of God's grace to extend to all.

In the context of contemporary religious pluralism, several theologians have reformulated the older doctrine of apokatastasis. Adherents of the newer pluralism are less committed to the finality of Jesus for the eternal salvation of non-Christians than were older thinkers such as Origen.[7]

The foundation of universalism. Many evangelicals find it difficult to understand how anyone who has read the Bible could embrace the doctrine of apokatastasis. Yet universalists are not at a loss for arguments in favor of their position. They garner support from theological, biblical, and pastoral considerations.[8]

(1) Universalists embrace this teaching because they find it to be the best reflection of certain theological considerations.

At the heart of the apologetic for universalism is an appeal to the divine love. Some universalists argue from the ultimate sovereignty of the God who is love,[9] whereas others refer to the persistency of the loving God.[10] God's love for all creation is so strong and so central to the divine being that God is unrelenting in pursuing the wayward. The God who is long-suffering and desires that all "come to a knowledge of the truth" could not rest in the enjoyment of eternity knowing that some humans were languishing in hell. Consequently, no one will eternally spurn the immense love of God. Origen suggested that even if it would require the creation of several universes like this one, God's love would pursue even the devil until he yields.

In addition to the divine love, universalists appeal to the triumph of Christ. According to the New Testament, Jesus' exaltation marked the installation of the one who had died for human sin and triumphed over all his enemies as the cosmic Lord. If Jesus is Lord of all, there can be no enclave in which his lordship does not operate, no realm

---

7. E.g., Paul Knitter, *No Other Name? A Critical Survey of Christian Attitudes toward the World Religions* (Maryknoll, N.Y.: Orbis, 1985), 143.

8. For this threefold categorization, see Stephen Travis, *I Believe in the Second Coming of Jesus* (Grand Rapids: Eerdmans, 1982), 200.

9. E.g., Langdon Gilkey, *Reaping the Whirlwind* (New York: Seabury, 1981), 298.

10. Nels Ferre, *Christ and the Christian* (New York: Harper, 1958), 247; *The Universal World: A Theology for a Universal Faith* (Philadelphia: Westminster, 1969), 258.

to which his death for sin and his triumph over the powers does not extend.

The presence of some in hell for all eternity would constitute just such an enclave where Jesus is not Lord. Hell would be a place beyond the reach of Jesus' reconciling work. It would be a realm over which death and sin rule as the antithesis of Jesus' claim to universal lordship.

(2) In addition to claiming that universalism best reflects these great Christian theological truths, proponents find direct biblical support for their position. Specifically, they appeal to texts which express God's desire that all be saved (1 Tim. 2:4; 4:10; 2 Pet. 3:9), proclaim that Christ's atonement is intended for all (2 Cor. 5:19; Titus 2:11; Heb. 2:9; 1 John 2:2), declare that God will bring all creation to its fullness in Christ (John 12:32; Eph. 1:10; Col. 1:16-23), or speak of a final restoration of all persons to God (Acts 3:19-21; Phil. 2:9-11).

Of the various texts that universalists cite, two stand out. Both come from Paul's pen and are connected to the theological theme of Christ's victory, for they draw out the universal implications of his work.

In the first text, the apostle draws a comparison between the first and second Adam in order to extol Jesus' victory over sin (Rom. 5:12-21). Whereas through disobedience the first Adam brought sin into the world, the second Adam won justification by his obedience. Paul appears to be envisioning a balanced parallel between the two. Just as Adam's sin brought condemnation to all humankind, so also the effects of Christ's obedience extend to all: "so also the result of one act of righteousness was justification that brings life for all men" (v. 18).

The second text emphasizes Christ's victory over death (1 Cor. 15:20-26a). Here Paul uses the same literary device with its apparent universalist implication (v. 22). Just as the first Adam brought death to humankind ("For as in Adam all die..."), so also the second Adam bestows resurrection life on all ("... so in Christ all will be made alive").

Some critics of universalism deny that Paul was speaking of a universal salvation. They see in the text merely a reference to the general resurrection. However, such an interpretation is improbable. In what sense could we properly declare that persons are "made alive" through Christ's resurrection, when they overcome physical death only to be banished to hell for eternity? In addition, the suggestion that the resurrection is the means whereby the dead are brought from the grave to the judgment is out of keeping with Paul's use of the term as a reference to the entrance into fullness of life.

(3) Finally, universalists display a pastoral concern for the unevangelized or for devotees of other religions. Proponents find it inconceivable that earthly choices should determine an irrevocable eternity apart from God, when so many people do not respond to the gospel in this life. This consideration leads these theologians to conclude that in the next life God will continue to draw all people to himself until everyone freely responds to his invitation and so participates in his new world.[11]

Difficulties with universalism. Critics of universalism claim that the view is neither biblically sound nor theologically necessary. Instead it is a serious distortion of Christian teaching.[12]

Critics fault proponents of apokatastasis for displaying a biblical exegesis that reads a universal homecoming into statements which actually declare the universal intent of a salvation that requires personal appropriation.[13] As Stephen Travis observed, "nearly all such 'universalist' statements occur alongside other statements about the need for faith in order to experience salvation."[14]

In addition, critics question the theological foundation of universalism. Some dismiss the doctrine on the basis that divine justice demands eternal punishment. This argument, however, is erroneous. As Berkouwer pointed out, "If the logic of vindicative and distributive justice did indeed have validity over against apocatastasis, not

---

11. For an example of this position, see John Hick, *Death and Eternal Life* (San Francisco: Harper and Row, 1976).

12. Hence, Travis, *I Believe in the Second Coming*, 201.

13. See, for example, Sanders, *No Other Name*, 107-8.

14. Travis, *I Believe in the Second Coming*, 202.

only would universal reconciliation have to be rejected, but any reconciliation at all would be impossible in principle."[15]

More germane is the suggestion that universalism fails to take seriously the limitation God has imposed on himself in creating humankind. Failing to acknowledge the vulnerable God of the Bible,[16] universalists simply go too far in their optimism for the outcome of the judgment. Travis declared, "Because love by definition must allow its object freedom to choose whether to respond or not, we *cannot* say that God's love will be successful in winning all."[17] Hans Schwarz offered a similar telling comment:

> [Universalism] does not take into account that the judgment is disclosure and finalization of our life attitude and not a transition to the universal love of God. If our life attitude runs counter to the love God extends, the result is a dichotomy that cannot be bridged through evolution or amelioration.[18]

Conditional Immortality

Some of the same theological considerations that lead thinkers to embrace universalism bring others to a second alternative. Like adherents of the doctrine of apokatastasis, proponents of "conditional immortality" or "annihilationism" take issue with any concept of eternal punishment that anticipates an unending conscious experience of torment for the unsaved. However, rather than optimistically declaring that God will eventually gather everyone into the eternal community, annihilationists anticipate that many will remain lost eternally. The unrighteous will not wallow outside the kingdom, however, but will be sentenced to extinction. Their fate will simply be cessation of existence.

Its presence in the church. Conditional immortality gained a sizeable number of adherents only in the late 1800s through the Seventh Day Adventists and later the Jehovah's Witnesses. Since 1960, however, several prominent British evangelicals have embraced this

---

15. Berkouwer, *The Return of Christ*, 394.

16. For this criticism, see Sanders, *No Other Name*, 110-13.

17. Travis, *I Believe in the Second Coming*, 203.

18. Hans Schwarz, *On the Way to the Future*, revised edition (Minneapolis: Augsburg, 1979), 262.

view, including Philip Edgcumbe Hughes,[19] Stephen Travis,[20] John Wenham,[21] and John Stott,[22] as well as the Canadian theologian Clark Pinnock.[23]

The foundation of annihilationism. Because their view is not accepted by the majority, evangelical proponents of conditional immortality spend much of their efforts attempting to show why they find the traditional teaching about hell unacceptable. To this end, they appeal to some of the same arguments raised by universalists.[24]

Rather than serving a useful purpose, eternal torment exhibits a vindictiveness incompatible with the loving God revealed in Jesus. In consigning some to hell, God acts in a manner that contradicts his goodness and offends our God-given sense of justice.[25] The presence of people in hell also interjects a metaphysical dualism into eternity which contradicts both Christ's victory and God's intention to reconcile all things in Christ and thereby to be all-in-all.[26]

Annihilationists add one additional criticism, however. They claim that the idea of eternal conscious punishment is the product of the intrusion of the Greek idea of the soul's immortality into biblical exegesis and Christian theology.[27] The biblical view, in contrast, is conditional immortality: We must receive immortality from God through participation in the resurrection.

To this critique of the idea of conscious eternal punishment, evangelical proponents of conditional immortality add a positive foundation from the Bible.[28] They find in the Old Testament the clear teaching that the end of the wicked is destruction (Ps. 37:2, 9-10, 20, 32; Mal. 4:1-3). This idea formed the context for the discussions of

19. Philip Edgcumbe Hughes, *The True Image* (Grand Rapids: Eerdmans, 1989), 402-407. These pages are reprinted as Philip Edgcumbe Hughes, "Conditional Immortality," in *Evangel* 10/7 (summer 1992): 10-12.

20. Travis, *I Believe in the Second Coming*, 198-99.

21. John Wenham, *The Goodness of God* (Downers Grove, Ill.: InterVarsity, 1974), 34-41.

22. David L. Edwards and John R. W. Stott, *Evangelical Essentials* (Downers Grove, Ill.: InterVarsity, 1988), 314-20.

23. Clark Pinnock, "The Conditional View," in *Four Views on Hell*, ed. William Crockett (Grand Rapids: Zondervan, 1992), 135-66.

24. See Travis, *I Believe in the Second Coming*, 199.

25. Pinnock, "The Conditional View," in *Four Views on Hell*, 149-54.

26. Ibid., 154-55.

27. Hence, ibid., 147; see also Travis, *I Believe in the Second Coming*, 198.

28. See, for example, Pinnock, "The Conditional View," in *Four Views on Hell*, 145-46.

the fate of the lost in the New. In keeping with the Old Testament background, Jesus used similar images to describe the situation of the wicked. They will be cast into the smoldering garbage heap of *gehenna* (Matt. 5:30) where they will be burned up (Matt. 3:10,12; 13:30,42,49-52) and destroyed in both body and soul (Matt. 10:28).

Annihilationists point to similar imagery scattered throughout the epistles. Paul spoke of the fate of the lost as death (Rom. 1:32; 6:23) and destruction (1 Cor. 3:17; Phil 1:28; 3:19). Peter used the same language (2 Pet. 2:1,3; 3:7; see also Heb. 10:39), likening the destruction of the ungodly to the burning of Sodom and Gomorrah (2 Peter 2:6; see also Jude 7) and the flood (2 Peter 3:6-7). And the seer envisioned the wicked consumed in the lake of fire, which he called "the second death" (Rev. 20:14-15).

Proponents acknowledge that certain New Testament texts do characterize the torment the wicked will suffer as "eternal." However, they caution us against coming to such texts with the presupposition that the soul is immortal. On this basis, Travis suggested an alternative understanding of the term *eternal* "may signify the permanence of the *result* of judgment rather than the continuation of the act of punishment itself."[29] Thus, "eternal punishment" means that the results of judgment "cannot be reversed."

Difficulties with annihilationism. Despite the influence of its evangelical advocates, the doctrine of conditional immortality has yet to displace the traditional view as the most widely held position among evangelicals. It is instructive to see why this is the case.

For many critics, the word *eternal* forms the Achilles' heal of annihilationism's biblical apologetic.[30] Interpretations such as Travis's lead to inconsistencies in the use of language. In several texts the same term refers both to the bliss of the righteous and to the punishment of the lost (Matt. 25:46). Further, because the judgment texts consign Satan to the same fate as the wicked, annihilationist exegesis leads to the conclusion that not only the unrighteous but also the devil and his cohorts will cease to exist. This seems to run counter to the

---

29. Travis, *I Believe in the Second Coming*, 199.

30. For a helpful discussion of the biblical materials, see Larry Dixon, *The Other Side of the Good News* (Wheaton, Ill.: Victor Books, 1992), 74-95.

expectation of the demons to whom Jesus spoke, for they anticipated an appointed time of torture (Matt. 8:29; Mark 5:7; for other uses of the same word, see Rev. 14:10; 18:7-8).

The idea that Satan is simply annihilated with those whom he held in bondage also runs afield in another manner. Several New Testament texts indicate that the unrighteous will suffer varying degrees of punishment. Those who have received greater opportunities for belief will suffer more severe condemnation (Matt. 10:15; 11:20-24; Luke 12:47-48). Conditional immortality, in contrast, anticipates only one ultimate destiny for all the wicked, an undifferentiated non-existence. This prospect both contradicts the teaching of Jesus and violates our sense of justice.

Conditional immortality runs into theological difficulties as well. The theory offers too simple a solution to a complex reality. Thereby it leads to two quite opposite problems.

On the one hand, simply passing out of existence seems to be an all-too-simple solution to the seriousness of the choices we make in life and our response to God's loving offer of community. Can we so easily escape the consequences of choosing alienation from God rather than reconciliation and fellowship with God? As Hans Schwarz asked, "how can there be an annihilation of anybody if there is no escape from God, since God is everywhere, even in death and beyond death?"[31]

On the other hand, annihilationism does not truly assuage the problems which lead its proponents to reject the traditional view. Ceasing to exist for all eternity is as permanent a consequence as conscious suffering in hell. For this reason, the annihilation of the lost ought to be equally offensive to evangelical sensibilities about what constitutes just punishment for decisions made during earthly life.

Despite these difficulties, at one central point annihilationism converges with the traditional view and stands against universalism. Proponents of conditional immortality do not chafe at the prospect of an eternal punishment for the unrighteous. They find problematic only the idea that the lost experience eternal conscious punishment.

---

31. Schwarz, *On the Way to the Future*, 262.

These sensitive Christians find the annihilation of the lost more in keeping with a gracious God.

This observation suggests that the difficulty between the two positions arises from attempts to pinpoint with too much detail the eternal situation of the lost. Annihilationists caution us against describing the eternal realm in present categories drawn from earthly existence. Just as we cannot envision what conscious bliss will mean to resurrected, spiritual bodies, so also we do not know what punishment will feel like to the eternally lost. While acknowledging the sad reality of hell, we must take seriously the concern annihilationists raise.

The Reality of Hell

Dominant throughout church history has been the anticipation of two eternal options lying beyond the judgment. The righteous enjoy unending fellowship in the community of God, whereas the unrighteous suffer eternal banishment from fellowship with their Creator.

The foundation of the doctrine. Proponents claim that the reality of two eternal conditions is the explicit teaching of the New Testament. Jesus spoke repeatedly about the two destinies and warned his listeners to avoid hell[32] (Matt. 13:42, 49-50; 22:13; 24:51; 25:10-13, 14-30, 46; John 5:29; see also Dan.12:2). The apostles echoed our Lord's teaching (2 Thess. 1:9; Heb. 6:2; Jude 7; Rev. 14:10-14).

In addition to explicit biblical statements, the possibility of eternal alternatives arises out of important theological considerations. Some proponents find such a theological foundation in the nature of human choice, specifically in the commonly held assertion that God has granted to humans the power of choosing whether to respond to God's love. Our capability to spurn reconciliation is as eternally consequential as our willingness to accept God's offer of fellowship. Hence, just as our acceptance of divine love is the gateway to eternal community, so also our rejection of that love means choosing a destiny apart from fellowship with God. God takes us so seriously that he will not force his will on anyone, not even in all eternity. As

---

32. For a recent discussion of the relevant texts, see Dixon, *The Other Side*, 121-47.

Travis correctly noted, "From the fundamental truth that God is love, it follows that he pays us the complement of treating all our actions as significant."[33]

This means, however, that God is engaging in a divine "experiment." He desires that humans freely respond to his love—that we enter into community with him, one another, and creation—and thereby that we truly become the image of the triune God. His desire, however, entails the possibility of our failure. Some of God's creatures may spurn God's love through all eternity and thus never realize our divinely-ordained destiny.

A more important theological basis for the possibility of two eternal options is our understanding of the divine love itself. Rather than being incompatible with God's love as some argue, the possibility of hell arises from a rigorous understanding of the nature of the God who is love.

God is an eternal lover. In keeping with his own nature, he loves his creation eternally, and he desires that humans respond to his love by enjoying unending fellowship with him. We dare not confuse God's love with sentimentality. As the great Lover, God is also the avenging protector of the love relationship. Consequently, God's love has a dark side. Those who spurn or seek to destroy the holy love relationship God desires to enjoy with creation experience the divine love as protective jealousy or wrath. Because God is eternal, our experience of God's love—whether as fellowship or as wrath— is also eternal. Just as the righteous enjoy unending community with God, so also those who set themselves in opposition to God's love experience his holy love eternally. For them, however, this experience is hell.

Hell: the eternal tragedy. The connection we have outlined between the two eternal alternatives and God's intention for his creatures points us to the manner in which we may understand hell. Ultimately, hell is the eternal tragedy, the eternal human failure.

Repeatedly Jesus spoke of the dark side of eternity as *gehenna*, a transliteration from the Hebrew *ge hinnom*. Hinnom was a valley south of Jerusalem where under Ahaz and Manasseh children were

---

33. Travis, 185.

sacrificed in fire to Molech (2 Kings 16:3; 21:6; 2 Chron. 28:3; 33:6). The prophets borrowed the term as a symbol for judgment (Jer. 7:31-32; 19:6) and later for the final judgment.[34] In Jesus' day, the valley was used as a burial place for criminals and for burning garbage. Located as it was outside the city of Jerusalem, it formed an appropriate metaphor for the destiny of the lost (Matt. 5:22,29-30; 10:28; 18:9; 23:33; Mark 9:43-47; Luke 12:5). Even in New Testament texts where the word *gehenna* is not present, the idea remains in the background of references to eternal punishment by fire.[35]

The New Testament writers repeatedly spoke of the fate of the unrighteous as exclusion, as eternal separation from community with God. This theme arose from our Lord himself. Jesus warned that at the judgment, the Son of Man will plainly declare to many, "I never knew you. Away from me you evildoers!" (Matt. 7:23). To those who have not cared for the needy, he will say, "Depart from me, you who are cursed, into the eternal fire prepared for the devil and his angels" (Matt. 25:41). In several of his parables, our Lord described the situation of the lost as exclusion, whether from a marriage feast (25:10-13) or from the master's house (25:30). In keeping with Jesus' words, Paul warned that those who are troubling the church will be "shut out from the presence of the Lord" (2 Thess. 1:9). At the climax of his vision, the seer of the Apocalypse described the eternal abode of the righteous as the Holy City, the new Jerusalem. But the unrighteous are banished outside the city (Rev. 22:15).

In the New Testament, exclusion from the eternal community received expression through images drawn from horrible experiences of earthly life: torture or torment (Rev. 20:10), outer darkness (Matt. 8:12; 22:13; 25:30), weeping and gnashing of teeth (8:12; 13:42; 22:13; 24:51; 25:30), eternal fire (18:8; 25:41; Jude 7), second death (Rev. 20:14). These images depict the sad Negative that lies outside the glorious Positive of the eternal community of God.

The biblical images suggest that hell is failure. The tragic truth is that in the case of some the cosmic experiment ends with a refusal to

---

34. Ladd, *The Last Things*, 94-95.

35. Otto Boecher, "gehenna," in the *Exegetical Dictionary of the New Testament*, ed. Horst Balz and Gerhard Schneider, English translation (Grand Rapids: Eerdmans, 1990), 1:240

live in accordance with God's intention. The gnawing despair represented by the biblical pictures of hell depicts the lost who realize that they missed the purpose for which God created them. The judgment marks the disclosure and finalization of the discrepancy between their personal narratives and the wonderful destiny God intended for them.

Consequently, hell is a place of burning fire. Although some interpret this figure literally,[36] we do well to follow the Reformers and understand the biblical pictures metaphorically.[37] The fire of hell is the anguish generated by the awareness that a person has invested his or her entire life in what is perishable and temporal rather than imperishable and eternal (Matt. 6:19-20; Luke 12:16-21). Because earthly life has ended and eternity has dawned, no opportunity to change directions remains. The failure of one's life is now eternally fixed and unalterable.

As the experience of failure, hell is also isolation. God's purpose for humans is community—the enjoyment of fellowship with the Creator, with one another, and with creation. The lost, however, fail to realize this destiny. Rather than living in fellowship with God through obedience to his will, they have expended their earthly lives in alienation. This failure in life leads beyond death to exclusion from the eternal community into the realm of isolation.

The Book of Revelation speaks of this experience as the "second death." This death is not physical—the cessation of the functioning of an organism. Rather, the picture refers to total separation from our destiny in the eternal divine community. The seer painted strong images in order to declare that the separation from the source of meaning and purpose—community with God—is now unalterably fixed.

As isolation, hell is marked by estrangement and loneliness. The biblical artists appropriately depicted this aspect as "outer darkness." Banished from the realm where believers bask in the light of God's presence, the unrighteous, who are shut up into themselves, can only grope in darkness.

---

36. E.g., John Walvoord, "The Literal View," in *Four Views on Hell*, 28.

37. For a statement of this position, see William Crockett, "The Metaphorical View," in *Four Views on Hell*, 44-76.

The failure and isolation of hell means that the unrighteous experience God's love in a terrifying manner. We must not think of hell in the popular manner, as the place of Satan's eternal sovereignty which lies beyond the pale of God's love.[38] Were that the case, hell would be "heaven" not only for the devil, but also for the unrighteous. What could be more desirous for those who spend their lives running from God than to be granted their chief wish after death? Rather than freedom from God's love, hell is the experience of the dark side of that love.

As the eternal Lover, God never withdraws his love from humankind, not even from those who spurn him. Beyond the judgment, the unrighteous remain the recipients of God's love. Yet in their alienation from the Lover they experience it in the form of wrath, because they have destroyed the covenantal love relationship God desires to share with all his creatures. Hence, those who reject God's reconciling love in this life must know that love as wrath in eternity. This is hell.

In short, then, there is a dark side to eternity. The cosmos entails a great tragedy, the exclusion of some from the eternal community. But thanks be to God that he is long-suffering. God's patience is not yet exhausted. The God who does not delight in the death of the wicked (Ezek. 18:23) and who desires that none should perish (1 Tim. 2:4) continues to offer pardon and grace to wayward humans. He continues to call sinful humans to enter into community with him.

The New Creation

The universe as we know it does not fully conform to God's purpose for his creation. One day, however, God will inaugurate the glorious new order in which all creation will reflect its divinely intended form.

The biblical writers spoke of this future reality as the new creation. Through Isaiah, for example, God declared, "Behold, I will

---

38. Larry Dixon is an example of those who separate God's wrath from his love. See *The Other Side*, 165-72.

create new heavens and a new earth. The former things will not be remembered, nor will they come to mind" (Isa. 65:17). This promise formed the foundation for John's vision of the future new order beyond the judgment with which the book of Revelation ends: "Then I saw a new heaven and a new earth, for the first heaven and the first earth had passed away" (Rev. 21:1).

We conclude our discussion of cosmic eschatology by looking more closely at this glorious vision.

The New Creation as the Renewal of the Cosmos

As the phrase "the new creation" indicates, the glorious future reality that God promises consists of the renewal of the entire cosmos. In chapter 21, we noted that the resurrection marks the culmination of our personal stories. In chapter 22, we described Christ's return as the culmination of the human story. The new creation that lies beyond the eschatological judgment lifts human life in both its personal and social dimensions into the life of the entire cosmos. Consequently, the anticipation of God's eschatological renewal stands at the apex of our eschatological vision.

Renewal as the completion of creation. As we concluded in our discussion of the doctrine of creation (chapter 4), God's act in creating the world is ultimately eschatological. God called the universe into existence "in the beginning." Nevertheless, his goal or purpose in creation remains unrealized until he fulfills his promise to "make all things new." This promise presupposes that creation is not yet as God intends. Because the cosmos does not conform to the Creator's design and destiny, it is not yet completely created. One day, however, the Creator will act definitively. He will liberate the cosmos from its present incompleteness and bring it into conformity with his design.

The biblical picture of the renewed cosmos differs from the vision many Christians articulate. They conceive of our eternal home as an entirely spiritual, non-material locale. To distinguish it from earthly, physical existence, they commonly call it "heaven."[39] Consequently, they picture eternity as a realm inhabited by purely spiritual beings.

As the texts we cited indicate, however, the prophets of both Testaments anticipated a new earth blanketed by a new heaven (Isa. 65:17; Rev. 21:1). Rather than resurrected believers being snatched away to live forever with God in some heavenly world beyond the cosmos, the seer of Revelation envisioned exactly the opposite. God will take up residence in the new creation (Rev. 21:3). The dwelling of the citizens of God's eternal community, therefore, will be the renewed earth.

The relationship of the new to the old. For the eternal God to dwell with his saints within creation, however, he must first inaugurate certain changes in the cosmos. In keeping with this, the biblical vision of the culmination of the cosmos entails an interplay of continuity and discontinuity with the present order.

(1) The eternal new creation will differ greatly from the old (discontinuity). The basic difference will occur as God banishes from the new order of all that is harmful or stands counter to his perfect design.

This includes the elimination of sin in its various forms. God will root sin out of our hearts. He will not only purge us of sinful acts but also of the "flesh"—our weakness in the face of sin, our disposition to fall into sin, and structures in our lives that do not measure up to God's ideal. God will expunge every trace of the alien power that now keeps us in bondage. And he will banish sin as a network or "kingdom of evil." No longer will the tempter, the architect of wickedness, be able to buffet us.

God's banishment of all that is harmful will likewise include the elimination of fallenness from the new creation. We will enjoy an environment free from decay, disease, and death (Rom. 8:21; Rev. 21:4). Relegated to the past will be all suffering. Because we will live in harmony with our environment, there will be no more want of the necessities that sustain life (Rev. 22:1-3a).

---

39. This tendency is visible in the title of a recently-written "history of the images Christians use to describe what happens after death." Colleen McDannell and Bernhard Lang, *Heaven: A History* (New Haven, Conn.: Yale University Press, 1988).

Incompleteness will likewise be absent from God's new world. No longer will we yearn to experience the fullness of life. Gone will be all uncertainty and insecurity (Heb. 11:10; 12:28) and any sense of anxiety or despair.

(2) The eternal new creation will also be the renewed cosmos (continuity). God's promise is that he will make all things new, not that he will begin anew. The judgment will not constitute a total annihilation of the cosmos followed by a new act of creation *ex nihilo*.[40] Rather than the total destruction of creation, the biblical authors spoke of its renewal and liberation (Rom. 8:20-22). The best of human culture may even flow into God's new world (Rev. 21:26).

The interplay between continuity and discontinuity means that the cosmos will undergo a transformation somewhat similar to our resurrection. The old will give way to something radically new. Yet it is *this* cosmos that God will transform into the new creation.

The implication of cosmic renewal. The biblical promise of the renewal of creation carries a grave implication for life in the present. God's intention to transform the physical world into our new dwelling means that the material universe—and consequently the material dimension of life—is important. For this reason, we rightly engage in "material" ministries as the eschatological community. Our task is to minister to whole persons. And our concern extends beyond human needs to include trusteeship within creation. The mandate of the church, then, includes seeking to model the future society of redeemed humanity living in harmony with creation, as far as is possible in the present age.

The New Creation as Fullness of Community

Ultimately, the new creation is the presence of the new community in its fullness. What will characterize this community? We offer several characteristics.

A place where God is present. The greatest statement we can make is that the eternal community will be a place where God is present. It

---

40. For a critic of the proponents of this disjunctive view, see Berkouwer, *The Return of Christ*, 219-25.

will mark the completion of the promise that runs throughout the entire Bible, namely, that God will be present among his people.

One of the most awe-inspiring and challenging visions of the entire Bible is the seer's anticipation that God himself will participate in the new creation: "And I heard a loud voice from the throne saying, 'Now the dwelling of God is with men, and he will live with them'" (Rev. 21:3). The God who is the lofty transcendent Creator of the universe will choose to become fully immanent in his creation. The renewed cosmos will be characterized by community in the highest sense, therefore, for it will be home not only to creatures but to the triune God himself. The One who throughout eternity is the community of Persons will grace the new community with his presence.

God's presence in the eternal community will facilitate our experience of fullness of fellowship with him. John described this in the poignant statement, "and there was no longer any sea" (Rev. 21:1). The sea represents the distance between God and creation. The inauguration of the new order will mean the elimination of creaturely separation from God.

At the same time, however, God will remain eternally distinct from creatures. Rather than being eliminated, the difference between creation and God will always remain an integral part of the eternal community.[41]

A place of fellowship. Because of the presence of God, the new creation will be a place of fellowship. Peace, harmony, love, and righteousness will reign everywhere.

Fellowship will characterize our experience as humans. Above all, we will enjoy eternal community with the God who makes his abode among us. Because we are reconciled with God, we will enjoy complete fellowship with each other as well, for the eternal community is a social reality. The experience of fellowship presupposes that we will recognize each other, just as the doctrine of resurrection indicates. We may remember the relationships that had characterized

---

41. Wolfhart Pannenberg, "The Significance of the Categories 'Part' and 'Whole' for the Epistemology of Theology," *Journal of Religion* 66 (1986):385.

our earthly lives, especially family connections such as parent, spouse, or offspring. Nevertheless, the former roles will not be carried into the new community (Matt. 22:30). They belong to temporal existence.

Our human experience in the eternal community will likewise include fellowship with all other creatures, for our abode will be the new earth. John drew from images of the primordial garden to describe the future harmonious relationship. He saw the tree of life in the middle of the city, yielding a bounty of fruit and providing leaves for healing. Also lying behind this picture is the biblical teaching concerning enmity with the earth we have experienced, the curse which arose from the primordial human fall into sin. In this penetrating manner, the seer asserted that the curse is "no more" (Rev. 22:2-3). Discord between humankind and nature will come to an end, and God's intention that Adam (and hence humankind) live in harmony with nature will finally be realized.

In addition to characterizing our experience as humans, fellowship in the form of harmony will mark all of creation. The prophets anticipated a day when even the animosity within the animal world will cease. Isaiah, for example, talked about the wolf learning to feed with the lamb (Isa. 65:25). No longer will fear and competition exist among any of God's creatures. Instead all creation will know the peace that results from the cosmic liberation from the effects of our alienation from God.

A place of glorification. Finally, the new creation will be a glorious place. The judgment will effect an eternal glorification in which all the inhabitants of the new community will participate.

In the new creation, we will experience glorification. As we noted in chapter 16, the Holy Spirit will bring us into perfect conformity with Christ, thereby effecting in us the fulfillment of God's purpose for humankind. However, there is more to eternal glorification than the eschatological perfecting of the saints.

In the eternal community we will glorify God as we offer him our praise. In fact, the redeemed will join all creatures in this act. On that great day, the Spirit will mold us into one great chorus of praise to the eternal Creator and Savior.[42] Through this act of worship we not only glorify God, however, we also experience our glorification. By bringing us to offer service and praise to God, the Spirit places us alongside of Jesus, who as the eternal Son glorifies the Father, just as he glorified him through the completion of his mission on earth (John 17:4).

Just as the Son glorifies the Father, however, the Father also eternally glorifies the Son. Through our union with Christ, the Father's lavish glorification of the Son overflows to us (John 17:24). In this manner, as the Spirit leads us to glorify the Father through the Son, the Father glorifies us in the Son.

Therefore, the eternal community ultimately means the participation of creation through the Spirit in the glory of, even in the life of, the triune God himself (2 Pet. 1:4). Our eschatological glorification will transpire together with the glorification of all creation. And it comes as the reciprocal dimension of our glorifying God through praise and service to him.

The participation of creation in the Son's glorification of the Father and in the Father's glorification of the Son marks the consummation of the Spirit's work. As the Spirit of the relationship between the Father and the Son, he is the completer of both the dynamic within the triune God and God's work in the world. In this way, the Spirit eternally glorifies the Father and the Son both within the divine life and by completing the mission of God in bringing creation to share in eschatological glorification.

What the Holy Spirit effects at the consummation is but the heightening of what he is already accomplishing in the brokenness of our present experience. Ultimately, therefore, the eternal community is the extension and renewal of our earthly enjoyment of fellowship. For us the eschatological judgment is the Spirit's radical perfecting of the community we now share.

Seen in this light, our glorious future does not come as a stranger, but as a mysterious yet welcomed friend. G. C. Berkouwer offered

---

42. Wolfhart Pannenberg, "Constructive and Critical Functions of Christian Eschatology," *Harvard Theological Review* 77 (1984):135-36.

this poignant conclusion: "The new earth is never a strange and futuristic fantasy, but a mystery that penetrates into this existence and will make itself manifest there, where steadfast love and faithfulness meet, where righteousness and peace kiss each other (Ps. 85:10), and where the lines that seem blurred to us now will come clearly into focus."[43] Or as the apostle Paul declared, "Now we see but a poor reflection; then we shall see face to face" (1 Cor. 13:12).

---

43. Berkouwer, *The Return of Christ*, 234.

24

The Significance of Eschatology

Therefore, my dear brothers, stand firm. Let nothing move you. Always give yourselves fully to the work of the Lord, because you know that your labor in the Lord is not in vain." (1 Cor. 15:58)

Outline

In the doctrine of last things we speak about the goal or purpose for God's activity in the lives of individuals, human history, and creation. Therefore, eschatology includes the systematic articulation of the events associated with the climax of personal, corporate, and cosmic history. Yet the fundamental purpose of the doctrine of last things entails more than setting forth the chronology of the consummation. Through this study, we seek to bring to light the deeper understanding of reality that underlies that chronology.

With this in view, therefore, we must raise a final question: In addition to the specific aspects of the future consummation of God's program, what does the Bible intend to teach by the eschatological orientation which flows through its pages? We reply that the doctrine of last things provides insight into our own age. It issues a call to action in the present. And it indicates how we ought to live in the light of the end.

Consideration of the deeper intention of biblical eschatology brings our entire systematic theology to a fitting conclusion. In delineating this dimension of God's promise to bring creation to its consummation we also set forth the central message of theology itself.

Eschatology as Insight into the Present

Building from the eschatological expectations of the Old Testament, the New Testament writers instructed believers about the significance of the age in which we are living. The biblical insight arises as we view the present in the light of God's activity in creation inaugurated in the past but completed only at the consummation.

The central motif of biblical eschatology is the assertion that the triune God is at work in history effecting the consummation of the divine reign by establishing community. The biblical perspective considers the history of the world in the context of the theological question of ultimate sovereignty. Is the Creator lord over creation, or is the universe self-existing and autonomous?

The first human attempt to answer this question, which came in the fall, offered a negative response. In transgressing the primordial divine command, Adam and Eve denied God's ultimate sovereignty and thereby introduced enmity and alienation into creaturely existence. To this day humans follow in the steps of our first parents. We attempt to manage our own lives apart from God, claiming that we are the authors of our own destinies. In so doing, we continue the pattern of alienation which began with the fall and led to expulsion from the Garden of Eden.

In the face of human estrangement, God seeks reconciliation and fellowship. According to the Bible, the focal point of God's action is Christ. At his first advent, Jesus proclaimed the reign of the sovereign God and invited his hearers to become God's friends. The story of Jesus, and with it the narrative of God's saving action in the world, remains incomplete. Its conclusion lies in the future, when God will establish community in its fullness and thereby bring his universal plan for creation to completion.

We boldly assert that before the end God has disclosed the future consummation of the divine program for creation—the climax to the story—in the resurrection and ascension of Jesus. The future consummation, therefore, is the public disclosure that Jesus is the center and focus of all creation.[1] At the eschaton, God will establish his ultimate program by publicly affirming the lordship of Jesus, who as the Son came as the bearer of the claim of God the Father to sovereignty. While focusing on the participation of individuals in the eternal community, this final chapter of the salvation narrative encompasses the social aspect of human existence as well. And it places human life in the context of the entire cosmos, for the consummation includes the consolidation of God's victory over the cosmic powers, even over death itself.

Since Christ's coming, we have been living in the in-between age, the last days, the time between the inauguration and completion of God's program. Although the consummation remains future, God's reign—the establishment of community—has broken into human history. The New Testament writers described this era as characterized by two opposite tendencies.

Ours is the time of tribulation and Antichrist. As John declared, "You have heard that an antichrist is coming. Let me tell you, that many antichrists have already gone out into the world and therefore

---

1. The thesis that eschatology focuses on Christ is ably defended in Adrio König, *The Eclipse of Christ in Eschatology: Toward a Christ-Centered Approach* (Grand Rapids: Eerdmans, 1989).

we know that this is the last hour" (1 John 2:18, see also 2 John 7). Yet in the midst of tribulation, the church of Jesus Christ moves forth triumphantly under the banner of the cross. Because the church acts under the mandate of the risen Lord (Matt. 28:19-20), the very gates of Hades cannot prevail against it (Matt. 16:18), and the gospel works like leaven in the world (Matt. 13:31-33). By providing insight into the nature of the present age in the light of God's future, eschatology sets forth the world view framework for the church's mission in the contemporary age.

Not only for the world but also for the faith community the present age is the era of the already-and-not-yet. Christians have tasted the goodness of the eternal community and even now experience fellowship with God through Christ. At the same time, we have not entered into the fullness of God's future community. This awareness deters us from all triumphalism.

Above all, eschatology—the word concerning the consummation of the already-inaugurated divine program—is a message of hope. Because we believe that one day God will publicly confirm Jesus as the meaning of all creation (hence, as the *Logos* or "Word"), we are a hopeful people. We live with assured confidence concerning the outcome of history and our participation in the eternal community of God.

Eschatology as God's Call in the Present

The doctrine of last things provides insight into the significance of the present age in the light of God's action in Christ and of God's future. As such, it embodies a multifaceted divine summons to us in the present. This call arises insofar as looking hopefully to the future consummation of God's program facilitates our speaking authoritatively in the present. As we understand God's future intentions for the world we can both hear and proclaim his word in the present, for we know that God's future has implications for living now.

The Foundation for God's Eschatological Call

Eschatology is God's call in the present in the light of his future. The basis of this understanding of the doctrine of last things lies in the Bible itself. Therefore, to comprehend this dimension we must look to its biblical foundation.

The biblical precedence. New Testament eschatology arose out of the Old Testament prophetic movement. Among the ancient Hebrews, prophets engaged in a twofold activity, the foretelling of God's future and the "forthtelling" of God's message. These two aspects did not stand on equal footing, however. The predictive component was always subservient to the declarative.

The focus of the prophetic ministry lay in the proclamation of God's message in the present, not in the prediction of the future. In fact, true prophets of God never foretold future events simply to tantalize the imagination of their hearers. Instead, their disclosure of God's future actions served as the basis for issuing a call to obedience in the present.

In its essence, then, biblical prophecy is the utilization of a word concerning God's future in order to speak God's call (the word of God) in the present. The message of the prophet followed a familiar pattern: "Because God is going to do that great thing, you must now respond to God in this way."

In the same way, the eschatological declarations of the Bible do not merely seek to inform us concerning details of the future. Rather, true eschatological insight leads us to appeal to the truth about the future consummation in order to issue God's call in the present. As G. C. Berkhouwer declared, "Eschatology is not a projection into the distant future; it bursts forth into our present existence, and structures life today in the light of the last days."[2]

The implications for theology. Cognizant of the biblical precedence, we direct our reflection in eschatology toward a practical goal. We declare the word concerning the *telos* of God's activity (the *logos* concerning the *eschaton*) in order to speak the word of God in the present.

---

2. C. G. Berkhouwer, *The Return of Christ*, trans. James Van Oosterom (Grand Rapids: Eerdmans, 1972), 19.

We do not attempt to discover those events which must come to pass in the end times in order to satisfy our curiosity. Rather we seek to understand God's intentions in order to challenge the hearts of people today in the light of God's future and the future of the world.

We may look to Jesus himself for the greatest example of this manner of speaking. According to Mark, our Lord aimed his message at invoking the proper response from his hearers in the light of God's eschatological action: "The kingdom of God is near. Repent and believe the good news!" (Mark 1:15). In keeping with the pattern of Jesus and the prophets, the final goal of contemporary eschatology is to issue a summons to people today in the light of the future.

Aspects of God's Eschatological Call

Eschatology is a call to action in the present based on God's future. To what exactly is God calling us? The New Testament writers suggested that eschatological reflection leads to a threefold summons.

A call to evangelism. One dimension of the eschatological message is a call to zeal in worldwide evangelism. Jesus' own proclamation is crucial in this context: "And this gospel of the kingdom will be preached in all the world and then the end will come" (Matt. 24:14).

Jesus' purpose in voicing this prophecy was not to encourage the disciples to enter into discussions concerning time and chronology. Rather, the Lord intended to instill confidence in his followers to fulfil a mandate under his authority. Jesus promised that the church will complete its task of carrying the good news throughout the world. Our awareness of his promise ought to produce in us zealous involvement in the evangelism mandate (Matt. 28:19-20; Acts 1:8). We can commit ourselves to proclaiming the gospel because we are confident that the Holy Spirit will accomplish this task through us before the end comes.

The ministry of the apostle Paul offers a vivid example of this principle. His expectation of the eschatological salvation of Israel motivated him to zealous engagement in evangelism. In fact, this perspective formed a basis for Paul's philosophy of missions (Rom.

9:1-3; 10:1; 11:13-14, 25-32). The apostle was zealous for the gospel because he believed that his mission to the Gentiles would result in the salvation of Israel before Christ's return. This vision likewise formed the basis for Paul's admonition to the Gentiles to avoid arrogance (Rom. 11:17-22). God is allowing salvation to come to them, ,e said, in order that the Jews might become jealous. Therefore, rather than becoming puffed up, they ought humbly to accept God's salvation.

A call to holiness. In addition to being a summons to zealous evangelism in the light of the end, eschatology is a call to holiness and right living. Repeatedly the New Testament authors sounded the alarm concerning the end of history and the eschatological judgment. They did not so much intend to offer data for charts depicting the chronology of future events as to produce proper conduct in the present.

Jesus himself linked eschatological truth to the importance of right living. In the parables of readiness in the Mount of Olive discourse, for example, he clearly declared that the future coming of the Son of man demands prepared watchfulness on the part of his disciples (Matt. 24:45-25:46).

In their preaching and writing his disciples followed our Lord's lead. According to Peter, for example, the message about the consummation of history should lead to "sane and sober living" in the present: "The end of all things is at hand. Therefore, be clear minded and sober so that you can pray." He then elaborated the meaning of such living in view of the end. It includes love for other believers, the practice of hospitality, and the use of spiritual gifts (1 Pet. 4:7-11).

Paul used the imagery of light and darkness in admonishing the Roman believers to "understand the present time." Because "the night is nearly over" and "the day is almost here," Christians should "put aside the deeds of darkness and put on the armor of light" (Rom. 13:11-14).

John believed that knowledge of Jesus' return issues a call to purity: "It is not yet revealed what we shall be but when he comes we will be like him for we will see him as he is. Everyone who has this hope in him, purifies himself just as he is pure" (1 John 3:2-3).

A call to steadfastness. The doctrine of last things encourages zealous evangelism. It demands holiness and preparedness. In addition, as the message concerning God's future, eschatology summons us to courage and steadfastness.

The call to courageous tenacity arises out of news which is both encouraging and discouraging. In the present era the church will continually face tragedy, persecution, and false prophets. This dark message reminds us that to be overcomers we must be steadfast in loyalty to Christ. As those who belong to the Lord we must stand firm in the face of persecution and apostasy, because he will one day return in judgment (Matt. 24-25; 2 Thess. 2:13-17).

The call to steadfast loyalty arises also through the joyous message concerning God's future. The New Testament writers spoke God's promise that we will one day experience resurrection and victory over death. This news ought to motivate us to courageous involvement in the tasks the Lord has given us.

In Paul's great chapter on the resurrection (1 Cor. 15), the apostle gave an example of how knowledge concerning the future summons believers to steadfastness in the present. In this text, the apostle set forth the nature of the resurrected body and presented proofs of its reality. But Paul did not articulate these grand assertions about our future to stimulate a quest for dates and places. He intended rather to encourage steadfast involvement in the work of the Lord, for he knew that present action carries eternal consequences. For this reason, the apostle concluded with a resounding call to action: "Therefore, my beloved brethren, be steadfast, unmovable, always abounding in the work of the Lord for you know that your labors in the Lord are not in vain" (1 Cor. 15:58, KJV).

This is eschatology at its biblical best. The message about God's future provides the foundation and motivation for proclaiming the word of God in the present. God reveals to us his promise of the future consummation in order to call us to proper attitude and action in the present.

Eschatology as Insight for Living

The doctrine of last things entails more than reflection on the events surrounding the consummation of God's program. Its goal lies in the question as to how we as the church of Jesus Christ ought to understand ourselves and our mission in the present age.

Stanley H. Gundry rightly pointed out how "time and again there seems to be a connection between eschatology and the Church's perception of itself in its historical situation....Eschatologies have been a reflection of the current mood or *Zeitgeist.*"[3] Our eschatological reflection, however, ought to move us in the opposite direction. In the in-between time, the era between the two advents of Christ, the message of God's future ought to lift us above the mood of our times to true biblical living—living in the light of the end. This realization leads us to ask, What characterizes true eschatological living?

Eschatological Living as Hopeful Involvement

Biblical assertions concerning the future are ultimately expressions of hope in what God will do. Eschatology sees our present in the light of God's future. Because we know that one day God's yet uncompleted program will arrive in its fullness, we wait eagerly and expectantly for the consummation of the divine plan.

According to the New Testament, eschatological hope does not allow us simply to sit back and wait for God's future. In fact, the apostles spoke out against this type of quietism (2 Thess. 3·6-13). We wait for the Lord's return, of course, but ours is an active waiting. Because we are certain that God will bring his plan to completion, we become actively involved in that program. In this way, hopeful living means living hopefully. Motivated by hope of the final consummation, we seek to fulfil our divinely given mandate in the world, proclaiming in word and action by the power of the Holy Spirit the good news about God's activity in the world.

Paul reminded his readers of the importance of such hopeful involvement (1 Cor. 15:58). Its importance arises in part from the con-

---

3. Stanley H. Gundry, "Hermeneutics or *Zeitgeist* as the Determining Factor in the History of Eschatologies," *Journal of the Evangelical Theological Society* 20/1 (1977): 50.

tingency of world events. The Lord will certainly return, and the eschatological consummation will be realized. At the same time, the future is, in certain respects, open. God has a program for the world, but many details are not fixed. As we noted in the previous chapter, creation is in some sense a divinely guided experiment, and as an experiment it involves risks.

The experimental nature of creation may form part of the basis for the divine joy. Some do respond to God's love. For them the experiment is successful, and all heaven celebrates this success: "there is more rejoicing in heaven over one sinner who repents than over ninety-nine righteous persons who do not need to repent" (Luke 15:7). The experimental nature of creation also offers a window on the divine sorrow. Some people choose not to be gathered into God's community. Just as the failure of some of God's creatures to respond to Jesus' ministry resulted in his suffering and death (Matt. 23:37-39), so also God grieves over those who reject his love (Isa. 65:2).

In so far as the future is open, God summons humans to participate in his program in creating that future. God's future will surely come, but we are invited to be involved in his historical work, bringing it to pass. Hence, Peter admonished his readers to live in such a manner so as to hasten the day of the Lord (2 Pet. 3:12).

In our involvement in the work of consummation we are motivated by eschatologically inspired hope, the vision of God's eternal community. Consequently, our mandate includes evangelism. Alienated sinners must hear the good news of God's reconciliation so that they too can participate in that grand eternal fellowship. God's community is a society of love, righteousness, and justice. Therefore, social action must also be a part of the church's agenda.

In all our actions, our awareness that God stands in the future beckoning us onward provides us with hope. In hope we can direct our efforts—which include our prayers[4] and our actions—toward the advance of God's program on earth. Because of hope, we can be steadfast in our efforts at each step en route to the consummation (1 Cor. 15:58).

---

4. See Stanley J. Grenz, *Prayer: The Cry for the Kingdom* (Peabody, Mass.: Hendrickson, 1988).

Eschatological Living as Realistic Engagement

Eschatological living entails hopeful involvement in the program of God. It also includes realistic engagement. The adjective "realistic" reminds us that our activity is both effective and penultimate.

Our actions as effective. We engage in our mandate confident that our activity is effective. Imbued with the vision of God's grand future, we are confident, because we believe the Holy Spirit links our efforts with God's program. Our sovereign God is actively bringing his purposes to pass. As a consequence, we are sure that in the cosmic battle we have joined the cause which in the end will be victorious. This God has invited us—through Christ even *commissioned* us—to participate in furthering the divine program. Knowing that we act under the authority of the Lord himself, we commit ourselves to work and pray, in order that his community may indeed be established—that his will be done on earth as it is in heaven.

The eschatological vision lifts our sight beyond what may from time to time appear to be the downward spiral of events. We perceive the grander, heavenly reality that forms the context for our ongoing mission in the world. As John Jefferson Davis asserted, "the key to the church's hope is faith in the sovereignty of God and the power of the Spirit, not in world conditions as such."[5]

Our actions as penultimate. While confident in our engagement, we must also keep in mind the penultimate nature of all our activities. We dare never conclude that we are the determiners of our history. Nor may we allow the proclamation of the coming of God's community as the goal of history to degenerate into human efforts to produce the kingdom of God within history. God, and not our feeble actions, is the final hope of the world. Likewise, the kingdom of God is ultimately a transcendent reality which always lies above every earthly configuration prior to the final transformation of creation. No earthly city can ever hope to become the New Jerusalem.

---

5. John Jefferson Davis, *Christ's Victorious Kingdom* (Grand Rapids: Baker, 1986), 127.

Eschatological Living in the Light of the Eternal

The doctrine of last things entails the reminder that this world must pass through the radical transformation of divine judgment before the eternal community arrives. Consequently, our eschatological vision lifts our sights above the present earth. It directs our attention to the glorious eternal reality of the new heaven and new earth.

The new creation alone completely fulfills the promises God gave to his ancient people. It alone fulfills His promise proclaimed in the New Testament that we will participate in eternal life. Only with the coming of the gloriously recreated cosmos will God make his dwelling with us. Only on the redeemed and transformed creation will we experience full community with nature, with each other, and most importantly with God our Creator and Redeemer.

Yet we also proclaim that this radically transcendent reality is at the same time radically immanent.[6] God has broken into our world. And he has brought us to participate in his already inaugurated explosion into the earthly realm. Therefore, in the midst of the brokenness of life we can celebrate the new life of the Spirit.

How can we maintain these two seemingly contrary themes in creative balance? Early in the twentieth century, the great Southern Baptist theologian E. Y. Mullins offered what remains excellent advice. We should cultivate the New Testament attitude of expectancy, Mullins said, always looking for the Lord's return "because he commanded it, and because we love him and trust him, and because all the future would be blank without him." At the same time, Mullins cautioned against becoming "absorbed in apocalyptic calculations and speculations." Instead the Baptist theologian enjoined believers to faithfulness in every dimension of our Christian duty:

> We should ever watch against temptation and pray for divine strength. We should cultivate a passion for righteousness, individual and social. We should work while it is day, knowing that the night cometh when no man can work. We should be so eager for the coming

---

6. This is the consensus reached by the newer research into the kingdom of God in the teaching of Jesus. See, Bruce Chilton, "Introduction," in *The Kingdom of God in the Teaching of Jesus*, ed. Bruce Chilton, *Issues in Religion and Theology* 5 (Philadelphia: Fortress, 1984): 25-26.

of our Lord, that if he should come tomorrow we would not be taken by surprise. We should so hold ourselves in restraint, that if his return should be delayed a thousand or ten thousand years, we would not be disappointed. And our hearts should be ever filled with joy at the prospect of his coming and the certain triumph of his kingdom.[7]

God's eternal community has dawned, is dawning, and will one day arrive in its fullness. The God who has reconciled us to himself through Christ will one day bring us into full participation in the grand eschatological community of his divine reign. This vision should inspire us in this in-between era to seek to be the eschatological community in the present, proclaiming in word and deed the good news of the coming eternal community in which God himself will dwell with us.

Ultimately, eschatology is the study of the Christian understanding of the glorious future God has for creation. As the study of God's overarching purpose, the doctrine of last things forms the proper climax of systematic theology. Eschatology leads us back to where we started. It brings us to the God who desires that all creation share in the community of his presence and thereby to participate in the eternal glory of the one God who is Father, Son, and Holy Spirit.

Ending as it does with the vision of God's program for creation, our entire systematic-theological reflection confronts us with a grave question: Will the vision of God's ultimate future motivate us to be about the work of the triune God in the present era until Christ comes in glory and splendor?

---

7. Edgar Young Mullins, *The Christian Religion in Its Doctrinal Expression* (Philadelphia: Roger Williams Press, 1917), 471-72.

Subject Index

Name Index

Scripture Index

Jeremiah

Ezekiel

Daniel

Hosea

Joel

Amos

Obadiah

Jonah

Micah

Mark

John

Acts

Romans

2 Corinthians

Galatians